Accelerating Digital Transformation with the Cloud and the Internet of Things (IoT)

Intelligent Data-Centric Systems

Accelerating Digital Transformation with the Cloud and the Internet of Things (IoT)

Yacine Atif
School of Informatics
University of Skövde
Skövde, Sweden

Sujith Samuel Mathew
College of Interdisciplinary Studies
Zayed University
Dubai, United Arab Emirates

Series Editor Fatos Xhafa
Universitat Politècnica de Catalunya (UPC), Barcelona, Spain

ELSEVIER

ACADEMIC PRESS
An imprint of Elsevier

Academic Press is an imprint of Elsevier
125 London Wall, London EC2Y 5AS, United Kingdom
525 B Street, Suite 1650, San Diego, CA 92101, United States
50 Hampshire Street, 5th Floor, Cambridge, MA 02139, United States

ISBN: 978-0-443-22217-7

For information on all Academic Press publications
visit our website at https://www.elsevier.com/books-and-journals

Publisher: Mara Conner
Editorial Project Manager: Emily Thomson
Production Project Manager: Selvaraj Raviraj
Cover Designer: Mark Rogers

Typeset by VTeX

Contents

PART 3 Cloud based IoT digital transformation in action!

PART 1

Cloud and IoT ecosystem

CHAPTER

Cloud-to-things continuum: technical challenges and economical opportunities

1

Introduction

Together, cloud computing and the Internet of Things (IoT) are unlocking innovative applications across various domains, including smart homes, industrial automation, healthcare, and transportation. IoT envisions networks of connected physical devices embedded with sensors, which enable them to collect and exchange data. Cloud computing provisions computing resources and services over the Internet, including storage, processing power, and software applications. The cloud-to-things continuum describes the integration and data flow between cloud-based services and connected devices in IoT. The integration of these two technologies has enabled businesses to process and analyze vast amounts of data generated by IoT devices and has created new data-centric opportunities for innovation and growth. In this chapter, we will provide a detailed definition of both IoT and cloud computing that encompasses IoT devices (Xhafa, 2021). The services operating across the cloud-to-things continuum layers work in tandem to transform raw data collected from IoT devices into abstract structures used by upper-layer applications of enterprise systems to create business value. We also discuss the benefits and challenges of IoT and cloud convergence and provide some motivational examples of how businesses are using this convergence to create value.

The cloud-to-things continuum is boosted by the rapid development of artificial intelligence (AI). These innovations are driving a host of improvements and novel efficient practices in business operations and customer experience across various industries, which this chapter brings light to. While the continuum involving IoT and cloud computing offers significant benefits, it also presents technical challenges, which we reveal in this chapter, as well. However, as IoT devices and cloud systems evolve and become more interconnected, ensuring effective communication, these challenges can be mitigated. Common standards are necessary to ensure that data is exchanged seamlessly across different network protocols within IoT and cloud ecosystems. Thus we review these standards and other key contributing factors to the cloud-to-things continuum, such as security and privacy to ensure the safety of sensitive data generated by IoT devices.

Accelerating Digital Transformation with the Cloud and the Internet of Things (IoT)
https://doi.org/10.1016/B978-0-44-322217-7.00007-4

There is an increasing number of IoT devices connected to cloud infrastructure creating potential vulnerabilities, and therefore IoT security concerns are important to sustain the continuum. The increased connectivity of physical devices increases possible cyber attack surfaces as further entry points are exposed for exploitation. The distributed nature of the IoT network also makes it more difficult to secure than in traditional computing environments. Hence, we outline robust authentication and authorization mechanisms to ensure that only authorized users and devices access IoT data; we do the same in regards to strong data encryption and privacy protections that prevent unauthorized access and data breaches in the cloud-to-things continuum.

Finally, as the number of IoT devices continues to grow, the generated volume of data that they generate grows as well. This endeavor poses a significant challenge to scalability prospects, as businesses are expected to manage and analyze large amounts of data in real-time. The ability to scale infrastructure as needed to accommodate changes that are in demand is the essence of cloud computing, which further provides sophisticated data management and processing tools. As an overview for subsequent chapters, this introductory chapter reveals these connectivity, security, and scalability challenges, and provides business contexts for successful solutions and use cases of IoT and cloud computing continuum.

1.1 From cloud to edge: the emergence of IoT in cloud computing

The rapid evolution of the world is driven by technological advances. The Internet of Things (IoT) promises exciting transformations ahead. Connecting everyday objects to the Internet allows them to collect and exchange data in real-time. New data sources are unfolded, which could have a profound impact on our daily life, working environment, and interactive environment. However, IoT devices generate large amounts of data, and processing this data in a secure, reliable, and scalable manner can be challenging for individual devices or on-premises systems.

Cloud computing overcomes these challenges with flexible and highly scalable data storage and processing solutions. By extending access to scalable computing resources, cloud computing enables businesses to focus on their core operations and disregard infrastructure considerations. Yet, as the number of connected devices grows, transmitting all devices' data to the cloud for processing and analysis becomes increasingly challenging too. Edge computing alleviates this challenge by offloading some of the processing tasks from the cloud and bringing them closer to the edge of the network, where the IoT devices are located. This alternative to the systematic transmission of all data to the cloud is particularly efficient in scenarios where real-time processing is required, or when cloud connectivity is intermittent.

The IoT, cloud computing, and edge computing continuum enables businesses to process data and run applications across a distributed architecture, from the cloud to the edge. This approach allows businesses to leverage the strengths of each technology and tailor their solutions to meet their specific needs. Next, we define the intervening elements in the clout-to-things continuum, and provide examples of how businesses are leveraging this continuum to improve their operations and gain a competitive advantage. We also discuss opportunities that open up new growth possibilities from this continuum.

1.1.1 The building blocks of the cloud-to-things continuum

As we discussed earlier, the cloud-to-things continuum spans a range of technologies, paradigms, and layers. Collectively, they unleash new data and further process it to feed innovative applications. IoT is a network of physical objects or "things" that are embedded with perception and communication capabilities. They capture environmental data and communicate with other devices and applications. Meanwhile, cloud computing enables an on-demand scalable and cost-effective infrastructure for storing and processing massive amounts of data generated by IoT devices. To fully appreciate the potential of the IoT and cloud computing continuum, we first explain the basic concepts and components of each technology. While defining IoT and cloud computing, we explore the opportunities and challenges raised by the cloud-to-things continuum. We will also introduce the concept of edge computing, which enhances the capability of cloud computing in IoT contexts by instrumenting the distribution of computational resources to be situated in close proximity to IoT devices and sensors.

IoT components and architecture

In a landmark article, Kevin Ashton first used the term "Internet of Things," while working at the MIT Auto-ID Labs, to describe a system where everyday objects could be connected to the Internet and communicate with each other without human intervention (Ashton, 1999). This article is often cited as foundational work to the concept of IoT and paved the way for its widespread adoption. However, earlier in 1991, Mark David Weiser's seminal work "The Computer for the 21st Century" developed a vision of "ubiquitous computing," which inspired the Internet of Things evolution by describing a world in which technology would seamlessly blend into our daily lives and be integrated into everyday objects (Weiser, 1991). While working as chief scientist at Xerox Park, he stated: "The most profound technologies are those that disappear. They weave themselves into the fabric of everyday life until they are indistinguishable from it." In this foreseeable future, devices interact with each other and anticipate our demands implicitly. This vision from Weiser inspired IoT developers and continues to do so, bringing a host of innovations.

Since the Internet of Things refers to a vision rather than a system, there is no single standardized IoT architecture, as the architecture of an IoT system can vary depending on the specific domain of application and related requirements. Nevertheless, some common patterns and frameworks are often used as a starting point for IoT architecture design, such as the IoT architecture reference models proposed by the International Telecommunication Union (ITU), the specifications of IoT architectures proposed by the Open Connectivity Foundation (OCF), or the guidelines formulated by the IEEE Standards Association. Some of these standardization efforts are illustrated in Table 1.1. However, this is by no means an exhaustive list as reference models exist for various functionalities and major application domains, such as smart cities. Furthermore, updated releases are being generated since the first versions.

For example, OCF Core Specification's current release mentioned in Table 1.1 dates back to October 2022 (referring to Version 2.2.6). The purpose of Table 1.1 is to sample out ongoing standardization efforts driven by the need to establish common protocols and frameworks. These efforts are meant to support the IoT industry of all sizes to take advantage of this transformative technology and lead the way to new business models and revenue streams, while reducing the costs and complexity associated with deploying diverse IoT systems.

Table 1.1 IoT architecture reference models.

Reference Model	First Release	Description
ITU-T Y.4000	2016	Provides an overview of the IoT ecosystem and identifies the key components and functional architecture of the IoT
IEEE P2413	2016	Provides guidelines for the development of IoT solutions, including interoperability, security, and privacy considerations
OCF Core Specification	2017	Defines a common framework for IoT devices and services, including discovery, connectivity, security, and data exchange
OCF Resource Type	2022	Provides a common way to represent and access data across different types of devices, platforms, and applications

Basically, a typical IoT architecture features three key components: (1) device or sensor specification, (2) connectivity protocol, and (3) communication protocol. These components make up the backbone of any IoT architecture and are specified in the form of three logical layers referred to respectively as Perception, Connectivity, and Application layers. The layers division facilitates maintenance by zeroing in on a particular layer to figure out the origin of issues when they occur. Note that there exist other standards with four or five layers, all inspired by the OSI conceptual model (Al-Fuqaha et al., 2015), used to introduce traditional telecommunication networks. The term "conceptual" here means that deployed networked systems may actually have different architectures, and so are IoT architectures (Abdmeziem et al., 2015; Čolaković and Hadžialić, 2018). The main cause behind the disparity of architectural layers lies in the wide range of domain applications. Fig. 1.1 illustrates the three-, four-, and five-layer architectures (Lombardi et al., 2021) as generic high-level abstractions found in common IoT architectures (Čolaković and Hadžialić, 2018).

As illustrated in Fig. 1.1, Perception, Connectivity, and Application layers are consistently featured. The 4-layer architecture adds a service layer used to operate devices via applications through service APIs (application programming interfaces) (Lee, 2019). The 5-layer architecture adds a middleware and a business layer. The

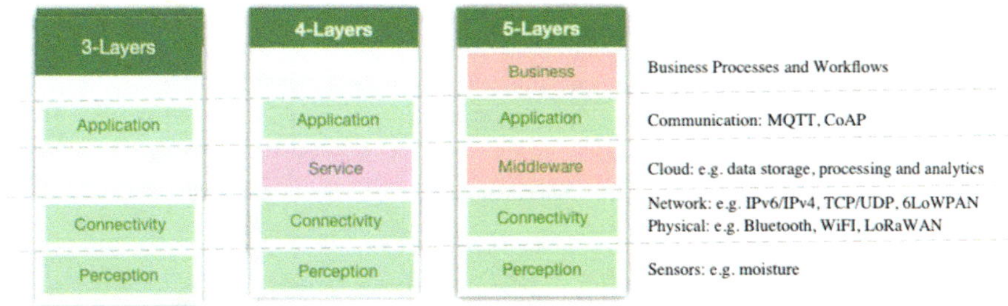

FIGURE 1.1

Common IoT architectures.

middleware layer integrates multiple IoT applications to enable communication and data exchange between them. This layer would then translate and transform data formats, protocols, and message structures to facilitate seamless communication. This form of integration is typically handy in enterprise business applications, where a middleware layer can be used to bridge the heterogeneity gap between them, allowing data to be transmitted and received by heterogeneous IoT applications. This is why this middleware-augmented architecture includes also a business layer, which manages the overall business logic and related processes across multiple IoT applications.

Next, we briefly describe the core components that are common to the three architectures, starting from the perception layers that accumulate employed sensors and devices in IoT systems. Then we reveal the underpinnings of the connectivity layer before emphasizing the communication protocols used at the application level.

Sensors and devices

The perception layer comprises sensors used to collect data about physical processes in the initial form of electrical signals, which can be transmitted to other devices. For example, in a smart home environment, physical fluctuations in temperature, humidity, light, and motion are captured by corresponding sensors, as illustrated in Fig. 1.2. More generally, IoT devices of the perception layer are the physical objects that are connected to the Internet and are used to collect data or control some physical processes, such as humidity diffusion through a humidifier, or operating a factory robot based on sensor inputs embedded in complex machinery. Thus IoT devices are Internet-connected physical objects augmented with sensors or actuator modules, which allow them to collect data and respond to changes in their environment. Application domains span various areas, such as monitoring environmental conditions, tracking the location of objects, or controlling home appliances.

However, it is worth mentioning that it is not the IoT device itself that is of interest to IoT applications but the physical material that it enables access to. For example, the motion sensor enables access to information on movements in the house area of Fig. 1.2. Similarly, it is the energy consumed by home appliances that are of interest rather than the Internet-enabled smart plugs used to connect them to power supplies.

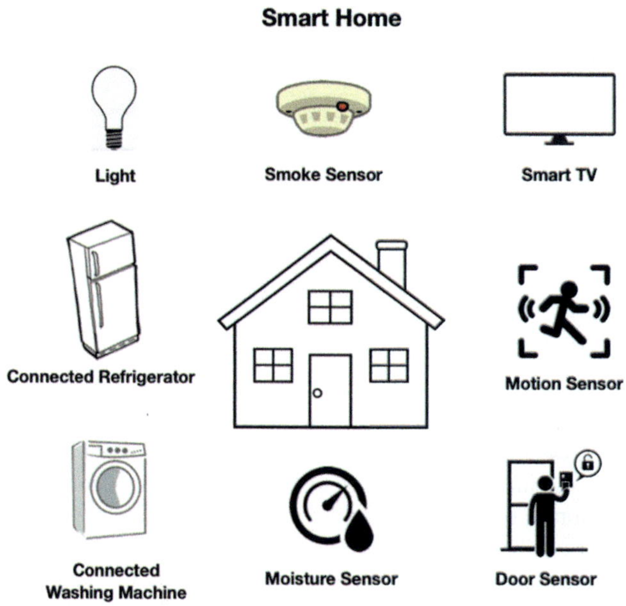

FIGURE 1.2

IoT sensors and devices.

To refer to a particular instance of a physical object, IoT devices need a unique identification. For example, this unique identification pinpoints a smart plug used in a particular home appliance, which energy consumption is of interest (Rokonuzzaman et al., 2021). Similarly, the motion or moisture sensors need to be uniquely identified to refer to particular house areas of interest. Thus the perception layer of IoT architectures, shown in Fig. 1.1, which comprises the physical sensors and IoT devices, assumes this primary identification function to track physical areas or objects of interest. This can be achieved through various technologies, such as RFID, which operates using radio signals over a short distance and is composed of an RFID tag, reader, and antenna (Finkenzeller, 2010; Duroc, 2022).

Connectivity protocols

For an Internet-based application to reach a device, a connectivity medium is required. This requirement is provided by a physical link in the form of electronic signals, which are directed by a set of rules, and which collectively are referred to as "protocol." Considering our smart home example of Fig. 1.2, a mobile phone app needs to reach a device such as the washing machine, which is equipped with a connectivity medium, to select remote washing programs and start a washing cycle. The mobile phone needs to use the same connectivity protocol to start a connection with the washing machine. Subsequently, a communication channel is established, allowing the mobile app to control the washing machine, via a communication protocol at the application layer.

Connectivity protocols in the middle layer of the 3-layer architecture in Fig. 1.1 define the way devices establish a connection with each other, and how data is subsequently transmitted through the set-up communication channel. These protocols also define how the devices are authenticated and authorized to communicate with each other. Connectivity protocols are typically associated with the physical and network layers of the IoT architecture. Thus the connectivity layer of Fig. 1.1 comprises two further layers: the physical layer and the network layer, which may both use several protocols as illustrated in Table 1.2.

In many deployment contexts, IoT devices are designed to be low-power, and may operate in remote or difficult-to-reach locations, where frequent battery replacement or recharging may not be practical. Furthermore, IoT devices may be deployed in large numbers, where even small differences in power consumption save overall energy when added up. Therefore IoT protocols are typically designed to minimize power consumption and extend battery life. Thus the disparity of protocols illustrated in Table 1.2 are distinguished by their level of power consumption (Barker and Hammoudeh, 2017).

Table 1.2 Connectivity and application layer protocols.

Layer		Protocols
Application		HTTP, CoAP, MQTT, DDS, AMQP, XMPP, REST
Connectivity	Network layer	IPv6/IPv4, TCP/UDP, RPL, 6LoWPAN, ZigBee (WSN)
	Physical layer	IEEE 802.15 series (e.g., Bluetooth, or sensor network), IEEE 802.11 series (e.g., WiFi), Z-WAVE, UWB, NB-IoT, LoRaWAN, NFC, LTE, 5G

Connectivity protocols enable devices to connect to a network and transmit data. As illustrated in Table 1.2, examples of connectivity protocols at the physical layer include Wi-Fi (IEEE 802.11), Bluetooth (IEEE 802.15.1), LoRaWAN, and cellular networks, such as 5G. These protocols are used to establish a physical network connection between devices, and subsequently provide reliable data transmissions over the established connection. This physical layer activity is concerned with the transmission of raw data over the connectivity medium. The subsequent network layer is responsible for managing the flow of data to ensure that it reaches its destination. It determines the best path for data to travel from the source to the destination device. This includes selecting the appropriate routing protocol and addressing scheme, managing network congestion, and handling any errors or data loss, which may occur during transmission. The network layer may also include security mechanisms to protect data as it travels between devices.

Communication protocols

Once the connection is established, the application protocol comes into play. This protocol specifies how two devices communicate and exchange information from their respective application perspectives. This results in application-to-application interaction, where, for example, the washing machine application might use a specific protocol to send information about its status, such as whether it's currently running a cycle or has completed a cycle. The receiving mobile phone app may use a different application protocol to send commands to the washing machine, for example, starting or stopping a cycle.

As illustrated in Table 1.2, IoT application layer communication protocols are designed to facilitate the exchange of application data between devices, but they still require an underlying connectivity protocol at the physical layer to establish and maintain the connection between the devices. Hence, IoT communication protocols at the application layer cannot work without using IoT physical layer connectivity protocols. Communication protocols include MQTT (message queuing telemetry transport), CoAP (constrained application protocol), HTTP (hypertext transfer protocol), DDS (data distribution service), and others illustrated in Table 1.2.

Fig. 1.3 illustrates the MQTT protocol, which uses the publish-subscribe model, that is, a messaging pattern, where senders of messages, called publishers, do not send messages directly to specific receivers, called subscribers. Instead, messages are published to topics or channels, and subscribers express interest in one or more topics by subscribing to them. The publishers and subscribers are decoupled from each other, as they do not need to know about the existence of each other. A flexible and scalable architecture is made possible by this decoupling, whereby multiple publishers send messages to a topic. Multiple subscribers receive messages associated with the same topic, as well.

For example, in the smart home of Fig. 1.2, the moisture sensor may publish the current level of humidity to a topic called "home/humidity," as illustrated in Fig. 1.3. The mobile app that displays the humidity at home can subscribe to the "home/humidity" topic and receive updates whenever the humidity changes. Another device, such as a dehumidifier, may subscribe to the same topic and adjust its settings based on the ambient moisture. A broker that runs the publish-subscribe model runs on a server on-premise, or in the cloud, and acts as a central hub, where publishers send messages and subscribers receive them.

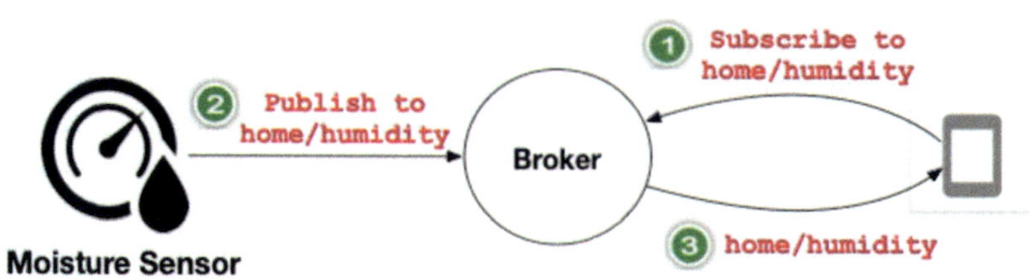

FIGURE 1.3

IoT publish/subscribe messaging protocol.

Note that the broker can be a standalone device, such as Amazon's Alexa or Samsung's SmartThings hub, or embedded in a smartphone app (Cavagnis, 2020) using open-source MQTT brokers, such as Mosquitto (Light, 2013), HiveMQ (HiveMQ, 2023), or RabbitMQ. These broker-based protocols can also be embedded in a single-board computer, such as Raspberry Pi or Arduino (FunTech, 2018). A broker can also be cloud-based, which provides a messaging service that supports MQTT, following the 4-layer IoT architecture model shown earlier in Fig. 1.1. Examples of cloud-based brokers include Amazon Web Services (AWS) IoT Core, Microsoft Azure IoT Hub, and IBM's Watson IoT Platform.

In terms of power consumption, CoAP is generally considered more efficient than MQTT, because it is designed to work on low-power devices. CoAP uses UDP instead of TCP, which is commonly used in MQTT as the underlying network protocol, and which contributes to CoAP's low amount of overhead data that needs to be sent. CoAP supports network layer protocols IPv4 and IPv6 networks and variants such as 6LoWPAN, illustrated in Table 1.2. This protocol is specifically designed for low-power and lossy networks prevalent in sensor networks, which use the IEEE 802.15.4 protocol at the physical layer. Additionally, CoAP has built-in support for power-saving features, such as sleepy nodes, which are wireless networked sensors that conserve power by turning off their radios and going into sleep mode for extended periods. These sensors may be placed in remote locations, where it is not practical to change batteries frequently, such as in environmental monitoring. For example, in smart agriculture contexts (Heble et al., 2018), wireless sensor networks (WSNs) with sleepy nodes can be used to monitor crop growth, soil moisture, and other environmental conditions. The sleepy nodes can be configured to periodically wake up, collect data, and transmit it to a base station or a gateway. Another application example of sleepy nodes relates to wildlife monitoring, where WSNs with sleepy nodes can be used to track animal movements, habitat use, and behavior (Ayele et al., 2018). The sleepy nodes can be attached to the animals and configured to wake up periodically to collect location and environmental data.

CoAP uses REST (representational state transfer) architectural style for resource manipulation and interaction, following HTTP request/response model. The RESTful principles define operations as web services commonly used in web applications, in a similar way to HTTP (hypertext transfer protocol). HTTP methods, such as GET, PUT, POST, and DELETE, are used by CoAP to interact with resources in an IoT environment, using resource identifiers (URIs) to address these resources. An example of CoAP using REST principles is to GET the humidity reading from a moisture sensor node, as illustrated in Fig. 1.4. In this example, the client would send a GET request in a CoAP message to the moisture sensor resource URI (uniform resource identifier) as coap://`192.168.0.101/humidity`. The sensor would then respond with the current moisture reading as the payload of a CoAP message. The payload can be encoded in a variety of formats, such as plain text or JSON. Assuming the requested format was JSON, then the reply format would be `{"humidity": { "value": 30, "unit": "%" } }`. Here, the value is 30, and the unit is "%".

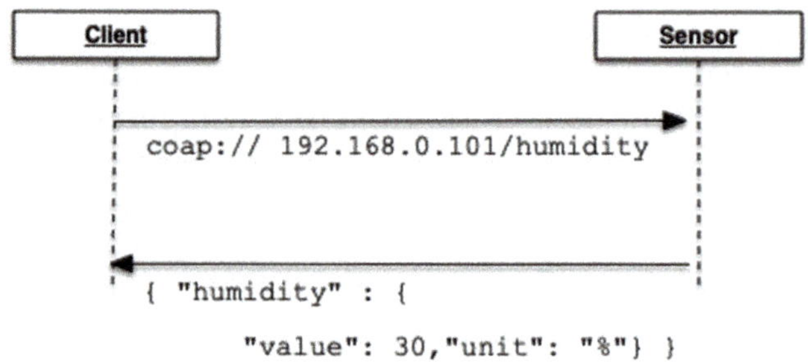

FIGURE 1.4

IoT request/reply messaging protocol.

Cloud computing: an overview

In cloud-based configurations, data generated by IoT objects is stored, processed, and analyzed through services made available from the cloud (Nazari Jahantigh et al., 2020). Cloud computing in the cloud-of-things continuum involves typically the use of cloud platforms and services. While these services are provided by major IT companies, such as Amazon Web Services (AWS) and Microsoft Azure, are potential providers of these cloud services, open-source alternatives are also available. Besides data storage, processing, and analytics, the provided services by these platforms may also include machine learning and artificial intelligence capabilities. Private and open-source cloud options, such as OpenStack (Rosado and Bernardino, 2014), CloudStack, and OpenNebula (Vogel et al., 2016), are popular options. IoT devices connect to the cloud through direct integration with cloud services via APIs, which use communication protocols, such as MQTT or CoAP, to send data to the cloud or through IoT platforms, which unifies the connection and integration of IoT devices with cloud services, as illustrated in Fig. 1.5.

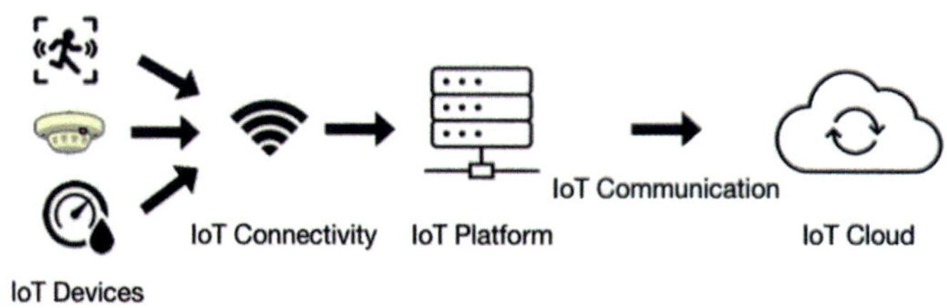

FIGURE 1.5

IoT platform.

A use-case for an IoT platform may be illustrated by a company that manufactures smart home devices, such as smart moisture sensors, motion detectors, and smoke detectors, as shown in Fig. 1.5. These devices are designed to be controlled and monitored by a mobile app. To enable this feature, the devices connect to the Internet to reach a cloud-based infrastructure that stores and processes data from the devices.

The company offers an onsite IoT platform device as a hub for smart homes, used as a common gateway to cloud services, such as AWS IoT or Microsoft Azure IoT. The platform provides the tools and services used to manage device connectivity and device status.

The platform may also provide additional services, such as software updates, remote configuration, and diagnostics. The company could further build custom applications and dashboards to monitor and control the devices, as well as to analyze the data for onsite optimizations. Note that the IoT platform could also be housed in the cloud, providing a direct cloud integration of IoT devices. This cloud-based IoT platform is a software service that allows IoT devices to connect and communicate with cloud services (Atif et al., 2016).

More generally, the US National Institute of Standards and Technology defines Cloud Computing as "a model for enabling ubiquitous, convenient, on-demand network access to a shared pool of configurable computing resources (e.g networks, servers, storage, applications, and services) that can be rapidly provisioned and released with minimal management effort or service provider interaction" (Peter Mell, 2011).

To qualify as a cloud computing facility, an infrastructure needs to possess essential cloud computing characteristics summarized in Table 1.3 (Peter Mell, 2011). These characteristics allow cloud computing to provide flexible, scalable, and cost-effective computing resources on demand, without requiring consumers to invest in their infrastructure.

Table 1.3 Essential cloud computing characteristics.

Characteristic	Description
On-demand self-service	A consumer can provision computing capabilities, such as server time and network storage, as needed automatically.
Broad network access	Capabilities are available over the network and can be accessed from a wide range of devices.
Resource pooling	Computing resources are dynamically allocated to serve multiple customers using a multi-tenant model (i.e., single resource serving multiple customers).
Measured service	Resource usage can be monitored, controlled, and reported, providing transparency for both the provider and consumer of the utilized service.
Rapid elasticity	Cloud computing resources can be scaled up or down quickly and easily to meet changing demands.
Ubiquitous access	Cloud computing services can be accessed from anywhere in the world with an internet connection.
Resilient computing	Cloud computing services are designed to be highly available and resilient, with built-in redundancy and failover mechanisms to ensure that services remain available, even in the event of hardware or software failures.

Virtualization

Although not all cloud computing platforms provide it, virtualization is a feature that provides virtual machines or containers, which can run multiple operating systems and applications on a single physical machine, as illustrated in Fig. 1.6. Virtualization can be used to create virtual sensors or virtual models of physical assets, used to manage and control the deployment of IoT devices. Often referred to as "Digital Twin" technology, virtualization simulates the behavior and performance of physical entities they represent, enabling analysis and testing of various scenarios without the need for physical experimentation. A cloud-based digital twin platform could use virtualization to dynamically provision computing resources on demand, allowing multiple digital twin applications to run on the same physical hardware.

As a use-case of digital twin applications, consider a manufacturer who creates a digital twin of a specific piece of equipment in the factory (Priyanka et al., 2021). This digital twin includes data such as temperature, pressure, and vibration on the machine's current condition, which are captured via embedded sensors into the live machine. By monitoring this data in real-time using the evolution of the virtual counterpart, the manufacturer can identify when the live machine is at risk of breaking down and proactively schedule maintenance before it actually fails. Thus downtime is minimized and repair costs are reduced (Gusselnikov and Brusakova, 2022). Besides the predictive maintenance and AI-based analytics, digital twins allow the manufacturer to identify trends and patterns in the machine's behavior and adjust maintenance schedules accordingly (Jagannath et al., 2022).

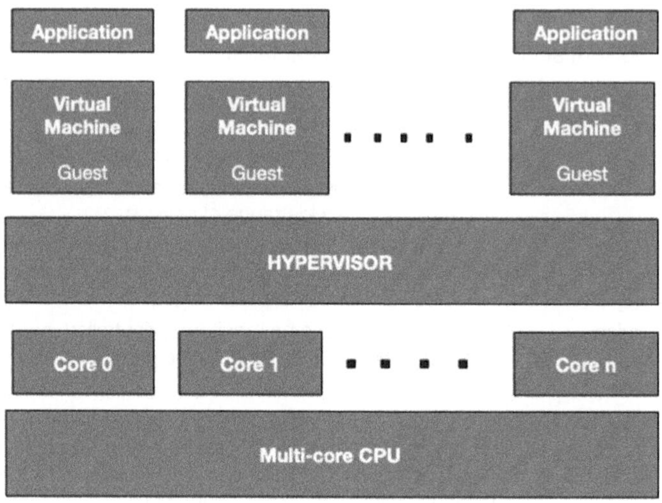

FIGURE 1.6

Hypervisor-based virtualization.

Provisioning

The process of configuring and setting up a virtual machine or container to deliver a specific application or service is referred to as provisioning. This process includes cloud computing resource allocations, such as processing and storage, installing the necessary software and libraries, and configuring network connectivity. As shown in Fig. 1.6, the hypervisor is software that makes up the virtualization layer between the physical hardware (host machine) and the virtual machines (guests). The hypervisor manages the resources of the physical machine and allocates them to the virtual machines on demand. This process ensures that each virtual machine has its own isolated environment running its own operating system and own applications.

Cloud service models

The different ways in which cloud computing services are delivered follow three main service models:

- Infrastructure as a service (IaaS): Consumers access virtualized computing resources, such as servers, storage, and networking. The management of the infrastructure is provided by the cloud provider, whereas the consumer is responsible for installing and configuring their own operating systems, applications, and data.
- Platform as a service (PaaS): Consumers are provided with a complete development environment, including the tools and libraries needed to build and deploy applications.
- Software as a service (SaaS): Consumers invoke software applications that are hosted and maintained by the cloud service provider. The consumer does not manage the underlying infrastructure, but instead uses the software through a client application or an API.

Edge computing: from cloud to distributed intelligence

The requirements of real-time applications that use cloud services, such as autonomous driving, remote healthcare, and digital twins, expect strict timeliness on latency. These applications facilitate AI in the cloud to process the ever-increasing amounts of data generated by these applications (Chang et al., 2021). Sending all data to the cloud for training or inference results in unpredictable data transmission latency. Edge computing reduces the amount of data that needs to be sent to the cloud, leading to faster response times and lower network traffic (Wu, 2021). In addition, by combining data from multiple edge nodes, distributed intelligence can provide more accurate and comprehensive insights than traditional cloud-based approaches (Filho et al., 2022).

Distributed artificial intelligence enables the training and inference of models to be performed in proximity to the sources of data, using a distributed approach rather than being sent to a central location in the cloud (Duan et al., 2023). This approach not only minimizes latency but also increases privacy and security. Typically, as shown in Fig. 1.7, an IoT-based distributed AI architecture starts with a first layer that consists of the end devices, which include various sensors, actuators, and other IoT devices.

This layer is essentially responsible for collecting data from the physical world, and that is the perception level of this layer. Then, the collected data is processed and transmitted, as part of the connectivity level task. Finally, the applications level assumes the role of running applications on the devices. These are the same three levels of common IoT architecture illustrated earlier in Fig. 1.1.

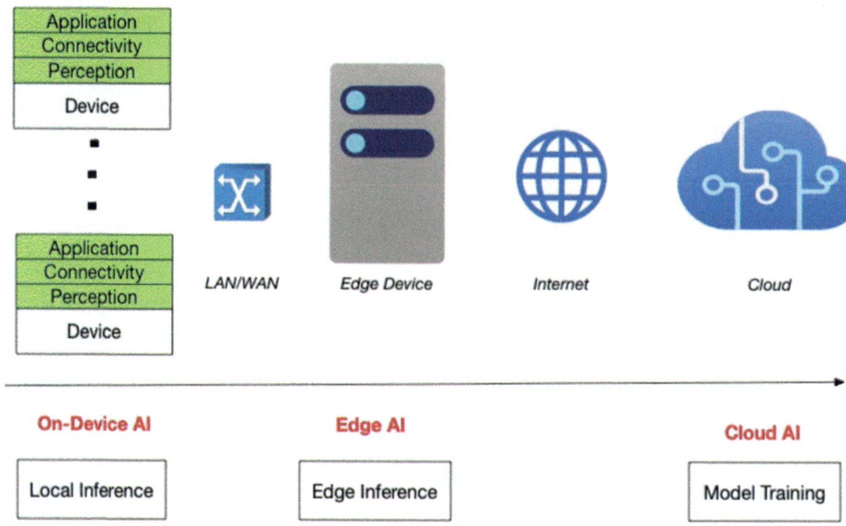

FIGURE 1.7

Distributed intelligence with edge computing.

On-device AI

With the increasing capabilities of IoT devices, it is possible to run on-device AI applications on the device itself as part of the first layer, which is also labeled the device layer or the end device layer, in IoT-based distributed AI architecture. These on-device AI applications can perform local data processing to infer decisions, without necessarily relying on cloud services or edge devices. Use cases depend on the application context and the capabilities of the IoT device. For example, on-device AI models can analyze image or video data captured cameras, to identify and localize objects of interest, such as people, vehicles, or objects. Use cases range from surveillance, or smart home security to industrial automation domains.

Other applications of on-device AI include anomaly detection, where the analysis of sensor data may reveal anomalies or deviations from normal patterns, indicating potential faults, or unusual behavior. Application domain use cases include predictive maintenance, network security, or environmental monitoring. On-device AI enables local automation, where sensor-captured data is analyzed to make local decisions or control actions based on predefined rules or policies. This is the case for autonomous vehicles, where an on-board AI system makes decisions and takes actions locally, without relying on cloud-based or external processing. Real-time decisions allow the vehicle's control system to infer acceleration, braking, steering, and navigation actions, without the need to send data to a remote cloud server for processing. Typical devices in this context include GPS, Lidar, radar, cameras, and other sensors, to perceive the surrounding environment, detect objects, identify road signs and markings, and track the vehicle's position, speed, and orientation. Machine learning algorithms, such as deep neural networks, process data to make decisions about the vehicle's actions, such as determining the optimal path, adjusting the speed, planning maneuvers, and ensuring overall safety measures.

Besides real-time processing benefits, on-device AI processing reduces privacy and security data breaches as well as unauthorized data access, as the generated data generated by the devices are processed locally without being transmitted to external servers. Continuous data transmission to the cloud is also reduced, resulting in lower data bandwidth requirements and potentially reducing the cost of data transmission. However, on-device AI can also have some challenges in some domains, such as limited processing power, memory, and energy constraints on IoT devices, as well as the need for effective management of AI models, updates, and security. For example, wearable IoT devices, such as smartwatches, fitness trackers, and other wearable devices, often have limited processing power, memory, and energy constraints. AI application domains, such as activity recognition, health monitoring, and gesture recognition, may face challenges in achieving real-time accurate inference, and energy-efficient operation.

Edge AI

Edge AI refers to the deployment of AI capabilities, such as machine learning and inference processing, at or near the edge of the network, where IoT devices are employed, to be close to data sources. This proximity is geographical, where IoT devices offload data processing tasks to edge devices, which are typically more powerful than end IoT devices to perform edge AI techniques. Edge devices may physically embed IoT devices in certain cases. This can occur in certain scenarios where the edge device and IoT device are designed as an integrated unit, or when the edge device is purpose-built to include specific IoT functionalities. This means that the edge device interfaces directly with IoT devices using some ad-hoc protocols. A typical example is discussed later as part of Fig. 1.9 illustration of embedded edge computing. These systems are commonly used in critical infrastructure control networks or industrial control systems, where embedded devices, such as programmable logic controllers (PLCs) and remote terminal units (RTUs) are used for real-time monitoring and control of sensors embedded in physical industrial processes. These embedded edge computing devices perform local data processing and decision-making to optimize the operation of the physical process efficiency (such as power flow) by instructing actuators to perform inferred actions.

Another example of embedded edge computing relates to smart cameras, which augment traditional camera functionality with edge computing capabilities, such as image processing, object detection, and video analytics. These cameras can analyze video streams locally and trigger events or alarms based on predefined rules, without the need for continuous video streaming to the cloud. Similarly, today smart appliances, such as smart refrigerators or smart washing machines often have embedded edge computing capabilities to optimize energy usage and perform personalized operations.

More generally, edge computing connects to IoT devices to run computing tasks, including the deployment of machine learning models or algorithms directly on edge devices. These tasks include transfer learning (Saggu and Azim, 2021), model compression (Wang et al., 2020b), and quantization (Chen et al., 2021) to optimize the size, complexity, and efficiency of machine learning models for deployment on edge devices with limited resources. Transfer learning is a machine learning technique, where a pre-trained model, typically trained on a large dataset for a task, is used to train another model for a different but related task using a smaller dataset. This is an alternative to train a model from scratch with a smaller dataset by instead transferring the knowledge and features learned from the larger dataset, for example, a pre-trained convolutional neural network (CNN) model, such as VGG. ResNet or Inception uses a large dataset, e.g., ImageNet for training (Krizhevsky et al., 2017; mageNet, 2022). This pre-trained model can subsequently be used as a feature extractor for another image recognition task with limited data to run on the edge device.

As an application instance, consider a pre-trained model for health monitoring use case, such as a physiological signal-based model for heart rate or blood pressure prediction, trained on a large dataset of physiological signals, which can be used as a starting point for health monitoring tasks on edge devices within a healthcare facility. On the other hand, model compression, also known as model optimization or model quantization, is the process used to reduce machine learning models' size and complexity, to deploy them on resource-constrained edge devices.

On-device-AI and edge-device-AI may collaborate to collectively infer decisions or perform tasks. For example, on-device AI in IoT devices can gather data from sensors, process it locally, and share relevant information with edge devices for further machine-learning processing and decision-making. In doing so, on-device AI offloads computationally intensive tasks to edge devices. This may entail also multiple IoT devices to capture different local contexts and perform specific features' extraction locally. And then this processed data is offloaded to an edge device for further analysis or inference. This distributed computation improves overall performance by leveraging the processing capabilities of edge devices.

Federated learning is a distributed AI approach, where models are trained collaboratively across multiple edge devices (Abreha et al., 2022). Federated learning trains models collaboratively, while keeping raw data locally on the respective edge devices. This approach contributes to addressing privacy concerns, lowers data transmission overhead, and enables diverse data sources to participate in distributed model training across edge devices. This distributed machine learning approach enables AI-capable edge devices to train models locally using their locally acquired data from connected IoT devices. The trained models from several edge devices are aggregated into a centralized model by averaging the model weights from multiple edge devices.

Thus a central server at the edge layer coordinates models' exchange and information updates. This approach allows edge devices to send only the updated model weights to the central server, rather than sharing the entire model or raw data. Thus privacy levels are raised as well as the security of local data on edge devices. The data is previously collected from sensors within the local environment of individual edge devices. The global model is shared back with edge devices for further local training iterations. This iterative training process enables edge devices and the central server to collaborate across multiple rounds, involving model updates and aggregation. Edge devices continuously train and update their local models based on the aggregated global model from the central server, and the central server updates the global model based on the received model updates from edge devices. This iterative process continues until the desired model performance is achieved.

These local models learn to capture patterns or trends of individual patients, and continuously update as new data is collected. The smartphones then participate in a federated learning process, where the local model updates, including the health insights learned from the edge-device AI, are securely shared and aggregated at a central server. The central server combines the aggregated updates with the global model, which incorporates knowledge from a large population of patients with chronic diseases, to generate an updated global disease management model.

The updated global disease management model is then shared back with the smartphones for further local training iterations, enabling the local models to benefit from the collective knowledge of the patient population, while maintaining data privacy and security. The smartphones may then provide personalized disease management recommendations, reminders, and interventions to individual patients, based on their unique health conditions, without exposing their sensitive health data to external parties.

As a federated learning example, consider a set of edge devices represented by smartphones that connect to IoT devices, which are equipped with sensors to collect raw health data, such as glucose levels, blood pressure, physical activity, and dietary information (see Fig. 1.8). This health monitoring approach is provided to some patients with chronic diseases, such as diabetes or hypertension. The smartphones process this raw health data locally using the edge AI capabilities of the smartphone to generate insights and predictions related to disease management.

The local models running on edge devices (i.e., smartphones) learn to capture patterns or trends of individual patients, and continuously update as new data is collected. The smartphones then participate in a federated learning process, where the local model updates, including the health insights learned from the edge-device AI, are securely shared and aggregated at a central server. The central server combines the aggregated updates with the global model, which incorporates knowledge from a large population of patients with chronic diseases, to generate an updated global disease management model. The updated global disease management model is then shared back with the smartphones for further local training iterations, enabling the local models to benefit from the collective knowledge of the patient population, while maintaining data privacy and security. The smartphones may then provide

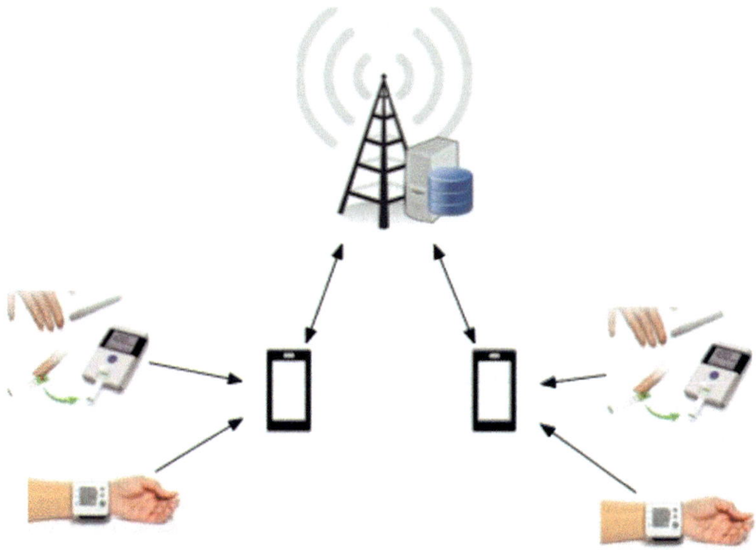

FIGURE 1.8

Distributed intelligence with edge computing.

personalized disease management recommendations, reminders, and interventions to individual patients, based on their unique health conditions, without exposing their sensitive health data to external parties.

Cloud AI

Data may further be sent from edge devices or IoT devices to remote cloud servers for processing, analysis, and inference. Cloud AI provides access to vast computing resources for centrally processing large-scale datasets. Algorithms with big data analytics capabilities are used to process such data. Besides computational capabilities, the key distinction between cloud AI and edge AI lies in the location where AI processing takes place. While cloud AI relies on remote cloud servers, edge AI leverages the local computing resources of edge devices. Also, edge AI is suited for tasks requiring low processing, real-time decisions, or privacy preservation. Cloud AI, on the other hand, is typically used for tasks that require complex algorithms and using large-scale data.

Edge AI complement cloud AI by offloading some processing tasks to the edge, reducing reliance on cloud resources and addressing bandwidth and latency constraints. Following the illustration of Fig. 1.8, AI processing is distributed across both edge devices and cloud servers to create an adaptive feedback loop, where edge devices feedback to the cloud about the performance of locally deployed AI models, which can be used to improve the models over time. This adaptive learning and feedback loop extends the federated learning at the edge layer discussed earlier to leverage the performance of cloud-based analytics.

It is important to note that there is no standard federated learning configuration, and the role of cloud AI can vary, depending on the specific implementation and requirements of the federated learning setup. However, cloud AI raises the scalability requirements of distributed AI, while reducing communication bandwidth by offloading some processing tasks to the edge AI layer. This tradeoff between the local processing capabilities at the edge and the scalable processing in the cloud is the subject of state-of-the-art research across deployment configurations in different application contexts (Janbi et al., 2022; Duan et al., 2023).

1.1.2 Overview of the cloud-to-things continuum

Drivers shaping the cloud-to-things continuum

The evolution of the cloud digital ecosystem, from its early stages to its current state, evolved through the integration of a diverse range of layers and systems, which span from cloud-based services to IoT devices and sensors. This trajectory has led to the emergence of the cloud-to-things continuum, which penetrates physical spaces to collect new data, which is further processed and analyzed across layers of the continuum (Distefano et al., 2012). This trajectory of cloud computing down to the level of IoT and sensor devices has been driven by several key factors illustrated in Table 1.4; we now explain this further:

Data explosion

With the increasing number of connected devices and sensors, the amount of data generated by IoT devices is growing exponentially (Bessis and Dobre, 2014; Ge et al., 2018). The massive amounts of data generated by a large number of connected devices led to a rapid growth of the generated data. This exponential growth in data has created significant challenges for businesses and organizations (Manyika et al., 2011). These IoT devices collect and transmit data in real-time, leading to a significant increase in the volume, velocity, and variety of data. This can create challenges for data storage, processing, and analysis, as well as the need for efficient data management techniques. Cloud computing provides the necessary storage and processing capabilities to handle this data explosion and subsequently unlock the value of data (Kalapesi, 2013; Banerjee et al., 2021; Philip Chen and Zhang, 2014; Elhoseny et al., 2018).

The cloud-to-things continuum allows for efficient handling and processing of the enormous amounts of data generated by IoT devices (Pizzolli et al., 2016; Ma et al., 2013). While cloud computing provides the necessary computational power to handle this data, IoT devices enable the collection of data from the physical environment (Liu et al., 2019). The cloud-to-things continuum allows for real-time, efficient handling and processing of the enormous amounts of data generated by IoT devices, including for more efficient decision-making. Furthermore, cloud-based IoT services offer a variety of data analysis solutions, including data filtering and aggregation, as

Table 1.4 Factors driving cloud-to-things continuum.

Factor	Issue	Cloud-to-things continuum-based solution
Data explosion	Connected devices and sensors generate an exponentially growing amount of data	Provides the necessary storage and processing capabilities to handle this data explosion
Real-time processing	Many IoT devices require quick decisions and take immediate action	Provides the computing power needed to process this data in real-time
Accessibility	Need to accommodate a growing number of devices and users	Provides secure transmission and interoperable applications to manage remote devices
Scalability	IoT data need to be accessed from anywhere and on any device	Provides elastic resources that automatically expand to meet the increased demand
Standardization	Different IoT devices and platforms use different protocols and standards	Provides a common platform for integrating different devices and related protocols
Cost savings	Expensive on-premise infrastructure, and associated costs of maintenance, upgrades, and security	Reduces the need for on-premises IT infrastructures through shared and robust resources
Security and privacy	IoT devices can be vulnerable to cyber-attacks and data breaches	Provides identity and access management to authenticate users and devices

well as data compression to further reduce storage and transmission requirements. (Emeakaroha et al., 2015).

Real-time processing

When data generated by IoT devices need to be processed and analyzed in real-time, decision-making processes and actions prompt another driving force for cloud-to-things continuum. Use cases include time-critical applications, such as industrial automation, healthcare monitoring, and autonomous vehicles. Using cloud-based processing, IoT devices can offload computation, allowing them to reduce the risk of overload or failure to meet real-time constraints due to limited processing capabilities. This is because cloud platforms can offer more powerful computing resources and scalability compared to individual IoT devices. To meet real-time processing, IoT devices delegate the computation to process the collected raw data to the cloud, instead of trying to perform all data computation on the device itself.

When IoT devices rely solely on their limited computational capabilities, processing the amount of collected data may result in overload or failure to meet real-time constraints. IoT devices have limited computational, memory, and storage resources; thus relying on the cloud for processing IoT devices' data can overcome these limitations and perform complex data analysis and processing tasks. As an example, consider the healthcare domain where IoT devices can be used to monitor patient indicators, such as heart rate, blood pressure, and oxygen levels (Akkaş et al., 2020). Processing the generated data from these devices in the cloud provides doctors with real-time alerts when any abnormalities are detected, allowing them to take immediate action (Ukil et al., 2016). IoT devices can also be used to remotely diagnose patients, reducing the need for in-person consultations. For example, wearable devices can collect data on a patient's movement, sleep patterns, or other physiological data to support remote diagnosis (Nancy et al., 2022). In clinical trial contexts, IoT devices can be used to collect data on patients' health and behavior. Identifying trends and patterns from this data in real-time helps researchers better understand the efficacy and safety of new treatments or vaccines (McNabb et al., 2020; Nagayo et al., 2023). Finally, IoT devices can be used to monitor patients' medication usage in real-time. For example, a smart pillbox can send alerts to patients, and can also notify doctors and caregivers (Latif et al., 2020; Srinivas et al., 2018; Ayshwarya and Velmurugan, 2021).

IoT in transportation systems features real-time data processing in a number of ways. Connected sensors can be embedded in vehicles to monitor various parameters, such as tire pressure, engine performance, fuel efficiency, and more (Bojan et al., 2014; Prasad et al., 2022). This data can be transmitted in real-time to cloud-based platforms, where it can be analyzed to detect potential problems and trigger maintenance or repair actions. Similarly, connected sensors can be used to monitor traffic flows in real-time, allowing transportation authorities to optimize traffic light timings, adjust toll booth rates, and provide real-time traffic updates to drivers (Ahmad et al., 2019; Javaid et al., 2018). Connected parking spots could reveal their availability in urban cores to the cloud and used by parking finder systems embedded in cars or running on mobile apps (Atif et al., 2016, 2020; Mathew et al., 2014).

Accessibility

Data generated from IoT devices can be accessed from anywhere using cloud services. Besides, a connected device can enable remote monitoring and management via cloud services. This means that users can access real-time device data from IoT devices, regardless of their location, and then use this information to make informed decisions and take timely actions. For example, smart grid operators can access the infrastructure data and remotely operate power components from anywhere using dedicated applications. IoT devices can be used to collect data from various points in the grid, such as power generation stations, distribution networks, and end-user consumption points (Bera et al., 2015). As illustrated further in Fig. 1.9, this data is collected via sensors in remote terminal unit (RTU) and further concentrated into master terminal unit (MTU) before it is transmitted to the operational layer through proprietary network protocols (i.e., SCADA) to nearby power substations for onsite operation control. Data flows further to remote control stations and enterprise layer stations via IP Networks, where cloud-hosted applications provide real-time analysis and processing for remote monitoring and management of the grid. This remote access to the power network control unit operations enables utilities to respond quickly to changes in the grid, such as fluctuations in demand or supply, and take appropriate actions to maintain a stable and reliable power supply (Hashmi et al., 2021).

Similar to smart grid operations, cloud-to-things continuum can be used to remotely monitor and manage oil pipeline networks (Priyanka et al., 2021) or water infrastructure (Priyanka et al., 2020), as well. This can help to increase the efficiency and safety of pipeline operations by providing real-time insights into pipeline performance, detecting leaks or other issues, and optimizing pipeline maintenance schedules. Cloud-based IoT platforms enable predictive maintenance and reduce downtime of infrastructure or manufacturing operations, leading to increased productivity and cost savings.

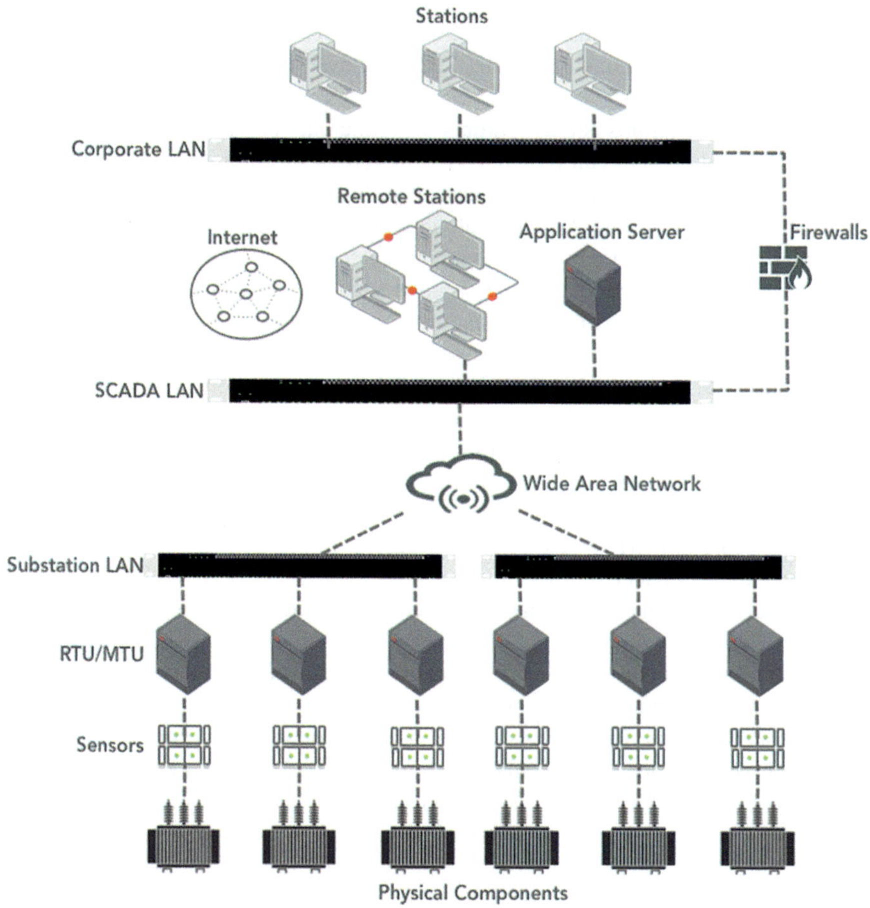

FIGURE 1.9

Remote operations of smart power grid networks.

Scalability

As the number of connected devices and the volume of data generated by these devices is rapidly increasing and even exponentially, traditional IT infrastructure and networks are unable to cope with the increasing demand for storage, processing, and analysis of data. IoT devices typically have limited processing power, memory, and battery life, which can limit their ability to handle large amounts of data or complex computations.

Scalability in IoT empowered by cloud resources harnesses load and traffic, which comes with a larger number of devices and data, without experiencing a decrease in performance or functionality. This allows a graceful expansion of computational resources to sustain operations effectively as the number of devices and generated data increases. Without scalability, the system may experience bottlenecks, delays, and even failure, which can negatively impact IoT user experience and business operations.

In an industrial setting, thousands of sensors and devices can be connected to a central platform. This platform may mediate between the design team and the production facility. In fact, this is one of the industrial Internet of Things (IIoT) benefits, whereby the design team can be located in a different location from the production facility and still be able to monitor the production process in real-time (Tan and Labastida, 2021). Better collaboration and coordination between the design team and the production team result from this approach. For example, a product design team in one country can plan a product, and the production team in another country can manufacture the product using IIoT-enabled infrastructure. The design team can monitor the production process in real-time and make adjustments to the design if necessary. This can help reduce production costs and time-to-market, while also improving the quality of the final product.

Furthermore, IIoT enables remote monitoring and control of production processes, which is especially useful in situations where there are limited resources or expertise on site. This concept of remote manufacturing using IIoT technologies is closely related to the Industry 4.0 framework (Munirathinam, 2020; Nagpal et al., 2019). Remote manufacturing using IIoT technologies is one of the key components of Industry 4.0, as it enables companies to create a more distributed and interconnected manufacturing system that can operate remotely and with greater flexibility. Industry 4.0 refers to the fourth industrial revolution, where IIoT and artificial intelligence enable smart factories to raise their level of efficiency, flexibility, and responsiveness to customer demands.

In the automotive industry, for example, it is common to have designers in one country sending their designs across the world to another country where manufacturing takes place (Shi and Kong, 2015). This global economy approach is justified by cost, as manufacturing products are cheaper in the Far East, in countries such as China, whereas designing can be done in Europe or the USA. A manufacturer may have its headquarters in a single country, with most or all of the design work being carried out in the same country. However, various manufacturers from around the world may supply the various standard and specialized parts, as illustrated in

Fig. 1.10. Several car plants in Europe, Asia, and South America may contribute to the manufacturing of a particular car model designed in a central headquarter (Mourtzis et al., 2021). IIoT can help create a more interconnected and collaborative global manufacturing network, enabling greater efficiency, flexibility, and agility in the production process, as partners contribute to manufacturing a product. IIoT enables real-time communication and data exchange among the factories. Sensors can be used to monitor production processes at each factory, providing real-time quality control data, which is analyzed in the cloud by the design team (Williams, 2020). This allows for a seamless flow of information between the different facilities, allowing them to collaborate and coordinate their operations in real-time.

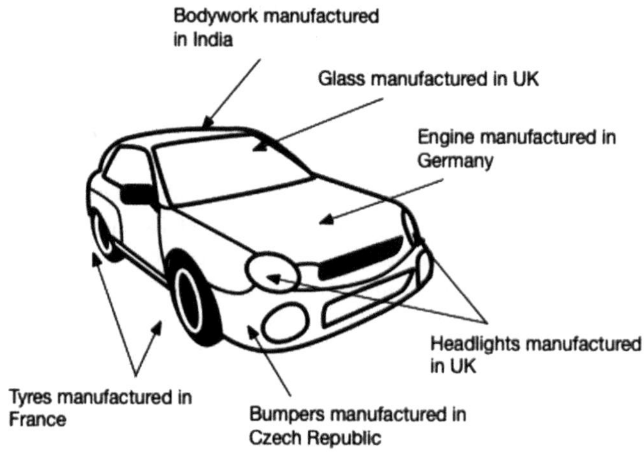

FIGURE 1.10

Remote vehicle manufacturing through an international network.

Interoperability and standardization

IoT devices use typically different communication protocols. For instance, different manufacturers may use different communication protocols in their IoT devices. A unified system that integrates these devices faces interoperability challenges. For example, one IoT device might use the MQTT protocol (Patil et al., 2020) to communicate with other devices, whereas another device might use CoAP (Almheiri and Maamar, 2021). MQTT is a layer over TCP, whereas CoAP works over UDP (see Section 1.1.1).

IoT Cloud can overcome interoperability challenges posed by different IoT communication protocols by providing middleware solutions, which act as a bridge between different communication protocols, enabling devices that use different protocols to communicate with each other. These middleware solutions illustrated earlier in the 5-layer IoT architecture of Fig. 1.1 can also perform protocol translation, transforming data from one protocol to another so that all devices can communicate seamlessly with the cloud (Razzaque et al., 2016).

To illustrate the interoperability issue and the IoT cloud solution, suppose a smart city wants to implement a system for monitoring air quality using IoT devices (Mandava et al., 2018). The smart city has sensors that use MQTT protocol to send data to the cloud, but there are also some sensors that use CoAP protocol. To overcome this interoperability challenge, the IoT cloud platform housed by the smart city supports both protocols and acts as a bridge between the two protocols. The IoT cloud platform processes the data from both protocols and provides a unified view of the air quality data to the city's environmental department. This can be done using a common data format, such as JSON or XML, which are supported by both protocols.

Cost savings

IoT-based solutions can involve various costs, such as the cost of hardware components, connectivity, data storage, security, and maintenance. These costs can be especially high for large-scale IoT deployments. Hardware costs include the cost of sensors, gateways, and other equipment required to connect devices to the network. Communication costs include expenses related to cellular or other communication medium used to transmit data from IoT devices. Additionally, the cost of processing power in cloud or edge computing, can be significant due to the need for scalable infrastructure to process the large volumes of data generated by IoT devices.

IoT devices often require regular maintenance to ensure they are functioning properly, including software updates, firmware upgrades, and hardware repairs or replacements. These maintenance processes can be challenging in large-scale IoT deployments as thousands of devices spread out over a wide geographic area are considered. The cost of hiring and training personnel, monitoring and managing device health, and coordinating repairs or replacements contribute to maintenance requirements. Security maintenance can also contribute significantly to this cost as the vulnerability of IoT devices may be routinely reported, which can compromise the privacy and safety of individuals and organizations. The cost of securing IoT devices includes implementing encryption protocols, securing communication channels, and monitoring and detecting security breaches. Therefore, investing in robust security measures is crucial to mitigating the risk of security breaches and reducing the associated costs. However, implementing in-house and robust security measures can increase the overall cost of IoT deployment.

Besides a reduction in storage costs, the cloud-to-things continuum can provide a range of tools and services to help manage and monitor IoT deployments, reducing the need for expensive in-house expertise (Kalmar and Kertesz, 2017). Finally, cloud-based solutions can also help reduce the upfront costs of hardware and connectivity by providing pay-as-you-go pricing models, such as those offered by Google Cloud IoT and other IoT platform vendors (Muhammed and Ucuz, 2020), which allow organizations to scale their IoT deployments as needed (Femminella et al., 2018).

Security and privacy

IoT devices collect and transmit data, some of which may contain sensitive information. Besides, these devices are often deployed in remote and unsecured locations, making them vulnerable to physical and cyber attacks. Attackers can exploit vulnerabilities in IoT devices to gain access to sensitive information or cause damage to infrastructure (Sahmim and Gharsellaoui, 2017). Since IoT devices are connected to the internet and other devices, they expose potential entry points to cyber attackers.

The cloud-to-things continuum cloud address these security and privacy issues by providing a centralized platform. By consolidating data in the cloud, it is easier to apply security measures and implement policies to protect against unauthorized access, malware, and other cyber threats. The cloud-based security solutions may further include advanced security features, such as encryption, access controls, and firewalls to prevent unauthorized access. In addition, cloud solutions can help to ensure data integrity by providing real-time monitoring and alerting of potential data tampering or anomalies (Belej et al., 2020).

1.1.3 Data flow in the cloud-to-things continuum

As illustrated earlier in Fig. 1.11, the main layers of the cloud-to-things continuum are the IoT layer, the edge layer, and the cloud layer. The IoT layer includes the IoT devices and sensors, which have the smallest processing capacity in the continuum. Next, the edge layer provides devices with higher processing capability and also assumes the role of a gateway to the cloud. Finally, the cloud layer provides the highest processing capacity. Each layer controls the data flow in terms of transmission frequency, volume, and sampling. For example, an edge device may relay data as-it-is to the cloud layer or preprocess it, and sample it further, or even run analytics algorithms to perform edge AI tasks before communicating the outcomes to the cloud layer. Thus data that originates from the IoT layer flows to the cloud via the edge layer in a rate-controlled manner.

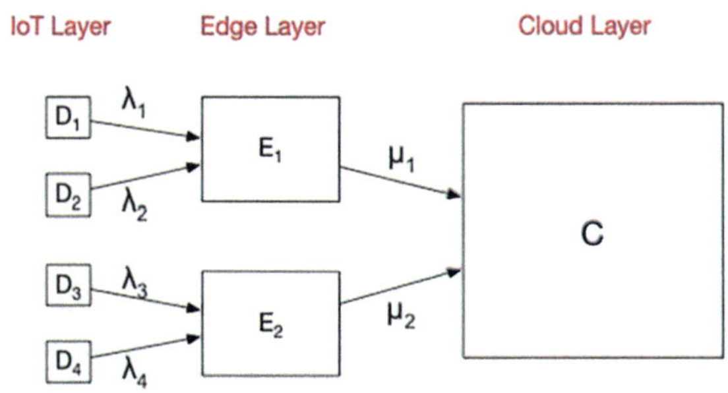

FIGURE 1.11

Data flow in the cloud-to-things continuum (Adapted from (Thekkummal et al., 2020)).

Being central in the data flow architecture, edge devices may send back control commands to IoT layer devices to balance the data load through sensors' transmission frequency configuration. Besides this traffic management role, which enables adaptive data flow schemes between IoT and edge layers, edge devices also enable messaging schemes for cloud servers that include data flows and commands as well

(Thekkummal et al., 2020). This edge-to-cloud interaction presents another level of dynamic flow configuration allowing further control of transmission frequency. Thus transmission includes data and control channels, where control channels convey commands to control flow rates at the edge and IoT layer levels. As part of the connection-establishment process, IoT devices register themselves at the corresponding edge device, thus enabling the data and control channels to be set up. Similarly, edge devices register themselves to designated servers at the cloud layer (Thekkummal et al., 2020).

The control information sent through commands to edge or IoT devices adjusts the data flow rates of the corresponding devices dynamically. The flow control algorithm may be centralized at the cloud level, where a map of the network is modeled as a graph and updated following some vents, such as adding additional IoT devices to an edge device, which can overwhelm the edge device, or a particular IoT device is highly solicited. This coordinated flow mechanism can be deployed to facilitate distributed deep learning algorithms, while reducing traffic (Wang and Wang, 2019).

1.1.4 Harnessing the power of cloud-to-things continuum: opportunities for social welfare, cost savings, and business growth

The continuum of cloud computing to IoT has paved the way for numerous opportunities that can bring significant benefits to society, businesses, and the economy at large. The integration of cloud computing and IoT technologies has given rise to new data sources that are processed in real-time by advanced analytics and machine learning algorithms to drive innovation, streamline operations, and improve decision-making. Next, we will introduce some of the key opportunities that arise from the cloud-to-things continuum, while enabling social welfare, cost savings, and business growth.

Improved efficiency and productivity

Cloud-to-things continuum leads to improved efficiency and productivity by streamlining processes, reducing waste, and automating tasks. With the ability to collect and analyze vast amounts of data from IoT devices, organizations gain insights into their operations to identify inefficiencies and optimize processes. AI and machine learning are subsequently enabled to predict maintenance and reduce downtime. Furthermore, the automation of tasks through the cloud-to-things continuum reduces the likelihood of errors, traditionally induced by human interventions, and frees up the workforce to focus on strategic functions. This work perception contributes to job satisfaction and employee retention.

Finally, the cloud-to-things continuum gives rise to new business models and revenue streams, including the sale of data-related services or the development of other new services based on IoT integration into physical spaces. Organizations are subsequently empowered to remain competitive in their respective industries and increase their level of profitability. As an example of successfully instrumenting the cloud-to-things continuum, consider Amazon's fulfillment centers, where robots utilize IoT sensors to track the movement of goods and optimize the picking and packing process (Girija et al., 2021). Furthermore, stock replenishing uses machine learning algorithms that predict demand and optimize inventory management.

Enhanced decision-making

The cloud-to-things continuum enhances decision-making by enabling organizations to gather and analyze vast amounts of data from IoT devices in real-time. Informed decision-making processes across various industries are subsequently enabled to identify trends, patterns, and insights. In the manufacturing industry, for instance, IoT devices can be used to collect data on machine performance, maintenance, and production efficiency. Using cloud services and predictive modeling, areas for improvement are identified to optimize production processes and reduce downtime. In the healthcare industry, IoT devices collect patient vitals data, medication adherence, and lifestyle behaviors to identify health risks and provide personalized treatment recommendations. The cloud-to-things continuum gathers and analyzes data from a wide range of sources, which are combined into a more comprehensive view of the operations and customers of a given organization, to empower them with informed decisions.

Enhanced customer experience

Cloud-to-things continuum enables businesses to create more personalized and responsive customer experiences, leading to increased customer satisfaction and loyalty. With the cloud-to-things continuum, businesses collect and analyze large amounts of data from various sources, including customer interactions, social media, and IoT devices. Advanced analytics and machine learning algorithms, give businesses an edge to discover customer preferences, and behavior patterns, and anticipate needs to provide personalized recommendations and services in real-time. A better understanding of customers increases customer satisfaction and loyalty. In doing so, a retail store that uses IoT devices to collect data on customer usage patterns can subsequently offer personalized recommendations and promotions to individual customers. For example, if the data analysis indicates that a user frequently uses their connected speaker to listen to music, the organization could send the user personalized recommendations for upcoming related concerts and sell tickets.

New revenue streams

The cloud-to-things continuum creates new revenue streams by enabling businesses to develop and offer innovative products and services. For example, a company that manufactures fitness trackers uses collected data from these devices to identify trends in customer behavior and preferences to develop new fitness programs or personalized coaching services. In another example, a smart home security company uses data from its connected security devices to offer personalized home insurance policies based on individual home security profiles. Additionally, by leveraging cloud-based services, businesses may further monetize collected IoT data through third-party partners for analytics and insights, or through data-driven marketing campaigns.

Novel innovative business models enabled by the cloud-to-things continuum may include subscription-based services, where customers pay for ongoing access to connected devices and their associated services, rather than a one-time purchase. This business model leads to more stable and predictable revenue streams for the company. Furthermore, customer behavior and preferences data can be used to create more targeted and personalized marketing campaigns. For example, a company that manufactures connected fitness equipment may, in addition, create personalized workout plans for its customers and offer ongoing virtual coaching services.

Lowered operational costs

The cloud-to-things continuum can significantly lower operational costs for businesses by enabling real-time monitoring and control of processes and optimizing resource allocation. IoT devices and sensors connected to cloud services deliver performance metrics, usage patterns, and potential anomalies in real-time, so businesses react quickly to address inefficiencies. Routine tasks are streamlined via the cloud-to-things continuum, enabling businesses to focus on higher-value strategic activities.

To illustrate this gain in operation costs, consider the case of Coca-Cola Bottling Company Consolidated (CCBCC) which is one of the largest Coca-Cola bottlers with over 16,000 employees and 13 production facilities. Operational efficiency is increased and costs are reduced through an IoT solution, which connected their vending machines to the cloud. The vending machines are equipped with IoT sensors that collect data on inventory levels and sales. This data is transmitted to the cloud, to be further processed and analyzed in real-time, enabling a timely restocking schedule of the vending machine, and improving the overall customer experience. CCBCC reduced operational costs by 28% as a result of IoT deployment. Additionally, by leveraging the data collected from the IoT sensors, CCBCC was able to develop new revenue streams by offering personalized promotions and discounts to customers based on their purchasing history.

Collaboration and innovation

The cloud-to-things continuum enables collaboration and innovation by bringing together diverse stakeholders, such as designers, developers, data scientists, and business analysts, to work on IoT deployment projects. This collaboration leads to innovative and practical solutions that meet specific business needs. Consider a company that produces smart home devices and collaborates with designers to create new products that meet the needs and preferences of their customers. The company collaborates with developers of applications for users to control their connected devices from their mobile phones. The company also collaborates with data scientists to discover devices' usage and patterns for product improvement. Finally, business analysts focus on the economic impact of the product to recommend pricing and marketing strategies.

The multitude of intervening stakeholders in the product development and improvement workflow makes room for greater innovation opportunities. By connecting devices to the cloud, data is shared and analyzed by different stakeholders, which breaks down data silos and provide a more comprehensive understanding of complex processes. The cloud-to-things continuum stimulates collaboration on projects by providing a platform for stakeholders to work together on common goals. This platform fosters a culture of innovation and experimentation, as stakeholders bring different perspectives and ideas to the table.

Addressing societal challenges

The cloud-to-things continuum has the potential to address a variety of societal challenges. The continuum enables innovative solutions that improve the quality of life for individuals and communities. In healthcare domains, IoT devices and cloud analytics enable remote patient monitoring, personalized treatments, and early disease detection, leading to improved health outcomes and reduced healthcare costs. For example, anticipating dementia by predicting related patterns can delay the disease through medication, which can be effective only with early symptom detection. Dementia prediction using unobtrusive IoT devices for monitoring the physical activities of elderly people can be achieved through motion sensors combined with data analytics based on cloud-based deep learning processing (Kim et al., 2022).

In connected transportation domains, vehicles and infrastructure share data to improve traffic flow, reduce congestion and carbon emissions, and further enhance road safety for all. In energy contexts, the smart grid reacts to changes in electricity usage in real-time to maintain a balance between power generation and consumption. The cloud-to-things continuum contributes to this response, to changes in energy demand and supply, to adapting to changing conditions, and ensuring efficient energy distribution. Cities as a whole are achieving a great level of efficiency and sustainability, and livability for citizens with the deployment of the cloud-to-things continuum is steadily advancing: traffic congestion is reduced in urban cores using a combination of traffic sensors and intelligent traffic management systems, and smart lighting systems save energy and enhance public safety. Garbage collection is optimized with the use of smart connected bins and water leaks are promptly detected (Maamar et al., 2019).

Smart agriculture uses IoT devices, such as sensors, drones, and satellite imagery to monitor crops, soil moisture, and weather conditions in real-time. Farmers are empowered to optimize water usage and minimize pesticide and fertilizer impact to improve crop yields. Soil moisture sensors and weather station data, including temperature, rainfall, and humidity, are transmitted to cloud-based analytics platforms, which can provide farmers with real-time insights into crop health, irrigation schedule, and other factors that affect crop growth.

1.2 Technical challenges of cloud-to-things continuum

1.2.1 Connectivity challenges: interoperability, standards, and protocols

The large number of devices and platforms in the IoT ecosystem raises significant interoperability challenges between different devices and networks is a significant challenge. The lack of standardized protocols and data formats exacerbates the complexity of data exchange between devices. Interoperability is defined as the ability of different IoT devices to communicate and exchange data with each other and with edge and cloud platforms, despite differences in hardware, application software, and communication protocols. Interoperability is crucial to ensure seamless connectivity between various devices across the cloud-to-things continuum layers, including edge and cloud platforms. Standards and protocols ensure data can be exchanged and understood across different devices of the continuum, regardless of their origins or configurations.

However, the lack of standardization is a significant barrier to interoperability. This challenge is especially relevant when dealing with legacy devices that may use proprietary communication protocols or when integrating multiple IoT devices from different vendors. To overcome these challenges, standardization bodies, such as IEEE, IETF, and W3C, are working towards creating standard protocols and data formats to enable seamless communication between IoT devices, edge, and cloud systems. The development of 5G networks and the expansion of LPWAN networks, such as LoRaWAN and Sigfox, are also addressing the connectivity challenges by providing reliable, low-power, and long-range communication networks for IoT devices. LPWAN refers to low-power wide-area networks and includes technologies such as LoRaWAN, Sigfox, and NB-IoT.

LoRaWAN stands for long range wide area network and is a communication protocol with the ability to support low data rates, long battery life, and long-range communication, even in dense urban environments. It is designed to enable the deployment of large-scale IoT networks, making it a popular choice for smart city applications and other IoT use cases. As illustrated in Fig. 1.12, LoRaWAN uses a star-of-stars topology, where multiple end nodes communicate with a central gateway, allowing scalable deployment and easy management. Additionally, LoRaWAN is an open standard, enabling interoperability between different vendors' devices and gateways.

Typically, LoRaWAN (and LPWAN networks at large) provides low-cost and low-rate connectivity to support simultaneously a large number of constrained devices (such as power consumption and processing capabilities). LoRa is the physical layer process that provides a low-power modulation technique over a communication link to transmit digital signals) as binary bits. End devices and receiving gateways are equipped with LoRa modules, which are devices that deliver connectivity via radio signals. The gateways use standard Ethernet/WiFi infrastructures or mobile internet (4G/5G) networks to reach a network server that filters out duplicate packets from gateways and implements security checks.

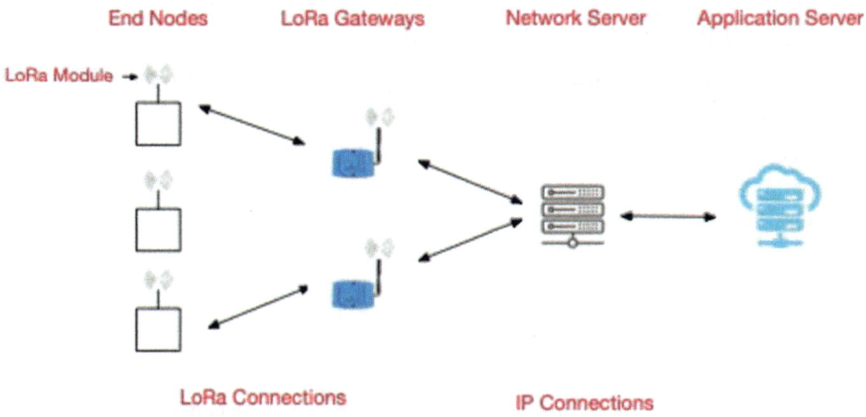

FIGURE 1.12

LoRaWAN architecture.

The network server generates packets intended for an application server and sends them to the corresponding application server. Thus LoRa modules deliver low-level, point-to-point connections between two such modules. LoRaWAN on the other hand uses the gateway that enables Internet-scale connection to extend end-nodes' visibility. Note that as part of LoRaWAN architecture, end nodes are associated with a dedicated gateway, which receives LoRa node signals and transmits them to cloud-based network servers. Note also that LoRa nodes may belong to three different classes A, B, and C, where class A represents the most energy-efficient nodes (may have years of battery life) transmitting only when necessary, whereas class C nodes maintain a continuous transmission window.

1.2.2 Security challenges: authentication, authorization, and data privacy

The basic security and privacy requirement of the cloud-to-things continuum is to ensure that the data transmitted between end devices, edge, and cloud servers are secure, private, and protected from unauthorized access or exploitation. Security mechanisms include secure communication channels and access control. Two techniques are used to provide secure communication channels, namely encryption and authentication. Encryption prevents unauthorized IoT data access and integrity breaches. Authentication, on the other hand, verifies the identity of both the device and the user accessing it. Access control determines what level of access is granted to users of IoT devices based on their identity, role, and preassigned permissions. Role-based access control (RBAC) refers to roles and permissions for users and authorized devices to limit access to sensitive IoT data and functions.

The above security mechanisms are implemented at every layer to ensure a holistic approach to protecting the cloud-to-things continuum. This includes security measures at the device, edge, and cloud layers. At the device layer, the above security mechanisms may be implemented, including encryption of data at rest and in transit, as well as secure boot to ensure only authorized firmware is loaded. Additionally, devices may implement secure enclave hardware, such as a trusted platform module (TPM). TPM technology is designed to provide hardware-level security (Tomlinson, 2017).

At the edge layer, security measures may include implementing firewalls, intrusion detection, and access control mechanisms. Edge devices should also have the ability to perform local analysis of data and enforce security policies, such as data filtering or blocking, before sending the data to the cloud. Thus edge layer may include firewalls to monitor incoming and outgoing traffic and prevent unauthorized access to edge device functions. Similarly, intrusion detection mechanisms prevent malicious activities, such as malware, denial of service attacks, and data filtration. Finally, locks and access controls can prevent unauthorized physical access to edge devices. For example, an edge device can be locked in a secure cabinet or room with access limited to authorized personnel only. Remote users require authorized access to edge devices as well. This access authorization is enforced through usernames and passwords, two-factor authentication, or biometric authentication.

At the cloud layer, security measures may include implementing identity and access management, data at rest and in transit encryption, and enforcing security policies for data access and usage. Additionally, cloud providers may also implement penetration testing, and security audits, and monitor security incidents via security information and event management (SIEM) systems. SIEM supports organizations to detect, analyze, and respond to security threats before infiltrating business operations. In doing so, SIEM collects logs of cloud storage, while performing a rapid security compliance analysis. This cloud vendor-manufactured platform automates security analytics and incident detection through comprehensive monitoring of event logs and real-time alerts.

The cloud-to-things continuum requires additional end-to-end considerations related to data privacy, even if the above security mechanisms are covered. Privacy concerns arise when personal data is collected, transmitted, and stored by IoT devices and related cloud services. In this context, privacy refers to the control and protection of personal information, such as personal health records. To address these privacy concerns over the cloud-to-things continuum may incorporate various techniques. Data minimization limits the amount of needed data collected from IoT devices to the necessary size to achieve the intended specific purpose. Data is subsequently anonymized or deleted, as long as it is not necessary. These techniques limit the collection and use of personal data to only what is necessary; this is to prevent the disclosure of personal data; combined with security access controls, they ensure that access to personal data is restricted to authorized parties only. By minimizing the amount of collected and retained data, the risk of data breaches and unauthorized access is reduced, and individuals' privacy rights are better protected. Therefore the cloud-to-things continuum needs to implement these additional privacy measures to protect personal data and maintain user trust.

As for security mechanisms, the above privacy-preserving techniques are applied at each layer of the cloud-to-things continuum. At the device layer, data minimization can involve reducing the amount of data that is collected or stored by the device, for example, sensors capture necessary information only or implement filtering mechanisms that eliminate irrelevant data. At the edge layer, data minimization involves processing data locally and only sending relevant information to the cloud, which reduces the amount of data that is transmitted and stored. At the cloud layer, data retention policies ensure that data is stored for as long as it is necessary only, and subsequently deleted once it is no longer needed.

Further privacy-preserving techniques may involve data masking at the device layer, besides anonymization, or pseudonymization (i.e., the identity of a subject is replaced by pseudonyms). And at the edge layer, privacy-preserving techniques may apply differential privacy which aggregates data in a way that protects individual privacy. And finally, at the cloud layer, data encryption and secure data storage further protect sensitive data.

1.2.3 Scalability challenges: handling massive amounts of data generated by IoT devices

The massive amounts of data generated by IoT devices can present scalability challenges for the cloud-to-things continuum. As the number of IoT devices and sensors increases, so does the generated data. Challenges include storage, processing, and analysis of this data, in addition to their transmission over long distances, leading to latency and bandwidth issues.

Scalability in the cloud-to-things continuum architecture combines vertical and horizontal scaling techniques. Vertical scaling involves adding resources to a single device or node in the architecture, such as expanding the memory or processing power of an edge node. This can increase the capacity and processing power of a device, but it may not be sufficient to handle the massive amounts of data generated by IoT devices.

Horizontal scaling involves adding nodes to the architecture layers, such as adding more edge devices, to distribute the workload across multiple edge devices. A larger volume of data and requests can thus be accommodated to improve the continuum's overall availability and fault tolerance. Cloud providers can leverage their ability to scale horizontally by deploying new edge devices or increasing their cloud capacity as the number of IoT devices in use increases. Furthermore, edge devices include built-in scalability features to automatically provision the services of new edge devices based on workload demands.

Further to vertical and horizontal scaling capabilities of the cloud-to-things continuum, cloud providers utilize other techniques, such as load balancing, caching, and content delivery networks (CDNs) to accommodate IoT devices' data. Load-balancing employs specialized devices or software to ensure that no single server becomes overwhelmed with traffic and becomes a bottleneck for the entire continuum. These "Load Balancers" are configured to distribute traffic evenly across all available servers, or can be set up to prioritize certain servers over others based on factors such as server health, geographic location, or other criteria (Chhabra and Singh, 2022).

Finally, auto-scaling is a technique that automatically provisions the required number of server instances based on changes in the demand (Verma and Bala, 2021). When the traffic increases, auto-scaling automatically adjusts additional server instances to handle the increased load. When traffic decreases, the extra instances are relinquished to save on costs. Auto-scaling can be implemented at various layers of the cloud-to-things continuum: from the device to the edge to the cloud. At the device level, auto-scaling can adjust the frequency of data transmissions based on the device's available resources and the current network conditions. At the edge level, auto-scaling can provision edge resources dynamically to handle increased traffic from devices. And at the cloud level, auto-scaling can allocate more computing resources to the data processing and storage systems as demand increases (i.e., on-demand horizontal scaling).

1.3 From connected devices to connected business: how cloud-to-things is enabling digital transformation?

The cloud-to-things continuum is revolutionizing the way businesses operate by connecting devices, data, and processes across the entire value chain. This convergence between physical and cyberspace enables companies to digitize their operations and transform their business models. Today's fast-paced digital landscape is prompting organizations across various industries to embrace digital transformation to change customer needs, improve operational efficiencies, and create new revenue streams. Digital transformation subscribes to the latest technology advances to fundamentally change the way a business operates, interacts with customers, and delivers value. The cloud-to-things continuum is paving the way for a new paradigm in digital transformation.

1.3.1 Digital transformation: why it matters and how cloud-to-things continuum can help?

The cloud-to-things continuum enables an organization to achieve digital transformation by deriving actionable insights that can drive business innovation and growth. The seamless flow of data across the various layers of the continuum architecture enables new gains and invaluable insights into the operations, customers, and markets of an organization.

For example, a hypothetical manufacturing company employs the cloud-to-things continuum to collect data from sensors about their production line, which could then be analyzed in real-time using machine learning algorithms to uproot inefficiencies and potential areas for optimization. Besides, the continuum provides new opportunities for revenue generation, whereby the same manufacturing company utilizes collected data from their production line to develop new services or products that address customer needs. These data-driven decisions develop innovative new products and services that drive growth.

With real-time data and insights at their fingertips, organizations can respond quickly to changes in the market and stay ahead of the competition. For example, a retailer instruments data from IoT sensors in their stores to optimize product placement and pricing, while a manufacturer uses real-time data from connected machines to improve production efficiency and reduce downtime.

For example, a hypothetical manufacturing company employs the cloud-to-things continuum to collect data from sensors about their production line, which could then be analyzed in real-time using machine learning algorithms to uproot inefficiencies and potential areas for optimization. Besides, the continuum provides new opportunities for revenue generation, whereby the same manufacturing company utilizes collected data from their production line to develop new services or products that address customer needs. These data-driven decisions develop innovative new products and services that drive growth.

With real-time data and insights at their fingertips, organizations can respond quickly to changes in the market and stay ahead of the competition. Two examples in this regard: a) a retailer uses data from IoT sensors in their stores to optimize product placement and pricing; b) a manufacturer uses real-time data from connected machines to improve production efficiency and reduce downtime.

In terms of innovation, consider a smart home security company that uses data from connected cameras and sensors to offer personalized security recommendations to customers, while a logistics company could use IoT devices and cloud analytics to optimize supply chain operations and reduce delivery times. In societal domains, such technologies can improve patient outcomes and reduce healthcare costs. Additionally, the continuum facilitates smart energy management, reduces waste and pollution, and enables sustainable urban planning, all of which contribute to environmental sustainability.

As an example of how the continuum enables digital transformation in urban planning, consider traffic sensors and cameras in connected transportation areas. Traffic flow patterns inferred from collected data contribute to planning urban cores to optimize traffic routes and reduce congestion. Similarly, air quality sensors provide real-time data on pollution levels, allowing city planners to make informed decisions about urban development and transportation as well. Successful deployments are already underway. Singapore has implemented a smart city project called "Smart Nation," which leverages cloud-to-things continuum technology to improve urban planning, transportation, healthcare, and education. The project includes initiatives such as a nationwide sensor network, smart traffic lights, and a mobile app for citizens to access government services (Ng, 2018). Smart waste management is another societal example that uses IoT sensors in waste containers to optimize garbage collection routes, reducing fuel consumption, and saving the city money. The data collected from the sensors is transmitted to the cloud, where it is analyzed to provide insights into waste management operations (Sosunova and Porras, 2022).

1.3.2 Harnessing the synergy of IoT and cloud computing to drive digital transformation

The integration of digital technologies into the physical space of organizations will fundamentally change how they operate and deliver value to customers. A shift in the organization's culture, processes, and strategies will create new capabilities and opportunities for digital transformation. IoT devices generate vast amounts of data that provide visibility into different aspects of an organization's operations, enabling better decision-making. Traditional data sources, on the other hand, typically come from a limited number of sources and are not as comprehensive as IoT data. This process is further supported by AI-based analytics provided by the power of cloud computing, which can store and process the large volume of data generated by IoT devices.

Furthermore, the combination of IoT and cloud computing enables new "as-a-service" business models, allowing a multitude of things "as-a-service" models. For example, a company may integrate IoT sensors to monitor the usage of its products and services, which are then advertised on a subscription basis. Cloud-based services manage the subscription model by tracking usage and providing billing and invoicing services. "Lighting as a Service" is an emerging trend provided by companies such as GE and Philips lighting industries. This transformation from commodity lamp supplier to strategic lighting partner allows lighting companies to provide smart lighting solutions to organizations' customers as a service, eliminating the need for customers to invest in and/or wonder about building their lighting infrastructure. This is a shift from the time when lamps are purchased routinely as a commodity to replacing existing ones as part of maintenance services. The cost induced by this replacement also adds up to the organization's operational expenditure. Instead, lighting is deployed with Internet connectivity in smart buildings and commercial areas on a subscription fee basis.

Transportation as a service is already widely adopted. However, the advent of autonomous vehicles and shared mobility will further increase the prospects of this business model to allow advanced fleet management: Cloud and IoT technologies allow fleet managers to optimize routing, scheduling, and maintenance of their vehicles more efficiently. This also enables the en route monitoring of goods such as food or medicine, thereby avoiding returns, wastage, or damage, in addition to increasing customer satisfaction. Personalized travel experiences, such as customized routes based on travelers' preferences and traffic conditions, are enabled. Finally, the synergy between cloud and IoT is crucial for the development of autonomous vehicles, which can significantly reduce human error and make transportation safer, faster, and more efficient.

1.3.3 IoT and cloud computing: key enablers for business agility and competitive advantage

IoT enables businesses to gather vast amounts of real-time data from sensors, devices, and machines, allowing them to gain greater visibility and distribution of their operations. Data is valuable only if it can be processed timely, which is leveraged by cloud computing scalability, flexibility, and cost-effectiveness. This processing speed allows businesses to quickly respond to changing market conditions and customer needs. Thus the cloud-to-things continuum empowers businesses to be more agile, innovative, and competitive, while driving growth and profitability in an increasingly digital world.

Examples of enabled business agility can be illustrated with smart inventory management. IoT-enabled sensors track inventory levels in real-time and automatically trigger replenishment when stock runs low. This reduces the risk of stock outages and ensures that businesses always have the products they need to fulfill customer orders. Data unleashed from IoT devices can be further turned into personalized marketing opportunities by gaining insights into customer behavior and preferences. Businesses develop targeted and personalized marketing campaigns, where, for example, customers equipped with a smartwatch get personalized recommendations when approaching a product. The smartwatch could communicate with the store's IoT sensors to determine which items are being viewed and utilizes the store's AI-powered recommendation engine to provide real-time suggestions, such as complimentary items or deals on similar products.

1.3.4 Real life applications

The cloud-to-things continuum is fundamentally transforming a wide array of real-life applications by bridging the gap between cloud, edge and IoT devices.

How cloud-to-things continuum is revolutionizing smart manufacturing?

The cloud-to-things continuum connects every aspect of the manufacturing process, from raw materials to the final product, through a network of intelligent devices and sensors. Manufacturers get complete visibility and control over their production process. IoT sensors collect data on machine performance, which feed machine learning algorithms in the cloud to predict maintenance schedules proactively.

Industry 4.0 facilitates cloud manufacturing, whereby machine operators are physically separated from machinery environments prompting decentralization, while events are tracked through sensors. The resulting data assist remote operators in making decisions that involve machines and physical processes in factories along the cloud-to-things continuum. This remote monitoring approach physically separates the machine location from the operator's location over a network that spans a wide geographical area. This network streamlines cooperation among intervening actors.

For example, a manufacturer of industrial equipment offers their machines as a service, where remote customers pay for the usage of the equipment on a per-hour or per-product basis. Machines' sensors enable usage monitoring and performance remotely through the continuum's cloud infrastructure. Customers benefit from reduced capital investment, increased flexibility, and the assurance of reliable machine performance. The manufacturer, on the other hand, benefits from a recurring revenue stream and increased customer loyalty.

The cloud-to-things continuum enables digital twins that create a virtual replica of a physical product, process, or system. The digital twin allows manufacturers to monitor, analyze, and optimize the performance of their machines and equipment in real-time. IoT devices collect data on the physical system for the digital twin to simulate various scenarios and provide improvement indicators for the manufacturing process. For example, a digital twin of a machine can provide real-time performance data, such as temperature, pressure, and vibration levels, which can be used to predict maintenance schedules. The digital twin may also be used to simulate different operating conditions to optimize the machine's performance and reduce downtime. Digital twins can also improve product design by simulating the behavior of a product in different environments and conditions. This allows manufacturers to identify potential issues early in the design process and make changes before the product is sent to production. This opportunity reduces reducing the risk of costly recalls or failures after deployment.

Connected healthcare and personalized medicine: enabling a new era of patient-centred care with IoT and cloud computing

Connected healthcare and personalized medicine are transforming the healthcare industry by shifting the focus away from the one-size-fits-all approach to a more patient-centered approach. IoT and cloud computing have generated new opportunities for healthcare providers. Patients' health is remotely monitored through real-time access to their health data, and personalized treatment plans. This customized care is based on individual patients' unique characteristics, medical history, and current health status. The increasing availability of health data leverages cloud-based analytics and AI-based comparisons to derive diagnosis and treatment plans that support healthcare providers in improving patients' health.

Wearable devices and related healthcare sensors are widely available to track vital signs and other health-related data in real-time. This data is sent to the cloud, where storage and processing handle the vast amounts of data streams generated by these devices, to analyze and extract meaningful insights. Cloud-based services use machine learning algorithms, which are trained on large datasets to identify patterns and make predictions about patients' health and support professionals with treatment plans. This approach to healthcare opens new ways of delivering healthcare services, which are more patient-centric, cost-effective, and efficient, as abnormalities are detected early, and timely interventions reduce the prospects of further treatment and care, which also saves on time and cost. Remote monitoring can be especially useful for patients with chronic conditions, who require regular monitoring and medication management. AI and ML algorithms can identify patterns and trends that would be impossible for humans to detect. However, these algorithms require data that the cloud-to-things continuum provides to support the development of treatment plans that are tailored to the individual patient's needs.

IoT devices can collect data on various healthcare parameters: from heart rate and blood pressure to sleep patterns and physical activity levels. This information is combined with the unique needs and lifestyles of patients to predict personalized treatments. The continued growth of telemedicine will allow patients to receive medical care remotely, reducing the need for in-person visits and allowing patients to receive care from the comfort of their own homes.

The recent evolution in connected medication, also known as smart pills or digital pills, is emerging in the healthcare industry as a promising technology, which assists patients to adhere to their medication plan and provide healthcare professionals with real-time data on patients' medication intake. These pills contain tiny sensors that are activated by stomach acid when ingested and transmit data to a wearable device or a mobile app. This data includes information such as when the medication was taken, the dosage, and the patient's heart rate, activity levels, and sleep patterns.

The use of connected medication can have several benefits. Firstly, it can improve medication adherence, which is a critical issue in healthcare. According to the World Health Organization, medication non-adherence can lead to poor health outcomes, increased hospitalizations, and higher healthcare costs (Brown and Bussell, 2011). Connected medication can send reminders to patients when it's time to take their medication, and can also notify healthcare professionals if a patient misses a dose. Another benefit of connected medication is that it can provide healthcare professionals with real-time data on patients' medication effects to adjust them as needed. For example, if a patient seems not to be responding to a particular medication, healthcare professionals can use the data to determine if the patient is taking the medication as prescribed or modifying the dosage.

Connected vehicles: transforming mobility with IoT and cloud computing

Current trends shaping next-generation driver support systems combine onboard sensors and connected surroundings' data to anticipate potential hazards and provide real-time feedback to drivers. These systems are intended to enhance the driver's situational awareness, provide alerts when necessary, and automate certain aspects of driving to reduce the risk of accidents and improve the overall driving experience. Collected data is shared in real-time via the cloud to connected road users and infrastructure. The outcomes of analyzed data feed vehicle-to-vehicle (V2V) communications to alert drivers about the behavior of other drivers, pedestrians, or cyclists, as well as vehicle-to-infrastructure (V2I) communications to notify drivers about road conditions, allowing route and speed adjustments.

An illustration of a cloud architecture that drives connectivity is shown in Fig. 1.13. Modern vehicles have access to greater computing power, which enables them to support a wide range of in-vehicle applications. However, new requirements are emerging, such as the need for novel driving support capabilities, dynamic traffic guidance, personalized human-vehicle interaction, and augmented reality (AR), which rely on powerful computing capabilities, massive data storage, fast data transfer and processing, and low latency for quick decision-making. Recent research proposes task offloading along vehicular and infrastructure edge nodes by creating resources that are typically operated in the central cloud platform. V2X communication technologies propelled by ultra-low latency and ultra-high reliability 5G networks are allowing different kinds of edge applications with little impact on security and data privacy.

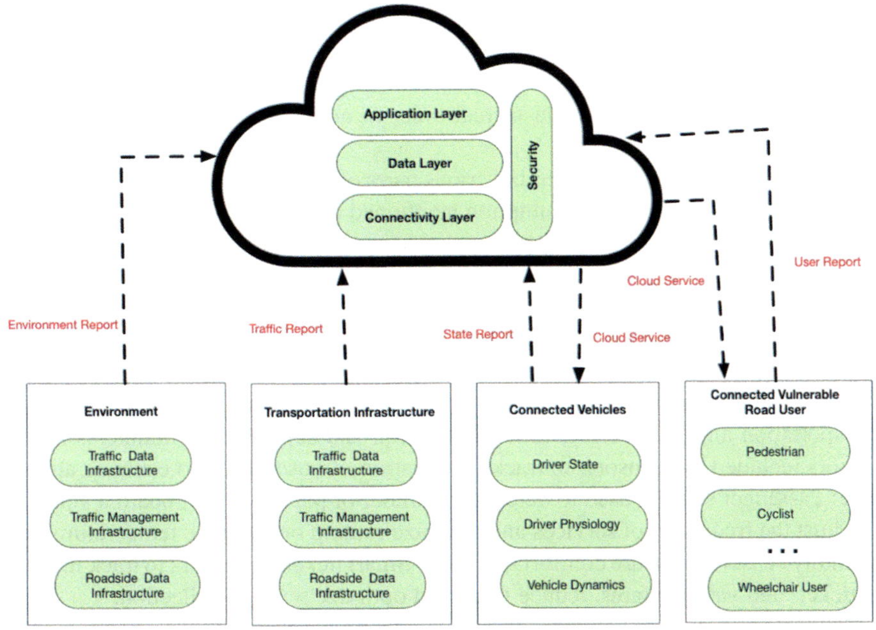

FIGURE 1.13

Cloud-based architecture for connected vehicles (Adapted from (SAMPATH, 2022)).

As the number of connected vehicles increases dramatically in the next decade with an increasing amount of data, a cloud-based platform is a viable option (SAMPATH, 2022). The bottom connectivity layer provides infrastructure as a service (IaaS) in the form of virtual servers designed to support different communication protocols. The middle data layer correlates multiple sources of data into a common platform as a service (PaaS) repository, whereas the top layer enables software as a service (SaaS) applications. Use cases of these services include data upload from the environment, transportation infrastructure or connected vehicles, and vulnerable road user domains. Other use cases include access to machine learning-based predictions, which enable proactive safety measures.

Smart cities: improving urban living and sustainability with IoT and cloud computing

Smart cities vision has gained significant attention in recent years, as many cities around the world are implementing a range of initiatives to empower citizens with improved urban living spaces with greater efficiency and sustainability indicators. These initiatives facilitate the cloud-to-things continuum as the backbone driver for gathering real-time data on a wide range of city indicators, such as traffic flow, air quality, and energy consumption. Subsequently, this information is used to optimize services and infrastructure, which lead to higher levels of resource efficiency, reduced environmental impact, and improved quality of life for citizens. The cloud-to-things continuum facilitates informed decisions and improves city services; the latter allows citizens to further thrive in smart cities by allowing the collection, processing, and analysis of vast amounts of data in real-time, to automate a range of community functions.

IoT sensors are being installed in various parts of smart cities to monitor air quality, traffic flow, and energy consumption mentioned earlier. But also noise sensors to measure noise pollution levels, water quality sensors to monitor the quality of water in rivers and lakes, and waste management sensors to monitor the levels of waste in containers and optimize waste collection schedules. Smart parking sensors are also installed to guide drivers to available parking spots, while smart lighting sensors are helping smart cities to optimize street lighting and reduce energy consumption. Furthermore, smart transportation systems are instrumenting sensors to manage public transportation and provide real-time information and support to commuters. These sensors include GPS sensors: to track the location of buses, used to estimate arrival time; Passenger sensors used to detect the number of passengers on board a vehicle, to adjust the frequency of services and optimize routing on demand; temperature and humidity sensors to ensure comfortable rides; Smart ticketing sensors to track the use of tickets and variable fares, reduce fraud and optimize revenue collection.

The integration of IoT sensors and cloud computing in smart cities makes it possible to track food from farm to table (Misra et al., 2022). Farmers use IoT sensors to monitor crop growth, soil moisture, and other environmental factors to optimize crop yields and reduce waste. Similarly, food suppliers and distributors ensure the quality and safety of the products during transportation and storage using an array of food freshness sensors. Grocery stores and restaurants monitor automatically food stock levels, expiration dates, and environmental factors that reduce waste and ensure the freshness of their products. Cloud services offered by the cloud-to-things continuum are used to enable data-driven strategies that promote efficiency, sustainability, and safety in the food industry.

Barcelona is considered as a pioneer smart city due to its innovative approach and successful implementation of various smart city projects since 2012. Its extensive use of technology to improve various aspects of urban life, including transportation, energy efficiency, waste management, and public safety has been acknowledged by several awards (Bibri and Krogstie, 2020). For example, Barcelona has implemented a bike-sharing program with thousands of bikes and hundreds of stations, as well as a smart bus system that instruments real-time data to optimize routes and schedules. In the bike-sharing project, bikes are equipped with a GPS device and sensors used to track traveled distances and bikes' condition. This data is then transmitted to a central system via wireless networks and cloud computing, to monitor the availability of bikes at different locations in real-time. Users access this data through mobile apps or websites to find available bikes and plan their routes accordingly. IoT is used to optimize bike usage, reduce the need for maintenance and repairs, and provide a more convenient and eco-friendly transportation option for citizens. The same experience has been replicated later with scooters, which were further optimized with strategic locations of charging stations. The project was called "eCooltra" which evolved into a company that provides electric scooter-sharing services in several European cities, including Barcelona. Users to rent electric scooters using a mobile application and the scooters' IoT sensors which are connected to the cloud, allow users to locate and unlock them using their smartphones.

Amsterdam is another city model that uses IoT sensors to implement several mobility services including shared electrical vehicles, and smart traffic management systems. The shared electric vehicle project called "We Drive Solar" uses IoT and cloud technologies to reduce emissions and promote sustainable transportation. A fleet of electric vehicles that are connected to the cloud and can be accessed through a mobile app has been deployed. The vehicles are equipped with sensors that provide the location, battery level, and vehicle usage. The data is further analyzed to optimize vehicle availability and charging infrastructure. The project has also innovated a smart charging solution that utilizes off-peak-hour prices. The project has been successful in reducing carbon emissions and increasing the adoption of sustainable transportation options in Amsterdam.

The city-state of Singapore has implemented an extensive network of sensors and cameras throughout the city to monitor traffic flow and adjust traffic lights dynamically to improve traffic management. In addition, Singapore has launched several sustainability initiatives, such as its "Zero Waste" campaign to incite recycling (Kerdlap et al., 2019). Singapore has implemented a smart waste tracking system that instruments RFID tags to track waste from its point of origin to its final disposal. This National Environment Agency (NEA) initiated project enables real-time monitoring of waste volumes and helps to identify areas where waste reduction efforts could be targeted. A mobile app that allows users to report littering and illegal dumping has also been deployed to leverage crowdsourcing for the cleanliness of public spaces.

Copenhagen is often regarded as a smart city for its ambitious goal to become carbon-neutral by 2025, and several innovative initiatives have been implemented initiatives to achieve this goal. For example, Copenhagen's advanced district heating system uses waste heat from power plants and other sources to heat residential homes and buildings throughout the city. The municipality of Copenhagen established a wireless parking sensor system to enable car drivers to find vacant parking spaces using their smartphones.

We can expect to see several future trends in Smart City development. These trends include self-driving vehicles becoming more prevalent in cities around the world. We can also expect more advanced smart grid technologies that leverage IoT sensors to predict demand and adjust supply accordingly. Smart cities will continue to invest in cloud-to-things-related technologies to enhance public safety, such as surveillance cameras, gunshot detection systems, and emergency response systems. Air pollution is a major concern for which smart cities will continue to integrate IoT sensors that monitor air pollution levels. Renewable energy sources are expected to expand further with the integration of IoT sensors and cloud computing systems. The cloud-to-things continuum enables the combination of renewable energy sources with other IoT-based implementations such as smart buildings and electric vehicles. For example, electric vehicles can be guided to renewable energy sources such as charging stations, and their batteries can even be used to store excess energy produced by those renewable sources.

1.4 Business challenges of cloud-to-things continuum

As the cloud-to-things Continuum gains prominence in various industries, organizations are encountering a set of unique challenges that must be addressed to fully leverage its potential. In this section, we will delve into the key business challenges associated with this transformative paradigm. From data ownership and governance issues to organizational silos, barriers to cloud adoption, and legal and regulatory hurdles, we will explore the complexities that organizations face in harnessing the power of the Cloud-to-Things Continuum. By understanding and effectively addressing these challenges, businesses can unlock the full benefits of this innovative framework and propel their digital transformation journey forward. Next, we delve into each of these challenges and explore strategies to overcome them.

1.4.1 Data ownership and governance issues in the IoT and cloud era

In the IoT and cloud computing landscapes, data ownership becomes a complex issue due to the distributed nature of data collection and storage. Traditional approaches to data ownership are challenged by the multitude of intervening sources, spanning IoT devices, sensors, and cloud platforms. One of the complexities lies in determining who owns the data generated by IoT devices. In many cases, multiple stakeholders may be involved, including device manufacturers, service providers, and end-users. Each stakeholder may have different rights and interests in the data, leading to potential conflicts. Besides, data ownership can be geared toward contractual agreements and service terms. Within this context, users often agree to terms and conditions that grant certain rights to the service or platform providers, which may impact data ownership. Hence, it is essential for organizations to carefully review and understand these agreements to ensure clarity on data ownership rights. Another challenge is the aggregation and integration of data from various sources.

As data is collected and shared across different devices and platforms, it becomes challenging to attribute ownership to specific data points. Additionally, data may be combined and analyzed with other datasets, raising questions about ownership and control over the derived insights. The complexities of data ownership in the IoT and cloud computing era necessitate the development of clear policies and legal frameworks. Organizations must establish data ownership guidelines and agreements that define the rights and responsibilities of all stakeholders involved. This includes addressing issues such as data access, sharing, retention, and disposal. In doing so, organizations should consider implementing data governance practices that ensure data privacy, security, and compliance with relevant regulations. This includes implementing measures to protect data from unauthorized access or breaches and ensuring that data handling practices adhere to privacy regulations. Overall, the complexities surrounding data ownership are harnessed by collaboration and clear communication between all stakeholders involved. Organizations need to establish transparent data ownership and governance frameworks to navigate through these complexities and build trust in the IoT and cloud computing platforms.

Personal and sensitive data collected from IoT devices can include health information, location data, and user preferences. To protect individuals' rights and maintain their trust, organizations need to have well-defined privacy policies that outline how this data is handled, who has access to it, and how long it is retained. Robust data governance frameworks help ensure that privacy regulations, such as the General Data Protection Regulation (GDPR), are adhered to. These data governance frameworks provide guidelines for ensuring compliance with standard regulations. This includes industry-specific regulations that maintain audit trails while conducting risk assessments and implementing appropriate data protection measures. Compliance with these frameworks, helps organizations to avoid legal penalties and reputation damage while fostering a culture of accountability, transparency, and trust.

1.4.2 Overcoming organizational silos: integration challenges of IoT and cloud in the business environment

In the context of IoT and cloud integration, organizational silos refer to the barriers that exist between different departments or business units within an organization. These silos can hinder the smooth integration of IoT and cloud technologies. Organizational silos often result in limited information sharing between departments. Each department may possess valuable data and insights that could contribute to the success of IoT and cloud initiatives, but without effective communication and collaboration channels, this information remains isolated within silos. The lack of information sharing hampers the ability to derive comprehensive insights and make data-driven decisions.

Silos lead to data fragmentation, where relevant data is scattered across various systems and databases. In the context of IoT, where data is generated from multiple devices and sensors, the presence of silos makes it challenging to consolidate and analyze data in a unified manner. This fragmentation hinders the ability to gain a holistic view of operations and limits the potential for valuable insights and actionable intelligence. Silos often result in duplicated efforts and redundant processes. Each department may independently invest in IoT and cloud solutions, leading to inefficiencies and increased costs. Without coordination and collaboration, different departments may unknowingly work on similar initiatives or utilize different technologies that do not integrate well with each other. This duplication of efforts not only wastes resources but also hampers the ability to achieve a cohesive and unified IoT and cloud ecosystem.

The absence of interdepartmental coordination poses challenges in implementing IoT and cloud projects. Integration efforts require collaboration between various teams, such as IT, operations, marketing, and finance. Silos can create communication gaps and resistance to collaboration, making it difficult to align goals, share resources, and coordinate activities effectively. This lack of coordination can delay project timelines, impede decision-making, and hinder the overall success of IoT and cloud integration initiatives.

Organizational silos can lead to resistance to change. Different departments may have their own established processes, systems, and ways of working. Integrating IoT and cloud technologies requires a shift in mindset, the adoption of new processes, and the willingness to embrace change. Thus, overcoming organizational silos requires a concerted effort to break down these silos, foster a culture of collaboration and knowledge sharing, and promote cross-functional teamwork. Subsequently, organizations can unlock the benefits of integrated IoT and cloud solutions, such as improved operational efficiency, enhanced decision-making, and the ability to deliver innovative products and services.

1.4.3 Barriers to cloud adoption for IoT applications

While the cloud-to-things continuum offers immense potential for organizations, there are several challenges that can hinder the seamless integration of IoT devices and cloud computing, hampering the realization of the full benefits of this transformative technology combination. Next, we reveal some of the key barriers that organizations may encounter when adopting cloud solutions for IoT applications. By understanding these barriers, organizations can pave the way for overcoming them to adopt a successful cloud-to-things continuum-based digital transformation.

Connectivity and network infrastructure pose significant challenges to the adoption of cloud solutions for IoT applications. These challenges primarily revolve around the need for robust, reliable, and scalable networks that can support the massive influx of data generated by IoT devices. A key challenge is ensuring seamless connectivity between IoT devices and the cloud. IoT devices often operate in diverse and dynamic environments, including remote locations, industrial settings, and urban areas with varying network coverage. Poor network connectivity can lead to data transmission delays, disruptions, or even complete data loss, hampering the effectiveness of IoT applications and cloud integration. Scalability of network infrastructure is another challenge to accommodate the growing number of IoT devices. Traditional network infrastructures may struggle to handle the sheer volume of data traffic and maintain optimal performance to face the rising number of connected devices. Resulting flaws include network congestion, reduced data transfer speeds, and increased latency, compromising the real-time capabilities and responsiveness of IoT applications. Deploying advanced networking technologies such as 5G, edge computing, and mesh networks (Sole et al., 2022) are expected to enhance connectivity and reduce latency to overcome these challenges.

IoT devices and network connectivity expose security vulnerabilities that pose significant barriers to cloud adoption. IoT devices have often limited computational capabilities and may lack built-in security features, making them vulnerable to cyber threats. Inadequate network security measures can expose sensitive data transmitted between IoT devices and the cloud, increasing the risk of data breaches and unauthorized access. Implementing stringent security measures, such as encryption, authentication protocols, and intrusion detection systems are potential safeguards of data transmitted over the network. Furthermore, collaborating with network service providers and adopting industry best practices for network security can mitigate the risks associated with IoT device connectivity.

1.4.4 Legal and regulatory hurdles in IoT and cloud computing

There are key legal and regulatory challenges that organizations face when deploying IoT and cloud computing technologies. The collection, storage, and processing of personal data by IoT devices and cloud services raise privacy concerns and data protection issues. Relevant regulations such as the General Data Protection Regulation (GDPR) ensure adequate security measures are in place to protect sensitive data, which organizations are expected to comply with. Certain industries have specific regulatory requirements that affect the use of IoT and cloud computing. Organizations must navigate through these industry-specific regulations, such as HIPAA (Health Insurance Portability and Accountability Act) (Herold and Beaver, 2014) or PCI DSS (Payment Card Industry Data Security Standard) (Ataya, 2010), prevalent in healthcare and finance domains respectively, to ensure compliance and secure the involved sensitive data.

It may happen that IoT devices and cloud services operate across multiple jurisdictions, organizations raising new challenges of cross-border data transfer. Different countries may have varying data protection laws and requirements, necessitating measures such as data localization or binding corporate rules. Furthermore, IoT deployments and related cloud services introduce new issues to liability and accountability terms. When data breaches, system failures, or other incidents occur, determining responsibility among various involved stakeholders in the IoT ecosystem may be challenging. Organizations must explore the legal implications and establish clear agreements and protocols to allocate liability and ensure accountability.

1.4.5 Business model innovation: creating new revenue streams with cloud-to-things continuum

A business transforms to meet the changes in socioeconomic demands while ensuring mutual benefits to its customers and its growth. The essence of such transformation is the value created by the transformation for the stakeholders. With the adoption of IoT and cloud technologies what value propositions can businesses expect? Earlier, physical things were embedded with technology to make them smart and thereby controlled or connected to a phone or computer. Today, in the digital transformation era the things around us have garnered the full capability and power of the Internet. These things are uniquely identifiable on the Internet, they can process and store information, and communicate across multiple platforms. These capabilities are being enabled by the increasing processing capabilities and decreasing dimensions of microprocessors, deployment of the 5G/6G networks, and increasing cloud service providers. With all these changes, the Cloud-To-Things Continuum is yet to be standardized.

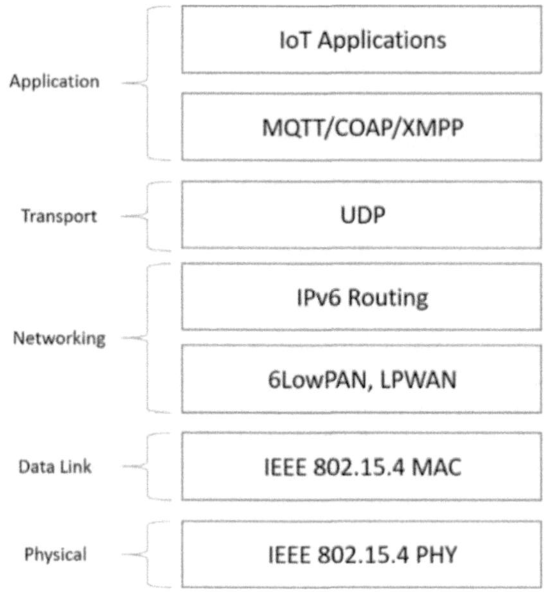

FIGURE 1.14

Generic IoT stack.

The value proposition starts with the choice of the IoT stack components. Fig. 1.14 provide a generic snapshot of an IoT stack. The stack is only the nuts and bolts of the whole system, but the decision of the layers of the IoT stack by the network engineer determines what back-end infrastructure would be an ideal fit for the business application at hand. In addition to the IoT stack, other embedded systems with sensors and actuators provide the ability to translate analog signals to digital data and transfer it over the networking infrastructure.

The value proposition is enhanced with the virtual representation of a physical thing in the cloud. Here the data is converted into information. The choice of cloud infrastructure decides the interfaces between the application and the physical entity. The virtual representation with the use of remote technologies would help the cloud engineer seamlessly design, access, and monitor the physical thing from the cloud. Fig. 1.15 depicts how a physical entity is represented in the cloud. The ability to plug in additional cloud technologies and services like storage, security, and web services provides better communication capabilities and an assurance to safely transact with the physical thing.

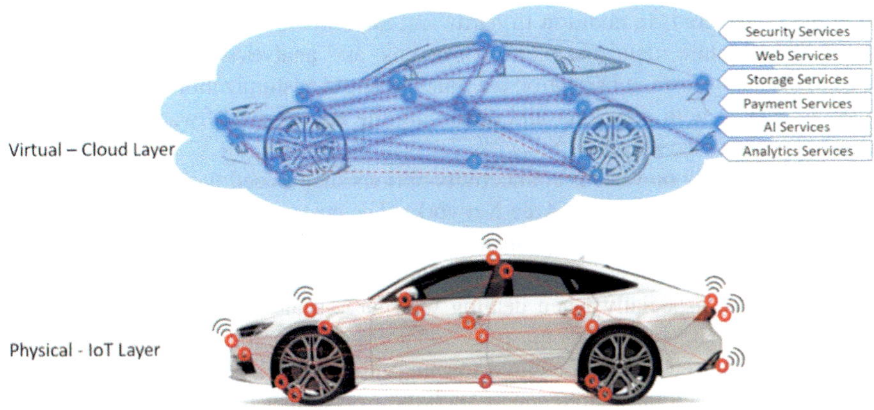

FIGURE 1.15

Representation of a real-world thing in the cloud.

An essential inclusion in the value proposition of any IoT-Cloud continuum is the provision of security and privacy across both layers of services provided, i.e. the physical and virtual. Here, the security engineer in collaboration with the network engineer and the cloud engineer ensures the integrity of the data exchanged in all spatiotemporal phases of the real-world thing's lifecycle. Translating information into actionable knowledge is now possible and adds to the value proposition. Additional cloud services like AI, analytics, and payment services plugged in at the cloud layer allows intelligent decisions to be made. AI and analytics provide the capability of reasoning and predicting actions in the physical world. For instance, weather reports from a web service may predict the possibility of rain, and the data from the car's tire sensors may be analyzed to deduce the possibility of the car skidding on the road. The AI model may reason the requirement to change the tires, place an order, and make a payment for standard tires that are road worthy. Overarching both the physical and virtual layers is the network infrastructure provider. The provider knits together all the physical and virtual layers again adding to the value proposition of the IoT-Cloud continuum.

1.4.6 Cost and resource allocation issues in implementing IoT and cloud solutions

The cost and resource allocation to implement IoT and cloud solutions need to be considered. Implementing IoT and cloud solutions requires investment in infrastructure, including IoT devices, cloud computing resources, networking, and data storage. IoT deployments often involve a wide range of hardware components, including sensors, actuators, gateways, and edge devices. These devices come with their associated costs, which vary depending on the functionality, quality, and scalability requirements. The selection of compatible, reliable, and cost-effective hardware needs to be carefully considered. In addition to hardware, the software includes IoT platforms, cloud infrastructure, data management systems, and analytics software. Issues related to licensing costs, subscription fees, and potential customization or development costs associated with acquiring and deploying the necessary software components, need to be addressed as well.

IoT devices rely on various connectivity options such as cellular networks, Wi-Fi, or LPWAN (Low-Power Wide-Area Network). The costs associated with data plans, network subscriptions, and data transmission charges induce various cost tradeoffs. An efficient data management and optimization strategy to minimize connectivity costs is needed, especially when dealing with large-scale IoT deployments. Other costs relate to maintenance, monitoring, and software upgrades that ensure optimal performance and security of the cloud-to-things continuum. An account of the costs associated with ongoing maintenance, including personnel resources, training, and support services needs to be established. Similar budgeting is expected for periodic hardware upgrades and software updates to keep up with evolving technologies and security requirements.

Cloud computing offers scalability and elasticity to the cloud-to-things continuum, allowing organizations to scale their IoT resources up or down based on demand. There are cost implications for scaling the infrastructure to accommodate increasing data volume, device connectivity, and user demands. The potential cost savings achieved through dynamic resource allocation and pay-as-you-go models that enable organizations to optimize costs based on actual usage are cost tradeoffs to be considered. Other cost optimization may include techniques such as data optimization and compression, workload consolidation, and leveraging serverless computing models (Wang et al., 2020a). The benefits of adopting cost optimization practices to maximize the value derived from the infrastructure while minimizing unnecessary expenses is an ongoing practice when budgeting for sustainable cloud-to-things solutions.

1.4.7 Balancing innovation and risk in IoT and cloud adoption

Embracing innovation and exploring the potential benefits of IoT and cloud technologies is paramount for organizations seeking to digital transformation to stay competitive in today's digital landscape. Cloud-to-things solutions can unlock a myriad of opportunities that drive improved efficiency, enhanced customer experiences, and the creation of new revenue streams for organizations. Connected devices provide valuable data for decision-support and predictive analytics over cloud-based platforms to identify patterns, anomalies, and optimization opportunities, leading to increased operational efficiency and cost savings. Furthermore, cloud-based platforms facilitate the collection, storage, and analysis of customer data retrieved from IoT devices to deliver customized experiences and build lasting customer relationships.

There are however inherent risks associated with the above advancements. A risk assessment study is essential to identify potential concerns, such as vulnerabilities that raise data security risks, as well as privacy and regulatory compliance issues, during the adoption of the cloud-to-things continuum. Indeed, IoT devices and cloud infrastructure expand attack surfaces and increase malicious opportunities for data breaches. Organizations must identify vulnerabilities and associated risks by conducting penetration testing, and vulnerability assessments, and implementing robust security measures such as encryption, authentication mechanisms, intrusion detection systems, network segmentation, and firewalls, to safeguard IoT devices, networks, and cloud infrastructure.

Besides IT risks, there is a need to balance innovation with business risks. Aligning IoT and cloud adoption with the organization's overall business objectives, and strategic priorities need to be discussed to develop a comprehensive risk management framework that incorporates IoT and cloud-specific risks into the broader enterprise risk management strategy. Different organizations have varying levels of risk tolerance based on their industry, size, and overall business strategy. Thus, continuous monitoring, evaluation, and assess the risks and rewards associated with the cloud-to-things continuum adoption need to be regularly reviewed for effective risk management, that adapts strategies as needed.

1.4.8 Maximizing ROI in IoT and cloud investments

Conducting a thorough cost-benefit analysis before making IoT and cloud investments is of significant importance. It allows organizations to evaluate the potential return on investment (ROI) and make informed decisions regarding the allocation of resources. Cost-benefit analysis provides expectations of the IoT and cloud investments' financial implications. It helps assess the costs associated with infrastructure setup, software implementation, data management, training, and ongoing maintenance. By comparing these costs with the anticipated benefits, organizations can determine if the investment aligns with their budget and financial goals. This exercise enables organizations to assess the potential return on investment. By quantifying cost savings, revenue growth, productivity gains, and operational efficiencies, organizations can estimate the financial impact of the investment. This assessment helps justify the investment and evaluate its viability compared to alternative digital transformation options.

By comparing different alternative digital transformation projects or solutions, organizations can determine which ones offer the highest value and align with their strategic objectives. This analysis ensures that resources are allocated to initiatives that deliver the greatest digital transformation benefits and contribute to the organization's long-term growth and competitiveness. This analysis helps also identify the payback period for the investment, estimate the potential cost savings or revenue growth over time, and assess the sustainability and scalability of the investment. This long-term perspective enables organizations to make strategic decisions that align with their future growth plans.

1.5 Conclusion

This chapter introduces the cloud-to-things continuum, its technical challenges, and the economic opportunities it presents. We have unveiled the emergence of IoT in cloud computing and how it has paved the way for a new paradigm of connected devices and businesses. We have discussed the technical challenges faced in implementing the cloud-to-things continuum, such as connectivity, interoperability, data management, and security.

Furthermore, we showed how the cloud-to-things continuum is enabling digital transformation by facilitating the integration of connected devices and business processes. We have explored the benefits of leveraging IoT and cloud technologies for improved operational efficiency, enhanced customer experiences, data-driven decision-making, and the development of innovative business models.

Additionally, we have addressed the business challenges associated with the cloud-to-things continuum, including data ownership and governance, organizational silos, barriers to cloud adoption, legal and regulatory hurdles, and the need to balance innovation with risk. These challenges highlight the importance of robust strategies, frameworks, and collaboration across various stakeholders to maximize the potential of IoT and cloud technologies.

Overall, the first chapter underscores the significant impact of the cloud-to-things continuum on the digital transformation of industries and organizations. It highlights the technical and business considerations involved in implementing IoT and cloud solutions, while also emphasizing opportunities and potential for innovation and growth. As we move forward through this book, we will delve deeper into the specific concepts sparsely introduced in this first chapter, while providing use cases, and real-world examples that demonstrate the transformative power of the cloud-to-things continuum in various domains, such as smart cities, healthcare, manufacturing, transportation, and more. In doing so, we aim to provide readers with a comprehensive understanding of the technical, economic, and societal implications of harnessing the cloud-to-things continuum to drive digital transformation.

References

Abdmeziem, M.R., Tandjaoui, D., Romdhani, I., 2015. Architecting the Internet of things: state of the art. In: Robots and Sensor Clouds. Springer International Publishing, pp. 55–75. https://doi.org/10.1007/978-3-319-22168-7_3.

Abreha, H.G., Hayajneh, M., Serhani, M.A., 2022. Federated learning in edge computing: a systematic survey. Sensors 22 (2). https://doi.org/10.3390/s22020450.

Ahmad, A., Jain, H., Singh, C.S., 2019. IoT (Internet of Things) enabled intelligent transportation system. In: Communication and Computing Systems. CRC Press, pp. 591–594.

Akkaş, M., Sokullu, R., Ertürk Çetin, H., 2020. Healthcare and patient monitoring using IoT. Internet of Things 11, 100173. https://www.sciencedirect.com/science/article/pii/S2542660520300147.

Al-Fuqaha, A., Guizani, M., Mohammadi, M., Aledhari, M., Ayyash, M., 2015. Internet of things: a survey on enabling technologies, protocols, and applications. IEEE Communications Surveys and Tutorials 17 (4), 2347–2376.

Almheiri, A., Maamar, Z., 2021. IoT protocols – MQTT versus CoAP. In: The 4th International Conference on Networking, Information Systems amp Security. ACM. https://doi.org/10.1145/3454127.3456594.

Ashton, K., 1999. That Internet of Things. RFID Journal 22.

Ataya, G., 2010. PCI DSS audit and compliance. Information Security Technical Report 15 (4), 138–144. Matchmaking between PCI-DSS and Security. https://www.sciencedirect.com/science/article/pii/S136341271100015X.

Atif, Y., Ding, J., Jeusfeld, M.A., 2016. Internet of things approach to cloud-based smart car parking. In: Procedia Computer Science. In: The 7th International Conference on Emerging Ubiquitous Systems and Pervasive Networks (EUSPN 2016)/The 6th International Conference on Current and Future Trends of Information and Communication Technologies in Healthcare (ICTH-2016)/Affiliated Workshops, vol. 98, pp. 193–198. https://www.sciencedirect.com/science/article/pii/S1877050916321603.

Atif, Y., Kharrazi, S., Jianguo, D., Andler, S.F., 2020. Internet of Things data analytics for parking availability prediction and guidance. Transactions on Emerging Telecommunications Technologies 31 (5), e3862. https://onlinelibrary.wiley.com/doi/abs/10.1002/ett.3862.

Ayele, E.D., Meratnia, N., Havinga, P.J., 2018. Towards a new opportunistic IoT network architecture for wildlife monitoring system. In: 2018 9th IFIP International Conference on New Technologies, Mobility and Security (NTMS), pp. 1–5.

Ayshwarya, B., Velmurugan, R., 2021. Intelligent and safe medication box in health IoT platform for medication monitoring system with timely remainders. In: 2021 7th International Conference on Advanced Computing and Communication Systems (ICACCS), vol. 1, pp. 1828–1831.

Banerjee, A., Datta, D., Gupta, S.K., 2021. Application of IoT in industry 4.0 for predictive analytics. In: Integration of Cloud Computing with Internet of Things. John Wiley & Sons, Ltd, pp. 165–182. Chapter 10. https://onlinelibrary.wiley.com/doi/abs/10.1002/9781119769323.ch10.

Barker, P., Hammoudeh, M., 2017. A survey on low power network protocols for the Internet of Things and wireless sensor networks. In: Proceedings of the International Conference on Future Networks and Distributed Systems. ACM. https://doi.org/10.1145/3102304.3102348.

Belej, O., Nestor, N., Polotai, O., Panchak, S., 2020. Developing a model of cloud computing protection system for the Internet of things. In: 2020 IEEE XVIth International Conference on the Perspective Technologies and Methods in MEMS Design (MEMSTECH), pp. 53–58.

Bera, S., Misra, S., Rodrigues, J.J., 2015. Cloud computing applications for smart grid: a survey. IEEE Transactions on Parallel and Distributed Systems 26 (5), 1477–1494.

Bessis, N., Dobre, C. (Eds.), 2014. Big Data and Internet of Things: A Roadmap for Smart Environments. Springer International Publishing. https://doi.org/10.1007/978-3-319-05029-4.

Bibri, S.E., Krogstie, J., 2020. The emerging data–driven smart city and its innovative applied solutions for sustainability: the cases of London and Barcelona. Energy Informatics 3 (1), 5. https://link.springer.com/content/pdf/10.1186/s42162-020-00108-6.pdf.

Bojan, T.M., Kumar, U.R., Bojan, V.M., 2014. An internet of things based intelligent transportation system. In: 2014 IEEE International Conference on Vehicular Electronics and Safety, pp. 174–179.

Brown, M.T., Bussell, J.K., 2011. Medication adherence: WHO cares? Mayo Clinic Proceedings 86 (4), 304–314. https://www.sciencedirect.com/science/article/pii/S0025619611600074.

Cavagnis, L., 2020. Android and MQTT: a simple guide. https://medium.com/swlh/android-and-mqtt-a-simple-guide-cb0cbba1931c.

Chang, Z., Liu, S., Xiong, X., Cai, Z., Tu, G., 2021. A survey of recent advances in edge-computing-powered artificial intelligence of things. IEEE Internet of Things Journal 8 (18), 13849–13875.

Chen, W., Qiu, H., Zhuang, J., Zhang, C., Hu, Y., Lu, Q., Wang, T., Shi, Y., Huang, M., Xu, X., 2021. Quantization of deep neural networks for accurate edge computing. ACM Journal on Emerging Technologies in Computing Systems 17 (4), 1–11. https://doi.org/10.1145/3451211.

Chhabra, S., Singh, A.K., 2022. Dynamic resource allocation method for load balance scheduling over cloud data center networks. https://arxiv.org/pdf/2211.02352.pdf.

Čolaković, A., Hadžialić, M., 2018. Internet of Things (IoT): a review of enabling technologies, challenges, and open research issues. Computer Networks 144, 17–39. https://www.sciencedirect.com/science/article/pii/S1389128618305243.

Distefano, S., Merlino, G., Puliafito, A., 2012. Enabling the cloud of things. In: 2012 Sixth International Conference on Innovative Mobile and Internet Services in Ubiquitous Computing, pp. 858–863.

Duan, S., Wang, D., Ren, J., Lyu, F., Zhang, Y., Wu, H., Shen, X., 2023. Distributed artificial intelligence empowered by end-edge-cloud computing: a survey. IEEE Communications Surveys and Tutorials 25 (1), 591–624.

Duroc, Y., 2022. From identification to sensing: RFID is one of the key technologies in the IoT field. Sensors 22 (19), 7523. https://doi.org/10.3390/s22197523.

Elhoseny, M., Abdelaziz, A., Salama, A.S., Riad, A., Muhammad, K., Sangaiah, A.K., 2018. A hybrid model of Internet of things and cloud computing to manage big data in health services applications. Future Generations Computer Systems 86, 1383–1394. https://www.sciencedirect.com/science/article/pii/S0167739X17322021.

Emeakaroha, V.C., Cafferkey, N., Healy, P., Morrison, J.P., 2015. A cloud-based IoT data gathering and processing platform. In: 2015 3rd International Conference on Future Internet of Things and Cloud, pp. 50–57.

Femminella, M., Pergolesi, M., Reali, G., 2018. IoT, big data, and cloud computing value chain: pricing issues and solutions. Annals of Telecommunications 73 (7), 511–520. https://link.springer.com/content/pdf/10.1007/s12243-018-0643-6.pdf.

Filho, C.P., Marques, E., Chang, V., dos Santos, L., Bernardini, F., Pires, P.F., Ochi, L., Delicato, F.C., 2022. A systematic literature review on distributed machine learning in edge computing. Sensors 22 (7), 2665. https://doi.org/10.3390/s22072665.

Finkenzeller, D., 2010. RFID Handbook: Fundamentals and Applications in Contactless Smart Cards, Radio Frequency Identification and Near-Field Communication. Wiley.

FunTech, 2018. Fun tech projects: RabbitMQ for IoT. https://funprojects.blog/2018/12/07/rabbitmq-for-iot/.

Ge, M., Bangui, H., Buhnova, B., 2018. Big data for Internet of things: a survey. Future Generations Computer Systems 87, 601–614. https://www.sciencedirect.com/science/article/pii/S0167739X17316953.

Girija, P., Mareena, J., Fenny, J., Swapna, K., Kaewkhiaolueang, K., 2021. Amazon robotic service (ARS). Engineering and Technology Management Student Projects. https://pdxscholar.library.pdx.edu/etm_studentprojects/2309.

Gusselnikov, S.P., Brusakova, I.A., 2022. Digital twin technologies for measurement virtualization process. In: 2022 Conference of Russian Young Researchers in Electrical and Electronic Engineering (ElConRus), pp. 1661–1663.

Hashmi, S.A., Ali, C.F., Zafar, S., 2021. Internet of things and cloud computing-based energy management system for demand side management in smart grid. International Journal of Energy Research 45 (1), 1007–1022. https://onlinelibrary.wiley.com/doi/abs/10.1002/er.6141.

Heble, S., Kumar, A., Prasad, K.V.V.D., Samirana, S., Rajalakshmi, P., Desai, U.B., 2018. A low power IoT network for smart agriculture. In: 2018 IEEE 4th World Forum on Internet of Things (WF-IoT), pp. 609–614.

Herold, R., Beaver, K., 2014. The Practical Guide to HIPAA Privacy and Security Compliance. Auerbach Publications.

HiveMQ, 2023. Develop efficient IoT solutions, retrieved on 13/05/2023. https://www.hivemq.com.

Jagannath, J., Ramezanpour, K., Jagannath, A., 2022. Digital twin virtualization with machine learning for IoT and beyond 5G networks. In: Proceedings of the 2022 ACM Workshop on Wireless Security and Machine Learning. ACM. https://doi.org/10.1145/3522783.3529519.

Janbi, N., Mehmood, R., Katib, I., Albeshri, A., Corchado, J.M., Yigitcanlar, T., 2022. Imtidad: a reference architecture and a case study on developing distributed AI services for skin disease diagnosis over cloud, fog and edge. Sensors 22 (5), 1854. https://doi.org/10.3390/s22051854.

Javaid, S., Sufian, A., Pervaiz, S., Tanveer, M., 2018. Smart traffic management system using Internet of things. In: 2018 20th International Conference on Advanced Communication Technology (ICACT), pp. 393–398.

Kalapesi, C., 2013. Unlocking the value of personal data: from collection to usage. Technical Report, World Economic Forum. https://www.weforum.org/reports/unlocking-value-personal-data-collection-usage/#:~:text=Download%20PDF-,Unlocking%20the%20Value%20of%20Personal%20Data%3A%20From%20Collection%20to%20Usage,flexible%2C%20adaptive%20and%20contextually%20driven.

Kalmar, E.E., Kertesz, A., 2017. Investigating operational costs of IoT cloud applications. In: Cloud Infrastructures, Services, and IoT Systems for Smart Cities. Springer International Publishing, pp. 141–150. https://doi.org/10.1007/978-3-319-67636-4_16.

Kerdlap, P., Low, J.S.C., Ramakrishna, S., 2019. Zero waste manufacturing: a framework and review of technology, research, and implementation barriers for enabling a circular economy transition in Singapore. Resources, Conservation and Recycling 151, 104438. https://www.sciencedirect.com/science/article/pii/S0921344919303337.

Kim, J., Cheon, S., Lim, J., 2022. IoT-based unobtrusive physical activity monitoring system for predicting dementia. IEEE Access 10, 26078–26089.

Krizhevsky, A., Sutskever, I., Hinton, G.E., 2017. ImageNet classification with deep convolutional neural networks. Communications of the ACM 60 (6), 84–90. https://doi.org/10.1145/3065386.

Latif, G., Shankar, A., Alghazo, J.M., Kalyanasundaram, V., Boopathi, C.S., Arfan Jaffar, M., 2020. I-CARES: advancing health diagnosis and medication through IoT. Wireless Networks 26 (4), 2375–2389. https://link.springer.com/content/pdf/10.1007/s11276-019-02165-6.pdf.

Lee, I., 2019. The Internet of things for enterprises: an ecosystem, architecture, and IoT service business model. Internet of Things 7, 100078. https://www.sciencedirect.com/science/article/pii/S2542660519301386.

Light, R., 2013. Mosquitto-an open source mqtt v3. 1 broker. http://mosquitto.org.

Liu, Y., Akram Hassan, K., Karlsson, M., Pang, Z., Gong, S., 2019. A data-centric Internet of things framework based on azure cloud. IEEE Access 7, 53839–53858.

Lombardi, M., Pascale, F., Santaniello, D., 2021. Internet of things: a general overview between architectures, protocols and applications. Information 12 (2), 87. https://doi.org/10.3390/info12020087.
Ma, M., Wang, P., Chu, C.-H., 2013. Data management for Internet of things: challenges, approaches and opportunities. In: 2013 IEEE International Conference on Green Computing and Communications and IEEE Internet of Things and IEEE Cyber, Physical and Social Computing, pp. 1144–1151.
Maamar, Z., Baker, T., Faci, N., Al-Khafajiy, M., Ugljanin, E., Atif, Y., Sellami, M., 2019. Weaving cognition into the Internet-of-things: application to water leaks. Cognitive Systems Research 56, 233–245. https://www.sciencedirect.com/science/article/pii/S1389041718303292.
mageNet, 2022. ImageNet & the rise of deep neural network architectures for image classification — AlexNet, inception, VGG, ResNet, ViT. https://ai.plainenglish.io/imagenet-the-rise-of-deep-neural-network-architectures-for-image-classification-alexnet-713df0500e7f.
Mandava, T., Chen, S., IST, O.I., 2018. An IoT middleware for air pollution monitoring in smart cities: a situation recognition model. In: Proceedings of the Information Science and Technology Conference.
Manyika, J., Chui, M., Brown, B., Bughin, J., Dobbs, R., 2011. Big data: the next frontier for innovation, competition, and productivity. McKinsey Digital. https://www.mckinsey.com/capabilities/mckinsey-digital/our-insights/big-data-the-next-frontier-for-innovation.
Mathew, S.S., Atif, Y., Sheng, Q.Z., Maamar, Z., 2014. Building sustainable parking lots with the web of things. Personal and Ubiquitous Computing 18 (4), 895–907. https://link.springer.com/content/pdf/10.1007/s00779-013-0694-7.pdf.
McNabb, T., Wicking, D.K., Myers, A.T., Lei, D.L., 2020. Optimizing Clinical Spatial Resources with IoT. In: Proceedings of the Australasian Computer Science Week Multiconference. ACM. https://doi.org/10.1145/3373017.3373047.
Misra, N.N., Dixit, Y., Al-Mallahi, A., Bhullar, M.S., Upadhyay, R., Martynenko, A., 2022. IoT, big data, and artificial intelligence in agriculture and food industry. IEEE Internet of Things Journal 9 (9), 6305–6324.
Mourtzis, D., Angelopoulos, J., Panopoulos, N., 2021. Design and development of an IoT enabled platform for remote monitoring and predictive maintenance of industrial equipment. In: Procedia Manufacturing. In: 10th CIRP Sponsored Conference on Digital Enterprise Technologies (DET 2020) – Digital Technologies as Enablers of Industrial Competitiveness and Sustainability, vol. 54, pp. 166–171. https://www.sciencedirect.com/science/article/pii/S235197892100161X.
Muhammed, A.S., Ucuz, D., 2020. Comparison of the IoT platform vendors, Microsoft azure, Amazon web services, and Google cloud, from users' perspectives. In: 2020 8th International Symposium on Digital Forensics and Security (ISDFS), pp. 1–4.
Munirathinam, S., 2020. Chapter six – Industry 4.0: Industrial Internet of Things (IIOT). In: The Digital Twin Paradigm for Smarter Systems and Environments: The Industry Use Cases, vol. 117(1), pp. 129–164. https://www.sciencedirect.com/science/article/pii/S0065245819300634.
Nagayo, A.M., Ajmi, M.Z.K.A., Guduri, N.R.K., AlBuradai, F.S.H., 2023. IoT-based telemedicine health monitoring system with a fuzzy inference-based medical decision support module for clinical risk evaluation. In: Lecture Notes in Networks and Systems. Springer Nature, Singapore, pp. 313–336. https://doi.org/10.1007/978-981-19-9228-5_28.
Nagpal, C., Upadhyay, P.K., Shahzeb Hussain, S., Bimal, A.C., Jain, S., 2019. IIoT based smart factory 4.0 over the cloud. In: 2019 International Conference on Computational Intelligence and Knowledge Economy (ICCIKE), pp. 668–673.

Nancy, A.A., Ravindran, D., Vincent, P.M.D.R., Srinivasan, K., Reina, D.G., 2022. IoT-cloud-based smart healthcare monitoring system for heart disease prediction via deep learning. Electronics 11 (15), 2292. https://doi.org/10.3390/electronics11152292.

Nazari Jahantigh, M., Masoud Rahmani, A., Jafari Navimirour, N., Rezaee, A., 2020. Integration of Internet of things and cloud computing: a systematic survey. IET Communications 14 (2), 165–176. https://ietresearch.onlinelibrary.wiley.com/doi/abs/10.1049/iet-com.2019.0537.

Ng, R., 2018. Cloud computing in Singapore: key drivers and recommendations for a smart nation. Politics and Governance 6 (4), 39–47. https://doi.org/10.17645/pag.v6i4.1757.

Patil, J., Bhiste, J.V., Pawar, D., Pawar, M.V., 2020. Framework for cloud based messaging system using MQTT. In: 2020 Advanced Computing and Communication Technologies for High Performance Applications (ACCTHPA), pp. 168–174.

Peter Mell, T.G., 2011. The NIST definition of cloud computing, retrieved on 13/05/2023. https://csrc.nist.gov/publications/detail/sp/800-145/final.

Philip Chen, C., Zhang, C.-Y., 2014. Data-intensive applications, challenges, techniques and technologies: a survey on big data. Information Sciences 275, 314–347. https://www.sciencedirect.com/science/article/pii/S0020025514000346.

Pizzolli, D., Cossu, G., Santoro, D., Capra, L., Dupont, C., Charalampos, D., De Pellegrini, F., Antonelli, F., Cretti, S., 2016. Cloud4IoT: a heterogeneous, distributed and autonomic cloud platform for the IoT. In: 2016 IEEE International Conference on Cloud Computing Technology and Science (CloudCom), pp. 476–479.

Prasad, G., Kanulla, L.K., Ijjagiri, V., Mary, S.S.C., 2022. Implementation and health monitoring system of vehicle by using IoT and cloud computing. In: 2022 6th International Conference on Electronics, Communication and Aerospace Technology, pp. 518–521.

Priyanka, E.B., Maheswari, C., Thangavel, S., 2021. A smart-integrated IoT module for intelligent transportation in oil industry. International Journal of Numerical Modelling: Electronic Networks, Devices and Fields 34 (3), e2731. https://onlinelibrary.wiley.com/doi/abs/10.1002/jnm.2731.

Priyanka, E.B., Thangavel, S., Madhuvishal, V., Tharun, S., Raagul, K.V., Krishnan, C.S.S., 2020. Application of integrated IoT framework to water pipeline transportation system in smart cities. In: Intelligence in Big Data Technologies—Beyond the Hype. Springer, Singapore, pp. 571–579. https://doi.org/10.1007/978-981-15-5285-4_57.

Razzaque, M.A., Milojevic-Jevric, M., Palade, A., Clarke, S., 2016. Middleware for Internet of things: a survey. IEEE Internet of Things Journal 3 (1), 70–95.

Rokonuzzaman, M., Mishu, M.K., Islam, M.R., Hossain, M.I., Shakeri, M., Amin, N., 2021. Design and implementation of an IoT-enabled smart plug socket for home energy management. In: 2021 5th International Conference on Smart Grid and Smart Cities (ICSGSC), pp. 50–54.

Rosado, T., Bernardino, J., 2014. An overview of openstack architecture. In: Proceedings of the 18th International Database Engineering & Applications Symposium – IDEAS'14'. ACM Press. https://doi.org/10.1145/2628194.2628195.

Saggu, D., Azim, A., 2021. Transfer learning on the edge networks. In: 2021 IEEE International Systems Conference (SysCon), pp. 1–8.

Sahmim, S., Gharsellaoui, H., 2017. Privacy and security in Internet-based computing: cloud computing, Internet of things, cloud of things: a review. In: Knowledge-Based and Intelligent Information & Engineering Systems: Proceedings of the 21st International Conference. KES-20176-8 September 2017, Marseille, France. In: Procedia Computer Science, vol. 112, pp. 1516–1522. https://www.sciencedirect.com/science/article/pii/S1877050917313923, 2017.

Sampath, D.A.M., 2022. Towards seamless edge computing in connected vehicles. TelematicsWire 22 (7), 13.

Shi, X., Kong, D., 2015. Application of IOT technology and remote control technology in industrial automation control. In: Advances in Computer Science Research. Atlantis Press. https://doi.org/10.2991/iccse-15.2015.63.

Sole, J.M., Nogues, S.M., Centelles, R.P., Freitag, F., 2022. Demonstration of a library prototype to build LoRa mesh networks for the IoT. In: 2022 IEEE 42nd International Conference on Distributed Computing Systems (ICDCS). IEEE. https://doi.org/10.1109/icdcs54860.2022.00150.

Sosunova, I., Porras, J., 2022. IoT-enabled smart waste management systems for smart cities: a systematic review. IEEE Access 10, 73326–73363.

Srinivas, M., Durgaprasadarao, P., Raj, V.N.P., 2018. Intelligent medicine box for medication management using IoT. In: 2018 2nd International Conference on Inventive Systems and Control (ICISC), pp. 32–34.

Tan, S.Z., Labastida, M.E., 2021. Unified IIoT cloud platform for smart factory. In: Intelligent Systems Reference Library. Springer International Publishing, pp. 55–78. https://doi.org/10.1007/978-3-030-67270-6_3.

Thekkummal, N.B., Jha, D.N., Puthal, D., James, P., Ranjan, R., 2020. Coordinated data flow control in IoT networks. In: Algorithmic Aspects of Cloud Computing. Springer International Publishing, pp. 25–41. https://doi.org/10.1007/978-3-030-58628-7_3.

Tomlinson, A., 2017. Introduction to the TPM. In: Smart Cards, Tokens, Security and Applications. Springer International Publishing, pp. 173–191. https://doi.org/10.1007/978-3-319-50500-8_7.

Ukil, A., Bandyoapdhyay, S., Puri, C., Pal, A., 2016. IoT healthcare analytics: the importance of anomaly detection. In: 2016 IEEE 30th International Conference on Advanced Information Networking and Applications (AINA), pp. 994–997.

Verma, S., Bala, A., 2021. Auto-scaling techniques for IoT-based cloud applications: a review. Cluster Computing 24 (3), 2425–2459. https://link.springer.com/content/pdf/10.1007/s10586-021-03265-9.pdf.

Vogel, A., Griebler, D., Maron, C.A.F., Schepke, C., Fernandes, L.G., 2016. Private IaaS clouds: a comparative analysis of OpenNebula, CloudStack and OpenStack. In: 2016 24th Euromicro International Conference on Parallel, Distributed, and Network-Based Processing (PDP), pp. 672–679.

Wang, I., Liri, E., Ramakrishnan, K.K., 2020a. Supporting IoT applications with serverless edge clouds. In: 2020 IEEE 9th International Conference on Cloud Networking (CloudNet), pp. 1–4.

Wang, L., Xiang, L., Xu, J., Chen, J., Zhao, X., Yao, D., Wang, X., Li, B., 2020b. Context-aware deep model compression for edge cloud computing. In: 2020 IEEE 40th International Conference on Distributed Computing Systems (ICDCS), pp. 787–797.

Wang, Z.-h., Wang, J., 2019. An IOT data collection mechanism based on cloud-edge coordinated deep learning. In: Guo, S., Liu, K., Chen, C., Huang, H. (Eds.), Wireless Sensor Networks. Springer, Singapore, pp. 76–89.

Weiser, M., 1991. The computer for the 21st century. Scientific American 265 (3), 66–75. http://www.ubiq.com/hypertext/weiser/SciAmDraft3.html.

Williams, R., 2020. Deploy IIoT sensors and networks in remote locations: IIoT adds value within a plant, but also is a natural ft for feld data gathering. Plant Engineering 74 (3), 12. https://link.gale.com/apps/doc/A628079248/AONE?u=anon~3a870fd2&sid=googleScholar&xid=f7c8b3b0.

Wu, Y., 2021. Cloud-edge orchestration for the Internet of things: architecture and AI-powered data processing. IEEE Internet of Things Journal 8 (16), 12792–12805.

Xhafa, F., 2021. Cloud services, storage and communications at large scale for reliable enterprise systems. Enterprise Information Systems 15 (2), 131–132. https://doi.org/10.1080/17517575.2020.1845812.

CHAPTER

Cloud-based IoT platforms for digital transformation

2

Introduction

Businesses and organizations are increasingly employing the Internet of Things (IoT) and cloud computing technologies to drive their digital transformation initiatives. The cloud-to-things continuum has given rise to powerful platforms that enable the seamless integration of connected devices, data analytics, and scalable infrastructure. Known as cloud-based IoT platforms, these platforms are revolutionizing the way cities create welfare for citizens, and the manner in which businesses create value for customers.

The motivation behind this chapter is to explore the transformative potential of cloud-based IoT platforms in driving digital transformation across various industries and domains. We will delve into the key features, benefits, and capabilities of these platforms, showcasing their role as a catalyst for innovation, operational efficiency, and business growth. Cloud-based IoT platforms unlock new opportunities for organizations to enhance customer experiences, and gain a competitive edge in today's dynamic marketplace.

Through real-world use cases and examples, we will highlight the diverse applications of cloud-based IoT platforms and their ability to address complex business challenges, while unfolding sustainable and scalable IoT solutions. We discuss the considerations that organizations have for selecting an IoT platform, to reshape its scalability, security, customization, and integration capabilities. By understanding these factors, businesses are empowered with informed decisions to embark on a successful digital transformation journey.

We conclude the chapter by highlighting the challenges and some future trends associated with cloud-based IoT platforms, while acknowledging the dynamic nature of technology and the need for continuous adaptation. As new advancements, such as artificial intelligence, blockchain, and edge computing are emerging, we explore their impact on, and further integration with IoT platforms, as well as their potential to further enhance digital transformation initiatives.

Accelerating Digital Transformation with the Cloud and the Internet of Things (IoT)
https://doi.org/10.1016/B978-0-44-322217-7.00008-6

2.1 IoT platform definition and overview

The cloud-to-things continuum has given rise to powerful platforms that revolutionize the way businesses harness the potential of connected technologies. Cloud-based IoT platforms have emerged as key enablers for organizations seeking to capitalize on the vast opportunities presented by the IoT ecosystem.

Next, we shed light on these platforms and explore their significance, capabilities, and impact on digital transformation. These platforms provide a robust foundation for managing and orchestrating IoT devices, capturing and analyzing data, and driving actionable insights by leveraging the scalability, agility, and data processing capabilities of the cloud.

We begin with an overview of cloud-based IoT platforms, highlighting their fundamental role as an integration layer that connects devices, sensors, and gateways to the cloud infrastructure. We delve into the key components and architecture of these platforms, emphasizing their ability to handle diverse types and volumes of data in real-time. Then, we explore the core features and functionalities offered by cloud-based IoT platforms. From device management and data collection to analytics and visualization, we show how these platforms empower organizations to monitor, control, and extract value from their IoT deployments. In doing so, we discuss the role of cloud services, such as data storage, computation power, and machine learning algorithms in enabling advanced analytics and predictive operation capabilities.

We showcase how businesses across various industries have leveraged cloud-based IoT platforms to improve efficiency, drive cost savings, and create new revenue streams. We also acknowledge the challenges and considerations associated with adopting cloud-based IoT platforms, such as security, privacy, interoperability, and vendor lock-in concerns, which organizations must address when selecting and implementing these platforms. We explore strategies for mitigating these challenges and emphasize the importance of robust data governance and security measures.

The fragmentation threat of the IoT industry hampers the integration of diverse technologies and limits the reusability of software and data. There is a growing need for handling data collection across diverse objects for effective and efficient application of robust reasoning systems. Furthermore, performance impairments may arise in scenarios where a large number of collaborating devices and technologies are involved. As the architecture of IoT technology is currently undergoing rapid evolution, there is still a lack of standardized and precise definitions. The plethora of hardware units, connection protocols, and low-level software languages, prompted an effort to bundle forces for streamlining these technologies, into a common platform. While certain companies adopt an open source approach that encourages transparency and collaboration, others choose to keep their APIs private. The latter group aims to retain customers within their proprietary technology, enabling them to generate revenue through license fees and potentially establish a dominant market position akin to a monopoly in the future. Thus interoperability is the main functionality of the IoT platforms to integrate versatile hardware and software standards.

Fig. 2.1 shows the variety of sub-components that make up a typical IoT platform. IoT platforms overcome the inherent heterogeneity in the IoT ecosystem due to the diverse nature of IoT devices, protocols, and technologies. IoT platforms accommodate this heterogeneity to effectively support the integration and interoperability of various devices and systems. By embracing the diverse sub-components, an IoT platform can provide a flexible and scalable infrastructure that can cater to a wide range of IoT applications and use cases. This allows organizations and developers to leverage different hardware units, connection protocols, and software languages, ensuring compatibility and seamless communication across diverse IoT devices and technologies. Supporting heterogeneity promotes innovation, fosters collaboration, and enables the development of comprehensive solutions, which can address the unique requirements and challenges of the IoT landscape. Hence the purpose of IoT platforms is to accommodate a wide range of sub-components.

The definition and functionality of IoT platforms have undergone significant changes due to the rising amounts and variety of data handled by IoT solutions. IoT analytics has adapted its definition of an IoT platform to reflect these changes to encompasses a range of sub-components, arranged into modular, and data-centric layers. These layers are the following (see Fig. 2.1):

1. **Device management:** Enables the capability to remotely configure, monitor, and oversee IoT devices, including the implementation of over-the-air updates.
2. **Communication management:** Enables telecommunications companies to effectively manage the seamless connectivity of IoT devices at a large scale.
3. **Data management:** Enables the capability to securely receive, store, and analyze data generated by IoT devices.
4. **Application management:** Facilitates agile development, efficient testing, and seamless management of IoT applications.

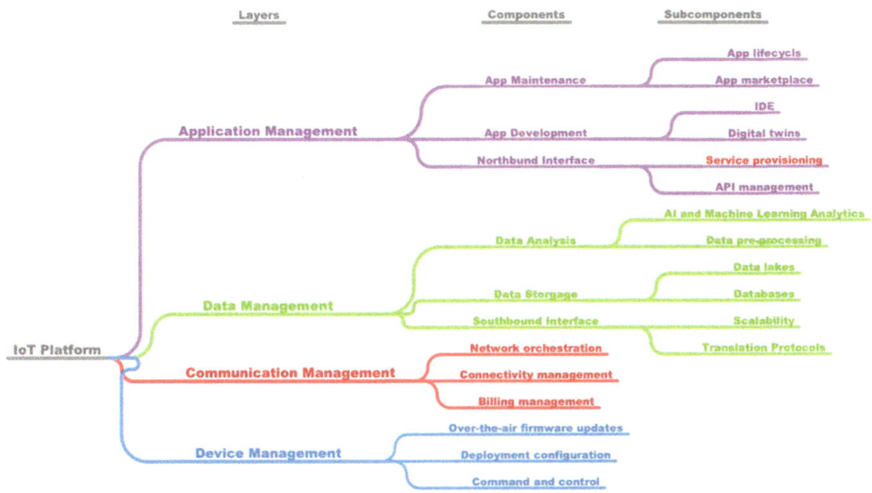

FIGURE 2.1

IoT platform definition (Adapted from (Wopata, 2021).

2.2 Key elements and features of IoT platforms

Understanding the key elements and features of IoT platform components is crucial for selecting a platform that fulfills desired functionalities. Organizations can make informed decisions regarding the selection, implementation, and optimization of their IoT platforms. It enables them to align their IoT strategies with specific business requirements, ensure interoperability across devices and systems, and enhance the overall functionality and efficiency of their IoT solutions. Additionally, this understanding allows organizations to address potential challenges and complexities associated with each component, such as data security, scalability, and integration properties, thereby facilitating the successful deployment and operation of IoT platforms.

2.2.1 Device management

The device management components in an IoT platform are used to oversee the connected devices throughout their lifecycle. They ensure the efficient operation, monitoring, and control of IoT devices. Typically, there are four main components: command and control, device monitoring, deployment configuration, and over-the-air firmware updates.

Command and control

The command and control component enables administrators or authorized users to have centralized control over the IoT devices. It provides a user interface or an application programming interface (API), through which device commands can be sent and executed. This component facilitates actions such as device activation, deactivation, rebooting, and resetting. Use cases include:

Device configuration

Administrators remotely configure the settings of IoT devices to modify parameters such as device identification, communication protocols, data sampling rates, thresholds, and other relevant configurations, which optimize device performance. For example, an IoT platform provider may offer a fleet management company a device configuration feature that allows them to remotely configure and customize the settings of the IoT devices installed in the vehicles. The fleet management company uses this feature to set parameters for data collection, such as specific collection data points by the IoT devices, related to location, speed, fuel consumption, and engine diagnostics. The frequency and granularity of data collection are configured to further optimize network bandwidth and storage requirements.

Real-time device monitoring

Administrators can monitor the real-time status of connected devices by accessing information such as device connectivity status, data transmission rates, power consumption levels, and environmental conditions. This real-time monitoring enables proactive monitoring, troubleshooting, and preventive maintenance. For example, in industrial settings, IoT devices monitor the performance of machinery in manufacturing equipment to provide real-time data on temperature, vibration, and other parameters. The IoT platform allows operators to detect abnormalities in real-time and facilitate scheduling preventive maintenance to avoid costly downtime.

Device activation and deactivation

Administrators can remotely activate new devices, associate them with the IoT platform, and configure their initial settings. Similarly, they can deactivate or decommission devices when needed, removing them from the network and terminating their functionalities. For example, in retail environments, IoT devices, such as RFID tags or barcode scanners, are used for inventory tracking and management. These devices need to be activated and associated with the respective inventory items or store locations. The IoT platform handles the activation process, ensuring that the devices are correctly configured and linked to the inventory management system. When items are sold, removed from inventory, or relocated, the platform allows for the deactivation and removal of the associated devices.

Command execution

Administrators can send commands or instructions to IoT devices. For example, they can initiate specific actions, such as turning on/off actuators, adjusting device parameters, initiating data collection or transmission, or triggering specific events based on predefined conditions. For example, in smart irrigation systems, the IoT platform used in agricultural applications can execute commands to control irrigation schedules, activate or deactivate specific sprinkler zones, or adjust water flow rates. The IoT platform processes these commands and communicates with the irrigation devices to carry out the requested actions, optimizing water usage, and promoting efficient irrigation practices.

Security and access control

Administrators need to authenticate and authorize users or applications to interact with devices, ensuring that only authorized entities can issue commands or access sensitive device functionalities. For example, when new devices are added to an IoT platform, security provisioning processes ensure that only trusted and authenticated devices can connect to the platform. This involves techniques such as device authentication, secure key exchange, and certificate-based authentication to establish a secure and trusted connection between devices and the platform (Khan et al., 2021).

Deployment configuration

The "deployment configuration" component of the device management layer in an IoT platform provides features and capabilities to facilitate the seamless deployment and configuration of IoT devices. Here are some typical features of the deployment configuration component:

Device provisioning

This feature enables the platform to automate the process of provisioning new IoT devices. It includes functionalities such as device registration, authentication, and enrollment into the IoT platform ecosystem. Device provisioning ensures that new devices can securely connect to the platform and start transmitting data. When a new IoT device is manufactured, it is pre-configured with unique identification credentials, such as a device ID or certificate. During the device provisioning process, the IoT platform automatically registers the device by associating these credentials with the device's profile in the platform's device registry. This process allows the platform to authenticate and establish secure communication with the device. Zero-touch provisioning allows devices to connect to the IoT platform and initiate the provisioning process automatically, particularly when IoT devices may be deployed in large numbers or in remote locations where manual configuration is impractical (Boškov et al., 2020).

Secure device enrollment

The enrollment process allows IoT devices to establish a trusted relationship with the IoT platform. This can involve mutual authentication, where the device presents its credentials to the platform, and the platform verifies the device's authenticity. Secure device enrollment ensures that only authorized devices can connect to the platform, enhancing overall security. Secure device enrollment methods commonly used in IoT are (1) public key infrastructure (PKI), where each device is assigned a unique public-private key pair, and during the enrollment process, the device's public key is securely registered with the IoT platform or service; (2) certificate-based authentication: a feature which issues digital certificates to devices during the enrollment process to verify the identity of the device and establish a secure connection with the IoT platform; and (3) one-time password (OTP), where devices enroll the platform with a one-time password to verify their authenticity before allowing the device to enroll.

Over-the-air firmware updates

OTA updates allow for remote firmware and software updates of IoT devices. The deployment configuration component enables the platform to securely deliver and install updates to the devices over the air. OTA updates help in enhancing device functionality, fixing bugs, and addressing security vulnerabilities without the need for physical intervention or device recalls. For example, IoT devices used in healthcare, such as wearable health monitors or connected medical devices, may receive OTA firmware updates to ensure they are operating with the latest security patches, bug fixes, and performance enhancements. These updates are crucial to maintaining the integrity and reliability of the devices, especially when they are involved in critical patient monitoring or treatment (Rajeesh Kumar et al., 2020). The features of OTA firmware updates provided by IoT platforms include:

Remote deployment

OTA firmware update services in IoT platforms enable the remote deployment of firmware updates to IoT devices without requiring physical access to the devices. This allows for convenient and efficient updates across a large number of devices. For example, car manufacturers can remotely deploy firmware updates to connected vehicles to enhance the vehicle's performance, introduce new functionalities, or address software vulnerabilities. This enables manufacturers to improve the vehicle's functionality and address potential safety concerns without the need for vehicle owners to visit a service center (Subke et al., 2020).

Secure delivery

OTA updates are designed to ensure secure delivery of firmware updates to prevent unauthorized access or tampering during the update process. Secure protocols and encryption techniques are often employed to protect the integrity and confidentiality of the update. Cryptographic signatures are used to allow digitally signed updates from the manufacturer using a private key. The device verifies the signature using the corresponding public key to ensure that the firmware has not been tampered with during transit and provides assurance of its authenticity. Similarly, encryption and access control mechanisms are used to securely store firmware update files. Secure delivery of OTA firmware updates may also involve mechanisms for code validation and verification, allowing the devices to further verify the update authenticity before initiating the installation process. This helps to prevent the installation of malicious or unauthorized firmware.

Version management

OTA firmware updates enable version management, allowing devices to track and manage different firmware versions. This facilitates the ability to roll back to a previous version if issues arise with the latest update. The IoT platforms may provide the capability to schedule firmware updates during periods of low device usage or minimal impact on critical operations, particularly since many IoT devices are designed to operate continuously. This helps ensure a smooth update process and minimizes disruptions to device functionality.

Reporting and monitoring

IoT platforms often provide reporting and monitoring capabilities to track the status of firmware updates across devices. This includes tracking the progress of updates, monitoring success rates, and identifying devices that may require additional attention or troubleshooting. The platform may provide visual representations of data collected from connected devices, which can include charts, graphs, and dashboards that offer real-time insights into device performance, usage patterns, and environmental conditions. Platforms can thus generate alerts and notifications based on predefined thresholds or specific events. For example, if a sensor detects an abnormal reading or a device goes offline, the platform can send notifications to designated users or system administrators for immediate action. Reports can include usage analytics to understand how devices are being utilized. This includes metrics such as device uptime, usage frequency, and user interactions. Such insights help in optimizing device deployments, identifying underutilized devices, and improving overall operational efficiency.

2.2.2 Communication management

As illustrated earlier in Fig. 2.1, the communication management layer of IoT platforms is responsible for enabling seamless connectivity and efficient communication between IoT devices, across different networks, and to versatile applications. This layer encompasses various components that play key roles in managing the communication aspects of an IoT ecosystem. These components include network orchestration, connectivity management, billing management, and service provisioning. Next, we will describe each of these components, while exploring their functionalities, importance, and how they contribute to the overall efficiency and effectiveness of IoT platforms. The efficiency of these components reflects on key performance indicators of IoT platforms, such as reliable data exchange, optimal network utilization, efficient billing processes, and streamlined service provisioning, all of which contribute to a solid foundation for successful IoT deployments. Let's explore further these key components of the communication management layer in detail.

Network orchestration

In the context of IoT platforms, network orchestration refers to the management and coordination of various network resources and components to enable seamless and efficient communication between IoT devices and systems. Network orchestration aims to streamline and automate network operations, such as the provisioning of network resources, such as IP addresses or virtual networks, while allowing IoT platforms to dynamically adapt to changing network conditions and requirements. Hence the term "orchestration" involves coordinating different network resources to ensure proper connectivity and data flow for IoT devices. Just like an orchestra maestro ensures that each musician plays their parts in harmony, network orchestration harmonizes network operations to ensure that network resources are utilized optimally, traffic flows smoothly, and security measures are effectively enforced.

The concept of network orchestration goes further beyond traditional network management approaches by incorporating intelligent algorithms, automation, and policy-based control. This concept enables IoT platforms to handle complex networking tasks, such as load balancing, failover mechanisms, and quality of service (QoS) enforcement. Next, we discuss the primary functions and capabilities of the network orchestration components.

Provisioning and configuration management

This component encompasses several key features, including automated resource allocation, which enables the automated provisioning of network resources required by IoT devices, such as IP addresses, subnets, VLANs (virtual local area networks), or virtualized network functions. The platform streamlines the process of resource allocation, eliminating the need for manual configuration.

Traffic management

Network orchestration helps in prioritizing and managing network traffic based on predefined policies, ensuring that critical IoT data is given higher priority for timely delivery to satisfy quality of service (QoS) for IoT, which is distinguished from general QoS for low-energy IoT devices (Tanganelli and Mingozzi, 2019). Traffic shaping policies refer to rules or configurations implemented by the platform in a network to control the flow of traffic and manage bandwidth allocation. These policies are designed to prioritize certain types of traffic or limit the bandwidth usage of specific applications or users. The primary purpose of traffic shaping policies is to optimize network performance, ensure fair resource allocation, and enforce quality of service (QoS) policies.

Network performance

Network orchestration provides continuous monitoring of network performance, including bandwidth utilization, latency, packet loss, and other metrics, to ensure optimal network operation. The IoT platform provides troubleshooting and diagnostics assistance in identifying and resolving network issues by providing diagnostic tools and analytics capabilities to pinpoint problems and take appropriate remedial actions. For example, the platform assists administrators to detect anomalies related to device malfunctions or connectivity issues through error logs and other relevant events generated by devices or system components. The platform enables remote access to connected devices, facilitating diagnostics and troubleshooting without physical intervention. It may provide remote control capabilities, allowing administrators to remotely investigate device configurations, perform tests, or apply fixes. Data analytics techniques may be used by the platform to analyze device data and identify patterns or anomalies that indicate potential issues. Visualizations and reports are generated in dashboard formats to provide insights into the overall system health and performance, making it easier to pinpoint and troubleshoot problems.

Integration with support systems

The IoT platform integrates with support ticketing systems or customer service platforms, enabling seamless communication and collaboration between administrators, support teams, and end-users. This integration facilitates efficient troubleshooting, issue tracking and resolution, ensuring timely support for IoT deployments. For example, the IoT platform can integrate with popular ticketing systems, such as JIRA, ServiceNow, or Zendesk. This integration allows support tickets to be automatically created and synchronized between the IoT platform and the support system. When an issue is reported or detected within the IoT ecosystem, a support ticket is generated, providing a centralized way to track, assign, and resolve the issue. This means also that the IoT platform can integrate with customer service portals, providing a self-service channel for customers to report issues, access knowledge bases, or request support. When an issue requires specialized expertise or needs to be escalated to a higher level of support, the IoT platform can initiate the escalation process within the support system, ensuring the appropriate team members are involved in resolving the issue.

Connectivity management

The connectivity management component ensures seamless connectivity between IoT devices and the underlying network infrastructure. A range of capabilities shapes this component that enables efficient management, monitoring, and control of device connectivity. Next, we explore these capabilities and their role in enabling reliable and scalable IoT deployments.

Device onboarding

Connectivity management facilitates the onboarding of IoT devices onto the network. Onboarding refers to device registration, authentication, and authorization. This feature streamlines the initial setup of devices and helps in managing device credentials securely.

Connectivity monitoring

Connectivity management continuously monitors the network connectivity status of IoT devices. Using this feature, IoT platforms track parameters such as signal strength, network availability, and latency to ensure IoT devices are properly connected and can communicate with the cloud infrastructure. The platform administrators are empowered with proactive identification of connectivity issues and prompt resolution. This feature is also used to assess and optimize the quality and performance of device connectivity. Factors such as data transfer rates, packet loss, and network congestion are monitored by the platform to ensure smooth and reliable communication between devices and the cloud. Troubleshooting tools are provided by the platform to identify connectivity issues, optimize network configurations, and enhance overall connectivity performance.

Roaming and handover management

In scenarios where devices move between different network environments or need to switch between different access points, connectivity management handles seamless network roaming and handover. Uninterrupted connectivity during transitions is ensured, while minimizing service disruptions and maintaining consistent data transmission. For example, in the context of smart transportation, IoT-enabled vehicles may need to switch between cellular networks as they move across different geographical areas. Network roaming and handover management provides a seamless transition between different network providers, ensuring continuous connectivity and uninterrupted access to vehicular services, such as real-time navigation, vehicle diagnostics, and remote monitoring. Another example is related to smart agriculture, where IoT devices, such as soil moisture sensors, weather stations, and crop monitoring systems may be deployed as mobile units across vast fields. As devices move within the field or encounter different network coverage areas, network roaming and handover management ensure smooth handover between cellular networks or wireless access points, maintaining continuous data collection and enabling timely decision-making for irrigation, fertilization, and crop management.

Billing management

The billing management component in IoT platforms instruments monetization issues for the provision of connectivity and other services to IoT devices. The main functionalities of this component are to accurately measure and track usage, generate invoices, and handle billing processes associated with IoT device deployments. Next, we explore some key features and benefits of billing management in the communication layer of IoT platforms.

Usage monitoring and metering

IoT platforms with billing management capabilities enable the measurement and monitoring of data usage, network traffic, and other relevant metrics associated with connected devices. This feature allows organized tracking and analysis of device and network-level usage patterns, facilitating accurate billing based on consumption. IoT platforms provide the flexibility to define and manage various pricing models and rate plans tailored to different customer requirements. This includes options such as flat-rate pricing, tiered pricing based on usage thresholds, pay-as-you-go models, and subscription-based plans. Billing management allows organizations to configure and manage these pricing models efficiently.

Invoice generation and payment processing

The billing management component automates the process of generating invoices based on usage data and predefined rate plans. The process involves the creation of detailed, itemized invoices that capture relevant information, such as device identifiers, usage duration, data volume, and associated costs. IoT platforms offer may customize billing and reporting based on specific customer needs. For example, organizations can generate customized invoices, reports, and financial summaries, providing detailed insights into usage patterns, costs, and revenue generation. This feature helps in transparent communication with customers and supports effective financial management. Furthermore, IoT platforms integrate payment gateways and related systems, to enable secure and convenient payment processing for customers.

Billing analytics and insights

IoT platforms with advanced billing management capabilities offer analytics and reporting features to gain valuable insights into revenue generation, customer behavior, and usage trends. These insights help organizations optimize pricing strategies, identify potential revenue opportunities, and make data-driven business decisions.

2.2.3 Data management

The data management component enables efficient and effective handling of IoT data. Next, we delve into some key components of the data management layer in IoT platforms, namely data analysis, data storage, and southbound interface, as further illustrated in Fig. 2.2. We explain how these components contribute to managing the vast volumes of data generated by IoT devices in a structured and valuable manner.

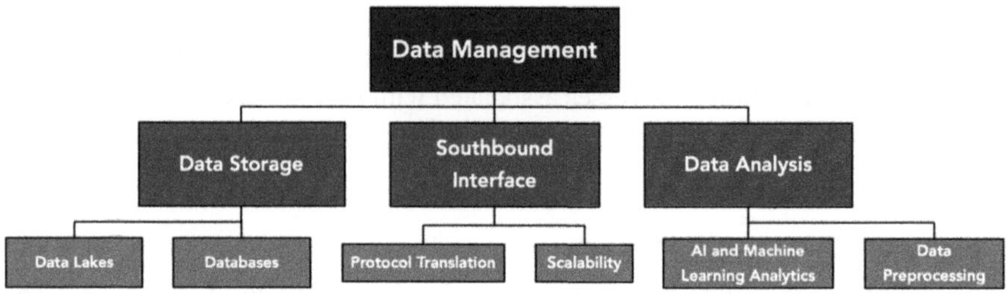

FIGURE 2.2

IoT platform data management.

Data storage

The IoT platform facilitates the collection of data from IoT devices in real-time through efficient and reliable data transmission protocols from devices to the IoT platform. Prior to storing collected data for further analysis, the data management layer of the platform may provide data validation and filtering capabilities to ensure data integrity and quality. These validation checks on incoming data may result in discarding or flagging invalid data and applying data filtering rules to reduce data noise and improve data accuracy.

Databases

Organizing and managing structured data in IoT platforms can be handled by traditional databases. IoT platforms leverage databases to store sensor readings, device metadata, and other structured data. Databases offer robust data integrity, transactional support, and advanced querying capabilities. However, this storage option is suitable only when the IoT data being generated has a well-defined structure and requires strict relational integrity. This storage option may not be suitable if IoT data includes diverse data formats, unstructured or semi-structured data, or if the data schema is bound to change. For example, IoT applications often involve multiple types and models of sensors. Each sensor may generate data with its specific attributes and schema. As new sensor models are introduced, or existing sensors are upgraded, the data schema may change to accommodate the new attributes or data formats. Yet, if an IoT application requires immediate data processing and real-time transactional operations, databases offer support for rapid query processing.

Data lakes

A data lake is a centralized storage repository designed to accommodate data from various IoT device sources, in different formats. Data is actually stored in its original form, whether structured, semi-structured, or unstructured, without the need for upfront data transformations. Large volumes of data, including big data, are efficiently processed in a flexible and scalable manner. Data lakes provide the capability to explore, refine, and analyze data using batch processing techniques, making it well-suited for advanced IoT analytics applications that use artificial intelligence (AI), machine learning (ML), and data science techniques. Thus companies can unlock valuable insights and derive actionable intelligence from their diverse IoT data sources. Hence, data lakes are used for both data storage and computation. Fig. 2.3 illustrates the data lake architecture, featuring various input sources from IoT data sensors. Collected data undergo subsequent cleaning and curation to correct inconsistencies, or deal with duplicates, and maintain the integrity of data over time. Data governance policies are implemented by the IoT platform around data lake processes, which lead to use cases, such as decision-support supported by analytics, machine learning algorithms, or visualization schemes.

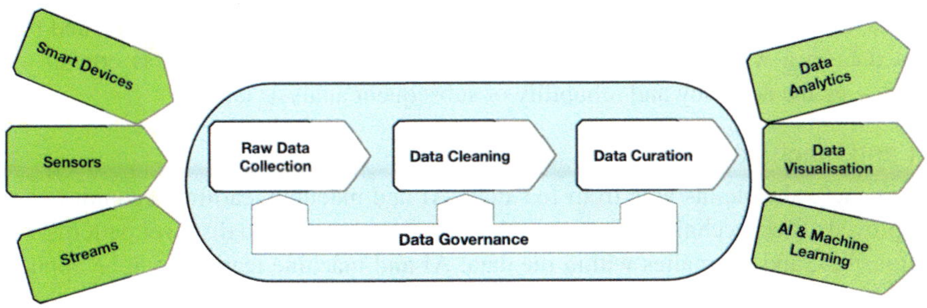

FIGURE 2.3

Data lake architecture.

Southbound interface

This interface ensures that the data generated by IoT devices can be efficiently transmitted, translated, and scaled for further processing and analysis. One of the main features of the southbound interface is protocol translation. IoT devices often use different communication protocols and standards to transmit data. The southbound interface facilitates the translation of data between these diverse protocols, enabling interoperability and smooth communication between devices and the data management infrastructure. This translation ensures that data can be seamlessly exchanged, regardless of the specific protocols used by different devices.

Another important feature of the southbound interface is scalability to accommodate the large number of devices that generate a vast amount of data. The southbound interface provides the data infrastructure to scale horizontally and vertically, ensuring that it can accommodate the increasing number of devices and the exponential growth of data. This scalability feature allows data to be processed, stored, and analyzed in a timely manner, to deliver real-time insights and actionable intelligence. This level of scalability is optimized using mechanisms such as load balancing, data partitioning strategies, and other distributed computing frameworks. These mechanisms ensure efficient data processing, storage, and analysis, even in highly dynamic and resource-intensive IoT environments.

Data analysis

The data analysis component encompasses various processes and technologies, which enable effective data utilization. Two key features of this component are data pre-processing and AI and machine learning. The goal is to unlock the value hidden patterns within the vast amount of data generated by IoT devices to make data-driven decisions, optimize processes, and drive innovation in organizations.

Data pre-processing

Before data can be analyzed, a pre-processing stage ensures its quality, completeness, and suitability for further analysis. Data pre-processing involves several steps, such as data cleaning, data integration, data transformation, and data reduction. These steps help to address data inconsistencies, handle missing values, remove outliers, and format data in a way that is suitable for analysis. Data pre-processing is crucial for improving the accuracy and reliability of subsequent analysis tasks.

AI and machine learning

To extract valuable insights from IoT data, AI and machine learning techniques are employed. These techniques leverage algorithms and models to discover patterns, relationships, and anomalies within the data. AI and machine learning can be applied to various IoT use cases, such as predictive maintenance, anomaly detection, optimization, and decision-making. These techniques involved three types of analytics, namely descriptive analytics, predictive analytics, and prescriptive analytics, which are illustrated in Fig. 2.4. The IoT data exploration process starts by gaining a deeper understanding of its characteristics through descriptive analytics, which summarizes data through aggregation, filtering, and basic statistical techniques.

The predictive analytics step follows by leveraging AI and machine learning techniques to forecast future outcomes and trends based on historical data. This step enables organizations to anticipate events or behaviors, facilitating proactive decision-making. The IoT data exploration process starts by gaining a deeper understanding of its characteristics through descriptive analytics, which summarizes data through aggregation, filtering, and basic statistical techniques. The predictive analytics step follows by leveraging AI and machine learning techniques to forecast future outcomes and trends based on historical data and current context, as illustrated further in Fig. 2.5. This step enables organizations to anticipate events or behaviors, facilitating proactive decision-making.

Finally, the prescriptive analytics step goes beyond predictive analytics by recommending optimal actions or strategies based on the analysis of IoT data. This step

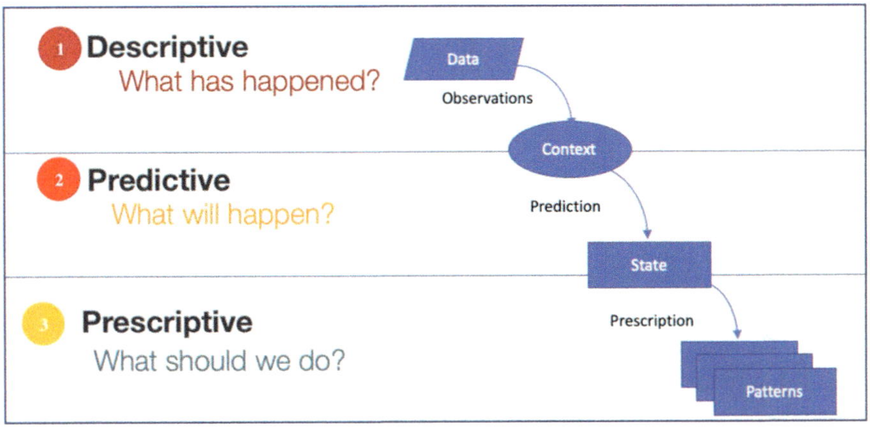

FIGURE 2.4

Data analytics.

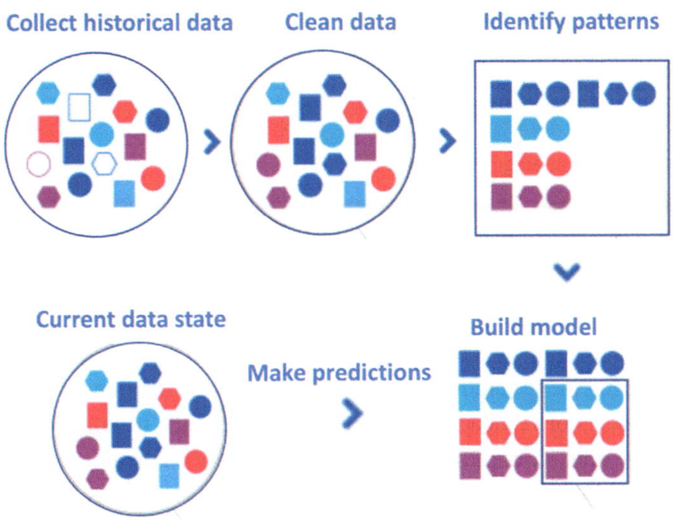

FIGURE 2.5

Predictive analytics.

utilizes advanced optimization algorithms and simulation techniques to prescribe actions. The machine learning process, illustrated further in Fig. 2.6, can be seen as a way of training a model to learn from data and make predictions, or prescribe decisions based on learned knowledge. The input is the data or observations, which are fed into the machine learning algorithm. As an analogy to the human brain, knowledge is acquired through input observations and experiences, which the brain processes over time to consolidate knowledge.

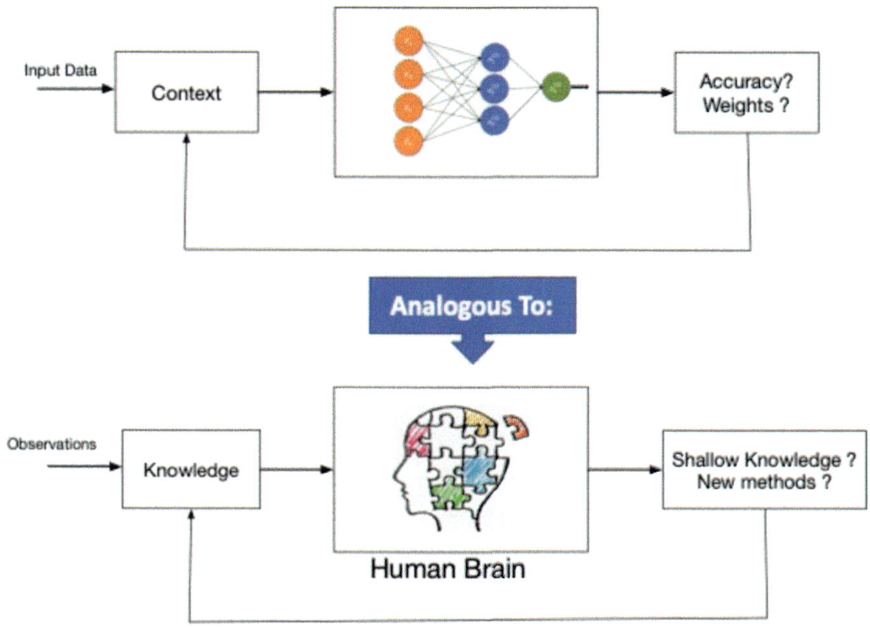

FIGURE 2.6

Machine learning and analogies with human brain.

Similarly, in machine learning, the algorithm takes in a set of observations or data as input. Through a series of computational processes, the algorithm refines and adjusts its internal parameters to learn patterns, relationships, and correlations within the data. The refinement iterations of the learning process may involve comparisons to known outcomes or feedback, and adjustments are made to improve accuracy or performance weights. These adjustments can again be seen as analogous to the brain's refinement methods, which enable the brain to update and revise its understanding of the world.

2.2.4 Application management

This layer acts as a bridge between the underlying IoT infrastructure and the applications that run on top of it. The "Application Management" layer, illustrated in Fig. 2.7, provides tools for managing and facilitating the development, maintenance, and integration of applications within the IoT platform. It encompasses tools for IoT applications' development, a framework for web services for connected objects, and a maintenance environment for monitoring deployed applications and resource optimization to ensure optimal application performance.

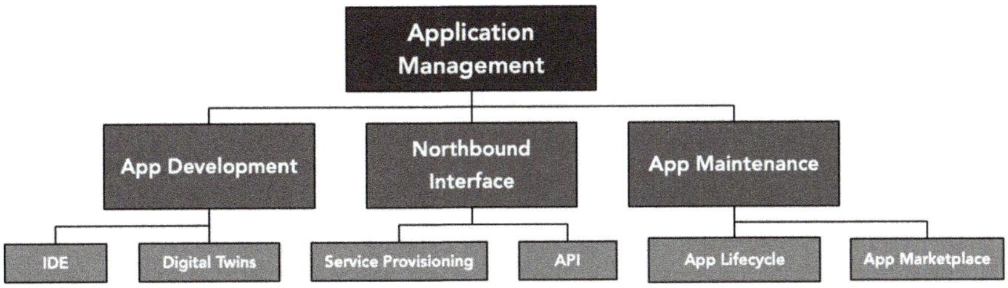

FIGURE 2.7

Application management components.

App development

This component provides the tools, frameworks, and resources necessary for developing IoT applications. Developers are enabled to create, test, and deploy applications using the platform's services and functionalities.

IDE

App development tools may include software development kits (SDKs) and integrated development environments (IDEs). These tools assist developers in building applications that can interact with various IoT devices and access data from sensors. An illustration of IDE is shown in Fig. 2.8. For example, PlatformIO is an open source, cross-platform IDE built specifically for IoT development. This platform supports multiple development standalone IDEs, including Arduino, Espressif IoT development framework (ESP-IDF) (Marwan and Wiklom, 2021), and Mbed (Tang and Zheng, 2023), among others. PlatformIO provides a unified development workflow, library management, and debugging capabilities, making it a popular choice for IoT developers working with different hardware platforms

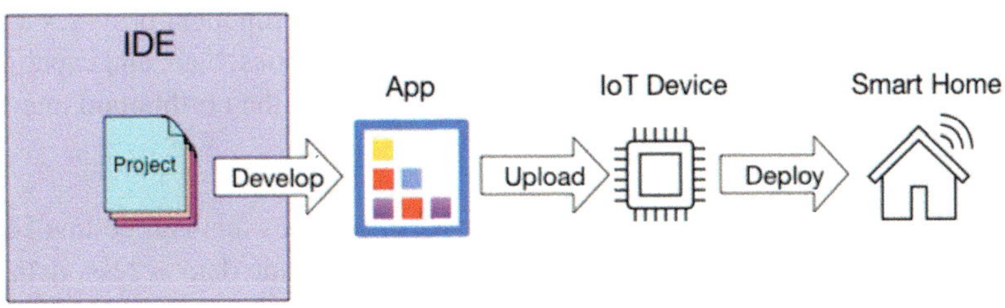

FIGURE 2.8

Integrated development environment (IDE) for IoT.

Digital twins

Creating and managing digital representations of physical objects, known as "digital twins," is a prominent IoT application that mirrors real-world physical objects, devices, or systems in the digital realm. Digital twins serve as virtual counterparts, providing a comprehensive view and real-time insights into the physical entities they represent. Next, we describe the functionalities and capabilities of the digital twins feature within the IoT platform, considering the following aspects:

- Digital twin creation: The IoT platform provides tools and interfaces for developers and administrators to create digital twins of physical assets or entities. These digital twins are typically modeled using standardized schemas or custom data structures that capture the relevant attributes, properties, and behaviors of the physical objects they represent. The platform may offer a visual interface or declarative language to define the structure and relationships of the digital twins.
- Real-time data synchronization: One of the key features of digital twins is their ability to synchronize and update real-time data with their physical counterparts. Data collected by the IoT platform is subsequently transmitted to the corresponding digital twin, ensuring that the virtual representation reflects the current state of the physical entity.
- Simulation and what-if scenarios: Digital twin simulations are used to explore different scenarios for physical assets. The IoT platform capabilities allow users to model and test various conditions, configurations, or operational strategies using digital twins. This feature helps stakeholders assess the impact of changes, evaluate potential risks, and optimize asset performance in a virtual environment before implementing them in the physical world. The IoT platform provides mechanisms to track and analyze data from digital twins, to assess some operational parameters and environmental conditions, which assist with predictive maintenance, anomaly detection, and performance optimization.

Northbound interface

The northbound interface component in the IoT platform enables seamless integration and interaction between the IoT platform and external systems, applications, or services. By provisioning services and API features, this component provides a gateway for external entities to access and utilize the functionalities, data, and capabilities of the IoT platform. Next, we explain these two features of the northbound interface:

Service provisioning

The northbound interface component offers a set of services that can be invoked by external systems or applications. These services may include data access, data processing, device management, event handling, security services, or any other specific functionalities provided by the IoT platform. External entities can leverage the capabilities of the IoT platform to enhance their own operation by invoking services provisioned by the platform. For example, the IoT platform may offer a notification service that allows external systems or applications to subscribe to receive event notifications, alerts, or alarms triggered by specific conditions of some IoT devices. This service enables external entities to stay informed about critical events detected by the IoT platform and to take appropriate actions based on these notifications.

Application programming interfaces (APIs)

APIs are programming interfaces that enable communication and interaction between the IoT platform and external systems. The northbound interface provides a well-defined set of programmatic ways to reach the available services and functionalities of the IoT platform. These APIs serve as the contract through which external developers can access, control, and retrieve data from the IoT platform through their own applications. APIs expose a standardized and structured way for applications or systems to communicate and integrate with the IoT platform.

App maintenance

This feature refers to the ongoing support and enhancement of deployed IoT applications, which typically include upgrading and app marketplace facilities. Upgrading support enables developers to continuously improve and upgrade their IoT applications over time. The platform provides mechanisms for version control, deployment, and seamless updates of applications running on the IoT platform, without disrupting the overall system or user experience.

The app marketplace facility on the other hand provides a centralized repository for managing and distributing IoT applications within the IoT ecosystem. It provides a hub, where developers can showcase and distribute their applications, and where users can discover and install the ones that meet their needs. The marketplace offers services such as application discovery, search, user reviews, ratings, and secure payment integration. This facility simplifies the process of discovering, installing, and managing applications for both developers and users, fostering collaboration, innovation, and growth.

2.3 IoT platform categories

The complexity of IoT platforms calls for ready-made packages that offer time and cost efficiency, rapid deployment, scalability, industry-wide adoption, integration capabilities, and application versatility. These benefits empower organizations to accelerate their IoT deployment initiatives, adapt to changing needs, and leverage a comprehensive set of pre-built features, ultimately enabling them to focus on their specific use cases and business goals.

Ready-made IoT platform packages come with pre-built features, functionalities, and tools that accelerate the development and deployment of IoT applications. This eliminates the need for organizations to build everything from scratch, saving time and reducing development costs. Several existing platforms provide a comprehensive set of capabilities, including device management, data analytics, security, and integration, which can be quickly leveraged without extensive development efforts. These existing platforms enable also the rapid deployment of IoT solutions. Organizations can leverage the platform's pre-configured components and frameworks to fast-track the development process. This speed-to-market advantage is particularly beneficial when there is a need for quick implementation or when to capitalize on time-sensitive opportunities is necessary.

Next, we discuss two main categories of IoT platforms: Commercial IoT platforms and open source IoT platforms. Each type offers distinct advantages and considerations, catering to different needs and requirements within the IoT ecosystem.

2.3.1 Commercial IoT platforms

Commercial IoT platforms are proprietary solutions offered by companies specializing in IoT or cloud technologies. These platforms are developed, maintained, and supported by commercial vendors, providing a comprehensive suite of tools, services, and features for IoT application development and deployment. Backed by dedicated vendors, commercial platforms include comprehensive support, such as technical assistance, training, and professional services. This level of support is valuable for organizations that require reliable guidance, quick response times, and accountability.

Some commercial platforms specialize in specific industries or use cases, offering domain-specific solutions and expertise. This industry focus caters to organizations that require tailored solutions with industry-specific features, compliance requirements, or integrations with existing enterprise systems.

Industry-specific IoT platforms

Industry-specific IoT platforms refer to a category of IoT platforms that are tailored to meet the unique needs and requirements of specific industries or verticals. These platforms are designed to address the challenges, compliance standards, and domain-specific use cases prevalent within particular industries. These platforms are developed with pre-built integrations and operational nuances that meet industry-specific analytics to optimize processes, enhance operational efficiency, and unlock new opportunities within the targeted industry. By aligning closely with the specific requirements of the industry, these platforms enable organizations to harness the full potential of IoT technologies in their domain. Next, we illustrate some commercial platforms in specific industries or use cases, offering domain-specific IoT solutions. We highlight their ability to deliver targeted solutions and value-added functionalities for specific sectors.

Automotive industry

These platforms focus on providing end-to-end solutions for the automotive industry, specializing in connected car solutions, fleet management, and telematics (Martínez de Aragón et al., 2018). IoT applications include remote vehicle diagnostics, predictive maintenance, and data analytics tailored to the automotive sector, for example, GSMA Automotive, Telit Cinterion, Ericsson connected vehicle cloud, and AWS connected vehicle solution.

Smart home industry

The smart home industry has witnessed significant growth with the proliferation of connected devices and IoT technologies. Smart home IoT platforms are transforming traditional homes into intelligent, automated, and interconnected environments. These platforms offer a range of features and capabilities tailored to smart homes, enabling homeowners to control and monitor various aspects of their homes remotely. They provide seamless integration with smart devices, such as thermostats, lighting systems, security cameras, and home appliances. Through intuitive interfaces and mobile applications, users can manage energy consumption, enhance security, automate tasks, and create personalized experiences. Prominent examples of IoT platforms catering to the smart home industry include Samsung SmartThings, Google Nest, Amazon Alexa, and Apple HomeKit. These platforms empower homeowners to create smarter and more convenient living spaces, increasing comfort, efficiency, and overall quality of life.

Building and facility management industry

The building and facility management industry relies on IoT platforms to optimize operations, enhance energy efficiency, and improve overall facility performance. IoT platforms designed for this industry enable real-time monitoring, control, and analysis of building systems and equipment. They integrate with sensors, meters, and building automation systems to collect data on energy usage, HVAC (heating, ventilation, and air conditioning), lighting, occupancy, and others. These platforms provide actionable insights, allowing facility managers to make data-driven decisions for efficient resource allocation, preventive maintenance, and cost savings. They enable remote monitoring and control of building systems, ensuring optimal performance and occupant comfort. Industry-specific IoT platforms, such as Siemens MindSphere, Schneider Electric EcoStruxure, Bosch Building Technologies, and Honeywell Forge, cater to the unique needs of building and facility management, offering features such as predictive maintenance, energy optimization, fault detection, and centralized control. By leveraging IoT platforms, the building and facility management industry can streamline operations, reduce energy waste, extend equipment lifecycle, and create sustainable and comfortable environments for occupants.

Smart cities and urban infrastructure industry

The deployment of IoT technologies within urban environments enables solutions for intelligent urban management, infrastructure optimization, and citizen-centric services. One key aspect of IoT platforms in the smart cities industry is the integration of diverse urban systems. These platforms facilitate the seamless connection and interoperability of different domains, such as transportation, energy, waste management, public safety, and water management. For example, with smart transportation systems, cities can monitor traffic conditions, optimize traffic flow, and provide real-time information to commuters. Energy management platforms allow cities to monitor and optimize energy consumption in street lighting, buildings, and infrastructure, reducing costs and carbon footprint. By monitoring the performance of critical infrastructure components, such as bridges, roads, and utility networks, cities can identify potential failures or anomalies in real-time and schedule maintenance activities more efficiently. This predictive maintenance approach reduces downtime, improves safety, and extends the lifespan of infrastructure assets.

For example, IBM Watson IoT for cities offers a comprehensive platform specifically designed for smart city initiatives (Umadevi and Amali, 2020; Marques and Pitarma, 2019), which integrates IoT data from various urban systems, including transportation, utilities, public safety, and environmental monitoring. The platform enables city authorities to gain insights, optimize resource allocation, and enhance the quality of life for citizens. Cisco Kinetic for cities provides a scalable and secure IoT platform tailored for smart cities, which enables seamless integration of various urban systems and data sources, such as traffic management, lighting, waste management, as well as public transportation. Particle IoT platform is another IoT platform with smart city applications that help cities to connect, monitor, and control various devices and sensors. Particle uses a full-stack PaaS (platform as a service) cloud infrastructure to connect urban objects (Particle, 2023).

General-purpose IoT platforms

General-purpose IoT platforms support diverse IoT applications across industries. These platforms offer a foundation for developing, deploying, and managing IoT solutions without being limited to specific use cases or industry verticals. They typically encompass capabilities such as device connectivity, data management, cloud services, analytics, and application development tools. These platforms empower organizations to design and implement IoT solutions tailored to the unique needs of organizations, regardless of the industry or specific use case.

AWS IoT Core

AWS IoT Core, provided by Amazon Web Services (AWS), is a leading general-purpose IoT platform that offers a robust and scalable infrastructure for connecting and managing IoT devices securely. The platform provides features such as device onboarding, secure communication, analytics engine, and device management. Given the seamless integration with other AWS services, organizations may further leverage cloud-based storage, analytics, and machine learning capabilities. AWS IoT Core also supports Amazon Sidewalk devices, which instrument low-power, long-range wireless devices that can extend the range of a home network and simplify device setup. These devices enable a (neighborhood) shared network that uses small private bandwidths. Sidewalk devices, which include a range of Amazon products, such as Amazon Echo devices, act as bandwidth relays to reach the AWS IoT Core platform, enabling novel neighborhood-network use cases.

For example, tracking lost pets when a pet wearing a compatible tracking device goes missing or wanders outside the range of the home Wi-Fi network. In this use case, other participating Sidewalk devices in the neighborhood can serve as potential signal relays, increasing the chances of locating the lost pet. In the same context, community pet owners may define virtual boundaries for their pets to enable geofencing capabilities for participating community members.

Microsoft Azure IoT Hub

This comprehensive IoT platform enables secure device connectivity and bidirectional communication between devices and the cloud. Features include device management, message routing, cloud-to-device messaging, and integration with other Azure services (Copeland et al., 2015). These services include query and data processing capabilities to gain insights from high-volume and high-velocity data streams, and serverless computing functionalities, which may trigger actions or execute custom logic in response to IoT events, such as receiving sensor data or device telemetry. This feature simplifies the process of building, deploying, and managing IoT solutions, as it provides a low-code approach for creating IoT applications, whereby the cloud provider takes care of infrastructure management, including scaling, patching, and availability, allowing developers to focus solely on writing and executing code.

Furthermore, Microsoft's Azure IoT Hub enables edge computing that allows organizations to deploy and manage cloud workloads, such as AI inferencing, analytics, and custom code, on edge devices (Ali and Ishak, 2020). Azure Stack Edge (formerly known as Azure Data Box Edge) is an appliance that combines edge computing, storage, and AI capabilities. This "box" acts as a gateway device, which brings Azure services to the edge, allowing local data processing, and thus reducing the need for data transfer to the cloud.

Oracle IoT cloud

This platform provides a range of services and capabilities to facilitate the development, deployment, and operation of IoT solutions, such as secure and scalable device connectivity and support of various IoT communication protocols, including MQTT, HTTP, and CoAP. Oracle IoT cloud also simplifies the management of large IoT device fleets through device provisioning, configuration, and firmware update services. Seamless integration with other Oracle Cloud services is provided, such as machine learning in Oracle Autonomous Database (Png and Helskyaho, 2022), Oracle Integration Cloud, and Oracle Mobile Cloud (Jakóbczyk, 2020). This integration allows organizations to leverage additional capabilities for data storage, integration, and mobile app development, to enhance IoT solutions.

2.3.2 Open source IoT platforms

Open source IoT platforms are developed and distributed under an open source license. These platforms provide a foundation for building and deploying IoT solutions by offering various features, functionalities, and tools that can be customized and extended by the community of developers. Thus open source platforms promote collaboration, transparency, and innovation by allowing users to access, modify, and distribute the source code freely.

Available open source IoT platforms are contributing significantly to IoT growth and democratization. They have empowered developers, researchers, and organizations to explore, experiment, and create IoT solutions without being tied to proprietary technologies or vendor lock-ins. Developers can benefit from a wide range of contributed plugins, libraries, and integration, which are shared by the wider community and that can be leveraged to extend the platform's capabilities or address specific use cases. An illustration of these platforms is provided in Table 2.1.

2.3.3 Hybrid IoT platforms

A hybrid approach to IoT platforms combines elements of both open source and commercial platforms, offering organizations a flexible and tailored solution to digital transformation. This approach allows organizations to address specific requirements and maximize customization, while benefiting from additional support and feature provided by both platforms. Table 2.2 outlines some possible tracks to hybrid IoT platforms, which are further elaborated on next.

Customized commercial platform

Organizations start with a commercial IoT platform as the foundation and customize it to meet their specific needs. This customization integrates additional open source components or involves the development of proprietary modules on top of the commercial platform to extend some functionalities or services. This level of customization aligns the platform with business processes that involve unique use cases for each organization. Organizations benefit from regular updates and bug fixes besides technical support services by well-established vendors.

Open source core with commercial enhancements

Customizing a commercial platform incurs costs such as fees for licenses and further maintenance. Furthermore, the commercial platform's design may restrict customization, or extensive development efforts are required for certain customizations. Adopting a commercial IoT platform followed by customization integrations may lead to vendor roadmap dependencies. Hence, when adopting a hybrid platform approach, vendor-related factors such as strategy and future commitment to customer needs are important selection criteria to weigh the likelihood of potential vendor lock-in against future organization developments. Finally, customizations may induce integration complexities, especially if the commercial platform lacks specific APIs or documentation for extending functionality. Organizations should thus carefully evaluate the ease of integration with existing systems and the availability of development resources to address any potential challenges.

Yet, there are important considerations surrounding this hybrid approach. Commercial enhancements of open source core functionalities may be challenging. A review of compatibility issues between the open source core and the intended commercial components or services to be incorporated needs to be drawn. Differences in architectures, programming languages, or dependencies may arise. Evaluation and

Table 2.1 Examples of open source IoT platforms.

Platform purpose	Features	Examples
General-purpose	- Capabilities can be utilized across different industries and use cases. - Offers device connectivity, data management, analytics, and application development tools.	- **ThingsBoard:** Scalable and customizable platform for connecting, managing, and analyzing IoT devices and data, with a rules engine and a community edition. - **Ubidots:** Offers a free tier with limited features and capacity, making it accessible to develop small-scale IoT projects.
Industry-specific	- Some open source IoT platforms are tailored to specific industries. - Provides pre-built solutions, protocols, and frameworks, which address the unique requirements of those industries.	- **Home Assistant:** Designed for smart home automation, with support of popular IoT communication protocols, enabling connectivity and interoperability with a range of smart home devices (Altherr and Grund, 2023). - **Eclipse Kapua:** An industrial platform (Kirkland and Carrer, 2017) that has been used in fleet management to build commercial IoT solutions (Eurotech, 2023).
Edge computing	- Enables the deployment and management of IoT workloads at the edge of the network, closer to the devices and data sources. - Provides edge analytics, local processing, and offline capabilities.	- **EdgeX Foundry:** Hosted by the Linux Foundation, and used in industrial IoT edge computing developments (Villali et al., 2021). - **Fledge:** Focuses on critical industrial control operations (Goethals et al., 2020).
Connectivity	- Focuses on providing robust connectivity for IoT devices. - Supports various protocols, gateways, and connectivity standards, such as LoRaWAN connectivity.	- **The Things Network (TTN):** A collaborative Internet of Things (IoT) platform that enables IoT connectivity solutions using LoRaWAN (www.thethingsnetwork.org). - **Eclipse Mosquitto:** Provides an MQTT broker, and tools for connecting MQTT clients (Eclipse Foundation, 2021).

continued on next page

Table 2.1 *(continued)*

Platform purpose	Features	Examples
Data analytics	- Provides tools and frameworks for processing, analyzing, and visualizing IoT data. - Offers real-time streaming analytics, machine learning, and data storage capabilities.	- **Apache Kafka:** A full-fledged event streaming platform to handling high volumes of data pipelines (Le Noac'h et al., 2017). - **InfluxDB:** Time series database (TSDB) for IoT sensor data, and real-time analytics (Gangadhar and Sowmya, 2021).

Table 2.2 Hybrid IoT platforms.

Platform configuration	Description	Evaluation
Customized commercial platform	- Start with a commercial IoT platform as the IoT platform foundation - Add or develop proprietary modules	- **Advantages:** Stability, support, extensibility, compatibility and customization - **Considerations:** Cost, flexibility limitations, vendor lock-in, integration complexity
Open source core with commercial enhancements	- Build IoT platform using an open source core - Enhance it with commercial components or services	- **Advantages:** Flexibility, customizability, cost-effectiveness and community support - **Considerations:** Integration challenges, compatibility, governance, vendor reliability, and development complexity
Hybrid integration	- Combine multiple IoT platforms, including both open source and commercial ones - For example, use an open source platform for data collection and analysis while integrating with a commercial platform for device connectivity and management	- **Advantages:** Best-of-breed selection, enhanced functionality, and scalability - **Considerations:** Integration complexity, interoperability, security, and maintenance.

testing practices are essential to ensure smooth integration. Commercial enhancements provided by third-party vendors induce the same lock-in issues mentioned in this previous option, although with a lower risk impact over long-term partnership prospects. Organizations need to establish some governance rules, which are guidelines, and protocols to ensure that the open source core and commercial enhancements are effectively integrated and maintained in a compliant and cohesive manner. Finally, building from an open source core may require a higher level of technical expertise and development resources compared to using a ready-made commercial platform. Organizations need to assess their internal capabilities and the availability of skilled developers or consider engaging external resources to handle the customization.

Hybrid integration

Multiple IoT platforms, including open source and commercial ones, may be combined. This approach leverages the strengths of different platforms along with specific use cases or functionalities. For example, data collection and device connectivity may involve diverse platforms. This hybrid integration approach offers the flexibility to choose the suitable platform for required use cases. Enhanced functionality and scalability distinguish this hybrid option. These levels of enhancements are due to the variety of features available across a range of potential platform candidates. This flexibility expands the possibilities that leverage emerging technologies.

But hybrid integration generates data synchronization issues, as well as interoperability, and communication challenges, as platforms may involve different storage models and communication protocols. Further integration efforts and additional development resources and expertise may be required. Proper data governance practices need to be established for data consistency and integrity, and potential security vulnerabilities introduced by integration points need to be mitigated. Finally, a hybrid integration approach may require ongoing maintenance and support from multiple platform vendors or service providers, which raises the complexity of managing multiple vendor relationships. Clear communication channels and well-defined support processes should be established to address these concurrent partnership issues.

2.4 IoT platforms for enabling digital transformation

At the forefront of the digital transformative journey are IoT platforms, which serve as the backbone for connecting, managing, and analyzing the vast array of IoT devices and data. IoT platforms offer seamless integration with existing business systems, such as enterprise resource planning (ERP) and customer relationship management (CRM), to scale the digitalization scope that unveils new data sources and use cases. As the number of connected devices expands, IoT platforms offer the scalability required to handle the growing volume and complexity of data, which fuel digitalization efforts. The flow of data between IoT devices and these systems enhances business processes, automates workflows, and drives data-driven decision-making. For example, the new flow of IoT data can be used to optimize inventory management, streamline customer service, and enable personalized marketing campaigns. Thus organizations that enrich their ERP and CRM data with real-time IoT data optimize their understanding of customer behavior, operational performance, and market trends. This level of understanding optimization leads to new levels of

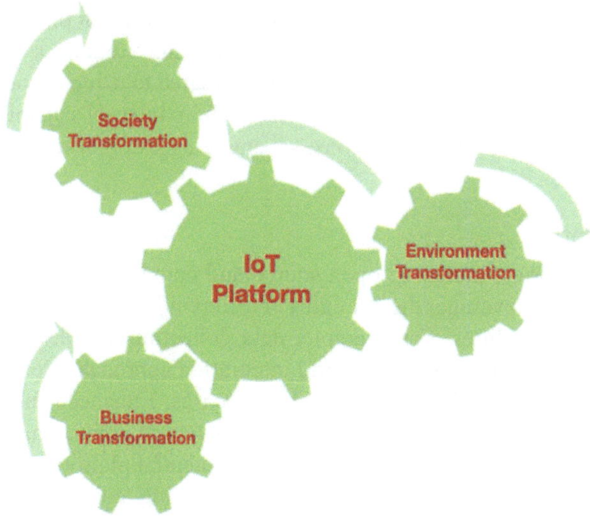

FIGURE 2.9

Digital transformation with IoT platforms.

process optimization, as collected data from IoT devices identify bottlenecks, and drive continuous improvement initiatives. For instance, IoT data can trigger automated actions inherently in ERP or CRM systems, such as initiating replenishment orders based on real-time inventory levels or generating personalized recommendations for customers.

Similarly, IoT platforms optimize citizens governance through scaling further the reach of urban resource management (URM). These systems emerged as a response to the increasing challenges faced by cities in managing their resources efficiently and sustainably (Volk et al., 2022), while optimizing citizen relations. Urban resource management (URM) systems refer to the holistic approach of effectively utilizing resources in urban environments through assisting governance with planning, monitoring, and efficient allocation of various resources, such as energy, water, transportation, waste, and infrastructure assets within a city. URM aims to enhance sustainability, improve citizen satisfiability and safety, and create livable and resilient urban spaces.

In addition to the business and societal impacts, the integration of IoT platforms can also have significant environmental benefits as part of the digital transformation journey (see Fig. 2.9). By integrating IoT sensors into environmental monitoring networks, pollution sources can be identified, and the effectiveness of environmental policies can be monitored. The insights gained from environmental monitoring enable proactive measures for environmental protection and sustainable planning.

Leveraging IoT platforms empowers organizations and communities to optimize processes, enhance services, and create sustainable and connected ecosystems. Data unleashed directly from their original sources enable organizations to identify bottlenecks, automate workflows, and implement predictive and proactive strategies, which result in improved operational efficiency, reduced costs, and enhanced productivity. IoT devices and sensors provide contexts for adaptive actions, proactive support, and tailored experiences.

2.4.1 IoT platforms for climate change

IoT platforms are contributing to digital transformation in environmental domains, specifically addressing climate change. IoT platforms are being used to monitor and collect data on various climate-related parameters and atmospheric conditions. This data is further instrumented to understand climate patterns, identify climate change impacts, and formulate effective adaptation strategies to alleviate global climate-related threats.

Weather underground

This IoT platform collects weather data from a network of personal weather stations worldwide. This data contributes to climate monitoring efforts and helps individuals, organizations, and policymakers make informed decisions related to climate change adaptation. The platform operates on the concept of crowdsourcing weather data, where individuals or organizations install personal weather stations in their locations and contribute real-time weather observations. These personal weather stations consist of sensors that measure temperature, humidity, barometric pressure, wind speed, and direction, among other parameters. The data collected by these stations is uploaded to the Weather Underground platform, which is based on the IBM Watson IoT platform to create a rich and extensive network of weather information (Masters, 2019). This rich data set is further shared with The Weather Company, which is another IBM subsidiary company that integrates satellite imagery and radar sensors data along with a network of over 250,000 stations in 195 countries, to provide accurate and reliable weather forecasting for various industries and applications across a platform that integrates other platforms (MacGillivray, 2016).

A key feature of Weather Underground is its interactive map interface that allows users to view weather conditions in a location of interest. The platform provides access to current weather conditions, forecasts, radar, and satellite imagery, as well as historical weather data. Users can customize their weather preferences, save favorite locations, and receive personalized weather alerts (see https://www.wunderground.com/wundermap/). Weather Underground not only serves as a reliable source of weather information for individuals, but it also contributes to climate monitoring efforts, scientific research, and weather forecasting. The data collected from personal weather stations is valuable for understanding microclimates, weather patterns, and local variations. Meteorologists and researchers can access this data to study weather phenomena, assess climate change impacts, and improve forecasting models.

ClimateCell

This platform offers a climate intelligence dimension that encompasses various features and capabilities, including detailed information on temperature, humidity, wind patterns, precipitation, and other relevant climate parameters. This platform leverages a combination of traditional weather data, satellite imagery, and IoT sensor data to enhance its accuracy in weather insights. The IoT component of ClimaCell's platform involves the integration of various sensors and devices that capture real-time weather data at a local level. These IoT sensors include environmental monitoring devices, which collected data and are combined with other data sources to improve the precision and accuracy of ClimaCell's weather forecasts. Rebranded as Tomorrow.io, it has recently announced that it will launch a fleet of radar-equipped satellites to improve its weather forecasting capabilities https://www.tomorrow.io/. The platform automates alerts for weather-related challenges to serve customers in various sectors, such as aviation, transportation, construction, mining, and logistics.

2.4.2 Smart city platforms for societal change

IoT platforms empower communities, organizations, and governments to address pressing societal challenges. There are ongoing initiatives of digital transformation to improve the lives of people and communities by using smart, connected devices. Some of the domains where IoT platforms are driving societal changes are the following:

Healthcare monitoring platforms

IoT platforms are enabling remote patient monitoring, telemedicine, and personalized healthcare solutions, while democratizing access to healthcare services. The latest COVID-19 pandemic has created an unprecedented demand for healthcare services and resources, as well as a need for social distancing and infection prevention measures besides the active quest for efficient vaccines. In this context, IoT platforms were used for enhancing the quality and accessibility of health care delivery, as well as in supporting public health efforts to contain and mitigate the spread of the virus (Bhardwaj et al., 2022). For example, smart devices, such as smartphones were used for proximity monitoring and alerting. Bluetooth, Wi-Fi, or GPS signals embedded in those devices alert their users if they are too close to others, or if they enter a high-risk area. For example, the Stop COVID app used in France is a contact tracing and exposure notification solution that uses Bluetooth signals and mobile devices to alert the users if they have been in close proximity to someone who has tested positive for COVID-19, or if they have visited a high-risk area. The app is designed to protect the privacy and data of the users, as well as to support the public health efforts to contain and mitigate the spread of the virus (Rowe et al., 2020; Min-Allah et al., 2021).

Healthcare monitoring IoT platforms connect medical devices, wearables, and sensors to gather real-time health data and transmit it securely to healthcare providers. This facilitates proactive healthcare management, early detection of health issues, and improved access to healthcare services. Examples include Philips HealthSuite and Medtronic CareLink, which enable remote monitoring and management of patients' health conditions. Philips HealthSuite is a cloud-based IoT platform that integrates with connected medical devices, enabling the collection and analysis of data from wearable or home-based remote medical-monitoring equipment (Philips, 2022). Medtronic CareLink is a remote monitoring system for patients with Medtronic implanted cardiac devices (Sharma, 2021). This IoT solution from Medtronic enables patients with implantable pacemakers to use their smartphones to transmit secure data from their pacemakers to their physicians. A related app is available for free on Android and Apple app stores, and works in tandem with a physician-prescribed portable device reader.

There is potential for using digital twin technology to improve the diagnosis, prognosis, and treatment of cardiovascular diseases. A digital twin in this context, is a virtual replica of a patient's heart, which can receive and analyze molecular, physiological, and lifestyle data, allowing for personalized and predictive interventions (Coorey et al., 2021). The opportunities of developing and implementing digital twin technology in these precision medicine contexts involve interdisciplinary collaboration, as well as regulatory frameworks to ensure ethical and equity aspects (Coorey et al., 2022).

Energy efficiency and sustainability

IoT platforms can help address the pressing challenge of energy consumption by promoting energy efficiency and sustainability. By connecting and monitoring devices, buildings, and energy systems, IoT platforms enable real-time energy monitoring, optimize energy usage, and facilitate the integration of renewable energy sources, contributing to a more sustainable and resilient energy infrastructure. Schneider Electric EcoStruxure IoT platform enables customers to optimize their energy consumption, reduce their carbon footprint, improve their resource efficiency, and achieve their sustainability goals (Schneider, 2023). Similarly, Siemens Navigator is an IoT platform that collects and analyzes data from sensors, meters, and energy systems, to monitor energy consumption, identify inefficiencies, and optimize energy usage (Ostroukh et al., 2021). Finally, C3.ai Energy Management is an enterprise-scale AI and IoT platform, which focuses on energy management and sustainability for various industries, to provide real-time visibility into energy consumption, identify energy waste, and optimize operations (C3 AI Energy Management, 2023).

IoT-enabled education

IoT platforms are transforming education by enabling interactive and personalized learning experiences. These platforms connect smart devices, sensors, and educational tools to create smart laboratories with virtual learning environments, empowering students to learn at their own pace and enhancing educational outcomes. These laboratories cover a wide spectrum of STEM domains (Rout et al., 2017; Prakash et al., 2021; Xie et al., 2021).

Education venues are also subject to transformation, whereby future academic institutions are expected to incorporate a multitude of sensors and automated processes.

The establishment of smart campus infrastructures that utilize IoT platforms leads to new opportunities (Li, 2021; Polin et al., 2023). The education impacts enhanced learning outcomes and experiences by leveraging personalized learning to support diverse learners and pedagogies (Atif et al., 2015). The outcomes of IoT platform-based smart campuses improve social inclusion and equity by ensuring access, affordability, and quality of education for all, regardless of gender, race, ethnicity, disability, or socioeconomic status (Acuña et al., 2021). Education changes go beyond smart campus vicinities by strengthening community engagement and partnerships through connecting with local and global stakeholders, sharing knowledge and resources, and contributing to social and environmental causes (Atif and Mathew, 2013).

Food security

IoT platforms enable precision agriculture. The health and well-being of livestock animals can also be monitored via the same technology, enabling holistic smart farming techniques. Furthermore, IoT platforms enable end-to-end tracking and monitoring of food products throughout the supply chain. Sensors and RFID tags can be used to monitor temperature, humidity, and other environmental conditions during storage and transportation to preserve food quality. This process includes the management of the cold chain. CropX offers an IoT platform, which uses soil sensors and cloud-based analytics to help farmers optimize irrigation, improve crop yield, and reduce water usage by providing guidance for successful and sustainable farming.

CropX uses various sources of data, such as soil sensors, satellites, weather stations, and farm machinery. CropX serves various crop types, such as corn, soybean, wheat, and potato (Quy et al., 2022). Rebranded as Herd-itt, a company named CattleSense has developed a remote monitoring system that combines artificial intelligence and an advanced IoT collar as well as a drone system for monitoring and managing large cattle herds. CattleSense's smart collar was designed to track the location, behavior, health, and productivity of cows using sensors, GPS, and solar panels. CattleSense also aimed to reduce costs and increase efficiency by using a drone to replace vehicles or horses for herd management (Herd-Itt, 2023).

2.4.3 Business transformation

IoT platforms usher in a new era of business transformation, where organizations are leveraging the power of interconnected devices, data analytics, and automation to drive innovation and operational improvements. Across various industries, businesses are embracing IoT platforms to optimize processes, enhance customer experiences, and unlock new revenue streams. Real-world examples abound, showcasing the tangible impact of these initiatives. Companies such as General Electric, Coca-Cola, Rolls Royce, Amazon, and Uber have harnessed the capabilities of IoT platforms to revolutionize their operations. Through predictive maintenance, intelligent vending machines, digital twin technology, cashier-less retail experiences, and real-time fleet management, these organizations have redefined the way they operate, transforming their business models and creating value in the digital age. By harnessing the potential of IoT platforms, businesses are poised to gain a competitive edge, improve efficiency, and deliver innovative solutions that meet the evolving needs of customers and markets.

Rolls Royce digital twin technology

Rolls Royce employs digital twin technology, powered by IoT platforms, to create virtual replicas of their complex assets, such as aircraft engines. By connecting the digital twin to real-time data from sensors, Rolls Royce can monitor performance, identify potential issues, and optimize engine operations, resulting in improved efficiency and reduced maintenance costs. Virtual replicas of physical objects or systems, aircraft engines support engineers to conduct real-time simulations before the actual creation of an object or system, enabling them to test and refine designs. Additionally, digital twins allow for real-time monitoring of the operation and performance of the corresponding physical object or system. By capturing and analyzing data from aircraft sensors, Rolls Royce engineers make informed decisions to optimize the overall performance (Girolam et al., 2021).

Amazon Go cashier-less retail experience

Amazon Go stores leverage IoT platforms that enable computer vision, sensor fusion, and machine learning, to provide a cashier-less shopping experience. IoT sensors track customer movements, item selection, and purchases, allowing them to simply grab what they need and leave the store without traditional checkout processes (Wankhede et al., 2018).

Aurora Driver

Aurora Driver is designed to enable autonomous driving capabilities in various types of vehicles, including trucks. IoT platforms integrate and process the sensor data collected by Aurora Driver for real-time analysis, interpretation, and contextual understanding of the driving contexts (Bogdoll et al., 2022). The Aurora Driver is expected to be used in trucking operations to provide a reliable and scalable driver supply for logistics companies and private fleets, as well as freight transportation, in partnership with several vehicle manufacturers and carriers, such as Volvo, Uber, Toyota, and FedEx (Aurora, 2023).

2.5 Considerations for selecting a cloud-based IoT platform

Selecting a cloud-based IoT platform contributes to successful digital transformation initiatives that unlock the full potential of connected devices and data. Factors to consider include the type of IoT platforms, deployment options, and strategic options for IoT application development and data handling. These considerations were addressed by actual government-level investigations seeking to take confident steps toward digital transformation goals by harnessing IoT the transformative capabilities of IoT platforms (Västra Göteland Region, 2022). With numerous options available in the market, it is essential to carefully evaluate and consider these factors to ensure that the platform aligns with specific requirements and business objectives. Next, we discuss these factors, which enable organizations to select an IoT platform that maximizes the benefits of IoT deployments and drives a successful digital transformation agenda.

There are key factors that organizations need to consider when choosing an IoT platform for their digital transformation initiatives. These factors encompass strategic, operational, and business alignments with the organization's goals and objectives. Evaluating these factors should include the specifics of each organization with respect to these alignments to choose well-suited IoT platform strategies that drive their digital transformation efforts. Table 2.3 provides a broad overview of selection criteria and related key considerations when choosing between open source, commercial, or hybrid IoT platforms for supporting digital transformation initiatives.

When choosing an open source IoT platform, Table 2.3 shows that several key selection criteria should be considered. Customization and flexibility factors allow organizations to tailor the platform to their specific needs and extend its functionality in a straightforward way. Development and maintenance considerations focus on the platform's community and its active involvement in maintaining and updating the platform with new features and bug fixes. Other factors involve compatibility and integration to ensure seamless interoperability with existing systems and IoT devices. Community engagement indicates an active and supportive community, which contributes to the platform's development and provides assistance when needed. License considerations provide the necessary elements to legitimate the platform's terms, while a governance model ensures compliance and long-term sustainability. Finally, security features ensure the platform's robustness against malicious vulnerabilities, and regular updates provide the necessary patches to protect against emerging threats.

Commercial IoT platforms induce key selection criteria as well; they are further outlined in Table 2.3. Features and functionality criteria reveals the necessary capabilities to meet specific requirements. Integration and compatibility ensure seamless integration with essential IoT tools, services, or third-party solutions. Scalability and performance considerations focus on the platform's ability to handle increasing data volumes and support of a growing number of IoT devices. Adaptability and configurability criteria are essential for tailoring the platform to unique use cases, while easily adapting to changing requirements. Vendor reputation and support should be evaluated to ensure reliable and responsive assistance throughout the implementation process. Security and compliance are critical to safeguard the platform assets and meet standard industry regulations. The total cost of the platform ownership involves assessing not only upfront costs but also ongoing expenses, considering factors such as maintenance, support, and training. Evaluating these selection criteria helps organizations to make an informed decision when selecting a commercial IoT platform that offers the desired features related to engaging digital transformation initiatives.

Specific selection criteria distinguish a hybrid IoT platform. Interoperability is a key factor, ensuring seamless integration between open source and commercial components. Modularity should be evaluated to ensure diverse components' integration

Table 2.3 IoT platform selection criteria.

Platform category	Selection criteria	Key considerations
Open source	- Customization and flexibility - Development and maintenance - Compatibility and integration - Community engagement - Documentation and support - License and governance - Security and updates	- Availability of development tools that enable customization (e.g., APIs & SDKs) - Activity strength of the open source community - Security features and robustness against potential vulnerabilities - Standard protocols that support interoperability are available - Governance rules establishment and internal development efforts are cost-effectiveness
Commercial	- Features and functionality - Integration & compatibility - Scalability and performance - Adaptability and configurability - Vendor reputation and support - Security and compliance - Total cost of ownership	- Capabilities include data management, device management, analytics, and security - Integration with essential IoT tools, services, or third-party solutions - Ability to handle anticipated data volumes, number of devices, and concurrent requests - Vendor's roadmap and commitment to continuous improvement - User-friendliness and learning curve
Hybrid	- Interoperability - Modular architecture - Management and orchestration - Vendor collaboration - Support and maintenance - Component selection flexibility - Future-proofing capabilities	- Interoperability between open source and commercial components - Plug-and-play approach: components can be added or replaced - Tools for open source and commercial components configuration, deployment, scaling, and lifecycle management are provided from a single point of control - Emerging standards are supported to safeguard future investments

into an open architecture. Management and orchestration capabilities should provide a centralized control and monitoring of the hybrid ecosystem, including commercial and open source components. Vendor cooperation between open source and commercial vendors ensures interoperability and ongoing support, while maintenance criterion ensures an inclusive support that accommodates the integration between open source and commercial components. Flexibility in component selection allows to choose the most suitable components in a plug-and-play way. Finally, future-proofing capabilities ensure compatibility with emerging technologies to accommodate and protect future investments.

2.6 Challenges and future trends in cloud-based IoT platforms

Along with the benefits and opportunities offered by IoT platforms for digital transformation, there are also challenges facing their implementation and obstacles that organizations encounter in fully utilizing their potential. Besides revealing these challenges, a subsequent section also explores the evolving trends and advances in IoT platform technologies, highlighting the exciting developments shaping the future of this field, considering emerging technologies, such as AI and blockchains. Below, the potential of these technologies to further enhance the capabilities and applications of IoT platforms is discussed.

2.6.1 Common challenges in implementing IoT platforms and utilization obstacles

From technical complexities and data management to ROI concerns and organizational readiness, these challenges require careful consideration and strategic planning. By understanding and addressing these challenges, organizations can navigate the complexities of IoT platform implementation, overcome utilization obstacles, and maximize the value of their IoT initiatives and related investment.

Various aspects may hamper the organization's readiness to embrace digital transformation initiatives through IoT platforms, including its culture, processes, infrastructure, and human resources, as discussed further.

Resistance to change

The unknown induces uncertainty about how the IoT platforms will impact employee roles, responsibilities, and daily routines. Addressing these concerns and providing clear communication about the benefits and opportunities offered by the adoption of IoT platforms can help alleviate fears and reduce resistance. Employees may be accustomed to traditional methods and resistant to adopting new technologies and processes. The leadership commitment can drive cultural change by creating an environment that fosters innovation, experimentation, and continuous learning.

Lack of trust

Resistance to change can also arise from a lack of trust in the organization's leadership or the digital transformation initiative itself. Employees may be skeptical about the potential benefits or have had negative experiences with previous change efforts. Building trust through open communication, transparency, and involving employees in the decision-making process can help gain buy-in and reduce resistance.

Skill gap

Implementing IoT platforms often requires new skills and competencies. Resistance can emerge when employees feel ill-equipped to handle the technology or lack the necessary training and support. Offering comprehensive training programs, upskilling opportunities, and providing ongoing support and resources can empower employees to embrace the changes and build confidence in their abilities.

Change management

Effective change management by (1) creating a structured plan for managing transition addresses concerns and questions; (2) involving employees in the process provides the necessary support and resources to navigate though the changes. A dedicated change management team or change management consultants can help facilitate the process and ensure a smooth transition.

Talent acquisition

Managing IoT platforms often requires a diverse set of skills and expertise, which may not be readily available within the organization. Organizations need to identify the specific IoT-related skills required for their digital transformation initiatives and develop a strategy for talent acquisition efforts accordingly. Professionals with hands on skills in IoT architecture, sensor technologies, connectivity protocols, data analytics, cybersecurity, and cloud computing are expected to run the IoT platform operations.

Managing IoT platforms requires collaboration between various disciplines, including IT, engineering, business, and domain-specific professionals. Thus project managers with the ability to work across these domains can bridge the gap between technical requirements and business objectives, facilitating effective communication and collaboration between different individuals and teams. Upskilling the existing workforce, or ensuring the recruitment of a knowledgeable team contributes to the success of IoT platform implementation and management.

ROI and cost-effectiveness

When organizations embark on digital transformation initiatives through IoT platforms, they face the challenge of assessing the return on investment (ROI) and ensuring cost-effectiveness. Key financial implications that determine the cost-effectiveness of digital transformation initiatives include upfront investment, scalability and expansion, operational costs, and total cost of ownership (TCO). Evaluating the TCO of implementing and maintaining IoT platforms reveals opportunities for cost-effectiveness in the initial investment, but also ongoing expenses related to maintenance, upgrades, security, data management, and training. Assessing TCO over the entire lifecycle of the IoT platform helps organizations understand the long-term financial implications and make informed decisions. Subsequently, calculating ROI involves comparing the anticipated benefits, against the expected TCO. Benefits may include cost savings, revenue growth, or improved customer satisfaction. However, other intangible benefits may include enhanced brand reputation, increased agility, or new business models.

Regulations and compliance

IoT platforms involve the collection, storage, and processing of vast amounts of data, including personal and sensitive information. Organizations must adhere to privacy regulations, such as GDPR in Europe or CCPA in the United States. Compliance with these regulations includes obtaining user consent, implementing robust data protection measures, and ensuring secure data storage and transmission.

2.6.2 Evolving trends and advances in IoT platform technologies

Integration of Artificial Intelligence (AI)

AI technologies, including machine learning, deep learning, and cognitive computing, are expected to propel IoT platforms to the next level, which enhances their decision-making and automation capabilities. AI unleashes the full potential of IoT by empowering networks and devices to learn from historical data, anticipate future behavior, and consistently enhance their performance and decision-making abilities (Dupon, 2022). Prominent IoT platform software providers, including Amazon, Oracle, and Microsof, are incorporating AI capabilities, such as advanced analytics powered by machine learning, to amplify the value proposition of their IoT offerings (Srivastava, 2022; Vinugayathri, 2023). AI and ML have been shown to improve the workload performance of industrial IoT platforms and enable edge AI-based initiatives (Columbus, 2021).

Edge computing and fog computing

These emerging computing paradigms bring computational capabilities closer to the edge of the network, reducing latency, improving response times, and enabling real-time processing and analysis of IoT data. By processing data at the network edge or within the fog layer, IoT platforms can enhance data privacy, reduce bandwidth requirements, and enable faster decision-making in time-sensitive applications. These computing paradigms complement cloud-based IoT platforms and facilitate distributed intelligence and localized decision-making (Singh and Gill, 2023; Tuli et al., 2023).

6G networks

The rollout of 6G networks is expected to have a significant impact on the future of IoT platforms (Amadeo et al., 2022). 6G networks enable new use cases and applications as well as new tactile interfaces (Gupta et al., 2023). Emerging applications, such as immersive extended reality in metaverse worlds, autonomous vehicles, and smart cities are expected to revolutionize further the potential of IoT platforms, which can leverage sensors and cameras to create accurate spatial maps of physical spaces. These maps can be used to align virtual objects and experiences with the real world, enabling users to interact with virtual elements in a spatially aware manner. IoT devices, such as depth cameras and motion sensors, can track the movements of users within the physical environment and translate them into corresponding actions in the virtual world. For example, Azure Kinect is a spatial computing developer kit with advanced AI sensors, including a depth sensor, a microphone array, and an RGB camera, which can be used to create mixed-reality applications that use computer vision and speech models to track and monitor user movements and interactions.

Blockchain technology

The decentralized, transparent, and secure framework for data exchange and transactions provided by blockchain technology enhances data integrity and immutability in IoT platforms, which raises their trust level among stakeholders. Blockchains enable secure and auditable data sharing, which facilitates peer-to-peer transactions and ensures data provenance and authenticity. Blockchain in IoT platforms finds applications in supply chain management, asset tracking, smart contracts, and data marketplace scenarios; the same applies to Industry 4.0 and Industrial IoT settings at large (Shammar et al., 2021).

References

Acuña, L.C., Narváez, R., Salas, C., Magre, L.A., González, M.J., 2021. Smart UTB: an IoT platform for smart campus. In: Communications in Computer and Information Science. Springer International Publishing, pp. 239–249. https://doi.org/10.1007/978-3-030-86702-7_21.

Ali, O., Ishak, M.K., 2020. Bringing intelligence to IoT edge: machine learning based smart city image classification using Microsoft azure IoT and custom vision. Journal of Physics. Conference Series 1529 (4), 042076. https://doi.org/10.1088/1742-6596/1529/4/042076.

Altherr, L.C., Grund, R.M., 2023. Development of an open source energy disaggregation tool for the home automation platform home assistant. Tagungsband AALE 2023.

Amadeo, M., Campolo, C., Ruggeri, G., Molinaro, A., 2022. Edge caching in IoT smart environments: benefits, challenges, and research perspectives toward 6g. In: Internet of Things. Springer International Publishing, pp. 53–73. https://doi.org/10.1007/978-3-031-15160-6_3.

Atif, Y., Mathew, S., 2013. A social web of things approach to a smart campus model. In: 2013 IEEE International Conference on Green Computing and Communications and IEEE Internet of Things and IEEE Cyber, Physical and Social Computing, pp. 349–354.

Atif, Y., Mathew, S.S., Lakas, A., 2015. Building a smart campus to support ubiquitous learning. Journal of Ambient Intelligence and Humanized Computing 6 (2), 223–238. https://link.springer.com/content/pdf/10.1007/s12652-014-0226-y.pdf.

Aurora, 2023. Autonomous freight is on the horizon. Available online at: https://aurora.tech. Retrieved on 10/07/2023.

Bhardwaj, V., Joshi, R., Gaur, A.M., 2022. IoT-based smart health monitoring system for COVID-19. SN Computer Science 3 (2), 137. https://link.springer.com/content/pdf/10.1007/s42979-022-01015-1.pdf.

Bogdoll, D., Orf, S., Töttel, L., Zöllner, J.M., 2022. Taxonomy and survey on remote human input systems for driving automation systems. In: Lecture Notes in Networks and Systems. Springer International Publishing, pp. 94–108. https://doi.org/10.1007/978-3-030-98015-3_6.

Boškov, I., Yetgin, H., Vučnik, M., Fortuna, C., Mohorčič, M., 2020. Time-to-provision evaluation of IoT devices using automated zero-touch provisioning. In: GLOBECOM 2020–2020 IEEE Global Communications Conference, pp. 1–7.

C3 AI Energy Management, 2023. AI powered energy management to reduce costs & GHG emission, C3 AI data sheet. Available online at: https://c3.ai/wpcontent/uploads/2020/10/C3-AI-Data-Sheet-Energy-Management.pdf. Retrieved on 08/07/2023.

Columbus, L., 2021. Realizing IoT's potential with AI and machine learning, CISCO. Available at: https://venturebeat.com/business/realizing-IoTs-potential-with-ai-and-machine-learning/. Retrieved on 12/07/2023.

Coorey, G., Figtree, G.A., Fletcher, D.F., Redfern, J., 2021. The health digital twin: advancing precision cardiovascular medicine. Nature Reviews Cardiology 18 (12), 803–804.

Coorey, G., Figtree, G.A., Fletcher, D.F., Snelson, V.J., Vernon, S.T., Winlaw, D., Grieve, S.M., McEwan, A., Yang, J.Y.H., Qian, P., O'Brien, K., Orchard, J., Kim, J., Patel, S., Redfern, J., 2022. The health digital twin to tackle cardiovascular disease—a review of an emerging interdisciplinary field. npj Digital Medicine 5 (1), 126.

Copeland, M., Soh, J., Puca, A., Manning, M., Gollob, D., 2015. Microsoft Azure. Apress. https://doi.org/10.1007/978-1-4842-1043-7.

Dupon, X., 2022. How AI is changing IoT, InfoWorld. Available at: https://www.infoworld.com/article/3663017/how-ai-is-changing-IoT.html. Retrieved on 12/07/2023.

Eclipse Foundation, 2021. Eclipse mosquitto. Available at: https://projects.eclipse.org/projects/IoT.mosquitto.

Eurotech, 2023. Everyware cloud users's hub. Available at: https://ec.eurotech.com. Retrieved on 05/07/2023.

Gangadhar, S., Sowmya, 2021. Real time environmental time series data analysis using influx DB. International Journal of Advanced Scientific Innovation. https://zenodo.org/record/4641703.

Girolam, M., Mair, R., Jans-Singh, M., 2021. Creating a virtual replica. Ingenia: Emerging Technology.

Goethals, T., Turck, F.D., Volckaert, B., 2020. FLEDGE: kubernetes compatible container orchestration on low-resource edge devices. In: Internet of Vehicles. Technologies and Services Toward Smart Cities. Springer International Publishing, pp. 174–189. https://doi.org/10.1007/978-3-030-38651-1_16.

Gupta, M., Jha, R.K., Jain, S., 2023. Tactile based intelligence touch technology in IoT configured WCN in B5G/6G-A survey. IEEE Access 11, 30639–30689.

Herd-Itt, 2023. Remote cattle monitoring system. https://www.herd-itt.com. Retrieved on 09/07/2023.

Jakóbczyk, M.T., 2020. Practical Oracle Cloud Infrastructure. Apress. https://doi.org/10.1007/978-1-4842-5506-3.

Khan, A., Tahir, S., Khan, F., Tahir, H., Zulkifl, Z., 2021. Enhancing security of cloud-based IoT systems through network access control (nac). In: 2021 International Conference on Communication Technologies (ComTech), pp. 103–108.
Kirkland, J., Carrer, M., 2017. Eclipse kapua: open IoT cloud platform. Eclipse Foundation. Available at: https://www.eclipse.org/community/eclipse_newsletter/2017/march/article4.php. Retrieved on 05/07/2023.
Le Noac'h, P., Costan, A., Bougé, L., 2017. A performance evaluation of Apache Kafka in support of big data streaming applications. In: 2017 IEEE International Conference on Big Data (Big Data), pp. 4803–4806.
Li, W., 2021. Design of smart campus management system based on Internet of things technology. Journal of Intelligent & Fuzzy Systems 40 (2), 3159–3168. https://doi.org/10.3233/jifs-189354.
MacGillivray, C., 2016. The platform of platforms in the Internet of things. IBM White paper available at: https://IoTslam.com/wp-content/uploads/2016/06/IDC-Study-IoT-Platform-of-Platforms.pdf. Retrieved on 07/07/2023.
Marques, G., Pitarma, R., 2019. Environmental quality supervision for enhanced living environments and laboratory activity support using IBM Watson internet of things platform. In: Lecture Notes in Computer Science. Springer International Publishing, pp. 680–691. https://doi.org/10.1007/978-3-030-22744-9_53.
Martínez de Aragón, B., Alonso-Zarate, J., Laya, A., 2018. How connectivity is transforming the automotive ecosystem. Internet Technology Letters 1 (1), e14. https://onlinelibrary.wiley.com/doi/abs/10.1002/itl2.14.
Marwan, W., Wiklom, T., 2021. Prototype development and performance evaluation of esp-wifi-mesh sensor networks for IoT. In: Proceedings of Asia Pacific Conference on Robot IoT System Development and Platform 2020, pp. 63–64. https://cir.nii.ac.jp/crid/1050011097134444544.
Masters, J., 2019. IBM introducing the world's highest-resolution global weather forecasting model. Available at: https://www.wunderground.com/cat6/IBM-Introducing-Worlds-Highest-Resolution-Global-Weather-Forecasting-Model. Retrieved 06/07/2023.
Min-Allah, N., Alahmed, B.A., Albreek, E.M., Alghamdi, L.S., Alawad, D.A., Alharbi, A.S., Al-Akkas, N., Musleh, D., Alrashed, S., 2021. A survey of COVID-19 contact-tracing apps. Computers in Biology and Medicine 137, 104787. https://www.sciencedirect.com/science/article/pii/S0010482521005813.
Ostroukh, A., Karelina, M., Filippova, N., Marusin, A., Evtyukov, S., 2021. Intelligent system for digital substation control. Transportation Research Procedia 57, 385–391. International conference of Arctic transport accessibility: networks and systems https://www.sciencedirect.com/science/article/pii/S2352146521006931.
Particle, 2023. IoT and the smart city: examples, applications, and goals. Available online at: https://www.particle.io/IoT-guides-and-resources/smart-cities-IoT/. Retrieved July 5, 2023.
Philips, 2022. Seven key success factors for digital transformation in healthcare. Philips Healthcare Informatics. Available online at: https://www.philips.com/a-w/about/news/archive/features/2022/20220413-seven-key-success-factors-for-digital-transformation-in-healthcare.html.
Png, A., Helskyaho, H., 2022. Oracle machine learning in autonomous database. In: Extending Oracle Application Express with Oracle Cloud Features. Apress, pp. 139–191. https://doi.org/10.1007/978-1-4842-8170-3_5.
Polin, K., Yigitcanlar, T., Limb, M., Washington, T., 2023. The making of smart campus: a review and conceptual framework. Buildings 13 (4), 891. https://doi.org/10.3390/buildings13040891.

Prakash, K.R., Santhosh, M.S., Purushothama, G.K., Ramya, M.V., 2021. An approach to convert conventional laboratories into IoT-enabled laboratories. International Journal of Web-Based Learning and Teaching Technologies 16 (5), 108–120. https://doi.org/10.4018/ijwltt.20210901.oa6.

Quy, V.K., Hau, N.V., Anh, D.V., Quy, N.M., Ban, N.T., Lanza, S., Randazzo, G., Muzirafuti, A., 2022. IoT-enabled smart agriculture: architecture, applications, and challenges. Applied Sciences 12 (7), 3396. https://doi.org/10.3390/app12073396.

Rajeesh Kumar, N., Arun, M.M., Baraneetharan, E., Stanly Jaya, Prakash J., Kanchana, A., Prabu, S., 2020. Detection and monitoring of the asymptotic COVID-19 patients using IoT devices and sensors. International Journal of Pervasive Computing and Communications 18 (4), 407–418. https://doi.org/10.1108/ijpcc-08-2020-0107.

Rout, K.K., Mishra, S., Routray, A., 2017. Development of an Internet of things (IoT) based introductory laboratory for undergraduate engineering students. In: 2017 International Conference on Information Technology (ICIT), pp. 113–118.

Rowe, F., Ngwenyama, O., Richet, J.-L., 2020. Contact-tracing apps and alienation in the age of COVID-19. European Journal of Information Systems 29 (5), 545–562. https://doi.org/10.1080/0960085x.2020.1803155.

Schneider, 2023. EcoStruxure for power and grid – power generation & smart grid solutions. Available online at: https://www.se.com/ww/en/work/solutions/for-business/electric-utilities/. Retrieved on 08/07/2023.

Shammar, E.A., Zahary, A.T., Al-Shargabi, A.A., 2021. A survey of IoT and blockchain integration: security perspective. IEEE Access 9, 156114–156150.

Sharma, A., 2021. A bibliometric analysis and visualisation of research trends in cardiac pacemaker battery. Annals of the Romanian Society for Cell Biology. Retrieved from: http://annalsofrscb.ro/index.php/journal/article/view/481.

Singh, R., Gill, S.S., 2023. Edge AI: a survey. Internet of Things and Cyber-Physical Systems 3, 71–92. https://www.sciencedirect.com/science/article/pii/S2667345223000196.

Srivastava, S., 2022. AI and IoT: two powerful entities that will change the way you do business. Appinventiv. Available at: https://appinventiv.com/blog/ai-and-IoT-in-business/. Retrieved on 12/07/2023.

Subke, P., Moshref, M., Erber, J., 2020. In-vehicle diagnostic system for prognostics and OTA updates of automated/autonomous vehicles. SAE International Journal of Advances and Current Practices in Mobility 2 (5), 2963–2968. https://doi.org/10.4271/2020-01-1373.

Tang, S., Zheng, Y., 2023. Implementation of an IoT system for environment monitoring and remote web control using ARM Mbed cloud and GUI. International Journal of Computer Applications in Technology 71 (1), 1. https://doi.org/10.1504/ijcat.2023.131061.

Tanganelli, G., Mingozzi, E., 2019. Energy-efficient IoT service brokering with quality of service support. Sensors 19 (3), 693. https://doi.org/10.3390/s19030693.

Tuli, S., Mirhakimi, F., Pallewatta, S., Zawad, S., Casale, G., Javadi, B., Yan, F., Buyya, R., Jennings, N.R., 2023. AI augmented edge and fog computing: trends and challenges. Journal of Network and Computer Applications 216, 103648. https://www.sciencedirect.com/science/article/pii/S108480452300067X.

Umadevi, K.S., Amali, D.G.B., 2020. Data visualization and analysis for air quality monitoring using IBM Watson IoT platform. In: Data Visualization. Springer, Singapore, pp. 15–32. https://doi.org/10.1007/978-981-15-2282-6_2.

Västra Göteland Region 2022. Internet of things (IoT) – crucial technology for digitization. Available online at Internet of Things (IoT) - crucial technology for digitization. Retrieved on 10/07/2023.

Villali, V., Bijivemula, S., Narayanan, S.L., Mohana Venkata Prathusha, T., Krishna Sri, M.S., Khan, A., 2021. Open-source solutions for edge computing. In: 2021 2nd International Conference on Smart Electronics and Communication (ICOSEC), pp. 1185–1193.

Vinugayathri, 2023. AI and IoT blended – what it is and why it matters?, Clarion technologies. Available at: https://www.clariontech.com/blog/ai-and-IoT-blended-what-it-is-and-why-it-matters. Retrieved on 12/07/2023.

Volk, R., Rambhia, M., Naber, E., Schultmann, F., 2022. Urban resource assessment, management, and planning tools for land, ecosystems, urban climate, water, and materials—a review. Sustainability 14 (12), 7203. https://doi.org/10.3390/su14127203.

Wankhede, K., Wukkadada, B., Nadar, V., 2018. Just walk-out technology and its challenges: a case of Amazon go. In: 2018 International Conference on Inventive Research in Computing Applications (ICIRCA), pp. 254–257.

Wopata, M., 2021. 5 things to know about the IoT platforms market. Available online: https://IoT-analytics.com/5-things-to-know-about-IoT-platforms-market/. (Accessed 23 June 2023).

Xie, C., Li, C., Ding, X., Jiang, R., Sung, S., 2021. Chemistry on the cloud: from wet labs to web labs. Journal of Chemical Education 98 (9), 2840–2847. https://doi.org/10.1021/acs.jchemed.1c00585.

CHAPTER

3 Enabling digital transformation with IoT cloud applications and services

3.1 Introduction

Digital transformation is a business paradigm that engages innovative digital technologies to revolutionize business models and operations. The transformation entails incorporating technologies into all aspects of a business. To achieve this, business organizations require leadership that fosters a mindset receptive to change and adaptable to the continual evolution of the digital landscape. The objective is to increase business performance and customer experiences by sustaining a competitive edge through enhanced operational efficiency in the rapidly evolving digital economy (Ciasullo and Lim, 2022).

Digitalization is the system-level restructuring of economies, institutions, and society, which happens through the diffusion of technologies. The increasing proliferation of technologies such as the Internet of Things (IoT) and cloud computing across organizations' business operations unfolded digitalization prospects. This digital transformation is propelled by advancements in processing power, storage capacity, and communication bandwidth (Legner et al., 2017).

IoT and cloud-based services are technologies that mutually reinforce and accelerate digital transformation by providing the infrastructure, tools, and capabilities necessary to harness the full potential of real-time sensory data. This infrastructure facilitates the utilization of AI models and analytics, empowering organizations to adopt an agile and data-driven approach in the swiftly changing digital landscape. The resulting opportunities allow businesses to sustain themselves, even in the face of unexpected disruptions.

However, organizations without robust digitalization strategies may struggle during unforeseen disruptions, while others manage to sustain themselves effectively. To stay competitive and thrive in today's swiftly evolving digital landscape, businesses must embrace digitalization (Warner and Wäger, 2019). Digitalization steps lay the groundwork for the comprehensive digital transformation journey.

Strategies for digital transformation are essential for any business looking to stay competitive in tomorrow's market. These strategies include revisiting IT governance processes and mechanisms to effectively leverage contemporary technologies, which

Accelerating Digital Transformation with the Cloud and the Internet of Things (IoT)
https://doi.org/10.1016/B978-0-44-322217-7.00009-8

drive digital transformation (Korachi and Bounabat, 2020). Companies can streamline operations and logistics with suitable approaches, improve customer experiences, and create new business models. By embracing digital transformation, businesses position themselves for long-term success and growth. The following sections of this chapter discuss the strategic vision and alignment required for businesses to embrace digital transformation. Enabling factors of digital transformation, including technology infrastructure, agile development and practices, and the creation of digital experiences are revealed.

3.2 Laying the foundation for scalability and flexibility: technology infrastructure

The technology infrastructure is the backbone of any organization's digital transformation strategy, and a robust technology infrastructure is crucial. This includes reliable and scalable hardware, software systems, networking capabilities, and cloud-based resources. In the process of digital transformation, systems such as ERP (enterprise resource planning), CRM (customer relationship management), and PIM (product information management) undergo substantial enhancements and integrations. Organizations must thoroughly evaluate these software solutions to guarantee they are good fit for their digital transformation requirements and can be smoothly integrated within the cloud-to-things continuum infrastructure. Next, we overview the possible evolutions of these solutions to support organizations' digital transformation, along this continuum.

3.2.1 Revolutionizing business operations with next generation ERP systems

Organizations are increasingly leveraging vast amounts of data to refine corporate operations, mitigate risks, and formulate strategic resource planning initiatives. In this context, the integration of the cloud-to-things continuum serves as a catalyst, facilitating real-time data processing and analysis. This seamless integration embodies the transition of the physical world into a virtual representation, facilitated by IoT networks, embedded sensors, application software, and networking devices. These networks enable real-time data acquisition and exchange, thereby realizing the expected revolution in business operations across multiple fronts.

In addition to IoT devices having the capacity to locally process and analyze data based on their capabilities, they also have the option to transmit substantial data volumes to IoT cloud-based platforms for further analysis. This interaction present challenges, given the limited capabilities of devices, which may affect data quality and security. Nevertheless, the incorporation of cloud-based services significantly mitigates these challenges, providing robust tools that are capable of fostering industry growth within the digital transformation spectrum.

Next-generation ERP systems stand at the core of this transformation, bringing together these technologies cohesively. These advanced systems, characterized by enhanced data analytics and machine learning algorithms, are advancing traditional business processes into intelligent operations, thus reshaping business into a more responsive and perceptive environment.

Acting as central hubs, next-generation ERP systems orchestrate the flow of information and enable smarter, data-driven decisions. In manufacturing plants, ERP systems can facilitate predictive maintenance by analyzing data from sensors to identify potential wear and tear of equipment, scheduling timely maintenance, and thereby reducing costs. In logistics sector, these systems integrate data from GPS trackers to streamline route planning, improving delivery times and customer satisfaction. Likewise, in retail business, next generation ERP systems further optimize the inventory levels by analyzing customer preferences and purchase patterns to ensure timely replenishment of commodities. Furthermore, in the healthcare sector, these systems instrument data from IoT-based wearables and sensors in real time, to optimize treatment plans. Next generation ERP systems are revolutionizing business operations by integrating with IoT devices and cloud services. This integration enhances efficiency, cuts down costs, and boosts customer satisfaction.

AI-driven analytics infer various operational and tasks' optimization opportunities in next generation ERP modules, such as customer support, sales, and marketing. The massive data collected through IoT devices, combined with the cloud's processing and storage capabilities, enable AI models to deliver timely strategies and business directions. These AI models understand customer behaviors, while recognizing and preventing fraudulent transaction patterns, which ultimately foster business continuity and minimize risks.

3.2.2 Harnessing the power of CRM through digital transformation

Integrating Customer Relationship Management (CRM) tools with IoT and cloud-based services allows businesses to collect and analyze a wider range of data to improve customer service, marketing strategies, and sale channels. Real-time analysis of customer loyalty via the social web and personalized preferences derived from IoT can be used to reach potential customers and thereby recommend opportunistic commercial transactions (Mathew et al., 2013).

Data collected from IoT devices about customers' behavior improve customer service, whereas retail stores with sensors to track customer footfall can identify areas within the store where customers are spending more time. This information could be instrumented to improve the layout of the store or to personalize marketing campaigns. Cloud-based services analyze large amounts of IoT data to gain insights into customer behavior in a way that would not be possible with traditional CRM systems. Using real-time data from IoT devices to analyze trends and patterns of customer behavior supports the development of customer engagement strategies and enhances sales across emerging markets (Yerpude and Singhal, 2021).

3.2.3 Enhancing product information flow with digital transformation: a paradigm shift

Product information management (PIM) involves using tools and procedures to gather, store, and handle data related to an organization's product inventory. It is a resource for businesses of any scale, as it enhances efficiency, productivity, and customer satisfaction. Additionally PIM aids in meeting obligations with regulatory authorities, while also reducing labor and infrastructure expenses.

The cloud-to-things continuum helps to improve product design, optimize production, and allow businesses to streamline their supply chain and gain insight into potential sales and marketing opportunities. Businesses can make better product development, marketing, and sales decisions by having access to a single source of truth (SSOT) of product data, which contribute to accurate, consistent, and curated product information. Utilizing IoT and cloud services, businesses can now provide an outlook over the entire product lifecycle: from initial design and development stages through to manufacturing and sales, in real time. This PIM evolution optimizes the entire supply chain but also significantly enhances the business's return on investment (ROI).

Leveraging IoT and cloud computing capabilities, modern PIM systems can now aggregate and analyze data from a myriad of sources in real time, facilitating a more responsive and data-driven approach to product management. These advances are boosted by the integration of artificial intelligence (AI) and machine learning algorithms, which refine product data analysis further. This innovative integration fosters enhanced business operations and customer satisfaction, prompted by efficient and intelligent PIM. Earlier PIM was largely confined to tracking static data, offering a snapshot of product information, which, while valuable, remained relatively stagnant and isolated from the dynamic forces shaping the market. The integration of IoT and cloud computing facilitates the continuous and real-time monitoring of the entire product lifecycle, prompting adaptability and responsiveness of business operations to market fluctuations. This shift is not just a technological advancement, but a paradigm shift that recognizes the fluid and interconnected nature of modern business. This transition from static to dynamic, from isolated to interconnected, describes the new horizons in PIM, paving the way for businesses to thrive in a digitalized and ever-evolving market environment.

3.2.4 Essential technology stack for effective digital transformation

Organizations must assess their cloud strategy, considering security, compliance, and data governance factors, to determine the most suitable deployment models (public, private, or hybrid) for their technology infrastructure. To orchestrate a successful digital transformation, organizations must adopt a holistic approach covering the entire technology stack, which integrates cloud strategies seamlessly with IoT deployments, to meet the demands of a rapidly evolving marketplace.

Cloud computing offers companies the flexibility and responsiveness required to navigate market environments. By leveraging cloud computing, businesses adjust resource allocation without the need for labor-intensive hardware upgrades. This level of improvement allows businesses to scale their operations and infrastructure quickly and efficiently, on demand. Similarly, IoT devices can be deployed and scaled to accommodate varying requirements for providing real-time data and sensory reports. This scalability and flexibility enable businesses to adapt quickly to changing market needs and seize new business opportunities. The synergistic relationship between cloud and IoT nurtures an environment where innovation thrives and industry paradigms are redefined.

To ensure efficient resource utilization and understand the scalability of the IoT and cloud ecosystem, it is imperative to monitor the digital infrastructure performance. This can be achieved by tracking the resource utilization percentage over time and comparing it to changing demands. To further gauge the efficacy of the digital transformation strategy, the number of IoT devices with successful cloud integration should be closely monitored. A performance indicator for measuring cross-platform collaboration could be the number of successful integration between different IoT cloud systems. This metric indicates the level of interoperability achieved and the ease of data exchange. Tracking the number of collaborative projects or initiatives enabled by the cloud-to-things continuum demonstrates the degree of innovation.

The technology stack must support digital initiatives and enable seamless integration and data flow across various systems. Collaboration with external partners, such as technology vendors, startups, industry experts, and research institutions, will accelerate digital transformation. These partnership opportunities provide organizations with access to expertise and resources, which support digital transformation strategies that enable agility and responsiveness to market changes (Manyika et al., 2015).

3.2.5 Key performance indicators (KPIs) to gauge scalability

Identifying key performance indicators (KPIs) to measure and monitor scalability and flexibility is mandatory to sustain long-term growth. Some important KPIs are the following:

- Revenue growth: Track the growth of the business's revenue over time after each digitalization process. This will help review how well the business adapts to changing market conditions and measure the impact of digitalization.
- Time to market: Track the time to launch new products or services after every digitalization initiative. This will help review the business's scalability and measure digitalization's impact.
- Customer retention: Track customer satisfaction metrics after every digitalization initiative. This will help review how well customer's needs are met and measure digitalization's impact.

Tools for KPI monitoring include real-time dashboards, which facilitate the dynamic tracking of various performance metrics, and analytics that present actionable insights to guide strategic decision-making processes.

3.3 Agile development and operations

Agile methodologies for development and operations (DevOps) production practices foster collaboration, speed, and flexibility in product or service development and deployment. They enable organizations to iterate quickly, respond to changing requirements, and release new features or products faster. Agile principles emphasize cross-functional teams, cross-functional training, continuous integration, automation, and iterative development cycles. Next, we reveal frameworks for agile practices for the cloud-to-things continuum development and operations.

3.3.1 Agile practices

A well-crafted agile framework can be an effective organizational model for complex environments. It encourages collaboration among all team stakeholders rather than assigning coordination and information-sharing responsibilities to a single role (Block, 2023). Some known frameworks, such as Scrum and Kanban, could be adapted to the cloud-to-things continuum (Guerrero-Ulloa et al., 2023).

Scrum

This is an agile framework designed to facilitate team collaboration on complex product development. This framework provides a set of principles and practices for team members to work together around developing solutions incrementally, focusing on delivering prioritized functionalities or features of a product (Zayat and Senvar, 2020). Small, manageable units of an organization, called sprints, carry out tasks over a period of usually two to four weeks, while promoting transparency and adaptation at regular intervals to ensure that the project is on track toward the product development goal.

IoT projects frequently entail systems in which the hardware (such as sensors and IoT devices) and software (including apps and data analytics tools) must operate seamlessly together. The iterative and incremental approach of Scrum can be particularly beneficial for IoT projects, because teams build, test, and improve IoT system components step-by-step, while reacting to changes in requirements as they progress. An IoT project team typically comprises members with varied expertise, including hardware engineers, software developers, data scientists, and others. Scrum emphasizes such cross-functional teams and promotes collaboration among these experts, fostering innovation and problem-solving.

Kanban

This visual tool helps to manage workflow and processes, aiming to maximize efficiency and agility (Zayat and Senvar, 2020). Originating from Japan, this methodology relies on a Kanban board, a tool that visualizes the workflow, where tasks move from one column to the next as they progress through different stages of the development process. This methodology can be instrumented in IoT developments, where a plethora of tasks, ranging from firmware development to integration with various devices, need to be managed efficiently.

Tasks related to hardware components of the IoT ecosystem can be visualized separately from software tasks, including firmware development, API integrations, etc. However, a separate column or lane is used to track the integration and testing tasks to ensure that components work seamlessly together. By utilizing Kanban in IoT developments, team development is visualized to assess efficiency and collaboration workflows, while ensuring timely delivery without compromising quality (Matsuo et al., 2019).

3.3.2 Overcoming Agile & DevOps challenges in cloud-to-things environments

When transitioning to Agile and DevOps methodologies using cloud computing and IoT, some challenges need to be addressed before digital transformation. These methodologies stress rapid development, frequent changes, and continuous integration and deployment, which may not align with traditional approaches.

Integration and automation

IoT systems have numerous devices and protocols, which must be integrated and work seamlessly with cloud-based applications, making it a complex process. DevOps practices require robust automation for managing these integrations. To overcome the complex integration and automation challenges in IoT systems, a unified development platform is advocated to facilitate the integration process. The platform may include automation tools that streamline integration processes and manage complex workflows efficiently.

Addressing scalability

Although cloud computing offers scalability advantages, it requires careful planning to ensure that applications and infrastructure can scale horizontally to accommodate IoT data influxes, which may involve using orchestration and containerization tools, such as Docker and Kubernetes. Docker is utilized for constructing microservices that enable scalable and flexible applications. Each microservice functions independently, which reduces failures and simplifies the management and updating processes of IoT systems. Kubernetes ensures load-balancing by distributing the load effectively across different containers based on their computing resource usage, which results in high availability of IoT applications.

Latency vs costs

IoT applications require low-latency responses and high reliability to ensure that the cloud infrastructure provide the necessary response times and reliability levels, while being continuously updated. While cloud computing is cost-effective, costs may still spiral out of control with high data volumes in IoT projects. Cost monitoring and control measures must be used to monitor these changes. This performance vs cost dilemma involves adopting a strategy that includes infrastructure and budget management. On the infrastructure side, implementing systems that can dynamically allocate resources based on the current demand can prevent over-provisioning and reduce costs. On the budget management side, setting up alerts to get notified when spending reaches certain thresholds ensures spending does not escalate beyond predetermined thresholds without necessary scrutiny and intervention.

Configuration consistency and security

Ensuring consistent configurations across IoT devices and cloud infrastructure components is crucial. Managing version control for IoT device firmware and cloud services can be complex. Furthermore, IoT devices may be vulnerable to cyberattacks. Thus transitioning to Agile and DevOps, while ensuring the security of IoT devices, cloud infrastructure, and applications, is challenging. Nevertheless, DevOps pipeline must integrate continuous security monitoring.

3.3.3 Enhancing operational efficiency and security in the cloud-to-things continuum

To ensure optimal performance and swift issue resolution, measuring the response time between detecting an event or anomaly and taking necessary action is valuable. This KPI can aid organizations in maintaining operational efficiency. Another useful KPI is the number of remote management operations performed through cloud-connected IoT devices. A significant number of operations could indicate higher automation and remote control, which potentially means fewer manual interventions and greater efficiency.

However, operational efficiency and the number of remote management operations KPIs are intrinsically linked to security and compliance within a cloud-connected IoT environment. The Cloud Security Alliance's (CSA) Security, Trust, and Assurance Registry (STAR) program plays a significant role in this context (Atieh, 2021). As organizations increasingly rely on remote management operations to maintain operational fluency and respond swiftly to any anomalies, the emphasis on securing these operations from potential cyber threats becomes paramount. The CSA STAR program stands as a beacon of trust and assurance, guiding organizations to partner with cloud providers, who are committed to maintaining high standards of security and compliance.

3.3.4 KPIs to gauge security compliance

Establishing and monitoring key performance indicators (KPIs) ensure the efficacy of security protocols and compliance with existing strategies. A robust framework safeguards sensitive information and ensures regulatory adherence. Some important KPIs for gauging security compliance, facilitating proactive measures, and fostering a culture of accountability and resilience within the organization are discussed next.

- Data breaches: Track the number of data breaches that occur to monitor the business strategies for data protection.

- Compliance with regulations: Track compliance with industry regulations to help monitor how well the business meets regulatory requirements.
- Security audits: Conduct regular security audits of the IT governance policies and the IT infrastructure, which will help in the early identification of vulnerabilities.

3.4 Creating digital experiences

Digital experiences are enhanced by intuitive data analysis. Utilizing deep-learning models to analyze data provides the intuitive digital interface to data and reshapes the dynamics of business operations as well as talent proficiency, and customer engagement, which result in enriched digital experiences that foster greater productivity and cost-efficiency.

3.4.1 Harnessing data and analytics: stimulus for digital transformation

An effective digital transformation requires a robust data strategy and analytics capability. In today's digital age, data is a crucial asset, which drives insights and innovation. A comprehensive data strategy involves capturing, managing, and utilizing data, while adhering to data governance practices, data quality management, and privacy regulations. Organizations must implement analytics tools and techniques to derive actionable insights from the new wealth of data generated from physical processes to unlock the actual value of data with the cloud-to-things continuum. Advanced analytics, including deep learning, but also predictive modeling and data visualization, empower organizations to make informed decisions, identify trends, and uncover hidden patterns. In doing so, organizations transform raw data into strategic assets, which drive informed decision-making and sustainable growth. By embracing data-driven decision-making, businesses optimize operations, personalize customer experiences, and identify new business opportunities.

Organizations take advantage of the cloud-to-things continuum to create new products and services by tapping into pre-built cloud services, which include machine learning and big data analytics (Atitallah et al., 2020). One way to measure the progress of data analytics in digital transformation experiences is the rate of data ingestion or the volume of data processed within a designated period. Additionally, analyzing the quality and quantity of insights gained from data analytics can help determine the effectiveness of using IoT data for decision-making. Key performance indicators for digital transformation may further include these factors, enabled by data analytics:

- Number of new products and services: Track the number of new products and services launched yearly, which germinated from the cloud-to-things continuum.
- Revenue growth: Track the growth of business revenue over time to monitor how well the business benefits from its digital transformation efforts.

- Customer satisfaction: Track customer satisfaction ratings over time to help monitor how well customers respond to new products and services.

3.4.2 Redefining leadership: skilled talent pool

Digital transformation requires a skilled workforce capable of leveraging digital technologies effectively. Organizations must assess their talent pool to identify skill gaps and provide training and development opportunities that upskill employees. New talents with expertise in emerging technologies, such as IoT, data science, cybersecurity, and digital marketing, may be solicited as well. This proactive response to the advancements in technology is also a strategic move that is aligned with the International Data Corporation (IDC) insights for skilled employees (Needham, 2023).

As a central hub, the cloud connects IoT devices, applications, and data sources, but also enables a shift in organizational mindset and culture among the organization's employees. Digital transformation project leaders use this platform to devise digital strategies, set achievable goals, and follow up with provisioning the necessary resources that support digital transformation initiatives. While doing so, they promote a digital-first mindset, foster innovation, and encourage experimentation and risk-taking.

Organizations must foster a culture that encourages learning, adaptability, and openness to new ideas from the organization's employees. This involves creating a safe environment for experimentation, empowering employees, and promoting cross-functional collaboration and knowledge sharing across the cloud platform featured by the cloud-to-things business layers.

Businesses today can explore new avenues for growth by creating innovative products and services and developing disruptive business models enabled by the cloud-to-things continuum. Engaging with external partners and suppliers across the cloud platform fosters real-time collaboration, co-creation, and value exchange in the digital space. In addition, cross-functional collaboration and training also foster a culture of continuous learning and innovation across partners. Lastly, focusing on delivering enhanced customer experiences through digital channels, personalized interactions, and targeted marketing enables customer centric business. Thus regularly collecting and analyzing data related to organizational talent and leadership will provide insights into the effectiveness of driving digital transformation initiatives. Strategies must be adjusted based on the trends and outcomes revealed by this employee-related KPIs.

- Digital skills development rate: A measure for businesses to track the rate at which employees develop new digital skills and competencies. This can be monitored by keeping tabs on training attendance, certification completion, or skills assessments.
- Employee engagement: Keep track of employees' engagement into digital transformation initiatives. This can be gauged by their level of involvement through conducting surveys, gathering feedback, and observing their participation in digital projects.

- Talent retention: It is imperative to closely monitor the organization's retention rate of vital digital talent. A significant turnover rate in digital positions could indicate severe problems with leadership or talent development.
- Digital leadership score: Create a scoring system to evaluate leadership's effectiveness in driving digital transformation. Metrics could include senior leaders' participation in digital training and the number of initiatives led.
- Time-to-fill digital roles: Measuring the time it takes to fill critical digital positions within the organization is imperative. A lengthy recruitment process can significantly hinder digital transformation efforts. Ensure that the process is efficient and streamlined to avoid any unnecessary delays.
- Innovation index: Develop an index to measure an organization's ability to foster innovation. This can include tracking the number of innovative ideas submitted, implemented, or resulting in revenue.

3.4.3 Increasing footfall: customer-centric approach

Putting the customer at the center of digital transformation efforts is vital. Organizations are expected to understand customer needs, preferences, and behaviors and design digital experiences that meet or even exceed their expectations. This includes leveraging customer data, conducting user research, implementing personalization strategies, and optimizing customer journeys across various digital touchpoints. The cloud-to-things continuum provides a customer-centric approach to digital transformation through gathered data, which enable organizations to optimize personalized operations.

Cloud platforms analyze customer data gathered from IoT devices, such as sensors, wearables, and smart appliances to derive actionable decisions, which tailor their products and services to customer needs. For instance, wearable fitness devices can provide customized exercise and health-related recommendations. Cloud-based customer relationship management (CRM) systems are empowered with analytics tools that enable businesses to segment their customer base and deliver a high level of personalized content, recommendations, and offers based on individual preferences.

The real-time communication with customers enabled by IoT devices provide proactive maintenance alerts, for example, when riding connected vehicles or receiving personalized notifications from smart home devices about security breaches or energy usage. By harnessing this data, businesses can respond quickly to customer inquiries and issues, ultimately enhancing the customer experience. Moreover, IoT sensors and devices contribute significantly to optimizing supply chain management, inventory control, and manufacturing processes. This efficiency can lead to cost savings, which can be passed on to customers. Cloud-based business process automation tools and enterprise resource planning (ERP) systems further improve operational efficiency, enabling faster order processing, better inventory management, and more accurate demand forecasting. Ultimately, all these benefits accrue to the customer, ensuring that they receive the best digital experience.

A comprehensive framework for monitoring the effectiveness of digital transformation efforts, which ensures a more customer-centric approach, is important. Some KPIs to monitor a customer-centric approach to digital transformation include:

- Personalization effectiveness: Track the success of personalization efforts using metrics like click-through rates, conversion rates, and customer satisfaction scores.
- Usage recommendation: Monitor the adoption of product or content suggestions offered to consumers based on their preferences.
- Customer segmentation accuracy: Measure the accuracy of customer segmentation to ensure relevant content and offers.
- Response time: The average response time to customer inquiries or alerts generated by IoT devices should be measured.
- Conversion rate: Track the percentage of customer interactions that result in a desired action, such as a purchase or issue resolution, to determine the conversion rate.
- Trust surveys: Implement surveys or feedback mechanisms to assess customers' trust and confidence in their data security. This can provide valuable insight into areas needing improvement and help ensure the customer feels secure and protected.

3.4.4 Embracing affordable strategies: cost efficiency

The cloud computing infrastructure of the cloud-to-things continuum, provide businesses cost-effective IT solutions. Upfront costs involved in buying and maintaining hardware and software are reduced, while fostering a reactive business environment through data insights derived and analyzed from physical processes.

Low-cost sensors and connectivity options make digital transformation accessible to organizations of all sizes, including startups and small businesses (Khan et al., 2022). Moreover, these technologies support accounting professionals to apply their skills within AI-analytics environments to assist with strategic financial decisions. This trend is in accordance with the earlier Sage's Practice Now report, published in November 2019, where 90 percent of accounting respondents believe there is a cultural shift in accountancy towards embracing digital transformation (Abd Razak et al., 2021).

To measure cost efficiency, a KPI emphasizes the total cost of ownership (TCO) reduction achieved through digital transformation initiatives enabled by cloud adoption. This metric considers factors such as infrastructure costs, maintenance, and operational expenses before and after implementing cloud solutions. A KPI for the IoT dimension of the cloud-to-things continuum could be IoT deployments' return on investment (ROI), comparing the cost savings or revenue generated through IoT-enabled processes with the initial investment. Key performance indicators (KPIs) for cost savings include:

- IT costs: Track IT costs over time to monitor how much money is saved with cloud computing services.
- Cloud usage: Tracks cloud usage over time to evaluate cloud resources' utilization.
- Return on investment (ROI): Calculates the ROI of cloud investments to monitor profits or savings enabled by cloud computing.

3.5 Data-driven decision-making

Digital transformation is driven by the ability to harness IoT data effectively. In this paradigm shift, data assumes a central role in shaping organizational strategies and operations. This process requires a comprehensive understanding of how IoT data can be effectively harnessed and analyzed to derive informed decisions that support organizations to navigate the complexities of contemporary business landscapes. A culture of data-driven decision-making emerges within organizations to foster new levels of innovation facilitated by the strategic utilization of IoT data (Model et al., n.d.).

3.5.1 Leveraging open datasets

Open datasets catalyze innovation with free availability and unrestricted access. These datasets span diverse IoT application domains, offering opportunities for organizations to enhance their decision-making initiatives. By integrating open data into their operations, companies foster collaborative innovation, while embracing open knowledge exchange.

Open IoT data in action

The transformative potential of open IoT data extends far beyond traditional data analytics, serving as a pivotal asset in the digital transformation. This data is derived from interconnected devices and sensors to offer unprecedented opportunities for enhancing real-time decision-making and operational efficiency across various sectors. Next, we explore the utilization of open IoT data within two evolving digital transformation areas, where the impact of data framework openness is illustrated.

Enabling digital transformation with open IoT data in public health

Open IoT data transforms public health management by providing training insights to automate assessments along health metrics, epidemic spread, and hospital resource allocation. This integration of open IoT data allows health authorities to predict trends, respond to emergencies swiftly, and improve community health services. Analyzing existing data previously collected from wearable devices, public sensors, and other IoT endpoints, stakeholders can lead to the development of targeted intervention applications and proactive health policies at national levels, which respond to the dynamic needs of citizens.

Consumer's wearable devices provide data which can be aggregated and anonymized for research (Dobson et al., 2023). PhysioNet offers a range of open datasets from such various wearable devices used in clinical and non-clinical settings, supporting research in health informatics (Goldberger et al., 2000).

A comprehensive array of physiological signals and time series data have been collected from thousands of human subjects in Physionet. This extensive data compilation is one of the largest open-access repositories, which includes recordings from a variety of sources, including wearable devices, hospital monitoring equipment, and other IoT devices used in both clinical settings and daily life. Key data category areas include:

- **Cardiopulmonary data:** These electrocardiograms or ECGs, data include respiratory signals, and other related measurements critical for assessing heart and lung function. These recordings are often obtained from wearable devices that patients can use outside traditional clinical settings, facilitating continuous monitoring without disrupting daily activities.
- **Neural data:** Electroencephalograms (labeled EEGs) and other neural recordings that monitor brain activity are essential for research into neurological conditions and can be collected via wearable technology designed for both clinical and research applications. Wearable technology for collecting EEG data has advanced significantly; they are designed to be less invasive and more user-friendly compared to traditional EEG systems, which typically require a clinical setting and extensive setup with gel-based electrodes. For example, devices such as the Emotiv EPOC+ (Nugraha et al., 2016) and NeuroSky MindWave (Morshad et al., 2020) use soft, polymer-based electrodes, which conform to the scalp. The Cognionics Quick-20 System is entirely wireless, allowing for full mobility, while collecting naturalistic human behavior data in various environments outside the lab (Marini et al., 2019).

Connecting transportation systems with open IoT data

In the evolving urban mobility landscape, the integration of open IoT data to improve connected transportation systems represents a significant leap toward smarter, more efficient urban environments. This integration extends to include advanced in-vehicle data systems as well, with the common vehicle signals specification framework, embraced by major automotive industry players. The VSS framework attempts to standardize the way vehicle data is collected and transmitted. The framework's openness enables interoperability between different manufacturers and devices. By openness, we mean both the specification framework illustrated in Fig. 3.1 and the advocated tooling services, which are designed to be publicly accessible and modifiable, fostering an environment of collaboration and continuous improvement (Wilms et al., 2021).

The VSS framework, illustrated in Fig. 3.1, is designed to provide a unified approach to handle connected-vehicle related data. VSS is based on a hierarchical structure of vehicle data, which includes various nodes and branches related to

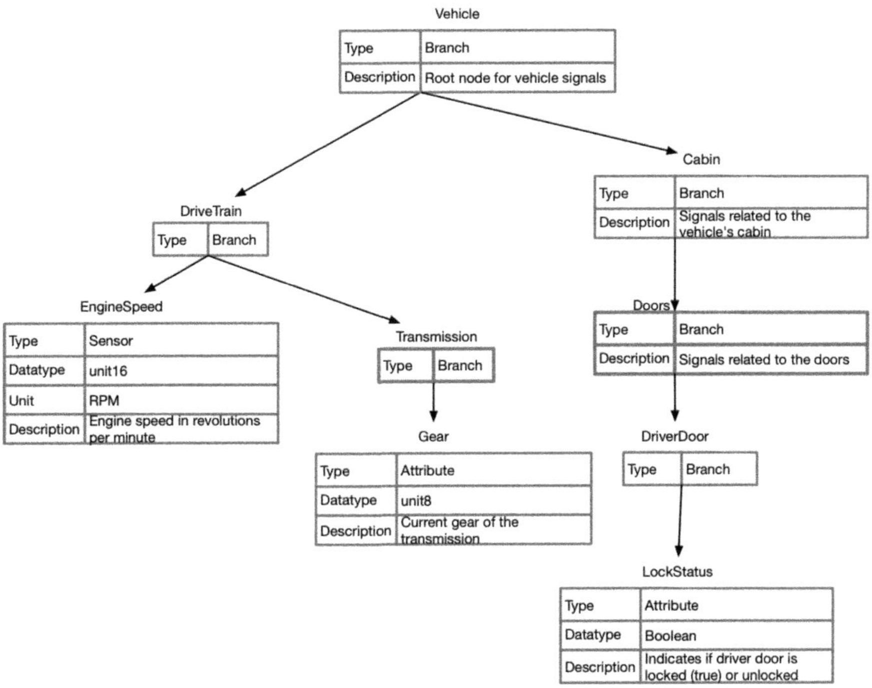

FIGURE 3.1

Vehicle signals specification.

vehicle functionalities. The vehicle node serves as the primary entry point, which branches into various subsystems. For example, EngineSpeed is classified as a sensor type, which records the engine speed in revolutions per minute or RPM. The data type uses a 16-bit unsigned integer format. A branch under the cabin represents data about doors and windows in the vehicle, for example. An attribute indicates whether the driver's door is locked or unlocked, utilizing a Boolean data type to represent this status (true or false).

The software industry is experiencing a growing need for common methods to communicate with individual vehicles or entire fleets. For example, insurance companies are keen to offer customized insurance models, which hinge on assessments of driver performance and driving scores. To meet this demand, a standardized vehicle API is being developed by the Connected Vehicle Systems Alliance (COVESA), which also initiated the undelying VSS project. As a result, data can be accessed by services or exchanged between on-board and remote vehicle systems, in a uniform way.

Developers and researchers can use simulation tools that model vehicle environments and generate data structured according to the VSS model. These tools can simulate various vehicle sensors and systems to produce open data for testing and development purposes (Aust, 2022).

Eclipse IoT is an umbrella project hosted by the Eclipse Foundation, which provides open source IDE for IoT solutions. This initiative covers a wide range of IoT needs. Eclipse Kuksa is part of the Eclipse IoT ecosystem, contributing specifically to the automotive and connected vehicle domains. This tool can simulate various vehicle sensors and systems to produce open VSS-structured data for testing and development purposes (Saarinen, 2022),

The combination of this tool with the open source traffic simulation suite Eclipse SUMO, which is a well-known traffic simulator, provides real-world telemetry data, which can further be sent to cloud via MQTT protocol to an IoT gateway of a connected vehicle ecosystem (Heisig et al., 2019). This allows the generation and communication of vehicle-specific simulation data to be stored and processed in a remote database.

Benefits and challenges of open IoT data

Open IoT data can lead to synergistic partnerships, which might not otherwise occur. For instance, data from connected vehicles can be used by city planners to model traffic light timing, reducing congestion and lowering emissions. Algorithms calculate the optimal timings for traffic lights, taking into account the number of approaching and interdependent vehicles in an intersection to reduce waiting times (Damadam et al., 2022).

Benefits of open IoT data

Open IoT data fosters a collaboration that empowers business research to innovate new solutions by democratizing access to information that was previously siloed or available only to large enterprises with the resources to collect it. The freedom offered by IoT open data allows developers to focus on creativity and problem-solving. Crossdomain synergies are further enabled. For instance, data from wearable health monitors might be combined with environmental data to study the impacts of air quality on public health.

Crowd-sourcing of solutions to shared problems is encouraged with open IoT data. When businesses and researchers face common challenges, open data bridges the collective gap for solutions to be developed collaboratively and shared within a community, which accelerates innovation. This is the case with the VSS data model for enabling innovations in connected vehicles, as specification is shared between the automotive industry and the research community (Aust, 2022).

Challenges of open IoT data

Though the wealth of IoT open data offers great potentials for innovation, it also introduces significant challenges. The volume, variety, and the velocity at which IoT data is produced raise challenges to safeguard privacy, ensure data integrity, and enable the successful utilization of IoT data in diverse applications. IoT devices are designed to be always connected, constantly sending and receiving data. This continuous connectivity ensures that devices can update their status and receive new instructions in real time. However, this also means that there are many more opportunities for unauthorized access. Each connected device potentially offers an entry point for attackers, and each data transmission can be intercepted.

When IoT data is made open, it is intended to be freely accessible for use, reuse, and redistribution by anyone. This openness is beneficial for innovation but increases the risk of exposing personal information. Data needs to be anonymized before it is made open using robust techniques that prevent re-identification opportunities. Techniques such as data aggregation and noise addition are commonly used, but they must be carefully balanced to maintain both privacy and data value (Jain and Kesswani, 2023).

3.5.2 Data analytics techniques

As IoT enable a wealth of open data, data analytics techniques are used to interpret the vast streams of generated data, which is openly shared across platforms. These techniques not only enable organizations to understand and predict trends; they also prescribe solutions that can lead to more informed decision-making and innovative outcomes.

Descriptive analytics

Descriptive analytics summarize raw data and present it in an interpretable format, which helps in identifying patterns based on historical instances. The data is visualized using statistical figures and graphical representations, making complex information easier to understand and accessible to decision-makers. This approach often utilizes measures of central tendency, such as mean, median, and spread, using measures such as standard deviation to provide a clear overview of data distributions and trends. Furthermore, charts, graphs, and heat maps are employed to depict these statistics visually, thereby enabling stakeholders to quickly grasp shifts and patterns in data, which might otherwise go unnoticed (Symeonides et al., 2019).

Predictive analytics

Predictive analytics harnesses machine learning models to use historical and current data for forecasting future events with a reasonable degree of accuracy. This analytical approach is particularly powerful in environments where past data patterns can help anticipate future outcomes. Organizations can proactively make decisions, optimize processes, and mitigate risks when predictions are determined with acceptable accuracies.

Machine learning algorithms can analyze vast datasets from multiple sources, such as healthcare IoT devices monitoring population health, environmental sensors tracking conditions linked to disease spread, and mobility data indicating human travel patterns. These models identify patterns and correlations, which often go unnoticed by traditional methods. For instance, machine learning can discern potential outbreak patterns based on changes in public movement and local health reports, long before traditional surveillance systems can do so (Rahman et al., 2020).

Prescriptive analytics

Prescriptive analytics goes beyond describing or predicting events to offer specific recommendations that guide decision-making processes. This advanced form of analytics combines past data patterns (descriptive analytics) and future predictions (predictive analytics) to suggest actions that can achieve desired outcomes (Lepenioti et al., 2020). For example, IoT devices are increasingly being integrated into various aspects of healthcare, ranging from wearable health monitors to smart inhalers and connected diagnostic tools. When combined with open data, such as epidemiological research repositories, this data can be used to tailor healthcare interventions.

Prescriptive analytics can advance diagnosis and treatment recommendations by using IoT-generated data to personalize medical care. For instance, data from a patient's wearable device could be analyzed in real time to adjust medication dosages or recommend lifestyle changes. As patient conditions evolve, these prescriptions are dynamically updated when new data becomes available, which ensures precise care, overtime (Mosavi and Santos, 2020).

3.5.3 Real-time data processing and analysis

Real-time data processing involves the immediate consumption, processing, and analysis of data as soon as it is acquired, which enable organizations to react swiftly to dynamically occurring conditions and formulate informed decisions instantly.

Data streaming technologies

Various tools and technologies have been developed to process data streams. Some prominent ones are the open source tools Apache Kafka, Apache Storm, and other streaming APIs.

- **Apache Kafka** is an open source stream-processing software platform. Kafka is a robust and highly scalable event streaming platform for handling real-time data feeds, which allows the publishing, subscribing, storing, and processing of data stream records in real time (Vyas et al., 2021).
- **Apache Storm** is another free and open source distributed real-time computation system. Unlike Kafka, which is primarily used as a message broker, Storm provides real-time data processing capabilities directly to process data streams with complex algorithms, which use directed acyclic graph representations. Storm provides the infrastructure needed for online machine learning algorithms, which update and adapt as new data arrives, without the need to reload the entire data set. Storm's distributed RPC capability is useful in scenarios where processing tasks need to be offloaded to a cluster, such as image or video processing tasks in social media applications. In such scenarios, users upload media, which is then processed in real time (Saxena and Gupta, 2017).

- **Streaming APIs** allow developers to handle continuous streams of data, such as tweets or live sports results, in real time. These APIs provide developers with the ability to connect to a data stream and receive live updates as they happen. A common use case of streaming APIs is in social media analytics, where companies monitor data on platforms such as Twitter or Facebook in real time to perform sentiment analysis or discover customer service-related issues as they arise.

In-memory data processing

In-memory computing platforms, such as Apache Spark provide accelerated data processing capabilities by leveraging the system's RAM, instead of slower disk drives. This approach eliminates the need for data retrieval from disk storage, reducing the I/O overhead and latency typically associated with large-scale data processing. Apache Spark utilizes in-memory computing to perform complex processing to support real-time stream processing, where data is sourced from various sensors or live streams (Fernández-Gómez et al., 2023).

3.6 Conclusion

Digital transformation enhanced with the cloud-to-things continuum and AI models reshapes future businesses and markets by promoting innovation, agility, data-driven decision-making, and enhanced customer experiences. These technologies empower businesses to adapt to changing market dynamics, gain a competitive edge, and explore new revenue streams, while effectively addressing concerns of compliance, sustainability, and efficiency. As a result, they are now essential for business longevity across various industries.

References

Abd Razak, S.N.A., Noor, W.N.B.W.M., Jusoh, Y.H.M., 2021. Embracing digital economy: drivers, barriers and factors affecting digital transformation of accounting professionals. International Journal of Advanced Research in Economics and Finance 3 (3), 63–71.

Atieh, A.T., 2021. Assuring the optimum security level for network, physical and cloud infrastructure. ScienceOpen Preprints.

Atitallah, S.B., Driss, M., Boulila, W., Ghézala, H.B., 2020. Leveraging deep learning and iot big data analytics to support the smart cities development: review and future directions. Computer Science Review 38, 100303.

Aust, S., 2022. Vehicle API and service catalog for next generation mobility. In: 2022 25th International Symposium on Wireless Personal Multimedia Communications (WPMC). IEEE, pp. 418–423.

Block, S., 2023. How to adapt and implement a large-scale agile framework in your organization. In: Large-Scale Agile Frameworks: Agile Frameworks, Agile Infrastructure and Pragmatic Solutions for Digital Transformation. Springer, pp. 65–168.

Ciasullo, M.V., Lim, W.M., 2022. Digital transformation and business model innovation: advances, challenges and opportunities. International Journal of Quality and Innovation 6 (1), 1–6.

Damadam, S., Zourbakhsh, M., Javidan, R., Faroughi, A., 2022. An intelligent iot based traffic light management system: deep reinforcement learning. Smart Cities 5 (4), 1293–1311.

Dobson, R., Stowell, M., Warren, J., Tane, T., Ni, L., Gu, Y., McCool, J., Whittaker, R., 2023. Use of consumer wearables in health research: issues and considerations. Journal of Medical Internet Research 25, e52444.

Fernández-Gómez, A.M., Gutiérrez-Avilés, D., Troncoso, A., Martínez-Álvarez, F., 2023. A new apache spark-based framework for big data streaming forecasting in iot networks. Journal of Supercomputing 79 (10), 11078–11100.

Goldberger, A.L., Amaral, L.A., Glass, L., Hausdorff, J.M., Ivanov, P.C., Mark, R.G., Mietus, J.E., Moody, G.B., Peng, C.-K., Stanley, H.E., 2000. Physiobank, physiotoolkit, and physionet: components of a new research resource for complex physiologic signals. Circulation 101 (23), e215–e220.

Guerrero-Ulloa, G., Rodríguez-Domínguez, C., Hornos, M.J., 2023. Agile methodologies applied to the development of Internet of Things (IoT)-based systems: a review. Sensors 23 (2), 790.

Heisig, P., Jeroschewski, S.E., Kristan, J., Höttger, R., Banijamali, A., Sachweh, S., 2019. Bridging the gap between sumo and kuksa: using a traffic simulator for testing cloud-based connected vehicle services. In: SUMO User Conference 2019. May 13-15 Berlin, Germany. EasyChair.

Jain, S.K., Kesswani, N., 2023. A noise-based privacy preserving model for Internet of Things. Complex & Intelligent Systems 9 (4), 3655–3679.

Khan, H.U., Ali, F., Alshehri, Y., Nazir, S., et al., 2022. Towards enhancing the capability of iot applications by utilizing cloud computing concept. Wireless Communications and Mobile Computing 2022.

Korachi, Z., Bounabat, B., 2020. General approach for formulating a digital transformation strategy. Journal of Computer Science 16 (4), 493–507.

Legner, C., Eymann, T., Hess, T., Matt, C., Böhmann, T., Drews, P., Mädche, A., Urbach, N., Ahlemann, F., 2017. Digitalization: opportunity and challenge for the business and information systems engineering community. Business & Information Systems Engineering 59 (4), 301–308. https://link.springer.com/content/pdf/10.1007/s12599-017-0484-2.pdf.

Lepenioti, K., Bousdekis, A., Apostolou, D., Mentzas, G., 2020. Prescriptive analytics: literature review and research challenges. International Journal of Information Management 50, 57–70.

Manyika, J., Chui, M., Bisson, P., Woetzel, J., Dobbs, R., Bughin, J., Aharon, D., 2015. Unlocking the potential of the Internet of Things. McKinsey Global Institute 1.

Marini, F., Lee, C., Wagner, J., Makeig, S., Gola, M., 2019. A comparative evaluation of signal quality between a research-grade and a wireless dry-electrode mobile eeg system. Journal of Neural Engineering 16 (5), 054001.

Mathew, S.S., Atif, Y., Sheng, Q.Z., Maamar, Z., 2013. Towards an efficient sales pitch with the web of things. In: 2013 IEEE 10th International Conference on e-Business Engineering. IEEE, pp. 377–384.

Matsuo, K., Kurita, T., Barolli, L., 2019. A new system for management of IoT sensors considering Agile-Kanban. In: Web, Artificial Intelligence and Network Applications: Proceedings of the Workshops of the 33rd International Conference on Advanced Information Networking and Applications (WAINA-2019) 33. Springer, pp. 604–611.

Model, F.D.C., Griffin, G.W., Holcomb, D., n.d., Building a data culture.

Morshad, S., Mazumder, M.R., Ahmed, F., 2020. Analysis of brain wave data using neurosky mindwave mobile II. In: Proceedings of the International Conference on Computing Advancements, pp. 1–4.

Mosavi, N.S., Santos, M.F., 2020. How prescriptive analytics influences decision making in precision medicine. Procedia Computer Science 177, 528–533.

Needham, M., 2023. Widespread adoption of cloud computing and modern development technologies will have a dramatic impact on the composition of IT teams, according to IDC. https://www.idc.com/getdoc.jsp?containerId=prUS50792523. (Accessed 29 August 2023).

Nugraha, B.T., Sarno, R., Asfani, D.A., Igasaki, T., Munawar, M.N., 2016. Classification of driver fatigue state based on eeg using emotiv epoc+. Journal of Theoretical and Applied Information Technology 86 (3).

Rahman, M.S., Peeri, N.C., Shrestha, N., Zaki, R., Haque, U., Ab Hamid, S.H., 2020. Defending against the novel coronavirus (Covid-19) outbreak: how can the Internet of Things (IoT) help to save the world? Health Policy and Technology 9 (2), 136.

Saarinen, M., 2022. A literature review on connected vehicle use cases.

Saxena, S., Gupta, S., 2017. Practical Real-Time Data Processing and Analytics: Distributed Computing and Event Processing Using Apache Spark. Flink, Storm, and Kafka. Packt Publishing Ltd.

Symeonides, M., Trihinas, D., Georgiou, Z., Pallis, G., Dikaiakos, M., 2019. Query-driven descriptive analytics for iot and edge computing. In: 2019 IEEE International Conference on Cloud Engineering (IC2E). IEEE, pp. 1–11.

Vyas, S., Tyagi, R.K., Jain, C., Sahu, S., 2021. Literature review: a comparative study of real time streaming technologies and apache kafka. In: 2021 Fourth International Conference on Computational Intelligence and Communication Technologies (CCICT). IEEE, pp. 146–153.

Warner, K.S., Wäger, M., 2019. Building dynamic capabilities for digital transformation: an ongoing process of strategic renewal. Long Range Planning 52 (3), 326–349.

Wilms, D., Alvarez-Coello, D., Bekan, A., 2021. An evolving ontology for vehicle signals. In: 2021 IEEE 93rd Vehicular Technology Conference (VTC2021-Spring). IEEE, pp. 1–5.

Yerpude, S., Singhal, T.K., 2021. "Custolytics" Internet of Things based customer analytics aiding customer engagement strategy in emerging markets–an empirical research. International Journal of Emerging Markets 16 (1), 92–112.

Zayat, W., Senvar, O., 2020. Framework study for agile software development via scrum and Kanban. International Journal of Innovation and Technology Management 17 (04), 2030002.

CHAPTER

Strategies for driving IoT data to the cloud in digital transformation initiatives

4

4.1 Introduction

The wealth of data generated by IoT devices is the heart of digital transformation, which empower organizations with unprecedented insights into the surrounding socio-economic environment. The real-time data unleashed from interconnected sensors, machines, wearables, and other smart objects unlock new business opportunities, while optimizing existing processes. Cloud IoT platforms serve as the backbone for analyzing massive volumes of IoT data. In this chapter, we reveal strategies that drive digital transformation initiatives from cloud IoT platform processed data. Additionally, we examine data collection techniques at the edge that prioritize and filter valuable data transmission to the cloud.

The integration of IoT data with cloud platforms is further illustrated across use cases that demonstrate the digital transformation outcomes. Understanding how IoT data and cloud computing act as catalysts for digital transformation, drive organizations to position themselves at the forefront of innovation. This data-intensive exploration of cloud IoT platforms shed light on the immense potential of the cloud-to-things continuum, which paves the way for a future, where organizations are more agile, responsive, and customer-centric. We show how the interplay between IoT data and cloud computing is shaping the transformative potential of organizations seeking to thrive in a data-driven world.

The chapter starts by highlighting the significance of IoT data as a transformative force. Section 4.2 delves into the power of cloud computing for effective IoT data management, discussing data scalability, integration, interoperability, and governance, within cloud environments. Section 4.3 sheds light on edge-to-cloud orchestration, while Section 4.4 highlights strategies for data collection and processing through intelligent edge computing techniques, which filter and prioritize data to be processed locally or referred to the cloud. Section 4.5 showcases organizations that extract meaningful insights from vast streams of IoT data using the array of techniques and technologies enabled by the cloud-to-things continuum. Finally, Section 4.6 concludes the chapter by summarizing the key takeaways and providing insights into the future trends and opportunities that lie ahead for harnessing the potential of data enabled through the cloud-to-things continuum in the pursuit of digital transformation excellence.

Accelerating Digital Transformation with the Cloud and the Internet of Things (IoT)
https://doi.org/10.1016/B978-0-44-322217-7.00010-4

By the end of this chapter, readers gain a comprehensive understanding of how IoT data and cloud computing play a pivotal role in digital transformation initiatives. These insights and best practices empower organizations to harness the potential of the cloud-to-things continuum to drive data-oriented innovations, which elevate operational excellence, and shape a future where data-driven decision-making is at the core of success. Section 4.3 sheds light on edge-to-cloud orchestration, highlighting how organizations can optimize data processing and analysis through intelligent edge computing.

4.2 IoT data in digital transformation

4.2.1 Types of IoT data

It is essential to understand the actual types of IoT data and their significance and impacts in driving organizational evolution. We reveal a broad categorization of IoT data and the sources they may originate from. This exploration is crucial to devise corresponding data and analysis collection methodologies. From sensor data capturing environmental variables to user-generated data from wearables, IoT uncovers a rich tapestry of information produced by versatile IoT devices. However, these devices generate distinct data types with distinct potential in reshaping industries and transforming business operations. Next, we explore these distinctive data empowerments that lead organization to enhanced productivity, streamlined processes, and enriched customer experiences.

Sensor data

Sensors are the front-line data collectors for capturing information about physical-world state or events. It is important to notice that it is the physical environment where sensors are embedded that is of interest. Sensors unleash novel data sources from the physical environment to form the foundation of IoT applications that drive digital transformation initiatives. Sensors extract a range of data points about living and inert entities, facilitating intelligent decision-making and automated actions. IoT applications across diverse industries use their constant vigilance and ability to capture data at high velocity. Vehicles with a high autonomy level use Lidar sensors to create 3D maps of their surroundings and measure distances to foreseeable obstacles. The rate of fluid flow in pipes or channels is conveyed by flow sensors in gas and oil industries. High-speed cameras capture images, and videos operate at extremely high frame rates, allowing them to detect fine-grain parameter values of fast-moving objects and related events.

Classification of sensors

Sensors can be classified into two broad categories outlined in Table 4.1. Active sensors propagate energy or signals externally, whereas passive sensors generate their own internal signal in reaction to external stimuli. Active sensor examples include

Lidar systems, which emits light pulses to measure the return time of the light signal to return, providing key data about distances. Similarly, sonar and radar devices emit sound waves and radio waves, respectively, analyzing the echoed return to calculate distance, size, and shape of objects. Similarly, radar devices emit radio waves to analyze the returned echos, which are further translated into distances, shapes, and sizes. Passive sensors respond to the changes in their environment. Microphones, for example, capture sound waves, which are converted into electric signals. Some touch sensors act as passive electric field sensors reacting to external influences that cause electrical field variations. Certain chemical sensors react passively to specific chemical reactions or biological activities by generating an electric potential or changing their resistance as a response. Table 4.1 classifications highlight further the diversity and adaptability of sensor data to a wide range of applications.

Characteristics of sensor data

Sensor data holds unique attributes that impact the significance implications on how data is collected, processed, and interpreted. First, sensors can generate an extensive volume of data, particularly when data is collected frequently or when multiple and scattered sensors cooperate to monitor a widely distributed area. Communication instances between these autonomous but interconnected sensors occur between adjacent nodes or sensors within the network, or with a sink node or IoT platform to convey data to an external system (Akyildiz et al., 2002). Intra-network communication uses specific protocols, such as Zigbee. External communication involves transmitting aggregated or processed data from the sensor network to an IoT platform. Longer-range communication protocols and methods are required in this case, which could include cellular networks or LoRaWAN. The justification of sensor networks span a range of use cases. For example, in precision agriculture multiple sensors are deployed across the field, creating a network that can provide detailed, granular data on soil moisture at multiple locations to paint a comprehensive picture of the field's condition.

Along with the volume, sensor data tend to be generated at high speed or velocity, particularly for sensors used in real-time applications. The sampling rate refers to this velocity that varies according to applications. Self-driving cars capture millions of data points per second with Lidar sensors to inform autonomous vehicles about their surrounding objects, whereas cameras capture frames at high rate to recognize road signs. In this example, high-speed data generation in real-time sensor applications ensure timely and accurate responses to dynamic environmental conditions. Drones use sensors, including cameras, Lidar, and GPS, besides gyroscopes as well as accelerometers among others, to collect data in large amounts with high rates for aerial mapping (Gupta and Fernando, 2022), as illustrated further in Fig. 4.1.

The previous illustration suggest also two characteristics of sensor data:e variety and variability. Sensors can collect various types of complex multi-dimensional data, which reflect changes overtime. Different sensors measure quantities for different modalities, such as temperature, pressure, light intensity, and chemical composition. The accuracy and reliability of these data, which together refer to the veracity char-

Table 4.1 Types of sensors.

Sensor type	Description	Examples
Active / passive	**Active sensors:** - Emit energy or signals into the environment to detect and measure the response - Require an external power source to function - Propagate electromagnetic or light waves, and then measure the reflected signals to determine the properties of the environment	- Lidar (light detection and ranging), uses laser light pulses to build a 3D map of the environment - Active infrared (IR) sensors emit infrared light to detect movements. - Radar (radio detection and ranging) emits radio waves to determine distance and velocity of objects
	Passive sensors: - Do not emit their own source of energy or light - Detect and measure ambient energy from the environment - Decodes signals transmitted by other devices	- Microphones detect sound waves and convert them into electrical signals - Temperature sensors measure the ambient temperature - Moisture sensors measure the amount of water
Detection mechanism	**Electric sensors:** detect changes in electrical properties, such as voltage, current, resistance, or capacitance	- Photodiodes convert light into electric signal - Touch sensors detect a change in the electrical capacitance or resistance of a material when touched - Thermocouples measure and convert voltage differences across conductive material into temperature reading
	Mechanical sensors: measure changes in mechanical properties, such as pressure, vibration, acceleration, displacement, or force	- Accelerometers detect orientation, motion and vibration - Gyroscopes measure the rotation and angular velocity - Pressure sensors react to the force of a process, creating an output signal
	Chemical/biological sensors: measure changes in electrical characteristics caused by chemical reactions or bioactive substances	- Gas sensors detect the presence and concentration of various gases, including pollutants, toxins, and combustible gases. - Biosensors interact with the substance of interest, such as glucose sensors, and DNA biosensors.

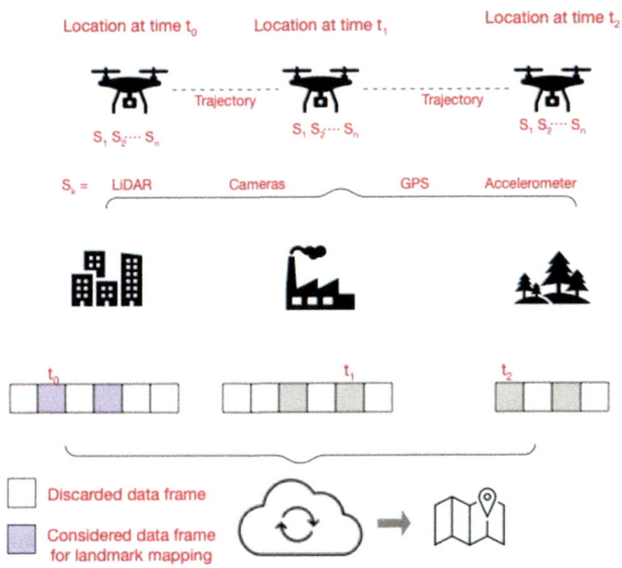

FIGURE 4.1

Sensor data from drones. Adapted from (Gupta and Fernando, 2022).

acteristic of sensor data are affected by sensor calibration, environmental conditions, and sensor degradation over time. The value characteristic of sensor data refers to its utilization or interpretation opportunities via actions or visualization schemes. Finally, sensor data is typically vulnerable to errors, noise, and even intentional tampering, which call for additional integrity and security supporting functions. These data characteristics contribute to designing appropriate systems for collecting, storing, and analyzing data generated by sensors in IoT applications.

Time-series data

The previous illustration about sensor data shows the relevance of time-series data, which is a sequence of data points collected over a period of time that follow a strict temporal order. Nearly all IoT devices generate these data points, which flow across a timeline. From smart home thermostats that generate temperature readings to the prospective delivery drones that generate GPS coordinates, these data points are recorded at periodic or sporadic instances, within a chronological order. They are used for various purposes, including predictive modeling and anomaly detection (Qi et al., 2023).

A time series is formulated as a set of variables $\{X_t : t \in T\}$, indexed by a parameter t which often represents time. Discrete time series represent values over equal intervals of time (like seconds, minutes, hours, days, and so on). This formulation allows various methods and models, whereby time series data result in identifying trends, cycles, or patterns as well as forecasting future insights or detecting anomalies. Working with time series data involving cleaning and preprocessing steps, as well as methodologies for filtering and discarding duplicates to prepare the data for further analysis or model building.

Data filtering

Removing unnecessary or irrelevant data from the time series is a preprocessing step to prepare the data for unleashing its true value. This step includes outlier removal. Some data points can significantly deviate from the typical range of values, which could be the result of measurement errors or genuinely unusual events. Depending on the context, outliers may need to be identified and removed to prevent a distorted analysis. Noise reduction is a subsequent data filtering operation used to smooth out short-term fluctuations to highlight patterns or cycles at longer terms. A vibration sensor in an industrial machine might use a noise reduction technique to ignore occasional large vibration readings caused by temporary disturbances. The raw temperature readings from a thermostat sensor might fluctuate slightly due to various factors, such as minor environmental changes or errors in measuring sensors. For example, the following temperature measurements are collected every minute 22.1 °C, then 22.3 °C, and then 22.0 °C. If the thermostat was set to react immediately to these minor fluctuations, it could lead to frequent and unnecessary activation of the heating or cooling system, resulting in energy waste and potential wear and tear on the system. To avoid this, the smart thermostat might calculate the average temperature over the last 5 minutes and use this averaged value to decide whether to activate the heating or cooling system.

Missing values imputation

In time series data, it is quite common to encounter instances where certain values are absent. There are techniques to substitute these missing values in time series data. Forward fill involves replacing the missing value with the last observed value prior to the missing one as it assumes the last known value would be similar to the missing one. When the next observed value is used, it is backward fill technique, which is suitable for filling missing data at the end of the series. Linear interpolation uses a straight line that spans through known data to guess missing values. More sophisticated approaches might involve building a statistical model, such as ARIMA (Shumway and Stoffer, 2017) and machine learning models based on discovered patterns and correlations from the observed data (Zhang et al., 2019).

Actuator data

Actuators serve as the mechanisms or parts that execute tasks or operations by following instructions or data received from an IoT control system. Their role is to transform signals into actions, such as switching on or off, adjusting positions, or controlling processes. For example, a temperature sensor which detects room temperatures may activate an actuator that controls air conditioning. There are kinds of actuators, each with its purpose of carrying out specific physical actions or tasks. In IoT systems, some utilized types of actuators include:

Electric actuators

These actuators utilize motors to transform electrical energy provided as input into movement. Solenoids create a magnetic field, which attracts or repels a metal core that causes a motion. Piezoelectric actuators produce a charge when exposed to stress, and, conversely, they undergo a deformation following an electric signal. Zinc oxide (ZnO) is an exceptional material that displays piezoelectric properties (Srikanth et al., 2021). Piezoelectric generators are energy harvesters; they convert normally wasted vibration energy in the environment to usable electrical energy. Bridges may integrate piezoelectric generators, which harvest vibration energy produced by traffic or wind. For example, consider a remote smart bridge equipped with various sensors to monitor its structural health. Alternative power sources would be the energy supplied by such generators to power these sensors.

Pneumatic actuators

These devices transform compressed air energy into mechanical energy. In an IoT environment, these actuators can be controlled remotely and integrated into a broader smart system for seamless operation (Brocker et al., 2022; Walker et al., 2020). They are often used in industrial automation to move objects in assembly lines repeatedly. Automated farming is another use case for seeding, harvesting, or sorting.

Thermal actuators

Changes in temperature can drive materials to expand and contract. Thermally responsive alloys change shape or size with temperature. Thermal actuators in smart HVAC systems can modulate airflow or radiator heat with IoT technologies, enabling energy-efficient climate control based on occupancy and preferences (Guo and Zhou, 2009).

4.2.2 Significance of IoT data

The collection and analysis of data from touchpoints present exciting possibilities for the creation of innovative business models and avenues to generate revenue.

Personalization and customer engagement

By gathering data from different customer touchpoints, businesses capture individual preferences, behaviors, and needs. Unleashing this understanding leads to increased personalization and tailored experiences, which further contribute to customer engagement. A retailer who uses in-store sensors and online browsing data offer customized promotions or recommendations to shoppers illustrates this business opportunity.

Optimization and efficiency

Data from various operations and logistics touchpoints can identify inefficiencies, or areas for improvement. By using RFID tags or sensors to monitor inventory levels in real time, companies can detect overstocking or shortages, optimizing inventory levels, dynamically. Similarly, GPS and telematics data can reveal delays or inefficiencies in transportation routes, enabling optimization of shipping paths. Within stores, the analysis of checkout wait times help in staff allocation during peak hours, enhancing customer satisfaction. In healthcare facilities, the usage of expensive medical equipment is better allocated to maximize utilization. Finally, IoT data that reveal consumption patterns of water or energy help in predicting demand and optimizing resource distribution.

New product and service development

Opportunities for new products or services are enabled from discovering unmet needs through IoT data analysis. Alternatively, prototyped new ideas can be tested via real-time IoT data to facilitate agile development. A healthcare company developing a wearable device that monitors vital signs or offers personalized health advice is a possible use case to test innovations in healthcare domains.

Data monetization models

Data as a service (DaaS) offers novel models for data monetization, transforming organizations' perspectives on data. IoT data offered via DaaS channels is an accessible avenue to generate revenues following subscription models or pay-as-you-go fees. From consuming organizations' perspectives, various types of data that reveal market trends, consumer behaviors, or industry-specific insights, are instrumented without having to collect and maintain it themselves.

DaaS empower collaboration between industries, enabling for example municipalities, transportation authorities, and technology companies to contribute new urban infrastructure services, which improve traffic management, optimize public transport schedules, and enhance the quality of life for citizens. Wearable tech manufacturers can share data about personalized healthcare solutions for remote patient monitoring. Finally, technology providers can also share energy consumption patterns with utilities for more efficient energy usage and distribution.

4.3 Cloud computing for IoT data management

Cloud IoT platforms enhances IoT data management, providing with a flexible and efficient environment for robust IoT applications. From scalable storage solutions to advanced data analytics and security, the platform drives digital transformation innovations with more intelligent IoT systems.

4.3.1 Adaptability to data fluctuation

IoT platforms are designed to handle data fluctuations and process vast amounts of information, which originate from various connected devices. Data fluctuations are handled collaboratively across IoT platform layers, namely sensing, data processing, analytics, and application layers, as illustrated in Fig. 4.2.

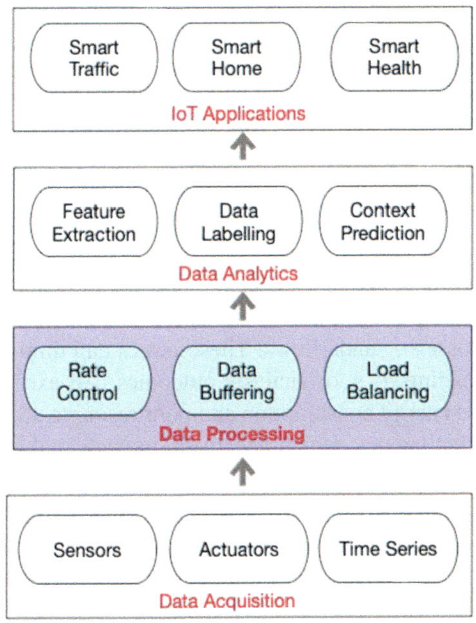

FIGURE 4.2

IoT data pipeline.

The diverse and dynamic nature of IoT data often lead to unpredictable and challenging fluctuations, which include surges due to a sudden increases in data volume or data rate. Many IoT devices may report data simultaneously or in a small time window. Data fluctuations can affect IoT platform systems' stability, efficiency, and responsiveness, necessitating robust mechanisms to address these data flow variations. The data processing layer of IoT platforms comprises rate control, data buffering, and load balancing modules, which synergize their functionalities to handle fluctuating data.

Rate control

IoT data generated by a multitude of sensors at different intervals and volumes may overwhelm IoT platform systems or lead to inefficient processing. Rate control helps in managing this influx of data by controlling or throttling the data transmission rate. Sensors, devices, and other components constantly communicate, sending various amounts of data. The different frequencies and quantities depend on device characteristics or environmental factors. Rate control addresses these challenges by dynamically adjusting the data transmission rate so that the system's capacity is aligned with incoming data flows. In doing so, incoming data rates are restricted by through intelligent controls (Truong et al., 2018; Abba and Garba, 2019).

Data buffering

A temporary storage allows data to be held until the system is ready to process to maintain the operations of a continuous and smooth data flow (Puschmann et al., 2017). In applications such healthcare or industrial monitoring, data buffering ensures that real-time data is processed smoothly without loss, even during high data influx. Smart transportation systems use data buffering to sustain data that originate from various sensors, including cameras, location, and traffic monitors, enabling efficient traffic management and control.

The size of the buffer space plays a significant role in managing IoT data effectively. If the buffer space is inadequately small, the related IoT platform system might be prone to packet losses or underflows. These issues can diminish the quality and reliability of data, leading to poor analysis outcomes. An excessively large buffer may lead to excessive energy consumption and poor resource utilization. These inefficiencies can increased latency, which negatively impacts real-time responsiveness. Adaptive buffer management for IoT devices uses a distributed algorithm to achieve a balance among IoT devices, edge nodes, and cloud resources in terms of their buffer sizes and utilities. Buffer sizes are adjusted by individual devices according to feedback from neighboring device nodes in the cloud-to-things continuum (Zhu et al., 2022). When some data is more critical than others, priority buffering can be used to ensure that essential data is processed first.

Load balancing

The process of distributing computational tasks across multiple servers or nodes is referred to as load balancing. The goal is resource optimization to minimize response times. Load balancing ensures that data processing does not overwhelmed any node in the cloud-to-things continuum. A load balancer coordinates requests across all servers capable of fulfilling those requests so that no server is overworked. Load balancing employs various algorithms. Techniques include round-robin distribution, least connections method, or even using more complex machine learning algorithms to predict the data load and distribute it optimally (Ramesh et al., 2021), as illustrated in Fig. 4.3.

4.3.2 Advanced data analytics

Positioned above the data processing layer and followed by the application layer, the data analytics layer in the IoT data pipeline is responsible for extracting insights. The inferred context from processed data enables the implementation of various IoT applications, as shown earlier in Fig. 4.2. The data analytics layer includes various modules, such as feature extraction, data labeling, and context prediction.

Feature extraction

In the stage of data analytics, we first focus on finding attributes or characteristics from the processed raw data. The aim is to extract context information relevant to IoT applications. However, IoT devices generate multidimensional data; each of them

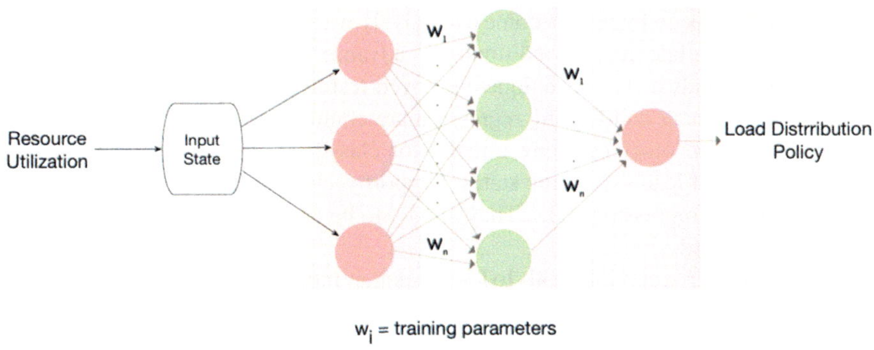

FIGURE 4.3

Deep learning for load balancing.

can be considered as a potential feature for analysis. However not all features carry the same level of relevant information. Techniques to reduce data into selected features include elimination, forward selection, and others, particularly used to reduce the number of variables that define these features. Many data contents are either redundant or irrelevant, and can thus be removed without incurring much loss of information. To improve the performance of training models in subsequent analytics steps, feature selection involves choosing which sensor readings to include in a model.

Data labeling

When employing supervised machine learning models, data labeling involves giving informative tags or labels to the features of instances, in the dataset. The goal of a supervised learning algorithm is to learn a function that connects these features to the labels. Let us consider a plant where various IoT sensors monitor aspects of their operation. Temperature, vibration, acoustics, and pressure features may be captured. Each sensor generates data streams representing feature values. A label could be an indication of whether the machine will fail within a future time frame. For each time frame there is a dimensional feature vector (representing sensor readings) and a binary label referring to the expected machine failure or not. Sensor readings are mapped to failure expectations by training a supervised learning methodology. This model can predict future machine failures given current data following a process that is analogous to the one illustrated earlier in Fig. 4.3.

Context prediction

The process of data labeling involves categorizing or tagging information, which acts as the ground truth for training supervised machine learning algorithms. On the other hand, context prediction takes a step further by identifying patterns, trends, and correlation within the data. This process make predictions about future states or changes in application contexts. For instance in a smart home scenario when the system anticipates that a room is on track to become excessively warm, it can autonomously adjust the blinds and regulate the air conditioning in advance to anticipate any discomfort.

Regression analysis is a technique employed to forecast numerical values using input features. Linear and logistic regression are commonly related techniques. Decision trees on the other hand are utilized for classification purposes to represent the conditions that lead to specific states. Support vector machines (SVMs) perform classification and regression tasks. They proved to be especially valuable, when data cannot be separated.

Let us consider a building with IoT sensors that monitor different environmental conditions, such as temperature, light intensity, CO2 levels, and noise levels. The goal of the building management is to organize areas within the building by using the data from sensors. This will help them implement energy-saving strategies. If a particular area is frequently unoccupied, they want to make lighting or HVAC adjustments for energy saving. However, data do not reveal a distinct pattern because of the complex interactions between various environmental factors. The temperature might rise when more people occupy a zone, but sunlight might also raise temperature. Since the zones are not easily separable by a linear boundary, SVM can classify different zones of the building (Shao et al., 2020).

4.3.3 Data governance in the cloud

Data governance involves the methods used to ensure that an organization's data remains trustworthy, accessible, and relevant. Setting standards, responsibilities, and roles related to acquiring, storing, analyzing, and sharing data, are typical data governance operations. Data governance also ensures compliance with these regulations and standards to meet business goals and alignment with the organization cloud-to-things continuum strategies (Lynn et al., 2020). Data governance methods in the context of the cloud-to-things continuum include data provenance, data quality, data security, and data privacy. Organizations can unlock the power of data for digital transformation by implementing data governance methods along the cloud-to-things continuum. These practices enable organizations to make decisions that improve operational efficiency, boost customer satisfaction, and generate social value (Laso et al., 2022).

Data provenance

Data provenance provides an architecture for gathering, preserving, and validating the lineage and origins of data in the continuum, which spans from cloud to IoT devices. This design allows tracking the journey of data since its inception for increased transparency. As data travels from IoT devices to the cloud and undergoes various transformations and analyses, knowing the data origin points, the changes that were made, and by whom, provide transparency for accountability and traceability purposes. Data provenance can also be used to demonstrate compliance with the organization or some accrediting agency guidelines in cloud-connected environments (Pasquier et al., 2018).

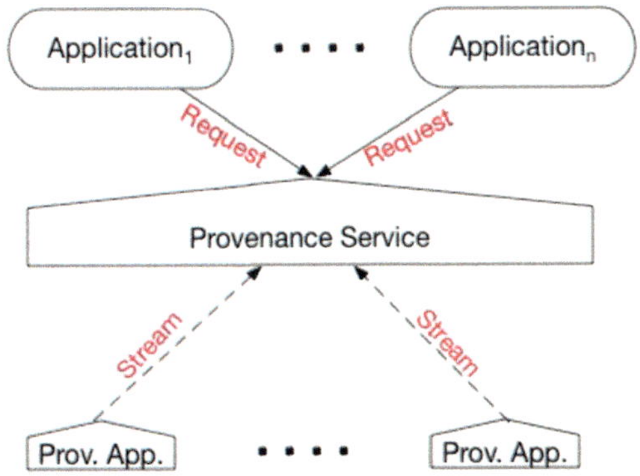

FIGURE 4.4

Data provenance service.

Provenance is a service provided by IoT cloud platforms, which facilitates tenants to track the exchange of data across the continuum devices, as shown in Fig. 4.4. Dedicated provenance applications stream captured provenance data to tenant applications, which may further process or store the data (Pasquier et al., 2017). The provenance information streamed by provenance applications across the continuum uses standard specifications, which can be used to assess data about its quality, reliability, or trustworthiness (Missier et al., 2013).

IoT and edge provenance applications

IoT devices constantly generate data and send it to the cloud. A provenance framework can be integrated at this level to capture the provenance of IoT data at the source itself by recording every transformation or operation that the data undergoes within the device. As the data travels from IoT devices to the cloud, it may pass through various intermediate nodes and gateways, where provenance applications record further information at these points as well.

Provenance applications play a role in ensuring adherence to specific data regulations at various stages of provenance data streams. If for example, there are laws in place that prohibit data from leaving a particular geographic region (due to data sovereignty regulations), the provenance application can promptly initiate alerts if this rule is violated at any node throughout the continuum.

Cloud provenance service

The provenance service at the cloud level provides interfaces for querying and analyzing underlying provenance data. Streamed provenance data is collected and organized by this cloud service. The cloud layer houses user applications that consume provenance data on demand. These applications trigger provenance requests for regulatory compliance, forensics, and security.

Data quality

The quality of data collected from IoT devices ensures reliable analysis. Accuracy, consistency, and completeness factors impact the effectiveness of deriving information from this data.

Accuracy

How accurately does the data gathered from IoT device reflect the actual condition of the phenomena being observed? Problems with the devices' sensors, such as calibration mistakes can result in misleading data. Accuracy can be optimized with regular calibration of sensors, ensuring they are working correctly, and that their measurements accurately reflect the real-world phenomena they are intended to capture. Implementing data checks at collection time could help detecting anomalies considering previous readings or some anomaly detection algorithms.

Timeliness

Timeliness pertains to the extent to which data remains current and accessible when required. Many IoT applications, including driving, smart manufacturing, and emergency response systems, rely on real-time or near real-time data processing to enable prompt decision-making. Therefore IoT data pipeline should be able to handle real-time data to maintain the timeliness of IoT data.

Furthermore, in many real-time applications, IoT data from multiple sources need to be combined or compared. Thus timestamping and synchronization data accurately maintain the correct sequence of events and associations throughout data sources and fulfill real-time processing requirements.

Completeness

Instances of data may be absent due to interruptions in the network, or periods when devices are not operational or problems with synchronization. Data loss induced by network disruptions or device malfunctions may be alleviated by buffering data for differed transmission. Imputation of missing values can be used with care, as they might introduce bias or inaccuracies into the data.

4.3.4 Edge-to-cloud orchestration

The growing need for response times, fast data processing, and protection of data privacy has accelerated the transition towards edge computing. This approach involves processing data in proximity of its origin. However, a standalone edge computing approach may be insufficient to manage the large volumes and high velocity of IoT data, necessitating a more integrated cloud-to-things continuum, which requires orchestrating data transmission from edge to cloud. This orchestration consists of coordinated data management operations across the continuum, which is aware of all available resources (both at the edge and in the cloud) and their current status, to enable dynamic resource allocation (Svorobej et al., 2020). There are several frameworks and strategies designed to manage, coordinate, and schedule computational processes and services in edge computing environments.

Distributed deployment

This paradigm consists in blending local data processing at the edge with broader orchestration across a continuum from edge devices to centralized cloud infrastructure. Orchestration ensures that relevant data is processed locally at the edge, minimizing latency and bandwidth. The paradigm executes applications or services across distributed edge nodes as close as possible to IoT devices or end-users, where data originate from.

KubeEdge

This is a framework for edge computing, which has been developed on top of Kubernetes open source platform for managing workloads and services that are encapsulated within isolated environments that package the application code and its dependencies, making them portable and consistent across different platforms (Bernstein, 2014). These containers, which are handled by a cluster of nodes along the cloud-to-edge continuum in a scalable through Kubernetes, was originally designed and developed by engineers at Google (Poulton, 2023).

EdgeX Foundry

Hosted by Linux Foundation, this open source platform provides a common framework for industrial IoT edge computing, which facilitates data collection and analytics across cloud connector services. The framework may run on top of Kubernetes to further enable container orchestration (Lee et al., 2021). EdgeX Foundry is vendor-neutral and platform-agnostic. Independent of hardware or operating system, this cloud-to-edge middleware enables data collection from sensors.

ETSI MEC (multi-access edge computing)

This framework facilitates the implementation by guaranteeing that applications operate at the most suitable position on the edge taking into account factors such as latency, bandwidth, and processing capability. Defined by the European Telecommunications Standards Institute (ETSI), this architecture brings cloud computing capabilities to the edge of cellular networks (Liyanage et al., 2021).

Scalability and flexibility

Cloud-to-things architectures are expected to handle growth, in terms of increased data volumes, the number of devices, or the complexity of operations. Scalability allows edge environment to expand, while the orchestration system continues to efficiently allocate resources and manage tasks without degradation in performance.

Flexibility assesses the orchestration architecture's ability to adjust itself according to different scenarios. These scenarios may include supporting different hardware, accommodating varied workload demands, and adapting to changing operational conditions. The key is to handle a range of scenarios without being limited to a particular configuration.

OpenFog Consortium

Fog computing is another decentralized computing paradigm, like edge computing, which brings computation and storage closer to data sources (i.e., IoT devices). However unlike edge computing, the processing takes place in the nodes situated between the cloud and the edge devices. These nodes encompass gateways, routers, or other intermediary points, which are capable of managing data processing and storage operations. By standardizing the fog computing paradigm, OpenFog facilitates scalability by allowing for the interoperation of multiple fog nodes, ensuring cohesive operation across large, distributed edge networks (OpenFog Consortium Architecture Working Group, 2017).

SORTS (supporting the orchestration of resilient and trustworthy fog services)

This approach to edge computing, which focuses on providing services, allows for the deployment of services according to real-time needs, The appropriate service is executed in the appropriate location and time (Velasquez et al., 2017).

SOAFI (service orchestration architecture for fog-enabled infrastructures)

This platform considers every node along the cloud-to-things continuum as a resource interface, controlled by a resource manager. The framework includes a Fog orchestrator (FO) and Fog agent (FA). FO manages the infrastructure of connected fog nodes, while FA's access to local resource is through the interface to FO. An initial working prototype of SOAFI is deployed within an IoT testbed (de Brito et al., 2017; Svorobej et al., 2020).

4.3.5 Data collection at the edge

Edge computing has the ability to schedule data transmission over off-peak period to reduce congestion. Furthermore, data that is processed locally is less exposed to notorious interception or breach risks associated with data transmission. Sensitive data can further be anonymized at the source before cloud transmission to address privacy concerns. Even when network outage or connectivity issue occur with the central server, edge devices can still continue their local operations without disruption, which supports operational resilience. All these benefits are associated with data collection strategies at the edge.

Strategies for effective data collection at the edge

Given the vast amount of data IoT devices can generate, distinguishing valuable data from noise is implemented by intelligent data filtering algorithms. Before data is sent to cloud, local data processing and analytics tasks are executed directly at the source of data generation or at nearby computing nodes (like gateways). Immediate decisions are inferred without the need to send raw data to cloud platforms. Data filtering, feature extraction, and pattern recognition are processed locally, enhancing application responsiveness. This means that multiple edge devices work in parallel, thus speeding up further overall data processing. By leveraging high-performance cloud computing resources, consolidated edge data optimize decision-making outcomes.

Edge data compression

To make data storage and transmission more efficient, compression techniques used at the edge can either be lossless or lossy. Delta encoding is commonly employed in edge data pipelines to transform data into the variance, that is, between the data and the preceding data, thereby diminishing the volume of transmitted information and enhancing overall performance (Hu et al., 2020). Minimizing the amount of transmitted data significantly extend the battery life of IoT devices. Devices placed in remote areas or those that do not have access to consistent power sources use this alternative for energy saving.

4.4 IoT data lifecycle in digital transformation

The lifecycle of IoT data encompasses the stages through which data is transformed: from its generation to its ultimate disposal or archiving. Understanding this lifecycle is paramount for effectively leveraging IoT data into digital transformation initiatives. Each stage of the lifecycle contributes to IoT integration into the digital transformation strategy, whereby data extracted from IoT sources generate actionable decisions. Digital transformation fundamentally relies on data-driven decision-making to drive operational efficiency and the ability to innovate rapidly.

The IoT data lifecycle provides a structured framework for managing the vast amounts of data generated by IoT devices. Understanding each stage of this lifecycle, empowers organizations to ensure that their IoT deployments impact positively the outcomes of their digital transformation goals. From the initial generation of data by IoT sensors to the sophisticated analysis that drives predictive insights, each step in the IoT data lifecycle contributes to building a responsive, intelligent, and agile organization. When properly managed, IoT data provide a significant competitive advantage to organizations by reducing operational costs, enhancing customer experiences, and opening up new revenue streams.

Effective data governance, security, and compliance are woven throughout the lifecycle to ensure that data remains trustworthy and compliant with regulatory standards. Moreover, the ability to orchestrate data between edge devices and cloud platforms within the cloud-to-things framework ensures that real-time analytics is processed efficiently, with an ability to scale to meet long-term strategic planning of organizations. The transformation of raw data into informed decision-making drives innovation. By meticulously managing the underlying lifecycle of this transformation, organizations can unlock the full potential of IoT towards creating a foundation for sustained growth within the digital transformation era.

4.4.1 Stages of the IoT data lifecycle

The IoT data lifecycle consists of interconnected stages, which form a continuous loop that ensures data is efficiently managed and utilized throughout its lifecycle. This cyclic process begins with data generation, where IoT devices collect raw data from various connected environments. The collected data is then transmitted and processed to ensure its accuracy and relevance. Next, the data is stored securely, making it accessible for analysis. Advanced analytics are applied to derive actionable decisions. These actions can further lead to new data generation, to trigger a new IoT data cycle. For example. connected vehicles generate data from various sensors and systems used to enhance safety and improve the driving experience. These systems shift the vehicle status to a new data landscape captured by the same sensors to consistently keep the driving experience safe and enjoyable.

Data generation

The IoT data lifecycle begins with data generation, where sensors, devices, and actuators collect raw data from various sources. Environmental sensors, wearables, industrial machinery, and home IoT devices are examples of such IoT devices. Following our earlier illustration related to connected vehicles, data generation begins with sensors and systems, such as the CAN bus, which monitors and records various parameters of the vehicle's operation, including speed and engine, as well as driver actions, such as steering and braking. Additionally, onboard cameras capture real-time video of the driver state to detect signs of drowsiness or distraction.

Data collection

Once generated, data is collected and transmitted to edge devices or cloud platforms. Data collection strategies at the edge include filtering, prioritization, and preliminary processing to reduce the volume of data sent to the cloud, thus optimizing bandwidth and ensuring timely data transfer. This state ensures that only relevant and valuable data reaches the next stages of the lifecycle. For example, the generated data from the CAN bus and onboard cameras is collected and transmitted to a central processing unit within the vehicle. This data collection is continuous, ensuring real-time monitoring of both the vehicle's performance and the driver's state.

Data processing

At this stage, the collected data undergoes various transformations to make it suitable for analysis. Data processing includes cleaning, normalization, and enrichment. Techniques such as data buffering, rate control, and load balancing are employed to manage the influx of data streams and ensure smooth processing. Edge computing plays a significant role here by performing real-time processing and reducing latency. Considering our connected vehicle scenario, the collected data is processed to filter out noise and irrelevant information. For instance, image processing algorithms analyze the video feed from the onboard cameras to detect facial features and eye movements that indicate drowsiness. Simultaneously, data from the CAN bus is analyzed to monitor vehicle performance and detect any anomalies.

Data storage

Processed data is then stored in databases, data lakes, or other storage solutions. Cloud platforms offer scalable storage options, which can handle large volumes of IoT data. Distributed storage systems and data compression techniques are data storage strategies that further optimize space and ensure data integrity. For example, processed connected-vehicle data is stored locally within the vehicle's onboard database, and also transmitted to a cloud platform for long-term storage and further analysis. This data storage architecture makes both real-time and historical data available for review and decision.making analysis.

Data analysis

Advanced analytics, including machine learning and artificial intelligence, are applied to stored data to identify patterns that reflect trends or reveal anomalies. Data analytics can be performed at the edge or in the cloud, depending on the requirements for speed and complexity. This stage of IoT data lifecycle converts raw data into actionable intelligence that drives informed decision-making. For example, machine learning models analyze patterns in the driver's eye movements and vehicle data to predict drowsiness state instances in connected vehicles. This analysis combines real-time data with historical data to improve accuracy.

Action

The actionable outcomes can range from automated responses, such as triggering actuators or sending alerts, to more strategic decisions. The feedback loop generated from these actions further refines the IoT data lifecycle, contributing to continuous improvement. For example. the HMI in the connected vehicle is triggered to alert drowsy drivers by activating an audible alert, vibrating the steering wheel, or displaying a warning message on the dashboard. The resulting change in driver state is captured in the next cycle of IoT data lifecycle. The onboard cameras and CAN bus continue to generate data about the driver's state and vehicle performance, creating a continuous loop of data generation, collection, processing, and action. This loop ensures ongoing safety improvements and adaptive responses to changing conditions.

Archiving and disposal

Finally, data that is no longer needed for immediate analysis or decision-making is either archived for future reference or securely disposed of. Data governance policies ensure that data retention and disposal comply with regulatory requirements and organizational policies.

4.4.2 The role of IoT data lifecycle in driving digital transformation

Each stage of the IoT data lifecycle is integral to the digital transformation journey. Next, we illustrate this interconnection.

- **Data-driven decision-making:** Effective IoT data generation and collection enable organizations to base their decisions on accurate, real-time data, thereby enhancing agility and responsiveness.
- **Operational efficiency:** Processing and storage strategies optimize resource utilization, ensuring that the infrastructure can handle the dynamic nature of IoT data. This optimization maintains operational efficiency throughout the digital transformation journey.
- **Innovation and value creation:** Advanced analytics uncover innovation patterns that lead to the development of new products, services, and business models. This stage directly impacts the creation of value from IoT data.
- **Regulatory compliance and trust:** Data governance, including provenance, quality, and privacy, ensures compliance with regulations and builds trust with stakeholders. This trust paves the way to the success of digital transformation initiatives.
- **Continuous self-improvement:** The feedback loop created by the action stage fosters a culture of continuous self-improvement, to consistently remain competitive in a rapidly changing digital landscape.

4.5 Real-life use cases of IoT data in cloud-driven digital transformation

As industries are becoming more aware of the possibilities that arise from combining IoT data and the computational capabilities offered by the cloud, they lead the industry innovations and gain a competitive edge. Next, some real-world examples are revealed to highlight how organizations are leveraging IoT data in cloud-driven digital transformations.

Smart agriculture with John Deere

John Deere, a leading company in the agricultural equipment manufacturing sector has incorporated sensors into their machinery. Data on soil conditions, crop health, and weather patterns are subsequently gathered and transmitted to the cloud (see Fig. 4.5). Farmers are subsequently able to access real-time insights, based on which they make decisions regarding irrigation, planting schedules, and harvesting strategies for optimal results (Haralayya, 2021).

John Deere launched the digital agriculture hub, a platform that offers digital information, insights, and learning resources to help growers use data in their operations. The hub covers subjects such as the significance of data in making informed decisions and techniques to gather and utilize data from farmland equipments to educate farmers about ways to access and leverage the John Deere digital ecosystem. Additionally, the hub highlights real-life resources, which have facilitated farmers effectively incorporating connected farming solutions, which resulted in enhanced efficiency and profitability. The hub's objective is to assist farmers in embracing,

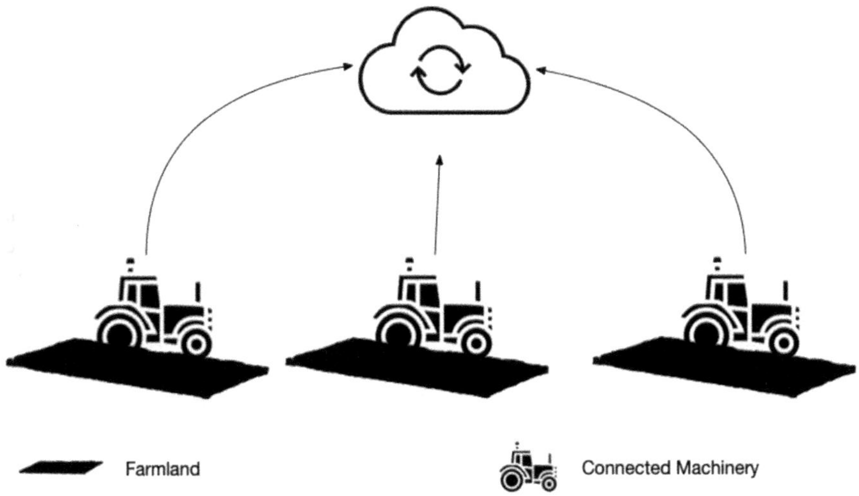

FIGURE 4.5

Connected agriculture.

implementing, and maximizing the benefits of technology in precision agriculture, while ensuring a favorable return on investment.

BMW's ConnectedDrive system

BMW has harnessed the power of cloud technologies to establish a smooth link between their vehicles and the drivers digital environment. Through cutting edge functionalities, such as up to the minute traffic notifications, remote diagnostics, and personalized concierge services, BMW's ConnectedDrive system embodies the transition aspects related to embracing digital transformation (BMW, 2023).

Furthermore the driver has the ability to retrieve and collaborate on information from the vehicle with external service providers, such as insurance companies, repair shops, or fleet managers. This information comprises details such as mileage, fuel usage, battery charge level, maintenance status, and error codes. Moreover, the driver can even ask for services, depending on the data collected, such as tailored insurance premiums or exclusive maintenance deals. This particular functionality employs data to ensure secure storage and transmission of the vehicles data through IBM cloud.

BMW has collaborated with IBM to leverage their computing platform to store and analyze the data gathered by ConnectedDrive. IBMs cloud platform, which includes IBM cloud foundry offers scalable storage capabilities for the collected data. Third-party developers can access this data through APIs hosted on IBMs cloud platform (Techerati, 2017).

In addition to BMW utilizing the IBM cloud to store and transfer vehicle data, the car manufacturer also leverages the Microsoft Azure cloud platform to instrument services from the open mobility cloud (OMC), which is a platform that connects car to drivers' devices, such as smartphones, smartwatches, and voice assistants. OMC enables services such as BMW's ConnectedDrive offering personalized mobility assistance and remote control across the cars functionalities (Microsoft, 2016).

The OMC architecture is designed to be flexible, allowing BMW to easily build new service experiences and incorporate partner content. This flexibility enables BMW to continuously enhance and expand the capabilities of the ConnectedDrive system, enabling further OMC to evolve into an intelligent mobility companion, which supports and learns the routine mobility needs of the car owners. Machine learning techniques instrument data to provide personalized recommendations and assistance to car owners, and performance enhancement opportunities to car manufacturers, such as improving maintenance processes and developing new services.

More recently, the BMW Group and Amazon AWS co-developed a cloud-based vehicle data platform that collects BMW vehicle signals and fleet intelligence data to provide insights to BMW engineers and developers (IoT World Today, 2022). BMW Group decided to re-architect and migrate its data lake to the scalable Amazon AWS cloud to innovate future needs. The scalable cloud technologies developed through this collaboration is expected to preserve the long-term availability of digitalized services in vehicular industry, which empower digital transformations of future mobility initiatives, at large (Amazon, 2022).

Schneider electric EcoStruxure

At the foundational layer of EcoStruxure cloud platform are the connected products, such as sensors, meters, switches, and more. These devices gather real-time data from different operational points, including machinery, or systems they monitor (Schneider, 2023), and span across multiple domains, such as buildings, manufacturing industries, and critical infrastructures. PLCs (programmable logic controllers) are components manufactured by Schneider, which control industrial machines or processes, and which have been augmented with data connectivity features of EcoStruxure. HMI (human-machine interfaces) are interfaces to a broad range of infractures to interact with machinery data in real time, and that also have been augmented with connectivity features of EcoStruxure. These connected products (and others) are examples of the devices that can be connected within the EcoStruxure platform, which delivers innovations at device, edge, and cloud levels, and integrated in over at least half a million installations connecting over 1 billion devices (Schneider, 2023).

4.6 Conclusion

IoT data and cloud computing stands at the forefront of transformative digital initiatives. As portrayed throughout this chapter, harnessing the steep increase in volume, velocity, and variety of IoT data is central to digital transformation operations. From sensors in manufacturing lines to wearables that monitor health metrics, IoT devices generate a vast array of data types. Leveraging IoT data, structured or unstructured, and acknowledging its value in the digital strategies of organizations are essential steps of digital transformation initiatives. These steps were discussed in this chapter as stepstones to operational efficiency and groundbreaking services and products.

The cloud's inherent capabilities, including scalability to accommodate data fluctuations, advanced analytics to extract meaningful insights, robust data governance structures, and seamless orchestration between edge and centralized systems, provide the infrastructure to empower organizations with the tools that derive actionable intelligence from IoT data data. With data processing increasingly happening at the edge, closer to where data is generated, orchestrating decentralized sources of data generation, and processing harmoniously with centralized cloud systems, set the stage for responsive and agile digital enterprises. The chapter concludes with some successful IoT data-based digital transformation initiatives. These real-world use cases brighten up the tangible benefits and reveal challenges experienced by some pioneering organizations in various economic sectors.

References

Abba, S., Garba, A.M., 2019. An IoT-based smart framework for a human heartbeat rate monitoring and control system. In: The 6th International Electronic Conference on Sensors and Applications. MDPI. https://doi.org/10.3390/ecsa-6-06543.

Akyildiz, I., Su, W., Sankarasubramaniam, Y., Cayirci, E., 2002. Wireless sensor networks: a survey. Computer Networks 38 (4), 393–422. https://www.sciencedirect.com/science/article/pii/S1389128601003024.

Amazon, 2022. BMW on AWS: case studies. https://aws.amazon.com/solutions/case-studies/innovators/bmw/. (Accessed 8 January 2023).

Bernstein, D., 2014. Containers and cloud: from LXC to docker to kubernetes. IEEE Cloud Computing 1 (3), 81–84.

BMW, 2023. BMW connected drive. Available at: https://www.bmw.com/en-au/offers-and-services/bmw-connected-drive/overview.html. Retrieved on 01/08/2023.

Brocker, A., Strüver, J., Voelker, S., Borchers, J., 2022. SoRoCAD: a design tool for the building blocks of pneumatic soft robotics. In: CHI Conference on Human Factors in Computing Systems Extended Abstracts. ACM. https://doi.org/10.1145/3491101.3519770.

de Brito, M.S., Hoque, S., Magedanz, T., Steinke, R., Willner, A., Nehls, D., Keils, O., Schreiner, F., 2017. A service orchestration architecture for fog-enabled infrastructures. In: 2017 Second International Conference on Fog and Mobile Edge Computing (FMEC), pp. 127–132.

Guo, W., Zhou, M., 2009. Technologies toward thermal comfort-based and energy-efficient HVAC systems: a review. In: 2009 IEEE International Conference on Systems, Man and Cybernetics, pp. 3883–3888.

Gupta, A., Fernando, X., 2022. Simultaneous localization and mapping (SLAM) and data fusion in unmanned aerial vehicles: recent advances and challenges. Drones 6 (4), 85. https://doi.org/10.3390/drones6040085.

Haralayya, B., 2021. Study on trend analysis at John Deere. Iconic Research and Engineering Journals 5 (1), 171–181.

Hu, Z., Wang, D., Li, Z., Li, J., Gao, Y., 2020. Delta compression optimisation for UAV-enabled mobile edge caching. IET Communications 14 (15), 2500–2508. https://ietresearch.onlinelibrary.wiley.com/doi/abs/10.1049/iet-com.2019.1214.

IoT World Today, 2022. AWS and BMW launch cloud-based vehicle data platform. https://www.iotworldtoday.com/transportation-logistics/aws-bmw-launch-cloud-based-vehicle-data-platform. (Accessed 8 January 2023).

Laso, S., Berrocal, J., Fernandez, P., García, J.M., Garcia-Alonso, J., Murillo, J.M., Ruiz-Cortés, A., Dustdar, S., 2022. Elastic data analytics for the cloud-to-things continuum. IEEE Internet Computing 26 (6), 42–49.

Lee, S., Phan, L.-A., Park, D.-H., Kim, S., Kim, T., 2021. EdgeX over kubernetes: enabling container orchestration in EdgeX. Applied Sciences 12 (1), 140. https://doi.org/10.3390/app12010140.

Liyanage, M., Porambage, P., Ding, A.Y., Kalla, A., 2021. Driving forces for multi-access edge computing (MEC) IoT integration in 5G. ICT Express 7 (2), 127–137. https://www.sciencedirect.com/science/article/pii/S2405959521000631.

Lynn, T., Mooney, J.G., Lee, B., Endo, P.T. (Eds.), 2020. The Cloud-to-Thing Continuum. Springer International Publishing. https://doi.org/10.1007/978-3-030-41110-7.

Microsoft, 2016. BMW launches digital mobility experience based on the open mobility cloud using Microsoft azure. https://news.microsoft.com/transform/bmw-launches-new-digital-mobility-experience-based-on-the-open-mobility-cloud-using-microsoft-azure/. (Accessed 8 January 2023).

Missier, P., Belhajjame, K., Cheney, J., 2013. The W3C PROV family of specifications for modelling provenance metadata. In: Proceedings of the 16th International Conference on Extending Database Technology. ACM.

OpenFog Consortium Architecture Working Group, 2017. OpenFog Reference Architecture for Fog Computing. OPFRA001 20817, p. 162.

Pasquier, T., Han, X., Goldstein, M., Moyer, T., Eyers, D., Seltzer, M., Bacon, J., 2017. Practical whole-system provenance capture. In: Proceedings of the 2017 Symposium on Cloud Computing, SoCC'17. Association for Computing Machinery, New York, NY, USA, pp. 405–418. https://doi.org/10.1145/3127479.3129249.

Pasquier, T., Singh, J., Powles, J., Eyers, D., Seltzer, M., Bacon, J., 2018. Data provenance to audit compliance with privacy policy in the Internet of things. Personal and Ubiquitous Computing 22 (2), 333–344. https://link.springer.com/content/pdf/10.1007/s00779-017-1067-4.pdf.

Poulton, N., 2023. The Kubernetes Book. Nigel Poulton LTD.

Puschmann, D., Barnaghi, P., Tafazolli, R., 2017. Adaptive clustering for dynamic IoT data streams. IEEE Internet of Things Journal 4 (1), 64–74.

Qi, Z., Xie, H., Shang, M., 2023. A predictive coding approach to multivariate time series anomaly detection. In: Database Systems for Advanced Applications. Springer Nature, Switzerland, pp. 188–204. https://doi.org/10.1007/978-3-031-30637-2_13.

Ramesh, R.K., Wang, H., Shen, H., Fan, Z., 2021. Machine learning for load balancing in cloud datacenters. In: 2021 IEEE/ACM 21st International Symposium on Cluster, Cloud and Internet Computing (CCGrid), pp. 186–195.

Schneider, 2023. EcoStruxure: IoT – Internet of things | Schneider electric USA. https://www.se.com/us/en/work/campaign/innovation/overview.jsp. (Accessed 8 January 2023).

Shao, M., Wang, X., Bu, Z., Chen, X., Wang, Y., 2020. Prediction of energy consumption in hotel buildings via support vector machines. Sustainable Cities and Society 57, 102128. https://www.sciencedirect.com/science/article/pii/S2210670720301153.

Shumway, R.H., Stoffer, D.S., 2017. ARIMA models. In: Springer Texts in Statistics. Springer International Publishing, pp. 75–163. https://doi.org/10.1007/978-3-319-52452-8_3.

Srikanth, K., Wazeer, A., Mathiyalagan, P., Vidya, S., Rajput, K., Kushwaha, H.S., 2021. Piezoelectric properties of ZnO. In: Awasthi, K. (Ed.), 'Nanostructured Zinc Oxide', Metal Oxides. Elsevier, pp. 717–736. https://www.sciencedirect.com/science/article/pii/B9780128189009000243.

Svorobej, S., Bendechache, M., Griesinger, F., Domaschka, J., 2020. Orchestration from the Cloud to the Edge. Springer International Publishing, Cham, pp. 61–77. https://doi.org/10.1007/978-3-030-41110-7_4.

Techerati, 2017. IBM cloud selected for BMW connected car. https://www.techerati.com/the-stack-archive/cloud/2017/06/19/ibm-cloud-selected-for-bmw-connected-car/. (Accessed 8 January 2023).

Truong, T.M., Harwood, A., Sinnott, R.O., Chen, S., 2018. Performance analysis of large-scale distributed stream processing systems on the cloud. In: 2018 IEEE 11th International Conference on Cloud Computing (CLOUD), pp. 754–761.

Velasquez, K., Abreu, D.P., Gonçalves, D., Bittencourt, L., Curado, M., Monteiro, E., Madeira, E., 2017. Service orchestration in fog environments. In: 2017 IEEE 5th International Conference on Future Internet of Things and Cloud (FiCloud), pp. 329–336.

Walker, J., Zidek, T., Harbel, C., Yoon, S., Strickland, F.S., Kumar, S., Shin, M., 2020. Soft robotics: a review of recent developments of pneumatic soft actuators. Actuators 9 (1), 3. https://doi.org/10.3390/act9010003.

Zhang, Y.-F., Thorburn, P.J., Xiang, W., Fitch, P., 2019. SSIM—a deep learning approach for recovering missing time series sensor data. IEEE Internet of Things Journal 6 (4), 6618–6628.

Zhu, J., Wang, D., Qin, S., Tao, G., Gui, H., Li, F., Ou, L., 2022. Towards network dynamics: adaptive buffer management with deep reinforcement learning. In: GLOBECOM 2022–2022 IEEE Global Communications Conference, pp. 4935–4940.

CHAPTER

Unlocking value with the cloud-to-things continuum

5

5.1 Introduction

In the age of digital transformation, the fast-paced changes in technology are adjusting the experiences and expectations of businesses. Real-world physical objects have been augmented with actuators, sensors, and even microprocessors to enable remote access and operation. The adoption of the cloud-to-things continuum has empowered real-world objects around us with the power of the Internet. These objects are enabled with processing, storing, and communication capabilities, while being uniquely identifiable on the Internet. Advances in microprocessor technology, 5G/6G networks deployment, and the increasing availability of cloud services are offering business excellent value propositions through this evolution. The primary factors to consider include the choice of the IoT stack and its integration with the networking infrastructure, then the virtual representation of a physical thing on the cloud, followed by the provision of privacy and security across the physical and virtual layers, and finally, the conversion of information into actionable knowledge by mining the IoT data, through the application of AI tools. Further developments in software-defined networking (SDN) facilitate these value propositions by allowing the network requirements to scale as needed, while reducing investment in physical infrastructure.

The exponential growth of Internet usage since the pandemic has put a burden on the Internet. The cloud-to-things continuum boosts the integration of SDN and IoT, providing a promising approach to ease this burden. The IoT, SDN Transport, and cloud computing provide a holistic approach to optimizing the processing and distribution of IoT data and analytics by leveraging SDN in the transport layer, along with cloud computing technologies. This integration aims to enhance efficiency in network resource utilization and improve real-time analytics processing for IoT applications. IoT devices generate vast amounts of data, and efficiently managing and analyzing this data is crucial for actionable insights in organizations that adopt digital transformation. Organizations can dynamically distribute IoT analytics by combining IoT devices with SDN-enabled transport networks and utilizing cloud computing resources. This ensures that analytics occur closer to the data source (edge) or in centralized data centers (cloud) based on real-time requirements, reducing latency and optimizing network resources.

Accelerating Digital Transformation with the Cloud and the Internet of Things (IoT)
https://doi.org/10.1016/B978-0-44-322217-7.00011-6

SDN facilitates intelligent and dynamic network traffic management, allowing for efficient routing and allocation of resources based on the specific demands of IoT analytics. Edge computing brings computation and analytics closer to the data source, minimizing data transit, and improving response times. Cloud computing provides the scalability and powerful processing capabilities required for complex analytics. Moreover, the deployment of AI-based SDN controllers expands the adoption of IoT because of the flexibility, programmability, and central control provided to the heterogeneous network architecture and QoS needs of IoT applications and infrastructure (Ja'afreh et al., 2022). Overall, this integrated approach aims to maximize the efficiency and effectiveness of IoT analytics by distributing processing tasks, utilizing network resources optimally, and ensuring timely and meaningful insights from IoT-generated data.

The following sections are dedicated to exploring how businesses can benefit from the cloud-to-thing value chain and data mining in the IoT landscape. The chapter examines data mining in detail, covering various aspects of data analysis to help businesses increase their value. This includes using data mining techniques, such as association, sequence, classification, clustering, and forecasting within the IoT domain to extract insights. Additionally, this chapter focuses on the value proposition, explaining how pain relievers can help alleviate discomforts and how gain creators can proactively generate benefits. The importance of leveraging IoT data mining and reaping the resulting value propositions are highlighted next.

5.2 Tracing the cloud-to-thing value chain

The market economy relies on the dynamic interaction between businesses and customers. Businesses provide various products and services to meet the demands of customers in a competitive market landscape. However, the cloud-to-things continuum has significantly transformed this exchange. It has amplified the value proposition for customers by offering them enhanced and tailored experiences. Fig. 5.1 shows that this augmentation results in a higher ROI for businesses. By leveraging data-driven insights, operations are optimized, which boost efficiencies and deliver personalized offerings. Competitive advantages in the market are thus enabled for the adopting organizations.

Businesses supply products and services based on consumers' demand. Multiple factors affect both supply and demand, causing fluctuations in price. In market dynamics, the interplay between product quantity, price, demand, and equilibrium price orchestrates a fundamental relationship depicted in Fig. 5.2. As the price of a product featured on the y-axis rises, demand experiences an associated decline following the x-axis, based on the fundamental law of supply and demand. However, decreased prices, generally lead to increased demands, reflecting the inverse relationship between prices and demand. This cyclic movement along the graph persists until an equilibrium price is reached. This is the point where supply and demand intersect,

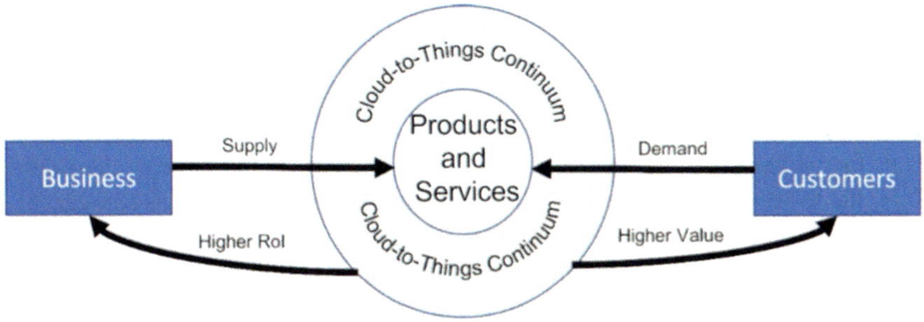

FIGURE 5.1

Cloud-to-things value and return on investment (RoI).

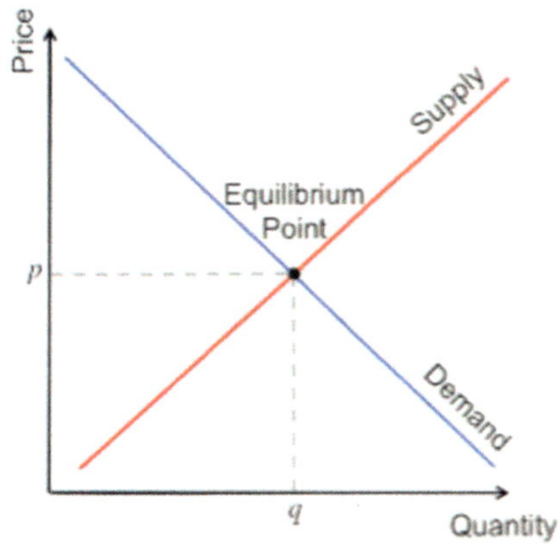

FIGURE 5.2

Inverse relationship between supply and demand.

marking quantity supplied equals to quantity demanded, and maintaining market stability.

The implications of this model are significant, as businesses optimize their pricing strategies in response to market shifts, while also influencing consumer behavior by aligning prices with demand elasticity. Consider technology companies introducing new models of their smartphones at reduced prices due to increased competition. The market often experiences an uptick in demand as consumers find these products more accessible and attractive. However, luxury brands deliberately maintain higher prices to create a perception of exclusivity, catering to a niche market, where low demand is associated with high profit margins. Understanding this inverse relationship empowers businesses to make informed decisions, tailor pricing strategies, and forecast demand, optimizing their market position and maximizing revenue potential by finding the delicate balance represented around the equilibrium price.

Enabling a product with IoT technology and cloud-based services incurs costs, including hardware, software, and networking, which must be retrieved for the business to have a better ROI. These investments seek to enhance the product's functionality, gather data, and facilitate connectivity, aiming to optimize performance and user experience. However, retrieving these costs and realizing a better ROI remains a challenge for businesses. Despite the added value from technology integration, businesses face a balancing act in pricing strategies. Increasing the price of the product solely due to the inclusion of new technology might seem intuitive to recover these costs. Yet, the economic model shown in Fig. 5.2 reveals a crucial caveat: raising prices often triggers a decrease in demand. Consequently, arbitrarily hiking prices due to technological advancements risks deterring potential consumers, diminishing market appeal, and subsequently hindering sales. Therefore businesses encounter a challenge; while they aim to recover investments, an abrupt price increase might result in reduced demand, impacting profitability and curtailing the potential for a favorable ROI.

Achieving a harmonious equilibrium between cost recovery and maintaining a price point that sustains or augments demand becomes pivotal in maximizing the returns on technological investments, while ensuring market competitiveness and consumer acceptance. For instance, consider a company that manufactures smart home devices, such as thermostats, equipped with IoT technology and cloud-based services for remote monitoring and control. Integrating these advanced features incurs substantial costs. Reaching a favorable ROI with these investments, may induce increasing the prices of these smart thermostats. If the company abruptly raises those prices solely due to the inclusion of IoT and cloud-based technology, it might carelessly deter potential buyers.

Imagine the increased price tag significantly surpasses the standard cost of regular thermostats without smart capabilities. This price hike could deter price-sensitive consumers, reducing the demand for these innovative devices. The company faces an interesting challenge, i.e., to balance the need to recover technological investments against maintaining a price point that does not reduce consumer demand. Finding the right equilibrium between cost recovery and market acceptance becomes essential. It entails strategizing pricing models, which navigate the balance between cost recovery, maintaining competitive prices, and stimulating demand, ultimately leading to sustained market penetration and profitability. Yes, technology does add value to the product or service, but does it add business value? A product must blend into the customer space and generate a demand for itself to have greater business value. An alternative approach would be to absorb some of the technology integration costs initially to competitively price the smart thermostats. Over time, based on economies of scale, the cost could be gradually adjusted, ensuring that it remains aligned with perceived value and consumer willingness to pay.

Value propositions are based on a combination of products and services, which create value for a segment of customers who put a demand on what a business can supply. ROI is positively impacted by the customer value (see Fig. 5.1). A higher value for customers is created when the cloud-to-thing continuum transforms data into useful knowledge driven by actionable data. Gathering such data from technology, converting it to information, and then analyzing it to create knowledge is the workflow whereby consumers perceive value.

Data collection, processing, analysis, and knowledge acquisition are essential components of a customer-centric product and services. By leveraging these transformations, businesses relieve their customers' pain points and create gains that push their growth forward. A commitment to data-driven solutions empowers companies to provide their customers with the awareness they need to make informed decisions and achieve success. By choosing a data-oriented approach, businesses can experience the transformative power of data (Osterwalder et al., 2015).

5.2.1 IoT data mining to increase business value

Data mining involves extracting knowledge from unprocessed data. Fig. 5.3 depicts the lifecycle of a data-driven value chain. Data consumers need to receive higher value from the cloud-to-things continuum. The data producers are the IoT devices and products. The cloud platform provides data storage, data mining, and analytics tools. The mining and analysis services provide different types of information from raw data (Zhao, 2012), including:

- `Associations`: occurrences triggered by a single event;
- `Sequences`: patterns of outcomes over time triggered by an event;
- `Classifications`: supervised categorization of distinct groups of items where the algorithm learns from the given data input;
- `Clusters`: unsupervised grouping of data points into patterns based on feature similarity, and
- `Forecasts`: prediction of future values based on existing data.

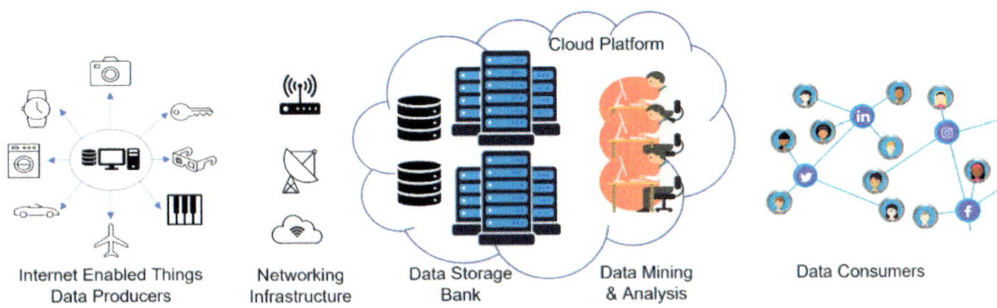

FIGURE 5.3

Life cycle of a data-driven value chain.

The business value resulting from these IoT data mining processes is multifold, including reduced downtime, lower maintenance costs, extended equipment lifespan, and improved overall operational efficiency. These benefits can be seen in smart agriculture, where IoT sensors are used to monitor soil conditions, weather, and overall crop health. Associations discover relationships between soil conditions, weather patterns, and crop yields to optimize planting and harvesting schedules. Sequences track the stages of crop growth in relation to environmental conditions to improve farming practices. Clusters can be used to group machinery with similar performance issues to streamline troubleshooting and repairs. And finally, forecasts predict the equipment failure likelihood or maintenance requirements to anticipate downtime with proactive maintenance schedules.

5.2.2 Value of association patterns in IoT data

Finding connections or patterns among variables within the data is known as association. When it comes to IoT this procedure helps uncovering correlations, between devices or sensor data. For example it can unveil patterns like whether certain sensor readings are linked to events or conditions as shown below.

- `Smart Retail`: Analyzing association patterns to identify frequently purchased items together in a retail store. For instance, customers who buy bread are likely to buy jam as well. Thus, items frequently purchased together are displayed in close proximity.
- `Energy Management`: Discovering associations between energy consumption patterns and external factors (e.g., weather conditions and location) to optimize energy usage in smart buildings or homes.
- `Supply Chain Optimization`: Identifying associations between product demand, delivery times, and supplier performance to streamline the supply chain process and enhance efficiency.

A less classical example relates to smart aquaculture to enhance fish farming practices (Prapti et al., 2022). IoT devices and sensors are utilized to monitor various environmental parameters, fish behavior, and equipment performance within fish farming operations. Association patterns within this IoT data enable aquaculture farmers to uncover valuable correlations that enhance fish health, optimize feeding practices, and improve overall farm management.

IoT sensors can monitor critical water quality parameters, such as pH, temperature, dissolved oxygen, and ammonia levels. The associations between these water quality metrics and fish health indicators (e.g., growth rates, disease incidence), can optimize water conditions for different fish species (Prapti et al., 2022). For example, there may be correlations between higher growth rates in salmon fish and a specific range of dissolved oxygen levels, enabling farmers to maintain these water conditions for improved fish health.

5.2.3 Sequence analysis in IoT data

This process involves discovering patterns or trends in ordered data, which is particularly relevant in IoT applications with time-series data. Discovering the sequences of events or actions taken by IoT devices facilitates predictive maintenance, behavior analysis, and process optimization, as illustrated next.

- `Healthcare monitoring`: Analyzing sequences of health data (e.g., body posture, blood pressure) to detect patterns leading to potential health issues and provide timely interventions.
- `Traffic management`: Studying sequences of traffic flow patterns to predict traffic congestion, enabling better traffic management and route optimization.
- `Manufacturing`: Analyzing sequences of machine operation data to predict potential equipment failures and schedule maintenance before a breakdown occurs.

Biotechnology labs associated with pharmaceutical companies, utilize IoT-enabled devices to monitor various factors critical to bioprocesses, such as temperature, pH, dissolved oxygen (O2), and glucose levels (Borgosz and Dikicioglu, 2024). The development lifecycle of biological sample expects a sequential data collection from these bioprocesses. Analyzing this data helps determining the optimal conditions for maximum growth and maintaining product integrity. This sequence analysis helps identifying deviations from optimal conditions in real time. For instance, IoT devices can detect a sudden change in pH or a drop in dissolved oxygen levels. Prompt corrective actions are subsequently undertaken to ensure that the bioprocess remains aligned with optimal output conditions.

5.2.4 Classification in IoT data mining

Categorizing data into predefined classes based on certain attributes is referred to as "classification." In an IoT environment, classification categorizes IoT data into meaningful groups, allowing for better decision-making. For instance, classifying sensor data to detect anomalies or predict system failures, as illustrated next.

- `Healthcare diagnostics`: Classifying medical imaging data to diagnose health conditions, such as diabetes, heart disease, or tumors.
- `Environmental monitoring`: Classifying sensor data from environmental monitoring devices to detect and predict pollution levels, natural disasters, or migrations.
- `Anomaly detection`: Classifying IoT device behavior to detect anomalies or potential cyber-attacks in IoT networks.

Farms and greenhouses utilize IoT-enabled devices to create a smart agricultural environment. These devices gather various data points from sensors and cameras; assess crop health based on attributes, such as soil moisture, temperature, light levels, and plant images. IoT devices continuously collect data on various parameters that affect crop health (Nayyar and Puri, 2016). This data is then classified into predefined classes (Vasavi et al., 2022). These categories could be namely healthy, nutrient-deficient, infected, or stressed, which may therefore require the following interventions:

- **Healthy:** the growth is optimal, and no changes are necessary.
- **Nutrient-deficient:** the system indicates the need for specific fertilizers.
- **Infected:** targeted treatments, such as pesticides, are applied.
- **Stressed:** specific interventions, such as adjusting water, light, or temperature.

5.2.5 IoT data clustering

This process involves grouping similar data points together based on their characteristics. In IoT, clustering can help in organizing and segmenting data from diverse IoT devices or sensors into clusters, aiding in understanding patterns and trends within different groups, as illustrated next.

- `Customer segmentation`: Clustering customer behavior data to segment customers based on purchasing patterns for targeted marketing strategies.
- `Smart agriculture`: Clustering soil and weather sensor data to group regions with similar agricultural conditions, aiding in personalized crop management.
- `Smart cities`: Clustering traffic and population data to identify areas with high congestion, assisting in urban planning and infrastructure development.

IoT data clustering can also be illustrated in the context of developing targeted marketing strategies to effectively explain how to group similar data points based on characteristics such as buying behavior, which can then inform more effective marketing campaigns. The aim is to respond to the needs of different customer segments. These segments can be based on various factors, such as demography, geography, buying behavior, lifecycle stage, or needs-based characteristics. Clustering such IoT data allows tailored marketing campaigns, which capture the attention of targeted customers, thereby enhancing engagement and increasing sales (Sholla et al., 2017). For example, to segment first-time parents, a marketing campaign can focus on promoting baby monitors with advanced IoT capabilities, which include smart home system integration (Joseph et al., 2021). These devices offer features such as reminders, feeding tracking, and sleep schedule monitoring. By combining the promotion of the advanced baby monitor with commonly purchased products, such as baby formula, businesses can create attractive bundled offers that encourage purchases. For example, offering a discount on baby formula with the purchase of a high-tech baby monitor can appeal to first-time parents looking for comprehensive solutions (Visvesvaran et al., 2021).

By further analyzing purchase data from first-time parents, businesses can identify patterns that form the basis of clusters (Wang et al., 2019). With the clustered data, a marketing campaign can be designed to highlight the benefits of an advanced baby monitor. This campaign could emphasize features such as integration with other smart home devices and additional functionalities tailored to first-time parents.

5.2.6 Forecasting with IoT data

Forecasting entails making predictions about trends or values using data from the past. In the context of IoT, this can be extremely advantageous for tasks such as maintenance to optimizing resources and anticipating customer demand or behavior by leveraging insights from previous observations. For instance,

- `Energy demand prediction`: Forecasting energy consumption patterns to optimize energy distribution and plan for future capacity needs based on IoT-connected devices embedded in power grid components.
- `Financial market prediction`: Forecasting market trends based on historical and real-time financial data to make informed investment decisions.
- `Demand forecasting in retail`: Forecasting consumer demand for specific products based on historical sales data, aiding in inventory management and supply chain optimization.

IoT devices in the form of augmented collars, ear tags, and leg sensors collect data on animal movement, heart rate, temperature, and activity levels in livestock farming. By leveraging historical and real-time data, farmers can forecast health issues and productivity trends, ensuring optimal animal care, and thus maximizing yield (Neethirajan, 2017). The data from these wearable sensors can also be combined with data from in-situ sensors placed in barns and pastures that monitor environmental conditions.

Historical data on animal health and productivity provide farmers with grounds to identify patterns and trends that match certain conditions. The integration of real-time data with historical trends allows dynamic forecasting of health issues, including early disease detections and overall productivity improvement, encompassing milk yield and weight gain. Forecasting health issues based on data from wearable sensors enables early intervention. For example, a rise in body temperature and reduced activity might indicate the onset of illness, prompting immediate veterinary attention (Nadimi et al., 2009). Similarly, predictive models can help farmers optimize feeding schedules, breeding programs, and overall farm management to maximize output. For instance, forecasting the best times for breeding based on historical data and current health indicators can improve reproductive success rates.

5.3 Enhanced business value through real-time IoT data

Businesses harness real-time data from IoT devices to enhance their products and services as well as to optimize production and operational processes, resulting in significant cost reductions. These savings allow competitive prices and increased profitability.

5.3.1 Real-time data utilization

The integration of machine learning algorithms with real-time data streamed from IoT devices ensures accurate demand forecasting. This capability enables businesses to effectively manage supplies, shipments, deliveries, orders, and allocations. An optimized supply chain management system, driven by real-time data generates substantial business value.

The need for real-time machine learning algorithms in IoT applications is justified by the continuous data generation by sensors. The ability to make forecasts within a fixed timeframe using machine learning algorithms is needed for various application domains, as illustrated next.

Real-time IoT data in action

Consider today's connected vehicles, which utilize IoT data from within and outside the vehicle to forecast hazards in real-time. On the one hand, cloud-based services are increasingly available to acquire real-time traffic and geospatial data. And on the other hand, the software-defined vehicle is transforming the automotive industry into software companies as vehicles are perceived as APIs (Aust, 2022).

Towards the foreseeable transformation, vehicles are expanding the scope of their advanced driver assistance systems (ADAS) to react proactively when traffic threats are forecasted. For example, as the vehicle approaches a busy junction, ADAS needs to forecast potential hazards, such as sudden stops by other vehicles, cyclists or pedestrians crossing, or connected changing traffic light conditions. External traffic actors can be captured and recognized by connected cameras, which monitor such busy junctions, providing IoT connectivity to notorious road networks for safety issues (Datondji et al., 2016). ADAS uses the outcomes of predictive machine learning algorithms to advocate proactive actions, such as issuing adaptive alerts to the driver, or even taking over vehicle operations to prevent imminent threats.

However, real-time inferences are expected by machine learning algorithms, which may run either on-board the vehicles, on edge devices, or in the cloud. With the advent of advanced cellular networks, latency is significantly minimized, making such distributed real-time processing more feasible and effective (Peltonen et al., 2021).

Real-time data processing for machine learning in IoT

To address the need for real-time processing in IoT, particularly in connected vehicles, three main real-time computing paradigms can be employed: contract-based, anytime, and progressive machine learning (ML).

Contract-based ML

This approach to real-time ML uses precompiled models to guarantee a certain level of deliberation within predefined timeframes. These models ensure that results are delivered within a specified duration, with different precision levels depending on the available computation time (Zhou and Yang, 2022). In a connected vehicle scenario, a contract-based ML model for hazard prediction might be designed to deliver forecasts within 500 milliseconds. During this time, the model can provide varying levels of detail about potential hazards, such as the likelihood of a pedestrian stepping into the crosswalk or the probability of a cyclist's trajectory getting close to the vehicle.

Contract-based machine learning models operate under predefined constraints to ensure results are delivered within specific timeframes. TensorRT, for example, is a high-performance deep learning inference library developed by NVIDIA, which illustrates this approach through its use of operator schemas (Zhou and Yang, 2022). These schemas define the input and output tensor types and recognized shapes for various operations. These schemas serve as a contract between the converters and the TensorRT engine, ensuring compatibility and accurate handling of tensor data. This contractual framework allows TensorRT to guarantee that ML models deliver results within the specified timeframes, achieving the desired balance between performance and precision.

Anytime ML

These models are expected to provide a usable result at any point during their computation. The precision of the result improves with more computation time, allowing for immediate but progressively refined predictions (Esmeir and Markovitch, 2011). For example, as a connected vehicle approaches a notorious junction, an anytime ML algorithm might estimate the risk levels in the immediate vicinity. As the vehicle gets closer and more data is processed, the algorithm refines its predictions, offering increasingly accurate hazard assessments, which ADAS can use to issue adaptive alerts or take proactive control actions, if necessary.

Progressive ML

Also known as online learning, this approach improves precision incrementally by processing more input data in each iteration. This approach continuously updates the model with new data, enhancing its accuracy over time (Fayek et al., 2020). A progressive ML model in a connected vehicle might continuously receive real-time traffic data and update its predictions about the junction. As new data from sensors and cloud sources is integrated, the model becomes more precise in identifying imminent threats and adjusting the vehicle's behavior accordingly, such as slowing down or preparing to stop.

Supporting real-time machine learning with heuristics

Real-time ML can be further enhanced by incorporating heuristics tailored to specific ML models. For instance, in a random forest algorithm, certain trees (those deemed more important based on prior data) can be prioritized during the forecasting process, ensuring faster and more relevant predictions (Krawczyk et al., 2017). Strategies for incorporating heuristics to optimize ensemble models, such as random forests in real-time applications, employ methods that streamline decision-making by focusing on the most promising options first. In a random forest model, not all trees contribute equally to the final prediction. During real-time inference, high-priority trees can be evaluated first, ensuring that the most informative and accurate predictions are available (Breiman, 2001).

5.4 Case studies of increased value proposition

The value proposition canvas introduces two categories known as "pain relievers" and "gain creators". This framework, developed by Alex Osterwalder et al. (Osterwalder et al., 2015), helps businesses gain an understanding of their customers needs and preferences. Pain relievers refer to the features or qualities of a product or service that alleviate specific problems customers may be facing.

These pain points can be anything that causes discontent or inconvenience. Pain relievers aim to provide solutions to these issues, making the customer's life easier and comfortable. Gain creators are the aspects of a product or service that generate additional benefits for the customers. These can be enhancements or added value, which go beyond just addressing existing pain points. Gain creators create new, valuable experiences for customers and help them achieve their goals or aspirations. We look at the value proposition gained by integrating cloud-to-thing projects in different areas and provide a synopsis of these projects and how they have contributed to providing increased value.

5.4.1 Education sector

The study by A. Uzelac, N. Gligorić, and S. Krčo (Uzelac et al., 2018) introduces an innovative cloud-to-things system designed to revolutionize education quality assessment. This system leverages smart devices to monitor and enhance the quality of lectures. Through sophisticated analysis of physical parameters extracted from these devices, the smart classroom system achieves an impressive accuracy, ranging between 70.7% and 83.9%, in classifying students' satisfaction with lecture quality. This groundbreaking approach using random forest modeling demonstrates its potential as a formidable tool for gauging educational effectiveness based on objective data, thereby providing educators with valuable insights into lecture quality.

The value creation resulting from this modeling approach extends far beyond accurate classification. By enabling educators to finely calibrate and optimize the educational process, the system fosters gain creation. Educators can leverage the insights derived from the cloud-to-things system to fine-tune teaching methodologies, identify strengths, and address weaknesses in lectures, ultimately empowering them to craft superior, more engaging content. Simultaneously, this technological innovation functions as a potent pain relief by alleviating the burden on students to learn from subpar content. Accurately assessing lecture quality eases the challenges faced by students forced to navigate and comprehend inadequate educational materials, thereby laying the groundwork for an environment conducive to enhanced learning experiences and improved academic outcomes.

5.4.2 Healthcare sector

Orthopedics

The research conducted by S. Liaqat, K. Dashtipour, K. Arshad, K. Assaleh, and N. Ramzan (Liaqat et al., 2021) introduces a cutting-edge cloud-to-things system focused on posture monitoring, which plays a crucial role in health management. This innovative hybrid posture detection framework combines machine learning (ML) and deep learning (DL) classifiers, showcasing remarkable success by achieving an impressive accuracy rate exceeding 98% in identifying various postures, such as standing, sitting, and walking. This accuracy underscores the system's efficacy in robustly recognizing different postures, positioning it as a pivotal tool for health monitoring and risk mitigation. The modeling approaches adopted, combining ML and DL classifiers, hold the potential for significant value creation. By leveraging this hybrid framework, the system offers gain creation in healthcare by providing early responses to avert potential health mishaps, especially for the elderly. The accurate and real-time posture detection aids in identifying any deviations or abnormalities, allowing for proactive interventions to prevent accidents or health risks, thus significantly improving the quality of healthcare for older adults.

Moreover, the system functions as an effective pain relief mechanism by facilitating early identification of potential health risks among the elderly. By recognizing posture deviations or irregularities, healthcare professionals can promptly detect emerging health issues, enabling timely interventions and personalized care plans to mitigate these risks. This proactive approach to healthcare, facilitated by the hybrid posture detection framework, minimizes the burden on elderly individuals by ensuring timely preventive measures and enhancing their overall health and well-being.

Cardiology

The study by F. Desai et al. (Desai et al., 2022) introduces an innovative cloud-to-things system aimed at monitoring the health status of heart patients, presenting a pivotal advancement in cardiac health management. This system leverages machine learning (ML) and cloud computing, specifically employing logistic regression modeling approaches to monitor and predict heart-related conditions effectively. Impressively, the research unveils logistic regression as the most responsive and accurate model among various ML models assessed, achieving an accuracy rate of 85.96%. This high accuracy underscores the system's effectiveness in robustly monitoring and predicting heart health, positioning it as a vital tool for proactive health management in cardiac care.

The application of logistic regression as a modeling approach holds significant value creation potential by contributing to gain creation in healthcare. By accurately predicting heart-related ailments and conditions, the system plays a crucial role in reducing the risk of heart failure, thereby averting potentially catastrophic cardiac events, such as cardiac arrests. The proactive monitoring facilitated by this system enables early detection of potential risks, empowering healthcare providers to implement preventive measures, administer timely interventions, and provide personalized care, ultimately improving patient outcomes and quality of life.

Moreover, this cloud-to-things system serves as a potent pain relief mechanism by enabling the early identification of heart ailments without the need for physical interaction with medical professionals. By proactively monitoring heart health parameters and swiftly identifying potential issues, the system alleviates the burden on patients and medical practitioners alike. Patients benefit from early detection, while healthcare professionals can act promptly, allowing for timely interventions and personalized treatment plans. This proactive and remote monitoring approach mitigates the stress associated with delayed diagnosis, enhancing patient safety and well-being, while optimizing healthcare resources.

Oncology

The research by A. A. Nayan et al. (Nayan et al., 2022) presents an innovative cloud-to-things system designed for the detection of brain tumors using magnetic resonance images (MRI). This system uses a deep learning technique called convolutional neural network (CNN), which analyzes MRI scan data to detect the brain tumors. The study demonstrates the system's capability to accurately identify and delineate abnormal cell growth within brain tissues, showcasing its potential to revolutionize diagnostic accuracy and early intervention in neurology. The utilization of CNN models as a modeling approach showcases the tremendous potential for gain creation in the medical domain.

By employing advanced deep learning techniques, the system enables precise diagnoses and early treatment plans for brain tumors detected from MRI scans. The system's ability to accurately identify and present abnormalities within brain tissues facilitates timely interventions. Subsequently, patients' life expectancy is improved and treatment outcomes are enhanced. Thus more effective medical interventions and personalized treatment plans are proactively advocated with this brain tumor detection and diagnosis technique, ultimately improving patient care and prognosis.

Furthermore, the cloud-to-things system serves as an instrumental pain relief mechanism by effectively detecting the growth of abnormal cells within brain tissues. The system's capability to identify and delineate brain tumors aids in early detection, enabling healthcare professionals to detect abnormal cell growth at its early stages. This proactive monitoring of abnormal cell growth within the brain tissues mitigates the challenges associated with delayed diagnoses and enables timely medical interventions. By facilitating early detection of brain tumors, the system contributes to alleviating the pain and uncertainties faced by patients, providing them with better chances of successful treatments and improved health.

5.4.3 Environment protection sector

Aquaculture

The study conducted by M. M. Islam, M. A. Kashem, and J. Uddin (Islam et al., 2021) introduces a novel cloud-to-things system aimed at predicting the survival of fish species in aquatic environments, which plays a pivotal role in aquaculture and environmental conservation. This innovative system employs a random forest modeling approach, showcasing its effectiveness in accurately predicting fish species in aquatic environments. Notably, this model outperforms existing methodologies, demonstrating higher accuracy, true positive rates, and kappa statistics. The system's ability to accurately forecast fish survival represents a significant breakthrough, offering substantial advantages in aquaculture management and ecological preservation.

The modeling approach utilizing random forest signifies considerable value creation by safeguarding the fish population and optimizing productivity, thus driving gain creation in aquaculture. By accurately predicting fish species' survival, the system facilitates proactive measures to protect and manage fish populations effectively. This proactive approach helps to maximize productivity in aquaculture by identifying species that thrive in specific aquatic environments, thereby ensuring a sustainable and thriving fish population.

Furthermore, the cloud-to-things system operates as a potent pain relief mechanism by aiding in the identification and selection of optimal fish species for aquaculture within specific aquatic environments. By leveraging predictive capabilities, this system alleviates the challenges of identifying suitable fish species and streamlines decision-making processes for aquaculture practices. This precision contributes to mitigating potential risks associated with introducing fish species that might struggle or be unsuitable for a particular aquatic environment, ultimately fostering a healthier and more productive aquaculture industry, while minimizing ecological disruptions.

Apiculture

The study by H. Nguyen Thi, T.-T.-H. Phan, and C. T. Tran (Nguyen Thi et al., 2023) introduce a novel cloud-to-things system focused on monitoring changes in beehives using audio classifications, signaling a significant advancement in apiculture and environmental conservation. This innovative system leverages the genetic programming (GP) algorithm as a modeling approach to effectively classify bee audio, enabling the detection of various conditions within beehives. This research demonstrates the system's capability to accurately identify and classify bee sounds, marking a crucial step towards proactive monitoring and maintenance of bee populations, as well as environmental preservation. The application of the genetic programming (GP) algorithm as a modeling approach holds tremendous potential for gain creation in the realm of apiculture and ecological balance.

Classifying bee audio with this cloud-to-things approach contributes to the protection of the honeybee population and to environmental sustainability and agriculture at large. The system's capability to detect changes or irregularities within beehives facilitates early responses to potential threats, ensuring timely interventions to safeguard honeybee colonies. Ultimately, this proactive approach enhances pollination processes, preserves ecosystems, and promotes agricultural productivity. Furthermore, the system functions as a vital pain relief mechanism by endeavoring to curtail the decline of honeybee populations, addressing the concerning decrease in bee numbers.

By accurately monitoring beehive conditions through audio classifications, this system assists beekeepers and environmentalists in identifying potential issues or stress factors affecting honeybee health. Early detection allows for prompt actions, enabling preventative measures and interventions to mitigate the factors contributing to the decline in honeybee populations. This proactive monitoring and protection of honeybees alleviates the decline in bee populations and the resulting detrimental impacts on agriculture, biodiversity, and ecological balance.

5.4.4 Precision agriculture

The study by S. K. Apat, J. Mishra, K. S. Raju, and N. Padhy (Apat et al., 2022) introduces an innovative cloud-to-things system tailored for planning and managing farming, underscoring a pivotal advancement in precision agriculture and smart farming practices. This system integrates the random forest modeling approach, emphasizing robustness and efficiency in decision-making for intelligent agricultural practices. By leveraging machine learning techniques within this cloud-to-thing framework, the system adeptly recommends suitable crops based on geographical and climatic parameters. This capability facilitates informed decision-making and crop planning, culminating in higher agricultural productivity, and optimized resource utilization.

The utilization of random forest as a modeling approach signifies substantial gain creation in agriculture by providing comprehensive recommendations for crop selection based on geographical and climatic parameters. By leveraging machine learning models, this cloud-to-things system assists farmers in making informed decisions regarding crop choices. The recommendations, considering geological and climatic conditions, aim to maximize agricultural productivity, aligning crop choices with environmental suitability. This proactive approach empowers farmers to optimize yields, mitigate risks associated with unsuitable crops, and ultimately enhance agricultural productivity and profitability.

Moreover, the cloud-to-things system functions as a potent pain relief mechanism by enabling farmers to circumvent adverse natural conditions, plant diseases, and demand-supply disparities prevalent in agriculture. The system's ability to recommend crops based on geological and climatic parameters assists farmers in avoiding potential adversities related to unsuitable crop choices.

By providing insights into optimal crop selections aligned with environmental conditions, the system aids in mitigating risks associated with natural calamities, diseases, or market fluctuations. This proactive decision-making capability supports farmers in minimizing losses and adapting to changing conditions, contributing to sustainable agricultural practices, and ensuring greater resilience in farming operations.

5.4.5 Cyber security sector

The research by A. Guezzaz, M. Azrour, S. Benkirane, M. Mohy-Eddine, H. Attou, and M. Douiba (Guezzaz et al., 2022) introduces an innovative cloud-to-things system aimed at detecting and isolating cyberattacks within industrial control systems (ICS), marking a significant advancement in industrial Internet of Things (IIoT) security. This system integrates the k-nearest neighbor (K-NN) and principal component analysis (PCA) as modeling approaches, forming a lightweight hybrid intrusion detection framework tailored for edge-based IIoT security. The integration of machine learning techniques within this framework enhances the abilities of the intrusion detection system (IDS) to diagnoze cyber security issues, while minimizing false alarms.

The hybrid intrusion detection framework enhances the IDS's ability to discern and react to cyber threats within industrial systems. By employing machine learning algorithms, this system refines the detection mechanisms, enabling reliable decisions that discern genuine cyber intrusions from false alarms. This proactive approach minimizes the occurrences of false positives, optimizing the IDS's accuracy and responsiveness, while reducing the impact of false alarms on industrial operations.

Moreover, the cloud-to-things system operates as a crucial pain relief mechanism by effectively detecting intrusions and undesirable activities within industrial control systems. The system's ability to identify and isolate cyberattacks within IIoT environments aids in mitigating security risks posed by potential intrusions. By promptly recognizing and responding to cyber threats, the system safeguards industrial systems from disruptive cyberattacks, ensuring the integrity and operational continuity of industrial control systems. This proactive security monitoring capability minimizes the impact of cyber intrusions, thereby enhancing the resilience and security posture of IIoT environments.

5.4.6 Energy management sector

The study conducted by A. Chahal, P. Gulia, N. S. Gill, and J. M. Chatterjee (Chahal et al., 2022) introduces a cloud-to-thing approach dedicated to predicting the stability of the energy grid, which is a critical aspect in the reliability and efficiency of smart grids. This system harnesses the power of an artificial neural network (ANN) optimized using the Adam optimizer to forecast the stability of the smart grid. This significant advancement in energy management systems utilizes machine learning techniques to optimize energy grid operations, while reducing human intervention, minimizing costs, and promoting a more sustainable mode of operation. The utilization of an optimized ANN signifies substantial gain creation by reducing human intervention and operational costs, while enhancing energy grid efficiency and sustainability.

By deploying machine learning-driven predictive models to optimize decision-making and reduce downtime, this proactive approach aids in balancing energy usage during peak demand conditions, such as different weather conditions. Furthermore, the cloud-to-things system functions as a crucial pain relief mechanism by effectively balancing usage during various weather conditions, and preventing potential outages. By accurately forecasting energy grid stability using an optimized ANN model, the system contributes to reducing energy wastage. This proactive energy management capability aids in maintaining grid stability, preventing potential outages, and ensuring continuous power supply, thereby alleviating the pain points associated with energy shortages, imbalances, and service disruptions.

5.4.7 Transportation sector

Aviation

The research by C. Sandamini et al. (Sandamini et al., 2023) delves into a cloud-to-things system dedicated to the indoor positioning of unmanned aerial vehicles (UAVs), presenting a significant stride in UAV localization for diverse indoor settings. This system embarks on a comprehensive comparison of various machine learning (ML) approaches and models to determine their efficacy in UAV localization, showcasing the versatility and adaptability of ML algorithms in indoor positioning. By examining multiple ML techniques, the research aims to optimize UAV localization in indoor environments, catering to diverse scenarios, such as warehouses, production lines, malls, and hangars. The exploration of different ML approaches and models signifies substantial gain creation by enabling predictive capabilities for congestion management and flow control in indoor settings.

Through the accurate localization of UAVs, the system facilitates predictive insights into potential congestion points or bottlenecks within indoor locations. This proactive approach aids in managing flow control in diverse environments, optimizing logistical processes, and enhancing operational efficiency. By leveraging ML-based predictive analytics, the system offers valuable insights for effective decision-making in diverse indoor settings, thereby streamlining operations and improving overall productivity.

Furthermore, the cloud-to-things system serves as a critical pain relief mechanism by accurately identifying issues in hazardous or dangerous locations without human intervention. The capability to precisely locate and assess potential issues or anomalies within hazardous indoor environments via UAVs provides a layer of safety and risk mitigation. By autonomously navigating and identifying issues in potentially dangerous areas, such as chemical plants or storage facilities, the system minimizes human exposure to hazardous conditions, ensuring timely responses to safety concerns. This proactive and automated surveillance capability enhances safety protocols and operational resilience in hazardous indoor locations, thereby minimizing risks and mitigating potential dangers.

Road transportation

The study by P. A. D. Amiri and S. Pierre (Amiri and Pierre, 2023) introduces a cloud-to-things system designed to revolutionize road transportation and traffic control by integrating ensemble learning using multiple machine learning (ML) approaches. This system focuses on forecasting network traffic in vehicular ad hoc networks (VANET), representing a significant leap forward in intelligent transportation systems. By instrumenting ensemble learning techniques with various ML approaches, the research aims to enhance the system's capability to manage road transportation efficiently and optimize traffic control measures.

The integration of ensemble learning techniques using diverse ML approaches signifies substantial gain creation by raising drivers' awareness regarding potential accidents or congestion on the roads. By leveraging ensemble learning methodologies, the system excels in forecasting network traffic patterns, providing insights into the likelihood of accidents or traffic congestion. This proactive approach aids in alerting drivers about potential road hazards or congested areas, fostering safer driving practices and enabling motorists to make informed decisions, thereby enhancing overall road safety. Moreover, the cloud-to-things system functions as a critical pain relief mechanism by improving traffic efficiency and road safety.

By accurately forecasting road traffic using ensemble-based ML models, the system contributes to optimizing traffic flow, mitigating congestion, and reducing the likelihood of accidents. This proactive traffic management capability leads to enhanced traffic efficiency, smoother traffic flow, and reduced instances of congestion, thereby alleviating the pain points associated with traffic delays, improving overall road safety, and promoting a more efficient transportation system.

5.5 Cloud-to-things continuum: adding value to digital transformation

The cloud-to-things continuum plays a crucial role in empowering businesses undergoing digital transformation across various sectors. The projects discussed in this chapter provide various examples of how the mining and analysis of data from the cloud-to-things continuum can provide higher value, either to relieve pain or create gain. Mining the data produced by IoT, processing, and analyzing the same in a cloud-based system provides a new or better way of providing greater value to the customers, and therefore, a better business ROI.

Enhanced efficiency and decision-making

Implementing systems with the cloud-to-things continuum, powered by machine learning (ML) algorithms or AI, enables businesses to enhance operational efficiency, as seen in smart farming, traffic control, or industrial systems. Optimized resource utilization, reduced costs, and improved decision-making processes result from this adoption.

Proactive problem identification and resolution

The continuum aids in early detection and resolution of issues, as illustrated in scenarios such as health monitoring, intrusion detection, or energy grid stability prediction. This proactive approach mitigates risks, reduces downtime, and enhances safety in various domains.

Improved productivity and resource management

Cloud-to-things systems assist in maximizing productivity and managing resources effectively, as seen in agriculture, industrial control, and energy management. This includes better crop selection, optimized production lines, and efficient energy utilization, which increase productivity and save costs.

Enhanced safety and quality of services

Applications such as healthcare monitoring, traffic management, and indoor positioning systems contribute to enhanced safety, improved service quality, and better decision-making in critical scenarios, thereby improving customer satisfaction.

Prediction and prevention

The systems' predictive capabilities, such as forecasting traffic, detecting brain tumors, or identifying beehive issues, allow for early problem detection and prevention, mitigating risks, and improving outcomes.

Reduced human intervention and costs

By utilizing AI-powered models and predictive analysis, companies can minimize the need for human involvement, lower operational expenses, and enhance resource allocation. This results in improved efficiency and an increased focus on sustainability.

Environmental impact

Cloud-to-things systems, such as those used in smart farming or energy grid stability, contribute to sustainability by optimizing resource usage, minimizing energy consumption, and reducing environmental impacts.

In summary the cloud-to-things continuum combines cloud computing, IoT, and AI to provide a range of benefits for different industries. As part of optimizing operations, decision-making processes, and resource management, the created value propositions offer efficient and a sustainable business environment, which promotes growth, innovation, and better services, while reducing risks and enhancing safety in a range of sectors.

References

Amiri, P.A.D., Pierre, S., 2023. An ensemble-based machine learning model for forecasting network traffic in vanet. IEEE Access 11, 22855–22870.

Apat, S.K., Mishra, J., Raju, K.S., Padhy, N., 2022. The robust and efficient machine learning model for smart farming decisions and allied intelligent agriculture decisions. Journal of Integrated Science and Technology 10 (2), 139–155.

Aust, S., 2022. Vehicle API and service catalog for next generation mobility. In: 2022 25th International Symposium on Wireless Personal Multimedia Communications (WPMC). IEEE, pp. 418–423.

Borgosz, L., Dikicioglu, D., 2024. Industrial Internet of Things: what does it mean for the bioprocess industries? Biochemical Engineering Journal 201, 109122.

Breiman, L., 2001. Random forests. Machine Learning 45, 5–32.

Chahal, A., Gulia, P., Gill, N.S., Chatterjee, J.M., 2022. Performance analysis of an optimized ann model to predict the stability of smart grid. Complexity 2022.

Datondji, S.R.E., Dupuis, Y., Subirats, P., Vasseur, P., 2016. A survey of vision-based traffic monitoring of road intersections. IEEE Transactions on Intelligent Transportation Systems 17 (10), 2681–2698.

Desai, F., et al., 2022. Healthcloud: a system for monitoring health status of heart patients using machine learning and cloud computing. Internet of Things 17, 100485.

Esmeir, S., Markovitch, S., 2011. Anytime learning of anycost classifiers. Machine Learning 82, 445–473.

Fayek, H.M., Cavedon, L., Wu, H.R., 2020. Progressive learning: a deep learning framework for continual learning. Neural Networks 128, 345–357.

Guezzaz, A., Azrour, M., Benkirane, S., Mohy-Eddine, M., Attou, H., Douiba, M., 2022. A lightweight hybrid intrusion detection framework using machine learning for edge-based IIoT security. The International Arab Journal of Information Technology 19 (5).

Islam, M.M., Kashem, M.A., Uddin, J., 2021. Fish survival prediction in an aquatic environment using random forest model. International Journal of Artificial Intelligence 2252 (8938), 8938.

Ja'afreh, M.A., Adhami, H., Alchalabi, A.E., Hoda, M., El Saddik, A., 2022. Toward integrating software defined networks with the Internet of Things: a review. Cluster Computing, 1–18.

Joseph, S., Kumar, A., Babu, M.H., et al., 2021. IoT Based Baby Monitoring System Smart Cradle. 2021 7th International Conference on Advanced Computing and Communication Systems (ICACCS), vol. 1. IEEE, pp. 748–751.

Krawczyk, B., Minku, L.L., Gama, J., Stefanowski, J., Woźniak, M., 2017. Ensemble learning for data stream analysis: a survey. Information Fusion 37, 132–156.

Liaqat, S., Dashtipour, K., Arshad, K., Assaleh, K., Ramzan, N., 2021. A hybrid posture detection framework: integrating machine learning and deep neural networks. IEEE Sensors Journal 21 (7), 9515–9522.

Nadimi, E.S., Jørgensen, R.N., Blanes-Vidal, V., Christensen, S., 2009. Monitoring and classifying the behavior of a herd of sheep using ad hoc wireless sensor networks and artificial intelligence. In: 7th World Congress on Computers in Agriculture Conference Proceedings. 22-24 June 2009, Reno, Nevada. American Society of Agricultural and Biological Engineers, p. 1.

Nayan, A.-A., et al., 2022. A deep learning approach for brain tumor detection using magnetic resonance imaging. Arxiv preprint: arXiv:2210.13882.

Nayyar, A., Puri, V., 2016. Smart farming: IoT based smart sensors agriculture stick for live temperature and moisture monitoring using arduino, cloud computing & solar technology. In: Proc. of The International Conference on Communication and Computing Systems (ICCCS-2016). https://doi.org/10.1201/9781315364094-121.

Neethirajan, S., 2017. Recent advances in wearable sensors for animal health management. Sensing Bio-Sensing Research 12, 15–29.

Nguyen Thi, H., Phan, T.-T.-H., Tran, C.T., 2023. Genetic programming for bee audio classification. In: Proceedings of the 2023 8th International Conference on Intelligent Information Technology, pp. 246–250.

Osterwalder, A., Pigneur, Y., Bernarda, G., Smith, A., 2015. Value Proposition Design: How to Create Products and Services Customers Want, vol. 2. John Wiley & Sons.

Peltonen, E., Sojan, A., Päivärinta, T., 2021. Towards real-time learning for edge-cloud continuum with vehicular computing. In: 2021 IEEE 7th World Forum on Internet of Things (WF-IoT). IEEE, pp. 921–926.

Prapti, D.R., Mohamed Shariff, A.R., Che Man, H., Ramli, N.M., Perumal, T., Shariff, M., 2022. Internet of things (IoT)-based aquaculture: an overview of IoT application on water quality monitoring. Reviews in Aquaculture 14 (2), 979–992.

Sandamini, C., et al., 2023. A review of indoor positioning systems for UAV localization with machine learning algorithms. Electronics (Basel) 12 (7), 1533.

Sholla, S., Kaur, S., Begh, G.R., Mir, R.N., Chishti, M.A., 2017. Clustering Internet of Things: a review. Journal of Science and Technology: Issue on Information and Communications Technology 3 (2), 21–27.

Uzelac, A., Gligorić, N., Krčo, S., 2018. System for recognizing lecture quality based on analysis of physical parameters. Telematics and Informatics 35 (3), 579–594.

Vasavi, P., Punitha, A., Rao, T.V.N., 2022. Crop leaf disease detection and classification using machine learning and deep learning algorithms by visual symptoms: a review. International Journal of Electrical and Computer Engineering 12 (2), 2079.

Visvesvaran, C., Nishanth, S., Sudha, R., Karthikeyan, J., et al., 2021. IoT based smart baby monitoring. In: 2021 Second International Conference on Electronics and Sustainable Communication Systems (ICESC). IEEE, pp. 1–6.

Wang, S.-C., Hsu, H.-W., Dai, C.-G., Ho, C.-L., Zhang, F.-Y., 2019. Use product segmentation to enhance the competitiveness of enterprises in the IoT. In: 2019 IEEE 10th International Conference on Awareness Science and Technology (iCAST). IEEE, pp. 1–6.

Zhao, Y., 2012. R and Data Mining: Examples and Case Studies. Academic Press.

Zhou, Y., Yang, K., 2022. Exploring tensorRT to improve real-time inference for deep learning. In: 2022 IEEE 24th Int Conf on High Performance Computing & Communications; 8th Int Conf on Data Science & Systems; 20th Int Conf on Smart City; 8th Int Conf on Dependability in Sensor, Cloud & Big Data Systems & Application (HPCC/DSS/SmartCity/DependSys). IEEE, pp. 2011–2018.

CHAPTER

IoT inter-cloud interoperability for sustainable digital transformation

6

6.1 Introduction

The anticipated convergence of cloud-IoT platforms into the inter-cloud space is the next frontier that is tailored for foreseeable IoT demands. Though individual cloud platforms have endeavored to cater to the needs of IoT applications, a single cloud infrastructure often falls short in addressing the multi-dimensional requirements of IoT ecosystems or discovering innovative links across inter-organizational data. The fusion of cloud-IoT platforms into a more integrated inter-cloud acknowledges the limitations of siloed cloud systems and emphasizes the collaborative potential of interconnected cloud environments, steering digital interconnectedness towards new, yet to be explored dimensions.

6.1.1 IoT and inter-cloud computing

The evolution of cloud computing provided a solution, but the multifaceted demands of IoT soon showcased the need for diverse cloud systems to interlink their strengths and mitigate their individual gaps. A singular cloud system may not be adept at efficiently handling both diverse data stream workloads that emerge from various IoT devices. Besides, IoT devices are globally dispersed and a centralized cloud system could introduce latency issues, which limits the prospects of real-time data processing. Multiple cloud systems strategically located, can offer low-latency solutions to geographically scattered IoT networks.

The concept of inter-cloud or multi-cloud is an ecosystem, where multiple cloud platforms collaborate, allowing data and processes to flow seamlessly between them. The inter-cloud paradigm ensures that specific workloads are handled by the most suitable cloud platform, optimizing for performance, cost, or other criteria. In an earlier section, we have seen, for example, the collaboration of the car manufacturing giant BMW with three major cloud service providers, namely IBM Cloud, Microsoft Azure, and Amazon Web Services.

Different cloud providers offer services with different pricing models and operational strengths. By utilizing the strengths of each provider for IoT functionalities,

Accelerating Digital Transformation with the Cloud and the Internet of Things (IoT)
https://doi.org/10.1016/B978-0-44-322217-7.00012-8

it is possible to achieve cost savings and improve performance. Additionally, when deploying solutions globally, there are considerations related to data sovereignty and regulatory compliance. The selection of the appropriate cloud provider within a specific jurisdiction when integrating cloud services in IoT deployments ensures that data generated in that region remains compliant with local regulations. For instance the European Union General Data Protection Regulation (GDPR), effective since May 2018, imposes requirements on the processing and movement of personal data belonging to EU citizens. An important requirement under GDPR restricts transferring data outside EU, whereby personal data can be transferred to only countries that guarantee a certain "level of data protection." This requirement challenges IoT systems, which frequently transmit data across international borders.

For example, consider an IoT-based health monitoring system that uses wearable devices of users in Europe constantly sending health metrics to a cloud for analysis. Data from these devices may include personal and sensitive information, so processing or storing this data in a cloud located outside the EU is potentially a breach to GDPR guidelines, unless specific conditions or safeguards are met (Georgiou and Lambrinoudakis, 2020). Through a well-orchestrated inter-cloud setup, the inter-cloud concept ensures that data generated by European users can be automatically directed to cloud platforms located within the EU or in regions recognized by the EU as having adequate data protection.

The inter-cloud strategy allows IoT deployments to make use of best-in-class services for tasks, such as managing devices, analyzing data, visualizing data, storing information, and implementing machine learning algorithms. And by distributing data across multiple cloud platforms, the inter-cloud model offers a higher degree of fault tolerance. If one cloud encounters issues, others can take over, ensuring uninterrupted IoT operations. Besides, the ability to dynamically allocate workloads based on the cost of computation or storage across different clouds can result in significant savings.

6.1.2 Interoperability in digital transformation

The ability of different IT systems and related software applications to communicate, and effectively utilize mutual data and processes is a keystone of digital transformation journeys. The diversity of devices, data formats, and cloud services prevalent in the context of the cloud-to-things continuum, raises the level of interoperability expectations. Varied systems need to "speak" the same language to ensure that data from one source can be comprehended and utilized by another without any friction. As businesses undergo digital transformation, they often retain legacy systems while integrating newer, cloud-based solutions. Interoperability allows these old and new systems to work in harmony.

Interoperable systems provide users with a common point of control experience. For instance, a smart home that houses different IoT device brands, each with its own software, protocols, and standards, is controllable using just one interface. Digital transformation is geared towards providing superior user-centric experiences. A user who is enabled to control various devices from a single interface, exemplifies this principle. The goal is to simplify and enhance the user's interaction with technology, through intuitive common interfaces.

In fact, interoperability leads to operational efficiency. Instead of operating, updating, or troubleshooting each device separately, users and administrators can manage them collectively, thereby saving time and effort. Thus interoperable systems enhance the value proposition to users. The smart home system with the ability to integrate devices or services from multiple brands is more appealing, especially for those customers who have already invested in certain IoT devices; in this case replacing already acquired IoT devices is unwanted.

Digital transformation is all about preparing organizations or systems for future trends in technology. An interoperable smart home system is more adaptable to future technologies or devices, which may be introduced, ensuring longevity and relevance in a rapidly evolving tech landscape. In this forthcoming horizon, data continues to be unleashed from new and diverse devices, unlocking new potentials for innovation and value creation.

6.2 Understanding IoT and inter-cloud computing

IoT and Inter-cloud Computing represent the forefront of the unprecedented rate by which technology is currently evolving. Their interaction with other technological developments, including Artificial Intelligence anticipates future trends and innovations, for which professionals need to prepare the necessary intellectual assets.

Indeed, businesses and cities are already becoming smarter and more connected, generating vast amounts of data, which requires a robust infrastructure. Inter-cloud computing offers a scalable solution to handle IoT-generated data, in this steadily increasing connectivity rate. As mentioned earlier, with global IoT deployments, issues related to data sovereignty and regulatory compliance will arise. Understanding how inter-cloud setups can navigate these intricacies, ensures that businesses remain compliant and avoid potential legal repercussions. It is all about strategic planning to position oneself or one's business for future success by understanding where the inter-cloud industry is heading.

6.2.1 Inter-cloud computing: features and characteristics

Inter-cloud computing is not just about using multiple cloud providers, but it is about these providers collaborating to deliver seamless services. This collaborative service provisioning matches IoT deployment requirements for diverse computational capabilities. Two facets characterize inter-cloud computing in IoT contexts: cloud federation and fog computing. At one end, cloud federation shapes the interconnection of diverse cloud platforms, allowing seamless data storage, processing, and transfer across multiple cloud service providers. This federated approach not only offers increased scalability and flexibility but also ensures that global IoT deployments can navigate the intricate maze of regional data regulations, thereby maintaining compliance through strategic data residency.

On the other hand, fog computing decentralizes and localizes data handling, while addressing real-time processing demands at the source, without the need for transmitting vast volumes of raw data. Together, these two facets form the backbone of the IoT inter-cloud framework, synergizing the real-time features of localized processing with the scalable and interoperable capacities of federated cloud environments (Celesti et al., 2016).

Cloud federation

In a federated cloud scenario, service providers may use the IoT services of other IoT cloud providers to complement their range of service offerings or expand their capacity to handle spikes according to a cloud bursting model (Guo et al., 2014). Federated cloud in IoT context refers to a collaborative model, where multiple IoT cloud providers combine resources to offer comprehensive IoT services, as illustrated in Fig. 6.1. Instead of operating in isolation, these providers interlink their services, thereby optimizing resource use and expanding their service offerings (Celesti et al., 2016).

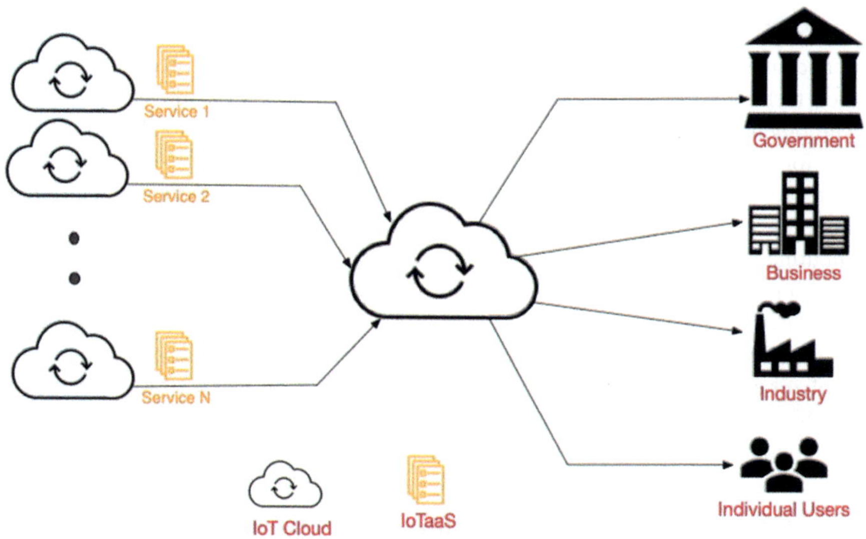

FIGURE 6.1

Cloud federation. Adapted from (Celesti et al., 2016).

Each IoT cloud provider is able to achieve an efficient use of IoT devices, while minimizing costs saved from onsite provisioning. Each IoT cloud platform builds its own IoT as service offerings (i.e., IoTaaS), which are provisioned on demand, without requiring investment or maintenance costs of the underlying infrastructure or software from consuming partners. For example, the service provider takes care of particular sensors, devices, networking, and software, while another provider does the same, and together they expand the range of services covered by the consuming IoT cloud platform. This model is similar to actual business models, such as the one adopted earlier by Dropbox, which offered storage services in the form of PaaS (platform as a service) and SaaS (software as a service), while using in the early years Amazon's IaaS (infrastructure as a service) in the form of Amason's VMs (virtual machines). However, Dropbox later transitioned to using its own infrastructure for a significant portion of its infrastructure needs (Amazon, 2020).

The National Institute of Standards and Technology (NIST) has been a source of references about the terminologies and structures of cloud computing. NIST released a version of the federated cloud reference architecture model, which outlines the guiding principles that dictate the roles and participants within a federated cloud setting (Lee et al., 2020).

The NIST cloud federation reference architecture consists of eleven components that collaborate to enable the federation of cloud resources. These components encompass aspects such as managing identities and access, discovering resources, data security, and implementing governance. The architecture places an emphasis on interoperability enabling different cloud providers and services to seamlessly collaborate through standard interfaces, data formats, and protocols that ensure compatibility and ease of integration (Bohn et al., 2022).

Fog computing

Fog computing and cloud federation represent complementary strategies to address the challenges and potentials of the IoT inter-cloud. Metaphorically, fog computing refers to an extended cloud closer to the ground. Fog encompasses the cloud-to-ground network, which ensures the interplay between cloud resources and edge ones, when driving data from edge devices to cloud data centers. Fog layers process data at multiple stages before it reaches the central cloud.

In a fog computing architecture, the idea is to distribute computing tasks appropriately across fog layers. Fog nodes are devices comprising the fog infrastructure, and they provide computing, storage, and network services between edge devices and computing data centers. Critical, time-sensitive tasks might be handled at the fog node/edge layer for swift response, while less urgent or more resource-intensive tasks could be offloaded to the cloud layer. This task distribution aims to provide efficient and real-time services, especially vital for applications such as autonomous driving. The OpenFog Consortium published a reference architecture for fog computing to help create and maintain fog computing systems (Mann, 2021), as abstracted in Fig. 6.2.

Fog nodes can be viewed as mini data centers positioned close to the network edge, catering to nearby edge devices (Mann, 2021). Like cloud systems, fog nodes employ virtualization techniques and associated technologies, such as containers, to execute applications from multiple tenants in a segregated manner. This setup promotes simplified application deployment, encompassing initiation, auto-scaling, and termination of IoT applications.

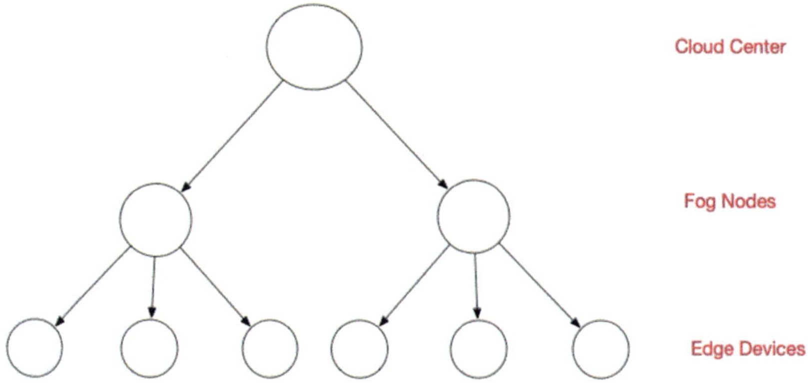

FIGURE 6.2

Fog computing abstract architecture.

6.2.2 IoT challenges in inter-cloud environments

Inter-cloud environments supporting the cloud-to-things continuum pose unique challenges that are specific to the integration of inter-cloud and IoT in cloud-to-things application scenarios.

Dynamic workload management

In cloud-to-things contexts, the dynamic nature of IoT workloads, with spikes in data during certain events or times, requires robust workload balancing across different cloud environments. Choosing which cloud to use for what purpose at which time becomes non-trivial. In modern IoT infrastructures, fog nodes may be connected to multiple cloud centers for increased resilience and efficiency. The orchestration across multiple clouds for dynamic resource provisioning is an imperative requirement for the seamless functioning of diverse applications.

Multi-cloud orchestration

Instead of relying on a single cloud provider, fog nodes coordinate resources allocation and workloads assignment across multiple cloud environments. Instead of relying on a single cloud provider, fog nodes coordinate resources allocation and workloads assignment across multiple cloud environments. Businesses can distribute their data and applications over several clouds, exploiting the unique capabilities of each cloud option for different tasks. Automating these processes through proper orchestration techniques is essential to avoid vendor lock-in, while increasing reliability, resource utilization, and complying with regulatory and data sovereignty requirements.

Fog nodes provide service, content, and container orchestration. Fog nodes improve QoS attributes, such as latency and availability. An optimization method ensures the required level of QoS, while requiring minimal resources from fog and edge devices by finding the best placement of services among available fog nodes.

A dynamic service orchestration deploys relevant services within specific fog nodes (Morkevicius et al., 2021). Fog nodes also orchestrate content across multiple clouds to ensure that the content is delivered with the expected quality of experience (Santos et al., 2020). Fog nodes orchestrate containers' deployment across multiple clouds to ensure that an application and its dependencies run consistently across different cloud environments (Wang et al., 2022).

Service discovery in dynamic environments

In cloud-to-things contexts, devices may frequently move or change their states. Discovering services across different clouds for these dynamic IoT devices requires sophisticated service discovery mechanisms. IoT devices can be mobile, just as wearables, vehicles, or drones. As they move, their optimal connection point or "nearest" cloud service might change. They may need to switch between local fog nodes, or even different cloud providers based on geographical proximity or service availability. This requires a service discovery mechanism that can swiftly detect the most appropriate service endpoint in real time (Achir et al., 2022).

In addition IoT devices have the ability to change their states. For instance, a sensor could transition from collecting data to entering a power saving sleep mode. Depending on the state, there may be different requirements for services or resources, and the service discovery mechanism must be able to adjust accordingly (Ariza et al., 2021). Many IoT, or even edge, devices are resource-constrained. Prolonged service discovery operations can drain their resources, including batteries. Fog nodes provide efficient and swift service discovery protocols when dealing with multiple cloud providers.

Edge-to-cloud coordination

Edge devices often process data locally before sending it to the cloud. In inter-cloud scenarios, deciding which cloud provider or environment is best suited for further processing or analytics can be complex, given the vast array of options available. The range of edge devices spans from IoT sensors to gateways to smartphones, with different capabilities to process data locally. For real-time applications, such as autonomous vehicles or health monitoring systems, waiting for data to travel to a centralized cloud and back might introduce unacceptable delays, which fog nodes alleviate by coordinating resource allocation to decide where to send the data from edge devices for further processing.

Depending on the nature of the data and the required analytics, the ideal cloud provider may vary. For instance, one provider might excel in machine learning analytics, while another offers better streaming data analysis. Another example refers to an edge device that usually sends a steady stream of data, and might suddenly experience a surge due to an event (e.g., a security camera detecting unusual activity). The chosen cloud environment must be able to handle these fluctuations, requiring dynamic scalability.

Data transfer and bandwidth constraints

Transferring data between multiple cloud providers and between edge devices and these providers can lead to bandwidth bottlenecks, especially when large volumes of IoT data are involved. For example, thousands of sensors monitoring temperature, humidity, vibration, and more, send data every few seconds, and create surges in bandwidth. The demand for higher bandwidth occurs with certain IoT devices, such as surveillance cameras or medical imaging devices, which produce high-resolution data. A multi-cloud environment exacerbates bandwidth requirements as data is potentially sent to multiple destinations. Inter-cloud data transfers occur sometimes when processed data or results from one cloud provider might need to be shared with another provider for further processing, leading to additional data transfers.

While cloud data centers have substantial bandwidth, the gateways or networks connecting edge devices might not, especially if they are in remote locations, use cellular connections, or rely on other constrained communication mediums. Transferring data between edge and multiple clouds, especially at high volumes, can also lead to significant financial costs. Cloud providers often charge for the data going out of their networks.

Unified data model creation

For analytics and insights, a unified data model across different cloud environments is crucial. Achieving this in an inter-cloud setup, especially with varied IoT data sources, can be challenging. For analytics and insights, a unified data model across different cloud environments supports interoperability. In many instances, organizations might have legacy systems or older IoT devices that still need to feed into the unified data model for seamless data flows, which originate from these older systems.

Even when metadata is used, managing and standardizing this metadata across multiple clouds adds another layer of complexity. This is because, different IoT devices might represent the same information differently. For instance, temperature data from two different sensors might use "Celsius" and "Fahrenheit," respectively. Ensuring semantic coherence and standardizing data nomenclature across diverse devices and clouds is essential. And there are several existing solutions and frameworks designed to address this diversity challenge.

Unified data model frameworks include Apache Avro, which is a framework for data serialization that is widely used in the field of big data processing, particularly in the Apache Hadoop ecosystem (Vohra, 2016). Apache Avro is language-neutral, with supporting libraries for various programming languages. Similarly, Google Protocol Buffers (labeled ProtoBuf) is a language-neutral and platform-neutral, extensible mechanism for serializing structured data, which is useful in developing a unified data model.

6.3 IoT inter-cloud interoperability

The proliferating deployment of IoT devices is continually generating vast data streams, demanding not just efficient storage but also a seamless ability to process data across diverse digital representations and supporting technologies. Yet, intricate data integration is rather challenging to maintain, requiring the establishment of standards or some brokering strategies to meet IoT inter-cloud interoperability requirements.

6.3.1 Standardization matters

The lack of universally adopted standards hampers the expanding landscape of IoT inter-cloud computing. Standardization ensures interoperability among devices, applications, and platforms in an increasingly fragmented IoT ecosystem. The representation uniformity promoted by standardization allows inter-cloud systems and applications to communicate and collaborate. This type of uniformity leads to reduced costs associated with integration, as developers and businesses won't need to invest significantly in custom solutions for each new cloud platform or IoT device. Standardized protocols and interfaces facilitate rapid deployments and scalability of IoT solutions across multiple clouds. Standardization also prevents vendor lock-in when proprietary solutions are deliberately developed in favor of open standards to keep their clientele dependent on their unique service offerings.

There are various standards that address different aspects of IoT inter-cloud, such as communication frameworks and data exchange. Some of the prominent standards organizations that are working on IoT inter-cloud standards are shown in Table 6.1.

6.3.2 Strategies for achieving inter-cloud interoperability in IoT

While no single solution is a universal remedy to interoperability challenges, a combination of several approaches can pave the way for a more interconnected, efficient, and responsive IoT inter-cloud ecosystem.

Interoperability with IoT data integration platforms

IoT data integration platforms connect different data sources together. They enable the creation of an IoT inter-cloud ecosystem, where data from various devices can be seamlessly combined, analyzed, and transferred to any application. Now let's delve into the process of data integration by examining the approaches used in certain existing data integration platforms.

Apache NiFi

Users are empowered with an attractive interface to fetch data from varied sources, be it databases, IoT devices, web services, or files (Apache, 2023). The intuitive drag-and-drop interface enables dataflow templates that cater to specific data integration requirements. This platform is a data integration tool that operates on a server using a Java machine; it automates the transfer of data among various applications. Although

Table 6.1 IoT inter-cloud standards.

Organization	Category	Standard examples
IEEE (IEEE, 2022)	**Network protocols:** - Methods of connecting IoT edge devices - Ensure interoperability, security, and efficient communication	- IEEE 802.15.4: serves as the foundation for various IoT communication and devices with limited power and processing capabilities - IEEE 802.11p (WAVE): enables communication for vehicles in smart cities
	Data protocols: - Seamless information exchange between IoT devices and cloud systems - Seamless data transfer among clouds	- IEEE 1451-99: interoperable data sharing for sensors and actuators - DDS (data distribution service): a data-centric protocol for device-to-device applications (Yim et al., 2017)
ISO/IEC (ISO, 2023)	**Foundation standards:** basic principles and frameworks of IoT	- SubCommittee (SC) 41 is tasked to ensure interoperability, consistency, and widespread adoption of IoT - SC 38 is focused on standardization in the area of cloud computing and distributed platforms - Working Group 10 performs smart city standardization
ETSI (ETSI, 2022)	**Inter-cloud interoperability and federation:** deals with the unification or collaboration of multiple cloud environments into a coordinated system	- oneM2M: standards for machine-to-machine (M2M) communications - GS NFV (network functions virtualization): a way to virtualize network services, such as routers and firewalls, which traditionally run on proprietary hardware

NiFi is an active open-source project, commercial support is currently offered by Cloudera (Cloudera, 2021).

Talend

This platform handles diverse data by converting disparate formats into a coherent shape that is suitable for analysis (Talend, 2023). Talend comes with a wide range of predefined connectors and components, which facilitate the connection to different data sources and applications. Each of these connectors can read and/or write in the format native to its respective source or target. For example, connectors for databases, cloud storage, APIs, etc., understand the inherent data structures and can convert data to/from these systems. Using a drag-and-drop interface, data transformation processes include parsing, string data transformation, type conversions, and other operations. With these tools, data can be transformed from its source format to a desired target format (Sreemathy et al., 2021).

Middleware solutions for interoperability

Middleware solutions enable interoperability within the IoT inter-cloud ecosystem by providing an intermediate layer that bridges gaps between disparate heterogeneous systems, to facilitate data exchanges and integrate operations, as illustrated in Fig. 6.3. Middleware channel data from the physical environment of IoT devices and networks to and applications in IoT platform servers. Different applications connect to device data via a high-level abstraction to facilitate their integration with a wide spectrum of physical data sources.

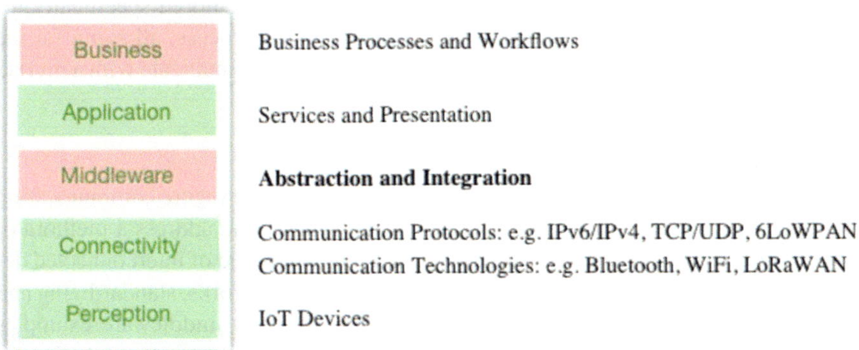

FIGURE 6.3

Middleware in IoT architecture.

Middleware cater to a diverse array of functionalities, for seamless integration of IoT data sources. This diversity of functionalities leads to middleware categories based on their primary functionalities or purposes. These categories range from managing communication between devices to processing and analyzing data, to ensuring robust security protocols. Each category plays a pivotal interoperability in IoT systems.

Communication middleware

Abstracting the complexities of device-to-device or device-to-application communication is provided through standard protocols, which ensure the uninterrupted flow of data transfer in IoT systems. For instance, MQTT (message queuing telemetry transport) is a popular choice for its lightweight publish/subscribe messaging system and is ideal for scenarios with limited bandwidth. Similarly, CoAP (constrained application protocol) is designed for resource-constrained resources, and provides an interface to users that resembles the HTTP model.

Database middleware

With a vast array of sensors and devices continuously collecting data, database middleware can efficiently store, retrieve, and query this vast amount of information. These middleware bridge raw data streams and applications that need to process or interpret this data. Specialized time-series databases, such as InfluxDB (Nasar and Kausar, 2019) or Cassandra (Mahgoub et al., 2017), have become increasingly prominent in this context, given they have been specifically designed to handle time-stamped data, which are prevalent in IoT applications.

Application enablement middleware

As IoT developments grow more complex, there are needs for standardized interfaces that can simplify the creation of robust and scalable IoT applications. Solutions such as ThingWorx and AWS IoT Core are examples of application enablement middleware, offering developers a suite of APIs, SDKs, and tools tailored specifically for IoT systems. These platforms streamline the development process, allowing for the quick deployment of interconnected applications that can communicate with a myriad of devices seamlessly (Machado, 2019).

Security middleware

The core purpose of security middleware in IoT is to facilitate secure communication channels, guarantee the privacy of data being transmitted, and address a plethora of other security-related challenges inherent to a system composed of interconnected devices. Given the heterogeneous nature of IoT devices and networks, standardizing and implementing security becomes even more critical. Security middleware examples include ARM mbed, a middleware to ensure secure device-to-device and device-to-cloud communications. On the other hand, Scandit, while primarily recognized for its barcode scanning solutions, also emphasizes secure data capture, ensuring the integrity and privacy of IoT systems data. Both of these middleware illustrate IoT industry's commitment to establish trust across IoT infrastructures, thereby further expanding the interconnected digital landscape (Xiao, 2018; Williams et al., 2022).

Integration middleware

As interoperability is paramount for IoT interconnectivity landscape, having the ability to integrate disparate systems is essential. It is not just about connecting devices; it is more about ensuring they can communicate and interoperate efficiently, regardless of their underlying architectures or protocols. Platforms such as MuleSoft's Anypoint (MuteSoft, 2023) and WSO2 (WSO, 2023) are examples of IoT integration middleware, which not only foster connectivity but also empower organizations to derive more value from their interconnected systems by ensuring that information flows smoothly and reliably across all touchpoints. Especially when these touchpoints are engineered independently from diverse vendors. Integration strategies for interoperability include protocol gateways to ensure compatibility among various communication methods. The burgeoning adoption of open-source integration middleware in IoT industry is rapidly growing (Behara and Naik, 2019) towards flexible, customizable, and cost-effective IoT integration solutions.

6.4 Sustainable digital transformation through IoT inter-cloud interoperability

The intricate web of devices and systems interacting across multiple cloud environments establishes a foundation for progressive, sustainable changes in various sectors. True sustainability in this context encompasses not just environmental considerations, but also economic and social factors, ensuring an inclusive, interoperable, and profitable digital transformation. Next, we explore three dimensions of sustainability enabled through IoT inter-cloud interoperability.

6.4.1 Economic sustainability: cost-effective integration

The combination of IoT and inter-cloud interoperability offers opportunities for significant economic benefits. By facilitating seamless communication between devices across different cloud platforms, businesses can achieve more streamlined operations and reduce integration costs. Interoperable IoT systems, by design, reduce redundancy and the need for repeated investments in similar technologies. Furthermore, the ability to leverage multiple cloud environments allows optimal resource allocation, while ensuring that organizations pay only for what they utilize, leading to cost-effective scalability. The long-term viability of digital transformation solutions lies in their economic sustainability, and the integration capabilities of IoT inter-cloud infrastructures contribute to this profitable horizon through various means outlined next.

Reducing integration and operational costs

Interoperability in IoT intercloud environments promotes plug-and-play processes rather than cumbersome custom coding. Furthermore, with protocol integration, troubleshooting is simplified by interventions limited to the integration points, thereby reducing system conflicts. This not only cuts down on operational delays but also reduces the costs associated with system downtimes and lengthy recovery resolutions.

Further cost-effective ways to integrate systems, include the adoption of open source solutions; these solutions are freely available and constantly improved by a community of developers. By adopting open source middleware or platforms, IoT businesses can significantly reduce their initial investment costs. Additionally, these solutions are regularly updated by the community, which means organizations can take advantage of the innovations without incurring additional expenses. Companies can further take advantage of open source solutions' flexibility to customize them according to their requirements, without subscription or other licensing fees.

Optimal resource allocation and scalability

Interoperability ensures optimal resource usage and offers the potential for seamless scalability in IoT intercloud environments, allowing businesses to utilize resources more judiciously. The need for redundancy is reduced by allowing IoT systems to share data directly due to interoperable standards. This approach illustrates how the need for duplicate storage or processing resources is eliminated.

The flexible pricing model with inter-cloud strategies allows organizations that invest in multi-cloud environments, to embrace "pay-as-you-go" models, where organizations only pay for the used resources. This flexibility can lead to substantial cost savings. Instead of overcommitting resources in anticipation of peak demands, businesses can dynamically allocate resources based on real-time needs.

Demands for resources can be sporadic in IoT applications. For instance, a retail business with smart shelves might experience high activity during promotional sales or holiday seasons when stock levels need constant monitoring. In such situations, effectively handling high demand periods requires cloud-based solutions that seamlessly allocate resources when needed and scale back during quieter periods. This dynamic resource allocation enhances user experiences to satisfy needs on-demand, while also being cost-effective.

6.4.2 Environmental sustainability: efficient resource utilization

By promoting resource optimization, IoT inter-cloud promotes also our collective endeavor to create a more sustainable relationship with our environment. Next, we discuss ways by which IoT inter-cloud aids in fostering environmental sustainability, throughout the sustainable digital transformation journey.

Moreover, by utilizing inter-cloud technology, IoT systems can locate data centers that are strategically positioned in areas, with access to renewable energy sources or where cooling expenses are naturally minimized. This approach effectively minimizes the carbon footprint and maximizes energy efficiency. Another energy optimization opportunity, which is enabled when utilizing inter-cloud solutions, is achieved by distributing data processing efficiently across multiple cloud servers globally, ensuring that no single server is overburdened and energy is used efficiently.

6.4.3 Social sustainability: enhanced user experience and inclusivity

IoT inter-cloud interoperability offers a unique opportunity to create a more cohesive and user-centric digital society. The intuitive user experience, which transcends traditional technological barriers, empowers all users. Whether it's an elderly person using a health monitor or a student accessing remote learning through an affordable IoT device, the aim is to provide an uninterrupted and blended experience across various platforms.

The broader implications of the integration brought by IoT inter-cloud interoperability go beyond mere convenience. One of the most profound impacts is its potential to democratize access. With interoperable systems, even areas with limited infrastructure can tap into global cloud resources. This inclusivity extends to marginalized or underserved communities, who, for the first time, might access vital services—be it telemedicine, online education, or digital financial systems. Such an approach ensures that the digital transformation does not leave anyone behind.

6.5 Real-life use cases

IoT inter-cloud interoperability is a transformative force shaping industries and improving lives, as interconnected devices in a federation of clouds or fog computing platforms proliferate. The true potential of this interconnectivity is realized when these devices can seamlessly communicate and share data, irrespective of the platform or service provider. Real-world applications of this interoperability are varied, stretching from healthcare to urban planning, and from manufacturing to agriculture. The practical uses of this interoperability can greatly gain from the smooth integration of data and services, across different cloud environments. Next, we illustrate specific use cases to gain a practical understanding of this transformation.

6.5.1 Healthcare: seamless data flow across multiple cloud providers

In healthcare systems, patient data often resides in disparate structures—ranging from hospital databases to wearable health trackers. IoT inter-cloud interoperability ensures that these varied data points communicate flawlessly, providing a holistic view of patient health. This integration facilitates a more collaborative approach to patient care from different care providers. Moreover, by securely connecting devices and platforms, it ensures that crucial health data is available to care providers anytime and anywhere, which enhances patient diagnosis and treatment, while placing the patient at the center of a cohesive healthcare ecosystem, which breaks down silos and fosters collaboration. A few tangible examples that can illustrate the transformative impact of IoT inter-cloud interoperability in healthcare are revealed next.

Remote patient monitoring

Patients who have conditions such as diabetes or cardiovascular diseases can benefit from the use of wearables that monitor health indicators, such as heart rate and blood pressure. When these devices are connected to inter-cloud platforms, communication channels involving healthcare professionals across different locations are established.

For example, a cardiologist in Paris and an endocrinologist in London can access patients data in real-time for collaborative interventions. Popular devices, such as Dexcom's G6 (Dexcom, 2023) and Abbott's FreeStyle Libre (FreeStyle, 2023), send real-time readings to a user's smartphone or dedicated receiver. With IoT inter-cloud interoperability, these readings can be sent to a cloud platform accessible by healthcare providers for real-time monitoring and timely intervention.

On the other hand, mobile applications, such as One Drop or MySugr, which allow diabetics to log their meals, medication, and blood glucose reading, can integrate with glucose monitoring devices to collect data that can be stored on IoT inter-cloud platforms. With patient consent, doctors can access this data for a more comprehensive view of the patient's condition between appointments. Telemedicine platforms, such as Teladoc (Health, 2023), which offers virtual consultations, can be extended to access this inter-cloud stored data to plan a telemedicine appointment or adjust treatment plans.

6.5.2 Smart cities: integrated urban management across platforms

The vision of a smart city is one where every municipality sector related to traffic, waste management, or public transportation works in a collaborative way to improve urban living. Devices and systems from various vendors need a) to integrate through IoT inter-cloud interoperability mechanisms; b) to synchronize the city's infrastructure elements in real-time; c) to deliver urban management solutions, such as optimizing traffic flow, reducing energy consumption, and ensuring public safety.

Smart bins that signal when they are full have seen several use cases. These bins can use different cloud service providers to send their status, considering private waste management company infrastructures. Through inter-cloud interoperability, the city's waste management system can efficiently plan waste collection routes by consolidating data from all bins, irrespective of their cloud platform. This scenario has actually been implemented by Seoul's municipality, which turned out to be a success story in improving urban living (Roy et al., 2022).

6.5.3 Manufacturing: streamlined supply chain with interoperable IoT

In the manufacturing sector, the journey of a product from raw material to the end-user involves multiple touchpoints. IoT inter-cloud interoperability can streamline this process. By ensuring that sensors, machines, and logistics systems can exchange data across different cloud platforms, manufacturers get a broad view of their supply chain. This real-time visibility allows predictive maintenance, efficient inventory management, and rapid response to market demands.

Consider a multinational company with manufacturing plants in various countries. Each plant might employ machinery from different vendors, each relying on its cloud infrastructure for reporting and analytics. Inter-cloud interoperability allows these different plants to integrate machinery data into a centralized system, enabling timely maintenance and ensuring reduced downtime. For instance, Bosch has partnered with various cloud providers, such as AWS, Microsoft Azure (Bosch, 2022), and Huawei Cloud (HUAWEI, 2018), to ensure that its IoT Suite is compatible and can integrate seamlessly with these platforms. This ensures data flow and process automation across different parts of a global supply chain. Similarly, using inter-cloud interoperability solutions, Toyota was able to unify data from machines sourced from different vendors, each coming with its own IoT ecosystem and cloud platform. This approach allows Toyota to preemptively address machine breakdowns, and ensure smooth operations. Although Toyota has its proprietary cloud infrastructure, this data integration across plants was necessary to monitor the performance of critical equipment and machinery, remotely (Qin et al., 2013).

6.6 Future directions in IoT inter-cloud interoperability

The evolving digital ecosystem demands a harmonious and meaningful exchange of data across diverse cloud platforms that support IoT ecosystems. This interplay between multiple cloud environments and IoT ecosystems, although complex, promises a more cohesive and integrated future of IoT diffusion, but only if the challenges of interoperability, data integration, and standards are addressed in a robust and efficient way. Advanced research and innovation are promising advancements in semantic interoperability, AI, and ML for seamless data integrations, and the anticipatory approaches towards the evolution of standards and protocols. Next, we reveal the roadmap driven by these innovations towards a truly interconnected digital tomorrow.

6.6.1 Advances in semantic interoperability

Semantic interoperability enables machine computable logic, inferencing, and data federation between systems, devices, and applications in a manner where the precise meaning of exchanged information is understandable without human intervention. Semantic interoperability is not just about packaging the data (syntax), but the simultaneous transmission of the meaning of the data (semantics). This is accomplished by adding data that describes the exchanged data (metadata), and linking each data element to a controlled, shared vocabulary. For example, the earlier semantic web introduced the RDF standard as a universally understood language, which links data pieces in a way that allows machines to interpret data using common specifications to interchange data on the web. Data carries not only information but is also linked to a context, transforming the web into a place where data items can be linked and integrated at a higher degree of abstraction. Similarly, web services was another semantic web revolution, which enabled agents capable of autonomously engaging in complex negotiations and transactions with other services over the web. Through a standard protocol, web services can retrieve the RDF, which describes data, interpret it, and carry out suitable actions for inferred data specifications (Pauwels et al., 2017).

In the context of IoT inter-cloud interoperability, semantic interoperability enhances exchanges between heterogeneous devices and platforms to occur at a higher level of abstraction by understanding the data that is being exchanged. Devices and platforms can comprehend the context of the data they are handling, and on that basis extract the appropriate actionable insights and make autonomously accurate decisions. The semantic web technologies facilitate interoperability between heterogeneous devices and cloud platforms. IoT-based semantic interoperability models employ semantic annotations of IoT data. For example, in precision agriculture, raw data generated by soil sensors, drones, and local weather stations use metadata to describe the accumulated value of information (Khatoon and Ahmed, 2022).

6.6.2 AI and ML for seamless data integration

Machine learning (ML) is a subfield of artificial intelligence (AI), which emerged as a powerful tool to transform the way data is integrated and utilized. ML algorithms, empowered with the ability to learn and adapt, are enhancing the efficiency, accuracy, and security of data integration processes, which foster interoperability across various IoT platforms. Through continuous learning from data patterns and structures, ML can automate the process of identifying and mapping similar data entities across different databases. This is a growing field that can help organizations automate data integration and accelerate data transformation. For example, Adeptia employs machine learning for inferring data mapping predictions from an existing library of tested and validated data maps. This dramatically reduces the effort and time required to create intelligent data mappings, by automating integration (Banga et al., 2020).

Octopai provides automated data mapping tools, which suggest data mapping using machine learning techniques. The tool analyzes metadata about fields/columns to draw conclusions on attributes or connections to other fields. This kind of platform is particularly useful in environments where data is dispersed across numerous systems and platforms. ML algorithms can sift through vast quantities of metadata generated by IoT devices and categorize them effectively. Platforms such as Octopai utilize such ML algorithms to automatically discover and analyze metadata across various data management tools. This facilitates streamlined data integration, ensuring accurate data lineage and tracking (Octopai, 2023).

6.6.3 Predicting the evolution of standards and protocols

The role of standards and protocols is bound to evolve further, given the increasing diversity of IoT networked devices and services. Anticipating the trajectory of these developments can grant organizations a competitive edge, facilitating smoother transitions and more integrated operations. The current IoT landscape is characterized by a myriad of standards and protocols, often leading to fragmentation and interoperability issues. In the foreseeable future, we can expect efforts to consolidate these into more unified, comprehensive standards that facilitate data exchange across diverse IoT cloud platforms (Lombardi et al., 2021). This is particularly relevant to mitigate security gaps, which may expose vulnerabilities across different standards (Sadhu et al., 2022).

The digital transformation is prompting network operators to shift into comprehensive digital service providers, which is expected to propel the necessity for uniform standards in the IoT landscape. This transformation involves new business models marked by the incorporation of a plethora of digital services that leverage data streams flowing through IoT networks, extending into content provision, cloud computing services, and big data analytics. Eventually, these services will converge into a holistic approach to interoperability, urging the industry to move towards unified standards. This expected evolution encourages a collaborative ecosystem, where digital service providers work with various stakeholders, including governments, enterprises, and developers, to shape an IoT landscape that is cohesive, and more inclusive (Cepal, 2021). Uniform standards would then be at the basis of this collaboration, fostering synergy and coordination.

6.7 Conclusion

As digital transformation is no longer merely a choice but a necessity, the implications of IoT inter-cloud interoperability have been highlighted as key enablers of this transformation. Traversing through the diverse, yet interconnected IoT inter-cloud environments is fundamentally driven by interoperability prospects. This chapter began with a foundational understanding of IoT and inter-cloud computing, emphasizing the synergies that can be forged between diverse IoT cloud platforms to foster a sustainable digital transformation. Features and characteristics of IoT inter-cloud platform were revealed, followed by some related challenges. Then, we explored the standardization domain for achieving successful IoT inter-cloud interoperability.

We then reflected on means to sustain digital transformation through IoT inter-cloud interoperability, across economic, environmental, and social dimensions. Moving from theoretical foundations to real-world applications, we revealed several use cases across varied sectors, including healthcare, urban management, and manufacturing. These use cases illustrate the transformative potential enabled by IoT inter-cloud interoperability, indicating a future that is more integrated and responsive. We concluded the chapter with a future outlook on the potential advances in semantic interoperability, AI, and ML integrations, and the evolution of standards and protocols to point out future developments, which promise innovation, driven by these emerging concepts.

References

Achir, M., Abdelli, A., Mokdad, L., Benothman, J., 2022. Service discovery and selection in IoT: a survey and a taxonomy. Journal of Network and Computer Applications 200, 103331. https://www.sciencedirect.com/science/article/pii/S1084804521003167.

Amazon, 2020. Dropbox migrates 34 PB of data to an Amazon S3 data lake for analytics. https://aws.amazon.com/solutions/case-studies/dropbox-s3/. (Accessed 10 August 2023).

Apache, 2023. Apache nifi overview. https://nifi.apache.org/docs/nifi-docs/html/overview.html. (Accessed 15 August 2023).

Ariza, J., Garcés, K., Cardozo, N., Sánchez, J.P.R., Vargas, F.J., 2021. IoT architecture for adaptation to transient devices. Journal of Parallel and Distributed Computing 148, 14–30. https://www.sciencedirect.com/science/article/pii/S0743731520303737.

Banga, J., Tyagi, M., Hans, S., 2020. B2b integration platform for next-gen business connectivity| adeptia. https://adeptia.com/. (Accessed 9 September 2023).

Behara, G.K., Naik, G., 2019. Open source IoT middleware for the integration of enterprise applications. https://www.opensourceforu.com/2019/10/a-primer-on-open-source-iot-middleware-for-the-integration-of-enterprise-applications/. (Accessed 20 August 2023).

Bohn, R.B., Chaparadza, R., Elkotob, M., Choi, T., 2022. The path to cloud federation through standardization. In: 2022 13th International Conference on Information and Communication Technology Convergence (ICTC), pp. 942–946.

Bosch, 2022. Bosch IoT device management: Bosch.IO to support device management together with major cloud providers. https://bosch-iot-suite.com/news/bosch-iot-device-management-boschio-to-support-device-management-together-with-major-cloud-providers/. (Accessed 27 August 2023).

Celesti, A., Fazio, M., Giacobbe, M., Puliafito, A., Villari, M., 2016. Characterizing cloud federation in IoT. In: 2016 30th International Conference on Advanced Information Networking and Applications Workshops (WAINA), pp. 93–98.

Cepal, N., 2021. Digital technologies for a new future.

Cloudera, 2021. Apache NiFi user guide. https://docs.cloudera.com/cfm/2.1.1/nifi-user-guide/nifi-user-guide.pdf. (Accessed 15 August 2023).

Dexcom, 2023. Dexcom G6 CGM system. https://www.dexcom.com/en-us/g6-cgm-system. (Accessed 26 August 2023).

ETSI, 2022. ETSI – Internet of things – IoT standards | machine to machine solutions (M2M). https://www.etsi.org/technologies/internet-of-things. (Accessed 14 August 2023).

FreeStyle, 2023. Continuous glucose monitoring (cgm). https://www.freestyle.abbott/us-en/home.html. (Accessed 27 August 2023).

Georgiou, D., Lambrinoudakis, C., 2020. GDPR compliance: proposed guidelines for cloud-based health organizations. In: Katsikas, S., Cuppens, F., Cuppens, N., Lambrinoudakis, C., Kalloniatis, C., Mylopoulos, J., Antón, A., Gritzalis, S., Meng, W., Furnell, S. (Eds.), Computer Security. Springer International Publishing, Cham, pp. 156–169.

Guo, T., Sharma, U., Shenoy, P., Wood, T., Sahu, S., 2014. Cost-aware cloud bursting for enterprise applications. ACM Transactions on Internet Technology 13 (3), 1–24. https://doi.org/10.1145/2602571.

Health, T., 2023. #1 telehealth & telemedicine provider. https://www.teladoc.com/. (Accessed 27 August 2023).

HUAWEI, 2018. Bosch IoT suite services launch on Huawei cloud. https://www.huaweicloud.com/intl/en-us/news/bosch-iot-suite-services-launch-on-huawei-cloud3.html. (Accessed 27 August 2023).

IEEE, 2022. IEEE Standards Activities in the Internet of Things (IoT). (Accessed 14 August 2023).

ISO, 2023. ISO/IEC JTC 1/SC 41 – Internet of things and digital twin. https://www.iso.org/committee/6483279.html. (Accessed 14 August 2023).

Khatoon, P.S., Ahmed, M., 2022. Importance of semantic interoperability in smart agriculture systems. Transactions on Emerging Telecommunications Technologies 33 (5), e4448. https://onlinelibrary.wiley.com/doi/abs/10.1002/ett.4448.

Lee, C.A., Bohn, R.B., Michel, M., 2020. The NIST cloud federation reference architecture. NASA Special Publication 500, 332.

Lombardi, M., Pascale, F., Santaniello, D., 2021. Internet of things: a general overview between architectures, protocols and applications. Information 12 (2), 87. https://doi.org/10.3390/info12020087.

Machado, G.C.P., 2019. Application developmente over IoT platform Thingworx. PhD thesis. Universidade de Coimbra, Portugal.

Mahgoub, A., Ganesh, S., Meyer, F., Grama, A., Chaterji, S., 2017. Suitability of NoSQL systems — Cassandra and ScyllaDB — for IoT workloads. In: 2017 9th International Conference on Communication Systems and Networks (COMSNETS), pp. 476–479.

Mann, Z.Á., 2021. Notions of architecture in fog computing. Computing 103 (1), 51–73. https://link.springer.com/content/pdf/10.1007/s00607-020-00848-z.pdf.

Morkevicius, N., Venčkauskas, A., Šatkauskas, N., Toldinas, J., 2021. Method for dynamic service orchestration in fog computing. Electronics 10 (15), 1796. https://doi.org/10.3390/electronics10151796.

MuteSoft, 2023. MuleSoft | automate anything. Empower everyone. https://www.mulesoft.com/. (Accessed 20 August 2023).

Nasar, M., Kausar, M.A., 2019. Suitability of Influxdb database for IoT applications. International Journal of Innovative Technology and Exploring Engineering 8 (10), 1850–1857.

Octopai, 2023. Automated data lineage, data catalog and discovery. https://www.octopai.com/. (Accessed 9 September 2023).

Pauwels, P., Zhang, S., Lee, Y.-C., 2017. Semantic web technologies in aec industry: a literature overview. Automation in Construction 73, 145–165. https://www.sciencedirect.com/science/article/pii/S0926580516302928.

Qin, E., Long, Y., Zhang, C., Huang, L., 2013. Cloud computing and the Internet of things: technology innovation in automobile service. In: Human Interface and the Management of Information. Information and Interaction for Health, Safety, Mobility and Complex Environments. Springer, Berlin Heidelberg, pp. 173–180.

Roy, A., Manna, A., Kim, J., Moon, I., 2022. IoT-based smart bin allocation and vehicle routing in solid waste management: a case study in South Korea. Computers & Industrial Engineering 171, 108457.

Sadhu, P.K., Yanambaka, V.P., Abdelgawad, A., 2022. Internet of things: security and solutions survey. Sensors 22 (19), 7433. https://doi.org/10.3390/s22197433.

Santos, H., Alencar, D., Meneguette, R., Rosário, D., Nobre, J., Both, C., Cerqueira, E., Braun, T., 2020. A multi-tier fog content orchestrator mechanism with quality of experience support. Computer Networks 177, 107288. https://www.sciencedirect.com/science/article/pii/S1389128620304448.

Sreemathy, J., Brindha, R., Selva Nagalakshmi, M., Suvekha, N., Karthick Ragul, N., Praveennandha, M., 2021. Overview of ETL tools and talend-data integration. In: 2021 7th International Conference on Advanced Computing and Communication Systems (ICACCS), vol. 1, pp. 1650–1654.

Talend, 2023. Data transformation defined | talend. https://www.talend.com/resources/data-transformation-defined/. (Accessed 15 August 2023).

Vohra, D., 2016. Apache avro. In: Practical Hadoop Ecosystem. Apress, pp. 303–323. https://doi.org/10.1007/978-1-4842-2199-0_7.

Wang, Z., Goudarzi, M., Aryal, J., Buyya, R., 2022. Container orchestration in edge and fog computing environments for real-time IoT applications. In: Computational Intelligence and Data Analytics. Springer Nature, Singapore, pp. 1–21. https://doi.org/10.1007/978-981-19-3391-2_1.

Williams, P., Dutta, I.K., Daoud, H., Bayoumi, M., 2022. A survey on security in Internet of things with a focus on the impact of emerging technologies. Internet of Things 19, 100564.

WSO, 2023. Create awesome digital experiences quickly, easily, and securely. https://wso2.com/. (Accessed 20 August 2023).

Xiao, P., 2018. Designing Embedded Systems and the Internet of Things (IoT) with the ARM mbed. John Wiley & Sons.

Yim, H.-J., Seo, D., Jung, H., Back, M.-K., Kim, I., Lee, K.-C., 2017. Description and classification for facilitating interoperability of heterogeneous data/events/services in the Internet of Things. Neurocomputing 256, 13–22. Fuzzy neuro theory and technologies for cloud computing. https://www.sciencedirect.com/science/article/pii/S0925231217304095.

CHAPTER

The Enterprise IoT

7

7.1 Introduction

The initial interest in IoT was focused not on creating new Internet-enabled real-world things but on augmenting existing things with sensing and computing capabilities. Data from these augmented things needed to be transferred to a place where it could be stored and analyzed. This led to the development of IoT platforms. Over time, this development evolved into enterprises adopting digital transformation initiatives where IoT platforms became an importantt part of the modern business infrastructure.

The adoption of IoT has brought significant transformation to enterprises' business. Philips Lighting, for instance, developed a lighting-as-a-service model that allows buildings and households to pay for light usage, whereas IoT-augmented lighting infrastructure and related maintenance are supplied by the company (Lacy and Rutqvist, 2015). The transformation was to sell light instead of light bulbs. Metromile is a San Francisco-based insurance company, which uses IoT to analyze driving data, assess risks and provide per-mile pricing for car insurance (Popelo et al., 2021). Their IoT-enabled idea was to have pay-per-mile car insurance by installing an IoT device in the insured vehicle. The device includes various sensors to collect and transmit data about driving attitude and vehicle operation. John Deere is an American corporation that manufactures agricultural machinery and partnered with an African-based agricultural technology company called Hello Tractor in Nigeria to enable small farmers to book IoT-enabled tractors (Daum and Birner, 2019). They moved from selling tractors to farmers to monitoring tractor usage.

In another IoT-enabled business model, HP enhances and optimizes its Instant Ink program with IoT (Ramaswamy, 2016). This helps HP in selling printer consumables by automatically tracking the ink level in its printers and shipping cartridges to its subscribers before the ink runs out. Many enterprises like these successfully embraced IoT-enabled business transformations, connecting their operations across industries and capitalizing on the advantages of integrating information with connected processes.

7.2 Consumer IoT vs enterprise IoT

The global direction is shifting towards a future that is increasingly interconnected, highlighting the importance of understanding the distinctions between systems for

Accelerating Digital Transformation with the Cloud and the Internet of Things (IoT)
https://doi.org/10.1016/B978-0-44-322217-7.00013-X

consumers and businesses. These distinctions play a crucial role in shaping future decisions, and significant benefits can be drawn from typical IoT aspects, such as scale, connectivity, security, analytics, and maintenance. By anticipating these future events, consumers can prepare for the changes enterprises enable to stay ahead in the rapidly evolving IoT industry.

7.2.1 Scalability aspects

Significant differences exist in scale and distribution between industrial and consumer applications of IoT technologies. Specifically, there is a stark contrast between industrial implementations' vast scale and distribution, which often encompasses thousands of interconnected devices across extensive factories, energy systems, and geographical regions, and consumer applications, which typically involve smaller networks of devices focused on enhancing personal convenience and home automation.

Industrial IoT (IIoT) turns large factory areas into networks, where thousands of devices operate together, far beyond the scale of consumer IoT applications. Although both focus on connecting devices, IIoT faces distinct challenges and possibilities because of its larger size, broader distribution, and longer-lasting operations.

Unlike a handful of smart home devices, IIoT deals with myriad sensors, machines, and actuators, each generating a vast array of data. Efficiently storing, processing, and analyzing this data flood is critical. It is key for IoT systems to filter out and act on the most important information. The other challenge is to oversee a vast network of devices widely spread apart. This task is analogous to coordinating a huge team from a distance, ensuring everything runs predictably and securely. This requires powerful tools for managing devices, strong security measures, and consistent ways for devices to communicate.

The above perspective requires robust device management capabilities, strong security measures, and consistent device communication protocols. Consider the impact of one malfunctioning device sending incorrect data, which could compromise the entire network's functionality. Ensuring the security and seamless communication of these extensive networks illustrates the spatial distribution challenge.

The answer to these challenges lies in decentralized designs brought by edge and fog computing, which distribute resources and intelligence throughout the network, enabling localized decision-making and resilience. By acknowledging these complexities and leveraging the opportunities they present, IIoT offers far-reaching benefits from increased efficiency and productivity. However, realizing this potential requires a paradigm shift from the familiar terrain of consumer IoT to the vast and complex domain of industrial systems, where large-scale integration of data and innovation meet effectively.

Digital transformation is being paved by the convergence of enterprise IoT and AI to integrate unprecedented levels of automation and efficiency into business operations, setting it apart from consumer IoT applications. Unlike consumer IoT, which often focuses on enhancing individual convenience and lifestyle, enterprise

IoT employs machine learning algorithms to automate intricate processes, predict maintenance needs, and dynamically adjust production based on real-time demand.

7.2.2 Connectivity aspects

Connectivity aspects are also contrasted between enterprise and consumer IoT segments. Enterprise IoT adopts advanced connectivity protocols, which exceed typical Wi-Fi and Bluetooth standards found in consumer settings. Enterprises often turn to cellular, low-power wide-area networks (LPWAN) and satellite communications to facilitate uninterrupted data flow over long distances, and through varied conditions for operations that stretch across remote areas.

On the other hand, consumer IoT devices are tailored for personal or home use, emphasizing usability through straightforward connectivity. These devices, such as smart home appliances and wearables, predominantly utilize standard Wi-Fi or Bluetooth for connectivity. This focus on simplicity is designed to allow users a seamless integration of IoT technologies into their daily routines without the complexities often associated with more advanced setups found in enterprise IoT.

7.2.3 Security aspects

Enterprise IoT must be safeguarded against a broad spectrum of cyber threats, protect sensitive data, and comply with stringent regulatory requirements. This involves deploying advanced security protocols alongside regular security patches. The implications of a breach can be vast, including substantial financial losses, operational disruptions, and damage to reputation.

Security remains a concern for consumer IoT. The scope is confined to preventing unauthorized access and data leakage. Consumers may be less aware that devices such as smart cameras and fitness trackers are vulnerable to hacking. Yet, the responsibility for security often falls on manufacturers to provide regular updates.

7.2.4 Data processing and analytics aspects

Analytics within enterprise IoT transform vast amounts of raw data into actionable patterns for strategic decision-making and operational efficiency. Enterprise IoT analytics features real-time monitoring capability for businesses to track the performance and condition of their assets on a continuous basis. Real-time data streams from embedded IoT devices in the enterprise processes identify trends, anomalies, and opportunities for improvement, enabling immediate responses to potential issues or optimization opportunities.

Predictive analytics leverages further historical data across machine learning algorithms to forecast the future, such as anticipating equipment failures. By predicting these events before they happen, businesses can schedule maintenance only when needed, avoiding unnecessary downtime and extending the life of their assets. The integration of IoT data with existing enterprise systems, such as enterprise resource planning (ERP) and customer relationship management (CRM) systems, refines business intelligence further. This integration facilitates operational processes and customer interactions with informed strategic decisions that drive business growth and innovation. New levels of operational optimization, cost reduction, and innovation are unlocked in product development and service offerings. The visibility needed to navigate the intricacies of modern markets is enhanced within enterprise IoT to quickly adapt to changing conditions, while maintaining a competitive edge.

In consumer IoT, analytics primarily enhance user experiences through personalization and usage inputs. Data collected from devices such as fitness trackers and smart home appliances provide users with information on their habits and preferences, enabling personalized feedback and recommendations. Although these analytics are less complex, they add a significant value to the user's experience with IoT devices.

7.2.5 Maintenance and device management aspects

Maintaining enterprise IoT devices is critical to ensure the reliability and longevity of business operations. Remote diagnostics, automatic firmware updates, and predictive maintenance are examples of these maintenance operations to prevent failures and minimize downtime of IoT deployments within enterprises. Maintenance for consumer IoT devices is focused on user convenience. This might include user-initiated updates or automatic updates pushed by manufacturers to improve functionality or security. Maintaining the performance of IoT devices is then carried out with no or little user intervention.

7.3 Cloud-to-things infrastructure in enterprise IoT platforms

Enterprise IoT platforms operate within a cloud-to-things continuum, integrating cloud services with edge computing to create a robust and scalable infrastructure. This continuum encompasses various layers, including cloud servers, edge devices, and IoT endpoints, to fulfil domain-specific operations of IoT solutions.

7.3.1 Cloud layer infrastructure

The cloud layer infrastructure provides centralized data storage, advanced analytics, and machine learning capabilities. This layer services support large-scale data processing and long-term storage. Platforms such as Microsoft Azure IoT Hub, AWS IoT Core, and Google Cloud IoT Core offer comprehensive enterprise cloud-to-things services. The cloud layer infrastructure typically consists of the following:

- **Storage services:** Amazon S3, Google Cloud Storage, and Azure Blob Storage offer highly durable storage for unstructured data, such as logs, images, and backups. MinIO (MinIO, 2024), Ceph (Ceph, 2024), and OpenStack Swift (OpenStack Swift, 2024) are open-source alternatives to storage infrastructure.

- **Database services:** Relational databases and NoSQL databases cater to structured and semi-structured data needs; examples include Amazon RDS, Google Cloud SQL, and Azure SQL Database for relational databases, and DynamoDB (Niranjanamurthy et al., 2014), Cosmos DB (Reagan and Reagan, 2018), and Firestore (Calderoni et al., 2022) for NoSQL databases. Open-source alternatives include PostgreSQL, an open-source alternative to an advanced relational database, which is known for its robustness and feature set. NoSQL open-source databases include Cassandra and MongoDB, which are widely used and known for their flexibility and scalability.
- **Data processing and analytics:** Cloud platforms offer powerful tools for processing and analyzing IoT data. Batch processing services, such as AWS Glue (Saxena et al., 2023), Google Cloud Dataflow (Ramuka, 2019), and Azure Data Factory (Rawat and Narain, 2018) enable the processing of large datasets in batch mode. Open-source alternatives include Apache Hadoop and Apache Spark (Mavridis and Karatza, 2017). Stream processing cater for real-time facilitated by services such as Amazon Kinesis (Bhartia, 2014), Google Cloud Pub/Sub, and Azure Stream Analytics (Basak et al., 2017). Open-source alternatives include Apache Kafka (Garg, 2013), Apache Storm (Bhartia, 2014), and Apache Flink (Carbone et al., 2015).
- **Machine learning and AI capabilities:** Advanced analytics and predictive insights are driven by integrated machine learning and AI services. AWS SageMaker, Google AI Platform, and Azure Machine Learning provide end-to-end solutions for building, training, and deploying machine learning models. Open-source alternatives include TensorFlow (Mengle and Gurmendez, 2019), PyTorch, and Apache MXNet.
- **Networking and connectivity:** Ensuring seamless and secure connectivity between IoT devices and the cloud is paramount. IoT hubs and gateways provided by services such as Azure IoT Hub, and AWS IoT Core manage communication between devices and the cloud. Open-source alternatives include Eclipse Kura and ThingsBoard (Ismail et al., 2018), which leverage MQTT/HTTP protocols to facilitate seamless communication and data exchange between IoT devices and cloud platforms. Eclipse Kura provides a Java/OSGi-based framework (Open Services Gateway Initiative), for building IoT gateways with edge computing capabilities, whereas ThingsBoard offers IoT device management services.
- **Security and compliance:** Robust security measures are essential to protect data and ensure regulatory compliance. Identity and access management (IAM) are security services to authenticate IoT devices offered by services such as AWS IAM, Google Cloud IAM, and Azure Active Directory to manage device identities and permissions (Kingsley, 2023). In addition to open-source user authentication alternatives, including Keycloak and OpenAM, which can be part of an IoT security infrastructure that manage authentication and authorization for devices and users, there are a few other options that have been adapted to support IoT use cases. Eclipse Hono provides a uniform API for interacting with devices (Eclipse Hono Developers, 2024). This API supports protocols commonly used in IoT, such as

MQTT, HTTP, and CoAP, but can also handle device registration and credentials management. Similarly, Apache NiFi is a data flow automation tool used in IoT environments to handle device data; it also includes features for securing data flow and device interactions (Apache NiFi Developers, 2024).

7.3.2 Edge layer infrastructure

The edge layer infrastructure includes devices such as gateways and edge servers, which process data closer to where it is generated, reducing latency and bandwidth usage. Edge computing enables real-time data processing and analytics for handling time-sensitive applications, such as road traffic considerations.

Edge gateways bridge the gap between IoT devices and the cloud. They perform several functions including (1) protocol translation, data aggregation to filter out and reduce the number of individual data streams sent to the cloud, (2) some local processing of data such as executing initial analytics and sending only relevant information to the cloud, and (3) implementing security measures to protect data in transit.

Edge servers provide additional computational resources and storage capabilities at the edge of the network. They offload computationally intensive tasks from IoT devices, enabling more complex data processing closer to the data source. Edge servers also offer temporary or long-term data storage, making data available, even when connectivity to the cloud is intermittent. Finally, applications that require low-latency interactions can be hosted by edge servers. These applications are involved in domains requiring real-time analytics, private machine learning inferences, and local decision-making algorithms. Several frameworks facilitate the development and deployment of edge computing solutions, including the following:

- **Eclipse Kura**: an open-source Java/OSGi-based framework for building IoT gateways with edge computing capabilities. Provided services include device management, data acquisition, and protocol translation (Desbiens, 2022).
- **Azure IoT Edge**: Microsoft's deploying cloud workloads, such as machine learning and AI, to edge devices. This platform supports containerized modules for flexibility and scalability. Containerization is a lightweight form of virtualization, which packages an application and its dependencies into a single, isolated unit called a container, thereby ensuring that applications do not interfere with each other (Morabito, 2017). This is particularly useful in edge computing, where multiple applications share the same hardware. Thus containers use the host system's kernel and resources, which make them more efficient than traditional virtual machines. This efficiency is particularly suitable for edge devices with limited resources (Morabito, 2017).
- **AWS Greengrass** is Amazon's edge computing service, which extends AWS capabilities to local devices, enabling them to act locally on the data they generate, while still using the cloud for management and analytics (Kurniawan, 2018).

7.3.3 Device layer infrastructure

This layer consists of IoT endpoints, including sensors, actuators, and embedded devices, which collect and transmit data. Effective device management and secure connectivity protocols support the integrity and functionality of the things in the cloud-to-things continuum ecosystem, where the seamless interaction between IoT devices and higher layers streamlines data flows and related operations.

The IoT endpoints of the cloud-to-things architecture feature devices that detect and measure physical properties, such as sensors and actuators, which perform actions based on the data received from sensors or commands from the upper layer in the architecture. Small computing devices with embedded systems may also act as IoT endpoints that process data from sensors and control actuators. These devices include microcontrollers and a single-board computer, such as those found connected vehicles.

Arduino boards are frequently used to interface between various sensors and controllers, collecting data from sensors and commanding actuators using preset firmware. In contrast, Raspberry Pi provides more processing power and memory to run more complex data processing and analytics. A Raspberry Pi can perform tasks that require higher computation power by aggregating data from multiple Arduino boards and other sensors (Bell, 2014). This configuration suits the role of an edge gateway to facilitate communication between the device layer and the cloud by fulfilling local data processing, storage, and analytics tasks.

7.3.4 Key enterprise IoT platforms

The seamless integration across all layers of the cloud-to-things continuum infrastructure—from cloud to edge to devices—facilitates operational efficiency and streamlines management procedures. Leading technology providers have developed sophisticated IoT platforms that consolidate these layers into unified frameworks. These platforms offer end-to-end solutions, ensuring that device management and edge and cloud computing are all handled within a cohesive system. Such key enterprise IoT platforms are highlighted next to illustrate this integrated approach towards a robust, scalable, and secure cloud-to-things infrastructure. By unifying various components under a single technology framework, these platforms enable businesses to streamline operations and secure their IoT ecosystems effectively.

Microsoft Azure IoT Hub

Azure IoT Hub provides a comprehensive cloud-to-things infrastructure, enabling extensive device management, advanced analytics, and edge computing support. This infrastructure supports multiple protocols and platforms and incorporates robust end-to-end security measures to ensure data confidentiality and integrity.

IBM Watson IoT Platform

IBM Watson IoT Platform focuses on cognitive intelligence and analytics, offering pre-built industry solutions and a strong partner ecosystem. This platform integrates an AI-powered engine for advanced analytics, providing significant benefits for enhancing IoT capabilities.

SAP Leonardo IoT platform

This platform is deeply integrated with SAP ERP systems, offering business process integration. Typical application support includes asset performance management and machine learning for predictive maintenance found in industrial environments.

Oracle IoT cloud platform

This platform offers strong security and scalability features, which are suitable for managing large deployments. The platform integrates seamlessly with Oracle enterprise applications and supports blockchain for secure data management.

7.3.5 Interoperability challenges in enterprise IoT cloud platforms

The key enterprise IoT platforms mentioned earlier, such as Microsoft Azure IoT Hub, AWS IoT Core, IBM Watson IoT Platform, SAP Leonardo IoT Platform, and Oracle IoT Cloud Platform, often implement proprietary protocols and technologies. Although these proprietary systems provide robust security features and optimized performance within their ecosystems, they pose challenges for interoperability with third-party devices and systems not explicitly designed to integrate with these platforms. For example, although AWS IoT Core supports standard protocols, such as MQTT and HTTP, achieving full functionality often requires leveraging AWS-specific services, such as AWS Lambda (Sbarski and Kroonenburg, 2017) or AWS Greengrass. This can limit interoperability with non-AWS systems and devices, requiring custom solutions for cross-platform integration.

Open-source platforms

Businesses must carefully consider their long-term interoperability needs when selecting an IoT platform, balancing the security and efficiency of a closed ecosystem with the flexibility and integration potential of open standards. **Kaa IoT Platform** is an open-source, highly flexible IoT platform for device management, data collection, processing, and visualization. Various IoT protocols are supported to facilitate the integration of devices from different vendors (Al Rasyid et al., 2020). **Home Assistant** is a platform that values privacy and local management, offering support for a range of smart home devices and services (Setz et al., 2021). **Zetta** is an open-source platform built on Node.js for creating IoT servers that bridge devices with applications using REST APIs and WebSockets (Amyx, 2017).

Middleware addressing interoperability challenges

Middleware can serve as a protocol translator, enabling devices and systems using different communication protocols to interact seamlessly. This is particularly important for integrating diverse IoT devices and platforms. For example, **Eclipse Kura** can translate between MQTT, CoAP, and HTTP, allowing devices that use different protocols to communicate with a unified backend (Amjad et al., 2021). Middleware can also be employed to aggregate data from various sources and normalize them into a consistent format. This helps overcoming the differences in data formats used by different devices and platforms. For example, the open-source platform **Node-RED** transforms data received from multiple sources into a standard format, which can then be routed to different endpoints across heterogeneous systems (Thuluva et al., 2020).

7.4 AI and IoT integration in enterprises

Today's IoT stacks in enterprises (Fig. 7.1) offer advanced integration of technologies, allowing companies to combine AI and the cloud-to-things continuum for improved advantages in the industry value chains and business processes, paving the way for Industry 4.0 with autonomous enterprises. Whereas IoT connects enterprise machines via various IoT devices and sensors, AI stimulates intelligent behavior and learning in those machines. Combining these technologies enables machine-to-machine communication and reasoning, enabling systems that autonomously interpret and act upon collected data.

This AI integration within enterprise IoT facilitates predictive maintenance, enhances operational efficiency, and drives innovation. AI algorithms continuously analyze data from sensors to detect patterns, anticipate failures, and dynamically optimize processes with no or minimal human intervention. As these technologies converge, smart enterprises that are more responsive to market dynamics emerge. The transition towards such interconnected and intelligent enterprise IoT systems marks a shift in data-driven strategies to new levels, where continuous (machine) learning and adaptation are embedded into the fabric of business operations, pushing further the boundaries of industrial automation and digital transformation.

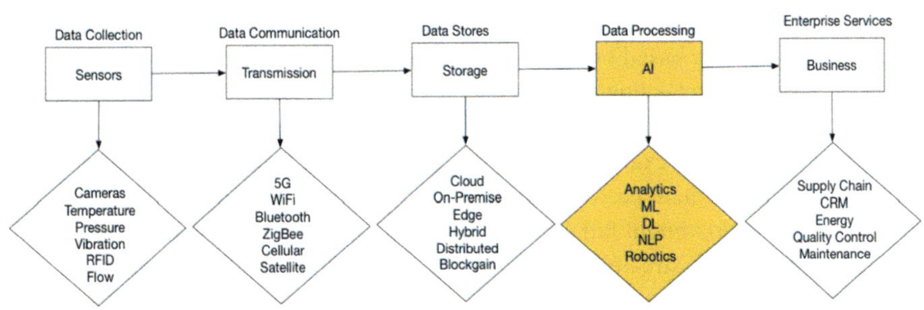

FIGURE 7.1

Integrating AI and the IoT stack.

The confluence of AI and IoT creates a powerful synergy that unlocks significant benefits for enterprises across various industries. This confluence provides several benefits for enterprise operations, as discussed next.

7.4.1 Predictive maintenance and reduced downtime

The potent alliance of IoT sensors and AI transforms industrial facilities into self-aware organisms. Consider a refinery where vibration sensors allow AI algorithms to diagnose an impending pump failure a day in advance. This advanced notice allows technicians to schedule a repair on their terms, preventing a breakdown that saves the enterprise production losses. Predictive maintenance, fueled by the real-time data collected from IoT sensors and analyzed by A algorithms, maximizes uptime and keeps operations within expected performance thresholds. It is this predictive capability that turns reactive maintenance strategies into proactive operational resilience.

7.4.2 Enhanced operational efficiency and optimization

Data-driven ecosystems orchestrated by AI-powered algorithms of IoT sensors continuously and dynamically adjust to changes in demand, supply chain disruptions, and even real-time shifts in consumer behavior. For example, IoT sensors in logistic vehicles combined with AI route optimization can lead to significant reductions in delivery times and fuel consumption. A manufacturing plant, where energy meters are connected to AI systems, enables energy savings over idle machinery. This intricate integration of data unleashed by IoT devices and AI adapts to fluctuating demand and efficiency opportunities.

7.4.3 Personalized customer experiences and improved products

The boundary between products and personal assistants is becoming increasingly blurred as IoT and AI integration is transforming how consumers interact with products, making these interactions more intuitive and responsive. Products are now equipped with smart assistive interfaces, which can anticipate customer needs and provide personalized services.

Envision a manufacturing floor where intelligent machinery adjusts production schedules in real time based on IoT sensor data and predictive AI analytics. For example, if sensors detect a slowdown in one part of the assembly line, AI systems can reroute tasks to other machines to maintain efficiency with no human intervention. Another enterprise IoT example pertains to an asset management system that uses IoT to monitor equipment performance across multiple facilities, with AI algorithms predicting when parts might fail and automatically ordering replacements, thus minimizing downtime and streamlining the supply chain (Mathew et al., 2022a).

When pairing logistics with AI, enterprise IoT systems can forecast stock needs, identify optimal storage conditions, and automate replenishment orders, thereby reducing manual errors and ensuring product availability. Similarly, an airline employs IoT devices to monitor aircraft health, with AI analyzing data to predict maintenance needs, allowing for repairs to be scheduled without disrupting flight schedules, thus improving fleet reliability and passenger or cargo service satisfaction (El Barachi et al., 2022).

7.4.4 Improved safety and security

AI and IoT sensors are weaving a safety net around businesses. For example, drones equipped with thermal cameras patrolling a refinery feed AI systems with data to detect anomalies in a storage tank, triggering an automated shutdown. From safeguarding critical industrial infrastructure to protecting sensitive data and detecting intrusions (Mathew et al., 2022b), the integration of AI with IoT sensors significantly enhances safety and security measures across various sectors.

Advanced AI algorithms analyze data from IoT devices in real time to identify patterns indicative of cyber threats or unusual activities. This allows businesses to address potential security breaches before they escalate preemptively. For instance, IoT sensors deployed across a network can monitor for suspicious network traffic, while AI assesses the risk level and automatically enforces security protocols, such as isolating affected systems or blocking unauthorized access attempts. Furthermore, this synergy enables continuous learning and adaptation to mitigate emerging threats, ensuring that security measures evolve with new cyber-attack techniques.

7.4.5 New business models and revenue streams

The traditional business model is being disrupted by digital transformation with the powerful combination of IoT and AI. Consider a business model where manufacturers evolve from selling machinery to providing subscription-based performance guarantees. This approach uses real-time data collected from connected equipment to enable service provisioning and performance levels to be continuously monitored and optimized. Service providers continuously gather operational data through IoT sensors, whereas AI algorithms analyze this information to optimize operational efficiency. This model allows customers to pay for the performance of the equipment rather than the physical hardware, transforming traditional sales using a service-oriented approach.

Insurance firms are also capitalizing on the convergence of IoT and AI by providing personalized risk assessments through data from connected home devices. This approach results in more accurate premiums and enhances customer satisfaction. The impact of this data-driven innovation extends across various sectors as well, enabling businesses to offer tailored products and service enhancements. Ultimately, the integration of IoT and AI opens novel revenue streams by transforming every piece of collected data into a potential for value creation.

7.5 Enterprise IoT in action: case studies

The joint evolution of AI and the cloud-to-things continuum rapidly reshapes digital transformation across diverse industries. The cloud-to-things continuum, empowered by AI's analytical prowess, is a driving force shaping the present and future of enterprises, whether it is in supply chain (Nahr et al., 2021), healthcare (Alowais et al., 2023), or smart cities (Kaginalkar et al., 2021). This section reveals case studies that illustrate practical enterprise IoT initiatives, demonstrating the synergy between AI and IoT to create innovative service models. Through these real-world scenarios, we explore the benefits and challenges of adopting enterprise IoT models and strategies that lead to successful digital transformation.

7.5.1 Environmental monitoring

Enterprise IoT models and strategies can foster a holistic, real-time understanding of urban environments. Harnessing resulting real-time data enables the automation of controls that enhance efficiency, resilience, and safety within urban landscapes. A compelling example of enterprise IoT in urban management is the ambitious endeavor of Copenhagen, the capital of Denmark, to address the sustainability challenge of becoming a carbon-neutral city by 2025 (Mathiesen et al., 2019). A network of environmental sensors across Copenhagen monitors environmental parameters, such as air-quality and temperature. The resulting real-time data is used to track pollution levels or identify sources of emissions and to inform policy decisions and public awareness campaigns.

The Royal Dutch Shell, the oil and gas organization, took safety to the next level by introducing AI-powered machines at their retail locations. These machines were fitted with cameras that captured potential hazards, such as detecting customers lighting cigarettes, a severe hazard, in real time. The images were processed at the edge, extracting crucial details, and then sent securely to the cloud via an online platform. AI models, trained on vast datasets of safety violations, scanned the images for danger patterns. A potential hazard triggers an immediate response to alert personnel, or shut down equipment. AI and IoT are thus leveraged by Royal Dutch Shell to create a safer environment for both employees and customers, through a commitment to innovation and a responsible use of technology.

Furthermore, Shell's application of reinforcement learning in its exploration and drilling programs represents another dimension of its commitment to leveraging enterprise IoT and AI. By optimizing the extraction processes, Shell aims to reduce operational costs, while maintaining its revenue from gas production. Enhancing safety at retail locations and improving efficiency in exploration and drilling illustrate how enterprise IoT and AI can transform traditional industries. This convergence can potentially drive significant improvements in safety protocols, operational efficiency, and cost management, paving the way toward smarter and safer business practices within the energy sector (Artificial Intelligence | Shell Global, n.d.).

7.5.2 Smart buildings and smart cities

Property owners increasingly leverage enterprise IoT technologies to achieve energy efficiency, comfort, convenience, safety, and security. HVAC infrastructures use real-time data and automation induced by enterprise IoT to adjust the temperature for optimum energy efficiency and comfort.

Building on the concept of smart management in property technology, the integration of IoT extends beyond common areas into personalized experiences within individual spaces, such as bathrooms. KOHLER's Konnect solution illustrates the next frontier in home automation: showers and faucets become intelligent agents that anticipate and respond to individual preferences (Özüdoğru et al., 2018). This system, powered by the Azure IoT Hub, illustrates IoT device networks in an intelligent environment, where analyzed data through Azure Stream Analytics, patterns, and potential issues, such as pressure or leaks, are detected, ensuring a seamless and responsive user experience. Voice control utilizing APIs further augments interaction with these smart systems intuitively, making it possible to adjust settings without manual intervention. KOHLER Konnect solutions continuously learn about users' habits and preferences to predict and adjust tailored bathroom experiences. This approach showcases the potential of enterprise IoT to transform living spaces into smart environments that anticipate and cater to individual preferences.

Enterprise IoT is transforming the landscape for safety service providers by enabling sophisticated home and commercial building safety solutions. These solutions leverage a network of connected cameras and sensors to offer real-time surveillance and proactive security measures. When these devices detect movement or specific activities, appropriate actions are taken to analyze collected data at a central IoT hub. For safety business providers, this means offering their clients a comprehensive safety ecosystem that automatically responds to potential threats by triggering alarms, locking doors, or even notifying law enforcement based on the severity of the detected activity. According to a 2023 report, the global smart building market was worth \$72.8 billion in 2022, and is deemed to reach \$304.3 billion by 2032 (Globenewswire, 2023). This enterprise IoT evolution is poised to further transform urban environments, making buildings smarter, safer, and more efficient.

PCL Construction, a leading name in the industry, pioneered a paradigm shift with its smart building initiative. This innovation leveraged enterprise IoT to lay extensive sensors that were strategically placed throughout construction sites to capture real-time environmental data, such as temperature, humidity, air quality, and worker activity. The data was seamlessly transmitted to a dedicated platform, where machine learning is used for predictive analytics. Equipment malfunctions, material shortages, or even safety hazards could thus be prevented. Predictive analytics also aimed to minimize downtime and optimize resource allocation, leading to cost savings and faster project completion (PCL, 2023).

In Norway, Powel's enterprise IoT project showcased advanced connectivity and analytics to optimize water distribution systems and efficiently address leakage issues, thereby yielding environmental and economic improvements. The enterprise IoT framework enabled early detection of leaks, allowing utility companies to quickly address issues, reduce water wastage and achieve significant cost savings. This initiative highlighted the critical role of enterprise IoT in enhancing water security and promoting resource sustainability. Collected IoT data are processed by algorithms trained to recognize deviations from normal flow patterns, indicative of potential leaks. This strategic application of enterprise IoT provided a more effective method for identifying and addressing leaks, illustrating the transformative potential of enterprise IoT in utility management and environmental conservation (Vuppalapati, 2019).

Compology is a waste management company, which introduced WasteOS, as a solution to utilize IoT and cloud technology for reducing waste collection costs (up to 40%). This system employs sensors and software to analyze data and plan the most efficient routes for the company's fleet of vehicles. Cameras installed within the bins capture images and transmit them over mobile networks, allowing the cloud-based system to calculate the fullness of each container in real time. These GPS-enabled sensors are battery-powered and built to withstand harsh conditions. Data collected from all serviced dumpsters is then used to optimize route planning and scheduling (Government Technology, 2016).

Additionally, drivers are equipped with tablets containing custom-built apps that provide real-time information on containers requiring service and the most efficient routes to reach them. WasteOS can also be used for predictive analysis of container status in areas with low connectivity and scattered data points. By optimizing routes and potentially reducing the truck fleet by 40%, WasteOS not only cuts costs but also leads to improved customer service, as haulers can anticipate service needs before customers even contact them (Government Technology, 2016).

Schindler elevators are widely used across the world. This 141-year-old company uses IoT to enhance their real-time maintenance. Systems connect sensor technology with mobile applications, creating a dashboard for the company's field workers. This allows their service engineers to correct the issue before customers notice it. The use of digital connectivity has led to improved maintenance and management of elevators, resulting in a more comfortable experience for passengers. A variety of controllers are available and compatible with Schindler Ahead. IoT and machine learning capture and analyze data stored in the cloud to optimize uptime and convenience (Weiss and Goldberg, 2018).

7.5.3 Employee productivity and customer services

Coca-Cola, as a pioneer in IoT technology, has connected its vending machines to the Internet. Through IoT, the company is able to fine-tune contextual engagement strategies, offer one-click self-service, understand customer purchasing behavior, reimagine customer loyalty, and trace spikes in consumption to improve targeted marketing. The data collected from IoT-enabled vending machines is crucial, as there are no humans present at the retail point to gather customer feedback. This data is used to locate the busiest locations, determine the most popular drinks, gauge inventory levels, and assess machine profitability. IoT technology enables cashless payments, personalized communications, stocks and refill notifications for management, performance and service data for suppliers, and a rewards loyalty program, where customers can pay via smartphones and accumulate points for a free drink all in one tap (Vyas et al., 2019).

Sociometric Solutions has developed cutting-edge tracking sensors for Bank of America, which are based on an idea developed at MIT. These advanced sensors are embedded in employee IDs and collect real-time data on various parameters, such as tone of voice, speaking speed, volume, movements, position, and posture during socializing with colleagues. The main objective behind this technology is to boost efficiency by identifying when and how productivity reaches its peak levels. The IoT-enabled employee tracking can be done without any legal issues or discomfort, as the sensors do not record conversations, and the connected software anonymizes all metadata. The devices were tested on 90 call center employees, and the results were nothing short of impressive. The study revealed that employees take time to solve workplace issues when taking breaks together. By changing the workplace culture, a remarkable 10 percent improvement in productivity was achieved (BusinessInsider, 2013).

7.6 Conclusion

Enterprise IoT refers to IoT deployments in a business context. The integration of AI and IoT within the enterprise environment is a shift in how businesses innovate to deliver new value propositions. Enterprise IoT fosters innovation and new business models derived from actionable intelligence through a vast network of connected devices. As businesses continue to explore and expand their IoT capabilities, the potential for transformation and growth of enterprise IoT is boundless.

References

Al Rasyid, M.U.H, Mubarrok, M.H., Hasim, J.A.N., 2020. Implementation of environmental monitoring based on kaa IoT platform. Bulletin of Electrical Engineering and Informatics 9 (6), 2578–2587.

Alowais, S.A., Alghamdi, S.S., Alsuhebany, N., Alqahtani, T., Alshaya, A.I., Almohareb, S.N., Aldairem, A., Alrashed, M., Bin Saleh, K., Badreldin, H.A., et al., 2023. Revolutionizing healthcare: the role of artificial intelligence in clinical practice. BMC Medical Education 23 (1), 689.

Amjad, A., Azam, F., Anwar, M.W., Butt, W.H., 2021. A systematic review on the data interoperability of application layer protocols in industrial IoT. IEEE Access 9, 96528–96545.

Amyx, S., 2017. Internet of things open-source systems. In: Internet of Things and Data Analytics Handbook, pp. 129–146.

Apache NiFi Developers, 2024. Apache nifi: a data logistics platform for automating the movement of data between disparate systems. https://nifi.apache.org/. (Accessed 23 May 2024).

Artificial Intelligence | Shell Global, n.d. https://www.shell.com/energy-and-innovation/digitalisation/shell-ai.html. (Accessed 27 February 2024).

Basak, A., Venkataraman, K., Murphy, R., Singh, M., 2017. Stream Analytics with Microsoft Azure: Real-Time Data Processing for Quick Insights Using Azure Stream Analytics. Packt Publishing Ltd.

Bell, C., 2014. Beginning Sensor Networks with Arduino and Raspberry Pi. Apress.

Bhartia, R., 2014. Amazon kinesis and apache storm. Amazon Web Service.

BusinessInsider, 2013. Tracking employees with productivity sensors. https://www.businessinsider.com/tracking-employees-with-productivity-sensors-2013-3?r=US&IR=T#:~:text=The%20sensors%20are%20intended%20to,whole%2C%20can%20work%20more%20efficiently. (Accessed 27 February 2024).

Calderoni, L., Maio, D., Tullini, L., 2022. Benchmarking cloud providers on serverless IoT back-end infrastructures. IEEE Internet of Things Journal 9 (16), 15255–15269.

Carbone, P., Katsifodimos, A., Ewen, S., Markl, V., Haridi, S., Tzoumas, K., 2015. Apache flink: stream and batch processing in a single engine. The Bulletin of the Technical Committee on Data Engineering 38 (4).

Ceph, 2024. Ceph: a scalable distributed storage system. https://github.com/ceph/ceph. (Accessed 23 May 2024).

Daum, T., Birner, R., 2019. African Agricultural Mechanization: Myths, Realities and an Emerging Research Agenda.

Desbiens, F., 2022. Edge computing. In: Building Enterprise IoT Solutions with Eclipse IoT Technologies: An Open Source Approach to Edge Computing. Springer, pp. 271–296.

Eclipse Hono Developers, 2024. Eclipse hono: IoT connectivity and messaging middleware. https://www.eclipse.org/hono/. (Accessed 23 May 2024).

El Barachi, M., Salman, S., Mathew, S., 2022. A sensor-embedded smart carton for the real-time monitoring of perishable foods' lifetime. In: 2022 7th International Conference on Smart and Sustainable Technologies (SpliTech). IEEE, pp. 1–8.

Garg, N., 2013. Apache Kafka. Packt Publishing, Birmingham, UK.

Globenewswire, 2023. Smart buildings market anticipated to surpass USD 304.3. https://www.globenewswire.com/en/news-release/2023/04/18/2649598/0/en/Smart-Buildings-Market-anticipated-to-surpass-USD-304-3-Billion-by-2032-with-a-sustained-CAGR-of-15-8-Market-us-Report.html#:~:text=New%20York%2C%20April%2018%2C%202023,15.8%25%20between%202023%20to%202032. (Accessed 27 February 2024).

Government Technology, 2016. 'Smart garbage' startup cuts city trash costs by 40 percent. https://www.govtech.com/civic/smart-garbage-startup-cuts-city-trash-costs-by-40-percent.html. (Accessed 27 February 2024).

Ismail, A.A., Hamza, H.S., Kotb, A.M., 2018. Performance evaluation of open source IoT platforms. In: 2018 IEEE Global Conference on Internet of Things (GCIoT). IEEE, pp. 1–5.

Kaginalkar, A., Kumar, S., Gargava, P., Niyogi, D., 2021. Review of urban computing in air quality management as smart city service: an integrated IoT, AI, and cloud technology perspective. Urban Climate 39, 100972.

Kingsley, M.S., 2023. Comparing aws, azure, and gcp. In: Cloud Technologies and Services: Theoretical Concepts and Practical Applications. Springer, pp. 381–393.

Kurniawan, A., 2018. Learning AWS IoT: Effectively Manage Connected Devices on the AWS Cloud Using Services Such as AWS Greengrass, AWS Button, Predictive Analytics and Machine Learning. Packt Publishing Ltd.

Lacy, P., Rutqvist, J., 2015. The product as a service business model: performance over ownership. In: Waste to Wealth: The Circular Economy Advantage. Springer, pp. 99–114.

Mathew, S.S., El Barachi, M., Kuhail, M.A., 2022a. Crowdpower: a novel crowdsensing-as-a-service platform for real-time incident reporting. Applied Sciences 12 (21), 11156.

Mathew, S.S., Hayawi, K., Dawit, N.A., Taleb, I., Trabelsi, Z., 2022b. Integration of blockchain and collaborative intrusion detection for secure data transactions in industrial IoT: a survey. Cluster Computing 25 (6), 4129–4149.

Mathiesen, B.V., Auken, I.M.M., Skibsted, J.M., 2019. This is how Copenhagen plans to go carbon-neutral by 2025, World economic forum. https://www.weforum.org/agenda/2019/05/the-copenhagen-effect-how-europe-can-become-heat-efficient/. (Accessed 23 February 2024).

Mavridis, I., Karatza, H., 2017. Performance evaluation of cloud-based log file analysis with apache hadoop and apache spark. The Journal of Systems and Software 125, 133–151.

Mengle, S.S., Gurmendez, M., 2019. Mastering Machine Learning on Aws: Advanced Machine Learning in Python Using SageMaker, Apache Spark, and TensorFlow. Packt Publishing Ltd.

MinIO, 2024. MinIO: high performance, kubernetes-native object storage. https://github.com/minio/minio. (Accessed 23 May 2024).

Morabito, R., 2017. Virtualization on Internet of Things edge devices with container technologies: a performance evaluation. IEEE Access 5, 8835–8850.

Nahr, J.G., Nozari, H., Sadeghi, M.E., 2021. Green supply chain based on artificial intelligence of things (aiot). International Journal of Innovation in Management, Economics and Social Sciences 1 (2), 56–63.

Niranjanamurthy, M., Archana, U., Niveditha, K., Jafar, S.A., Shravan, N., 2014. The research study on dynamoDB—NoSQL database service. International Journal of Computer Science and Mobile Computing 3 (10), 268–279.

OpenStack Swift, 2024. OpenStack Swift: a highly available, distributed, eventually consistent object store. https://github.com/openstack/swift. (Accessed 23 May 2024).

Özüdoğru, A.G., Ergün, E., Ammari, D., Görener, A., 2018. How industry 4.0 changes business: a commercial perspective. International Journal of Commerce and Finance 4 (1), 84–95.

PCL, 2023. Leveraging smart construction when building manufacturing 4.0 facilities. https://www.pcl.com/us/en/insights/leveraging-smart-construction-when-building-manufacturing-facilities. (Accessed 27 February 2024).

Popelo, O., Dubyna, M., Kholiavko, N., 2021. World experience in the introduction of modern innovation and information technologies in the functioning of financial institutions. Baltic Journal of Economic Studies 7 (2), 188–199.

Ramaswamy, S., 2016. Using IoT data to understand how your products perform. Harvard Business Review.

Ramuka, M., 2019. In: Data Analytics with Google Cloud Platform. BPB Publications.

Rawat, S., Narain, A., 2018. Understanding Azure Data Factory: Operationalizing Big Data and Advanced Analytics Solutions. Apress.

Reagan, R., Reagan, R., 2018. Cosmos db. In: Web Applications on Azure: Developing for Global Scale, pp. 187–255.

Saxena, M., Sowell, B., Alamgir, D., Bahadur, N., Bisht, B., Chandrachood, S., Keswani, C., Krishnamoorthy, G., Lee, A., Li, B., Mitchell, Z., Porwal, V., Chappidi, M.R., Ross, B., Sekiyama, N., Zaki, O., Zhang, L., Shah, M.A., 2023. The story of aws glue. In: VLDB 2023. https://www.amazon.science/publications/the-story-of-aws-glue.

Setz, B., Graef, S., Ivanova, D., Tiessen, A., Aiello, M., 2021. A comparison of open-source home automation systems. IEEE Access 9, 167332–167352.

Sbarski, P., Kroonenburg, S., 2017. Serverless Architectures on AWS: with Examples Using Aws Lambda. Simon and Schuster.

Thuluva, A.S., Anicic, D., Rudolph, S., Adikari, M., 2020. Semantic node-red for rapid development of interoperable industrial IoT applications. Semantic Web 11 (6), 949–975.

Vuppalapati, C., 2019. Building Enterprise IoT Applications. CRC Press.

Vyas, S., Jain, S.S., Choudhary, I., Chaudhary, A., 2019. Study on use of AI and big data for commercial system. In: 2019 Amity International Conference on Artificial Intelligence (AICAI). IEEE, pp. 737–739.

Weiss, E.N., Goldberg, R., 2018. Schindler Elevator Corporation. University of Virginia. https://doi.org/10.2139/ssrn.3159657. Darden Case No. UVA-OM-1593. Available at SSRN: https://ssrn.com/abstract=3159657.

PART 2

IoT cloud security

CHAPTER

IoT cloud security in digital transformation

8

8.1 Introduction

The convergence of Internet of Things (IoT) and cloud computing is driving digital transformation forward across several industries. This integration fosters businesses to embrace a future where intelligent interconnected devices become ubiquitous. However, this transformation is intricately linked to the assurance of security. As organizations embark on this transformation journey, they encounter a diverse array of security threats that could potentially disrupt operations, inflict financial damage, and lower trust in the organization services. The pervasive connectivity of IoT devices expands the attack surface, while cloud computing introduces intricacies in data governance and protection. The critical role of security in this landscape is not merely about defensive measures but about enabling the safe harnessing of the transformative potential of cloud-to-things integration. By embedding security at the core of digital transformation strategies, businesses foster resilience, ensure compliance with standard regulations, and forge a reliable path forward in the digitized marketplace.

As mentioned earlier, the integration of IoT and cloud computing has expanded the potential for systemic innovation, while simultaneously increasing the vulnerability to sophisticated cyber attacks. Next, we examine some major security breaches to not only shed light on the types of threats organizations face in this domain, but also to provide valuable lessons for preventing such incidents. Below is an analysis of several notable IoT-cloud security breaches and the critical takeaways from each incident:

The Mirai Botnet attack (2016)

The Mirai Botnet is a malware that targets consumer devices, such as smart cameras and home routers, turning them into a network of remotely-controlled bots. The malware exploits vulnerabilities in IoT devices to launch cyber attacks, such as DDoS attacks on websites and servers, as illustrated in Fig. 8.1. This malicious ware aims to overwhelm a website or server with a large amount of traffic from multiple sources, which results in disruptions of their normal functioning (Zhang et al., 2020).

The Mirai botnet targets devices that have security settings, such as open ports or default login credentials. When it finds these devices, it exploits them to gain access and installs its malicious code. Subsequently, the infected devicc joins the Mirai botnet network used by the attacker to further spread and control devices, such as webcams, smart TVs, IP cameras, and home routers. All connected devices within

Accelerating Digital Transformation with the Cloud and the Internet of Things (IoT)
https://doi.org/10.1016/B978-0-44-322217-7.00015-3

FIGURE 8.1

Mirai botnet operation.

a network can be infected, leading potentially to large-scale attacks, with devastating outcomes. Cybercriminals use Mirai botnets to target computer systems in large DDoS attacks, and their attacks could not be tied back to a single user or group. Robust security on IoT devices, including changing default credentials, implementing regular software updates, and network segmentation, is a necessity to prevent the spread of malware (Jaramillo, 2018).

Capital one data breach (2019)

The capital one data breach in 2019 was a significant cybersecurity incident, which was not directly linked to IoT security breach. Instead, it was primarily a cloud security issue involving a misconfiguration in a web application's firewall on Amazon Web Services (AWS). However, IoT devices are cloud-connected in a cloud-to-things context, which may involve countless connected devices, and which could be exploited to gain unauthorized access to IoT data. The lessons learnt from this major cloud security incident highlighted the importance of strict access controls and continuous monitoring of configurations in cloud environments to ensure they remain secure against such unauthorized access. (Khan et al., 2022).

Verkada camera hack (2021)

In March 2021, Verkada, a Silicon Valley-based security startup that provides cloud-based security camera services, suffered a major security breach. Hackers gained access to the video feeds of 150,000 security cameras in jails, hospitals, schools, and companies, such as Tesla, all managed through a cloud-based admin panel. This incident highlights the critical need of securing remote access to IoT devices, utilizing strong authentication methods, and regular auditing of access logs to detect anomalies (Cecil, 2023).

St. Jude Medical's cardiac devices (2017)

St. Jude Medical manufactures a variety of devices, such as cardioverter defibrillators and pacemakers. In 2017, security researchers discovered vulnerabilities that could allow a hacker to remotely access these devices (Campbell, 2017). Vulnerabilities in the IoT-connected cardiac devices could allow hackers to deplete the batteries or administer incorrect pacing or shocks, although there were no reports of these vulnerabilities being exploited in the real world. The company released firmware updates since then to patch these vulnerabilities. However, it is worth mentioning that the company had legal issues related to the sale of defective heart devices.

From this incident, medical devices ought to have end-to-end encryption, robust authentication, and the ability to receive secure software updates to mitigate risks. It is also noted that security should be implemented from the earliest design stages of IoT devices rather than as an afterthought. Continuous scanning for vulnerabilities and the deployment of patches is also crucial to defend against emerging exploits.

8.2 Information security background

Interconnected systems brought by the evolution of IoT and cloud form the backbone of digital transformation transition. However this evolution may be hampered by security incidents, and thus understanding the foundational elements of information security is crucial to drive safely through this transition. The core components that constitute the landscape of information security include the concepts of vulnerabilities, threats, cyber attacks, and risk evaluation. Each of these elements plays a distinct role in the ecosystem of cybersecurity, and their interplay defines the challenges and strategies in protecting information assets, as seen in Fig. 8.2.

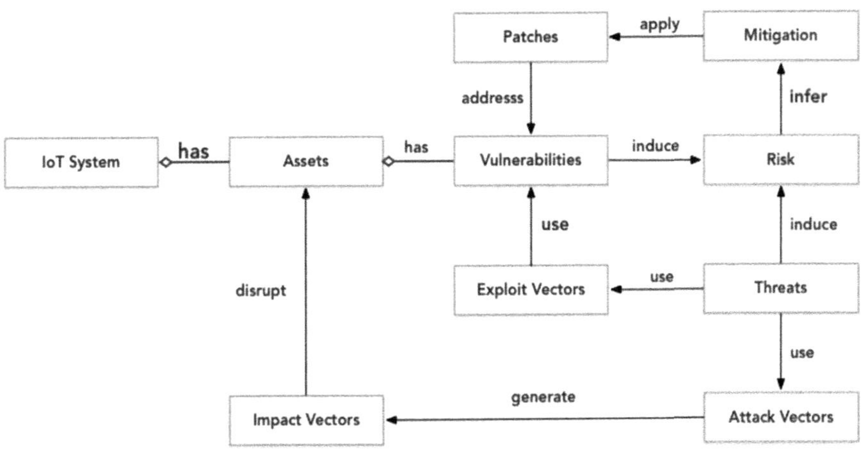

FIGURE 8.2

Security concepts.

At the base of Fig. 8.2 is an IoT system, which comprises various assets, and which are essential service-providing equipment, such as sensor or cloud services. These assets represent multiple components across the cloud-to-things layers, including embedded software, network, and edge, each integral to the asset's functionality. Inherent to these components are vulnerabilities, which are weaknesses or flaws that can be exploited, such as those found in software or operating systems. Exploits, or exploit vectors, are methods or sequences of actions that utilize these vulnerabilities for malicious purposes, often involving commands or open-source kits. These exploits are materialized by threats into attack vector instances.

Threats are hypothetical scenarios, where attackers could leverage vulnerabilities. Threat models categorize exploit vectors that represent different ways to exploit a particular vulnerability. When a threat transitions from a theoretical risk to a real occurrence, it materializes a cyber attack, executed by an actor such as a hacker or cybercriminal. Unlike threats, which are possibilities, an attack is a concrete event that requires the involvement of an actor. The outcomes of these attacks can lead to tangible physical impacts, quantifiable in terms of various losses, such as power disruptions or financial setbacks due to activities like ransomware. This structure highlights the complexity and interdependence of cybersecurity concepts within IoT systems, from the foundational assets to the eventual realization of security risks. The level of risk infers the mitigation actions that an operator may need to undertake to patch the vulnerability.

8.2.1 Vulnerability assessment

When it comes to the security of IoT, we refer to vulnerabilities as weaknesses or flaws that can be found across the cloud-to-things layers. These vulnerabilities can be exploited by cyber attackers to gain access, cause disruptions, or carry out other malicious activities. Vulnerabilities may affect different components, including device hardware, software, network connections, or even in the operational procedures featured by cloud services.

Key features of vulnerabilities

Key vulnerability issues are related to authentication and authorization, where weak methods for verifying identities and granting access can leave IoT devices and networks vulnerable to unauthorized use. This includes the use of weak passwords, the absence of multi-factor authentication, and insufficiently implemented authorization protocols.

The lack of robust encryption practices, or the failure to encrypt data altogether, lead to sensitive information being exposed and susceptible to interception and further misuse. This concern is exacerbated by the default settings under which IoT devices are shipped with, and which may not prioritize security, such as generic passwords or open network ports. Without proper configuration upon deployment, these devices become easy targets for exploitation.

Furthermore, IoT devices security is not only contingent on the devices themselves, but also on the processes behind their conception. The intricate supply chains involved in the production of IoT devices may introduce vulnerabilities at various stages, including design, manufacturing, or software development and distribution stages. This complex web of production and supply underscores the multifaceted nature of IoT vulnerabilities, highlighting the need for a comprehensive approach to IoT security that spans the following categories:

Software vulnerabilities

These are weaknesses or glitches in the software or firmware of a device. These vulnerabilities can be exploited by actors to take control of the device, steal data, or disrupt its normal functioning. Unpatched software, insecure software design, or outdated firmware, contribute to the emergence of vulnerabilities. The limited computational abilities and hardware limitations contribute to IoT devices vulnerabilities in the form of weak or hardcoded passwords, insecure update mechanisms, and insecure communication interfaces. These vulnerabilities can allow cybercriminals to gain unauthorized access to sensitive data, launch sophisticated cyberattacks, and disrupt the services offered by IoT devices. Open-source components used by manufacturers to build IoT devices create a complex supply chain, potentially inheriting vulnerabilities known to attackers. Robust security measures need to be implemented to mitigate these vulnerabilities, including using devices from manufacturers with a good track record of releasing timely updates and ensuring the protection of data transmissions between devices (Butun et al., 2019).

Hardware vulnerabilities

Weaknesses in the physical components of IoT devices, such as processors, sensors, or interfaces, can be exploited by adversaries, allowing them to manipulate the device's environment to extract sensitive data. IoT devices are often deployed in outdoor, public, or remote areas where monitoring and protection are limited, making it easier for attackers to tamper with them. Physical attacks can involve unsoldering the target device and reading out contents of flash memory, attacking the device's microcontroller chip, and attempting to exfiltrate sensitive information by measuring opportunistic hardware emissions (Hu et al., 2020).

Network vulnerabilities

IoT devices are often interconnected and communicate over networks. Vulnerabilities in network protocols or the implementation of these protocols may prompt unauthorized access or data interception. IoT devices are made vulnerable by outdated, unencrypted, or poorly configured network protocols used by IoT, which can lead to attacks such as denial-of-service. IoT devices that use insecure protocols, such as Telnet, which transmits data in plain text, allow transmission interceptions by malicious attackers (Barcena and Wueest, 2015). However, updated network protocols, such as SSH, HTTPS, or MQTT, are more secure for IoT devices as alternative mitigation schemes of these network vulnerabilities (Kim, 2020).

Vulnerability metrics

Vulnerability assessment requires a prioritization scheme to gauge concurrently occurring vulnerabilities against a scale of severity levels. This is to adjust security investments to focus on prioritizing specific patching mechanisms. Standard vulnerability assessment metrics use the common vulnerability scoring system (CVSS), which is a standardized framework for evaluating the severity of security vulnerabilities in software, hardware, and network protocols. CVSS provides an open method to rate these vulnerabilities using a set of criteria for assessing the likelihood of exploiting a vulnerability, and the potential impact of such exploitation. Here is a breakdown the CVSS scheme to score vulnerability severities.

CVSS metrics

CVSS assigns a score to a vulnerability based on metrics, which fall into three main groups: base, temporal, and environmental. The base metrics are constant over time and across user environments, unlike the two other metric categories whose valuation may vary across time or deployment environments. The base metrics include the following (Walkowski et al., 2021):

- Attack vector (AV): How the vulnerability is exploited (e.g., locally, through adjacent network, wider network, or physically).
- Attack complexity (AC): The difficulty faced by the attacker to exploit the vulnerability.
- Privileges required (PR): The level of privileges an attacker must possess before successfully exploiting the vulnerability.
- User interaction (UI): Whether the vulnerability requires user participation to be exploited.
- Scope (S): Whether a successful exploit impacts resources beyond the vulnerable component.
- Impact metrics (confidentiality, integrity, availability): Measure the direct impact of the exploit on the system's confidentiality, integrity, and availability.

The temporal metrics involve variables that can change over time but are not dependent on a particular user's environment. They include

- Exploit code maturity (E): The level of availability and maturity of exploit code or techniques.
- Remediation level (RL): The level of the available fix (e.g., official fix, temporary fix, workaround).
- Report confidence (RC): The degree of confidence in the truth of the vulnerability report.

The environmental metrics which allow customization of the CVSS score depend on the importance of the affected IT asset to a user's environment. They include

- Collateral damage potential (CDP): Potential for loss due to damage.
- Target distribution (TD): The proportion of vulnerable systems.
- Security requirements (confidentiality, integrity, availability): The importance of these three aspects to the user.

Calculating CVSS score

The CVSS score is computed by combining the above metrics (Kai et al., 2021). The resulting score ranges from 0 to 10, where higher scores indicating greater severity of the vulnerability. Organizations use CVSS scores to prioritize response and remediation actions for known vulnerabilities based on the severity. This approach facilitates resource allocation and risk management.

8.2.2 Threat modeling

Threats are potential ways to exploit vulnerabilities. In the context of IoT, a threat refers to any possible malicious activity that can capitalize on vulnerabilities within IoT devices, networks, or related cloud systems. Threat modeling is a proactive approach for categorizing threats, and understanding the corresponding exploit and attack vectors that adversaries might use to exploit vulnerabilities and induce impacts. This structured analysis enables developers and security professionals to anticipate and prepare for potential security issues. The process involves assessing the IoT ecosystem, from individual devices to the broader network, and evaluating the potential impact of identified threats. Typically, this exercise involves mapping the network and data flow to threat models, which support the identification of potential vulnerabilities and attack entry points, while analyzing the information that flows across the system. Subsequently, threats are prioritized based on their likelihood and impact, to plan mitigation efforts and investments. impact (Mahak and Singh, 2021). Effective threat modeling in IoT guides the design of more secure systems and keeps an account of ongoing security measures, to ensure a consistent alignment with the evolving nature of threats in this interconnected and dynamic environment. The integration of threat modeling into the development and maintenance of IoT systems, enhances significantly organizations' defensive posture and resilience against potential cyber attacks.

8.2.3 Cyber attack

A cyber attack is not merely a hypothetical threat, but the actual materialization of the threat. When a vulnerability within an IoT system is exploited, the potential threat evolves into an active attack, often with varying magnitudes of consequences.

The spectrum of a cyber attack

The spectrum of consequences arising from cyber attacks in IoT systems ranges from data breaches, which compromise sensitive information, to more severe outcomes, such as service disruptions, affecting system availability and reliability. Attack vectors represent these dimensions of losses involving IoT devices that control physical machinery. These attacks can lead to actual physical damage, posing significant safety risks. Beyond these immediate impacts, cyber attacks can also inflict reputational damage on organizations and lead to substantial financial losses due to the costs associated with mitigation, legal liabilities, and lost business opportunities. This spectrum illustrates the multifaceted nature of risks associated with cyber attacks in the IoT context.

The following are tools for understanding and mitigating these risks in IoT security:

Attack tree

A key tool for understanding and mitigating these risks in IoT security is the use of attack trees, which is a methodical conceptual framework that provides a visual representation of potential attack scenarios on an IoT system. This attack model is structured as a branching hierarchy, where each branch represents a different attack vector or method to materialize a threat. The root of the tree represents the primary goal of the attacker, whereas the subsequent branches represent the various steps to achieve this goal. An illustration of an attack tree targeting a sensor node is illustrated in Fig. 8.3. In this case, a sensor may be damaged through jamming or changing the environment, such as placing a heat source for a temperature source to falsify readings.

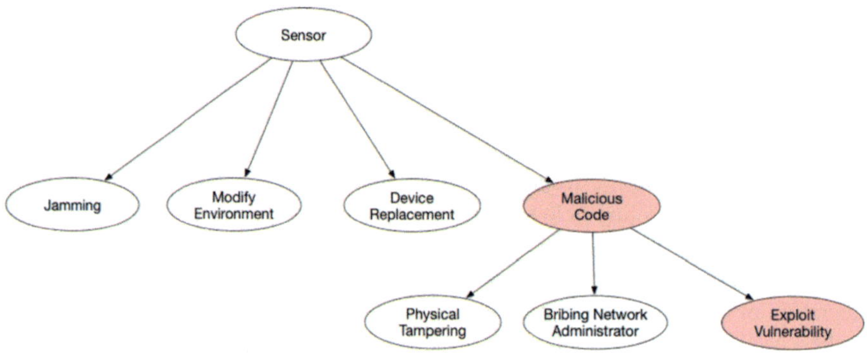

FIGURE 8.3

Attack tree illustration (inspired from (Fantacci et al., 2019)).

8.2.4 Risk analysis

Risk analysis is critical to effectively manage IoT security. Evaluating potential risks involves quantifying vulnerabilities that could be exploited and the societal impact of such exploits. Subsequently, risk can be conceptualized as a function of the vulnerability score, and a measure of its impact, if the vulnerability is successfully exploited. That is,

$$Risk = f(VulnerabilityScore, QuantifiedImpact)$$

The above risk function might involve a simple multiplication of the vulnerability score with the quantified impact or a more complex calculation, depending on the organization's risk posture and tolerance. However, a comprehensive risk management of IoT security further involves the identification of vulnerabilities, potential threats, and a way to evaluate their impacts to assess the associated risks with IoT devices and related cloud systems. The calculated risk values are used to prioritize which vulnerabilities require immediate attention. Higher risk values indicate a more significant threat to the organization. This risk assessment leads to the development of appropriate mitigation strategies that address high-risk vulnerabilities. Remediation processes may include patch management, configuration changes, authentication, and authorization schemes, or other security controls. It is important to acknowledge that the IoT landscape is dynamic, and new vulnerabilities may emerge while others become less relevant. Hence risk analysis is not a one-time activity, but a continuous activity.

Cybersecurity testbeds that include infrastructure simulators or empowered by digital twin technology enable the creation of realistic, controlled environments, where the impacts of potential cyber attacks can be evaluated to quantify risk using the above formulation. Testbeds may be physical or virtual environments that replicate real-world IoT networks and systems. They provide a safe and controlled setting for conducting cybersecurity experiments, including the triggering of mock cyber attacks. By exploiting a known vulnerability in the testbed's IoT setup, researchers can observe the attack's progression and impact in real time to understand the potential cost, consequences, and efficiency of different mitigation strategies.

Infrastructure simulators are software tools that model the behavior of complex IoT networks and systems. They can simulate network traffic, device interactions, and even the behavior of attackers. Use cases include simulators that can model a vulnerability exploitation in progress to discover spreading stages of malware through a network or a denial of service (DoS) attack magnitude over the system availability.

Fig. 8.4 illustrates a framework of a cybersecurity testbed that aggregates different modules to evaluate risk, including an infrastructure modeler, a threat modeler, and a simulator that is relevant to the infrastructure, to evaluate the impact of a given attack vector. This could be a power flow simulator for a smart grid infrastructure, for example. In this case, the components of the smart grid are retrieved from the provided model to assess and rank their CVSS-based scores, which forms the second parameter of the risk assessment formula suggested earlier. The first parameter was the quantified impact resulting from the power flow simulator, which may show the magnitude of power loss following a fictional cyber attack that may shutdown some power generators or SCADA components within a specific power substation.

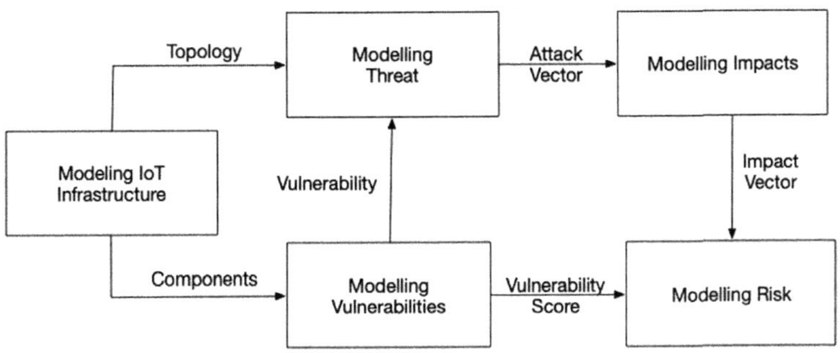

FIGURE 8.4

Cybersecurity testbed framework.

8.3 IoT vulnerabilities and their cloud implications

There are vulnerabilities inherent to the cloud-to-things architecture. This architecture encompasses cloud platforms, a myriad of IoT devices, and the edge layer that acts as an intermediary. The resulting complex network enables security lapses in one component to have cascading effects throughout the architecture layers. Detecting and addressing IoT vulnerabilities within this architecture prevent compromised IoT data integrity and privacy breaches. Moreover, these vulnerabilities, if exploited, can extend into the cloud layer, leading to significant data breaches and service disruptions. Given the vast data flow and the interconnected nature of the cloud-to-things architecture, vulnerabilities pose not just isolated risks but platform-wide threats.

8.3.1 Understanding IoT vulnerabilities

Vulnerabilities can exist at any level of the cloud-to-things ecosystem, including hardware (devices), software (applications, operating systems), network (communication protocols).

Hardware vulnerabilities in IoT devices represent a significant concern in IoT cybersecurity. These vulnerabilities arise from flaws or weaknesses in the physical components of IoT devices, such as microchips, sensors, circuit boards, and other embedded systems. Defects or inconsistencies in hardware components may introduce vulnerabilities at manufacturing stage. For instance, a microchip with a design flaw might be prone to overheating, leading to system failures or being easier to physically tamper with.

For example, sensors that lack proper shielding or isolation can be susceptible to tampering or eavesdropping. Attackers can exploit hardware vulnerabilities through physical access. This could involve manipulating the device's hardware to bypass security measures, extract sensitive data, or implant malicious components. More sophisticated techniques allow attackers to extract sensitive information from a system by analyzing hardware performance characteristics, such as power consumption.

8.3.2 Cloud-specific threats in an IoT-integrated environment

Besides threats that can escalate from IoT devices into significant cloud security issues along the cloud-to-things framework, the massive volumes of data that are transmitted to and from the cloud is a lucrative target for cyber attacks aiming to breach into IoT data. The variety of IoT devices connected to the cloud, each with its own security posture, creates multiple entry points for cyber attackers. Devices ranging from simple sensors to complex industrial machinery can present unique vulnerabilities (Li and Liu, 2021).

The APIs and interfaces used to connect IoT devices with cloud services are other potential entry points. Insecure APIs or interfaces can be exploited for unauthorized data access or manipulation (Altayaran and Elmedany, 2021). This is because APIs connect IoT data to enterprise applications in cloud. Insecure APIs can be exploited to compromise or steal sensitive and private data. Insecure web applications, backend API, cloud services, or mobile interfaces in the cloud-to-things ecosystem outside IoT or edge devices can be sources of significant vulnerabilities. Many IoT-related cloud services suffer from inadequate authentication mechanisms. This means they do not effectively verify the identity of users or devices trying to gain access, making them vulnerable to unauthorized access. API users or developers often leave default passwords unchanged, creating opportunities for unauthorized invocations.

Alongside authentication, the process of granting appropriate access levels (authorization) is often not stringent. This can lead to users or devices having more access privileges than needed, posing a risk of data breaches or malicious operations. Furthermore, some IoT-cloud services use weak or no encryption protocols, making data exchange across service invocations susceptible to interception and unauthorized access during its transfer between IoT devices and cloud servers (Kumar and Goyal, 2019).

8.3.3 Potential attacks in IoT cloud networks

As the cloud-to-things infrastructure integrates diverse IoT devices with cloud computing services, the potential for cyber attacks is significantly amplified. Next, we discuss various types of attacks, supported by case scenarios that illustrate real-world implications.

Data breaches

Consider the case where a cloud storage service used by multiple IoT devices is compromised due to weak authentication protocols. This could lead to substantial data breach, which exposes sensitive user data. Besides compromising user privacy, these incidents also affect trust in IoT systems, with legal and reputational repercussions for the involved organizations. For example, the Verkada security camera breach, which occurred in 2021, allowed hackers to gain unauthorized access to over 150,000 of the company's cameras, including those installed in various sensitive locations, such as Tesla factories, Cloudflare offices, Equinox gyms, hospitals, jails, schools, and police stations. The breach exposed live surveillance camera feeds and the full video archive of Verkada's customers, raising significant concerns about privacy and security (Al Allaf and Totonji, 2023).

Due to authentication weaknesses, the hackers were able to gain "Super Admin"-level access to Verkada's surveillance system, which raised concerns about the security of cloud-connected cameras and the potential risks associated with related breaches. This breach highlighted the importance of robust security measures, including secure authentication protocols and access controls, to protect cloud-based surveillance systems from unauthorized access and potential compromises. Proactive measures to safeguard sensitive data are needed to prevent privacy leakages in cloud-to-things-based environments (Almohri et al., 2022).

Man-in-the-middle

Attackers may secretly intercept and potentially alter the communication between IoT devices and the cloud. This type of attack, called man-in-the-middle attack, can have severe consequences in a cloud-to-things architecture due to the critical role that cloud services play in IoT operations. Weak passwords for both IoT devices and linked cloud services continue to contribute to successful data breaches. Attack vectors may include altering DNS entries to redirect IoT devices' data traffic to a malicious server, enabling interception and manipulation (Hesselman et al., 2020). Enterprises can effectively address cloud-related IoT threats by identifying the assets and data to protect, for which security measures are devised, and continuous monitoring controls are implemented.

Firmware and software tampering

Outdated or unpatched firmware versions provide attackers opportunities to control IoT devices or intercept their data, or even install malicious updates (i.e., malware) in IoT devices via the cloud. Such tampering can turn devices into bots for further attacks, stealing data, or causing device malfunctions. Firmware vulnerabilities, such as those discovered in URGENT/11, Ripple20, and NAME:WRECK, allowed attackers to embed malware on devices, leading to persistent access and limited ability to detect and remediate infections (Seri et al., 2019).

8.4 Best practices for ensuring IoT-cloud security

Next, we delve into the best practices for safeguarding IoT-cloud environments, spanning various critical aspects from risk evaluation to compliance with security standards.

8.4.1 Risk evaluation of IoT-cloud systems

The regular assessment of vulnerabilities is essential for robust security. A comprehensive risk assessment strategy that is tailored to the unique challenges posed by IoT and cloud integration includes identifying and evaluating vulnerabilities continuously in both IoT devices and cloud systems. This process facilitates timely updates and patching of IoT devices and cloud systems. Monitoring the edge and the core of the network, which make up the cloud-to-things infrastructure, ensures a comprehensive visibility and control over the entire edge environment, in addition to addressing the challenges and opportunities associated with edge computing.

Subsequently, methods to evaluate the potential impact of the above vulnerabilities and the likelihood of exploiting threats are outlined and their impacts are quantified. Penetration testing is a proactive approach, which involves simulating cyber attacks to assess the security of a system. Ethical hackers attempt to breach the security defenses of IoT-cloud systems. This helps in uncovering vulnerabilities that might not be apparent during routine security assessments. Penetration testing also helps in understanding the broader impact of a breach on business operations, customer trust, and compliance with standard regulations. Following a penetration test, organizations receive detailed reports on the findings, including specific vulnerabilities and how they were exploited. This guides the development into prioritizing remediation strategies (Yadav et al., 2019).

8.4.2 Security protocols for IoT-cloud systems

In the cloud-to-things ecosystem, data encryption is used for securing sensitive data at rest and in transit. As data travels across networks from IoT devices to cloud servers, it is susceptible to malicious interception. Encryption prevents intercepted data from malicious access. The security of data transmission utilizes SSL (sockets layer) or TLS (transport layer security) protocols. These protocols prevent malicious access to data in transit, including potential personal details. Stored data, or data at rest—whether on a cloud server or an IoT device—is also vulnerable. AES (advanced encryption) is suitable and efficient for securing data at rest, stored in IoT devices or servers in cloud (Mehmood et al., 2019).

8.4.3 IoT device software/firmware maintenance

The maintenance of software and firmware in IoT devices is a critical best practice for IoT security and optimal functionality. Regular updates patch vulnerabilities that could be exploited by cyber attackers. As new threats emerge, updates provide necessary fixes and security enhancements. Over-the-air (OTA) update mechanisms enable remote updates to ensure both security and functionality in IoT ecosystems on the fly, eliminating the need for physical access to each device. A primary role of OTA updates is to swiftly address security vulnerabilities. IoT devices are quickly patched by updates that are dynamically pushed.

8.4.4 Regulatory compliance and security standards

Regulatory compliance in the IoT-cloud security ensures that this data is handled in a manner that respects privacy rights and safeguards against unauthorized access and breaches. Regulations such as GDPR set stringent guidelines for data handling, enforcing principles, for example, data minimization, consent, and the right to be forgotten. Such compliance with established regulations also builds trust, which is crucial for the adoption and continued use of IoT technologies.

Standardized frameworks for security compel organizations to adopt robust security measures. This includes encrypting data, securing data transmissions, and ensuring that both IoT devices and cloud platforms have strong security protocols in place. Organizations that do not comply with these regulations may incur fines and penalties. Furthermore, organizations can suffer reputational damage. As cyber threats evolve, so do regulations. Compliance ensures that organizations regularly update their security practices to protect against latest threats.

8.5 Securing critical infrastructures in IoT-cloud environments

Critical infrastructures encompass the assets that support life-sustaining and essential services to citizens and the economy. The integration of IoT and cloud technologies into these infrastructures offers enhanced efficiency, real-time monitoring, and advanced analytics, propelling digital transformation across various sectors. However, this transformation also exposes assets to security threats, which need to be mitigated to ensure their protection.

Various societal sectors rely on the physical and cyber assets in critical infrastructures, as illustrated in Fig. 8.5. Assets in critical infrastructures include the following:

- **Physical facilities**: These are the tangible structures, such as power plants, water treatment facilities, and transportation hubs.
- **IT hardware**: This comprises servers, routers, and other physical components essential for data processing and communication.
- **Software**: Includes cyber components, such as applications and operating systems that manage and control critical infrastructure operations.
- **Networks**: The communication pathways that connect devices, systems, and users, facilitating data exchange and coordination.

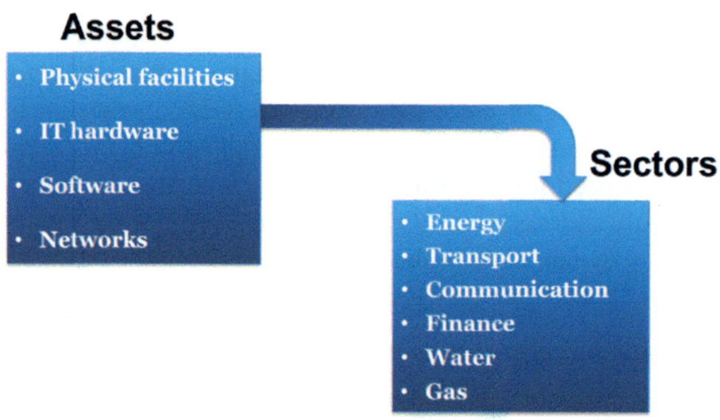

FIGURE 8.5

Critical infrastructure domains.

Examples of critical infrastructure domains include the energy sector, which relies on the above assets to ensure the generation, transmission, and distribution of electricity. The transportation sector encompasses roads, railways, and public transit systems. The communication sector involves telecommunication systems and networks, which enable information exchange. The water sector covers water supply and wastewater management systems. Finally, the gas sector encompasses the infrastructure for natural gas distribution.

IoT and cloud integration within the above sectors improve critical infrastructure capabilities as part of digital transformation by analyzing the resulting data for monitoring the infrastructure assets. However, this interconnectedness also broadens the attack surface, making these infrastructures vulnerable to cyber threats.

8.5.1 Cybersecurity workflow in critical infrastructure protection

As hinted earlier, IoT and cloud technologies enhances critical infrastructures operational efficiencies but also introduces significant security challenges. Understanding the cybersecurity workflow is essential for protecting these infrastructures against potential threats. Fig. 8.6 illustrates the comprehensive process involved in identifying, assessing, and mitigating risks in critical infrastructure systems. The cybersecurity workflow for critical infrastructure protection depicted in the figure involves components that are the individual elements that make up the assets, such as hardware (processors, sensors), software (applications, operating systems), and networks (communication protocols).

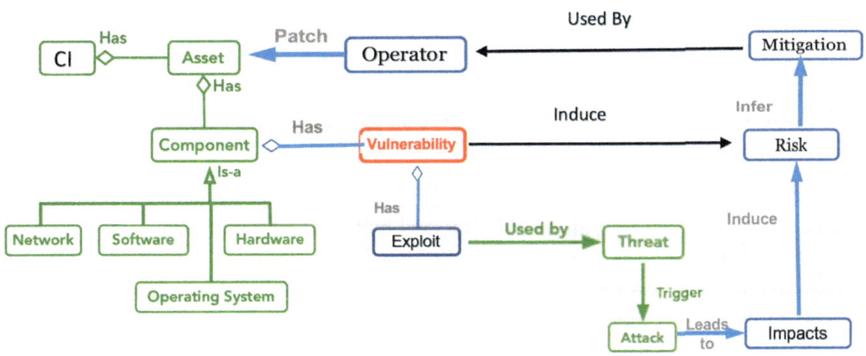

FIGURE 8.6

Critical infrastructure protection.

The components of an asset can expose weaknesses, prompting attackers to create and employ methods to gain entry, disrupt services, or steal sensitive information. These techniques together with the potential impacts of triggered attacks, represents a threat. Attacks materialize threats in the form of impact vectors that quantify the magnitude of loss in infrastructure services or data breaches. The potential attack impacts and the severity of the related vulnerability quantify the level of induced risk on the infrastructure.

Subsequently, mitigation strategies and controls are employed to reduce the identified risks by patching vulnerabilities or segmenting the infrastructure network to lower the cascading effect of potential attacks. The cybersecurity process used to protect critical infrastructures is continuous, whereby operators consistently refine their strategies to address emerging vulnerabilities and changing threats.

8.5.2 Critical infrastructures are at risk!

The increased integration of IoT and cloud technologies in critical infrastructures enhances operational efficiency data-driven decision-making, but exposes these vital systems to significant cybersecurity risks. The pressing need for securing critical infrastructures is illustrated by real-world cyber attacks on energy grids, transportation systems, and healthcare networks.

For example, a cyber attack on Ukraine's power grid in 2015 caused widespread power outages, affecting hundreds of thousands of people. This multistep attack began with spear-phishing emails that installed malware through macros in Microsoft Office documents. The attackers then progressed through various stages, including reconnaissance, brute-force attacks on active directory, and gaining access to the control network via compromised VPN credentials. The attackers manipulated circuit breakers through human-machine interfaces (HMIs), resulting in a six-hour power outage that affected 230,000 people and overwhelmed internal telephony with bogus calls. This incident underscores the importance of stringent security measures to protect energy grids from similar attacks.

8.6 Threats and mitigation strategies in IoT-based digital transformation

The very characteristics that make IoT systems advantageous, such as connectivity, data collection, and integration with various technologies, including cloud computing, make them exposed to a unique set of security threats. Unlike traditional IT environments, IoT systems are characterized by a range of connected devices, often operating in unsupervised environments. This diversity and ubiquity expand the attack surface with threats such as unauthorized access or intercepting data transmission, but also more serious attacks, such as sabotage of critical infrastructures.

The interconnectivity of IoT devices and their integration with cloud services, create further opportunity for to the security threats to materialize into cyber attacks. Each node in an IoT network, from sensors to gateways, can be a potential entry point for attackers (Tariq et al., 2021). The scale of IoT deployments further amplifies the impact of any single point of compromise.

IoT devices are typically resource-constrained, lacking the computational power or memory to support robust security measures (Rana et al., 2023). This limitation often leads to opportunistic threats that compromise the implementation of security protocols, making devices vulnerable to sophisticated threats. As IoT technology continues to evolve, so do the associated security threats.

Advanced techniques, such as AI-induced attacks and ransomware targeting IoT devices, are becoming more prevalent, requiring equally advanced countermeasures (Ahanger et al., 2023). Traditional cybersecurity strategies often fall short in addressing the unique challenges posed by cloud-to-things systems. There is a need for specific security approaches that consider the diverse, distributed, and dynamic nature of IoT networks (Jurcut et al., 2020).

In this chapter, we discuss IoT security threats in the cloud-to-things continuum, addressing risk assessment via threat modeling, analyzing of targeted cyber attacks, and proactive mitigation strategies. The chapter ends with real-world case studies, offering insights into overcoming these security threats to digital transformation.

8.6.1 The evolving threat landscape in IoT

As IoT devices increasingly invade our daily lives and integrate with cloud computing landscape, a spectrum of sophisticated security threats emerge. These threats are not static but constantly evolving, shaped by advances in technology, and IoT networks expansion and complexity. Next, we highlight the nature and characteristics of these emerging threats, emphasizing their implications in IoT systems integrated within cloud environments. The necessity of robust security measures discussed in subsequent sections is based on understanding the groundwork that makes up the threat landscape.

8.6.2 Emerging threats in the cloud-to-things model

Unauthorized access due to weak cloud interfaces, and the resulting potential attacks on data integrity enable threats to exploit the connectivity and data flow between IoT devices and cloud platforms through vulnerabilities that are unique to this model. Many IoT devices have inherent security weaknesses, such as inadequate password protection, unsecured wireless connections, or outdated firmware. Once inside the network, attackers can move laterally, exploiting the interconnected nature of devices. They can gradually make their way to more critical systems or data stores, following the advanced persistent threat (APT) model.

APTs are characterized by their stealthy, continuous, and targeted nature, which pose unique challenges due to their focus on long-term infiltration and data exfiltration (Steffens, 2020). In this model, attackers typically exploit vulnerabilities in IoT devices as entry points, and then move laterally to cloud systems, maintaining a persistent presence to gather valuable data over time. The interconnected nature of IoT and cloud services makes it challenging to detect these threats early, as APT actors skillfully blend their activities within normal network traffic. APTs often involve state-sponsored or highly organized criminal entities, equipped with advanced tools and strategies (Javed et al., 2022). This can lead to substantial data breaches, intellectual property theft, and even critical infrastructure sabotage.

Fig. 8.7 illustrates the multi-level attack surfaces exposed by a SCADA network, which is a cyber physical system (CPS), and which like the cloud-to-things architecture integrates computational (cyber) elements and physical processes. The APT attack on SCADA CPS, which affected Ukraine power grid 2015, allowed cyber attacker to infiltrate the corporate, operation and control subsystems (Lee et al., 2016).

The attack reportedly began with a phishing campaign that targeted the power companies' corporate networks. Employees unknowingly compromised their systems by opening infected email attachments, allowing attackers to gain access to the corporate network. This initial breach is a classic APT move, using seemingly benign methods to penetrate the network. Once inside the network, the attackers moved laterally, identifying and compromising additional systems. This phase involved the reconnaissance to move into a privilege escalation phase, and subsequently gain administrative access, through a brute force attack involving the active directory server. With administrative privileges, attackers access the VPN network of the power grid operations. Once inside the VPN, the attackers could access the SCADA system, which is the central framework for managing the power grid.

SCADA systems typically include HMI (human-machine interface) that provides a graphical overview of the system, allowing operators to interact with the SCADA system, monitor processes, and input control commands. Gaining access to HMI would allow attackers to view and potentially manipulate operational data. The master terminal unit (MTU) acts as a central hub in SCADA systems, communicating with RTUs, which collect and change the state of power grid data. Access to MTUs would enable attackers to disrupt these communications or send false commands. Compromising RTUs leads to direct manipulation of physical processes within the power grid, such as opening circuit breakers. Attackers could execute various disruptive actions to shut down power distribution, causing blackouts, and damaging equipments.

Addressing APTs requires a layered security approach, encompassing strong encryption, rigorous access controls, continuous monitoring, and proactive threat intelligence to detect and mitigate these sophisticated attacks.

Threat types

Threats to information systems at large and cloud-to-things subsystems particularly can manifest in numerous forms, each with unique implications for security. Interception threat involves an unauthorized party gaining access to services or data. This can take the form of eavesdropping over a network to monitor program activities, while listening to private communications without consent. Another significant threat is interruption, which compromises the availability and functionality of services or data, as seen in denial-of-service (DoS) attacks, where resources are overwhelmed to the point of inaccessibility.

A third threat type is modification, which involves unauthorized alterations of data or services, such as false data injection, where legitimate information is tampered with, leading to potentially disastrous decisions or actions based on false information. Lastly, fabrication, introduces additional data or activities that would otherwise not exist, creating a falsified reality within the system. An example of this is a replay attack, where an adversary trick a receiver into accepting a legitimate message that has been maliciously retransmitted, potentially leading to unauthorized actions or access. Each of these threats poses a distinct challenge, requiring tailored strategies to detect, mitigate, and protect against potential cyber risks. These threat categories are illustrated in Fig. 8.8, where Alice and Bob are the good guys, whereas Chuck and Eve usually represent the bad guys.

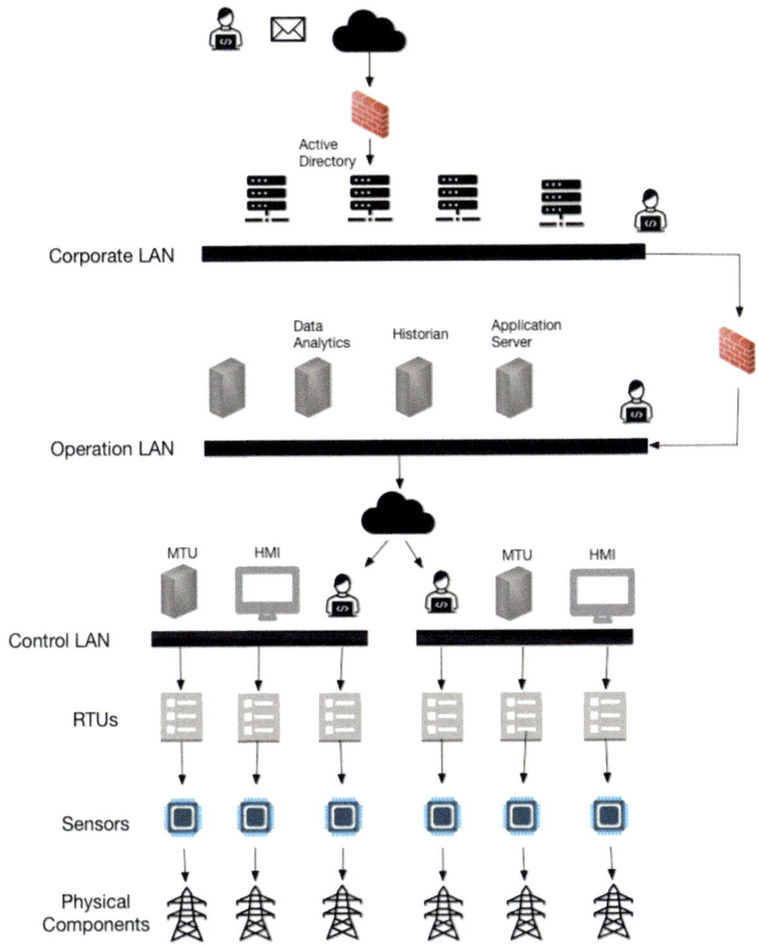

FIGURE 8.7

APT threat to SCADA layers.

8.6.3 Threat modeling in IoT

Threat modeling is an essential practice in cybersecurity, especially within the intricate cloud-to-things continuum, which characterizes modern interconnected systems. This practice represents the structured approach of identifying, assessing, and preparing for potential security threats. The basic principle of threat modeling within the cloud-to-things continuum is to ensure a thorough understanding of the system architecture. This understanding encompasses the identification of all assets, including physical devices, data stores, and communication pathways. By mapping data flows across the IoT ecosystem and into the cloud, security professionals attempt to anticipate threats that might emerge and cascade through the system (Islam et al., 2019).

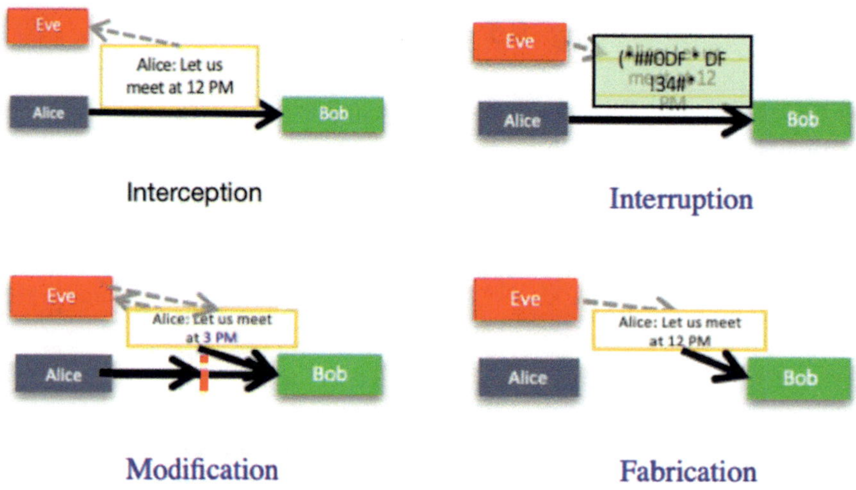

FIGURE 8.8

Threat types.

Threat modeling concepts

The significance of threat modeling lies in its preventative nature. Instead of reacting to security incidents after they occur, threat modeling proactively identifies weak points in the system's architecture, such as unsecured data transmission channels or vulnerable endpoints. The magnitude of threats is measured through likelihood and impact parameters to assist prioritizing security efforts and related resource allocation (Casola et al., 2019).

A threat is conceptualized through several dimensions, which quantify its potential to cause harm to an information system, as illustrated in Fig. 8.9. This multi-dimensional approach is essential in understanding and preparing for possible security incidents within the cloud-to-things continuum.

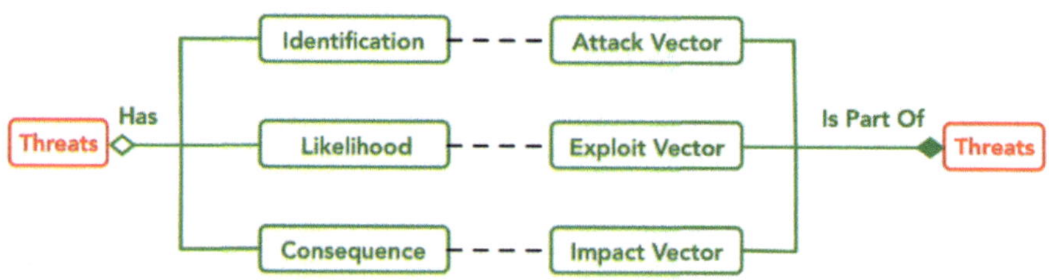

FIGURE 8.9

Threat modeling.

Identification – attack vector

The first step in the threat modeling process is the identification of a threat, which aligns with the attack vector that materializes its occurrence. The attack vector is the pathway by which an attacker gains access to the system assets. This could range from direct attacks on the IoT devices, such as physical tampering or via network-based attacks like phishing or exploiting software vulnerabilities. In the cloud-to-things continuum, attack vectors reflect the propagation of a threat throughout the interconnectivity between devices and cloud services.

Likelihood – exploit vector

Once a potential attack vector is identified, the next dimension to consider is the likelihood, which corresponds to the exploit vector. This involves assessing how probable it is that a threat actor will successfully utilize the identified attack vector. The factors that could influence this assessment measure the complexity of the attack, the level of skill required, the availability of the resources needed to materialize the attack, and the presence of existing safeguards that could prevent the attack. The exploit vector essentially measures how easy a vulnerability can be turned into an actual breach.

Impact – impact vector

The third dimension of a threat model is the impact, which is mapped into a vector that measures the potential consequences of an attack, should the threat materialize. The impact can vary widely, from data loss or theft and service disruption to physical damage or safety hazards in IoT devices. Furthermore, the organization's reputation damage, financial loss, or legal consequences are also potential consequences. In a connected infrastructure, such as the cloud-to-things framework, assessing the impact involves not only the immediate effects of a cyber incident but also the cascading effects that might occur within the interconnected cloud-to-things ecosystem.

Measuring the post-effects of a threat as part of preventing it may appear contradictory, but infrastructure simulators can be used to quantify the effects of disruptions. For example, a smart grid infrastructure may instrument power simulators, such as the open-source PyPower (Lincoln, 2017) or several other commercial tools. Fig. 8.10 shows an approach to simulate power failure following an artificially triggered cyber attack as part of a threat modeling framework. The first step of the simulation involves modeling the power flow using PyPower, followed by simulating the role of a cyber threat actor, which translates a cyber attack into a physical outcome. Step 3 involves the use of the power simulator again to calculate the new power load that results from shutting down a power generator, while Step 4 evaluates the resulting power loss.

Threat categorization

The cloud-to-things seamless integration expands threat horizons. The cloud's vast storage and computational power, coupled with the IoT's extensive sensory and actuation capabilities, introduce new potential entry points for attackers, and accurate threat identification may span across multiple physical and virtual domains.

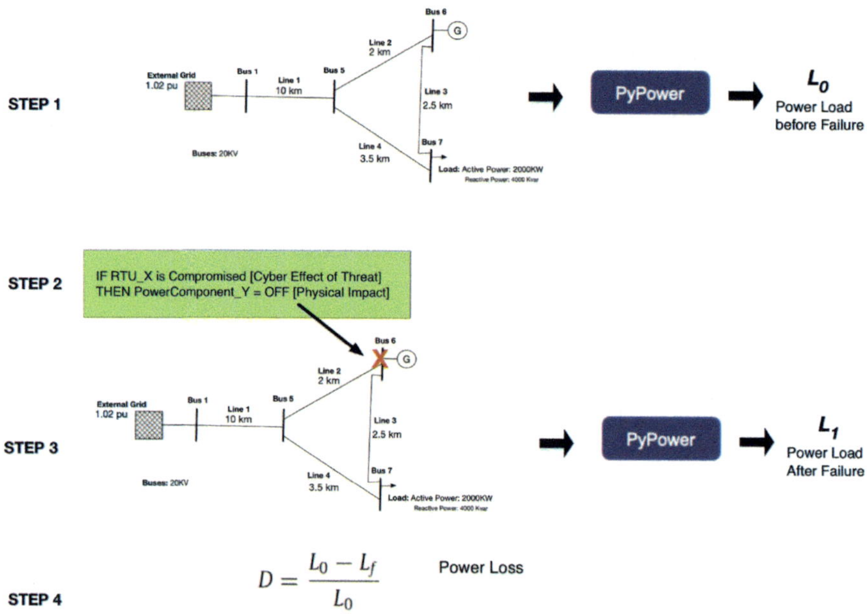

FIGURE 8.10

Impact modeling example.

The classical threat modeling approach developed by Microsoft, which uses the mnemonic "STRIDE," suggests six categories (Johnstone, 2010). This systematic approach to categorizing security threats in software systems can also be used in cloud and IoT integrations. Next, a breakdown of STRIDE components is presented and their relevance to the cloud-to-dhings continuum is discussed.

Spoofing identity

Spoofing involves an attacker impersonating another user, device, or component. In the context of cloud and IoT, this could refer to an unauthorized entity pretending to be a legitimate device to gain access to the cloud. An attacker masquerades itself as a legitimate user or device to gain access to resources and information. As numerous devices are constantly communicating with cloud services, spoofing may threaten the cloud-to-things continuum through different ways.

Device impersonation might create a device that claims to be a legitimate part of the IoT network. This device could then send false data to the cloud, leading to incorrect decisions based on this data. For example, a spoofed temperature sensor could report overheating, triggering unnecessary cooling systems to activate. Credential theft involves stealing credentials, such as digital certificates or API keys; an attacker can gain access to the cloud's backend as if they were an authentic IoT device. Once inside the continuum infrastructure, attackers can access sensitive data, inject malicious code, or disrupt services.

Man-in-the-middle (MitM) attacks is a spoofing approach, where the attacker intercepts communications between the IoT device and the cloud. The attacker can then alter or record the data before passing it along. Both parties believe they are communicating safely with each other, and the interceptions is invisible to them. DNS spoofing compromises the domain name system (DNS) to redirect IoT devices to fraudulent endpoints. Devices that attempt to connect to cloud services may be directed to attacker-controlled servers, who can then capture data or issue malicious commands.

Tampering with data

Tampering threats relate to unauthorized alterations of data in transit or at rest. In IoT systems, this could manifest as altered sensor readings sent to the cloud or unauthorized changes to data stored on cloud platforms, which can lead to incorrect analytics, decision-making, and actions.

In an integrated IoT and cloud environment, the integrity of data is used to directly influence the analytics, decision-making processes, and automated actions. Altered sensor readings of IoT devices, such as sensors, either by physically manipulating the sensors or intercepting and altering the data in transit, can lead to false conclusions or trigger inappropriate actions. For example, a tampered temperature sensor in an industrial setting might report extreme temperatures, causing the automated system to unnecessarily shutdown equipment, leading to operational disruptions.

Data stored on cloud platforms can also be a target for tampering. Malicious access to the cloud storage, can alter historical sensor readings, configuration settings, or user information. Such alterations can have a cascading effect, leading to incorrect data analysis, flawed business intelligence, or erroneous strategic decisions. In many IoT applications, decisions and actions are automated based on data analysis. Tampered data leads to incorrect decisions. For example, misallocating resources in smart cities, misdiagnosing patients in healthcare systems, or triggering false alarms in security systems. The impacts can range from minor inconveniences to severe operational, financial, or safety-related consequences.

In interconnected systems, such as the cloud-to-things continuum, the effects of tampered data can propagate beyond the initial point of compromise. For instance, compromised data in one IoT device can affect the overall analytics performed in the cloud, impacting other devices and systems relying on that data. The Ukrainian power grid cyber attack started from initially infiltrating the power grid's network through phishing emails followed by accessing remote devices. In this scenario, the IoT devices can be considered as the grid's operational technology (OT) components. Once the attackers gained access to the control network access, they were able to compromise these OT devices.

Repudiation

Involves an attacker denying their actions, making it difficult to trace and hold the perpetrator accountable. In cloud-IoT paradigms, without proper logging and auditing measures, it is challenging to discover the authenticity of transactions, which is important for maintaining trust and integrity. Blockchain technology can create an immutable ledger of transactions and system logs. Blockchain's inherent tamper-evident design ensures that once data is written, it cannot be altered unnoticed, thus enhancing the trustworthiness of the log data (Iftekhar et al., 2020).

Information disclosure

Unauthorized access and exposure of sensitive information are significant concerns. IoT devices often collect personal data, which, if disclosed, could lead to privacy violations. Data leaks in the cloud is amplified resulting in a vast amount of sensitive data exposed to the public or to adversaries. For example, numerous instances of Amazon Ring security cameras were hacked in 2019, resulting in unauthorized individuals accessing live feeds from inside homes (Fleishman, 2023). A lawsuit that followed combined complaints from more than 30 people in 15 families who claimed their devices were hacked and used to harass them.

Denial of service (DoS)

DoS attacks aim to disrupt service availability provided by IoT applications that rely on real-time data and cloud services for operation. A successful DoS attack could incapacitate smart devices, or even entire segments of the data provisioning IoT networks.

A distributed denial of service (DDoS) threat in IoT networks involves multiple compromised systems that become controlled by a malicious actor, who floods the bandwidth targeted system, such as a server or IoT network or a website, with a excessively high Internet traffic. IoT devices are particularly vulnerable to these attacks due to weak security. A notorious example of a DDoS attack in 2016 leveraged IoT devices of a major DNS provider named Dyn. Linked to the Mirai botnet, this incident involved millions of IoT devices, including surveillance cameras, which were hijacked and used to flood with traffic Dyn networks (Liu et al., 2018).

Elevation of privilege

This threat category involves an attacker gaining higher access rights than intended, allowing them to execute commands or access data that should be restricted. In the cloud-to-things model, this could allow attackers to take control of IoT devices or cloud resources, leading to widespread system compromise.

Healthcare systems have increasingly become targets for elevation of privilege (or EoP) attacks, especially through IoT medical devices. These attacks often start with a breach in a seemingly less critical IoT device and escalate to gain wider network access. One of the notable examples in the healthcare sector is the series of attacks known as "MedJack" (medical device hijack). Attackers targeted older medical devices with outdated operating systems, including diagnostic equipment (e.g., X-ray machines, MRI scanners) and medical workstations (Meggitt, 2018).

Threat modeling tools

The proactive identification and mitigation of potential threats are indispensable for protecting cloud-to-things infrastructures. The integrated complex systems, spanning from on-premise networks IoT and edge devices to cloud environments, require sophisticated threat modeling tools. These tools represent the front line in the battle against cyber threats, offering a blend of strategic foresight and technical precision (Shi et al., 2021).

A taxonomy of existing threat modeling tools suggest two categories: diagram-based and text-based tools. Diagram-based tools are more intuitive and with user-friendly interfaces, which make system modeling more accessible. These tools, often favored by commercial entities, enable a visual representation of system architecture and related data flows to understand and communicate the security aspects of a system. Features such as drag-and-drop elements further simplify the process of building system models, streamlining the threat modeling process. Examples of such tools include Microsoft threat modeling tool and OWASP Threat Dragon, as well as IriusRisk and SecuriCAD (Shi et al., 2021).

On the other hand, text-based tools cater to a different set of needs. They require users to define the system model using a structured language, such as Python or YAML. This approach is particularly suited for formal analysis and allows for extensions and customizations through text-processing scripts. Text-based tools excel in scenarios where version control and the reusability of system components are important. They offer a more granular level of control over the threat modeling process, which can be essential for detailed and complex system analyses. An example of an existing text-based threat modeling tool is OWASP pytm and Threagile (Shi et al., 2021).

Threat modeling tools allow organizations to anticipate, understand, and prepare for potential security threats. By simulating various attack scenarios and analyzing the possible exploitation of vulnerabilities, these tools provide a detailed assessment of potential security flaws (Verheyden, 2018). There exist a plethora of such tools. Each tool, with its unique capabilities and features, caters to different aspects of threat modeling, from identifying vulnerabilities in software code to analyzing network vulnerabilities and simulating attack scenarios. Next, we explore some tools, from open-source solutions, such as OWASP Threat Dragon to comprehensive platforms, for example, Microsoft Threat Modeling Tool and IriusRisk, offering a preview into their functionalities, applications, and how they fit into the broader context of cybersecurity strategy in cloud-to-things contexts.

Microsoft threat modeling tool

This free tool, offered by Microsoft, is designed to help software architects and developers identify potential security threats at the design stage of software development by creating threat models. The tool helps threat modelers identify classes of threats they should consider based on the STRIDE model. A plugin is provided into issue-tracking systems to enable developers to progressively refine their threat model (Potter, 2009).

The tool provides a graphical interface for creating and analyzing threat models. Users can visually map out their system's architecture, including data flows and entry points, which is particularly helpful in complex IoT ecosystems. Predefined templates are provided for various types of systems and applications, including templates that can be tailored to IoT scenarios. These templates guide users through the threat modelling process, ensuring no critical component is overlooked. This tool helps IoT developers understand potential security issues early in the development process, enabling proactive measures rather than reactive ones. Once threats are identified, the tool provides mitigation guidance. This is particularly useful in IoT contexts, where standard security measures may need to be adapted to suit the unique requirements of IoT devices and networks.

OWASP threat dragon

This open-source tool from the OWASP (Open Web Application Security Project) community provides a web-based interface for modeling threats in web applications and IoT systems. Diagrams of data flow and their analysis for potential security threats are facilitated by the tool, which also has a desktop version with a flexible deployments. Users can visually map out data flows within their systems to identify potential security issues, especially in complex IoT environment. Similar to Microsoft's tool, Threat Dragon utilizes the STRIDE methodology to identify potential threats. This methodical approach is particularly effective in breaking down and analyzing the security of IoT systems, where different components may have varied vulnerabilities. However, Microsoft's tool is more detailed and comprehensive, whereas OWASP Threat Dragon is more user-friendly and simpler (Bygdas et al., 2021).

After a system analysis, Threat Dragon generates an interactive report, which identifies threats but also suggests mitigations. This is particularly useful for IoT systems, which often involve a mix of physical devices, network interfaces, and cloud-based components. OWASP Threat Dragon's flexible in models of threats adapt to the diverse and interconnected nature of IoT architectures.

SecuriCAD

Developed by the Swedish company foreseeti, SecuriCAD is an advanced cybersecurity modeling and simulation tool. It is particularly adept at handling the complexities of IoT and cloud computing systems. Users can create detailed models of their infrastructure, including interconnected networks and cloud environments. The tool then uses these models to identify potential vulnerabilities and attack paths. SecuriCAD allows users to simulate various cyber attack scenarios against their modeled infrastructure to understand attacker's exploit vectors, providing valuable insights into weak points that need to be mitigated (Mao et al., 2019).

The tool also offers a comprehensive analysis of the potential impacts of various security threat, providing quantifiable insights and enabling prioritization of security measures. Users can examine different security scenarios, such as the effect of implementing certain security controls or the impact of new system integrations. This feature supports planning and management of security, especially in dynamic environments, such as IoT.

OWASP pytm

This tool requires users to create a Python object for each system component, utilizing predefined Python classes. After defining these components, the tool generates a system diagram and identifies threats from the text-based model. A detailed and programmatically structured model is further generated into a visual representations of the model system diagrams. The tool includes a thorough library with information on each potential threat, including attributes for threat identification, such as "likelihood" and "severity".

This approach to threat modeling is particularly suitable for formal analysis and allows for deliberate extensions and customization using text-processing scripts. The structured text format of the system model and the threat library also facilitates version control and model reusability.

8.6.4 Mitigation strategies

Methodologies aimed at anticipating and neutralizing threats before they materialize into tangible risks are elaborated as preventive measures. Various approaches exist, including early threat detection, regular system audits, and the implementation of predictive security models. The need for continuous monitoring and regular updates to security protocols cannot be overstated to ensure that IoT and cloud systems remain resilient against emerging threats.

The bow-tie diagram of Fig. 8.11 visualizes mitigation strategies considering both preventive and reactive measures, including respective cybersecurity and resilience controls. On the left side of the diagram, we have preventive measures aimed at addressing the causes that could lead to a security incident. These causes are vulnerabilities or weaknesses that could be exploited by threats. Cybersecurity controls prevent these causes from developing into active threats. Examples of such controls include the following:

- Strong authentication and access control measures to prevent unauthorized access.
- Regularly updating and patching software to eliminate known vulnerabilities.
- Conducting continuous security assessments to identify and mitigate potential risks proactively.
- Using encryption to protect data in transit and at rest from being intercepted or accessed by unauthorized parties.

On the right side of the diagram, we see the potential effects of a security event, which are the consequences or impacts if a threat materializes. Reactive measures are resilience controls to minimize the impact of a security event following its occurrence. Examples of such measures are

- Incident response plans to quickly address breaches and restore normal operations.
- Data backup strategies to recover lost or corrupted data.

- Disaster recovery plans to ensure business continuity in the event of severe incidents.
- Regular drills and training to prepare the organization for responding to security incidents effectively.

At the center of the diagram of Fig. 8.11, the "Event" represents the incident or the point at which a threat exploits a vulnerability to trigger an actual cyber attack. The goal preventive measures are expected to stop the threat from reaching this point. If the preventive measures fail, the reactive measures or resilience controls come into play to manage and mitigate the effects of the event. The integration of cybersecurity controls with resilience controls forms a comprehensive defense and response strategy. Whereas cybersecurity controls aim to prevent incidents, resilience controls are designed to manage and recover from them. Together, they provide a layered mitigation approach to prevent security incidents and recover from them.

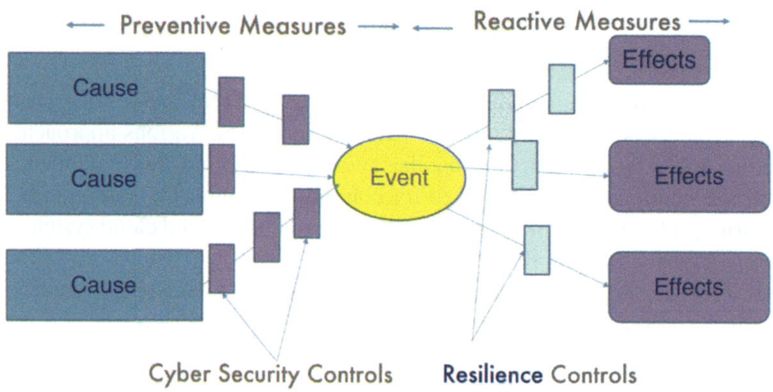

FIGURE 8.11

Preventive vs reactive measures.

8.6.5 Case studies: overcoming IoT security threats

There is an array of real-world scenarios that illustrate the resilience of IoT systems against cyber threats. Next, we discus incidents where security threats looming over IoT infrastructures were mitigated. In addition to these case studies providing a historical account of threats, they serve also as a rich source of strategic guidance for prevention and resilience against cyber security threats.

Real-world IoT security threats

Home automation hacks

Cybercriminals exploit vulnerabilities in smart home devices to gain unauthorized access to home networks. The Mirai botnet of 2016 triggered the most disruptive

DDoS attacks back then using a large number of consumer IoT devices, including home routers and IP cameras.

Exploited vulnerabilities include weak default passwords and unsecured network connections. For example, the Mirai malware exploited weak default usernames and passwords on IoT devices, which many users failed to change. Once infected, these devices were controlled remotely to launch DDOS attacks.

The resulting impacts include privacy invasion, data theft, and unauthorized control over home devices. In the Mirai botnet case, major websites and services were taken down, resulting in widespread internet outages and disruption of services. The attack highlighted the vulnerabilities in consumer IoT devices and the magnitude of damage from such attacks.

The advocated mitigation strategy considers the implementation of strong, unique passwords for devices and networks, regular firmware updates, use of network segmentation to isolate IoT devices, and the adoption of two-factor authentication where possible. In the Mirai botnet case, the following mitigation strategies were implemented:

- Password hygiene: Users were urged to change default credentials on all IoT devices to strong, unique passwords.
- Firmware updates: Vendors released firmware updates to patch the exploited vulnerabilities and improve security measures.
- Network segmentation: Users and businesses were advised to segment their networks, isolating IoT devices from critical segments to contain any potential breaches.
- Multi-factor authentication: The implementation of multi-factor authentication added an extra layer of security, raising the difficulty of gaining unauthorized access.

Industrial IoT (IIoT) compromise

Attackers target industrial control systems connected to IoT for espionage or sabotage. In 2017, a petrochemical plant in Saudi Arabia was targeted by a new kind of malware known as Triton (Di Pinto et al., 2018). This malware specifically targeted the safety instrumented systems of the plant, which are designed to monitor the likelihood of catastrophic events and shut down industrial processes if they detect harmful conditions.

The exploited vulnerabilities include outdated systems without proper security patches, lack of encryption, and insufficient network monitoring. In the Triton case, the attackers took advantage of certain vulnerabilities in the SIS controllers, which were not timely patched. The lack of robust network segmentation and monitoring allowed the malware to reach and interact with these industrial infrastructure.

The resulting impacts include potential disruption of critical infrastructure, financial loss, and compromise of sensitive industrial data. The malicious software Triton had the capability to cause harm to infrastructure by disabling safety systems that are designed to prevent industrial accidents. This could have resulted in loss of life, extensive ecological harm, and significant disruption to energy supply networks.

The advocated mitigation strategy involves rigorous patch management policies, end-to-end encryption for data in transit, continuous network monitoring for unusual activity, and employee training on security best practices. The mitigation strategies applied to face Triton malicious outcomes included the following:

- Patch management: Following the incident, there was an immediate call for updating and patching all systems, particularly those deemed critical for safety and operation.
- Encryption and secure communications: Implementing robust encryption standards for communications to and from IIoT devices became a priority.
- Network monitoring and segmentation: Enhanced monitoring capabilities were deployed to promptly detect any suspicious activity. Networks were segmented to isolate critical systems from general networks, minimizing the potential attack surface.
- Training and awareness: Staff members were educated on the latest cyber threats and the importance of following security protocols to safeguard industrial systems.

Healthcare IoT device breaches

Medical devices, such as pacemakers and insulin pumps, are hacked, potentially causing harm to patients. In 2019, vulnerabilities were found in certain insulin pumps. These vulnerabilities allow unauthorized wireless connections to the pump and alter its settings, leading to over- or under-delivery of insulin to diabetic patients (Klonoff and Han, 2019).

The exploited vulnerabilities include unencrypted wireless communication and insecure device interfaces. The primary vulnerability in the insulin pump case lay in the wireless communication protocol used by the pumps, which lacked proper authentication and encryption mechanisms. This weakness allowed unauthorized users to intercept and potentially manipulate the communication between the pump and its controlling devices.

The resulting impacts involve health risks to patients, loss of confidential medical data, and loss of trust in healthcare providers. If exploited, the vulnerability in the insulin pump leads to severe health implications for patients, including hypoglycemia or hyperglycemia, both of which can be life-threatening. The breach of such sensitive healthcare devices would further undermine public confidence in connected medical devices.

The advocated mitigation strategy considers encrypting device communications, securing interfaces, conducting routine security audits, and incorporating security by design in medical IoT devices. Some of the applied mitigation strategies in the insulin pump case included

- Secure communications: In response, the insulin pump manufacturer recommended that patients switch to models with more secure communication protocols and issued guidelines on maintaining the security of their devices.

- Routine security audits: Healthcare providers were urged to conduct frequent security checks on medical IoT devices to identify and address any emerging vulnerabilities.
- Security by design: The incident highlighted the critical need for embedding robust security features during the design and development phases of medical IoT devices, rather than relying on post-market patches and fixes.

8.7 Conclusion

The progress towards the cloud-to-things era brings with it a complex array of security challenges, which must be addressed with diligence. The incidents analyzed in this chapter, from the Mirai botnet attack to the Verkada camera hack, serve as stark reminders of the inherent vulnerabilities and the dire consequences of security oversights. Comprehensive security protocols, regular software and firmware maintenance, and adherence to regulatory standards cannot be overstated. Encryption, both of data in transit and at rest, are fundamental practices to secure IoT-cloud environments, ensuring that sensitive information remains protected against unauthorized access. OTA updates provide proactive management of IoT device security for timely patching vulnerabilities.

Moreover, the significance of regulatory compliance and alignment with security standards fosters a culture of trust and reliability. Throughout the digital transformation journey, security is not a hindrance but a catalyst, enabling organizations to unlock new horizons of innovation and efficiency, while ensuring the integrity and trustworthiness of their IoT-cloud infrastructure.

We have unveiled the evolving threat landscape that shadows IoT systems, emphasizing the need for robust security measures. We have described the attributes of threat modeling, offering a blueprint for identifying, assessing, and mitigating potential security threats in IoT systems. The chapter analyzed cyber attacks, clarifying their mechanisms and impacts, and showcased proactive mitigation strategies.

The presented case studies illustrate the resilience of IoT systems against cyber threats, drawing lessons from real-world scenarios, where security threats were not only confronted but ultimately overcome. They serve as testimonials to the reliability of cybersecurity strategies in safeguarding the digital transformation journey powered by IoT and cloud technologies.

References

Ahanger, T.A., Tariq, U., Dahan, F., Chaudhry, S.A., Malik, Y., 2023. Securing IoT devices running pureos from ransomware attacks: leveraging hybrid machine learning techniques. Mathematics 11 (11), 2481. https://doi.org/10.3390/math11112481.

Al Allaf, A., Totonji, W., 2023. In: Exploring IoT Security Threats and Forensic Challenges: A Literaturereview and Survey Study.

Almohri, H., Watson, L., Evans, D., Billups, S., 2022. Dynamic system diversification for securing cloud-based IoT subnetworks. ACM Transactions on Autonomous and Adaptive Systems 17 (1–2), 1–23. https://doi.org/10.1145/3547350.

Altayaran, S., Elmedany, W., 2021. Security threats of application programming interface (API's) in Internet of Things (IoT) communications. In: 4th Smart Cities Symposium (SCS 2021), vol. 2021. IET, pp. 552–557.

Barcena, M.B., Wueest, C., 2015. Insecurity in the Internet of Things. In: Security Response, Symantec, vol. 20.

Butun, I., Österberg, P., Song, H., 2019. Security of the Internet of Things: vulnerabilities, attacks, and countermeasures. IEEE Communications Surveys and Tutorials 22 (1), 616–644.

Bygdas, E., Jaatun, L.A., Antonsen, S.B., Ringen, A., Eiring, E., 2021. Evaluating threat modeling tools: Microsoft tmt versus owasp threat dragon. In: 2021 International Conference on Cyber Situational Awareness, Data Analytics and Assessment (CyberSA), pp. 1–7.

Campbell, K.R., 2017. Just how safe are medical devices? Protecting patients from cyber attacks. EP Lab Digest 17 (3).

Casola, V., De Benedictis, A., Rak, M., Villano, U., 2019. Toward the automation of threat modeling and risk assessment in IoT systems. Internet of Things 7, 100056.

Cecil, C., 2023. Cybersecurity of the Cloud and IoT Devices.

Di Pinto, A., Dragoni, Y., Carcano, A., 2018. Triton: the first ics cyber attack on safety instrument systems. In: Proc. Black Hat USA 2018, pp. 1–26.

Fantacci, R., Nizzi, F., Pecorella, T., Pierucci, L., Roveri, M., 2019. False data detection for fog and Internet of Things networks. Sensors 19 (19), 4235.

Fleishman, G., 2023. Take Control of Home Security Cameras. alt concepts.

Hesselman, C., Kaeo, M., Chapin, L., Claffy, K., Seiden, M., McPherson, D., Piscitello, D., McConachie, A., April, T., Latour, J., et al., 2020. The DNS in IoT: opportunities, risks, and challenges. IEEE Internet Computing 24 (4), 23–32.

Hu, W., Chang, C.-H., Sengupta, A., Bhunia, S., Kastner, R., Li, H., 2020. An overview of hardware security and trust: threats, countermeasures, and design tools. IEEE Transactions on Computer-Aided Design of Integrated Circuits and Systems 40 (6), 1010–1038.

Iftekhar, A., Cui, X., Hassan, M., Afzal, W., 2020. Application of blockchain and Internet of Things to ensure tamper-proof data availability for food safety. Journal of Food Quality 2020, 1–14.

Islam, M.J., Mahin, M., Khatun, A., Roy, S., Kabir, S., Debnath, B.C., 2019. A comprehensive data security and forensic investigation framework for cloud-IoT ecosystem. GUB Journal of Science and Engineering 4 (1), 1–12.

Jaramillo, L.E.S., 2018. Malware detection and mitigation techniques: lessons learned from mirai ddos attack. Journal of Information Systems Engineering & Management 3 (3), 19.

Javed, S.H., Ahmad, M.B., Asif, M., Almotiri, S.H., Masood, K., Ghamdi, M.A.A., 2022. An intelligent system to detect advanced persistent threats in industrial Internet of Things (I-IoT). Electronics 11 (5), 742.

Johnstone, M.N., 2010. Threat Modelling with Stride and Uml.

Jurcut, A.D., Ranaweera, P., Xu, L., 2020. Introduction to IoT security. In: IoT Security: Advances in Authentication, pp. 27–64.

Kai, S., Zheng, J., Shi, F., Lu, Z., 2021. A cvss-based vulnerability assessment method for reducing scoring error. In: 2021 2nd International Conference on Electronics, Communications and Information Technology (CECIT). IEEE, pp. 25–32.

Khan, S., Kabanov, I., Hua, Y., Madnick, S., 2022. A systematic analysis of the capital one data breach: critical lessons learned. ACM Transactions on Privacy and Security 26 (1), 1–29.

Kim, H., 2020. 5g core network security issues and attack classification from network protocol perspective. Journal of Internet Services and Information Security 10 (2), 1–15.
Klonoff, D., Han, J., 2019. The First Recall of a Diabetes Device Because of Cybersecurity Risks.
Kumar, R., Goyal, R., 2019. On cloud security requirements, threats, vulnerabilities and countermeasures: a survey. Computer Science Review 33, 1–48.
Lee, R., Assante, M., Conway, T., 2016. Analysis of the cyber attack on the Ukraine power grid. In: E-ISAC and SANS. TLP: White, Washington, DC.
Li, Y., Liu, Q., 2021. A comprehensive review study of cyber-attacks and cyber security: emerging trends and recent developments. Energy Reports 7, 8176–8186.
Lincoln, R., 2017. PyPower.
Liu, Y., Wang, Z., Li, N., 2018. Characterizing the impact of ddos attack on inter-domain routing system: a case study of the dyn cyberattack. In: 2018 International Conference on Computer Science, Electronics and Communication Engineering (CSECE 2018). Atlantis Press, pp. 79–82.
Mahak, M., Singh, Y., 2021. Threat modelling and risk assessment in Internet of Things: a review. In: Proceedings of Second International Conference on Computing, Communications, and Cyber-Security: IC4S 2020. Springer, pp. 293–305.
Mao, X., Ekstedt, M., Ling, E., Ringdahl, E., Lagerström, R., 2019. Conceptual abstraction of attack graphs-a use case of securiCAD. In: Graphical Models for Security: 6th International Workshop. GraMSec 2019, Hoboken, NJ, USA, June 24, 2019. In: Revised Papers 6. Springer, pp. 186–202.
Meggitt, S., 2018. Medjack Attacks: The Scariest Part of the Hospital.
Mehmood, M.S., Shahid, M.R., Jamil, A., Ashraf, R., Mahmood, T., Mehmood, A., 2019. A comprehensive literature review of data encryption techniques in cloud computing and IoT environment. In: 2019 8th International Conference on Information and Communication Technologies (ICICT). IEEE, pp. 54–59.
Potter, B., 2009. Microsoft sdl threat modelling tool. Network Security 2009 (1), 15–18.
Rana, M., Mamun, Q., Islam, R., 2023. Enhancing IoT security: an innovative key management system for lightweight block ciphers. Sensors 23 (18), 7678.
Seri, B., Vishnepolsky, G., Zusman, D., 2019. Critical vulnerabilities to remotely compromise vxworks, the most popular rtos. White Paper, ARMIS, URGENT/11.
Shi, Z., Graffi, K., Starobinski, D., Matyunin, N., 2021. Threat modeling tools: a taxonomy. IEEE Security & Privacy 20 (4), 29–39.
Steffens, T., 2020. Advanced persistent threats. In: Attribution of Advanced Persistent Threats: How to Identify the Actors Behind Cyber-Espionage. Springer, pp. 3–21.
Tariq, N., Khan, F.A., Asim, M., 2021. Security challenges and requirements for smart Internet of Things applications: a comprehensive analysis. Procedia Computer Science 191, 425–430.
Verheyden, L., 2018. Effectiveness of threat modelling tools. PhD thesis, Master thesis.
Walkowski, M., Oko, J., Sujecki, S., 2021. Vulnerability management models using a common vulnerability scoring system. Applied Sciences 11 (18), 8735.
Yadav, G., Allakany, A., Kumar, V., Paul, K., Okamura, K., 2019. Penetration testing framework for IoT. In: 2019 8th International Congress on Advanced Applied Informatics (IIAI-AAI). IEEE, pp. 477–482.
Zhang, X., Upton, O., Beebe, N.L., Choo, K.-K.R., 2020. IoT botnet forensics: a comprehensive digital forensic case study on Mirai Botnet servers. Forensic Science International: Digital Investigation 32, 300926.

CHAPTER 9

Discovering and analyzing IoT-cloud vulnerabilities

9.1 Introduction

The digital transformation shaped by the integration of IoT and cloud computing leverages vast amounts of data generated by IoT devices, which are further processed by the cloud's scalable computational capabilities. By harnessing this synergy, businesses are unlocking unprecedented levels of efficiency, innovation drivers, and smarter operational models. However, vulnerabilities within either the IoT or cloud component of this ecosystem can significantly threaten the success of digital transformation initiatives.

Security violations have demonstrated their potential to cause considerable setbacks in innovation and the adoption of the cloud-to-things approach for digital transformation. Incidents where IoT devices have been hijacked for large-scale DDoS attacks have raised serious concerns about the security of these devices (Ekwo, 2021). In the cloud domain, unauthorized access to sensitive information stored on cloud servers raised data breach concerns, which justified the need for robust security protocols and practices (Van Houten, 2020; Prasanna Balasooriya et al., 2017).

Thus vulnerabilities in this interconnected environment can significantly hinder the progress of digitalization, posing threats not only to operational efficiency but also to the innovative potential of IoT and cloud integrations. Data breaches or system compromises can lead to substantial disruptions, eroding confidence in these transformative technologies. A comprehensive vulnerability analysis involves a process to systematically identify, evaluate, and address potential security weaknesses that can compromise data integrity and undermine user trust. By proactively analyzing vulnerabilities, organizations can safeguard critical data and sustain trust in the successful adoption and growth of cloud-to-things continuum technologies, which pave the way towards a transformative digital endeavor.

The process that entails a comprehensive examination of the entire IoT-cloud framework pinpoints and evaluates potential weaknesses that could be exploited by cyber threats. A methodical approach to this process is discussed in this chapter to derive proactive cybersecurity measures that transform security from a reactive task to a strategic, integrated component of the cloud-to-things framework. Additionally, prioritizing vulnerabilities to be analyzed adjusts security budgets and efforts to focus on most pressing security measures. Thus the scoring mechanism used to streamline vulnerabilities along standard scales is revealed in this chapter.

Accelerating Digital Transformation with the Cloud and the Internet of Things (IoT)
https://doi.org/10.1016/B978-0-44-322217-7.00016-5

The subsequent sections of this chapter are designed to guide readers through the intricate process of identifying, assessing, and managing vulnerabilities. We will explore a range of topics, from the lifecycle of vulnerabilities in IoT-cloud environments to real-world case studies, which illustrate the consequences of security oversights and the effectiveness of mitigation strategies. Cutting-edge tools used to streamline vulnerability analysis and management are also discussed.

9.2 Understanding IoT-cloud vulnerabilities

IoT-cloud environments are particularly prone to security challenges and their vulnerabilities differ from those found in traditional IT settings. Next, we explain further these challenges and nuances.

9.2.1 IoT-cloud vulnerability challenges and specific risks

The unique vulnerabilities inherent in IoT-cloud environments make them particularly susceptible to security threats. As shown in Table 9.1, the key points include the complex interconnectivity nature of the IoT-cloud ecosystem, the diversity of IoT devices and their computational constraints, as well as other data and software aspects; the latter are further explained next.

The complex interconnectivity challenge in IoT cloud environments exposes a wide range of vulnerabilities from interconnecting devices, systems, and cloud services. This intricate web of connections increases the attack surface, providing more opportunities for malicious actors to exploit vulnerabilities. Specific attack vector scenarios can seize these vulnerabilities, as illustrated in Table 9.1.

Consider a scenario where attackers identify a poorly secured IoT device within a network, such as an unsecured smart thermostat. They use this device as an entry point to access the broader network, moving laterally to more sensitive data stores or control systems in the cloud. In another scenario of IoT-cloud-related vulnerability challenges illustrated in Table 9.1, consider a network that consists of various IoT devices from different manufacturers, each with its own security protocols. More opportunities are present for an attacker to target devices with known vulnerabilities, such as older models of smart cameras, to infiltrate the network. The diverse plethora of IoT devices allow attackers to find and exploit the weakest link in the IoT ecosystem.

Further, Table 9.1 raises the typical IoT-cloud vulnerability issue whereby several IoT sensors in an industrial setting have limited processing power and cannot support advanced encryption. An attacker who intercepts the data transmission can gain access to sensitive operational data. In doing so, the hypothetical attacker capitalizes on the devices' ineffective encryption, leading to information disclosure and potential operational manipulation. Moving up through the network of the cloud-to-things continuum, Table 9.1 illustrates the vulnerability category, where a cloud storage service used by IoT devices contains a vast amount of personal user data. When an attacker

Table 9.1 Vulnerabilities inherent in IoT-cloud environments.

Vulnerability category	Scenario	Attack vector
Interconnectivity exploits	An attacker identifies a poorly secured IoT device within a network.	The attacker exploits the interconnected nature of devices and systems, using one vulnerable point to compromise the entire network.
Device diversity	There exists various IoT devices from different manufacturers, each with its security protocols.	The attacker leverages the lack of uniform security standards across diverse devices to find and exploit the weakest link in the cloud-to-things continuum.
Computational constraints	IoT sensors have limited processing power, and cannot support advanced encryption.	The attacker takes advantage of poor encryption to gain access to sensitive operational data.
Data services	An attacker hacks a cloud data service through a security flaw, leading to a significant data leak.	The attacker emphasizes the cloud component of the Cloud IoT ecosystem, where valuable data are stored.
Remote accessibility	An IoT-based home security system allows remote access	The attacker takes advantage of weak authentication protocols, to operate IoT device functionality for malicious purposes.
Firmware updates	IoT devices receive irregular firmware updates, leaving gaps of unpatched operating system vulnerabilities.	The attacker uses known software vulnerabilities, which are unaddressed due to inconsistent update mechanisms, to hijack IoT devices.
Legacy integration	An older building management system is integrated with new IoT-based monitoring devices, where the legacy system lacks modern security features.	Attackers exploit gaps that arise from integrating advanced IoT devices with outdated legacy systems, to disrupt building operations.

breaches into the cloud service through a security flaw, a significant data leak occurs. In doing so, the attacker focuses on the cloud service component of the IoT ecosystem, where large volumes of valuable data are stored to maximize harmful impacts.

To illustrate an instance of remote accessibility vulnerabilities category compiled in Table 9.1, consider an IoT-based home security system that allows remote access for convenience purposes. However, due to weak authentication protocols, an unauthorized user gains access and disables the security alarms. This attack instance takes advantage of weak remote access security, manipulating IoT device functionality for malicious purposes. Similarly an instance of firmware and software vulnerabilities may relate to an IoT device that receives irregular firmware updates, and a known vulnerability in its operating system remains unpatched. The attacker uses known software vulnerabilities, which are unaddressed due to inconsistent update mechanisms, to hijack IoT devices.

9.2.2 Vulnerability lifecycle

The vulnerability lifecycle is a concept in cybersecurity that tracks the evolution of a security vulnerability from its inception to resolution (Dumitraş, 2015). Understanding this lifecycle is essential for managing risk effectively within any technological ecosystem, especially one as dynamic and complex as IoT-cloud environments. This lifecycle underscores the evolving nature of risk in the IoT-cloud environment, as illustrated in Fig. 9.1.

At the outset, a vulnerability is created, often inadvertently, during the development or deployment phase of an IoT-cloud system. This stage is characterized by the vulnerability's obscurity, since it remains unknown to stakeholders and potential attackers. As such, its risk is unmeasurable.

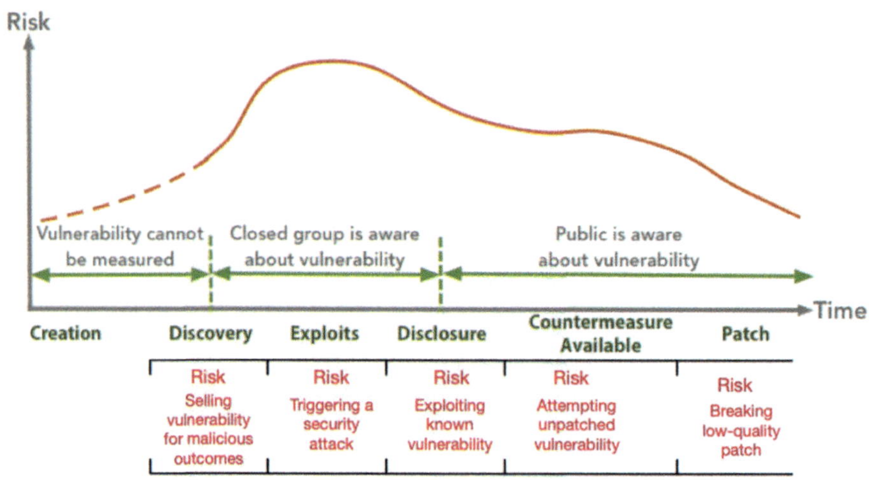

FIGURE 9.1

Vulnerability lifecycle.

Discovery stage of the vulnerability timeline marks a pivotal turn in the lifecycle. The vulnerability is identified either by internal security teams conducting audits or by external entities potentially with malicious intentions. Once discovered, the knowledge of the vulnerability might initially circulate within a limited group, but the associated risk begins to increase and the information about the vulnerability may be sold to circles with malicious agendas.

The exploitation phase is where the risk reaches its highest level, as attackers actively leverage the vulnerability to compromise the components associated with the cloud-to-things continuum systems. This period is the most dangerous, as the vulnerability is exposed and potentially manipulated to breach into the continuum, leading to exfiltrating sensitive data, or disrupting the IoT-cloud services.

Following the initial awareness about vulnerability, its disclosure to the public initiates its decline in risk. As awareness proliferates to the public, the development of countermeasures is prompted leading to the development of temporary fixes or security practices to mitigate the vulnerability.

When countermeasures are made available, they offer a buffer against the vulnerability, further diminishing the risk, as organizations begin to implement these protective measures. As indicated in Fig. 9.1, the final stage of the vulnerability lifecycle is the release and application of a formal patch, aimed at mitigating the vulnerability for significantly reducing the associated risk. Yet, not all systems are patched promptly, leaving some elements of the infrastructure vulnerable, which highlights the importance of rapid and widespread patch deployment to minimize the window of opportunity for attackers.

9.2.3 Common types of vulnerabilities

Understanding the various types of vulnerabilities that can afflict IoT-cloud ecosystems is key for establishing robust security measures. Common types of vulnerabilities can be broadly categorized into software flaws, hardware limitations, and network vulnerabilities. Each category has unique challenges and specific potential entry points for attackers, leading to tailored mitigation requirements. Next, we discuss these common vulnerability types; they are supported by real-world case studies to illustrate the incurred risks and the efficiency of responsive countermeasures.

Software flaws

Software vulnerabilities are often due to mistakes in coding or oversights in design. The scale of these weaknesses ranges from minor glitches to significant security breaches, which cybercriminals can exploit. The Heartbleed bug is a software vulnerability example that affected the OpenSSL cryptography library, which is extensively used for securing Internet communications (Carvalho et al., 2014). Uncovered back in 2014, Heartbleed enabled attackers to access the memory of servers utilizing versions of OpenSSL potentially exposing sensitive information. Addressing software flaws in IoT devices and cloud systems is a multi-layered task, which involves a variety of strategies and tools.

Countermeasure strategies

Organizations need to implement robust countermeasure strategies to address and mitigate software flaws. These strategies ensure the integrity and reliability of both devices and data in the cloud-to-things continuum. They range from proactive measures, such as secure coding practices to reactive solutions, for example, timely patch management, all aimed at fortifying the software against potential breaches. These strategic layers are complemented by a suite of analytical tools that continuously monitor, detect, and resolve vulnerabilities.

- **Secure coding:** Implement secure coding guidelines to prevent vulnerabilities at the source. Organizations, such as OWASP, provide comprehensive resources to adopt secure code writing practices (Lala et al., 2021; Sane, 2020).
- **Software updates and patch management:** Up-to-date software ensures that the latest patches are applied. There exist automated patch management tools to help with timely updates. For example WSUS (Windows Server Update Services) which is a Microsoft product that allows administrators to manage in a corporate environment, the distribution of updates released through Microsoft update to computers (Henderson, 2018). Automox is a cloud-native platform that is relatively new on the market compared to traditional patch management solutions. This cloud-based patch management platform automates the patching process for Windows, macOS, and Linux systems, also third-party software (Ebbers, 2022).
- **Vulnerability scanners:** These automated tools are used to regularly scan the infrastructure for known vulnerabilities. These static application security testing (SAST) tools can analyze source code for potential security flaws without executing the program. The OWASP-SANS is a collaborative reference document, which outlines some of the most effective security controls to mitigate the risk from common cybersecurity threats. The list is a result of collaboration between the SANS Institute, a research and education organization, and the OWASP Project (Li, 2020).
- **Penetration testing:** This practice can identify runtime vulnerabilities and simulate attacks to test defenses (Johari et al., 2020). One of the most widely used penetration testing framework is Metasploit, which helps security teams identify and validate vulnerabilities, develop and execute exploit code, and simulate attacks. This tool assesses system vulnerabilities at runtime against a vast database of known vulnerabilities (Kennedy et al., 2011). Mirage is a Metasploit-like penetration testing framework specifically designed for IoT (Cayre et al., 2019).

Hardware limitations

There are inherent weaknesses and constraints that are often found in IoT devices, and they contribute to the overall vulnerability of IoT cloud ecosystems. Unlike traditional computing hardware, many IoT devices are designed with minimalistic principles for cost-effectiveness, energy-efficiency, and space-saving. Processing power, memory, and storage are inherently limited, which expose IoT devices to security threats, ranging from physical tampering to remote exploitation.

- **Processing power:** Many IoT devices are equipped with low-power processors to conserve energy, which restricts the complexity of security algorithms that can run advanced encryptions schemes or comprehensive antivirus software on these devices. A study of smart home devices revealed that some devices could not support advanced encryption protocols due to their limited processing capabilities, leaving communications vulnerable to eavesdropping (Kim and Suh, 2021).

- **Memory and storage:** IoT devices may not have the capacity to store extensive security logs or update patches, making them vulnerable to attacks that exploit outdated software or firmware. For example, security cameras with insufficient storage that use outdated firmware versions can be exploited to run botnets for launching DDoS attacks (Bobrovnikova et al., 2022).
- **Physical security:** IoT devices are often deployed in easily accessible or remote locations, making them vulnerable to physical tampering or substitution with compromised devices. As an illustration, consider an industrial setting, where an attacker physically accesses a sensor node and replaces it with a compromised device that sent false data to the central monitoring system.

Network vulnerabilities

Network vulnerabilities emerge from weaknesses in communication protocols or network configurations, which can be exploited to intercept or reroute data. KRACK (key reinstallation attacks) vulnerability, which was discovered in 2017, affected the WPA2 protocol, which is used to secure Wi-Fi networks. KRACK allowed attackers to eavesdrop on Wi-Fi traffic and to inject ransomware into websites (Alhamry and Elmedany, 2022). Certain communication protocols used in IoT, such as MQTT, CoAP, might lack built-in security features. Being lightweight and not having encryption by default, they have been exploited for eavesdropping or injection of malicious payloads (Shapsough et al., 2018).

Network vulnerabilities in IoT ecosystems present significant risks that extend far beyond individual devices. These vulnerabilities can lead to widespread consequences, impacting entire IoT-cloud systems, often with severe repercussions. They can cascade within an IoT ecosystem, whereby a single compromised device can act as a gateway for broader network exploitation. With initial access, attackers can exploit further vulnerabilities to gain higher privileges. This escalation can allow them to access more critical systems or sensitive data, increasing the severity of the breach. A malware can spread across compromised IoT devices through the entire network (Aman et al., 2021).

- **Strong encryption:** Data in transit protection makes use of encryption protocols, which includes transport layer security (or TLS) and secure sockets layer (or SSL). All exchanged data between IoT devices and cloud servers is encrypted to prevent interception and unauthorized access. Encryption algorithms are expected to be regularly updated to counter emerging decryption techniques.
- **Authentication mechanisms:** Robust authentication protocols protect device-to-device and device-to-cloud communications. This involves a multi-factor authentication (MFA), wherever feasible, to add a layer of security that goes beyond traditional password protection. Regular management and updating of credentials are important practices, particularly in replacing default passwords with strong,

unique alternatives. These practices ensure that access to devices and cloud services is tightly controlled and resistant to unauthorized intrusion.

- **Network segmentation:** Adopting a segmented network approach consists of dividing the network into smaller, isolated segments, whereby the risk of widespread breaches is significantly reduced. This strategy involves ensuring that IoT devices operate within their own dedicated network segment, distinct from critical business systems. Such segregation enhances security and helps in containing any potential breaches within a limited scope. Additionally, strict access controls should be enforced between different network segments. These controls act as barriers, limiting the ability of potential attackers to move laterally within the network.
- **Intrusion detection:** Advanced network monitoring tools detect unusual network activities, which may indicate potential breaches. Intrusion detection systems (IDS) are tailored to identify specifically IoT network threats (Elrawy et al., 2018). Additionally, regular analyses of network logs help in early identification of security incidents, enabling prompt and effective responses to potential threats (Cheng et al., 2019).

9.3 Discovering vulnerabilities

The methodologies and tools for discovering vulnerabilities within IoT and cloud systems are contrasted between automated and manual alternatives, each with unique advantages and limitations. Techniques specifically tailored for vulnerability scanning in these complex environments are effective to discover relevant vulnerability patterns. Next we explain these methodologies and tools, and then emphasize the critical role of testbeds in unearthing hidden vulnerabilities, demonstrating their importance through practical examples and case studies.

9.3.1 Vulnerability discovery methods

Whereas automated methods leverage sophisticated software tools for scanning and identifying vulnerabilities, manual methods involve hands-on analysis by cybersecurity experts.

Automated discovery methods

Automated tools, such as vulnerability scanners, can quickly scan large networks and systems, covering more ground than manual methods. They are particularly efficient for routine checks and in environments with a vast number of IoT devices and cloud services. Automated scans ensure consistent and regular monitoring of systems, which is particularly useful in dynamic environments, where new vulnerabilities can rapidly emerge. However, although automated vulnerability discovery tools are excellent for identifying known vulnerabilities, they may not always effectively uncover complex, multi-step attack scenarios or zero-day vulnerabilities that require human expert perspective methods.

Manual discovery methods

Manual methods offer deeper insights into specific vulnerabilities. Experienced cybersecurity professionals can interpret and contextualize findings, giving rise to understanding the intricate implications of each vulnerability. Manual testing can be tailored to unique system architectures, especially where specific IoT configurations or custom cloud setups are in place. Besides, human experts can adapt and change their approach in real-time during the discovery process, something that automated tools can't replicate.

Combined discovery methods

An optimal approach involves a combination of both methods. Automated tools can quickly identify known vulnerabilities and provide a baseline security posture, whereas manual methods can involve the deeper view of an expert into critical or complex areas. In fast-paced environments with frequent updates, such as cloud-based services, automated tools are essential for keeping pace with changes. However, for critical components, particularly in industrial IoT or areas with high data sensitivity, manual testing is indispensable for a comprehensive security coverage. Automated methods are ideal for continuous monitoring throughout the lifecycle of IoT and cloud systems. Manual methods, on the other hand, are instrumental during the development phase, major updates, or post-incident analyses to provide detailed perceptions and expert recommendations.

9.3.2 Tools for discovering vulnerabilities in IoT and cloud systems

There is a spectrum of tools designed for discovering vulnerabilities in IoT and cloud systems, each equipped with distinct features tailored for the intricacies of the cloud-to-things continuum.

- **Nessus**: This is a widely-used tool, which specializes in scanning for vulnerabilities, offering a comprehensive database of known security weaknesses (Rogers, 2011). Nessus is known for its fast scanning process and low false positive rate, which helps to save time and reduces the number of false alarms. Nessus has the deepest and broadest vulnerability coverage in the industry, ensuring that a wide range of vulnerabilities are detected. Nessus provides a scripting language to extend tests into user-defined contexts. The Nessus team updates the list of vulnerabilities to check for daily, ensuring that users can detect new vulnerabilities as they emerge. When Nessus detects a vulnerability, it can often suggest appropriate remediation steps.
- **Qualys**: This tool provides cloud-based vulnerability management, delivering continuous monitoring and comprehensive reporting (Moncy, 2023). It has the ability to integrate with various cloud services, making it particularly suitable for cloud-to-things environments, which may use it as a monitoring service. Qualys' continuous security platform enables detection, identification, and classification of vulnerable systems and applications.

- **OpenVAS**: This is an open-source alternative that offers a broad range of tests, constantly updated from community contributions. It is well-suited for scanning both IoT devices and cloud infrastructures, but known to be a resource-intensive tool that consumes substantial memory and CPU (Rahalkar and Rahalkar, 2019). OpenVAS supports both unauthenticated and authenticated testing. Unauthenticated testing checks the target systems, including IoT devices or cloud services, without any special access privileges. This test simulates an external attacker exploiting vulnerabilities that have been exposed on the Internet, without requiring any credentials to log into the system. These vulnerabilities may be as open ports or outdated software versions.
  Authenticated testing involves scanning the target system with authorized credentials. This means the scanner logs into the system as a legitimate user allowing to simulate an insider attack or an external attacker who has gained access credentials. This test helps in identifying vulnerabilities that are not visible to unauthenticated scans, such as misconfigurations, which could be exploited by someone who has bypassed the initial layers of security. This is like having the key to the house and checking internal security measures, which provides a broader range of vulnerabilities, including internal application bugs and issues with user permissions.
- Shodan: This tool locates and provides information about devices connected to the Internet, including potentially vulnerable IoT devices. By discovering devices that are publicly accessible and potentially vulnerable to attacks, Shodan uses related metadata to understand the distribution of devices globally, identifying security loopholes, and mitigating potential risks (Albataineh and Alsmadi, 2019).
- IoTSeeker: This tool is specifically designed for IoT devices, scanning for weak passwords and known vulnerabilities common in these devices. Unsecured IoT devices can be scanned, and even logins using default usernames and passwords can be attempted for penetration testing (Chu and Lisitsa, 2018). By finding these devices, administrators can take steps to secure them. However, though intended for use by security professionals to improve network security, tools such as IoT Seeker (and Shodan) can also, theoretically, be used by malicious actors to identify vulnerable devices.

9.3.3 The role of testbeds in discovering vulnerabilities

Testbeds simulate real-world IoT and cloud infrastructure environments, providing a safe platform to conduct rigorous testing without risking actual systems or data. By mimicing actual operational conditions of IoT and cloud systems, software and network configuration scenarios that closely resemble their intended use are investigated. This process identifies dependencies found in real IoT and cloud ecosystems, which facilitate the discovery of vulnerabilities that might only emerge under specific conditions or through complex interactions between various system components.

Testbeds provide a secure environment, where potentially destructive experiments can be conducted without the risk of impacting actual operations. This is particularly useful when checking for weaknesses that could result in consequences such as security breaches or system malfunctions. Beyond just discovering vulnerabilities, testbeds are instrumental in validating the effectiveness of countermeasures. By simulating attacks and breaches, organizations can evaluate the resilience of their systems and refine their defense strategies accordingly.

- **IoT-LAB (France):** This large-scale IoT testbed located in France can be used by researchers and companies to test and experiment with IoT technologies. The testbed consists of 2728 wireless sensor nodes spread across 6 different sites in France (Fambon et al., 2014). The nodes use various IoT hardware and wireless technologies, such as ZigBee and 6LoWPAN. Access, control, and programming IoT nodes remotely is provided to conduct experiments at scale on things such as wireless protocols, distributed algorithms, and security. IoT-LAB provides tools and services to inject faults to experiment vulnerability hacks. Registration is open for any researcher/academic associated with a university, research institute, or public organization. Commercial entities can also gain access through research collaborations.
- **IoT@Cork (Ireland):** This testbed is developed by the Tyndall National Institute and offers a real-world environment for the deployment and evaluation of IoT technologies, focusing on applications such as agriculture, maritime, and smart buildings. Researchers can access the IoT nodes remotely and try to hack into them to test the robustness of their security protections (O'Grady et al., 2012). They can manipulate the sensor data being transmitted to evaluate vulnerabilities, for example, eavesdropping, spoofing, and alteration of sensor readings.
- **MONICA (EU):** This testbed conducts large-scale pilot demonstrations to showcase the potential of IoT technologies in various applications, such as smart cities, healthcare, and industrial automation. MONICA provides an open-access platform for researchers, developers, and organizations to test and develop IoT solutions in real-world environments (Guillén et al., 2022). Monica enables the use of a range of IoT devices and sensors in real-life situations, allowing researchers to observe how these devices function in different scenarios, including identifying possible security vulnerabilities.

9.4 Analysis and classification of vulnerabilities

9.4.1 Methods for analyzing the identified vulnerabilities

Vulnerability analysis can involve static or dynamic processes. Static analysis involves examining the codebase of IoT applications and cloud services without executing them. This process, often automated, scans the source code, binaries, or byte code to identify security flaws, coding errors, and vulnerabilities. This code review for IoT applications is essential for reviewing the security of IoT device firmware and applications. Vulnerabilities such as buffer overflows, SQL injection, or insecure library use before deployment can be identified.

Dynamic analysis involves testing and evaluating the software in a runtime environment. This method detects vulnerabilities that become apparent only during the execution of the application. Testing IoT devices in real-world scenarios is thus enabled to monitor their behavior under various conditions, and hence identify runtime vulnerabilities. IoT devices interaction with cloud services are tested to ensure that APIs and service endpoints handle data securely and respond correctly to unexpected inputs or conditions.

Another vulnerability testing method involves penetration testing, which is a simulated cyber attack to check for exploitable vulnerabilities. In the context of IoT and cloud computing, this examination encompasses both the physical evaluation of IoT devices and the virtual assessment of cloud services. Analyzing the impact of cyber attacks on devices involves examining how these devices react to such attacks. The goal is to identify any vulnerabilities in their firmware and network interfaces. Evaluating the strength of cloud infrastructure against attacks is determined through cloud service penetration. This evaluation includes conducting tests to identify weaknesses in web applications, databases, and server configurations.

9.4.2 Classifying vulnerabilities

Classifying vulnerabilities is essential for prioritizing security efforts and budgets. Given the extensive range of potential vulnerabilities in IoT cloud environments, identifying which vulnerabilities pose the greatest risk is paramount. The potential impact of each vulnerability is assessed to help understand which vulnerabilities could lead to severe data breaches, service disruptions, or even physical harm in IoT deployments. By classifying vulnerabilities, organizations can allocate their resources more efficiently. High-risk vulnerabilities require immediate attention and resources, whereas lower-risk issues might be scheduled for later remediation.

Prioritizing high-risk vulnerabilities ensures that the most critical issues are addressed first, optimizing the use of limited security resources and reducing the overall cost of security management. This proactive approach to security helps in identifying potential threats before they are exploited, reducing the likelihood of successful cyber attacks. Classification allows for clearer reporting to stakeholders, including management and regulatory bodies, about the security posture and the actions taken to mitigate risks.

Assessing vulnerabilities: severity-based exploitability and impact

Vulnerabilities are typically classified according to their level of severity. This classification uses the consequences and likelihood of exploitation metrics of the vulnerability. An approach to measure these severity metrics of vulnerabilities instruments CVSS (the common vulnerability scoring system). This method involves categorizing vulnerabilities based on their severity scores reflecting software flaws, hardware limitations, or network vulnerabilities.

Machine learning algorithms can be trained to recognize patterns and anomalies, which may indicate vulnerabilities. By analyzing vast datasets of network traffic, system logs, and past vulnerabilities, these algorithms can identify potential new threats. Advanced machine learning models have been instrumented to predict the likelihood of vulnerability exploitation (Hulayyil et al., 2023). Historical data are assessed to forecast vulnerabilities that are likely to be exploited.

Standard security repositories

Common vulnerabilities and exposures (CVE) system

The Common vulnerabilities and exposures (CVE) system provides standardized identification of known vulnerabilities. This system allows an effective communication and management of vulnerabilities. CVE assigns unique identifiers, known as CVE IDs, to each publicly known cybersecurity vulnerability. Each CVE ID follows a standard format to allow security professionals referencing specific vulnerabilities (Blinowski and Piotrowski, 2020). CVE identifiers are frequently utilized alongside security databases, such as the National Vulnerability Database (NVD), to augment the range of information available on vulnerabilities. This correlation allows for a comprehensive assessment of vulnerabilities by providing severity scores (CVSS) and impact evaluations.

National Vulnerability Database (NVD)

The NVD is the U.S. government's repository of standards-based vulnerability management data and is directly synchronized with CVE. It enhances the information in CVE entries with additional analysis, impact scores (using the common vulnerability scoring system, CVSS), and links to detailed vulnerability reports and mitigation advice. NVD can be used alongside CVE to understand the severity and potential impact of vulnerabilities in software components, including IoT device software (Nerwich et al., 2020).

Common platform enumeration (CPE)

CPE is a structured naming scheme for information technology systems, software, and packages. This repository is closely integrated with CVE and NVD and provides a standardized method for identifying and matching software components to known vulnerabilities. Correlating CPE identifiers with CVE entries allows for more precise identification of vulnerable software components (Cheikes et al., 2011).

Software assurance reference dataset (SARD)

Managed by NIST, SARD provides a comprehensive set of software test cases, including those that contain known vulnerabilities. This can be correlated with CVE data to evaluate the effectiveness of software testing tools in detecting vulnerabilities. The primary purpose of SARD is identifying vulnerabilities using a comprehensive set of test cases. A wide range of test cases across various programming languages are included in this security data repository. Vulnerability types and their location in codes are provided along other detailed information (Al-Boghdady et al., 2022).

Open Web Application Security Project (OWASP)

The Open Web Application Security Project (OWASP) is a data repository dedicated to web application security, and providing resources, tools, and community-driven projects aimed at identifying, understanding, and mitigating common vulnerabilities. Perhaps the most well-known contribution of OWASP is the "OWASP Top Ten," a regularly updated report outlining the top ten most critical web application security risks (Miessler, 2015). This ranking lists risks and related examples of vulnerabilities, in addition to practical recommendations for mitigation. Developers are offered a benchmark to guide them in prioritizing security efforts and raising awareness about prevalent web security issues.

9.5 IoT-cloud vulnerability management

A comprehensive approach to managing vulnerabilities within IoT and cloud ecosystems is illustrated in Fig. 9.2, which shows a hierarchical model for understanding and managing vulnerabilities.

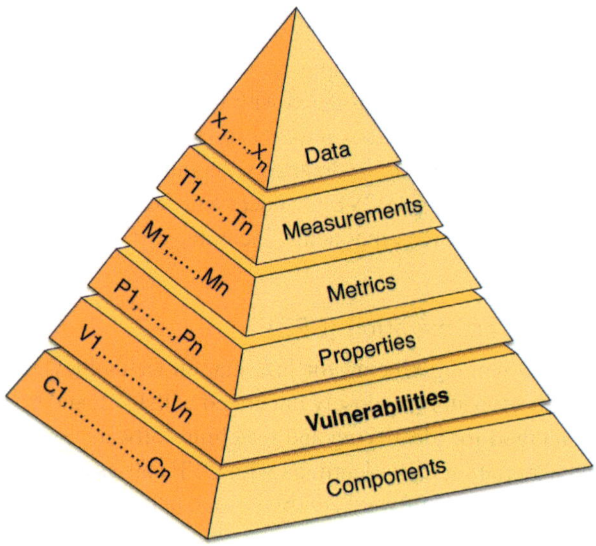

FIGURE 9.2

Vulnerability data management.

At the base of the pyramid are the foundational components of IoT and cloud systems, such as devices, applications, and networks. The "Vulnerabilities" layer represents component weaknesses that could potentially be exploited by attackers. Each vulnerability has standard "Properties" used to refers to the specific characteristics of this vulnerability. Ease of exploitation property, the impact of an exploit, and the conditions under which a vulnerability can be exploited are instrumental for assessing the severity score of each vulnerability, such as CVSS scoring mechanism. The "Metrics" layer combines these properties of vulnerabilities to infer a level of severity and prioritize them accordingly. Finally, "Measurements" performed at the top of pyramid along these metrics use actionable "Data," such as versions- and vendor-related data and other sources of information collected from security alert repositories.

9.5.1 Strategies for managing vulnerabilities in IoT cloud environments

A systematic approach to managing vulnerabilities within the cloud-to-things continuum is illustrated in Fig. 9.3. The process is a cycle that involves several key steps to maintain a robust security posture in dynamic and complex IoT cloud environments.

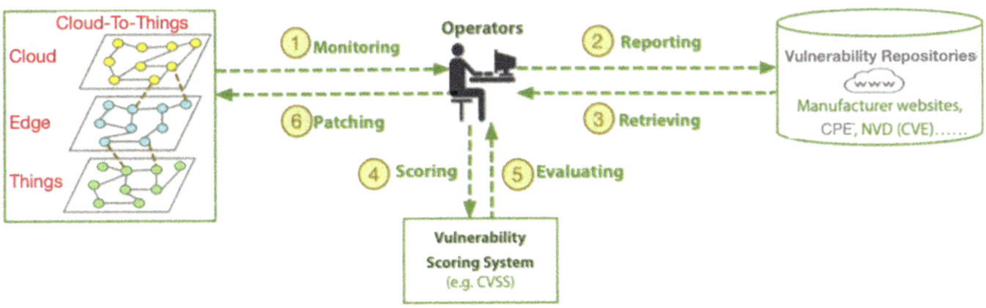

FIGURE 9.3

Vulnerability management operations.

A continuous surveillance is part of the monitoring step to detect any anomalies or signs of potential vulnerabilities. Real-time monitoring of devices, network traffic, and system logs across the cloud, edge, and IoT layers is part of this surveillance operation. Automated systems assist security operators by generating alerts of unusual activity, which may indicate a vulnerability. Following an alert of a potential issue, the relevant data is retrieved from vulnerability repositories, such as NVD or CVE, as well as manufacturer websites.

The identified vulnerabilities are then scored using a vulnerability scoring system, such as CVSS, to assesses the severity of the vulnerabilities based on various factors, including their impact and the ease with which they can be exploited. Security operators rank the scored vulnerabilities, taking into account the specific context of their IoT-cloud environment. This evaluation determines the urgency and the necessary response to each vulnerability. The final step in the vulnerability management process is remediation, which often takes the form of patching. This process involves deploying fixes to the identified vulnerabilities to secure the systems against potential exploitation.

9.5.2 Patch management and regular updates

As part of the systematic vulnerability management, the process of identifying, acquiring, testing, and installing updates on the components of the IoT infrastructure corrects vulnerabilities and improves security. The lifecycle of patch management is a continuous process that includes several key stages.

Identification of patches

The initial stage involves identifying available patches for all the software and hardware components within the IoT-cloud ecosystem. This is typically facilitated by automated vulnerability scanning tools that alert administrators to available updates for their systems.

Patch acquisition

After identifying a patch, it is downloaded from the website of the software vendor or developer ensuring its authenticity and integrity.

Patch testing

Before widespread deployment, patches should be tested in a controlled environment. This step verifies that the patch does not introduce new issues or incompatibilities with existing system functionalities.

Deployment scheduling

Deployment of patches should be planned to minimize impact on operations. This includes scheduling updates during off-peak hours or in stages to avoid downtime in critical systems.

Automated patch management tools help organizations streamline the process of updating systems with the latest security patches. For example, Microsoft WSUS and SCCM (system center configuration manager) provide comprehensive management solutions, including patch deployment, inventory, and compliance reporting. Red Hat Satellite is a patch management tool designed for managing Linux Red Hat systems with automated updates and configuration. Automox is a cloud-based patch management solution used to automate the patching process on any OS, given any endpoint, and in any location (Ebbers, 2022).

9.5.3 Data-driven vulnerability management

Unleashing data from physical environments enhances operational and decision-making solutions, but weaknesses in how data is collected, transmitted, stored, and processed within IoT-cloud environments do arise, leading to security gaps or vulnerabilities. Examples include insecure communication channels induced by weak encryption of data in transit.

Analyzing access logs, user actions, and data movement trends, through data analytics methods, such as machine learning, can help pinpointing data usage irregularities, highlighting suspicious behaviors that require deeper risk analysis. However, immense volumes of data are generated in IoT-cloud environments, and they are continuously growing. Security operation centers (SOCs), which are at the forefront of analyzing this data, can quickly run through several gigabytes of security events per day, which include logs from network traffic, user activities, device communications, and application performance metrics.

The challenge is exacerbated by the need to analyze and uncover weaknesses across this vast amount of data in a timely manner. Traditional methods of assessing vulnerabilities typically follow a schedule for analysis, such as monthly checks. However sticking to this routine can lead to delays between the vulnerability occurrence, its discovery, and the implementation of necessary patches. IoT-cloud dynamic environments require timely data analytics. Automating security analytics via advanced machine learning techniques allows a continuous monitoring and prompt response to security events.

Machine-learning-based security analytics

There is an increasing consensus among cybersecurity experts that machine learning (ML) techniques can support a continuous assessment of vulnerability data sources, and hence alleviate unfolding cyber threats' changing landscape. ML algorithms excel at analyzing vast amounts of data in real time, identifying patterns, and predicting potential security threats. By training on historical data, these algorithms can recognize normal behaviors and quickly detect deviations that may indicate a security breach (Jiang and Atif, 2021).

For instance supervised learning models can be taught to categorize occurrences as either typical or unusual using labeled data for training. Unsupervised learning techniques, such as clustering can bring events together, pointing out any cases that might need closer evaluation. Furthermore, reinforcement learning is able to adjust to emerging risks, enhancing its ability to detect threats continuously.

Analyzing access logs and user actions

Records of access logs and user activities document all efforts to access a system, regardless of their outcome capturing information, such as timing, location, and the type of access. Through a review of these records ML algorithms can pinpoint suspicious actions, such as multiple unsuccessful login tries from unfamiliar places or access trends that differ from typical patterns.

For example, if an IoT device is usually accessed from a specific location, an alert is triggered when it is accessed from a different location. Likewise, an excessive number of access requests to devices might signal a possible insider threat. By linking these streams of data with ML techniques, security teams can better focus their mitigation operations.

Data movement trend analysis

Tracking data movement trends entails monitoring how information moves within and across systems, revealing locations where data is accessed, transferred, or altered. This analysis helps detecting unusual traffic patterns, which may signify a security threat. For example, an unexpected spike in data transfer volume or data being sent to an unrecognized external IP address can be indicative of a data exfiltration attempt.

Thus ML algorithms have the ability to examine traffic patterns by comparing them to baseline models. Further scrutiny operations are prioritized according to levels of detected variations from these standards, such as data transfer spikes or unauthorized device access. The reasons for accessing data, the access frequency, and the specific tasks carried out on data, are all factors to consider. For instance, unnecessary data retrieval, frequent access during odd hours, or altering data that should remain unchanged are key features for ML algorithms to reason about.

9.6 Case studies: vulnerabilities and mitigation strategies

Real-world incidents serve as case studies on the challenges faced by industries, whereby each exploited vulnerability offers some unique perspectives into inherent interconnected systems, such as the cloud-to-things continuum. Past breaches provide lessons on the need for robust security protocols and the importance of continuous system monitoring. From healthcare to industrial manufacturing, these real-world scenarios provide a roadmap for securing the pervasive cloud-to-thing integration that underpins digital transformation.

The hypothetical scenarios discussed next illustrate the potential vulnerabilities and mitigation strategies related to IoT deployment settings. These case studies do not refer to a specific real-world incident, but represent the kind of security challenges that IoT application providers may face when integrating IoT devices into their operations.

9.6.1 Healthcare IoT: protecting sensitive data

The increasing reliance on IoT devices in healthcare settings brought efficiency and patient care personalization. However, this technological integration has also introduced new vulnerabilities, as evidenced by a significant data breach at a well-known healthcare providers.

A major hospital network suffered a data breach when cybercriminals exploited security weaknesses in IoT-enabled medical devices. The attackers accessed a vast amount of sensitive patient data, which included health records, treatment plans, and personal identification information. The breach not only compromised patient privacy but also exposed the hospital to regulatory inspection and financial penalties.

Investigations revealed that the breach was facilitated by a combination of unpatched software vulnerabilities and insecure device configurations. These IoT medical devices, which ranged from patient monitoring systems to insulin pumps, were operating on outdated firmware that contained known security gaps. Moreover, default passwords and lack of encryption in device communications made them easy targets for the attackers, who were able to inject malicious payloads and intercept data transmissions.

In response to the breach, the healthcare provider swiftly implemented emergency patches to the affected devices and temporarily restricted network access to essential medical personnel only. The IT department rolled out mandatory updates to strengthen firewall protections and initiated a complete review of all IoT device configurations across the network.

To prevent future incidents, the healthcare organization overhauled its IoT security policies. This included the adoption of secure communication protocols for all IoT devices and the enforcement of regular password updates and two-factor authentication for device access. The hospital also introduced a continuous monitoring system to detect and respond to suspicious activities promptly. In addition, staff training programs were enhanced to instill best practices for IoT device management and data privacy adherence.

9.6.2 Smart city infrastructure: addressing systemic weaknesses

A smart city initiative aimed at leveraging interconnected IoT systems for urban management faced a series of sophisticated cyber attacks. These incidents exposed critical weaknesses that challenged the city's ability to provide reliable services. The smart city's infrastructure, designed for optimal efficiency and resource management, inadvertently introduced vulnerabilities.

The analysis revealed that the tightly coupled nature of the IoT systems allowed for a single point of failure to potentially compromise the entire network. Intrusion detection was initially hampered by the lack of specialized monitoring tools capable of detecting anomalies across such a diverse and complex ecosystem. In response to these challenges, the smart city project implemented several key mitigation strategies:

Network segmentation

Dividing the broader network into smaller, more manageable segments, enables the city to contain potential breaches. This segmentation facilitates more focused security protocols tailored to the unique needs of each segment, while reducing overall attack surface.

Advanced threat monitoring

The city deployed advanced threat monitoring systems that leveraged AI and machine learning to identify unusual patterns of behavior indicative of a cyber attack. These systems provided real-time alerts and automated responses to potential threats.

Regular vulnerability assessments

To proactively manage risks, the smart city adopted a schedule of regular vulnerability assessments. These assessment exercises, carried out by both automated tools and human experts, helped to identify and patch vulnerabilities before they could be exploited by attackers.

9.6.3 Industrial IoT (IIoT): securing operational technology

In the heart of an advanced industrial plant, a series of operational disruptions unfolded, tracing back to a series of compromised IoT devices. This case study investigates vulnerabilities that affected the plant's IIoT infrastructure and the comprehensive measures taken to secure it further against future threats.

A detailed analysis identified multiple vulnerabilities. These included outdated firmware on several critical devices, unsecured network communication channels, and inadequate access control measures. The lack of sufficient security protocols left the plant's operational technology exposed to cyber threats, leading to several instances of system malfunctions and data integrity issues. The interconnected nature of the IIoT devices meant that a breach in one node could potentially cascade through the entire network, magnifying the impact.

To countermeasure these vulnerabilities and safeguard the operational technology, the plant adopted multiple steps:

Robust firewalls

The plant's network was equipped with advanced firewalls designed to filter and monitor incoming and outgoing traffic. These firewalls were specifically configured to protect against common IIoT threats and to isolate the operational network from the public internet.

Real-time anomaly detection

Implementing real-time anomaly detection systems enabled the plant to monitor unusual activities or deviations in the regular system's operation. These systems used machine learning algorithms to learn from regular network patterns and quickly identify potential breaches or malfunctions.

Regular security audits

The plant affirmed a policy of regular, comprehensive security audits. These audits included a thorough examination of all IIoT devices and network systems, ensuring that any new vulnerabilities were quickly identified and addressed. These audits also served as a platform for continuous improvement of the plant's cybersecurity.

9.6.4 Cloud integration: strengthening the IoT backbone

The rapid adoption of cloud services led to a series of security breaches targeting IoT-cloud services. These incidents not only disrupt operations but also raises concerns about the vulnerability of cloud-integrated IoT systems.

A thorough investigation into the breaches revealed that the business's cloud infrastructure had several cloud-specific vulnerabilities. The primary issues included misconfigurations, which left cloud storage buckets exposed, and weak API security, which allowed unauthorized access to IoT data streams. These vulnerabilities were compounded by the complexity of the cloud environment, which made consistent security configurations challenging.

In response to these findings, the business took decisive steps to fortify its cloud infrastructure:

Advanced encryption

The company implemented advanced encryption standards for both data at rest and in transit. If data was intercepted, it would then remain unreadable without the proper decryption keys.

Authenticated access controls

Access controls were significantly tightened, with the principle of least privilege being applied throughout the system. Users and devices were only granted the minimum levels of authenticated access that is necessary for their functions, which helped to limit the potential damage from any single compromised account or device.

Continuous monitoring

The business invested in automated monitoring systems. These systems utilized machine learning algorithms to detect and alert on anomalous behavior, which could indicate a security incident, thus enabling a swift response.

9.7 Conclusion

This chapter explored the vulnerability landscape in IoT-cloud environments, emphasizing the importance of understanding, discovering, and managing security weaknesses. The key takeaways and future outlooks, in addition to remaining challenges are discussed next.

IoT-cloud ecosystems are particularly susceptible to a range of vulnerabilities, from software flaws and hardware limitations to network vulnerabilities. The chapter emphasized the critical role of both automated and manual methods in discovering vulnerabilities. Tools such as Nessus, Qualys, and OpenVAS, alongside testbeds, for example, IoT-LAB and MONICA, are illustrated in identifying potential security gaps. We discussed various strategies to mitigate these vulnerabilities, including network segmentation, real-time anomaly detection, and regular security audits. The case studies provided practical insights into the application of these strategies in typical scenarios, and across various domains. Managing vulnerabilities requires a systematic and effective approach, as illustrated in the discussed models. Classifying vulnerabilities based on their severity and potential impact helps to prioritize remediation efforts.

As IoT and cloud technologies continue to evolve, so do the associated security threats. Future trends may include more sophisticated cyber attacks exploiting AI and machine learning, increased focus on securing edge computing components, and the rise of quantum computing, which could render current encryption methods obsolete (Raheman, 2022). Proactive vulnerability management remains a critical strategy. Anticipating future security challenges involves staying aware of technological advances, understanding the changing threat landscape, and continuously evolving security protocols.

The integration of IoT and cloud computing will continue to challenge traditional cybersecurity models. Organizations must adapt by investing in advanced security tools, fostering a culture of security awareness and engaging in continuous monitoring and assessment.

References

Al-Boghdady, A., El-Ramly, M., Wassif, K., 2022. Idetect for vulnerability detection in Internet of Things operating systems using machine learning. Scientific Reports 12 (1), 17086.

Albataineh, A., Alsmadi, I., 2019. IoT and the risk of Internet exposure: risk assessment using shodan queries. In: 2019 IEEE 20th International Symposium on "A World of Wireless, Mobile and Multimedia Networks"(WoWMoM). IEEE, pp. 1–5.

Alhamry, M., Elmedany, W., 2022. Exploring wi-fi wpa2 krack vulnerability: a review paper. In: 2022 International Conference on Data Analytics for Business and Industry (ICDABI). IEEE, pp. 766–772.

Aman, M.N., Javaid, U., Sikdar, B., 2021. IoT-proctor: a secure and lightweight device patching framework for mitigating malware spread in IoT networks. IEEE Systems Journal 16 (3), 3468–3479.

Blinowski, G.J., Piotrowski, P., 2020. Cve based classification of vulnerable IoT systems. In: Theory and Applications of Dependable Computer Systems: Proceedings of the Fifteenth International Conference on Dependability of Computer Systems DepCoS-RELCOMEX. June 29–July 3, 2020, Brunów, Poland 15. Springer, pp. 82–93.

Bobrovnikova, K., Lysenko, S., Hurman, I., Kwiecien, A., 2022. Machine learning based techniques for cyberattacks detection in the Internet of Things infrastructure. In: IntelITSIS, pp. 411–420.

Carvalho, M., DeMott, J., Ford, R., Wheeler, D.A., 2014. Heartbleed 101. IEEE Security & Privacy Magazine 12 (4), 63–67.

Cayre, R., Nicomette, V., Auriol, G., Alata, E., Kaaniche, M., Marconato, G., 2019. Mirage: towards a metasploit-like framework for IoT. In: 2019 IEEE 30th International Symposium on Software Reliability Engineering (ISSRE). IEEE, pp. 261–270.

Cheikes, B.A., Cheikes, B.A., Kent, K.A., Waltermire, D., 2011. Common Platform Enumeration: Naming Specification Version 2.3, US Department of Commerce. National Institute of Standards and Technology ….

Cheng, X., Zhang, J., Chen, B., 2019. Cyber situation comprehension for IoT systems based on apt alerts and logs correlation. Sensors 19 (18), 4045.

Chu, G., Lisitsa, A., 2018. Penetration testing for Internet of Things and its automation. In: 2018 IEEE 20th International Conference on High Performance Computing and Communications; IEEE 16th International Conference on Smart City; IEEE 4th International Conference on Data Science and Systems (HPCC/SmartCity/DSS). IEEE, pp. 1479–1484.

Dumitraş, T., 2015. Understanding the vulnerability lifecycle for risk assessment and defense against sophisticated cyber attacks. In: Cyber Warfare: Building the Scientific Foundation. Springer, pp. 265–285.

Ebbers, F., 2022. A large-scale analysis of IoT firmware version distribution in the wild. IEEE Transactions on Software Engineering 49 (2), 816–830.

Ekwo, S., 2021. Strategies to Protect against Security Violations during the Adoption of the Internet of Things by Manufacturers. PhD thesis. Walden University.

Elrawy, M.F., Awad, A.I., Hamed, H.F., 2018. Intrusion detection systems for IoT-based smart environments: a survey. Journal of Cloud Computing 7 (1), 1–20.

Fambon, O., Fleury, E., Harter, G., Pissard-Gibollet, R., Saint-Marcel, F., 2014. Fit IoT-lab tutorial: hands-on practice with a very large scale testbed tool for the Internet of Things. In: 10èmes journées francophones Mobilité et Ubiquité, UbiMob2014.

Guillén, S., Sala, P., Fico, G., Arredondo, M.T., Cano, A., Posada, J., Gutiérrez, G., Palau, C., Votis, K., Verdouw, C., et al., 2022. IoT European large-scale pilots–integration, experimentation and testing. In: Cognitive Hyperconnected Digital Transformation. River Publishers, pp. 221–282.

Henderson, B.M., 2018. Custom windows patching methodology-comparative analysis.

Hulayyil, S.B., Li, S., Xu, L., 2023. Machine-learning-based vulnerability detection and classification in Internet of Things device security. Electronics 12 (18), 3927.

Jiang, Y., Atif, Y., 2021. A selective ensemble model for cognitive cybersecurity analysis. Journal of Network and Computer Applications 193, 103210.

Johari, R., Kaur, I., Tripathi, R., Gupta, K., 2020. Penetration testing in IoT network. In: 2020 5th International Conference on Computing, Communication and Security (ICCCS). IEEE, pp. 1–7.

Kennedy, D., O'gorman, J., Kearns, D., Aharoni, M., 2011. Metasploit: the Penetration Tester's Guide. No Starch Press.

Kim, M., Suh, T., 2021. Eavesdropping vulnerability and countermeasure in infrared communication for IoT devices. Sensors 21 (24), 8207.

Lala, S.K., Kumar, A., Subbulakshmi, T., 2021. Secure web development using owasp guidelines. In: 2021 5th International Conference on Intelligent Computing and Control Systems (ICICCS). IEEE, pp. 323–332.

Li, J., 2020. Vulnerabilities mapping based on owasp-sans: a survey for static application security testing (sast). arXiv preprint: arXiv:2004.03216.

Miessler, D., 2015. Securing the Internet of Things: mapping attack surface areas using the owasp IoT top 10. In: RSA Conference, vol. 2015.

Moncy, M.M., 2023. Vulnerability management in practice: Contribution of qualys to the access project for enhanced cybersecurity.

Nerwich, M., Gauravaram, P., Paik, H.-y., Nepal, S., 2020. Vulnerability database as a service for IoT. In: International Conference on Applications and Techniques in Information Security. Springer, pp. 95–107.

O'Grady, M.J., Angove, P., Magnin, W., O'Hare, G.M.P., O'Flynn, B., Barton, J., O'Mathuna, C., 2012. Enabling Intelligence on a Wireless Sensor Network Platform. Springer, Berlin, Heidelberg, pp. 299–306. https://doi.org/10.1007/978-3-642-28762-6_36.

Prasanna Balasooriya, L.N., Wibowo, S., Grandhi, S., Wells, M., 2017. The impact of security concernson personal innovativeness, behavioural and adoption intentionsof cloud technology. Software Networking 2017 (1), 265–290. http://dx.doi.org/10.13052/jsn2445-9739.2017.013.

Rahalkar, S., Rahalkar, S., 2019. Openvas. In: Quick Start Guide to Penetration Testing: With NMAP, OpenVAS and Metasploit, pp. 47–71.

Raheman, F., 2022. The future of cybersecurity in the age of quantum computers. Future Internet 14 (11), 335.

Rogers, R., 2011. Nessus Network Auditing. Elsevier.

Sane, P., 2020. Is the owasp top 10 list comprehensive enough for writing secure code? In: Proceedings of the 2020 International Conference on Big Data in Management, pp. 58–61.

Shapsough, S., Aloul, F., Zualkernan, I.A., 2018. Securing low-resource edge devices for IoT systems. In: 2018 International Symposium in Sensing and Instrumentation in IoT Era (ISSI). IEEE, pp. 1–4.

Van Houten, J., 2020. Relationship Between Specific Security Concerns and CIO Intention to Adopt Cloud. PhD thesis. Walden University.

CHAPTER

IoT security best practices 10

10.1 Introduction

The challenge of securing a myriad of interconnected devices and systems in the cloud-to-things continuum emerges as a critical framework for IoT security. As IoT devices proliferate across industries, from smart homes to industrial control systems, the complexity and scope of securing these devices expand rapidly.

Cloud-to-things continuum security represents a holistic, integrated approach designed to protect the entire spectrum of IoT interactions: from the cloud, where data is processed and stored, down to the individual things, including sensors, edge nodes, and other connected devices. This continuum approach emphasizes the necessity of seamless security integration, ensuring that protective measures are uniformly applied, regardless of the entry point or layer within the IoT ecosystem.

This inherent interconnectedness of IoT systems may propagate vulnerabilities that can occur in one layer by compromising the integrity of the entire network. By adopting a security strategy that spans the entire spectrum of the continuum, organizations can establish a robust security attitude that addresses the multifaceted risks associated with the IoT's diverse components, and throughout the entire lifecycle of induced data flows. This chapter uncovers these associated advanced considerations to IoT security with a cloud-to-things framework, focusing on the cutting-edge solutions and methodologies designed to enhance the security of IoT systems across various domains and applications.

As the entry point for securing devices and data, authentication stands as a critical barrier against unauthorized access. However, the traditional username and password approach often falls short in IoT security contexts, due to the scale, diversity, and inherent limitations of IoT devices (Sasi et al., 2023). This chapter reveals advanced authentication methods that are gaining traction in the IoT security space. These methods significantly increase the difficulty for attackers to compromise security. The principles behind these approaches are discussed and their application in IoT contexts are shown, as well as how they can be integrated into the cloud-to-things continuum security strategy.

Advanced encryption is the cornerstone of data protection to ensure that information remains confidential and intact as it moves across cloud-to-things networks, as well as when residing in storage nodes. Where data often traverses multiple nodes and environments, robust encryption methods are paramount. This chapter explores these advanced encryption techniques tailored for IoT ecosystems, including end-to-end

Accelerating Digital Transformation with the Cloud and the Internet of Things (IoT)
https://doi.org/10.1016/B978-0-44-322217-7.00017-7

encryption schemes, lightweight cryptography for resource-constrained devices, and quantum-resistant algorithms poised to address future threats. By examining these techniques, the chapter aims to provide guidance into how organizations can implement strong encryption standards to safeguard their IoT data against interception and tampering.

The dynamic and distributed nature of IoT-based systems makes them challenging to monitor and protect using traditional intrusion detection and prevention approaches. However emerging solutions are made more effective by technology advancements. This chapter highlights these advancements tailored for IoT, including anomaly-based detection, which leverages machine learning to identify unusual patterns indicative of a security breach. Additionally, the integration of network segmentation strategies and how they play a pivotal role in limiting the spread of an attack within cloud-to-things ecosystems are also discussed. These advancements represent a leap forward to respond to security incidents in real time, offering a more resilient defense against evolving cyber threats.

As organizations increasingly rely on interconnected devices to drive innovation and operational efficiency, the complexity and volume of security threats have surged. Traditional security measures are no longer sufficient to safeguard the intricate and expansive IoT ecosystems. This chapter further emphasizes security strategies that are informed by real-time data and aligned with the specific risk profiles of different IoT systems. The vast amounts of data generated by IoT devices, networks, and systems is analyzed to proactively identify patterns, trends, and anomalies that signify potential security threat and vulnerabilities, enabling organizations to prioritize security measures. The chapter explores tools and technologies that facilitate the application of security-relevant data, including advanced analytics, and security information and event management (SIEM) systems (Maggiolo, 2021).

10.2 Securing IoT devices

IoT devices have become more than integrated into our daily lives and core business operations, and thus ensuring their security is not just about protecting data, but also about safeguarding the functionality and reliability of essential services. Next, we discuss the crucial aspects of securing IoT devices, focusing on three foundational pillars: device identity and management, advances in authentication mechanisms, and automated firmware/software updates of IoT devices.

10.2.1 Device identity and security management

As IoT ecosystems expand, the number of devices can quickly grow from dozens to thousands, or even millions. Effective identity management enables administrators to keep track of device statuses, updates, and security configurations. In IoT ecosystems, the structure of device identifiers extends beyond traditional IP addresses to encompass unique device-specific identifiers, including serial numbers, MAC addresses, and digital certificates that utilize public key infrastructure (PKI) for IoT to enable secure communication.

At the heart of IoT security, device identity requires that each IoT device to have a unique identity to be recognized as a specific node in the broader network. Managing these identities effectively is paramount to accurately authenticate a device when it attempts to communicate with other devices. Advanced authentication and access control mechanisms ensure that only authorized devices can access the network and exchange data.

Device identity management is the first step towards a secure cloud-to-things ecosystem, whose significance in terms of security management spans several critical security areas, including authentication, authorization, integrity, non-repudiation, and scoping privileges. These elements are essential in creating a robust security framework that ensures only legitimate devices can interact within an IoT ecosystem.

Authentication

Authentication refers to the procedure of confirming the identity of a device that attempts to gain access to the network. Through device identity management, devices' unique identifier is used to ensure that only verified identities can connect to and communicate within the cloud-to-things ecosystem. Besides preventing unauthorized access, effective authentication mechanisms mitigate also impersonation attacks (Papathanasaki et al., 2022).

The illustration of Fig. 10.1 captures the essence of digital signature-based authentication in a public key infrastructure (PKI), which is one of the fundamental techniques for verifying identities and ensuring that a message has been sent by a legitimate sender. The illustrated authentication process between devices A and B starts by Device A's intention to send a secure message to Device B. B's challenge is ensure that the message he receives is indeed from A and not an impersonator, that is, no tampering or forgery was introduced by an intruder.

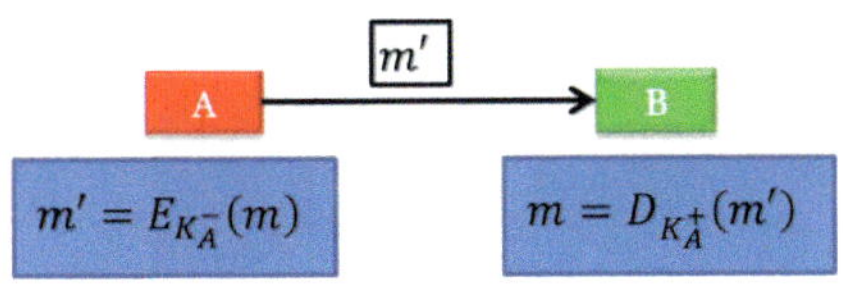

FIGURE 10.1

Authentication lifecycle.

1. Device A writes its message m and encrypts it using the device's private key K_A^-. The result of this encryption is a digital signature, denoted as "m.". This digital signature is unique to both the message and A's private key, ensuring that only Device A could have created it.
2. Device A sends the original message m along with the digital signature m' to Device B.
3. Upon receiving the message and the digital signature, Device B uses A's public key K_A+ to decrypt m'. The process of decryption allows B to retrieve a version of the original message m.

4. Upon receiving the message and the digital signature, Device B uses A's public key K_A+ to decrypt m'. The process of decryption allows B to retrieve a version of the original message, denoted as m''.
5. Device B now compares the decrypted message m'' with the original message m that he received. If m'' matches m, Device B can be assured that the message has indeed come from Device A. The match confirms that the digital signature was created with A's private key, which only Device A possesses.

This process not only authenticates Device A as the sender but also ensures the integrity of the message, as any tampering would be detectable by Device B. In real-world situations, it is worth noting that the alternative to encrypting the entire message is applying a cryptographic hash of the message that is typically encrypted to produce the digital signature. Subsequently, the encrypted hash and a hash of the received message are compared to assert its authenticity and integrity. But how to ensure that only "Device B" gets the message? This is the scope of the autorization security service, explained next.

Authorization

Authorization refers to the rules that determine who is allowed to access resources or receive data messages. In an IoT system, these policies should be dynamic, to adapt to the changing states and roles of devices. By encrypting a message with the recipient's public key, only the recipient can decrypt it and read it using their private key, ensuring secure communication., the recipient is the only legitimate device that can decrypt and read the message, using the recipient private key, as illustrated in Fig. 10.2.

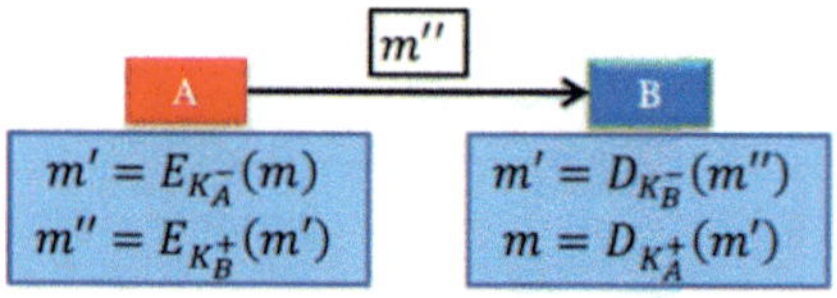

FIGURE 10.2

Authorization lifecycle.

The process blends confidentiality and authentication to ensure that only Device B can access and read the message (confidentiality). Moreover Device B has the capability to verify the message's authenticity, assuring that it was truly sent by Device A (authentication). Device A encrypts m', which results from applying Device A's private key K_A^- using Device B's public key K_B+ to create m''. This ensures that only Device B can decrypt it.

In IoT systems, role-based access control (RBAC) serves as a protocol that grants devices access privileges according to their designated roles (Barka et al., 2015). RBAC enforces the boundaries of access for each Device's role, ensuring that devices have only the necessary permissions to perform their designated functions.

Each role in an RBAC system is defined according to the functions within the cloud-to-things continuum, which require access to the continuum data. Permissions to access certain resources are assigned to roles, not individual devices. These permissions are carefully scoped to include only the access necessary for the role to function effectively. A role example might be the privilege to read data from a sensor but not to change its configuration. The permissions linked to the role, rather than individual device permissions, determine data access privileges. This approach simplifies consistent access controls across devices with the same role.

Attribute-based access control (ABAC) uses policies that combine multiple attributes, which could be device attributes and environmental attributes. Device type, location, current network status, or access time, are examples of such attributes (Bhatt and Sandhu, 2020). Sensitivity of a device is another example of device attribute used to classify the device in terms of confidentiality and impact, such as public, internal, confidential, or secret. The present load on a device, which might affect whether additional processes or access requests can be safely handled, represents another example of environmental attribute.

The combination of the above attributes means that even if a device has the right identity and role, access can be denied if the request comes from an unexpected location or outside of designated times, given that the request is made during regular business hours (environmental attribute). This granularity makes ABAC particularly well-suited to the variability of IoT environments, where contextual factors can significantly impact security considerations (Bhatt and Sandhu, 2020).

Non-repudiation

Non-repudiation ensures that a device cannot deny the authenticity of the data it sends or the actions it performs. This is achieved through digital signatures and secure logging, tied to the unique identity of each device. Device identity management attributes every action to a specific device, which results in an audit track, which can be used for forensic analysis, as well as compliance purposes and resolving possible disputes.

10.2.2 User access control in IoT devices

The imperative to control access to devices is not just a matter of data security. Operating the device by users requires safety and privacy preservation. IoT may even control critical systems, where unauthorized access can lead to dire consequences, including breaches of confidentiality, alterations of device functionality, and disruptions of essential services. Beyond device-to-device authentication discussed earlier, user access control devices' participation in secure and trustworthy IoT environments.

However, it is no longer adequate to rely on basic security measures that have become all too vulnerable to sophisticated cyber threats. The traditional username and password approach is increasingly seen as a weak link in the face of advanced phishing attacks, social engineering tactics, and brute force methods (Alkhalil et al., 2021). To address these challenges and protect against unauthorized use, IoT devices require novel access control layers that adapt to the complexity of IoT networks and the evolving landscape of cyber threats.

Biometric verification

Physiological traits are used to confirm user identity, making unauthorized access more challenging (Wu et al., 2018). Fingerprints are common and widely used biometric methods as individual's fingerprint pattern is unique, providing a reliable way to confirm identity. Smartphones and tablets became equipped with fingerprint sensors that allow users to unlock their devices, authorize payments, and sign into applications. Personal laptops and PCs feature also built-in fingerprint scanners that users can use to log in to their devices. Smart locks that provide access to residential and commercial security systems often utilize fingerprint recognition as well to control access to properties. Such smart locks can replace traditional keys and increase security by only allowing entry to registered fingerprints. Workplaces use fingerprint-based time attendance systems to track employees' working hours and ensure accurate attendance records.

Facial recognition utilizes a person's facial features to create a corresponding digital model. These methods analyze the structure, shape, and contours of the face, even accounting for variations in expression or lighting, to identify users. Considering the unique patterns in the colored ring of the eye, iris scanning offers a highly secure form of biometric authentication. It is less likely to be affected by external factors, such as dirt in fingerprint scans. Voice recognition can be used in hands-free authentication scenarios (Hayashi and Ruggiero, 2022).

An emerging biometric method, gait analysis identifies individuals by the way they walk (Patil et al., 2016). Behavioral biometrics, such as these are less intrusive and can be used in continuous authentication scenarios (Wu et al., 2018). This method is part of a broad category of any biometric authentication method that utilizes user's behavior, including gesture patterns, and other interactions that can be subtly distinctive.

Multi-factor authentication (MFA)

This approach layers multiple authentication factors, significantly reducing the likelihood that an unauthorized user can gain access to IoT devices. MFA adds layers of security by requiring two or more verification methods from independent categories of credentials to authenticate the user's identity. This process reduces the risk of unauthorized access, as even if one factor is compromised, a malicious user faces another security layer. However, additional considerations are required for integrating MFA as an authentication method, namely

- User knows a password or PIN.
- User has a mobile device, smart card, or security token that can generate or receive a one-time password (OTP).
- Biometric characteristics, such as fingerprint, facial recognition, or voice patterns can be supplied
- Geolocation data that ensures access is granted only when the user is at a specific location.

10.2.3 Automated firmware updates

The ability to maintain and enhance device security through timely firmware and software updates is paramount. Automated firmware updates ensure up-to-date IoT devices with the latest features, and patched against emerging vulnerabilities. Best practices for automating updates securely involves several key practices that protect the devices during the update process and ensure that updates themselves do not become vectors for attacks (Bettayeb et al., 2019).

- **Secure transmission:** Updates should be transmitted over encrypted channels to prevent interception by malicious actors. Digital signatures and hashing can be used to verify the authenticity and integrity of the update packages to ensure no tampering occurred during transmission.
- **Integrity checking:** Before applying an update, devices should perform integrity checks to confirm that the update package is complete and unaltered. This integrity validation step can verify digital signatures or checksums provided by the update server.
- **Rollback mechanisms:** If an update introduces instability or compatibility issues, devices should have the capability to revert back to a previous, stable firmware version. This rollback mechanism keeps devices operational and secure, even if a planned update does not meet the expected behaviour.

10.3 Network security

The network security of data traffic forms the backbone of a comprehensive security strategy throughout the cloud-to-things continuum data flows. Robust intrusion detection and prevention mechanisms and the strategic implementation of network segmentation strategies, such as microsegmentation (Klein, 2019) and zero trust models (Samaniego and Deters, 2018) are essential components for detecting and neutralizing threats, and ensuring the resilience and integrity of IoT networks against sophisticated attacks.

10.3.1 Intrusion detection and prevention

The dynamic and distributed nature of IoT networks, combined with the criticality of the services they provide, necessitates advanced intrusion detection and prevention solutions (IDPS). Modern IDPS solutions leverage advanced data analytics and machine learning algorithms to sift through and analyze large datasets generated by IoT devices. These technologies enable the identification of patterns and anomalies indicative of a security threat. Learning from historical data adapt these developments to new and evolving threats more efficiently than traditional, rule-based systems (Prajapati et al., 2021).

Enhanced data analytics and machine learning

Advanced data analytics and machine learning (ML) algorithms have been integrated into IDPS for IoT networks to identify and mitigate cyber threats, as illustrated next:

- **Anomaly detection in smart home networks:** Smart thermostats, or lighting systems, and security cameras are connected to the network in a smart home environment. Each device exhibits a pattern of normal behavior based on user interactions and automated routines. An IDPS equipped with ML algorithms analyzes the network traffic and device behavior to establish a baseline of "normal" activity for each device. Over time, the system learns to differentiate between routine activities and anomalies enabling security threat detection, such as unusual outbound traffic from a smart thermostat, indicating a potential compromise (Al-Masri et al., 2022; Illy et al., 2022).
- **Industrial IoT (IIoT) protection:** Industrial IoT environments, such as manufacturing plants, utilize a wide range of connected devices to monitor production processes. These environments are often targets for sophisticated cyber attacks aiming to disrupt operations (Tsiknas et al., 2021). An IDPS designed for IIoT environments can use data analytics and ML to monitor the operational data from machinery and sensors continuously. Identified patterns related to equipment performance, operational efficiency, and safety protocols follows a training step to recognize deviations that might indicate malicious incidents. These incidents may originate from intentional sabotage, which may materialize into sudden changes in machinery speed or unauthorized access to control systems (for e.g., Stuxnet (Trautman and Ormerod, 2017)).

Protocol diversity and compatibility

IoT networks often utilize a wide range of communication protocols, including MQTT, CoAP, and Zigbee. Recent innovations in Intrusion Detection and Prevention Systems (IDPS) have led to the development of protocol-agnostic systems, which are capable of analyzing traffic across a diverse protocol landscape. This monitoring process ensures a comprehensive coverage and protection, regardless the specific protocol technologies employed by the IoT devices within the network.

Deep packet inspection (DPI) techniques analyze the payload and header information of network traffic, regardless of whether it is MQTT for lightweight messaging or CoAP for constrained nodes and networks, are employed as IoT communication protocols (Rescio et al., 2021). This capability allows the system to detect anomalies such as unexpected message payloads or abnormal communication patterns indicative of a cyber threat across any protocol used within the network (Owusu and Nayak, 2020).

IDPS solutions are integrated directly with IoT-cloud management platforms, providing a seamless security layer that is protocol-agnostic by design. These platforms can orchestrate security policies, perform real-time monitoring, and execute defensive actions across the entire cloud-to-things continuum, regardless of the specific protocols each device uses (Alghamdi, 2022). This integration ensures that security measures are consistently applied and managed from a central point, enhancing the overall security posture of the continuum (Javadpour et al., 2023).

Scalability and flexibility

IDPS solutions have evolved with the exponential growth of IoT devices to be highly scalable and flexible, capable of securing networks that range from a few devices to millions. This scalability is achieved through cloud-based architectures and distributed processing techniques, allowing the IDPS to expand its monitoring and analysis capabilities as the network grows. For example, Cisco's Stealthwatch Cloud leverages the cloud to provide visibility and security analytics across the entire network of IoT deployments (Alatalo, 2022). Cloud-based processing and storage enable Stealthwatch Cloud to scale when analyzing traffic from millions of devices, detecting anomalous behaviors and sophisticated threats in real-time without the need for on-premises hardware.

Microsegmentation and zero trust models

Microsegmentation and zero trust models aim to minimize lateral movement within networks, thereby limiting the potential damage that can be caused by cyber threats (Arifeen et al., 2021). By breaking down a network into smaller, more manageable segments and enforcing strict access controls, organizations can significantly reduce the attack surface.

- **Microsegmentation:** Microsegmentation involves dividing a network into distinct security segments down to the individual workload or device level. Each segment can have its own security policies and controls. This granularity allows for more precise control over traffic flows and more effective isolation of potential threats, preventing an attacker who has compromised one device from easily moving to others (A Al-Ofeishat and Alshorman, 2023). For example, critical devices can be separated from the rest of the network. The segmentation may be functional, whereby, for example, an HVAC system in a smart building can be segmented from lighting controls so that a vulnerability in one system does not expose the other system to the same cyber risk (Ewing et al., 2023).
- **Zero trust:** The belief that organizations should not automatically trust anything inside or outside their perimeters is called "Zero Trust" (Li et al., 2022). Organizations ought to verify everything that tries to connect to their systems before granting access. This approach is distinguished from traditional network security models, which often rely on a strong perimeter defense, assuming that everything inside the network is safe. Thus with the zero trust model, only authenticated and authorized users and devices can access network resources since zero trust recognizes that threats can originate anywhere, making internal network security just as important as external. Access decisions are made dynamically based on the context of each access request, including user identity, device health, and location.

  In IoT contexts, this approach is particularly relevant due to devices often operating beyond an organization's traditional network perimeters. Zero trust architecture in IoT involves microsegmentation to create smaller, manageable, and secure network zones, continuous verification of all devices and users, ensuring authenticated and authorized access at all times and centralized management to enforce security policies efficiently from a single point of control. Using smart contracts to automate and enforce access policies directly within the network, blockchains have been suggested as a viable methodology (Dhar and Bose, 2020).

10.3.2 Advanced encryption techniques for IoT

Advanced encryption techniques for IoT are designed to secure data transmission across devices and networks, while accommodating the unique constraints of IoT ecosystems, such as limited processing power and the need for real-time processing. Next, we review some advanced encryption techniques that are particularly relevant for IoT.

Lightweight cryptography

Designed for devices with limited computational resources, lightweight cryptography (LWC) offers a balance between security and performance using algorithms optimized for small code size, low power consumption, and efficient processing. AES (Advanced Encryption Standard) with simplified modes of operation (e.g., smaller key sizes, such as AES-128) (Tsai et al., 2018), PRESENT (Chatterjee and Chakraborty, 2020), and SIMON and SPECK cipher suites (Yustiarini et al., 2022), are explicitly designed to address the challenges in environments where traditional cryptographic algorithms would be too resource-intensive.

Quantum-resistant algorithms

The advent of quantum computing poses security risks to traditional encryption methods, such as RSA (Sharma et al., 2021) and ECC (Liu et al., 2024), which prompted the development of quantum-resistant or post-quantum cryptographic algorithms that can secure communications against an adversary equipped with a quantum computer. The potential for quantum computers to break these encryptions necessitates a shift towards developing and implementing quantum-resistant cryptographic standards to protect data in the future quantum era. This ongoing transition underscores the need for proactive adaptation in the field of cryptography to safeguard information security against evolving technological advances (Chawla and Mehra, 2023).

10.4 Edge and cloud security

The distributed nature of the cloud-to-things continuum architecture expands the attack surface, and hence requires comprehensive security measures that span the cloud-to-edge level of the architecture. Next, we explore security practices essential for safeguarding IoT infrastructures across cloud and edge computing environments.

Implementing consistent security policies across cloud and edge components of the continuum architecture is a basic requirement to ensure uniform protection against threats as data resides or is processed across these two IoT cloud layers. This protection scheme ensures that data is encrypted both in transit and at rest, with robust encryption standards applied uniformly across the cloud and edge layers.

10.4.1 Security as a service for edge-enabled IoT systems

Cloud-provided security services are an emerging concept, offering a centralized, robust security framework, which edge nodes can request on-demand. This model ensures that even the most resource-constrained edge devices benefit from advanced security measures. Thus a uniform security posture across the IoT ecosystem is maintained by outsourcing security measures to a consistent source of management.

The traditional approach of on-premises security solutions is rapidly giving way to more agile, flexible, and scalable cloud-based security solutions, broadly referred to as security as a service (SECaaS). Recent market analysis projects SECaaS industry to reach USD 68.33 billion by 2031 (ADROIT Market Research, 2021), as illustrated in Fig. 10.3. This upward trajectory underscores a paradigm shift in cybersecurity strategies, where the demand for cloud-based security services reflects the changing dynamics of threat landscapes and organizational capabilities.

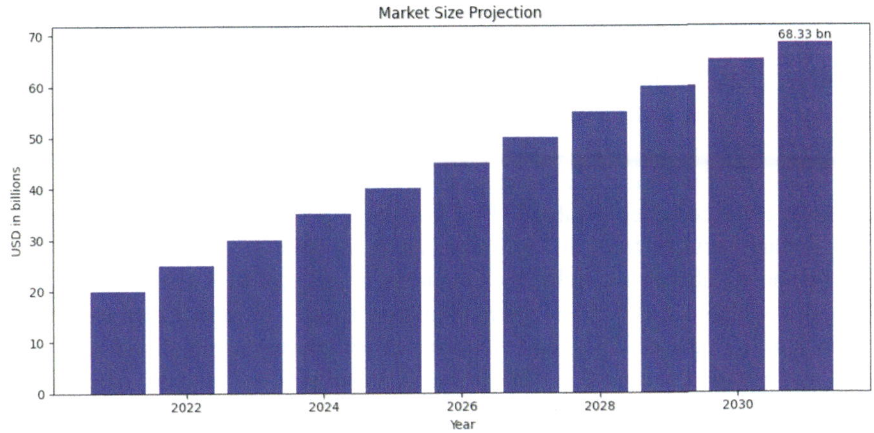

FIGURE 10.3

Projected SECaaS market share (Adapted from (ADROIT Market Research, 2021)).

SECaaS offers a compelling suite of advantages that resonate with the needs of modern digital infrastructures. SECaaS cloud-native nature provides a wide array of security tools and services on demand to organizations, without the overhead of managing and maintaining extensive security hardware and software (Ranaweera et al., 2020; Tourani et al., 2019). This approach optimizes cost efficiency and ensures that businesses can swiftly adapt to the latest security threats and security compliance requirements (Saxena and Nisha, 2021).

Moreover, the SECaaS model democratizes access to robust security measures, making state-of-the-art defenses accessible to smaller organizations, which may lack the resources for extensive in-house security operations. Building on SECaaS momentum, the deployment and management of security at the edge of networks can also leverage SECaaS. As organizations push computing power outwards to the edge to enhance responsiveness and reduce latency, the need for on-demand, cloud-delivered security services is appealing (Boudi et al., 2019).

Lightweight virtualization can be leveraged to implement SECaaS at the network edge as well using containers and microservices. In doing so, organizations can deploy essential security measures, such as intrusion detection systems, firewalls, and malware scanners, directly where data processing and collection occur (Boudi et al., 2019). By processing and securing data locally, edge computing can mitigate the risks associated with data transmission over potentially insecure networks, thereby aligning with stringent data protection regulations.

10.4.2 Federated identity management

Managing the identities of a myriad of interconnected devices and services presents a formidable challenge. The traditional, siloed approach to identity management falls short in addressing the complex requirements of IoT ecosystems, requiring a more dynamic, scalable, and secure solution. Federated identity management (FIM) emerges as a cohesive framework for seamless identity verification across diverse platforms. FIM facilitates a cloud-based infrastructure to identity management used by devices, users, and services for authentication needs across various domains securely (Fremantle and Aziz, 2018).

One of the fundamental advantages of adopting cloud-based FIM in IoT environments is enhanced interoperability. FIM bridges disparate identity systems, allowing devices and services from different manufacturers or service providers to communicate and collaborate securely. The cloud-based nature of FIM solutions inherently supports scalability as well, a critical requirement given the anticipated exponential growth of IoT devices. The cloud platforms can efficiently handle the authentication and authorization of countless devices, while adapting to the dynamic nature of IoT networks (Fremantle and Aziz, 2018).

10.5 Leveraging data for security

The proliferation of interconnected devices has exponentially increased the complexity and volume of data traversing cloud-to-things continuum ecosystems. This surge underscores the need to leverage advanced data analysis and analytics for bolstering cybersecurity measures. Although used interchangeably, data analysis and data analytics for cybersecurity are distinguished by their methods and goals. Data analysis in cybersecurity refers to the process of inspecting, cleansing, transforming, and modeling data with the objective of discovering useful information, informing conclusions, and supporting decision-making. Data analysis uses a) historical data for "incident analysis" to understand how a breach occurred or b) forensic analysis, which examines logs to uncover the timeline and method of a cyberattack.

Analytics extends analysis to include machine learning techniques to model and predict future outcomes. Thus data analysis is typically aimed at understanding and interpreting historical data, while analytics is about predicting future outcomes and trends. Using analytics techniques to identify potential future threats and vulnerabilities before they result in breaches is a typical forecasting activity. Similarly, quantifying security risks based on the likelihood is an analytics activity that helps organizations allocate resources effectively.

Data-driven strategies for securing IoT ecosystems against a backdrop of sophisticated cyber threats have become the norm in cybersecurity (Tariq et al., 2023; Lal et al., 2023). Data analytics, coupled with security information and event management (SIEM) systems have emerged as efficient enablers for transforming vast amounts of raw data into actionable intelligence. By adopting a proactive action from data analytics, organizations can anticipate threats, ensuring the integrity, confidentiality, and availability of IoT infrastructures data. Next, we discuss best practices in deploying data analysis and analytics to safeguard IoT ecosystems from the myriad of cybersecurity challenges they face.

10.5.1 Data-driven security with SIEM

In IoT cybersecurity, the transition from historical data analysis to predictive analytics represents a critical shift towards a more proactive and preemptive security activity. Analyzing past incidents reveal vulnerability indicators and attack patterns, serving as a foundation for predictive modeling. For instance, by examining the sequence of events in a data breach, security teams can identify specific weaknesses in their network that were exploited. Leveraging these informational relationships, analytics can then forecast potential future attack vectors, enabling organizations to reinforce their defenses against similar or evolving threats before they materialize.

The integration of security information management (SIM) and security event management (SEM) technologies led to the development security information and event management (SIEM) systems (Díaz López et al., 2018). SIEM system provides a comprehensive view of an organization's information security by aggregating data from multiple sources, as well as analyzing this data for patterns of normal and suspicious behavior, based on which real-time alerts on potential security incidents are raised (Scarfone, 2015).

As illustrated in Fig. 10.4, SIEM combines data for analysis using predefined correlation rules used to identify potential security incidents. This architecture emphasizes the comprehensive SIEM approach to security management, integrating a wide range of data sources to secure an organization's network.

Fig. 10.4 shows that logs from various cloud-based applications, edge and device data flows, including from intermediary points between the core network and the edge of the network. These logs are correlated with context data, including information from vulnerability scans or databases, detailing potential security weaknesses within

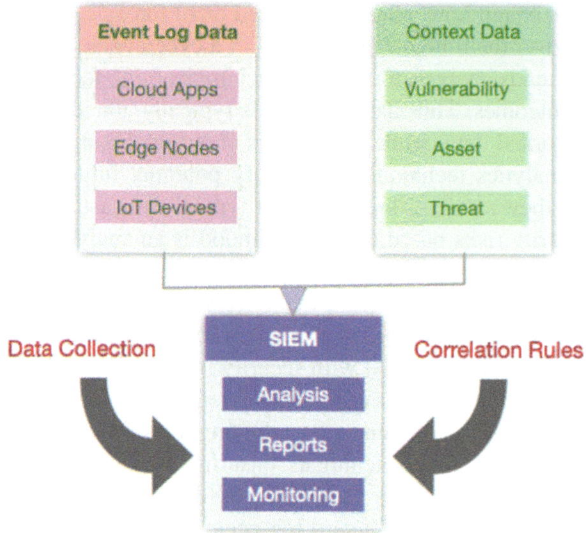

FIGURE 10.4

SIEM architecture.

the system and assets inventory within the network, in addition to data from threat landscape, to inform SIEM about known attack vectors.

The integration of AI/ML with SIEM systems enhances their ability to detect and respond to anomalies. Machine learning algorithms that are trained on historical data to recognize patterns of normal behavior can identify deviations, which may indicate a security threat. Response to certain types of incidents can also be automated with AI/ML, enabling a prompt and more efficient resolution.

10.5.2 AI for anomaly detection and network monitoring

Historical data serves as the foundation for training AI and ML models. By analyzing past security incidents and network traffic patterns, AI models learn to discern between normal operations and potential threats. This historical data analysis is not just a preliminary step but a continuous process, as AI systems must evolve with the ever-changing landscape of cyber threats. Therefore a dataset covering a wide range of scenarios improves the accuracy of anomaly detection over time (Xu et al., 2023).

The complexity and scale of IoT ecosystems require a comprehensive approach to security by facilitating the understanding of past, present, and future datasets. Subsequently, as illustrated in Fig. 10.5, three types of analytics are employed: predictive, descriptive, and prescriptive.

These three core analytics types are applied in cybersecurity domains, specifically within IoT security frameworks. This first level of analytics involves the collection and examination of event data logs, to understand and interpret security events that

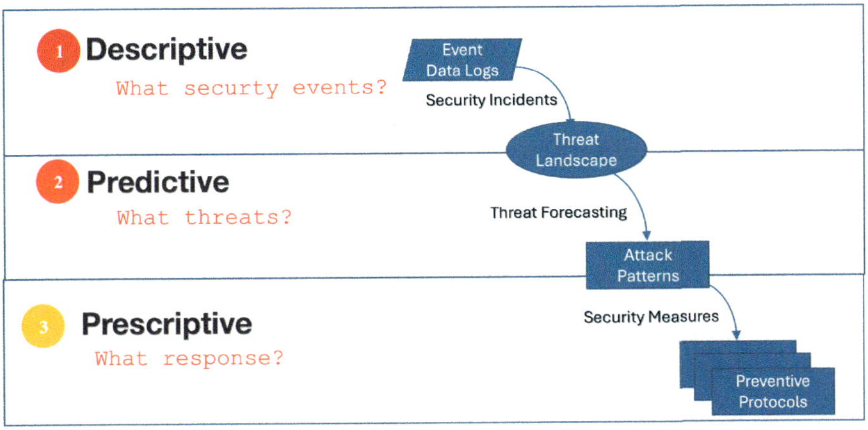

FIGURE 10.5

Cybersecurity data analytics.

have already occurred. This process supports the detection of various security incidents or vulnerabilities.

Descriptive analytics

This first level of analytics focuses on understanding what security events are being considered and interpret them by first collecting and examining related event data logs, which reveal features related to security incidents (Wolniak, 2023). These logs serve as records of all actions and events within the network, providing cybersecurity professionals with valuable information. This is a key step toward enabling further AI processing in subsequent cybersecurity analytics (Saleem and Chishti, 2019).

Descriptive analytics begins by clarifying which types of security events need attention. This could range from unauthorized access attempts to unexpected changes in system configurations. The process continues with the systematic collection of logs that record network activities, transactions, and events. By examining these logs, cybersecurity professionals can uncover features that are distinctive data points or attributes indicative of security incidents. These features could include timestamp patterns of access attempts, IP addresses, user IDs, system calls, etc. Identified features are instrumented for training machine learning models (Abri et al., 2019). They serve as inputs for algorithms that will learn to classify events, predict threats, or even suggest countermeasures. They also enable AI algorithms to discern between normal and suspicious behavior (Elsayed and Zulkernine, 2020).

Predictive analytics

Historical data analyzed by descriptive analytics are further employed by predictive analytics across various statistical models and machine learning algorithms to predict future security threats (Sarker et al., 2021). Considering the threat landscape that includes known vulnerabilities and attack patterns, predictive analytics can forecast potential future attacks. Predictive analytics takes the features identified in the descriptive analytics step and uses them to train machine learning algorithms. These algorithms analyze patterns within the data to predict potential future security events. This could include a) predicting phishing attacks by identifying email characteristics or b) anticipating DDoS attacks by monitoring traffic flow patterns (Ali et al., 2023).

Trained model used by predictive analytics anticipate attacks before they occur, allowing preemptive measures to be taken (Hulayyil et al., 2023). If the predictive model identifies a pattern similar to a historical data breach, a cybersecurity team is alerted to investigate and alleviate exploits. Machine learning models are not static; they constantly learn and adapt based on new data and feedback from the outcomes of previous predictions (Samanpour et al., 2018). This means that predictive analytics processes improves over time, becoming more accurate and reliable in forecasting threats (Chen et al., 2022).

Prescriptive analytics

Building upon both descriptive and predictive analytics, prescriptive analytics suggests concrete actions or security measures that organizations should take. The focus is on formulating preventive protocols and responses to either avert the predicted threats or mitigate their impact. This branch of analytics is action-oriented and seeks to guide decision-makers in implementing the most effective security strategies (Eschweiler, 2018).

AI models do more than just predict; they can also be trained to suggest mitigation strategies. By analyzing the outcomes of past decisions and their effectiveness, the best course of action to face a given threat scenario can be AI-enhanced. Prescriptive analytics can introduce automated responses to certain types of security threat (Sarker, 2023). For example, if a potential attack vector is identified, firewall rules are inferred and automatically implemented to block suspicious traffic or isolate affected network segments.

10.5.3 Data-centric risk assessment

The variability of IoT devices, the complexity of networks, and the uniqueness of data interactions in a cloud-to-things continuum demand a dynamic security strategy. Risk-based security customizes security measures to the distinctive challenges in the diverse IoT landscape. Conducting a risk assessment identifies vulnerabilities specific to different devices and their operational environments.

The subsequent data classification process evaluates the criticality of the data each device handles, assigning levels of protection commensurate with the sensitivity and value of that data. By closely aligning security measures with data classification, organizations can focus their resources on shielding the most critical and vulnerable assets. This methodology is proactive, focusing on preemptive measures for high-risk areas, while also responding promptly to new threats as they emerge. This agile security approach reacts or anticipates continuously as it develops effectiveness against the evolving cyber threat environment.

Data classification involves categorizing data based on its sensitivity and the potential impact should it be compromised. For example, data can be classified into categories such as public, internal, confidential, and highly Confidential. Public data might include marketing materials with no restrictions on access. Internal data could consist of internal emails, requiring limited access. Confidential data might encompass customer information, necessitating strict access controls. Highly confidential data could include intellectual property or financial records, which if compromised, could significantly harm the organization. Through such classification, security measures can be aligned with the sensitivity of the data, ensuring that the most critical data receives the highest level of protection.

Next, we discuss specific use case scenarios within the cloud-to-things continuum context, considering application domains tailored to highlighting the application of a data-centric risk-based security strategy.

Smart healthcare

In a healthcare IoT ecosystem, devices range from wearable health monitors to hospital equipment. A risk-based approach would classify patient data as highly confidential, requiring the highest security measures, including encryption and access controls, to protect against data breaches that could have severe privacy implications.

Industrial IoT (IIoT) in manufacturing

Sensors and machines on a factory floor are interconnected to optimize production. Risk assessment identifies vulnerabilities in operational technology (OT) environments. Data classification ensures that proprietary manufacturing data is protected as highly confidential, with rigorous security protocols to prevent industrial espionage.

Integrating a data-centric risk assessment within the layered security approach of the cloud-to-things continuum security involves identifying and classifying data based on its sensitivity across the continuum layers. This approach ensures comprehensive protection across all IoT devices, edge nodes and cloud services, dynamically adjusting depending on evolving threats and vulnerabilities in this IoT ecosystem (Al-Salem et al., 2023).

The process begins by systematically identifying all types of data generated or processed across IoT devices, edge nodes, and cloud services. Then this data is classified based on sensitivity levels (e.g., public, internal, confidential, highly confidential). A thorough vulnerability assessments for each layer is conducted to identify potential security weaknesses that could impact the classified data and appropriate security measures tailored to the sensitivity of the data at each layer are applied. For highly confidential data, strict access controls, encryption in transit and at rest, and rigorous authentication mechanisms are advocated (Sicari et al., 2018).

10.6 Physical security

Physical security ensures the physical integrity of IoT devices, safeguarding devices from tampering, theft, or damage, and maintaining their operational functionality against environmental challenges. Next, we discuss device hardening, environmental protections, surveillance strategies, and overall best practices for building a resilient IoT ecosystem that can withstand not just cyber threats but physical ones as well.

10.6.1 Device hardening and environmental protections

Physical security of IoT devices serves as the first line of defense to protect these devices from environmental hazards, to maintain their operational integrity, and safeguard the data they collect and process. Strategies for device hardening include the following:

- **Enclosure design:** The utilization of robust enclosures for IoT devices is advocated, especially those deployed in harsh environmental conditions, with the aim to protect against factors such as moisture, dust, extreme temperatures, and electromagnetic interference. Consider agricultural sensors used in precision farming. Their outdoor deployments expose them to harsh environmental conditions, including rain, dust, as well as high or low temperatures, and potential interference with farming equipments. In this case, the agricultural sensor is encased in a waterproof and dustproof enclosure, ensuring it remains operational during rainstorms or in dusty conditions. The enclosure should be designed with shielding techniques, using materials that block or reduce the penetration of electromagnetic fields.
- **Tamper detection:** Mechanisms that alert administrators to any unauthorized physical interactions with the devices are implemented, such as when the device casing is opened. For example, ATMs that are deployed across various locations, including remote areas, are equipped with sensors and security mechanisms to detect and alert administrators of any unauthorized access attempts, including the opening of the machine's casing.

10.6.2 Access control and surveillance

Unauthorized physical access to IoT components requires another security layer against potential intruders. Biometric access systems and keycard protocols can create a robust defense mechanism that ensures only authorized personnel interact with critical IoT infrastructure.

Surveillance mechanisms monitor and react to physical security breaches. The deployment of CCTV systems, motion sensors, and environmental monitoring tools extends the security perimeter, offering real-time surveillance and incident response capabilities.

10.7 Conclusion

This chapter has outlined a spectrum of best practices for safeguarding the cloud-to-things continuum. Advanced authentication mechanisms, automated firmware updates, and encryption establish a foundation upon which robust IoT security can be built. Network security emphasized the critical adoption of intrusion detection and prevention systems enhanced by data analytics and machine learning. The innovative model of security as a service (SECaaS) as part of the advancing paradigm shift towards more agile and scalable security solutions has been explained. Leveraging data for security emerged as a cornerstone strategy, highlighting how SIEM systems and AI/ML technologies transform vast datasets into actionable solutions for preemptive security measures. The often-overlooked aspect of physical security for device hardening and environmental protections, alongside comprehensive access control and surveillance mechanisms have been highlighted for creating resilient incident response plans.

References

A Al-Ofeishat, H., Alshorman, R., 2023. Build a secure network using segmentation and micro-segmentation techniques. International Journal of Computing and Digital Systems 14 (1), 1–16.

Abri, F., Siami-Namini, S., Khanghah, M.A., Soltani, F.M., Namin, A.S., 2019. Can machine/deep learning classifiers detect zero-day malware with high accuracy? In: 2019 IEEE International Conference on Big Data (Big Data). IEEE, pp. 3252–3259.

ADROIT Market Research, 2021. Security as a service market size. https://www.adroitmarketresearch.com/industry-reports/security-as-a-service-market. (Accessed 5 February 2024).

Alatalo, M., 2022. Cisco secure network analytics (stealthwatch).

Alghamdi, S.A., 2022. Novel trust-aware intrusion detection and prevention system for 5g manet–cloud. International Journal of Computer Science and Information Security 21 (3), 469–488.

Ali, T.E., Chong, Y.-W., Manickam, S., 2023. Machine learning techniques to detect a ddos attack in sdn: a systematic review. Applied Sciences 13 (5), 3183.

Alkhalil, Z., Hewage, C., Nawaf, L., Khan, I., 2021. Phishing attacks: a recent comprehensive study and a new anatomy. Frontiers of Computer Science 3, 563060.

AlMasri, T., Snober, M.A., Al-Haija, Q.A., 2022. Idps-sdn-ml: an intrusion detection and prevention system using software-defined networks and machine learning. In: 2022 1st International Conference on Smart Technology, Applied Informatics, and Engineering (APICS). IEEE, pp. 133–137.

AlSalem, T.S., Almaiah, M.A., Lutfi, A., 2023. Cybersecurity risk analysis in the IoT: a systematic review. Electronics 12 (18), 3958.

Arifeen, M., Petrovski, A., Petrovski, S., 2021. Automated microsegmentation for lateral movement prevention in Industrial Internet of Things (IIoT). In: 2021 14th International Conference on Security of Information and Networks (SIN), vol. 1. IEEE, pp. 1–6.

Barka, E., Mathew, S.S., Atif, Y., 2015. Securing the Web of Things with Role-Based Access Control. Springer International Publishing, pp. 14–26. https://doi.org/10.1007/978-3-319-18681-8_2.

Bettayeb, M., Nasir, Q., Talib, M.A., 2019. Firmware update attacks and security for IoT devices: survey. In: Proceedings of the ArabWIC 6th Annual International Conference Research Track, pp. 1–6.

Bhatt, S., Sandhu, R., 2020. Abac-cc: attribute-based access control and communication control for Internet of Things. In: Proceedings of the 25th ACM Symposium on Access Control Models and Technologies, pp. 203–212.

Boudi, A., Farris, I., Bagaa, M., Taleb, T., 2019. Assessing lightweight virtualization for security-as-a-service at the network edge. IEICE Transactions on Communications 102 (5), 970–977.

Chatterjee, R., Chakraborty, R., 2020. A modified lightweight present cipher for IoT security. In: 2020 International Conference on Computer Science, Engineering and Applications (ICCSEA). IEEE, pp. 1–6.

Chawla, D., Mehra, P.S., 2023. A roadmap from classical cryptography to post-quantum resistant cryptography for 5g-enabled IoT: challenges, opportunities and solutions. Internet of Things, 100950.

Chen, Z., Liu, J., Shen, Y., Simsek, M., Kantarci, B., Mouftah, H.T., Djukic, P., 2022. Machine learning-enabled IoT security: open issues and challenges under advanced persistent threats. ACM Computing Surveys 55 (5), 1–37. https://doi.org/10.1145/3530812.

Dhar, S., Bose, I., 2020. Securing IoT devices using zero trust and blockchain. Journal of Organizational Computing and Electronic Commerce 31 (1), 18–34. https://doi.org/10.1080/10919392.2020.1831870.

Díaz López, D., Blanco Uribe, M., Santiago Cely, C., Vega Torres, A., Moreno Guataquira, N., Morón Castro, S., Nespoli, P., Gómez Mármol, F., et al., 2018. Shielding IoT against cyber-attacks: an event-based approach using siem. Wireless Communications and Mobile Computing 2018.

Elsayed, M.A., Zulkernine, M., 2020. Predictdeep: security analytics as a service for anomaly detection and prediction. IEEE Access 8, 45184–45197.

Eschweiler, J., 2018. Progressing towards a prescriptive approach on cyber security–adopting best practices and leverage technical innovation. In: Cybersecurity Best Practices: Lösungen zur Erhöhung der Cyberresilienz für Unternehmen und Behörden, pp. 339–347.

Ewing, J., Farr, R., Hughes, W., 2023. Creating a smart building strategy. Corporate Real Estate Journal 12 (3), 216–223.

Fremantle, P., Aziz, B., 2018. Cloud-based federated identity for the Internet of Things. Annals of Telecommunications 73, 415–427.

Hayashi, V.T., Ruggiero, W.V., 2022. Hands-free authentication for virtual assistants with trusted IoT device and machine learning. Sensors 22 (4), 1325.

Hulayyil, S.B., Li, S., Xu, L., 2023. Machine-learning-based vulnerability detection and classification in Internet of Things device security. Electronics 12 (18), 3927.

Illy, P., Kaddoum, G., Kaur, K., Garg, S., 2022. Ml-based idps enhancement with complementary features for home IoT networks. IEEE Transactions on Network and Service Management 19 (2), 772–783.

Javadpour, A., Pinto, P., Ja'fari, F., Zhang, W., 2023. Dmaidps: a distributed multi-agent intrusion detection and prevention system for cloud IoT environments. Cluster Computing 26 (1), 367–384.

Klein, D., 2019. Micro-segmentation: securing complex cloud environments. Network Security 2019 (3), 6–10.

Lal, B., Ravichandran, S., Kavin, R., Kumar, N.A., Bordoloi, D., Kumar, R.G., 2023. IoT-based cyber security identification model through machine learning technique. In: Measurement: Sensors, vol. 27, p. 100791.

Li, S., Iqbal, M., Saxena, N., 2022. Future industry Internet of Things with zero-trust security. Information Systems Frontiers, 1–14.

Liu, T., Ramachandran, G., Jurdak, R., 2024. Post-quantum cryptography for Internet of Things: a survey on performance and optimization. arXiv preprint: arXiv:2401.17538.

Maggiolo, N., 2021. IoT oriented SIEM tools. PhD thesis. Università degli Studi di Padova. https://thesis.unipd.it/handle/20.500.12608/10638.

Owusu, A.I., Nayak, A., 2020. An intelligent traffic classification in sdn-IoT: a machine learning approach. In: 2020 IEEE International Black Sea Conference on Communications and Networking (BlackSeaCom). IEEE, pp. 1–6.

Papathanasaki, M., Maglaras, L., Ayres, N., 2022. Modern authentication methods: a comprehensive survey. In: AI, Computer Science and Robotics Technology, vol. 2022, pp. 1–24. https://doi.org/10.5772/acrt.08.

Patil, J., Nandur, D., Mellikeri, M., Naik, K., Kulkarni, P., 2016. Integrated sensor system for gait analysis. In: 2016 International Conference on Electrical, Electronics, and Optimization Techniques (ICEEOT). IEEE, pp. 2298–2301.

Prajapati, P., Bhatt, B., Zalavadiya, G., Ajwalia, M., Shah, P., 2021. A review on recent intrusion detection systems and intrusion prevention systems in IoT. In: 2021 11th International Conference on Cloud Computing, Data Science & Engineering (Confluence). IEEE, pp. 588–593.

Ranaweera, P., Imrith, V.N., Liyanag, M., Jurcut, A.D., 2020. Security as a service platform leveraging multi-access edge computing infrastructure provisions. In: ICC 2020-2020 IEEE International Conference on Communications (ICC). IEEE, pp. 1–6.

Rescio, T., Favale, T., Soro, F., Mellia, M., Drago, I., 2021. Dpi solutions in practice: benchmark and comparison. In: 2021 IEEE Security and Privacy Workshops (SPW). IEEE, pp. 37–42.

Saleem, T.J., Chishti, M.A., 2019. Data analytics in the Internet of Things: a survey. Scalable Computing: Practice and Experience 20 (4), 607–630.

Samaniego, M., Deters, R., 2018. Zero-trust hierarchical management in IoT. In: 2018 IEEE International Congress on Internet of Things (ICIOT). IEEE, pp. 88–95.

Samanpour, A.R., Ruegenberg, A., Ahlers, R., 2018. The future of machine learning and predictive analytics. In: Digital Marketplaces Unleashed, pp. 297–309.

Sarker, I.H., 2023. Machine learning for intelligent data analysis and automation in cybersecurity: current and future prospects. Annals of Data Science 10 (6), 1473–1498.

Sarker, I.H., Furhad, M.H., Nowrozy, R., 2021. Ai-driven cybersecurity: an overview, security intelligence modeling and research directions. SN Computer Science 2 (3), 173. https://link.springer.com/content/pdf/10.1007/s42979-021-00557-0.pdf.

Sasi, T., Lashkari, A.H., Lu, R., Xiong, P., Iqbal, S., 2023. A comprehensive survey on IoT attacks: taxonomy, detection mechanisms and challenges. Journal of Information and Intelligence. https://www.sciencedirect.com/science/article/pii/S2949715923000793.

Saxena, S., Nisha, T., 2021. Augmentation of secaas model with eciso in cloud-based security services: a comprehensive study. Journal of Physics. Conference Series 1964, 042013.

Scarfone, K., 2015. Introduction to siem services and products.

Sharma, M., Choudhary, V., Bhatia, R., Malik, S., Raina, A., Khandelwal, H., 2021. Leveraging the power of quantum computing for breaking rsa encryption. Cyber-Physical Systems 7 (2), 73–92.

Sicari, S., Rizzardi, A., Miorandi, D., Coen-Porisini, A., 2018. A risk assessment methodology for the Internet of Things. Computer Communications 129, 67–79.

Tariq, U., Ahmed, I., Bashir, A.K., Shaukat, K., 2023. A critical cybersecurity analysis and future research directions for the Internet of Things: a comprehensive review. Sensors 23 (8), 4117.

Tourani, R., Bos, A., Misra, S., Esposito, F., 2019. Towards security-as-a-service in multi-access edge. In: Proceedings of the 4th ACM/IEEE Symposium on Edge Computing, pp. 358–363.

Trautman, L.J., Ormerod, P.C., 2017. Industrial cyber vulnerabilities: lessons from stuxnet and the Internet of Things. U. Miami L. Rev. 72, 761.

Tsai, K.-L., Huang, Y.-L., Leu, F.-Y., You, I., Huang, Y.-L., Tsai, C.-H., 2018. Aes-128 based secure low power communication for lorawan IoT environments. IEEE Access 6, 45325–45334.

Tsiknas, K., Taketzis, D., Demertzis, K., Skianis, C., 2021. Cyber threats to industrial IoT: a survey on attacks and countermeasures. IoT 2 (1), 163–186.

Wolniak, R., 2023. The concept of descriptive analytics. In: Scientific Papers of Silesian University of Technology. Organization & Management/Zeszyty Naukowe Politechniki Slaskiej. Seria Organizacji i Zarzadzanie, vol. 1(172).

Wu, G., Wang, J., Zhang, Y., Jiang, S., 2018. A continuous identity authentication scheme based on physiological and behavioral characteristics. Sensors 18 (1), 179.

Xu, H., Sun, Z., Cao, Y., Bilal, H., 2023. A data-driven approach for intrusion and anomaly detection using automated machine learning for the Internet of Things. Soft Computing 27 (19), 14469–14481.

Yustiarini, B.Y., Dewanta, F., Nuha, H.H., 2022. A comparative method for securing Internet of Things (IoT) devices: aes vs simon-speck encryptions. In: 2022 1st International Conference on Information System & Information Technology (ICISIT). IEEE, pp. 392–396.

PART

3

Cloud based IoT digital transformation in action!

CHAPTER

Smart citizenship through IoT-cloud adoption

11

11.1 Introduction

Smart cities represent the forefront of integrating the cloud-to-things continuum within urban management ecosystems to enhance citizens' quality of life, sustainability, and efficiency. This digital transformation is driven by smart citizenship, which emphasizes the development of individual competences to thrive in such technologically advanced environments. As smart cities evolve, the need for smart citizenship competences underpins the capacity of citizens to engage with, contribute to, and benefit from the cloud-to-things continuum integration into smart city ecosystems (de Waal and Dignum, 2017).

IoT and cloud technologies, driven by the cloud-to-things continuum, serve as the backbone of smart cities, enabling functionalities that redefine public services, safety, and sustainability. The integration of data from connected devices and infrastructures, including energy systems and transportation networks or environmental sensors, facilitate proactive responses to urban challenges. For instance, energy management with smart grids adjusts to consumption patterns, while intelligent transportation systems optimize traffic flow and reduce congestion. Moreover, environmental monitoring improves air quality and water management operations, contributing to healthier urban environments.

Digital transformation significantly impacts civic engagement by providing platforms for more direct participation in governance and community development (Liu and Zowghi, 2022). Digital platforms enable citizens to voice their opinions, contribute to decision-making processes, and engage with local governments and community initiatives more effectively. Yet, this transformative potential challenges the digital divide, for it aims to ensure equitable access to technology. Addressing disparities in digital literacy unlocks the full potential of smart citizenship to thrive in digitally transformed societies (Rêgo et al., 2023).

Educational initiatives and public programs foster the culture of innovation and continuous learning within education forums and among general citizens. By empowering individuals with the competences needed for smart citizenship, these initiatives and programs promote a resilient, inclusive, and participatory smart city (Sá et al., 2021). Next, we explore the foundational elements of smart citizenship, before revealing innovative education models for fostering these competences and discussing such practical initiatives in the context of case studies that highlight the path towards achieving smart citizenship through cloud-to-things continuum adoption.

Accelerating Digital Transformation with the Cloud and the Internet of Things (IoT)
https://doi.org/10.1016/B978-0-44-322217-7.00019-0

11.2 Foundational elements of smart citizenship

Smart citizenship encapsulates the idea that citizens are not just passive beneficiaries of technological advancements but active participants in shaping their urban environments. These foundational elements are necessary, for fostering smart citizenship requires specific skills, knowledge areas, and technological competencies; the latter are logically essential in cloud-to-things-enabled smart city contexts (Ferronato and Ruecker, 2018).

A smart citizen requires a multifaceted skillset, beginning with digital literacy. Understanding how to navigate smart city ecosystems effectively ensures that citizens can leverage technology for personal and community benefit. Beyond mere usage, digital literacy for smart citizenship empowers individuals to make informed decisions, safeguard their data, and engage with cloud-to-things digital platforms responsibly.

Civic engagement in cloud-to-things ecosystems takes on new dimensions that offer novel interaction opportunities for participation in governance, public service improvement, and community initiatives (Hamm, 2022). This enhanced interaction between citizens and city administrators creates a collaborative environment, where feedback and initiatives can be shared more freely and efficiently.

However, the digital divide poses a significant challenge to realizing the full potential of smart citizenship. Addressing this divide involves not only enhancing access to cloud-to-things continuum ecosystems equally but also ensuring that all citizens have the necessary skills to participate fully in these ecosystems (Van Deursen and Mossberger, 2018b). Strategies to overcome these barriers target inclusive smart city development resources (Shin et al., 2021).

Furthermore, the security of personal information and the ethical use of data and IoT devices are important consideration for smart citizenship. Next, we explore the importance of such secure practices, data privacy awareness, and ethical considerations in building public trust to thrive in ecosystems transformed by the cloud-to-things continuum. These elements are integral to creating a secure and trustworthy environment in these ecosystems, where citizens feel confident in their interactions with smart city digital services.

11.2.1 Civic engagement

The bridge between citizens and their urban environments enabled by IoT provides a level of connectivity that was previously unattainable, fundamentally transforming the dynamics of civic engagement and governance. The vast network of devices embedded within the city's infrastructure collect data on everything: from air quality and traffic patterns to energy usage and public safety. The resulting real-time data collection and sharing empower city administrators with agile governance tools used to promptly respond to citizen needs (Hamm, 2022).

Moreover, IoT technologies open new avenues for civic involvement, empowering citizens to interact with their urban environment in innovative ways. Mobile applications provisioned by IoT platforms enable residents to report issues, access information about city services, and easily participate in public consultations. Engaging with city governance is encouraged with proactive and informed processes. The constant flow of information between citizens and their physical environments promotes a culture of transparency, efficiency, and participation.

The CorkCitiEngage project provided information for local authorities and stakeholders on where to invest to enhance citizen engagement in smart city initiatives (Pham et al., 2016). Through surveys, the project explored the inter-correlation between citizen engagement, smart city issues, and crowdsourcing methodologies, collecting responses from 3,599 participants in Cork, Ireland. Subsequently, citizen engagement areas have been identified to successfully implement smart city initiatives. These areas include the following:

- Stimulating engagement through volunteering practices
- Providing various platforms and mechanisms for citizens to participate in smart city initiatives
- Generating engagement based on issues that concern citizens to increase their involvement
- Offering better and free services that facilitate access to digital tools to increase citizen participation
- Developing apps specific to the city to encourage citizens to interact more with relevant smart city initiatives

11.2.2 Overcoming the digital divide

There is a need to address the new digital divide emerging from the gap induced by the cloud-to-things continuum-related skills. This divide not only refer to access to technology but also involves the differentiated skills and resources required to effectively utilize IoT technologies. A new dimension of the digital divide is taking shape, one that extends beyond the traditional access and usage gaps to encompass a skills divide, which could significantly impact social equality. As IoT technologies promise to revolutionize aspects of daily life, the benefits risk to be unevenly distributed, favoring those with the necessary digital skills, while leaving others behind (van Deursen and Mossberger, 2018a).

According to van Deursen and Mossberger & (van Deursen and Mossberger, 2018a), the core of the IoT skills divide lies in the unique characteristics of IoT technologies: their autonomous operation, the volume and complexity of data they generate, and the strategic knowledge required to navigate through the cloud-to-things continuum. Whereas operational and formal skills required for traditional internet usage may see a reduced emphasis in an IoT context, the demand for new levels of information and certain communication skills is significantly increased. These skills are essential for understanding, managing, and safeguarding citizens' interaction with IoT systems, in addition to maximizing the potential benefits and mitigating associated risks.

Policy and educational interventions

To bridge this new digital divide, targeted policy and educational interventions across all societal groups are advocated to ensure that individuals are equipped with the knowledge to make informed decisions about IoT usage. Understanding the implications of data sharing and effectively managing privacy and security risks entail developing comprehensive educational programs that address IoT-specific skills, through awareness campaigns about the benefits and challenges of IoT technologies, and access to IoT learning resources.

In addition to formal education, community-based initiatives foster a broader understanding of cloud-to-things continuum technologies. Besides libraries, community centers, and non-profit organizations, practice-based learning, involving hands-on experiences and accessible venues for IoT skill development, such as workshops that cater to diverse community needs are necessary to foster smart citizenship.

Fostering inclusive innovation

Overcoming the IoT skills divide also requires the involvement of industry stakeholders in creating more user-friendly and transparent IoT solutions. Designing IoT devices and systems with intuitive interfaces, clear privacy settings, and easily accessible information about data usage can help demystifying the cloud-to-things continuum for the average user, reducing the skill barrier for effective engagement.

Furthermore, inclusive innovation processes that involve users from varied backgrounds in the design and development of cloud-to-things-related services contribute to addressing the needs and concerns of a broader population, which enhance the societal benefits of the cloud-to-things continuum.

11.2.3 Security practices

The security implications of cloud-to-things-induced digital transformation must be rigorously addressed. A variety of security challenges, particularly concerning citizens' roles in this transformation need to be considered. A holistic approach to managing these security risks involves the implementation of several key strategies that smart cities can adopt to enhance their cybersecurity posture and protect the privacy and integrity of citizen data. These practices aim to create a secure cloud-to-things environment by advocating the following (Karabatak et al., 2023):

- **Strong passwords:** Advocates for the creation and use of complex, unique passwords for different cloud-to-things services to prevent unauthorized access.
- **Phishing awareness:** Emphasizes education on recognizing and avoiding phishing attempts, which trick users into divulging personal information.
- **Secure networks:** The use of secure, encrypted networks is encouraged to protect against eavesdropping and data breaches.
- **Regular updates:** Stresses the importance of keeping software and devices updated to protect against known vulnerabilities.
- **Privacy settings:** The careful management of privacy settings on social media and other online platforms is advised to control the visibility of personal information.

- **Two-factor authentication:** Using two-factor authentication for an additional layer of security beyond just a password is recommended.

11.2.4 Awareness of data privacy

Data is the modern world's most valuable resource. This change underscores the critical role data plays in the functioning of cloud-to-things continuum within smart cities, containing sensitive and personal information, such as bank details, medical records, passwords, and location data. The accessibility of this data through hacking or social engineering highlights the ongoing threat posed by cyber attackers, requiring constant vigilance (Almubark and Masmali, 2022).

User privacy concerns with IoT devices

Privacy concerns arise from the amount of data gathered by IoT, pertaining to a range of information, including location details, usage patterns, and personal data, without the users' complete awareness or comprehension (Lee and Kobsa, 2016). Transparency and informed consent play an important role to build trust; the purpose of gathered data and who can access it are to be clarified. Users should be able to decide how their collected data is utilized and shared. Trust issues arise when users grant permissions without understanding the consequences making them susceptible to misuse of their data.

User access and control

Frequently, individuals face challenges in accessing or altering their own data stored by IoT firms. This lack of transparency poses obstacles in ensuring these companies uphold data handling practices and respect users' privacy rights.

Profiling for targeted advertising

IoT data raise concerns about the potential manipulation and exploitation induced by building detailed profiles of users based on their habits and preferences. In doing so, companies can target them with intrusive advertising and potentially influence their behavior in undesirable ways. This lack of accountability undermines user trust, hindering their ability to fully benefit from IoT-induced digital transformation.

The right to be forgotten

GDPR (the General Data Protection Regulation) in the European Union established the right for personal information held by organizations to delete it upon user's request (Barati et al., 2019). This privilege is valid in situations such as when the data is no longer needed for its original intent or if the user revokes their permission for its use (López, 2022).

However, data collected by IoT devices might be distributed across various databases and systems, making it challenging to locate and erase all relevant information (Politou et al., 2022). Besides, many IoT devices constantly collect data, requiring ongoing monitoring and erasure processes. Finally, some IoT devices run typically in low power mode or have limited storage capacity, which could hamper an efficient implementation of erasure requests (Ramos and Skármeta, 2020).

11.2.5 Ethical considerations and public trust

In smart cities, the ethical use of data centers around principles such as consent, transparency, and accountability. Ethical considerations require that city administrations and IoT providers prioritize the privacy of citizen data. This involves implementing robust data protection measures, ensuring data is collected with informed consent and used in ways that are transparent to and understood by citizens. Additionally, accountability mechanisms must be in place to address any misuse of data or technology, with clear avenues for citizens to report concerns and seek corrections.

- **Informed consent:** People using IoT devices ought to be able to manage the data gathered with straightforward choices to either agree or decline participation in data collection procedures. This agreement should be well informed, ensuring that individuals are completely aware of the types and purposes of data being collected, and who can access it (O'Connor et al., 2017).
  Informed consent in IoT must address the complexities of obtaining informed consent through control policies tailored to the user and the context. This process incorporates privacy-friendly practices using pseudonyms to associate policies with users, IoT service providers, and IoT devices. This enhanced EULA approach protects personal data flow from IoT sensors by informed consent mechanisms in the IoT domain to ensure privacy and data protection (Neisse et al., 2015).
- **Public trust:** Transparency is a fundamental building block of trust, especially when collecting data from or about citizens. By facilitating informed decision-making and mitigating privacy concerns early on, trust between authorities and citizens involved in smart city initiatives can be established. Building trust and confidence among all stakeholders, including the public, is considered to be essential to gain acceptance and ensure continued development of IoT, where transparency is a key component of trust (Jacobs et al., 2022).

11.3 Open Data for smart citizenship empowerment

For more than a decade, many governments at national and city levels have been driving the Open Data Initiative. This commitment to transparency and public access to information is illustrated by the EU strategy to promote the re-use of public sector information, which led to the Open Data portal as a comprehensive source of datasets from EU institutions (de Juana-Espinosa and Luján-Mora, 2019). This portal aims to foster innovation, economic growth, and government accountability by making data freely available, reusable, redistributable, and machine-readable within a legal and secure framework for anyone to use. Such initiatives underscore governments commitment to empower citizens through transparent enactments and data-evidenced decision-making.

Data is considered "Open" when it is free, reusable, redistributable, and machine-readable, within a legal and secure framework, accessible to anyone. Open Data enables citizens to access a wide range of information, including weather reports, traffic conditions, emergency services, and legal resources. Furthermore, Open Data initiatives have the potential to optimize government services, alleviate poverty, and enhancing public safety. As the widespread impact of Open Data becomes increasingly apparent and new applications emerge, such as IoT driven initiatives, governments are eagerly expanding their open data programs. This growing adoption of Open Data is a key component of digital transformation efforts aimed at creating smarter, more connected communities (Damiani et al., 2017).

11.3.1 Open Data catalogs for smart city digital transformation

A list of datasets made available as open data is called a data catalog. Essential elements of a data catalog include searching, metadata, clear license information, and access to the datasets themselves. Typically, a data catalog is the online centerpiece of an Open Data initiative. Open Data catalog management may be decentralized to one or more contributing smart ministries, as shown in Fig. 11.1. Each smart ministry may have its own data catalog or support APIs to directly access the central data catalog hosted by the government. The data storage is managed separately, with the metadata exchanged to enable synchronized access and searching. This model can be adopted by ministries that have the capacity and experience to manage their own open data. Alternatively, ministries may choose to directly provide access to the central data catalog.

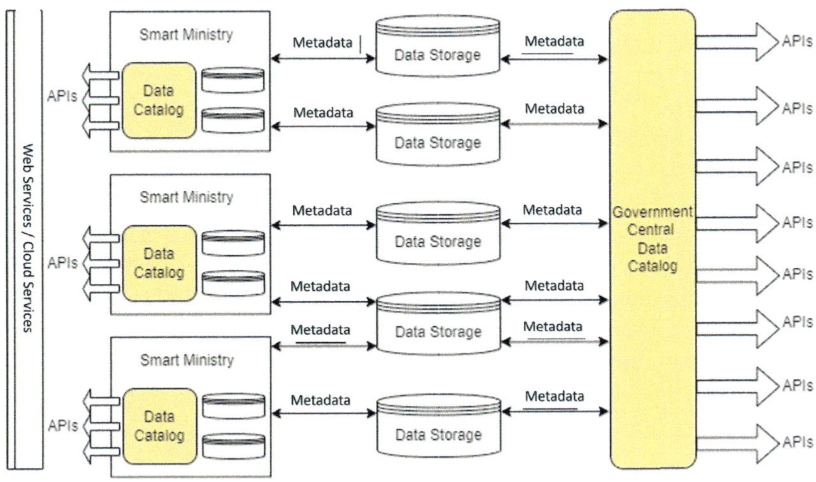

FIGURE 11.1

Federated data catalog management.

Some of the most widely used open data catalogs around the world are listed below:

- **Data.gov:** The central repository for open data published in the US. Users can find datasets on various topics, including weather, healthcare, and economics.
- **Data.gov.uk:** Access to UK government open data, where users can explore data on public services, education, and transportation.
- **Data.gov.au:** The Australian government's open data platform, which features datasets on agriculture, science, and social welfare.
- **Data.gouv.fr:** The French open data portal offers datasets on public spending, legislation, and the environment.
- **Data.gov.in:** The Indian government's open data portal. Users can find datasets on agriculture, education, and health.

11.3.2 Technologies enabling Open Data platforms

An Open Data platform is a portal that provides online services (Web services or cloud services) for users to access all resources available. These platforms offer a wealth of information for citizens and authorities alike. These portals function as online hubs, providing access to various datasets and resources, typically for asking questions, technical support, and feedback. Additionally, there is a knowledge base of background and training materials, along with a blog for communication and outreach. The services within a platform are often implemented with a suite of technologies. Some of the widely used technology suites for these platforms are listed here.

CKAN

An open-source data catalog platform that serves as an online library specifically for datasets. It is used by government agencies, research institutions, and NGOs to publish, share, and manage their datasets. CKAN is python-based, easy to set up and to customize due to its modular architecture, and is supported by the Open Knowledge Foundation to enable robust solutions for managing open data (Winn, 2013).

DKAN

An open-source, Drupal-based data catalog platform, which is a popular content management system (Ali et al., 2022). Like CKAN, DKAN is used for publishing, sharing, and managing datasets by leveraging Drupal's vast library of open-source modules for customization; it is supported by a large developer community. Additionally, API compatibility with CKAN allows easy data exchanges. DKAN is written in PHP.

Junar

A cloud-based SaaS (software as a service) open data platform, which offers a subscription-based service that manages open data and provides access through a data catalog or APIs (Lutchman and Hosein, 2015). Junar is an alternative solution for organizations that want to delegate the management of their own data infrastructure to third-pary service providers.

OpenDataSoft

Another cloud-based SaaS open data platform with visualization tools. This a one-stop shop to publish data, create visualizations, and share them with the public; it is used by government agencies, businesses, and NGOs to share data. Tools to easily create data visualizations are provided to enhance the understanding of published data (Ali et al., 2022).

Socrata

A cloud-based software as a service (SaaS) platform for open data catalogs, which offers tools for manipulating data publishing and visualizations to explore the data interactively (Kalinin et al., 2022). Similar to DKAN and CKAN, Socrata is commonly used for sharing and publishing open data. What sets it apart is its advanced data visualization features, which enhance the analysis process. The platform is user friendly, equipped with built-in tools for manipulating data and unique visualization options, which make it a valuable resource for data projects.

Swirrl

A cloud-based SaaS open data platform built on linked data technologies, designed for maximum data discoverability and interoperability using semantic technologies (Dodero et al., 2011). Swirrl's linked data approach benefits organizations that work with complex datasets or need to ensure the highest level of data findability. The platform achieves 100% compliance with the 5-star Open Data model, making data highly discoverable and reusable by machines and applications, thus maximizing its utility and impact.

ArcGIS Open Data

Is a cloud-based platform that is tailor-made for exploring into spatial as well as nonspatial data. Government agencies, utility companies, and environmental organizations use this tool to publish, share, and analyze data. The platform seamlessly integrates with ArcGIS services and tools, making it easy for users to explore and analyze types of data all in one spot. Besides the open source technologies used to manage geospatial data, this platform comes free, with an ArcGIS online subscription.

Geonode

A platform that is a resource for creating geospatial information systems (GIS), offering a base for developing customized GIS applications and organizing infrastructure data accordingly. Government agencies, NGOs, and research institutions utilize Geonode to build GIS apps, which cater to specific requirements. This platform can be personalized extensively and seamlessly integrates with existing systems, making it a preferred choice for developers looking to construct intricate GIS applications on a flexible and reliable foundation.

11.4 Innovative education models for smart citizenship

Novel educational strategies aimed at enhancing smart citizenship competencies need to be emphasized when developing educational initiatives that equip citizens with the skills needed for active participation in smart cities. The evolution of e-learning and u-learning (for ubiquitous learning), and deployment of ambient learning spaces are shaping this educational transformation towards a future where learning is more integrated into our daily environments, adaptive to our needs and contexts.

These modern educational strategies, by integrating these innovative learning methodologies, educational initiatives can effectively equip citizens with the necessary skills, ensuring they are well-prepared to engage with and contribute to the development and sustainability of smart urban environments (Atif et al., 2015).

11.4.1 E-learning and u-learning

Digital educational platforms propelled e-learning by offering flexibility and accessibility to learning resources online, enabling learners to access educational content anywhere, anytime. Technologies such as learning management systems (LMS) (Turnbull et al., 2020), multimedia content (Atif et al., 2003), and virtual classrooms (Atif, 2013) have shaped e-learning era. The advent of IoT transitions e-learning to u-learning (ubiquitous learning) (Atif et al., 2015), enhancing e-learning models with ubiquity, context-awareness, and personalization. IoT integration into educational environments transforms learning experiences, making them more interactive, personalized, and responsive to the learners' environment and needs, thus elevating learning practices to be more intuitive and embedded in daily practices.

Connected IoT devices are attached to physical objects and linked to web or mobile applications, which collect and curate data, while providing interaction interfaces with the objects. This physical and virtual convergence depends on learners' engagement within smart environments through appropriate learning strategies. For example, in energy domains, household energy-data could be seamlessly collected to reflect real-time self-assessment of energy management, and link-up with power retailers' programmes and incentives to balance energy-load, as illustrated in Fig. 11.2.

Consumers' engagement is key to smart grids evolution to involve users into excess energy redistribution, as an alternative for power-retailers to buy shortages from energy suppliers or to build new power distribution infrastructures. However, these adjustments in energy distribution require consumers' education and engagement to build this level of smart digital citizenship across a new educational continuum (Atif et al., 2018a).

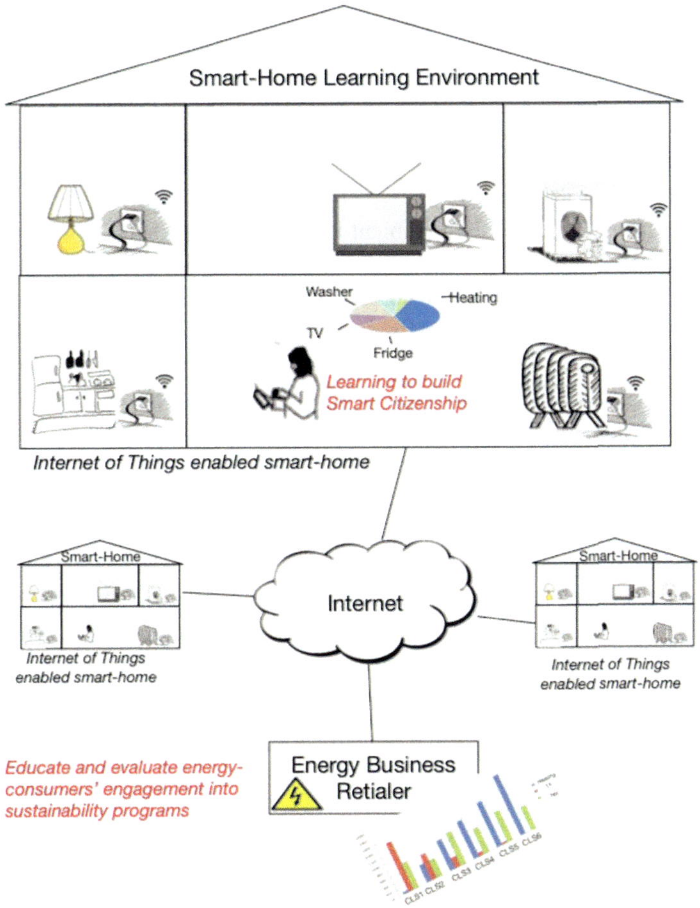

FIGURE 11.2

Smart citizenship learning in smart home environments (Atif et al., 2017)).

Using cloud-to-things such as infrastructures, power-consumption data from physical home-appliances is analyzed to customize education programs provided by energy retailers. Uneducated consumers reduce their engagement expectation, and subsequently delay citizenship responsibilities, such as commitment to sustainability. IoT-induced energy data can identify patterns to educate consumers on appropriate use of energy in cooperation with power retailers (Abdel-Basset et al., 2019). Although it is not common practice for retailers to incorporate "smart educational" features in their devices such as smart meters, this model could be hypothetically offered to smart homes, and also to workplaces and public venues, to promote smart citizenship competences (Atif et al., 2018b).

11.4.2 Ambient learning spaces

Ambient learning refers to embedding educational content and experiences within physical environments, allowing for seamless and situated learning as part of daily life. Ambient learning spaces utilize IoT devices and related cloud services to create smart, interactive environments that foster citizen education and engagement (Kanagarajan and Ramakrishnan, 2018).

As citizens navigate through ambient learning spaces, such as smart classrooms, intelligent office buildings, or connected urban environments, they access contextualized learning content relevant to their current situation and needs (Koren and Klamma, 2015). For instance, walking through a historic district may automatically deliver to passersby information that pop-up on their mobile devices about architectural details via a location-aware mobile app. Or an employee entering a conference room could be guided through a quick tutorial on how to use the room's smart display and collaboration tools (Atif et al., 2015).

Ambient learning aligns with the goals of smart citizenship, providing just-in-time learning embedded within daily routines and environments. Fig. 11.3 shows a mode-based representation of ambient learning, where data is exchanged across cloud services in JSON format. Citizens are members of a social community that aggregates physical objects and their users. Social interactions are triggered by model-defined rules, which shape actor interactions in the community, as illustrated in Fig. 11.4.

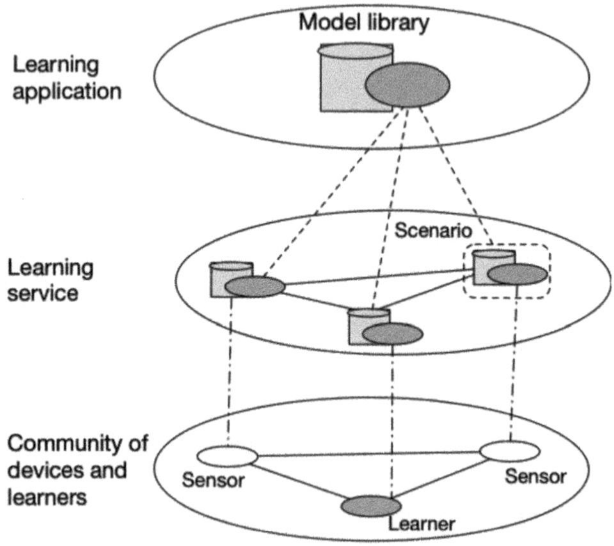

FIGURE 11.3

Social IoT learning community.

The sequence diagram of Fig. 11.4 integrates educational content and experiences within a person's daily environment, facilitated by IoT and related cloud services. The diagram illustrates the interaction among a user, a mobile application, and smart objects within an ambient learning space, which is part of a framework aimed at enhancing smart citizenship through just-in-time education. The sequence diagram features the following elements and interactions:

- **User:** This is the person engaging with the ambient learning environment through a mobile app.
- **Sensor/actuator (smart object):** These are IoT-enabled devices within the physical environment that interact with the user and the learning model.
- **Educator (learning model):** This represents the intelligent system or educational model that processes information and personalizes the learning experience.

The diagram outlines a loop, where the learning path is determined by reading and updating the learner's profile and the object's profile. This dynamic and adaptive learning process responds to the learner's actions and the context provided by smart objects.

This scenario could translate in real world to users of smart home devices, seeking to optimize energy patterns of home appliances. This model-based representation illustrates how data flows within an ambient learning space tailor learning experiences and respond to the individual's immediate context and actions. The sequence diagram is a visual representation of the underlying processes that enable ambient learning in smart citizenship education environments (Atif et al., 2018a).

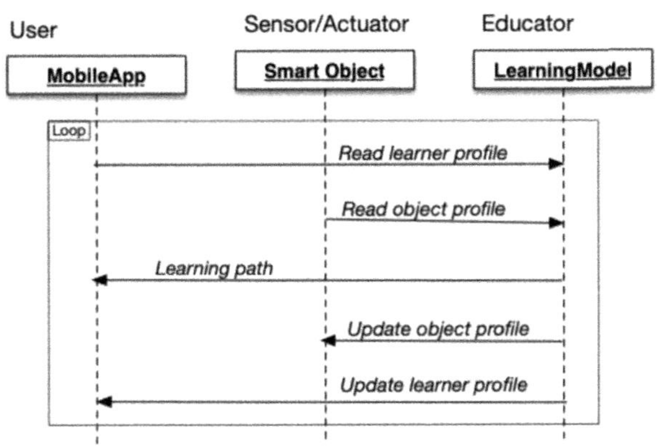

FIGURE 11.4

Learning interactions.

11.5 Practical initiatives and campaigns

Although the potential of smart citizenship is still being realized, many communities worldwide have already implemented impactful initiatives to increase citizen participation, digital literacy, and inclusion within cloud-to-things continuum as part of digital transformation initiatives. Next, we highlight some on-the-ground campaigns and projects that are cultivating smart citizenship through community education, grassroots innovation, and public-private partnerships. These campaigns could frame a diverse range of further smart citizenship initiatives, including the following:

- Digital literacy programs for underserved populations, such as low-income youth, seniors, and immigrants.
- Community hackathons and innovation challenges to develop IoT and cloud-based solutions to local problems.
- Smart city pilot projects emphasizing citizen co-creation and user-centric design.
- Public digital infrastructure programs expanding access to high-speed internet and devices.
- Cities utilizing IoT-related developments to increase civic participation and government transparency.

Each case study discussed next describe the background, objectives, and outcomes of the initiative, providing perspectives into real-world implementations of smart citizenship. The analysis leverages cloud-to-things continuum to engage local communities along best practices and lessons learned that can inform future efforts worldwide. By highlighting these on-the-ground initiatives, we aim at inspiring readers to launch their own smart citizenship campaigns. The diverse examples of citizen-centric innovation and collaboration showcase how communities globally are already pioneering smart citizenship principles to create more inclusive, participatory, and IoT-enabled societies.

11.5.1 Making Sense (Barcelona, Spain)

The Making Sense project in Barcelona aimed to empower residents with data about noise levels in their living environment, using open-source digital hardware combined with community participation techniques (Coulson et al., 2021). The project sought to enable the local community to monitor noise levels, and then use the data to advocate measures to reduce noise nuisance.

Background and objectives

Citizen sensing has emerged as an effective approach for fostering grassroots smart citizenship through community-driven data collection and civic action. This EU project was implemented from 2016 to 2017 in Barcelona, Spain. The initiative equipped local residents with noise-monitoring sensors to understand pollution issues in their neighborhoods. The core objectives were to (Coulson et al., 2021)

- Enable citizens to gather granular environmental data in their communities.
- Build public awareness and engagement around urban pollution.
- Develop grassroots proposals to address local noise problems.
- Establish an inclusive, collaborative model for citizen science, where residents collectively gather and interpret hyperlocal data.
- Promote public understanding of IoT and urban data.

By pursuing these goals, the project sought to activate citizens as urban scientists and civic participants leveraging IoT for positive community impact.

Outcomes and lessons learned

The Barcelona Making Sense project engaged 130 residents who were trained in using the sensors through 12 workshops. Thirty (30) different locations were monitored over a year, producing 100,000 data points, and 2 interactive maps were created to publicly showcase the localized data. Finally a community proposal was developed by residents to reduce motorbike noise (Coulson et al., 2021).

This initiative also demonstrated important lessons for participatory sensing, including

- Hands-on training and support is crucial to build confidence with IoT-related tools.
- Sustained motivation requires tangible applications of IoT data.
- Community partnerships are key to translating IoT data into action.

Overall, the Barcelona case study illustrates how participatory sensing can increase civic participation in sustainability issues, while building critical IoT-engagement literacies among urban residents. By providing localized data directly to communities, the ability of grassroots citizen in science initiatives is enhanced to drive progress in smart citizenship.

11.5.2 Smart Citizens Lab (Amsterdam, Netherlands)

Beyond traditional top-down approaches, innovative projects, such as the Amsterdam Smart Citizens Lab, are emerging, harnessing the power of IoT and community participation to empower residents and contribute to urban improvement. Similarly to the Barcelona project, by leveraging open-source tools and citizen science principles, this project explores the potential of smart citizenship enablement by focusing on air quality. The air we breathe in cities significantly impacts health and well-being. Recognizing the gap of localized mapping in air quality, the Amsterdam Smart Citizens Lab took an innovative step towards empowering residents to become active participants in monitoring and improving their city's air quality (Veenkamp et al., 2020). This innovative project was launched in 2015, where open-source sensor kits to measure key air pollutants are supplied to participants. Engaging residents in data collection and analysis aims to raise awareness, support policy decisions, and, ultimately, create a healthier Amsterdam for all.

Background and objectives

The bustling canals and historical charm of Amsterdam often mask a hidden threat: air pollution. From traffic emissions to industrial activity, the city faces challenges in maintaining healthy air quality, impacting the health and well-being of its residents. In this context, the Amsterdam Smart Citizens Lab emerges as a breath of fresh air, quite literally. Instead of relying solely on experts, the lab envisioned residents as active participants, transforming them into citizen scientists.

The project empowers citizens to collect real-time data from their own neighborhood to foster a sense of urban responsibility, but also provided an education practice to engage in IoT-induced smart citizenship. The lab's ambitions didn't stop at data collection, but actively promoted collaborative learning, and community engagement throughout the process. Workshops and data analysis sessions allowed participants to share their findings, learn from each other, and gain insights into the science behind air quality. These core principles translated into several key objectives:

- **Connect:** Provide citizens with affordable and accessible open-source sensor kits to connect their neighborhood with cloud-based urban management applications, such as air quality monitoring services.
- **Empower:** Enable citizens to foster trust and understanding of IoT-induced urbanism strategies by collecting their own data and reflect on it.
- **Engage:** Promote community engagement, breaking down silos and bridging the digital divide, while building collective action.
- **Inform:** Utilize citizen-generated data to make informed policy decisions and advocate for solutions that improve urban issues for all.

By following these objectives, the Amsterdam Smart Citizens Lab aimed to breathe life into a more citizen-centric approach to improving air quality, offering valuable lessons for other cities seeking to engage their communities in tackling smart-citizenship challenge.

Outcomes and lessons learned

The project demonstrated the power of community engagement in urban governance. By equipping residents with the tools to collect and interpret environmental data themselves, Making Sense engage community knowledge and collective action towards addressing an urban issue. This case underscores the importance of citizen participation in urban problem-solving and highlights the need for IoT-induced solutions to be embedded within participatory frameworks.

11.5.3 GammaSense (Netherlands)

Nuclear power plants often spark anxieties about invisible dangers looming from radiation leaks and potential accidents. Though safety measures are in place, many residents living near these facilities crave for more information and involvement in monitoring their environment. In response, the GammaSense project emerged, not as a passive solution, but as an approach to smart citizen empowerment (Bucur and Kjærgaard, 2008).

Background and objectives

Launched in the Netherlands, GammaSense recognized the limitations of traditional methods solely relying on official monitoring stations. These often offer sparse data and leave residents feeling uninformed. The project's vision aimed at democratizing science and technology by equipping citizens with the tools to measure nuclear radiation themselves. By providing participants with user-friendly Geiger–Müller tubes and a cloud-based platform, GammaSense empowered them to collect and share real-time radiation data directly from their own homes.

This shift from passive recipients to active knowledge producers fostered a sense of responsibility for radiation safety. GammaSense aggregates citizen-generated data on an online map, creating a transparent and accessible tool for all. This crowd-sourced data offered a more comprehensive picture of radiation levels across the region, potentially revealing localized variations not captured by official monitoring systems. The project's goals translated into key objectives:

- **Connect:** Provide citizens with affordable, user-friendly radiation detection tools.
- **Empower:** Equip citizens with skills to interpret data and understand radiation safety.
- **Engage:** Foster community engagement, collaboration, and knowledge sharing.
- **Inform:** Create a transparent online platform that aggregates citizen data and informs residents and policymakers.

Outcomes and lessons learned

GammaSense highlighted the challenges and opportunities of citizen-led environmental monitoring. The project faced difficulties in mobilizing citizens to discuss technical topics that were harnessed with increased user accessibility tools. However, the project successfully produced institutional knowledge on the governance of gamma radiation. This case study illustrates the need for smart city initiatives to balance technical precision with user accessibility and to foster spaces where citizens meaningfully contribute to discussions on urban environmental issues.

11.5.4 COVID-19: integrated contact tracing systems (South Korea and Singapore)

As the COVID-19 pandemic surged across the globe, traditional contact tracing methods often proved to be slow and resource-intensive. In response, several countries explored innovative solutions, harnessing IoT power to enhance tracking, improve efficiency, and, ultimately, mitigate the spread of the virus. South Korea and Singapore have been widely recognized for their best practice integration and promotion of IoT-enabled contact tracing systems during the COVID-19 pandemic (Jahmunah et al., 2021). They successfully engaged citizens into IoT devices and applications to curb the spread of the virus, while addressing privacy challenges (Garg et al., 2020).

Background and objectives

Faced with a rapidly spreading virus, South Korea sought a fast and accurate way to identify and isolate potential COVID-19 cases, whereas Singapore aimed to complement manual contact tracing efforts with digital solutions to improve accuracy and speed. In Korea's case, the existing extensive network of CCTV cameras in public spaces was leveraged to track the movements of individuals who had tested positive for COVID-19 or were close contacts of confirmed cases. This data helped in identifying potential exposure locations and trace movement patterns. Data was anonymized before analysis and utilization, ensuring individual privacy was protected. Access to this data was also restricted to authorized personnel directly involved in the contact tracing process. And finally, a legal framework was established to regulate data collection, storage, and usage, ensuring adherence to privacy regulations.

Singapore, addressed the limitations of traditional manual contact tracing methods to contain the virus's spread by embarking on a pioneering initiative to enhance both the accuracy and speed of contact tracing. This exploration materialized in the form of the TraceTogether program, aimed to address the shortcomings of traditional methods. At its core, the program sought to leverage Bluetooth technology to automatically log encounters between individuals, providing valuable data for tracing potential contacts in the case of a positive COVID-19 diagnosis.

However, public trust and privacy considerations are addressed through the implementation of secure data management within the program, whereby collected data went through a mobile phone app collected by way of wearable tokens equipped with Bluetooth technology. The data remained encrypted and stored locally on individual devices, accessible only to health authorities upon a confirmed positive test. This approach aimed to strike a balance between the program's effectiveness and individuals' right to privacy (Seto et al., 2021). The wearable tokens equipped with Bluetooth technology were employed in the TraceTogether program to ensure that even those without smartphones could participate in the program.

Outcomes and lessons learned

Both countries demonstrated the potential of IoT for rapid contact tracing, thereby potentially preventing wider outbreaks. However, extensive data collection raised privacy concerns, which were addressed in both case studies. The main outcomes of these initiatives are the following:

- IoT enables swift contact tracing, offering valuable time for interventions.
- Transparency and robust data security reinforced public engagement.
- Inclusive solutions can effectively address the digital divide for wider smart-citizenship adoption.

Though IoT-enabled contact tracing offers promising tools for pandemic management, its successful implementation hinges on addressing privacy concerns, building public trust, and integrating IoT technologies within a comprehensive public agency strategy. The experiences of South Korea and Singapore provide valuable indications of public engagement in smart citizenship initiatives to embrace future digital transformation advancements.

11.6 Conclusion

Smart citizenship is a journey through IoT-cloud adoption, where technology, community, and governance converge to redefine urban living. The exploration of innovative education models, practical initiatives, and relevant case studies revealed a multidimensional approach to fostering smart citizenship. Furthermore, the integration of IoT and cloud technologies catalyzes the development of smart cities, enabling functionalities that enhance civic engagement. However, this digital transformation journey is marked by challenges such as the digital divide, privacy concerns, and the need for ethical considerations in data usage.

Ensuring equitable access to technology and fostering digital literacy among all citizens enable smart cities to prioritize inclusive policies and programs that empower every citizen to navigate and contribute to the digital ecosystem. As cities become smarter, the collection and analysis of data escalate, while the privacy of citizen data is harnessed with transparent policies, supported by citizen awareness programs that maintain public trust in digital transformation initiatives. The latter make it evident that the ethical implications of IoT and cloud technologies require ongoing dialogue among policymakers, technology suppliers, and citizens.

Ethical frameworks that guide the development and deployment of smart city initiatives evolve with continuous learning and adaptation to new situations through innovative education models. Ambient learning spaces and u-learning environments play a significant role in equipping citizens with the skills needed for future digital transformations, while active participation of citizens in shaping their urban environments enhance the sense of ownership and responsibility towards the community.

As we envision the future of smart cities, the role of citizens evolves from passive beneficiaries to active participants and co-creators of their urban ecosystems. Empowering citizens with the competences to thrive in digitally transformed societies is part of the successful journey towards smart citizenship, where the cloud-to-things continuum offers endless possibilities for enhancing the quality of life, sustainability, and efficiency of urban spaces.

References

Abdel-Basset, M., Manogaran, G., Mohamed, M., Rushdy, E., 2019. Internet of things in smart education environment: supportive framework in the decision-making process. Concurrency and Computation: Practice and Experience 31 (10), e4515.

Ali, M., Alexopoulos, C., Charalabidis, Y., 2022. A comprehensive review of open data platforms, prevalent technologies, and functionalities. In: Proceedings of the 15th International Conference on Theory and Practice of Electronic Governance, pp. 203–214.

Almubark, H., Masmali, O., 2022. The awareness of Internet of Things (IoT) privacy risk: a survey study. In: Proceedings of the Future Technologies Conference. Springer, pp. 174–190.

Atif, Y., 2013. Conversational learning integration in technology enhanced classrooms. Computers in Human Behavior 29 (2), 416–423.

Atif, Y., Berri, J., Benlamri, R., 2003. An adaptive multimedia approach to e-learning. In: 10th IEEE International Conference on Electronics, Circuits and Systems. ICECS 2003. Proceedings of the 2003, vol. 3. IEEE, 2003, pp. 1224–1227.

Atif, Y., Mathew, S.S., Lakas, A., 2015. Building a smart campus to support ubiquitous learning. Journal of Ambient Intelligence and Humanized Computing 6, 223–238.

Atif, Y., Sergis, S., Sampson, D., 2018a. Digital smart citizenship competence development with a cyber-physical learning approach supported by Internet of Things technologies. In: Digital Technologies: Sustainable Innovations for Improving Teaching and Learning, pp. 277–300.

Atif, Y., Sergis, S., Sampson, D., 2018b. Digital Smart Citizenship Competence Development with a Cyber-Physical Learning Approach Supported by Internet of Things Technologies. Springer International Publishing, pp. 277–300. https://doi.org/10.1007/978-3-319-73417-0_16.

Atif, Y., Sergis, S., Sampson, D., Mathiason, G., 2017. A cyberphysical learning approach for digital smart citizenship competence development. In: Proceedings of the 26th International Conference on World Wide Web Companion, pp. 397–405.

Barati, M., Petri, I., Rana, O.F., 2019. Developing gdpr compliant user data policies for Internet of Things. In: Proceedings of the 12th IEEE/ACM International Conference on Utility and Cloud Computing, pp. 133–141.

Bucur, D., Kjærgaard, M.B., 2008. GammaSense: infrastructureless positioning using background radioactivity. In: European Conference on Smart Sensing and Context. Springer, pp. 69–82.

Coulson, S., Woods, M., EU, M.S., 2021. Citizen sensing: an action-orientated framework for citizen science. Frontiers in Communication 6, 629700.

Damiani, E., Kowalczyk, R., Parr, G., 2017. Extending the outreach: from smart cities to connected communities.

de Juana-Espinosa, S., Luján-Mora, S., 2019. Open government data portals in the European Union: considerations, development, and expectations. Technological Forecasting & Social Change 149, 119769.

de Waal, M., Dignum, M., 2017. The citizen in the smart city. How the smart city could transform citizenship. IT - Information Technology 59 (6), 263–273. https://doi.org/10.1515/itit-2017-0012.

Dodero, J.M., Ruiz-Rube, I., Palomo-Duarte, M., Vázquez-Murga, J., 2011. Open linked data model revelation and access for analytical web science. In: Metadata and Semantic Research: 5th International Conference. MTSR 2011, Izmir, Turkey, October 12–14, 2011, Proceedings 5. Springer, pp. 105–116.

Ferronato, P., Ruecker, S., 2018. Smart citizenship: Designing the interaction between citizens and smart cities.

Garg, L., Chukwu, E., Nasser, N., Chakraborty, C., Garg, G., 2020. Anonymity preserving IoT-based COVID-19 and other infectious disease contact tracing model. IEEE Access 8, 159402–159414.

Hamm, A., 2022. The civic Internet of Things as a socio-technical object. Studies on community-based environmental monitoring, sustained civic engagement and new opportunities in journalism. PhD thesis. University of Berlin.

Jacobs, N., Loveday, F., Markovic, M., Cottrill, C.D., Zullo, R., Edwards, P., 2022. Prototyping an IoT transparency toolkit to support communication, governance and policy in the smart city. Design Journal 25 (3), 459–480.

Jahmunah, V., Sudarshan, V.K., Oh, S.L., Gururajan, R., Gururajan, R., Zhou, X., Tao, X., Faust, O., Ciaccio, E.J., Ng, K.H., et al., 2021. Future IoT tools for COVID-19 contact tracing and prediction: a review of the state-of-the-science. International Journal of Imaging Systems and Technology 31 (2), 455–471.

Kalinin, A.A., Palanimalai, S., Zhu, J., Wu, W., Devraj, N., Ye, C., Ponarul, N., Husain, S.S., Dinov, I.D., 2022. Socrat: a dynamic web toolbox for interactive data processing, analysis and visualization. Information 13 (11), 547.

Kanagarajan, S., Ramakrishnan, S., 2018. Ubiquitous and ambient intelligence assisted learning environment infrastructures development – a review. Education and Information Technologies 23, 569–598.

Karabatak, S., Ay, S., Karabatak, M., 2023. The relationship between digital citizenship and information security achievement. In: 2023 11th International Symposium on Digital Forensics and Security (ISDFS). IEEE, pp. 1–5.

Koren, I., Klamma, R., 2015. Smart ambient learning with physical artifacts using wearable technologies. In: Intelligent Environments (Workshops), pp. 325–332.

Lee, H., Kobsa, A., 2016. Understanding user privacy in Internet of Things environments. In: 2016 IEEE 3rd World Forum on Internet of Things (WF-IoT). IEEE, pp. 407–412.

Liu, C., Zowghi, D., 2022. Citizen involvement in digital transformation: a systematic review and a framework. Online Information Review 47 (4), 644–660. https://doi.org/10.1108/OIR-04-2022-0237.

López, M.S., 2022. Violation of the right to be forgotten on the Internet: legal overview of tort law aspects. In: International Conference on Autonomous Systems and the Law. Springer, pp. 25–40.

Lutchman, S., Hosein, P., 2015. An open source real-time data portal. Journal of ICT 2 (3), 289–302.

Neisse, R., Baldini, G., Steri, G., Miyake, Y., Kiyomoto, S., Biswas, A.R., 2015. An agent-based framework for informed consent in the Internet of Things. In: 2015 IEEE 2nd World Forum on Internet of Things (WF-IoT). IEEE, pp. 789–794.

O'Connor, Y., Rowan, W., Lynch, L., Heavin, C., 2017. Privacy by design: informed consent and Internet of Things for smart health. Procedia Computer Science 113, 653–658.

Pham, L., Mai, T.T., Massey, B., 2016. Key factors for effective citizens engagement in smart city: the case of cork city. In: AIS Pre-ICIS Workshop on "IoT & Smart City Challenges and Applications".

Politou, E., Alepis, E., Virvou, M., Patsakis, C., 2022. Privacy and Data Protection Challenges in the Distributed Era, vol. 26. Springer.

Ramos, J.H., Skármeta, A., 2020. Security and Privacy in the Internet of Things: Challenges and Solutions, vol. 27. IOS Press.

Rêgo, B.S., Lourenço, D., Moreira, F., Pereira, C.S., 2023. Digital transformation, skills and education: a systematic literature review. Industry & Higher Education, 09504222231208969.

Sá, M.J., Santos, A.I., Serpa, S., Ferreira, C.M., 2021. Digital literacy in digital society 5.0. Academic Journal of Interdisciplinary Studies 10 (2), 1–9.

Seto, E., Challa, P., Ware, P., 2021. Adoption of COVID-19 contact tracing apps: a balance between privacy and effectiveness. Journal of Medical Internet Research 23 (3), e25726.

Shin, S.-Y., Kim, D., Chun, S.A., 2021. Digital divide in advanced smart city innovations. Sustainability 13 (7), 4076.

Turnbull, D., Chugh, R., Luck, J., 2020. Learning management systems, an overview. In: Encyclopedia of Education and Information Technologies, pp. 1052–1058.

van Deursen, A.J.A.M., Mossberger, K., 2018a. Any thing for anyone? A new digital divide in Internet-of-Things skills. Policy & Internet 10 (2), 122–140. https://onlinelibrary.wiley.com/doi/abs/10.1002/poi3.171.

Van Deursen, A.J., Mossberger, K., 2018b. Any thing for anyone? A new digital divide in Internet-of-Things skills. Policy & Internet 10 (2), 122–140.

Veenkamp, J., Kresin, F., Kortlander, M., 2020. Smart citizens in Amsterdam. In: The Routledge Companion to Smart Cities.

Winn, J., 2013. Open data and the academy: an evaluation of ckan for research data management.

CHAPTER

12 Driving change and innovation with IoT-cloud-based digital transformation

12.1 Introduction

The seamless connection, between the cloud and everyday devices is driving the shift towards innovations that address global challenges, such as urban growth, environmental sustainability, embracing digital commerce, and responding to climate change. For example, rapid urbanization is straining city infrastructure and resources, such as water and energy. One method of addressing this socio-economic challenge is to use IoT sensors embedded in building infrastructures to monitor water leakages and energy consumption. This data is further analyzed in the cloud to enable predictive maintenance and energy optimization. The "Array of Things" project in Chicago (DeMedeiros et al., 2024) is a compelling example of an innovative urban sensing initiative. This project involves deploying a network of interactive, modular sensor boxes around the city. Real-time data on ambient sound intensity, carbon emission, barometric pressures, and traffic of pedestrians and vehicles are collected from sensors. This data is subsequently used across a broad spectrum of applications to improve urban living and urban planning, making cities more livable and sustainable.

Optimal allocation of resources, such as water and energy, along with waste minimization, shape a sustainable tomorrow. Cloud-based analytics of IoT data can identify areas where efficiency can be improved. For instance, smart irrigation systems use IoT sensors to monitor soil moisture in India (Murthy et al., 2023) and automatically adjust water usage, reducing waste and contributing to sustainable practices. Similarly, Aclima mitigates impacts on climate change by monitoring oil and gas emissions (Aclima, 2024) through environmental sensors. IoT and cloud-based technologies can be leveraged to track these environmental changes and provide effective strategies to develop and promote a sustainable future (Biz4Intellia, 2022).

Cloud platforms act as a central hub for IoT data exchange, to enable businesses leveraging the power of data from any location. Ride-sharing apps, such as Uber and Lyft, rely on IoT and cloud connectivity to link potential passengers with drivers in real time, which contributes to digital sharing economy (Mnyakin, 2023). Whereas IoT allows businesses to remotely monitor and manage physical assets and infras-

Accelerating Digital Transformation with the Cloud and the Internet of Things (IoT)
https://doi.org/10.1016/B978-0-44-322217-7.00020-7

tructure, cloud-based analytics can identify areas of waste and inefficiency, and AI algorithms can further optimize resource allocation, predict maintenance needs, and develop new, sustainable practices. This saves costs and promotes environmental sustainability within the digital economy.

In light of the above examples, the theory of change framework (Taplin and Clark, 2012) emerges as an essential framework for navigating and capitalizing on the cloud-to-things continuum. Mapping out the pathways from technological deployment to tangible benefits, reflects the strategic role of this theory, which dictates necessary interventions to face the complexities of rapid urbanization, sustainability challenges, and the evolving digital economy. In essence, the theory of change offers a blueprint for action to work towards a future where IoT and cloud data drive sustainability throughout communities and economies.

12.2 Managing change: towards digital transformation

A theory of change (ToC) is used in business and social programs, as well as international developments, to explain how a specific transformation can be achieved. This theory outlines essentially the steps and assumptions to reach a desired outcome, like a roadmap (Colby et al., 2013).

12.2.1 Theory of change (ToC)

ToC impacts digital transformation in multiple ways. Clarity to the transformation plan is through the steps and assumptions underlying the transformation approach. Furthermore, potential gaps in the plan are identified before implementation. Secondly, a well-developed ToC promotes communication and alignment among stakeholders by providing a shared understanding of the goals, activities, and expected results. Ultimately, a ToC serves as a baseline to gauge the initiative's progress. This standard is utilized to assess the actions that contribute to the desired results and adjust strategies as needed. Establishing a link between actions and their consequences enhances the likelihood of reaching desired objectives.

The ToC framework, by (Taplin and Clark, 2012) lays out the actions to reach defined objectives and pinpoint signs of progress. It proves useful in crafting strategies that require various stages, involvement of multiple parties, and continuous feedback loops. To implement digital transformation through the integration of IoT and cloud technologies, we propose the following ToC elements:

- **Long-term goals:** The initiative's ultimate aim is to achieve targeted outcomes.
- **Preconditions or intermediate outcomes:** Necessary conditions that need to be in place for long-term goals to be achieved.
- **Interventions:** Actions or events initiated to realize the preconditions or outcomes.
- **Assumptions:** Beliefs on how interventions will lead to desired outcomes.

- **Indicators:** Metrics or signs used to assess whether the preconditions, interventions, and outcomes are being achieved.

12.2.2 Driving change through IoT-cloud integration

The convergence of cloud and IoT technologies presents a transformative opportunity for organizations to unlock a new era of operational efficiency, sustainability, and business growth. This ultimate ToC goal requires a well-defined roadmap. The ToC framework guides the integration of cloud and IoT as instruments for achieving specific, measurable outcomes into a reality that delivers lasting value and societal benefit.

Long-term goals

Integrating IoT and cloud technologies aims to optimize further operational efficiency, sustainability, and business growth. These advances in technology have the potential to improve city living standards and support sustainability by optimizing the use of resources. Moreover they can boost development through a competitive economy that encourages and supports digital marketplaces.

Preconditions or intermediate outcomes

For the long-term goals to be realized, intermediate outcomes form the path to achieve the integration of IoT and cloud technologies.

- Widespread adoption of technology: Integrating sensor technology across various sectors and establishing robust cloud computing capabilities.
- Effective data analysis: Leveraging big data analytics to process the data generated by IoT devices for actionable output.
- Policy and infrastructure: Developing supportive policies and investing in infrastructure to accommodate advances in IoT and cloud applications.
- Stakeholder engagement: Engaging public and private sectors alongside communities to ensure the solutions meet the needs of all stakeholders.

Interventions

These are specific actions undertaken to achieve the intermediate outcomes as outlined next.

- Innovative deployment of IoT and cloud technologies, such as sensor technology in GE Aviation's jet engines for real-time performance monitoring (Adamopoulou and Daskalakis, 2023) and Siemens' use of cloud-based analytics for factory optimization (Annanth et al., 2021).
- Edge computing allows for processing data closer to its source, reducing latency and bandwidth requirements. Wind farms use edge devices to analyze sensor data from turbines for predictive maintenance, minimizing downtime, and ensuring optimal energy production (Durbhaka et al., 2021).

- Cloud and IoT innovations enable organizations to optimize resource utilization. For instance, a city government can analyze data on energy consumption from smart meters installed in buildings to identify inefficient buildings and implement targeted energy-saving measures (Wang et al., 2023).
- Retailers can leverage data on customer purchase history and browsing behavior to personalize product recommendations and marketing campaigns (Trivedi et al., 2022). Cloud-based analytics platforms can process customer data to identify trends and preferences, allowing businesses to offer targeted promotions and recommendations, increasing customer satisfaction and loyalty.
- Capacity building and training: Enhancing skills in data analytics and IoT system management to utilize these technologies effectively.
- Collaborative projects and policies: Initiating smart city projects, such as the "Array of Things" in Chicago and adopting policies that encourage digital transformation.

Assumptions

ToC for IoT and cloud integration relies on several assumptions, elaborated further next.

- Seamless integration of IoT devices with existing infrastructure is possible and effective.
- Data generated through IoT devices, when analyzed, will provide insights that can lead to operational improvements and innovative solutions. For example, a manufacturing plant can deploy IoT sensors on production lines to monitor machine performance, temperature, and vibration (Javaid et al., 2021). This real-time data is expected to provide insights into potential issues before they escalate into costly breakdowns.
- Stakeholders, including government bodies, private companies, and the public, are willing to adopt and adapt to these new technologies.
- The interventions will lead to the intended intermediate outcomes without unintended negative consequences. For example, an agricultural company can equip its fields with moisture sensors and weather stations that collect data continuously (Kayad et al., 2021). This data is then uploaded to the cloud, where advanced analytics tools can analyze soil conditions and weather patterns and predict optimal irrigation schedules, maximizing crop yield and water conservation.

Analyzing the context of transformation

The subsequent step of ToC for digital transformation with cloud and IoT involves analyzing the context and situation. This analysis identifies areas where these technologies can drive significant change. Some key activities enabled by IoT and cloud technologies are listed next.

- **Data-driven decisions:** Cloud and IoT enable data-aware decisions by providing real-time and historical data from IoT devices to inform decision-making across various sectors. For instance, a healthcare provider deploys wearable health monitors for patients with chronic conditions. Cloud-based processes analyze this healthcare data, enabling doctors to proactively identify potential health risks and personalize treatment plans (Shafi et al., 2024).

- **Process automation:** Cloud-to-things continuum automates repetitive tasks within processes. IoT devices' collected data is fed into cloud-based workflows. These workflows can then trigger actions and automate tasks, reducing the need for manual intervention. For example, a logistics company can use IoT sensors in trucks to track location and cargo status (Muñuzuri et al., 2020). Cloud platforms can integrate this data with route planning software. A delivery route that changes due to traffic or weather conditions is automatically recalculated based on cloud-based analytics, which saves time and optimize resources, while also improving delivery efficiency.
- **Demand forecasting:** Cloud and IoT can be leveraged for demand forecasting by employing machine learning algorithms on historical sales data and real-time sensor data from customer-facing stores. This allows for predicting customer demand for products with greater accuracy. For example, a grocery store chain utilizes smart shelves equipped with weight sensors (Falcão et al., 2020). Combining this data with past sales information stored in the cloud allows for accurate demand forecasting.
- **Resource optimization:** Cloud and IoT technologies optimize resource consumption, such as energy and water, using data from embedded IoT devices, such as smart meters, to track energy use across production lines (Hoyer et al., 2020). Cloud platforms can then analyze this data to identify areas of high consumption. The utility company can then inform commercial consumers about targeted energy-saving measures by adjusting machine settings or using energy-efficient lighting.
- **Predictive maintenance:** Predictive maintenance involves analyzing sensor data from equipment to predict potential failures before breakdowns occur (Namuduri et al., 2020). For example, an airline company equips its aircraft with sensors that monitor engine performance parameters. Cloud-based analytics analyze this data, allowing for predictive maintenance, preventing in-flight emergencies, and ensuring optimal aircraft operation.

Indicators

Success in the integration of IoT and cloud technologies can be measured by specific indicators. Two of those indicators are:

- **Operational efficiency and innovation:** Achievements such as enhanced operational efficiency, the introduction of new revenue streams, and the optimization of resource utilization are direct outcomes of the interventions. These include real-time monitoring for predictive maintenance and data analytics for process improvements.
- **Customer experience enhancement:** The use of IoT and cloud data to personalize customer experiences represents another critical outcome, leading to higher customer satisfaction and loyalty.

Through the combination of IoT data with cloud workflows, organizations can automate many repetitive tasks within their processes. Sensor data from devices is collected and fed into cloud-based workflows. These workflows are then enabled to trigger automation actions, which reduces the need for manual intervention. The benefits include reduced manual errors, faster turnaround times, and streamlined operations. For example, a pharmaceutical company can automate quality control processes by deploying IoT sensors on production lines (Arden et al., 2021). Potential defects are identified in real time by cloud-based analytics. Immediate corrective action empower organizations to minimize production delays and improve overall efficiency.

Data-driven decisions based on IoT and cloud analytics, along with predictive maintenance practices, can significantly reduce overall operational costs. By analyzing sensor data and historical trends, organizations can make informed decisions about resource allocation, identify areas for optimization, and predict potential equipment failures. Predictive maintenance supports proactive maintenance scheduling, prevents costly breakdowns, and extend the lifespan of equipment. Further reduction in operational expenses is enabled by real-time data from IoT devices, which optimize resource consumption, such as energy and fuel.

Cloud and IoT technologies can improve customer engagement by enabling personalized recommendations and real-time support. By leveraging customer purchase history stored in the cloud, retailers can recommend personalized styles and offer targeted promotions. Customers can also utilize smart fitting rooms that analyze body measurements and suggest suitable clothing options, leading to a more engaging and personalized shopping experience. Similarly, a manufacturing company may use connected devices to provide real-time support to customers. For example, a customer experiencing issues with a product may receive remote assistance through a mobile app (Hoyer et al., 2020), while communicating the state of the connected product, inherently. This personalized approach to customer support enhances customer experiences, increases customer satisfaction, and fosters brand loyalty.

The above ToC activities, which focus on the desired organizational outcomes, leverage cloud and IoT to achieve significant improvements in operational efficiency, reduce costs, enhance customer engagement, and contribute to a more sustainable future. The specific activities and desired outcomes may vary, depending on each organization goals and industry. However, cloud and IoT transformative potential are retained across a wide spectrum of organizational contexts and industries.

12.2.3 Societal impact of digital transformation

Digital transformation, empowered by cloud computing and IoT, extends beyond driving business success. It unlocks significant societal benefits, promoting sustainability, smarter urban planning, and improved quality of life for citizens. A key principle is to consider environmental impact alongside business outcomes when developing a theory of change (ToC) framework for digital transformation. For example, a "remote equipment monitoring" service for manufacturers can also track energy usage and suggest efficiency improvements. This approach translates business benefits, such as cost savings, into environmental benefits by reducing energy consumption. Similarly, a "precision irrigation" service in agriculture can be adapted for urban landscaping. By optimizing water usage in parks and green spaces, this service contributes to more innovative city planning and promotes sustainable resource management. Digital transformation enhanced with cloud and IoT directly impacts society in several ways, as discussed next.

Sustainable smart cities

The influence of cloud technology and IoT convergence, affects communities significantly with enhanced urban solutions. These innovative approaches combine sensor networks from IoT with cloud services to establish a more efficient, sustainable, and livable urban environment. Examples include smart grid projects that allocate energy based on real-time demand, smart parking applications that optimize parking availability, or waste management systems with real-time bin fill level monitoring, eliminating the need for outdated schedule-based collection routes. These applications offer a multitude of benefits:

- **Increased operational efficiency:** Smart city solutions streamline operations across various city services, reducing costs and resource utilization.
- **Minimized impact, on the environment:** Real-time data analysis enable optimized energy use, waste management, and traffic flow, leading to a more sustainable city.
- **Enhanced public safety measures:** Sensor networks can monitor noise levels and air quality, and even detect gunshots. This empowers authorities to respond proactively to incidents, improving public safety for all.

Barcelona, Spain showcases a demonstration of smart city initiatives. The city has installed sensors, over urban areas to keep track of traffic patterns, brightness of streetlights, garbage bin capacity, availability of parking spots, air quality, and noise levels. Cloud platforms analyze data from these sensors and provide actionable decisions for optimizing these urban operations. For example, Barcelona's smart parking system uses sensors to detect and direct drivers to available parking spaces, reducing congestion caused by cars circling in search of parking. Similarly, the city's noise monitoring system identifies areas with excessive noise levels. This data allows authorities to enforce noise ordinances and take targeted measures for noise reduction in specific areas.

Fostering economic growth

Cloud services empower cities to outsource the management of various smart city service portfolios to local companies. This business model offers several advantages:

- **Expertise and innovation:** Local companies may encompass specialized knowledge and expertise in smart city-related technologies and their management. This expertise allows cities to fit the city's unique needs in the advocated transformation solutions.

- **Cost efficiency:** Outsourcing can save costs by utilizing existing personnel and infrastructure locally, which reduces the city's need to invest in additional resources.
- **Economic development:** The city's growth is partly quantified by its capacity to generate employment opportunities and boosting the industry for further smart city solutions. Outsourcing contributes also to these socio-economic opportunities, which in turn attracts additional investments.
- **Agility and adaptability:** Domestic small businesses are often more agile to respond quickly to changing needs and willing to experiment new technologies than larger corporations.
- **Public-private partnerships:** Private partnerships promote cooperation between the government and private companies, combining their expertise to create more sustainable solutions for urban development.

Defining metrics and consistently tracking their performance guarantee the success of city outsources services. Here are some key indicators that should be kept under observation:

- **System uptime, data quality, and accuracy:** These measures guarantee that smart city solutions are up and running, easily accessible to users, and offer data for obtaining actionable insights and improving city services.
- **Assessing performance:** Decreased traffic jams or enhanced air quality are examples of indocators to monitor the effectiveness of smart city solutions.
- **Citizen satisfaction:** Survey public perception of smart city solutions.
- **Return on investment (ROI):** Evaluate the financial benefits of smart city solutions against costs to manage outsourcing initiatives.
- **Innovation and job creation:** Quantify instances of new solutions implemented by outsourced service providers, as well as the related number of jobs created by domestic companies that manage smart city solutions.

Establishing objectives and holding service providers accountable for meeting the associated performance metrics, along with maintaining communication and collaboration channels between the city and the service providers, ensure the long-term success of smart city initiatives.

12.3 Business model transformation

Integrating cloud services and IoT using the theory of change (ToC) framework can bring about opportunities for reshaping business models. This shift has the potential to spark creativity in service offerings and broaden market reach beyond what was thought possible. Cloud platforms serve as the groundwork for introducing data-powered services, and IoT sensors provide the information wealth, which can pave the way for brand service solutions. The prospects for fostering innovation and expanding business horizons are truly remarkable.

12.3.1 Predictive maintenance as a service (PdMaaS)

Predictive maintenance as a service (PdMaaS) is transforming equipment management by leveraging IoT power and related cloud analytics services. These innovative services embed sensors in equipment to collect real-time data on various performance parameters. The collected data is transmitted to cloud platforms, where advanced analytics and machine learning algorithms process it to predict potential failures and maintenance needs. This proactive approach allows organizations to address issues before they escalate further. PdMaaS are utilized by Rolls Royce through a cloud-based AI and machine learning platform to analyze data from aircraft engine sensors. By adopting this strategy maintenance, needs are predicted to enhance engine efficiency and reduce airline disruptions. In doing so, airlines plan maintenance activities during scheduled flights to ensure aircraft availability and lower downtime expenses.

The PdMaaS platform offers users comprehensive tools for proactive equipment management. Dashboards allow users to visualize sensor data and monitor equipment performance in real time. Alerts and notifications are generated when sensor data indicates potential issues that require operational attention. Besides predicting equipment failures, advanced analytics recommend optimal maintenance schedules. Data-driven reports are further generated to oversee equipment health trends and develop maintenance interventions.

PdMaaS can be provided as a subscription service, with various pricing options. These pricing plans take into account variables such as the quantity of devices being monitored, the intricacy of the machinery, and the preferred service level. Entry level packages may involve monitoring and notifications, whereas higher tier plans might provide predictive maintenance analytics and tailored reports.

Providers of PdMaaS can collaborate with partners for outsourced services to support their effective implementation and operation. Sensor installation and maintenance can be outsourced to companies with sensor deployment and data quality management expertise. Establishing collaborations with data science firms create and maintain machine learning algorithms that can analyze sensor data effectively to predict equipment failures. Working together with experts in domain industries leads to customized recommendations, which match the equipment and maintenance needs of each specific industry. PdMaaS offers a win-win solution for both users and platform providers. Real-time data and advanced analytics employed by PdMaaS promote maintenance practices that reduce equipment breakdowns and downtime. This leads to improved efficiency and productivity for businesses. Moreover PdMaaS helps to cut down maintenance costs by enabling users to plan maintenance tasks during scheduled downtimes, avoiding disruptions and optimizing resource allocation for maintenance teams. The subscription model also ensures a reliable income stream for the platform provider.

However, this business model depends on tackling key hurdles. It is important to integrate sensor protocols and data formats from different types of equipment across various industries. Strong security measures are needed to protect equipment data and following relevant data privacy legislations. Additionally, it is important to address user concerns about the cost and value of PdMaaS to encourage its adoption.

By showing businesses return on investment (ROI), in terms of cost savings and operational efficiency improvements, platform providers can persuade them to embrace PdMaaS and enjoy its advantages.

12.3.2 Remote equipment monitoring as a service (REMaaS)

REMaaS (Remote Equipment Monitoring as a Service) harnesses the capabilities of IoT and cloud analytics to transform equipment management practices. This approach monitors and assesses equipment performance operational conditions and environmental influences in different sectors, such as manufacturing, construction, transportation, and utilities.

REMaaS utilizes cloud-based services that fuse data from sensors implanted in different devices. These sensors offer information on the health of equipment, its operational status and the environmental conditions around it. The system support users with a range of tools for remotely monitoring and managing the equipment. This capacity enable users to

- **Visualize real-time data:** Users can keep track of equipment performance with dashboards that spot any issues promptly, through a display of sensor data.
- **Set up alerts and notifications:** Users get alerts and notifications that inform them of issues or changes in equipment performance, enabling them to act proactively.
- **Analyze historical trends:** Users can browse data to examine how equipment has performed over time and comprehensively spot trends that might reveal potential issues.
- **Utilize predictive maintenance tools:** Experienced users have the option to utilize the platform's machine learning capabilities for maintenance. These algorithms examine sensor data to anticipate equipment malfunctions in advance, allowing users to plan maintenance activities during scheduled downtime.

REMaaS could be provided on a subscription basis with pricing tiers. These pricing plans take into account factors such as the quantity of devices being monitored, the level of data analysis complexity needed (for instance basic monitoring, versus maintenance), and the range of features included. This adaptive strategy enables REMaaS usage to adjust to users' requirements and financial resources.

REMaaS business model offers service outsourcing opportunities throughout the entire value chain. Here are some potential partnership options for outsourcing:

- **Sensor installation and maintenance:** Partnering with specialized companies ensures proper sensor deployment, data quality, and ongoing functionality of the sensor network.
- **Data analysis and machine learning:** The provider of the platform can work together with companies that have expertise in machine learning and data science for in-depth analysis of data, especially in applications related to predictive maintenance. These collaborations guarantee the development and maintenance of algorithms for examining sensor data and forecasting potential equipment failures.

- **Industry-specific expertise:** Partnerships with experts in specialized sectors relevant to unique equipment and maintenance needs offer guidance and suggestions to users based on their equipment data to guarantee that the REMaaS solution remains pertinent and beneficial across a variety of industries.

The REMaaS model offers advantages to both users and the platform provider. It empowers users with maintenance strategies that reduce equipment downtime and repair expenses. By detecting problems early, users can plan maintenance during scheduled downtimes, preventing costly disruptions to operations. Furthermore, proactive maintenance helps to extend the lifespan of equipment by preventing breakdowns. Furthermore, real-time data insights from REMaaS enable users to optimize equipment utilization and workflow planning, enhancing overall operational efficiency. The platform provider benefits from the subscription model's predictable and recurring revenue stream.

REMaaS implementation is susceptible to encounter some obstacles. Sensor protocols and data formats must incorporate data from different types of equipment and sectors. A uniform integration simplifies the process of collecting and analyzing data from a variety of equipment, irrespective of the manufacturer or sector. Robust security measures are also required to safeguard sensitive data collected from equipment. Compliance with relevant data privacy regulations ensure user trust in the REMaaS platform's ability to protect their data. Finally, overcoming user adoption challenges necessitates addressing initial hesitancy regarding costs and potential security risks. Platform providers can effectively address these concerns by demonstrating the return on investment (ROI) through cost savings and improved operational efficiency. By highlighting the financial benefits and emphasizing the robust security measures, platform providers can convince businesses to embrace REMaaS and unlock its numerous advantages.

Addressing these obstacles and harnessing the benefits of outsourcing enable REMaaS to transform the way equipment is managed in several sectors. Companies can anticipate operational performance, experience less downtime, and have longer lasting equipment, while the service provider sets up a reliable business model with ongoing income.

12.3.3 Precision agriculture as a service (PAgaaS)

Precision agriculture as a service (PAgaaS) leverages IoT and cloud analytics to enable data-informed decisions that improve farming practices. This innovative service model empowers to increase yields, reduce waste, and enhance environmental sustainability. For instance, the "Precision Agriculture for Development" initiative utilizes IoT sensors and satellite imagery to provide farmers in Asia and Africa with data-driven tools for optimizing crop yields and water usage (Stone, 2022).

PAgaaS utilizes a network of sensors strategically placed in agricultural fields. These sensors gather data on soil moisture, temperature, and nutrient levels. The data is transmitted to a secure cloud platform, where advanced analytics generate comprehensive insights for farmers. An interesting example of PAgaaS in action is the Climate Corporation's FieldView platform. This platform utilizes soil sensor data and weather information to provide farmers with recommendations for planting schedules, irrigation optimization, fertilizer application, and pest control. The outcomes led to increased yields and reduced water usage. The cloud platform can further integrate data from various sources beyond sensors, creating a holistic view of the farm's ecosystem. This includes data from farming equipment, drones, and high-resolution satellite imagery. PAgaaS platform empowers farmers with a level of decision-support that guides them in making informed agricultural operations. These insights include the following:

- **Field-specific recommendations:** The system examines information to offer suggestions of customized features across various sections in a plot. This approach supports watering, fertilizing, pest management tactics, and planting selections.
- **Yield prediction:** The platform evaluates data and examines the current condition of the fields to provide farmers with forecasts regarding crop yields. This enables farmers to make informed decisions about resource allocation throughout the growing season and to plan harvest and storage operations effectively.
- **Proactive risk management:** By combining up-to-date data with weather predictions and environmental indicators, farmers can detect risks such as frost, drought, or pest infestations in advance. This empowers them to proactively safeguard their crops against harm.
- **Marketplace integration:** The platform connects farmers with suppliers for seeds, fertilizers, and other necessary agricultural inputs by integrating with various marketplaces. This feature provides farmers with competitive prices and tailored recommendations based on their specific data and requirements.

PAgaaS can operate on a subscription model, offering flexibility and affordability for farmers. Tiered subscription plans cater to diverse needs, with basic plans providing access to essential data and analytics, while premium plans offer advanced features, such as yield forecasting or AI-powered risk management tools. This model unlocks opportunities for outsourcing crucial services. Specialized companies can manage the sensor networks across farms, ensuring reliable data collection and quality. Collaborating with agricultural data science firms enables the creation of analysis tools that produce practical recommendations customized to the unique requirements of farmers. Additionally the system can connect with experts in soil management and crop production, who provide consultations with agricultural knowledge based on following data-driven guidance. The effectiveness of this model relies on establishing trust with farmers and showcasing the value of PAgaaS for small-scale farmers, who have limited resources or technical knowledge. Monitoring crop yields evaluate PAgaaS enhancements in agricultural outcomes.

To earn the confidence and engagement of farmers who have limited resources or technical knowledge, it is crucial to show the tangible advantages of PAgaaS. By ensuring that the platform is easy to use and accessible, through mobile devices or web interfaces, technological challenges faced by farmers with varying levels of digital skills can be addressed. Furthermore, introducing subscription options and financial rewards can enhance the affordability and attractiveness of PAgaaS for a wider group of farmers.

12.3.4 Healthcare as a service (HCaaS)

The healthcare sector is being transformed by healthcare as a service (HCaaS), which utilizes IoT and cloud analytics. This contemporary approach to healthcare automates care plans and personalize overall patient experience. Healthcare as a service (HCaaS) offers services that transform healthcare through automated care plans and personalized remote patient monitoring (RPM). Central to RPM are wearable devices and connected medical equipment. The collected data is later uploaded to a cloud platform for further analysis.

People have the option to join health monitoring programs and book healthcare services. Healthcare professionals can utilize patient data and related analysis tools, as well as population health management strategies, to keep track of the health status of their patient communities. Insurance companies can make use of HCaaS to focus on preventing diseases and managing risks, which could lead to reduced premiums for policyholders, who take charge of their health through HCaaS. This method also opens up possibilities for outsourcing services throughout the healthcare system.

HCaaS can help enhance services for adults receiving care. By examining data from IoT devices and sensors in homes, HCaaS can spot possible health concerns and trigger responses from qualified healthcare experts. This process may involve managing medications remotely, monitoring patient conditions, or notifying emergency services if there are falls or other urgent situations that require prompt interventions. Furthermore, HCaaS could support communications between elderly patients and caregivers, offering an emotional backing and social connections. However it's vital to make sure that HCaaS works alongside caregivers for aged cares, rather than replacing it. Human contact remains an important part of caring for seniors and HCaaS should improve the current care provided by family members or professional caregivers. Various other potential collaborative opportunities are outlined next.

- **Data analytics:** Healthcare professionals might not have the expertise internally to effectively analyze intricate patient data. Collaborating with data analytics firms guarantees the extraction of practical insights from patient data.
- **Remote patient monitoring (RPM) services:** By collaborating with firms that focus on RPM services, the HCaaS platform can make use of their skills in setting up these services, managing devices that gather patient data, and safeguarding data privacy.
- **Telemedicine integration:** With a connection to telemedicine services already set up, patients can easily access virtual consultations through the HCaaS platform, which provides them various healthcare choices.
- **AI-powered healthcare solutions:** Incorporating AI-driven healthcare systems enables assessments and treatment suggestions rooted in the analysis of patient data. This can greatly support healthcare professionals in making informed decisions in their clinical practice.

The HCaaS model is advantageous to patients, healthcare professionals, and insurance companies alike. By giving patients the tools to take control of their health with up-to-date data analysis, HCaaS lowers rates of hospital readmissions. Moreover, remote patient monitoring and telemedicine features can simplify healthcare processes. HCaaS makes also resource allocation more efficient for healthcare providers, which could potentially decrease healthcare expenses for patients and insurers by allowing interventions and preventive care.

The key to the success of healthcare as a service (HCaaS) lies in overcoming some challenges. One crucial aspect is maintaining security measures to protect patient confidentiality. HCaaS platforms must adhere to regulations to build and maintain trust with patients. Another obstacle is enabling data sharing within HCaaS ecosystem. The healthcare sector often faces issues with data and compatibility problems among different healthcare systems and devices. Implementing HCaaS requires integration and effective analysis of data from various sources. Moreover, democratizing access to HCaaS reduces healthcare disparities. The HCaaS model should be affordable and easily accessible to all patients, regardless of their status or location.

The concept of healthcare as a service (HCaaS) driven by IoT and cloud technology presents an outlook for the future of healthcare provision. The prospect of enhancing patient care, boosting effectiveness, and cutting down expenses positions HCaaS as a business model that opens up substantial avenues for partnerships and subcontracting in the healthcare sector. Through tackling existing obstacles, HCaaS stands to transform healthcare delivery by empowering patients streamlining care services and establishing a viable healthcare framework.

12.3.5 Supply chain tracking as a service (SCaaS)

Maersk, as a leading shipping company, utilizes blockchain technology to track containers throughout the global supply chain, enhancing transparency and streamlining logistics processes (Wagner and Wiśnicki, 2019). Supply chain tracking as a service (SCaaS) manages logistics to harness the capabilities of IoT and cloud analytics. Through cloud platforms, businesses can monitor shipment status and effectively manage logistics operations proactively. Maersk also utilizes a logistics platform that integrates IoT sensors with cloud-based analytics.

The sensor data gathered is sent to a cloud-based SCaaS platform. This platform uses APIs (application programming interfaces) to enable smooth data sharing among all parties involved in the supply chain. Real-time visualization dashboards offer authorized users access to information on shipment whereabouts, stock levels, and environmental factors. This level of transparency allows businesses to make informed choices and enhance their logistics processes. The SCaaS service functions on a subscription system to meet the different requirements of businesses regardless their size. Subscription packages provide levels of access to real-time tracking options, data analysis tools, and route optimization capabilities. This adaptable strategy guarantees cost effectiveness and easy availability for all involved in the supply chain community.

- Improved visibility and transparency: Users, with authorized credentials have the ability to access inventory levels and oversee the environmental conditions of shipments as they progress along the supply chain.
- Optimized logistics and reduced costs: The data analysis tools on the platform can be used to enhance routes, reduce delays, and pinpoint areas of congestion. This results in deliveries with lower transportation expenses and better overall operational efficiency.
- Predictive maintenance and proactive risk management: Using sensor data can anticipate vehicles and machinery maintenance requirements, leading to less downtimes and lower expenses. Additionally, real-time data aids in risk management, allowing individuals to proactively address potential threats, such as extreme weather, to safeguard goods.
- Enhanced collaboration and problem-solving: The platform enhances communication and cooperation among supply chain participants, allowing them to share information and quickly address issues as they arise.

The owners of the SCaaS platform can monetize it in various ways. They can generate income through subscription fees, which offer a continuous source of revenue. Furthermore, the platform has the option to provide premium services, such as data analytics tools, route optimization software, or insurance products designed for real-time risk evaluations. The effectiveness of SCaaS relies on overcoming significant challenges. Ensuring smooth data sharing across the platform necessitates data formats across the entire supply chain. It is essential to implement security measures to safeguard sensitive information and support trust among users. Defined guidelines on data ownership and privacy need to be set up to address any potential concerns. Additionally, the platform should be user friendly and seamlessly integrate with the enterprise systems utilized by logistics providers and clients.

By using IoT cloud analytics and open collaboration, SCaaS offers a new perspective on the future of managing the supply chain. Through real-time visibility insights based on data and a team-oriented approach, companies can improve their logistics operations, save money, and boost the efficiency of their supply chain. SCaaS has the power to bring about changes in how logistics work, benefiting everyone involved in the supply-chain, and making the global supply chain more organized and efficient.

12.4 Strategies for implementing change

Digital transformation fueled by cloud and IoT technologies presents an opportunity for businesses to achieve significant improvements in efficiency, cost reduction, and customer satisfaction. However, navigating this transformation requires a well-defined strategy that considers the human and cultural dimensions of change, besides technological dimensions. This section explores key strategies for implementing change, focusing on fostering leadership and stakeholder engagement to overcome common challenges and establish clear metrics for long-term success and sustainability of IoT and cloud-driven digital transformation initiatives.

12.4.1 Identifying change agents

Successful digital transformation with IoT and cloud requires strong leadership, a culture of innovation, and active stakeholder engagement.

Leadership

Executive sponsors who champion transformation provide a clear vision, allocate resources, and drive cultural change are essential. For example, GE CEO Jeffrey Immelt played a crucial role in driving the company's "Industrial Internet" initiative, leveraging IoT and cloud to transform GE from a traditional manufacturer into a digital industrial leader (Joshi, 2021).

Culture

An organization needs a culture that embraces experimentation, learning from failures, and adapting to new technologies. Training programs, hackathons, and open communication channels encourage employee participation. For example, Siemens established a culture of innovation through its "Next47" venture capital arm (Cozmiuc and Petrisor, 2020), which invests in and collaborates with startups developing cutting-edge IoT and cloud solutions.

Stakeholder engagement

All stakeholders are expected to actively engage, including employees, customers, and partners, throughout the transformation process. Following this level of engagement, everyone understands the goals and benefits of the changes. For example, Rolls Royce uses a co-creation approach, working with airlines to develop cloud-based engine monitoring and analytics solutions (Eigner and Stary, 2023). This collaborative approach ensures the solutions meet the airlines' specific needs and fosters buy-in from key stakeholders.

12.4.2 Overcoming challenges

Several common barriers can hinder the successful implementation of IoT and cloud solutions.

Resistance to change

Communicate transformation benefits, addressing employee concerns about job security and retraining needs. Pilot projects showcasing the positive impact of the technology can help overcome resistance. For example, Walmart addressed employee concerns about job displacement by retraining store associates to operate new in-store automation technologies, ensuring a smooth transition (FasterCapital, 2024).

Technological hurdles

Carefully assess existing infrastructure and invest in necessary upgrades and training to ensure secure and efficient integration of IoT and cloud solutions. Partnerships with experienced technology providers can help navigate these technical complexities. For example, Mahindra & Mahindra, an Indian automaker, partnered with Qualcomm and Amazon Web Services (AWS) to leverage the Snapdragon Digital Chassis Solution's cloud-connected services platform for Mahindra's upcoming SUVs in India (McDowell, 2024).

Security concerns

Prioritize data security by implementing robust authentication, access controls, and encryption protocols. Continuous security monitoring is paramount to identify and address potential vulnerabilities. For instance, Amazon Web Services (AWS) offers security services and functionalities throughout its computing platform to emphasize data security for its clients and their applications (Amazon Web Services, 2024).

12.4.3 KPIs and metrics

Defining and measuring key performance indicators (KPIs) and metrics is essential to evaluate the success of IoT and cloud initiatives. These should align with your overall transformation goals.

Operational efficiency KPIs

Track metrics such as reduced downtime, faster turnaround times, and improved resource utilization after implementing IoT-enabled predictive maintenance or cloud-based process automation.

Cost reduction KPIs

Measure the impact on operational costs by monitoring metrics such as reduced energy consumption or minimized material waste, achieved through IoT-based resource optimization or data-driven outcomes from cloud analytics.

Customer satisfaction KPIs

Track customer satisfaction through surveys and feedback after implementing new data-driven customer services or personalized recommendations powered by cloud and IoT data.

Sustainability KPIs

For initiatives focused on sustainability, measure metrics such as reduced carbon emissions or minimized water usage achieved through IoT-based environmental monitoring or cloud-based optimization of resource management systems.

To ensure the long-term sustainability of the digital transformation journey with cloud and IoT, a focus on continuous improvement, employee engagement, and innovation is essential. Regular reviews and refinement ToC framework based on learnings and stakeholder feedback are essential. A culture of continuous learning and upskilling equip employees with the necessary skills to operate and maintain new technologies. Resources must be dedicated to explore new applications of cloud and IoT to maintain a competitive edge with further innovations. By prioritizing these elements, the transformation efforts deliver lasting value and position the organization for success in the ever-evolving digital landscape. Successful implementation requires a holistic approach, which considers leadership, culture, stakeholder engagement, and continuous improvement.

12.5 Enabling readiness to change

Businesses can leverage the benefits of IoT and cloud technologies by promoting ongoing learning, nurturing an environment that encourages creativity, and establishing valuable partnerships. Effectively implementing transformations necessitates a clear plan, supported by effective leadership and an adaptable culture. To improve their preparedness for change, companies should concentrate on the following five elements outlined below:

Leadership and vision

Leaders have an important role in driving change. It is crucial for leaders to fully support the change and clearly explain the vision behind it. They need to lead the change effort, communicate its advantages to the team, and motivate them to embrace ways of working. When there is no vision and commitment from leadership efforts, bringing about change may struggle due to a lack of guidance and employee engagement.

Collaborative change management

A well-defined change management strategy outlines the steps for implementing the change, addresses potential challenges, and provides a roadmap for successful adoption. This strategy should involve employees at all levels. Actively seeking employee input during the planning stages fosters a sense of ownership and increases buy-in. The strategy should also consider potential resistance to change and outline communication plans to address employee concerns.

Transparent communication

Open and clear communication are paramount over transition periods. It is important for staff to grasp the rationale behind changes, especially in regards to how they affect their responsibilities and the implementation plan. Providing updates helps to keep employees in the loop and involved, easing any uncertainties or concerns. Leaders should utilize communication platforms to guarantee that information is effectively distributed, thereby promoting an atmosphere of openness and confidence among all stakeholders.

Building a culture of adaptability

Successful organizations thrive on being adaptable and constantly striving to improve. Creating a work environment that values learning, experimentation, and taking calculated risks is crucial for embracing change. It is important for employees to feel at ease when asking questions, sharing feedback, and exploring strategies. Nurturing this culture by recognizing achievements, incentivizing creative thinking, and acknowledging that obstacles are a normal part of the transformation journey, shape the leader's role over the transformation journey.

Empowering employees

Engaging employees during times of change by encouraging them to voice their thoughts, worries, and skills help cultivate a feeling of responsibility and boosts their commitment. Empowering employees involves providing them with the abilities and understanding to excel in the evolving settings induced by change. Offering training sessions on technologies, procedures, and work approaches guarantees that employees are well equipped to prosper in the changing work environment.

Effectively carrying out change management requires keeping track of progress and adapting approaches as required. Here are some key techniques to take into account:

1. **Track key performance indicators (KPIs):** Identify measures that are in line with the objectives of the transformation effort. These measures, also known as key performance indicators (KPIs), can be either quantitative or qualitative. Quantitative KPIs may encompass how readily employees embrace technologies, enhancements in operational efficiency, gauged by time or cost reductions or levels of customer satisfaction. Qualitative KPIs could include employee attitudes towards the change, the caliber of communication received, or the perceived effectiveness of training schemes. Regularly monitoring these metrics offers perceptions regarding the progress of the transformation and sheds light on areas that require fine tuning.
2. **Monitor communication effectiveness:** Clear, consistent, and two-way communication is critical for successful change adoption. Monitor communication channels to ensure messages reach all employees and the intended meaning is understood. Gather feedback through surveys, focus groups, or informal discussions to assess employee comprehension of the change and identify any areas of confusion. Addressing communication gaps promptly ensures everyone is on the same page and minimizes resistance.
3. **Assess employee engagement:** To make a change initiative, it is important to get employees on board and actively involved. Keep an eye on how employees feel during the change process to spot any resistance or worries. Conduct surveys, hold focus groups, also have casual chats with employees to measure their involvement. Dealing with employee concerns from the start can help prevent them from snowballing into problems, which might hinder the change process.
4. **Evaluate training effectiveness:** Providing employees with the required skills and knowledge is crucial for embracing change. Evaluate the impact of training

initiatives through performance appraisals, skill evaluations, or feedback questionnaires. Seek input from employees regarding the training materials quality, how relevant the content is to their roles and their capacity to implement knowledge. Utilize this feedback to enhance training programs and ensure they adequately prepare employees for success in the intended transformation.

5. **Track return on investment (ROI):** Enhancing efficiency or effectiveness and evaluating cost reductions or revenue increase leads to return on investment (ROI), which can also be evaluated by customer happiness, boosted employee satisfaction, or improved brand image. Monitoring ROI aids in validating the change investment and showcasing its outcomes to stakeholders.
6. **Continuous learning:** Encourage a learning environment in the company to ensure employees stay updated on the technologies by offering training sessions, workshops, and chances to participate in industry gatherings.
7. **Innovation culture:** Encourage a culture of experimentation and risk-taking to explore emerging technologies. Innovation hubs, hackathons, and internal innovation challenges can facilitate the development of this culture.
8. **Strategic partnerships:** Collaborate with tech companies and academic institutions to keep up-to-date on relevant advances, and tap into specialized knowledge. For example, Siemens teams up with startups and research centers via its "Next47" investment division enhancing its innovation initiatives in cloud technologies (Siemens, 2024).

By taking these aspects into account and applying monitoring methods, companies can enhance their preparedness for change, and guarantee a smooth shift to new technologies, procedures, or business frameworks.

12.6 Conclusion

This chapter explored the transformative potential of cloud and Internet-of-Things (IoT) integration, highlighting its impact on business models and society. The theory of change (ToC) framework provides a foundation for managing digital transformation. Real-world examples showcase innovative business models. These illustrate the potential for IoT and cloud across industries. The chapter then dives into practical strategies for implementing change within organizations. Identifying change agents and overcoming challenges such as resistance to change are crucial. Clear communication, leadership commitment, and KPIs are essential for success. Beyond implementation, fostering a culture receptive to change is vital. This requires leadership commitment, a culture of adaptability, and transparent communication. A culture of innovation unlocks the full potential of cloud and IoT. Organizations can ensure lasting value by monitoring emerging technologies, such as 5G, AI/ML, and blockchain and partnering with technology providers. Successful digital transformation hinges on strong leadership, stakeholder engagement, and clear communication. Organizations can ensure initiatives deliver the intended outcomes by overcoming challenges and establishing KPIs. Organizations that proactively monitor trends and embrace innovation will be best positioned to leverage the transformative power of cloud and IoT to revolutionize business models, foster societal progress, and improve quality of life.

References

Aclima, 2024. Aclima. https://www.aclima.io. (Accessed 21 March 2024).

Adamopoulou, E., Daskalakis, E., 2023. Applications and technologies of big data in the aerospace domain. Electronics 12 (10), 2225.

Amazon Web Services, 2024. Cloud security at aws. https://aws.amazon.com/security/. (Accessed 21 March 2024).

Annanth, V.K., Abinash, M., Rao, L.B., 2021. Intelligent manufacturing in the context of industry 4.0: a case study of Siemens industry. Journal of Physics. Conference Series 1969 (1), 012019.

Arden, N.S., Fisher, A.C., Tyner, K., Lawrence, X.Y., Lee, S.L., Kopcha, M., 2021. Industry 4.0 for pharmaceutical manufacturing: preparing for the smart factories of the future. International Journal of Pharmaceutics 602, 120554.

Biz4Intellia, 2022. Why consider IoT a best platform for environmental monitoring? https://www.biz4intellia.com/blog/why-consider-iot-a-best-platform-for-environmental-monitoring/. (Accessed 21 March 2024).

Colby, D., Collins, E., Taplin, D., 2013. Theory of change technical papers: a series of papers to support development of theories of change based on practice in the field. Technical report. Center for Human. Environments https://www.actknowledge.org/resources/documents/ToC-Tech-Papers.pdf.

Cozmiuc, D.C., Petrisor, I.I., 2020. Innovation in the age of digital disruption: the case of Siemens. In: Disruptive Technology: Concepts, Methodologies, Tools, and Applications. IGI Global, pp. 1124–1144.

DeMedeiros, K., Koh, C.Y., Hendawi, A., 2024. Clustering on the Chicago array of things: spotting anomalies in the Internet of Things records. Future Internet 16 (1), 28. https://doi.org/10.3390/fi16010028.

Durbhaka, G.K., et al., 2021. Convergence of artificial intelligence and Internet of Things in predictive maintenance systems–a review. Turkish Journal of Computer and Mathematics Education (TURCOMAT) 12 (11), 205–214.

Eigner, A., Stary, C., 2023. The role of Internet-of-Things for service transformation. SAGE Open 13 (1). https://doi.org/10.1177/21582440231159281.

Falcão, J., Ruiz, C., Pan, S., Noh, H.Y., Zhang, P., 2020. Faim: vision and weight sensing fusion framework for autonomous inventory monitoring in convenience stores. Frontiers in Built Environment 6, 568372.

FasterCapital, 2024. Responsible sourcing initiative. https://fastercapital.com/keyword/responsible-sourcing-initiative.html. (Accessed 21 March 2024).

Hoyer, W.D., Kroschke, M., Schmitt, B., Kraume, K., Shankar, V., 2020. Transforming the customer experience through new technologies. Journal of Interactive Marketing 51 (1), 57–71.

Javaid, M., Haleem, A., Singh, R.P., Rab, S., Suman, R., 2021. Significance of sensors for industry 4.0: roles, capabilities, and applications. Sensors International 2, 100110. https://www.sciencedirect.com/science/article/pii/S2666351121000310.

Joshi, Y.V., 2021. Digital Transformation, Ecosystem Design, and Platform Strategy: an IIoT Perspective. PhD thesis. Massachusetts Institute of Technology.

Kayad, A., Sozzi, M., Gatto, S., Whelan, B., Sartori, L., Marinello, F., 2021. Ten years of corn yield dynamics at field scale under digital agriculture solutions: a case study from North Italy. Computers and Electronics in Agriculture 185, 106126.

McDowell, S., 2024. Qualcomm's new automotive platform, partnership with aws & expanded reach into auto oems. https://www.forbes.com/sites/stevemcdowell/2023/09/06/qualcomms-new-automotive-platform-partnership-with-aws--expanded-reach-into-auto-oems/?sh=149cc40480f2. (Accessed 18 March 2024).

Mnyakin, M., 2023. Applications of AI, IoT, and cloud computing in smart transportation: a review. Artificial Intelligence and Society 3 (1), 9–27.

Muñuzuri, J., Onieva, L., Cortés, P., Guadix, J., 2020. Using IoT data and applications to improve port-based intermodal supply chains. Computers & Industrial Engineering 139, 105668.

Murthy, K.R., et al., 2023. IoT Based Smart Irrigation System Using Sensors: A Revolutionary Idea in the Field of Agriculture in India. Recent Developments in Electronics and Communication Systems: Proceedings of the First International Conference on Recent Developments in Electronics and Communication Systems (RDECS-2022), vol. 32. IOS Press, p. 222.

Namuduri, S., Narayanan, B.N., Davuluru, V.S.P., Burton, L., Bhansali, S., 2020. Reviewâdeep learning methods for sensor based predictive maintenance and future perspectives for electrochemical sensors. Journal of the Electrochemical Society 167 (3), 037552. https://doi.org/10.1149/1945-7111/ab67a8.

Shafi, I., Din, S., Farooq, S., Díez, I.d.l.T., Breñosa, J., Espinosa, J.C.M., Ashraf, I., 2024. Design and development of patient health tracking, monitoring and big data storage using Internet of Things and real time cloud computing. PLoS ONE 19 (3), e0298582.

Siemens, 2024. next47: Siemens founds separate unit for startups. https://press.siemens.com/global/en/feature/next47-siemens-founds-separate-unit-startups. (Accessed 18 March 2024).

Stone, G.D., 2022. Surveillance agriculture and peasant autonomy. Journal of Agrarian Change 22 (3), 608–631.

Taplin, D.H., Clark, H., 2012. Theory of Change Basics: A Primer on Theory of Change, vol. 844. ActKnowledge, New York, NY, p. 845.

Trivedi, S.K., Patra, P., Srivastava, P.R., Zhang, J.Z., Zheng, L.J., 2022. What prompts consumers to purchase online? A machine learning approach. Electronic Commerce Research, 1–37.

Wagner, N., Wiśnicki, B., 2019. Application of blockchain technology in maritime logistics. In: DIEM: Dubrovnik International Economic Meeting, vol. 4, No. 1, pp. 155–164.

Wang, R.-G., Ho, W.-J., Chiang, K.-C., Hung, Y.-C., Tai, J.-K., Tan, J.-C., Chuang, M.-L., Ke, C.-Y., Chien, Y.-F., Jeng, A.-P., et al., 2023. Analyzing long-term and high instantaneous power consumption of buildings from smart meter big data with deep learning and knowledge graph techniques. Energies 16 (19), 6893.

CHAPTER

Digital transformation with IoT and cloud in healthcare

13

13.1 Introduction

The term "digital transformation" in healthcare encapsulates a comprehensive restructuring and digitalization of all aspects of healthcare practices, from patient care to backend operations, leveraging the power of advanced technologies. This transformative process reshapes care delivery to engage with patients through data-informed medical interventions and healthcare service operational improvements. This approach transforms raw health data into a powerful tool that enhances treatment protocols and streamlines hospital management practices (Belliger and Krieger, 2018). The gap between data collection and clinical action is bridged by agile responses to individual patient needs, rather than the rigid door-to-door or phone followups, which are both inflexible and frequently inconvenient.

The aim of healthcare is to enhance accessibility, efficiency and personalization, with the combined goal of improving treatment results and lowering associated expenses. Digital transformation encompasses a wide range of technologies, including electronic health records (EHRs), telehealth services, AI as an aid to diagnosis and followup, and machine learning analytics as aid to analyze clinical trials for discovering new health protocols.

These technologies are fundamentally changing the interactions between healthcare researchers, professionals and patients (Andreassen et al., 2018), streamlining processes and opening new avenues for treatment and diagnosis decisions. For example, telehealth has broken down geographical barriers for patients to consult specialists without the need for physical travels.

Similarly, wearable devices and health apps enable real-time health monitoring and personalized health support made directly available at patient fingertips, fostering having more engaged and informed patients. IoT devices can monitor patient health metrics continuously, while cloud computing provides the infrastructure necessary to store, process, and make this data available across healthcare applications. Together, IoT and cloud technologies have the potential to support healthcare towards more proactive, predictive, and personalized care models that are both effective and cost-efficient, as well as accessible to a broader population (Akkaş et al., 2020; Coulby et al., 2020).

https://doi.org/10.1016/B978-0-44-322217-7.00021-9

Today the healthcare industry is dealing with challenges that the integration of IoT and cloud technologies can address efficiently. For instance, with the aging population and increasing cases of related chronic illnesses associated with the low resources in medical personnel and related assistance services, it has become essential to monitor patients outside of conventional healthcare facilities. Home health devices and wearables connected through IoT and cloud services can monitor patients health data in real time to allow remote monitoring and timely interventions when needed (Perera et al., 2021).

13.2 Healthcare IoT

Through an array of devices, sensors, and the seamless connectivity with cloud computing, the mechanisms by which IoT enhances patient care is redefining the operational capacities of healthcare providers. Next, we provide a comprehensive overview of how IoT technologies are applied within healthcare sector. In doing so, we emphasize the critical role of cloud computing in managing the large volume of healthcare data and the transformative potential of integrating IoT with cloud platforms for real-time health data analysis (Dimitrov, 2016).

The global shortage of medical personnel is a pressing issue, characterized by insufficient healthcare workers to meet the growing demands of patient care. We show innovative approaches enabled through the capabilities of IoT technologies, which automate routine monitoring, remote care options, and data-driven decision-making, to fill the gaps left by the shortage of healthcare professionals. These approaches offer a sustainable solution to overburdened medical staff, while extending the reach of healthcare services to diverse patients who receive equally timely and efficient care (Darwish et al., 2019).

13.2.1 An overview of IoT devices and sensors for healthcare

Connected health is characterized by the integration of technology into medical care at large, to enhance healthcare delivery and streamline healthcare operations. Connected health leverages a comprehensive network of devices, sensors, and cloud solutions to facilitate the remote delivery and management of healthcare services (Pattichis and Panayides, 2019). Connected health integrates wearable technologies, telehealth, mobile health applications, and remote patient monitoring systems to create a seamless, patient-centered healthcare experience. The scope of connected health stretches to bridge the gap between the healthcare provider and the patient's living environment for continuous, proactive care management beyond the scope of hospitals and clinics.

We suggest classifying IoT devices according to deployment contexts to facilitate analyzing their influence on healthcare, as illustrated in Fig. 13.1. This approach helps understanding the contribution of different IoT devices in healthcare environments and the specific roles each category plays in improving patient care. By grouping devices into deployment scenarios, we can better capture the challenges they address and the services they offer to patients, healthcare professionals, and the healthcare system (Rhayem et al., 2021).

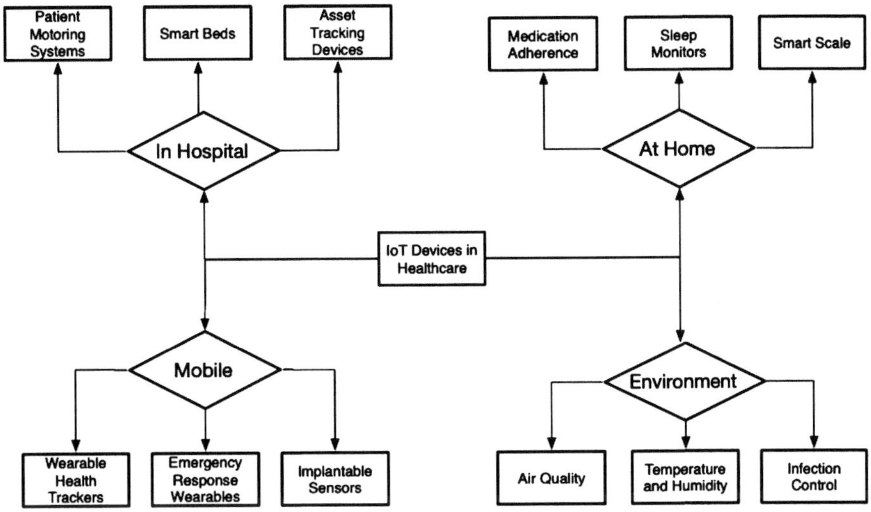

FIGURE 13.1

IoT devices in healthcare.

In hospital sensors

Modern hospitals are equipped with IoT devices to monitor a wide range of variables: from patient health metrics to asset location. Patient monitoring sensors measure continuously vital signs, including heart rate, blood pressure, oxygen saturation, and temperature. They are located in fundamental hospital structure areas, such as emergency rooms, intensive care units, and general wards. RFID tags and readers track the location and status of medical equipment, supplies, and even staff and patients within the hospital. This helps in optimizing asset use, preventing loss, and improving response times in critical situations. Smart beds can detect when a patient is attempting to get up, reducing the risk of falls by alerting nursing staff to provide assistance (Bacchin et al., 2022). Additionally, some smart beds are capable of tracking sleep quality and patterns (Laurino et al., 2020).

At home sensors

Managing and monitoring health conditions outside traditional healthcare settings use devices that empower patients and caregivers with tools to maintain health and safety within the home, while ensuring ongoing care and monitoring chronic conditions, elderlies, or individuals undergoing rehabilitation. Typical devices include the following:

- **Smart pill dispensers:** These devices remind patients about the time to take their medications and dispense the correct doses. These devices can track medication usage and alert caregivers or healthcare providers if doses are missed, helping to maintain the prescribed treatment regimen.
- **Activity and fall monitors:** Sensors placed around the home to detect movement; these devices can alert caregivers or emergency services if unusual patterns are detected, such as a lack of movement, which might indicate a fall or health issue episode.
- **Smart scales:** Measure weight but also body composition, including body fat percentage, muscle mass, and water content, which provide a comprehensive health overview.

MobileSensors

These sensors offer a flexible approach to health monitoring and management outside traditional settings. Leveraging the ubiquity of smartphones and wearable devices, these sensors offer real-time health data collection and analysis, enabling immediate feedback and interventions. Next, we discuss mobile sensors used in healthcare:

- **Fitness bands and smartwatches:** Designed with physical activity or heart rate monitoring are advanced models that can monitor blood oxygen levels, stress levels, and even produce electrocardiograms (ECGs). These devices are expected to be worn continuously to provide ongoing health metrics to users and remote healthcare professionals.
- **Handheld blood analysis devices:** Immediate blood testing for a range of markers are made possible to providing critical information for disease management, such as blood glucose levels for diabetes.
- **Emergency response wearables:** Automatic detection mechanisms that can send alerts to emergency services or designated caregivers in case of a fall, accident, or sudden health issue are crucial for elderly individuals, or anyone at risk of medical emergencies. The goal is to ensure quick response times as GPS trackers are often integrated into these handheld devices, enabling emergency services to quickly locate the individual in need. This feature is particularly valuable for patients with dementia or other conditions that may lead to disorientation and wandering.
- **Implantable sensors:** The transformative advancement in healthcare technology is merging the capabilities of medical monitoring and intervention directly within the human body. These tiny, sophisticated devices are surgically placed inside the body to provide continuous, real-time data on various health metrics or to deliver therapeutic interventions for a range of chronic conditions (Li et al., 2020). Their applications span across numerous medical fields, including cardiology, endocrinology, which require continuous data collection with high precision without impacting daily activities (Khanna and Khanna, 2016). Research and development in implantable sensors are poised to aid in identification of health concerns and to tailor treatment strategies to individuals in a manner that enhance well being and lifespan of patients globally (Yang, 2018).

Environmental sensors

Ensuring the well being and comfort of patients may involve utilizing sensors to track elements of the surrounding areas. These sensors include those that track air quality, temperature, and humidity, to reduce the risk of infections. For example, asthma affected individuals need to avoid areas that pose high rate of allergens. Air quality sensors can identify these areas and steer sensitive individuals away from areas with poor air quality or high levels of allergens (Kaffash-Charandabi et al., 2019).

13.2.2 The role of cloud computing in healthcare data integration and analysis

Cloud computing integrates real-time data generated by IoT healthcare devices. Processing these data streams in real time is paramount within healthcare domains, where timely decisions can significantly impact patient outcomes. The power of cloud computing supports healthcare providers with access, analysis, and prompt action upon health data as it is collected, ensuring that patient care is both proactive and responsive. This preventive care, where early detection and intervention can lead to better health outcomes, reduces the need for extensive medical interventions, which may pose a burden on healthcare resources.

Through the automation of data collection, analysis, and alert systems, the cloud-to-things continuum enables healthcare providers to extend their reach and enhance their efficiency, effectively multiplying the impact of each healthcare professional. This integration allows for remote monitoring and management of patient conditions, reducing the need for constant physical presence and enabling healthcare workers to focus on cases that require direct intervention.

Cloud computing ensures that medical personnel can prioritize their workload more effectively, intervening when IoT devices signal a need for urgent care (Feng et al., 2021). This approach optimizes the use of scarce human resources in the medical sector, while improving patient outcomes by ensuring timely medical attention. Moreover, the cloud-to-things continuum enhances telehealth experiences, which can significantly alleviate the strain on healthcare facilities. This gain in human resource is associated with access to care from patients' comfort zones, such as their homes. The synergy between cloud computing and IoT devices presents a sustainable solution to the challenge of medical personnel shortages, thereby promising a more efficient and responsive healthcare system.

Data is consistently gathered from IoT devices, assessed, and acted upon. A significant application is remote patient monitoring, in which case wearable sensors and home monitoring devices regularly communicate health data to cloud-based systems (Mohammed et al., 2014). For instance, heart rate monitors, glucose monitors, and blood pressure cuffs collect vital signs and send this information to the cloud, where it is analyzed in real time. This allows healthcare providers to monitor patients' conditions remotely, adjust treatments promptly, and intervene immediately when anomalies suggest potential health risks. Managing chronic conditions, such as diabetes and heart disease, can leverage this digital monitoring approach to significantly reduce hospital readmissions, which results in improved patients' care and quality of life (Iranpak et al., 2021).

13.3 Enhancing patient care with IoT and cloud

The paradigm shift towards a more connected, intelligent, and patient-centric healthcare system harnesses the power of IoT devices to gather real-time health data and leveraging the cloud's computational and storage capabilities. As a result, the healthcare industry is witnessing improvements in care delivery, efficiency, and patient outcomes. Next, we explores the transformative potential of IoT and cloud integration across various aspects of healthcare, starting from examining remote patient monitoring and telehealth solutions, which are extending care beyond the confines of hospital walls. These solutions ensure continuous patient engagement, while facilitating access to healthcare services irrespective of geographical constraints or medical personnel availability. These technologies democratize healthcare through accessible and reduced disparities in care delivery, while lessening strains on physical healthcare facilities and personnel resources (Demetriou et al., 2023).

13.3.1 Remote patient monitoring and telehealth solutions

Remote patient monitoring and telehealth emerged as viable solutions in extending healthcare beyond traditional clinical settings. IoT devices, such as wearable health monitors, smart medical devices, and home monitoring equipment, collect vital health data in real time. As data is transmitted to cloud-based platforms, healthcare providers monitor patients' health remotely. Cloud-augmented telehealth solutions offer virtual consultations, allowing patients to receive medical advice, diagnosis, without the associated drudgery to move into specific physical facilities. This cloud access to healthcare services enhances patient engagement and adherence to treatment plans when combined with IoT data evidences.

Integration of wearable technologies and cloud analytics

Wearable devices track health indicators, such as a) fitness trackers that utilize accelerometers, b) and heart rate monitors, c) glucose monitors that sense blood sugar levels, or d) blood pressure cuffs that use pressure sensors to measure blood pressure (Vijayan et al., 2021). These devices typically incorporate connectivity technologies to transmit collected data. Health data is continuously streamed from the wearable device to a paired smartphone or directly to a cloud platform. Real-time analysis leverages the cloud performance to run sophisticated algorithms, including machine learning to identify patterns, trends, and anomalies. For instance, a sudden spike in heart rate or a drop in blood glucose levels can trigger alerts. Predictive analytics can also be applied to foresee potential health issues based on historical data and current trends.

Cloud platforms often provide dashboards and reports accessible by healthcare providers and patients. Real-time health metrics, historical data, and analytical patterns, make it easier to track health progress and build informed decisions. Based on the analysis, the cloud platform can generate notifications and alerts for both patients and healthcare providers when, for example, blood pressure readings exceed safe thresholds. The severity of the alerts is analyzed by machine learning algorithms to prompt whether a medical action is expected from physicians, such as medication adjustments or medical consultation (Bharadwaj et al., 2021).

Patient engagement and self-management tools

Mobile apps that integrate with IoT devices and cloud services can provide patients with tools for self-management, health tracking, and direct communication with healthcare providers when needed. Besides, cloud algorithms analyze IoT-generated data to send personalized health notifications via mobile apps, as well as reminders for medication, and tips for lifestyle adjustments to individual patients. Patients can also view a comprehensive dashboard on their mobile app, displaying real-time health data collected from wearable IoT devices. Patients embrace a proactive role in their own health management, when provided with this level of individual access to health information (Cruz-Ramos et al., 2022).

Beyond reminders and alerts, mobile apps integrated with IoT and cloud services offer tailored educational content to patients to educate themselves about their own specific health condition. Based on their health data, patients receive relevant articles, videos, and tips, empowering them with knowledge about their health and how to accept treatment that manage it effectively. Some apps may even incorporate gamification features and behavioral incentives, such as rewards or challenges, to encourage healthy habits. These features motivate patients to reach their health goals, maintain regular medication intake, or achieve a certain level of physical activity, or even following some dietary recommendations (Johnson et al., 2016b; Sardi et al., 2017).

13.3.2 Personalized medicine through data analytics

The convergence of IoT with cloud-based data analytics created more opportunities in personalized medicine, transforming patient care into a tailored experience that accounts for individual differences and preferences.

Genetic data collection and integration

The complexity and volume of genetic data pose significant challenges in terms of storage, processing, and analysis. Cloud computing, with its scalable storage solutions and computational power capabilities, alongside IoT devices for real-time health monitoring, shares a synergistic framework to unlock the potential of genetic information in healthcare (Prasad, 2023). Furthermore, the analysis of genetic data to derive indicators requires substantial computational resources, provisioned by cloud services, which run complex algorithms and bioinformatics tools to identify genetic markers, understand predispositions to diseases, and predict responses to medications (Rahman et al., 2022).

Proactive and predictive healthcare

Studies have shown that predictive analytics can significantly improve outcomes in cancer treatment. For example, cloud-based analytics has been instrumented to analyze genomic data alongside clinical health records, leading to the discovery of patterns that predict patient responses to chemotherapy. Subsequently, prescribed treatments are personalized considering response differences (Lau et al., 2022).

Wearable devices in cardiac care

Wearable devices can monitor heart rates and activity levels, which when combined with cloud-based predictive models have shown to successfully identify early signs of heart failure in patients with cardiac conditions (Umer et al., 2022). Preemptive adjustments are enabled by these models to formulate personalized treatment plans, such as medication adjustments or personalized lifestyle interventions before the patient experiences critical health episodes.

13.4 Healthcare operational efficiency and cost reduction with IoT and cloud

As healthcare organizations struggle with increasing cost pressures and the demand for high-quality care, the integration of IoT and cloud emerges as a potential strategy to streamline operations of healthcare services. Next, we explore how the IoT and cloud convergence acts as a catalyst for operational efficiency in healthcare. We review relevant applications that redefine hospital and facility management, automating complex healthcare processes and reducing cost, while increasing operational efficiency.

13.4.1 IoT and cloud in hospital and facility management

The dynamic capabilities of IoT technology in real-time asset tracking and management within healthcare settings represent a paradigm shift in how hospitals oversee and utilize their critical assets, including medical equipment and supplies. When integrated with cloud analytics, these capabilities extend the lifecycle of valuable healthcare assets, as discussed further immediately below.

Real-time asset tracking

Medical equipment and supplies are fitted with IoT-enabled tags and sensors, which continuously transmit data about their location, status, and condition. These tagging facilities range from simple RFID tags for tracking location to sensors that can monitor the asset condition (e.g., temperature, sterilization status) of sensitive medical supplies (Ranjbar et al., 2019).

Lifecycle optimization

IoT devices can monitor various parameters indicating the health and operational status of medical equipment, from usage patterns to critical condition indicators, such as battery levels, temperature, or mechanical wear. Cloud analytics process the data collected from IoT devices to predict when equipment might fail or require maintenance. These patterns of predicted anomalies support hospitals to shift from reactive to predictive maintenance strategies, servicing equipment before breakdowns occur, thereby extending asset lifecycles and ensuring equipment reliability.

Automated inventory tracking

IoT devices track medical supplies inventory levels. Sensors can detect when supplies are running low and automatically trigger replenishment orders, ensuring that hospitals maintain optimal stock levels without manual intervention. Cloud algorithms run supply chain analytics: analytics to further analyze usage data, as a way to understand trends in supply usage. By considering lead times, hospitals can reduce excess inventory, minimize storage costs, and ensure that supplies are available when needed (Essila, 2023).

Operational cost savings

Predictive maintenance, optimized inventory management, and improved asset utilization collectively lead to significant cost savings for hospitals. Integrating these IoT and cloud solutions within existing hospital information systems enables a seamless flow of data across systems, enhancing decision-making and operational workflows. Hospital staff are notified about maintenance schedules, inventory levels, and asset deployment through mobile apps or dashboards, enabling swift action and coordination. By employing these methods, the frequency and impact of equipment failures are reduced, while and assets' utilization is optimised leading to more cost-effective operations, while ensuring that patients receive timely and effective care.

13.5 IoT data management in healthcare

The IoT and cloud evolution brings with it new challenges in data management, particularly privacy and security of patient information and complying with stringent healthcare regulations. As healthcare organizations embrace the IoT-driven digital transformation, the imperative to manage the large flows of data generated by a myriad of IoT devices arise. Next, we discuss the challenges of IoT data management in healthcare, exploring strategies to safeguard patient privacy, while ensuring robust data security and compliance with the complex structure of regulatory measures.

13.5.1 Challenges in healthcare data management

The volume, velocity, and variety of data generated from IoT devices in healthcare domains bring a set of challenges and opportunities for healthcare delivery and management. This vast influx of data from IoT devices encompasses everything from patient vital signs monitored in real time by wearable devices to the operational data generated by smart hospital systems. These characteristics necessitate advanced data management solutions capable of harnessing the complexity and scale of the data for improved patient care and operational efficiency.

Cloud-enabled data lakes for large volume storage and analytics

The amount of information produced by healthcare IoT devices is substantial. MRI device can produce as much as 1 terabyte of data daily, whereas portable devices consistently report health indicators, such as heart rate, blood sugar levels, and sleep patterns for millions of individuals (Banerjee et al., 2020).

To manage this volume, healthcare organizations are turning to cloud-enabled data lakes that offer scalable storage solutions. In this scenario, a hospital employs a cloud-based data lake to aggregate and store vast amounts of data from various IoT devices. The data lake provides a repository for this data and supports advanced analytics and machine learning algorithms. As part of the data lake structure, patterns that might indicate a patient's deteriorating condition before it becomes critical are discovered.

The speed of data generation

Consider a situation where wearable IoT devices keep track of patients with heart conditions. These devices stream data to a cloud infrastructure at high velocity. Real-time analysis is applied on this data flow to identify any anomaly occurrences related to heart rhythms or sudden decreases in blood pressure.

The diversity of data types

The variety of data types generated by IoT devices in healthcare adds another layer of complexity. Data can range from structured numerical data to unstructured data, such as images from digital pathology, notes from voice-to-text applications, and video from patient consultations. For example, a cloud-based integrated health record system can aggregate and analyze diverse data types, such as structured health metrics from wearable devices and unstructured data from doctor's notes or radiology images.

Integration and interoperability

Integrating IoT data with existing healthcare information systems requires interoperability across various platforms and devices. Different manufacturers often use proprietary protocols and data formats, making it difficult to integrate data across systems seamlessly. Data aggregation with existing healthcare information systems is exacerbated by the diversity and scale of IoT data. Many healthcare organizations rely on legacy systems that were not designed to interact with IoT devices. Upgrading these systems to support IoT integration may incur substantial costs and time, requiring significant adjustments within the organization.

Ensuring patient privacy and data security

The privacy of individual patients and the healthcare processes are fundamental to establishing trust in IoT adoption. The interconnected nature of IoT devices, which collect, transmit, and store vast amounts of health data, introduces significant vulnerabilities. To prevent their exploitation, healthcare organizations must enforce secure data transmission protocols, advanced encryption techniques, and robust access control mechanisms. Encryption serves as the first line of defense in protecting patient data, ensuring that information is readable only by authorized parties. Encryption should span data origin and destination, whereby data is encrypted at its origin and decrypted only at its final destination. Enforcing this end-to-end security protocol over all data transmitted by IoT devices and within cloud platforms should be part of the healthcare organizations' security policy.

Data in transit as it travels between devices, cloud platforms, and healthcare systems and data at rest when stored at intermediary collection points within the cloud-to-things continuum, need to be protected. All connecting points across the continuum need to employ secure communication protocols, such as TLS, when transmitting data. Role and permission definitions in healthcare settings confine access rights to data to legitrimate devices and individuals. Biometric authentication methods, such as fingerprint scans or facial recognition, provides a secure way to ensure that access to patient data is restricted to those specific individuals.

13.5.2 Data-driven analytics in healthcare

The combination of IoT and cloud technology has revolutionized the healthcare sector by transforming data-related operations, starting from the way it is gathered, to storage and evaluation approaches, enabling a move towards accessible and personalized healthcare. Real-time data from various sources, such as wearable devices, patient monitoring systems, and hospital management tools are now seamlessly integrated and analyzed to improve patient care and operational efficiency.

The integration of advanced analytics techniques, such as machine learning supports the continuous improvement in real-time of healthcare services. Furthermore, generative AI opens new possibilities for enhancing diagnostic imaging and automating report generation as outcomes of more data-centric healthcare models.

Healthcare datasets

Various categories of healthcare data from IoT devices, patient health records, medical imaging data, operational data regarding the use of hospital resources, and patient movements, are relevant datasets for analytics. Data-driven analytics are continuously enhancing the healthcare sector offering efficient solutions that contrasts from healthcare practices.

Continuous data from wearable devices

Wearable devices, such as heart rate monitors, glucose meters, and fitness trackers generate continuous data streams that provide datasets into patients' health status.

These data streams allow real-time monitoring and analysis when integrated with analytics algorithms running in cloud platforms. Some of the open datasets used by analytics techniques feature the MIMIC III waveform database matched subset (Gow et al., 2023), which contains waveform information, such as ECGs from patients in intensive care units. This data can be utilized for creating and evaluating real-time monitoring solutions.

Electronic health records (EHRs)

Electronic health records (EHRs) contain patient details, ranging from information and medical background to care strategies and health progress. Cloud-hosted EHR platforms enable effortless retrieval and exchange of data among healthcare professionals. The medical information mart for intensive care (MIMIC-III) database contains de-identified health data associated with over thousands critical care patients, supporting advanced analytics and research (Johnson et al., 2016a).

Imaging data

Detailed images obtained from MRI, CT scans, and X rays play are pivotal for diagnosing patient conditions and devising effective treatment strategies. A collection of images used for cancer studies, including MRI and CT scans, is available at the Cancer Imaging Archive (TCIA). This data repository support researchers to develop image analysis algorithms that run the cloud (Clark et al., 2013).

Operational data

Healthcare costs and usage databases are made available for analysis by the Healthcare Cost and Utilization Project (HCUP) (Steiner et al., 2002). The continuous data-driven progress is creating healthcare solutions that anticipate such diseases through the use of devices and cloud computing. Healthcare analytics can use this vast amount of patient data and operational efficiency to identify patterns, detect anomalies, and predict health outcomes.

Machine learning in predictive healthcare

An example of this healthcare approach is researchers utilizing historical datasets, such as MIMIC-III, to develop models to predict ICU patient, improving treatment plans and resource allocation. Linear regression, regression, and support vector machines (SVM) have been instrumented in healthcare domains to improve patient care outcomes and streamline operational processes. (Kansagara et al., 2011). Significant factors for prediction analysis include age, existing health conditions, and prior medical background.

Supervised learning

SVM has the capability to categorize individuals into varying risk groups by examining their records and present health information. For instance, SVM can differentiate between patients at risk and those at risk for ailments such as stroke or heart attack, allowing for tailored preventative actions.

Linear regression

Assessing the probability of a patients return to the hospital aids in crafting aftercare strategies and lowering readmission rates. Linear regression can be used to predict the likelihood of a patient being readmitted. Analyzing cost records and patient details with linear regression models can also anticipate expenses of treatments. This helps healthcare providers, with budgeting and financial planning (Gregori et al., 2011).

Logistic regression

Logistic regression techniques are used to diagnose illnesses, including diabetes and heart conditions. (Rahimloo and Jafarian, 2016). Logistic regression models employs factors such as blood pressure, glucose levels, and lifestyle, to evaluate the likelihood of illnesses. In clinical trials, logistic regression can also assert the effectiveness of new treatments. By comparing patient outcomes between treatment and control groups, this technique determines the success rates of interventions.

Leveraging IoT and cloud for predictive healthcare analytics

IoT devices continuously monitor patient conditions, such as heart rate, blood pressure, and glucose levels. This data is subsequently transmitted in real time to cloud platforms, where with its integration with historical datasets, such as MIMIC-III, machine learning models, including linear regression and SVM, can predict potential complications. In doing so, timely interventions and improved treatment plans are enabled.

This implies that health measurements can be quickly analyzed and responded to with prompt care actions. Simultaneously, healthcare data stream processing and storage are handled by cloud systems in a scalable way. Scalability techniques that are employed in this context include the following:

- **Auto-scaling:** Auto-scaling cloud services can automatically adjust computational resources for applications to satisfy their current loads (Heinze et al., 2014). For example, AWS auto-scaling, Azure scale sets and Google Cloud auto-scaling are able to manage varying levels of data without any manual interventions. These auto-scaling techniques involve monitoring the workload and streamlining the provisioning or de-provisioning process of resources to maintain performance and cost-efficiency. For instance, AWS auto-scaling can automatically increase the number of EC2 instances (which are revirtual servers provided by Amazon Web Services or AWS), when incoming data from IoT devices surges, and decrease the instances during lower demand periods.
- **Load balancing:** Load balancing techniques in IoT-cloud contexts distribute incoming network traffic across multiple servers dynamically (Kanellopoulos and Sharma, 2022). This distribution prevents any single server from becoming a bottleneck, thereby allowing high availability of IoT applications. Load balancing techniques include round-robin load balancing, which involves distributing requests sequentially across a pool of servers. Each server receives a request in turn, ensuring an even distribution of the load. This simple method is effective

for scenarios where all servers have similar processing capabilities. An enhancement of the round-robin technique, also known as weighted round-robin, assigns weights to each server based on their processing power or current load capacity. The servers with higher weights receive more requests, allowing a distribution scheme that considers server capabilities.

- **Edge computing:** By decentralizing data processing, edge computing enhances the scalability of IoT-cloud environments. The latency required for data transfers is crucial for healthcare monitoring, where edge nodes filter data locally to reduce the amount of data that needs to be transmitted to the cloud (Sonkoly et al., 2020). This optimization decreases both latency and the bandwidth requirements and alleviates network congestion, thereby facilitating further scalability.
- **Serverless computing:** Serverless computing involves on demand resource assignments to run code based on triggers such as sensor data changes. This new approach is suitable for IoT applications, offering scalability and efficient resource utilization by allocating computing power when functions are activated (Cassel et al., 2022). Healthcare IoT devices continuously monitoring patient vitals can trigger serverless functions only when anomalies are detected, thereby conserving resources while maintaining high responsiveness. Serverless platforms integrate seamlessly with other cloud services, enabling complex data processing workflows that leverage the full suite of cloud capabilities. Thus an IoT healthcare application can integrate serverless functions with cloud-based machine learning services to analyze patient data and provide predictive analytics, thereby enhancing patient care.

13.6 Case studies of successful IoT integration in healthcare

IoT integration within the healthcare sector is part of the digital transformation trend in patient care, aiming at enhancing operational efficiency and opening new avenues for medical research. IoT has demonstrated significant potential in addressing some of the most pressing challenges faced by healthcare providers today. Next, we reveal some case studies of successful IoT integration projects in healthcare. We discus their impactful outcomes and the obstacles they overcame. By exploring these real-world examples, we aim to draw valuable lessons learned and identify best practices, which can guide future IoT integration in healthcare settings. The goal is to inspire and inform healthcare organizations embarking on their digital transformation journeys about the transformative possibilities offered by IoT when effectively harnessed.

13.6.1 Analysis of successful digital transformation projects in healthcare

Remote patient monitoring systems

In this case study, we focus on the implementation of remote patient monitoring systems by a healthcare providers aiming to improve care for chronic disease patients. Such systems utilize wearable IoT devices to continuously monitor vital signs and transmit this data to cloud-based platforms for analysis, enabling timely interventions and reducing hospital interventions or costly readmissions. One tangible example of a successful IoT implementation in remote patent monitoring is the Philips eCareCoordinator and eCareCompanion remote patient monitoring system.

Philips Healthcare designed eCareCompanion as part of its telehealth solutions to enable healthcare providers to monitor patients remotely. The eCareCompanion serves as a patient application, typically running on a tablet at the patient's home, allowing patients to input daily health metrics and communicate with their care teams. Simultaneously, the eCareCoordinator is a clinical dashboard used by healthcare professionals to monitor their patients' health status remotely (Roden et al., 2017).

Philips Healthcare platform integrates with various wearable IoT devices that patients use at home, such as blood pressure monitors, weight scales, and pulse oximeters. These devices continuously gather vital health data and transmit it to the cloud-based telehealth platform (Amanatidou et al., 2015). Through cloud-based analytics, the system analyzes the collected data to identify trends and flag potential health deteriorations. Healthcare providers receive alerts about any concerning changes in a patient's condition, enabling them to intervene promptly to adjust medication, provide specific health recommendations, or escalating the level of care.

The implementation of Philips' remote patient monitoring system has demonstrated significant success in managing chronic conditions. For example, Banner Health, a large non-profit healthcare system in the U.S., integrated this telehealth solution into its care management program for patients with complex chronic conditions. The results included a 45% reduction in hospital readmissions and a 27% reduction in cost of care, showcasing the substantial impact of IoT in enhancing patient outcomes and optimizing healthcare costs (Philips Healthcare, 2023).

The key success factors of Philips eCareCoordinator and eCareCompanion systems include the following:

- Seamless device integration: The smooth integration of various wearable IoT devices with the cloud-based platform was crucial for the continuous and reliable collection of patient health data.
- Patient engagement: The user-friendly design of the eCareCompanion app facilitated patient engagement, encouraging regular health monitoring and communication with care providers.
- Data-driven decision-making: By utilizing real-time data analysis, Philips platform enables healthcare professionals to gain pertinent information and make relevant interventions for each patients' unique requirements.

Smart hospital infrastructure

Another case study highlights the transformation of a hospital into a "smart" facility through IoT integration. Smart sensors were installed to monitor environmental conditions, manage energy use, and track the location and availability of medical equipment. This integration resulted in improved asset utilization and significant cost savings.

A tangible example of transforming a hospital into a "smart" facility through IoT integration is the implementation of the GE Healthcare digital solutions at the Johns Hopkins Hospital. This initiative integrated IoT technologies to enhance operational efficiency, patient care, and resource management within one of the most prestigious medical care in the United States. The initiative focused on enhancing the efficiency of patient flow and optimizing medical assets management within the hospital. Johns Hopkins Hospital has subsequently launched a Capacity Command Center powered by GE Healthcare's command center software and analytics solutions (GE Healthcare Command Center, 2023b).

The Capacity Command Center aims to improve patient flow, increase bed availability, and enhance operational efficiency. IoT and AI capabilities of GE Healthcare's command center were used to provide real-time data related to patient flow and bed occupancy. The command center has substantially improved the hospital's operational capabilities, including patient transfers, ambulance pickup times, and the speed at which patients are assigned beds.

This solution has also facilitated a more efficient discharge process, thereby improving patient flow and access to care. Utilizing predictive analytics, the command center can anticipate and manage patient volumes and movements more effectively. This approach also proved instrumental during the COVID-19 pandemic, assisting in decision-making for virus trends and resource allocation (GE Healthcare Command Center, 2023a).

13.6.2 Lessons learned and best practices

Integrating IoT technologies into healthcare has paved the way to both challenges and successful endeavors. Based on successful case studies, critical lessons alongside best practices underscore the essence of effective IoT deployments in healthcare environments.

Ensuring interoperability

Leveraging integration platforms that act as intermediaries between IoT devices and healthcare information systems can streamline data exchange, while ensuring seamless communication. The above Philips HealthSuite is a cloud-based platform that illustrates interoperability. This cloud intermediary enables the connection and exchange of data among medical devices, applications, and existing healthcare systems. By adhering to global health data standards, such as HL7 FHIR (Bender and Sartipi, 2013), the HealthSuite ensures that data from Philips' IoT device can be seamlessly integrated into hospital systems. Similarly, GE Healthcare's platform enhances interoperability by supporting standard healthcare protocols and providing robust APIs, to utilize data from IoT devices within existing hospital systems.

Engaging patients and staff

The integration of IoT technologies in healthcare by Philips and GE Healthcare highlights the importance of engaging both patients and healthcare staff in the transformation process. Through user-centric design and comprehensive education and training programs, these solutions set benchmarks in the successful adoption and effective engagement of relevant stakeholders. The design of Philips' patient monitoring systems focuses on intuitive interfaces and seamless interactions, making it easier for patients to manage their own health conditions and for clinicians to monitor patient data effectively. GE Healthcare's platform emphasizes ease of use through intuitive interfaces and robust training.

13.7 Conclusion

The integration of IoT and cloud technologies in healthcare represents a significant step forward in healthcare services delivery and management. This chapter uncovered the landscape of IoT and cloud implications in healthcare domains. The exploration of IoT devices and sensors showcased their role in collecting real-time health data, thereby facilitating transition towards proactive and personalized patient care. Cloud computing manages the large flows of data generated by IoT devices to enable a data-driven approach to healthcare. Some case studies were discussed to highlight IoT and cloud integration in optimizing hospital operations, asset management, and patient monitoring, leading to significant cost savings and operational efficiencies. IoT for remote health monitoring is expected to become ubiquitous, as healthcare is extending its reach and becoming more inclusive. Cloud analytics will further enhance the ability to tailor treatments to individual genetic profiles, lifestyle factors, and real-time health data, advancing the field of personalized medicine. Innovative solutions to protect patient privacy and secure health data will become increasingly critical as the future will see a more integrated healthcare ecosystem fostering greater interoperability and collaboration across the healthcare sector.

References

Akkaş, M.A., Sokullu, R., Çetin, H.E., 2020. Healthcare and patient monitoring using IoT. Internet of Things 11, 100173.

Amanatidou, P.S., et al., 2015. A unified quality measure engine for the Philips healthsuite digital platform.

Andreassen, H.K., Dyb, K., May, C.R., Pope, C.J., Warth, L.L., 2018. Digitized patient–provider interaction: how does it matter? A qualitative meta-synthesis. Social Science & Medicine 215, 36–44.

Bacchin, D., Pernice, G.F., Sardena, M., Malvestio, M., Gamberini, L., 2022. Caregivers' perceived usefulness of an IoT-based smart bed. In: International Conference on Human-Computer Interaction. Springer, pp. 247–265.

Banerjee, A., Chakraborty, C., Kumar, A., Biswas, D., 2020. Emerging trends in IoT and big data analytics for biomedical and health care technologies. In: Handbook of Data Science Approaches for Biomedical Engineering, pp. 121–152.

Belliger, A., Krieger, D.J., 2018. The digital transformation of healthcare. In: Knowledge Management in Digital Change: New Findings and Practical Cases, pp. 311–326.

Bender, D., Sartipi, K., 2013. Hl7 fhir: an agile and restful approach to healthcare information exchange. In: Proceedings of the 26th IEEE International Symposium on Computer-Based Medical Systems. IEEE, pp. 326–331.

Bharadwaj, H.K., Agarwal, A., Chamola, V., Lakkaniga, N.R., Hassija, V., Guizani, M., Sikdar, B., 2021. A review on the role of machine learning in enabling IoT based healthcare applications. IEEE Access 9, 38859–38890.

Cassel, G.A.S., Rodrigues, V.F., da Rosa Righi, R., Bez, M.R., Nepomuceno, A.C., da Costa, C.A., 2022. Serverless computing for Internet of Things: a systematic literature review. Future Generations Computer Systems 128, 299–316.

Clark, K., Vendt, B., Smith, K., Freymann, J., Kirby, J., Koppel, P., Moore, S., Phillips, S., Maffitt, D., Pringle, M., et al., 2013. The cancer imaging archive (tcia): maintaining and operating a public information repository. Journal of Digital Imaging 26, 1045–1057.

Coulby, G., Clear, A., Jones, O., Young, F., Stuart, S., Godfrey, A., 2020. Towards remote healthcare monitoring using accessible IoT technology: state-of-the-art, insights and experimental design. BioMedical Engineering Online 19, 1–24.

Cruz-Ramos, N.A., Alor-Hernández, G., Colombo-Mendoza, L.O., Sánchez-Cervantes, J.L., Rodríguez-Mazahua, L., Guarneros-Nolasco, L.R., 2022. mHealth apps for self-management of cardiovascular diseases: a scoping review. Healthcare 10 (2), 322.

Darwish, A., Hassanien, A.E., Elhoseny, M., Sangaiah, A.K., Muhammad, K., 2019. The impact of the hybrid platform of Internet of Things and cloud computing on healthcare systems: opportunities, challenges, and open problems. Journal of Ambient Intelligence and Humanized Computing 10, 4151–4166.

Demetriou, D., Mathabe, K., Lolas, G., Dlamini, Z., 2023. Internet of things in society 5.0 and the democratization of healthcare. In: Society 5.0 and Next Generation Healthcare: Patient-Focused and Technology-Assisted Precision Therapies. Springer, pp. 111–130.

Dimitrov, D.V., 2016. Medical Internet of Things and big data in healthcare. Healthcare Informatics Research 22 (3), 156–163.

Essila, J.C., 2023. Strategies for reducing healthcare supply chain inventory costs. Benchmarking: An International Journal 30 (8), 2655–2669.

Feng, Y., Pan, Z., et al., 2021. Optimization of remote public medical emergency management system with low delay based on Internet of Things. Journal of Healthcare Engineering 2021.

GE Healthcare Command Center, 2023a. The johns Hopkins capacity command center rises to the challenge. https://www.gehccommandcenter.com/press-coverage/The-Johns-Hopkins-Capacity-Command-Center-rises-to-the-challenge. (Accessed 4 September 2024).

GE Healthcare Command Center, 2023b. Johns Hopkins hospital launches capacity command center to enhance hospital operations. https://www.gehccommandcenter.com/press-coverage/johns-hopkins-hospital-launches-capacity-command-center-to-enhance-hospital-operations. (Accessed 4 September 2024).

Gow, B., Pollard, T., Nathanson, L.A., Johnson, A., Moody, B., Fernandes, C., Greenbaum, N., Berkowitz, S., Moukheiber, D., Eslami, P., et al., 2023. Mimic-iv-ecg-diagnostic electrocardiogram matched subset. Type: Dataset.

Gregori, D., Petrinco, M., Bo, S., Desideri, A., Merletti, F., Pagano, E., 2011. Regression models for analyzing costs and their determinants in health care: an introductory review. International Journal for Quality in Health Care 23 (3), 331–341.

Heinze, T., Pappalardo, V., Jerzak, Z., Fetzer, C., 2014. Auto-scaling techniques for elastic data stream processing. In: Proceedings of the 8th ACM International Conference on Distributed Event-Based Systems, pp. 318–321.

Iranpak, S., Shahbahrami, A., Shakeri, H., 2021. Remote patient monitoring and classifying using the Internet of Things platform combined with cloud computing. Journal of Big Data 8, 1–22.

Johnson, A.E., Pollard, T.J., Shen, L., Lehman, L.-w.H., Feng, M., Ghassemi, M., Moody, B., Szolovits, P., Anthony Celi, L., Mark, R.G., 2016a. Mimic-iii, a freely accessible critical care database. Scientific Data 3 (1), 1–9.

Johnson, D., Deterding, S., Kuhn, K.-A., Staneva, A., Stoyanov, S., Hides, L., 2016b. Gamification for health and wellbeing: a systematic review of the literature. Internet Interventions 6, 89–106.

Kaffash-Charandabi, N., Alesheikh, A.A., Sharif, M., 2019. A ubiquitous asthma monitoring framework based on ambient air pollutants and individuals' contexts. Environmental Science and Pollution Research 26 (8), 7525–7539.

Kanellopoulos, D., Sharma, V.K., 2022. Dynamic load balancing techniques in the IoT: a review. Symmetry 14 (12), 2554.

Kansagara, D., Englander, H., Salanitro, A., Kagen, D., Theobald, C., Freeman, M., Kripalani, S., 2011. Risk prediction models for hospital readmission: a systematic review. JAMA 306 (15), 1688–1698.

Khanna, V.K., Khanna, V.K., 2016. Implantable sensors. In: Implantable Medical Electronics: Prosthetics, Drug Delivery, and Health Monitoring, pp. 249–265.

Lau, C.W., Qu, Z., Draper, D., Quan, R., Braytee, A., Bluff, A., Zhang, D., Johnston, A., Kennedy, P.J., Simoff, S., et al., 2022. Virtual reality for the observation of oncology models (vroom): immersive analytics for oncology patient cohorts. Scientific Reports 12 (1), 11337.

Laurino, M., Arcarisi, L., Carbonaro, N., Gemignani, A., Menicucci, D., Tognetti, A., 2020. A smart bed for non-obtrusive sleep analysis in real world context. IEEE Access 8, 45664–45673.

Li, J., Liang, J.Y., Laken, S.J., Langer, R., Traverso, G., 2020. Clinical opportunities for continuous biosensing and closed-loop therapies. Trends in Chemistry 2 (4), 319–340.

Mohammed, J., Lung, C.-H., Ocneanu, A., Thakral, A., Jones, C., Adler, A., 2014. Internet of things: remote patient monitoring using web services and cloud computing. In: 2014 IEEE International Conference on Internet of Things (IThings), and IEEE Green Computing and Communications (GreenCom) and IEEE Cyber, Physical and Social Computing (CPSCom). IEEE, pp. 256–263.

Pattichis, C.S., Panayides, A.S., 2019. Connected health.

Perera, M.S., Halgamuge, M.N., Samarakody, R., Mohammad, A., 2021. Internet of Things in healthcare: a survey of telemedicine systems used for elderly people. In: IoT in Healthcare and Ambient Assisted Living, pp. 69–88.

Philips Healthcare, 2023. Telehealth: Access to care. https://www.usa.philips.com/healthcare/government/our-approach/perspectives/telehealth-access-to-care. (Accessed 4 September 2024).

Prasad, D.D., 2023. An IoT-based computational intelligence model to perform gene analytics in paternity testing and comparison for health 4.0. Journal of Theoretical and Applied Information Technology 101 (14).

Rahimloo, P., Jafarian, A., 2016. Prediction of diabetes by using artificial neural network, logistic regression statistical model and combination of them. Bulletin de la Société Royale Des Sciences de Liège 85, 1148–1164.

Rahman, M.J., Morshed, B.I., Harmon, B., Rahman, M., 2022. A pilot study towards a smart-health framework to collect and analyze biomarkers with low-cost and flexible wearables. Smart Health 23, 100249.

Ranjbar, E., Sedehi, R.G., Rashidi, M., Suratgar, A.A., 2019. Design of an IoT-based system for smart maintenance of medical equipment. In: 2019 3rd International Conference on Internet of Things and Applications (IoT). IEEE, pp. 1–12.

Rhayem, A., Mhiri, M.B.A., Drira, K., Tazi, S., Gargouri, F., 2021. A semantic-enabled and context-aware monitoring system for the Internet of medical things. Expert Systems 38 (2), e12629.

Roden, S., Nucciarelli, A., Li, F., Graham, G., 2017. Big data and the transformation of operations models: a framework and a new research agenda. Production Planning & Control 28 (11–12), 929–944.

Sardi, L., Idri, A., Fernández-Alemán, J.L., 2017. A systematic review of gamification in e-health. Journal of Biomedical Informatics 71, 31–48.

Sonkoly, B., Haja, D., Németh, B., Szalay, M., Czentye, J., Szabó, R., Ullah, R., Kim, B.-S., Toka, L., 2020. Scalable edge cloud platforms for IoT services. Journal of Network and Computer Applications 170, 102785.

Steiner, C., Elixhauser, A., Schnaier, J., 2002. The healthcare cost and utilization project: an overview. Effective Clinical Practice 5 (3).

Umer, M., Sadiq, S., Karamti, H., Karamti, W., Majeed, R., Nappi, M., 2022. IoT based smart monitoring of patients' with acute heart failure. Sensors 22 (7), 2431.

Vijayan, V., Connolly, J.P., Condell, J., McKelvey, N., Gardiner, P., 2021. Review of wearable devices and data collection considerations for connected health. Sensors 21 (16), 5589.

Yang, G.-Z., 2018. Implantable Sensors and Systems: From Theory to Practice. Springer.

CHAPTER

IoT-cloud for social good in municipality services 14

14.1 Introduction

The Internet-of-Things (IoT) is rapidly transforming various businesses and industries, and the public sector is no exception. Government bodies around the world are increasingly recognizing the potential of IoT to address urban and community challenges, improve public utilities, and enhance citizen well-being. A growing global movement towards using IoT for societal benefits is being witnessed as urban areas, communities, and public entities embrace this trend, within municipalities, regions, and public sectors to instill smarter and more sustainable communities. The combination of IoT and cloud empower the governments to enhance public services, creating value for the community. Adopting these services further fosters trust in public authorities, while nurturing citizens' positive attitudes and behaviors regarding government operations (Chohan and Hu, 2020).

Amsterdam addressed overflowing trash challenges and high waste collection costs by introducing a network of smart bins equipped with fill-level sensors. This public service innovation optimizes collection routes and significantly cut down unnecessary pickups, which also reduced traffic congestion caused by collection trucks and lowered induced air pollution. These solar-powered bins, which further compact waste, reduced the waste collection frequency by up to 85% (TheMayor.EU, 2020). A similar approach was adopted in the Kingdom of Saudi Arabia and a study showed 46% enhancement in the performance of waste-collection truck management (Rosil, 2022; Abdullah et al., 2022). Another inspiring public service example comes from Singapore's "Smart Nation" initiative, which harnesses IoT and cloud for sustainable urban management. This project utilizes IoT sensors to collect data on and energy, optimizing traffic light patterns and reducing energy waste in public buildings (Ferro-Escobar et al., 2022).

The growing focus on environmental sustainability is addressed by IoT sensors deployed to monitor air and water quality, track greenhouse gas emissions, and other environmental conditions. Policy decisions are made to, for example, monitor water usage in parks and public gardens, enabling more efficient irrigation practices and conserving precious water resources. Public safety is further enhanced by deploying a range of IoT-based solutions, such as smart lighting systems, gunshot detection sensors, and video surveillance cameras, equipped with facial recognition technology, to deter crime. Overall, the integration of IoT and cloud technologies prompt public

Accelerating Digital Transformation with the Cloud and the Internet of Things (IoT)
https://doi.org/10.1016/B978-0-44-322217-7.00022-0

sector entities to foster increased efficiency and satisfaction within communities (El Barachi et al., 2022b).

Yet it is paramount to adhere to data protection regulations, such as GDPR in the EU and similar regulations in other areas for the effective deployment of these technologies, to safeguard citizen data privacy and security. Supporting activities such as limiting data gathering to only needed information and maintaining transparency in data utilization contribute to building public confidence in IoT solutions aimed at societal benefits.

14.2 Environmental sustainability with IoT and cloud

As the global community copes with environmental challenges, such as climate change and lack of resources, the public sector is increasingly turning to the fusion of IoT and cloud for innovative solutions. Next, we discuss case studies that use this fusion to support greener urban prospects.

14.2.1 Preserving habitats and resources: sensor-driven environmental monitoring

The fight against environmental degradation requires a comprehensive understanding of complex ecosystems and resource usage.

Wildlife monitoring and conservation

A successful application of IoT and cloud for habitat preservation involves wildlife monitoring. Conservation organizations in Africa are deploying camera traps equipped with cellular connectivity and AI image recognition software to capture wildlife activity, and track population trends. These efforts support the development of targeted strategies for protecting endangered species (Perera et al., 2019; NextBigThing, 2022).

Marine life preservation

Marine biologists have deployed a network of underwater sensors in the Australian Great Barrier Reef to observe salinity levels, and coral health. This data track the impact of environmental changes on the reef ecosystem by identifying areas of coral bleaching. With this information, conservationists prioritize areas in need of coral restoration efforts and gather evidence to support budgeting and advocacy for stronger policies to safeguard the reef's long-term preservation (Jahanbakht et al., 2021).

Water resource management

Beyond wildlife and marine ecosystems, cities such as San Francisco are deploying smart water meters equipped with leak detection capabilities to enhance water management and conservation effort. These meters can detect even small leaks in pipes, allowing for timely repairs and minimizing water waste (Government Technology, 2023). These meters utilize low-frequency radio signals to collect hourly water usage data, which is then transmitted multiple times a day to a cloud-based billing system. Furthermore, sensor networks monitor water levels in reservoirs and rivers, enabling authorities to optimize water allocation and irrigation practices during periods of drought. A proactive management of water resources ensure the sustainability of cities' water supplies and a way to safeguard aquatic ecosystems. IoT and cloud technologies empower authorities to make data-driven decisions, which contribute to the preservation of precious resources and preserve biodiversity (Maamar et al., 2019).

14.2.2 Traffic safety

Driver behavior analysis

IoT devices can collect a) data on driver state, such as levels of drowsiness or inattention, and b) driving patterns, such as harsh braking, sharp turns, or erratic driving. This information can be analyzed to identify risky driving behaviors and inform targeted safety campaigns or individual driver feedback systems.

Among IoT devices that have been deployed for driver monitoring are onboard cameras to track drivers' eye gaze and body posture, assessing driver's state and level of attention to the driving task (Albadawi et al., 2023; Li et al., 2023).

Advanced driver monitoring systems (DMS) harness the power of these onboard cameras alongside cutting-edge computer vision and AI algorithms to assess drivers' physiological and behavioral indicators. These systems constantly observe drivers' eye gaze, blink rate, head position, and body posture to gauge their attention and alertness levels. By continuously monitoring for signs of fatigue and distraction, advanced DMS provide a layer of safety, which can save lives by alerting drivers to risks before they lead to accidents.

Friction detection algorithms for road infrastructure

The friction coefficient is the level of grip between tires and the road, which influences vehicle stability, braking distance, and overall safety. Traditionally, assessing road friction relied on intermittent manual inspections and subjective evaluations, following rain, snow, or icy patch inspections. Advanced sensor technologies coupled with cloud-based data analytics are transforming this process. By embedding sensors capable of measuring friction coefficients directly into road surfaces, municipalities and transportation agencies act promptly to safeguard the dynamic conditions of their road networks (Šabanovič et al., 2020).

Furthermore, connected vehicles themselves can communicate friction index information. Through various onboard sensors and communication technologies, such as GPS, accelerometers, and vehicle-to-vehicle or vehicle-to-infrastructure communication systems, gathered data about road conditions can be supplied to cloud for computing the friction index. This centralized cloud-based platform aggregates and analyzes the friction index, which is then shared with vehicles o the road and transportation authorities. In doing so, connected vehicles contribute to a collective intelligence of road conditions, enhancing overall road safety (Chu et al., 2021).

Pedestrian safety systems

The application of IoT technologies in enhancing pedestrian safety is gaining traction in various cities globally. One notable innovation is the smart crossing, a responsive road surface developed by Umbrellium in collaboration with Direct Line. This system can differentiate between vehicles, pedestrians, and cyclists, adjusting its markings and signals in real time to ensure safety and learn from road users' behaviors over time. The smart crossing can widen the crossing space when needed, provide extra warnings to cyclists when pedestrians are hidden by vehicles, and alert drivers about distracted pedestrians stepping onto the road (The NBS, 2023).

Another advanced application comes from Applied Information in Suwanee, Georgia, which introduced a configurable IoT pedestrian crossing safety system (PCSS). This system enhances road crossing safety through features such as push-button activated flashers, IoT connectivity, and connection to the TravelSafely smartphone app. The system can alert both pedestrians and approaching motorists of potential dangers, improving safety at crossings. This IoT solution demonstrates a significant step toward creating safer urban environments for pedestrians with IoT-enabled solutions (IoT M2M Council, 2022).

Smart parking

Sensors can detect vehicle occupancy in parking spaces and provide real-time information on available parking spots. The time drivers spend searching for parking is reduced, while safety hazards induced by navigating to a parking spot are minimized, and air quality is maximized in urban cores (Mathew et al., 2014; Atif et al., 2020). For instance, San Francisco has implemented a network of smart parking sensors that provide real-time parking availability information (Rodier and Shaheen, 2010).

14.2.3 Enhancing urban life

Streamlined waste management and the rise of smart trash bins

Urban areas face the challenge of managing increasing amounts of waste, efficiently. This issue is exacerbated by traditional waste management systems struggling to keep pace with the surge in waste generated by growing populations, leading to overflowing bins, inefficient collection schedules, and higher operational costs. Moreover, these outdated systems contribute significantly to environmental degradation induced by harmful gases from landfills and increasing fuel consumption due to inefficient collection routes. The health risks associated with poorly managed waste, such as overflowing bins and possibly contaminated water sources, require more efficient waste management solutions. Economically, the inefficiency of traditional waste management systems challenge municipalities, rounding up costs associated with fuel, labor, and maintenance, which divert resources from other essential services (Herranz, 2020; SmartSight, 2020).

IoT technology offers a transformative solution to these challenges (Shukla and Hait, 2022). Smart waste management systems utilize a network of sensors and other IoT devices to monitor waste levels in bins in real time, enabling waste management companies to optimize collection routes and schedules. This smart system ensures that waste is collected at the optimal time, preventing overflow and reducing the frequency of collections when bins are not full, thereby saving significant operational costs and fuel consumption besides significantly lowering environmental impacts.

The lessons learned from successful adoptions of smart waste management by way of cities such as Amsterdam, Barcelona, and Seoul illustrate the potential for further innovation that extends beyond just monitoring and collection optimization (Ringenson and Höjer, 2016). Predictive analytics, powered by machine learning algorithms, can further forecast waste generation patterns, allowing for even more precise scheduling of waste collection (Bakhshi and Ahmed, 2018). This can lead to further improvement in urban living conditions by ensuring a cleaner and more hygienic urban environment.

Food safety in schools with IoT-powered student meals

Access to safe and nutritious meals is a basic requirement for student health, which support their academic performance. However, traditional methods of school food inventory management is prone to errors and waste. A study showed that food waste was the largest fraction of Florida school cafeterias waste streams, ranging from 47% to 58% (Wilkie et al., 2015).

An innovative solution equips refrigerators and freezers in school kitchens with smart sensors that track food temperature and expiration dates (Bonaccorsi et al., 2017), sending alerts to kitchen staff when food is nearing its expiration. A game-theoretic decision-making model has been proposed to maintain and assess the food parameters of such food outlets and restaurants (Bhatia and Ahanger, 2021). This proactive inventory management prevents food spoilage and ensures students have access to fresh and safe meals in school cafeterias.

Another application involves the use of barcode or QR-code scanners and cloud-based inventory management software. School staff can scan food items upon receiving them, thereby automatically updating inventory levels and facilitating real-time tracking of stock. This allows schools to optimize their ordering processes, reducing the risk of stockouts and ensuring a consistent supply of essential ingredients for nutritious meals. Moreover, the students can scan these codes or use nutrition kiosks in dining halls to access the nutritional value and ingredients used in the food items. This can help students with dietary intolerances to make safe choices (Xie et al., 2022).

Schools typically have breakfast programs, where the food served includes milk and fruits. Due to weather conditions, delays, or unconventional handling of food during transportation, it is possible that fruits or milk may have perished or decayed before it reaches the schools. IoT technology can play a vital role in ensuring early detection of such food that is perishing. Sensor-embedded cartons are able to accurately detect the spoilage of even a single item of food in real time, thereby enabling timely intervention and prevent contamination of the rest of the items. This allows the accurate and real-time monitoring of perishable food, facilitates inventory management, and minimizes food safety and waste concerns (El Barachi et al., 2022c).

Leveraging IoT technologies allow schools to create safer, more efficient, and more responsive food service environments. These advances reduce food waste and save costs, ultimately contributing to the well-being and academic success of students. As we move forward, the continued integration of IoT solutions holds immense potential for further innovation and improvements within school meal programs.

Pollution fighters

Air and noise pollution pose significant health risks to urban residents, impacting respiratory health, cardiovascular function, and general well-being. Smart cities use IoT technologies to proactively monitor and manage pollution levels to facilitate creating healthier urban environments. Air quality verification sensors deployed in cities measure and report variations in air quality. The collected data from these sensors is aggregated and visualized to online platforms and mobile applications to support daily activity decisions, such as planning outdoor events (Kaginalkar et al., 2021). Studies on air quality management systems have shown that the emissions can be monitored by deploying IoT-based sensors network, enabling them informed decisions about health and well-being (Gupta et al., 2019; Bhangale et al., 2023). A study performed in Delhi showed that air quality can be substantially improved by using IoT-based sensing system to forecast urban air quality (Barthwal and Acharya, 2021).

Another effective strategy involves utilizing noise pollution sensors. These devices can be mounted on light poles, or integrated into existing street infrastructure (Gunatilaka, 2021). They continuously monitor noise levels and can be configured to identify and report excessive noise violations. The collected data enforce programs towards areas with chronic noise pollution problems and promote responsible behavior among citizens (Patil, 2017).

14.3 Measuring success: challenges and value proposition

IoT and cloud technologies integration in the public sector is a shift towards more responsive and citizen-centric services. Municipality services promise to address longstanding challenges ranging from streamlining waste management to enhancing public safety and promoting environmental sustainability. However, the mere deployment of IoT and cloud solutions is not the endpoint, but the beginning of a digital transformation towards maximizing their social good potential for enhancing citizens' welfare.

To truly harness the benefits of IoT and cloud technologies, municipalities must not only implement these solutions but also rigorously measure their success and navigate the challenges that accompany their adoption. Strategies for evaluating the effectiveness of IoT initiatives are drawn to ensure they deliver tangible benefits in service delivery, cost efficiency, and citizen satisfaction,

14.3.1 Success definition

When adopting IoT for social good, municipalities' definition of success extends beyond traditional metrics of operational efficiency and cost-effectiveness. A further broad spectrum of outcomes that collectively contribute to the well-being of the community and the sustainability of the environment is encompassed in assessing the community as a basis for the successful implementation of this adaption. Specific objectives that are tailored to the unique needs and aspirations of the community need to be established.

Improved service efficiency

At the core of IoT initiatives is the drive to enhance the efficiency of public services. Metrics to quantify successful attainments include reduced response times to public inquiries, increased accuracy in service delivery, or streamlined operational processes that leverage IoT and cloud technologies.

Cost savings

Financial metrics remain a decisive component of success, with cost savings from optimized resource allocation, reduced waste, and lower operational expenses serving as key indicators. These savings reflect the economic benefits of IoT initiatives and the resulting potential to redirect financial resources towards other public service areas.

Enhanced citizen satisfaction

Perhaps the most revealing indicator of success is the level of citizen satisfaction and engagement with IoT-enhanced public services. Surveys, feedback mechanisms, and participatory platforms can provide valuable measurements into how citizens perceive IoT improvements in quality of life.

Environmental impact

With the growing emphasis on sustainability, the environmental impact of IoT initiatives gains significance as a metric of success. Decreased pollution levels and improved management of natural resources are tangible outcomes that municipalities can measure to evaluate the environmental benefits of their IoT projects.

The challenge, however, lies in developing a framework that effectively captures these diverse criteria for success, while aligning technological capabilities with human and environmental considerations, in balanced way. Setting clear, measurable outcomes and continuously monitoring their progress against the abovementioned benchmarks support municipalities to navigate through the intricacies of IoT deployment for social good, ensuring that the technology truly serves the public interest and paves the way for a more sustainable, inclusive, and connected future.

14.3.2 Value proposition

The value proposition of IoT and cloud in municipal services underscores a set of strategic advantages, which are distinct from success metrics. Instead, the broader transformative impacts to redefine the essence of municipality governance and community living are emphasized via the following strategies:

Strategic innovation

The integration of IoT and cloud technologies introduces an era of strategic innovation within public services. This innovation extends beyond incremental improvements, venturing into creating novel solutions that address longstanding urban challenges in unprecedented ways. It is about reimagining urban life with a forward-looking vision that aligns with future societal needs and technological developments.

Sustainability and resilience

While environmental sustainability forms a part of the measurable outcomes, the value proposition emphasizes the role of these technologies in fostering a resilient urban ecosystem. This resilience is crucial to face climate change and urbanization challenges, ensuring that cities can adapt, survive, and thrive despite adversities. This strategy ensures today's urban centers remain viable, while committing to preserving the planet for future generations.

Economic development and attractiveness

IoT and cloud technologies serve as catalysts for economic development. Enhancing the city's infrastructure with smart technology makes municipalities become more attractive to businesses and investors as well as tourists, driving economic growth and job creation. This economic development raises cities' profile as competitive entities, capable of attracting and retaining talents.

Equitable access and inclusion

A significant part of the value proposition lies in using IoT and cloud technologies to bridge digital, economic, or social divides. IoT and cloud technologies can democratize access to services, ensuring that benefits reach all citizens, including the most vulnerable. Municipalities can develop a more inclusive society through with solutions that meet diverse needs and eliminate access barriers.

Governance transparency

Enhancing governance through increased transparency and accountability forms an important value proposition in public services. Data and analytics IoT and cloud technologies enable municipalities to operate with greater transparency, offering citizens accounts regarding decision-making processes. This transparency builds trust and invites citizen participation, creating a more engaged and informed community.

14.3.3 Evaluation in real-world settings

Whereas the potential benefits of IoT and cloud technologies are vast, rigorous evaluation in real-world settings ensure they deliver the above tangible value propositions for the intended beneficiaries. Conducting user surveys with focus groups is a possible approach to gather feedback directly from users about their experiences with the implemented solution. Another approach involves collecting and analyzing usage data. IoT and cloud platforms often generate vast amounts of data on user interaction and system performance. By analyzing this data, areas for improvement are identified. For example, in Singapore, researchers evaluated the effectiveness of a smart waste management system by analyzing data, which brought further ease in the collection and treatment of waste and improved environmental indicators (Ferro-Escobar et al., 2022).

Tracking the impact of an IoT and cloud solution over time to assess its long-term effects on user behavior and broader societal outcomes is conducted in a study using both qualitative and quantitative measures on the readiness of smart city citizens to continuously use smart city public services (El Barachi et al., 2021a). The study reveals technology readiness as a personality trait in shaping user satisfaction and intention to continue using smart city public services. Furthermore, the study proposed a new scale and model for measuring users' readiness to adopt and continuously use smart city public services. The proposed model informs the design of future public services and ensures their sustainable and successful adoption by citizens.

Conducting cost-benefit analyses evaluate the financial costs associated with implementing and maintaining these solutions alongside the quantifiable benefits they generate. For example, a cost-benefit analysis of an innovative irrigation system in a drought-stricken region might consider the cost of sensors and network infrastructure to show that it is viable for overall lower costs, better product quality and quantity, and increased sustainability, making it an attractive area for investment and growth (Acharya et al., 2023).

This user-centric approach, involving evaluation of the extent and how well IoT and cloud solutions for social good are meeting user needs, ensures that these solutions address the real-world challenges faced by the community. This approach results also in more effective and impactful interventions contributing to measurable improvements.

14.4 Data protection and ethical considerations in IoT implementations

Incorporating IoT into public services has led to citizen data protection requirements. Regulations such as the General Data Protection Regulation (GDPR) in the European Union and similar laws elsewhere around the world, establish guidelines to protect data privacy. These regulations emphasize limiting data collection to its purpose and ensuring transparent data management.

14.4.1 Key principles of data protection

Robust data protection in public sector IoT services should follow data protection principles that help municipalities protect citizen privacy and establish trust with the public. This could be achieved by adhering to legal regulations, such as the General Data Protection Regulation (GDPR) in the EU. These principles guide secure data management, while ensuring responsible and efficient use of IoT technologies for enhancing public services and improving urban living.

Data minimization

IoT solutions should gather the essential data needed to accomplish their objectives, lowering the chances of data breaches and alleviating privacy concerns for individuals. For example, in waste management IoT solutions, information gathered should be restricted to waste quantities and pick up timetables, while refraining from obtaining details about individuals.

Transparency

Government agencies should openly share information about the data they gather and its purposes by offering means for citizens to understand their rights regarding collected data. Transparency fosters public trust, while motivating public involvement in smart city projects.

Consent

Citizens should have the option to decide whether they want to take part in data gathering without experiencing any outcomes. By providing consent, citizens can comprehend and approve of the ways their information will be utilized. This concept holds higher significance for data activities, such as assessing driver behavior and monitoring patient health conditions.

The right to be forgotten

The concept of the right to be forgotten is a principle in safeguarding data privacy. It allows individuals to request the removal of their information from digital databases once it is no longer needed for the initial reasons it was collected. This privacy aspect is relevant to IoT applications, where extensive data gathering, storage, and analysis take place. Municipalities and public agencies need to make sure that people have a way to ask for their personal information to be removed from IoT-based systems. This covers information gathered from sensors, public monitoring, and other IoT-based services. Putting this idea into action includes the following:

Data access and rectification

Citizens should be able to view their information and ask for changes if there are any mistakes. This helps to make sure that the details are correct and current, thereby building confidence into IoT-based applications.

14.4.2 Ethical considerations in IoT implementations for public services

As IoT technology continues to integrate into public services, it is important to consider the ethical implications of related application. Ethical concerns related to IoT encompass a range of topics, including data confidentiality, security measures, openness, and the societal consequences of data gathering. In the public domain, where IoT has a significant impact on urban living, addressing these issues is essential for gaining public confidence and ensuring that technology serves the community well. Next, the values and standards that ought to be adhered to when responsibly introducing IoT solutions, in public services, are discussed.

Ethical data use

When developing IoT solutions, it is important to think about ethics and how data can be used for the greater good of society, making sure it does not lead to discrimination or harm against people. For example, information gathered from intersections should focus on enhancing pedestrian safety, while respecting individuals privacy.

Privacy by design

Privacy should be a by-design factor in IoT systems right from the start. This method, referred to as "privacy by design" guarantees that privacy and data protection are accounted for in the system development process.

Impact assessments

Regularly performing data protection impact assessments (DPIAs) is essential for recognizing and minimizing risks linked to handling data. DPIAs prove valuable in situations involving high risk tasks, such as surveillance and health monitoring.

Ethical governance

Governance structures that deploy IoT systems should endorse societal values and adhere to legal requirements. This involves setting up committees or boards for overseeing data ethics and ensuring compliance with all regulations.

14.5 The future of IoT in public sector services

Harnessing the full power of IoT and cloud computing in the public sector demands a distinctive approach, which balances technological advances, user needs and preferences, societal benefits, and ethical considerations. Realizing this vision involves the ethical use of data. Developing comprehensive privacy guidelines that ensure data protection and foster a culture of transparency are foundational to the responsible deployment of these technologies. Looking ahead, the future of public sector IoT lies in striking a balance between innovation and ethical responsibility, ensuring that technological advances serve the broader goals of society.

14.5.1 Striking a balance: innovation, user focus, and societal benefit

IoT in the public sector trajectory is drawn by the fusion and the harmonious balance of technological innovation, user-centric design, and the pursuit of societal benefits. This integration is essential for crafting IoT solutions that meet the requirements of diverse community members, and not just showcasing technological prowesses.

To achieve the above equilibrium, a continuous and open dialogue among technology developers, policymakers, and the community at large is established. This collaborative approach ensures that IoT initiatives contribute to the broader objectives of enhancing the quality of life, fosters inclusivity, and encourages inclusive participation. The public sector can employ these principles to engage into the transformative power of IoT, which streamlines operations and improves public services, making the communities more connected and supportive of digital transformation projects.

14.5.2 Privacy guidelines for ethical and responsible implementation

The collection of personal data raises significant ethical concerns, considering privacy issues. Smart cities implementing IoT-based solutions should be transparent and clearly communicate these details to users through accessible channels. Individuals should have the right to opt-in or opt-out of data collection without repercussions (Tsesis, 2019).

Citizens are empowered to control their personal information, which fosters trust in organizations and institutions that introduce new smart services. Data security measures safeguard personal data throughout its lifecycle: from collection and storage to transmission and use. These security implementations include regular security audits, data encryption protocols, and secure disposal practices to minimize the risk of unauthorized access, breaches, or misuse (Badii et al., 2020).

Finally, IoT solutions should collect only the minimum amount of data necessary to achieve the intended purpose. This reduces the risk of data breaches and minimizes privacy concerns for or by citizens. These ethical principles establish clear privacy guidelines, enabling public authorities to foster public trust in IoT solutions for social good. Transparency, user consent, and data minimization practices (Makker, 2016) constitute a responsible approach to data collection and utilization, besides the implementation of robust security measures.

References

Abdullah, N., Al-wesabi, O.A., Mohammed, B.A., Al-Mekhlafi, Z.G., Alazmi, M., Alsaffar, M., Baklizi, M., Sumari, P., 2022. IoT-based waste management system in formal and informal public areas in mecca. International Journal of Environmental Research and Public Health 19 (20), 13066. https://doi.org/10.3390/ijerph192013066.

Acharya, U., Ramaprasad, B.S., Kate, N., Srivastava, A., 2023. The adoption of smart agriculture technologies based on the perception of the farmers in the Indian context. In: 2023 Second International Conference on Smart Technologies for Smart Nation (SmartTechCon). IEEE, pp. 586–593.

Albadawi, Y., AlRedhaei, A., Takruri, M., 2023. Real-time machine learning-based driver drowsiness detection using visual features. Journal of Imaging 9 (5), 91. https://www.mdpi.com/2313-433X/9/5/91.

Atif, Y., Kharrazi, S., Jianguo, D., Andler, S.F., 2020. Internet of things data analytics for parking availability prediction and guidance. Transactions on Emerging Telecommunications Technologies 31 (5), e3862.

Badii, C., Bellini, P., Difino, A., Nesi, P., 2020. Smart city iot platform respecting gdpr privacy and security aspects. IEEE Access 8, 23601–23623.

Bakhshi, T., Ahmed, M., 2018. Iot-enabled smart city waste management using machine learning analytics. In: 2018 2nd International Conference on Energy Conservation and Efficiency (ICECE). IEEE, pp. 66–71.

Barthwal, A., Acharya, D., 2021. An iot based sensing system for modeling and forecasting urban air quality. Wireless Personal Communications 116 (4), 3503–3526.

Bhangale, S.C., Varade, H.P., Thorat, S.R., Roy, D.K., William, P., Verma, A., 2023. Air quality hotspot monitoring with trajectories of iot in smart city implementation. In: 2023 3rd International Conference on Pervasive Computing and Social Networking (ICPCSN), pp. 1274–1279.

Bhatia, M., Ahanger, T.A., 2021. Intelligent decision-making in smart food industry: quality perspective. Pervasive and Mobile Computing 72, 101304.

Bonaccorsi, M., Betti, S., Rateni, G., Esposito, D., Brischetto, A., Marseglia, M., Dario, P., Cavallo, F., 2017. 'highchest': an augmented freezer designed for smart food management and promotion of eco-efficient behaviour. Sensors 17 (6), 1357.

Chohan, S.R., Hu, G., 2020. Success factors influencing citizens' adoption of iot service orchestration for public value creation in smart government. IEEE Access 8, 208427–208448.

Chu, W., Wuniri, Q., Du, X., Xiong, Q., Huang, T., Li, K., 2021. Cloud control system architectures, technologies and applications on intelligent and connected vehicles: a review. Chinese Journal of Mechanical Engineering 34 (1), 139.

El Barachi, M., Abu Salim, T., Nyadzayo, M.W., Mathew, S.S., Badewi, A., Amankwah-Amoah, J., 2021a. The social dimension of smart cities: Impact of readiness on citizens' intention to continuously use smart city services. In: Munyaradzi, W., Mathew, Sujith Samuel, Badewi, Amgad, Amankwah-Amoah, Joseph (Eds.), The Social Dimension of Smart Cities: Impact of Readiness on Citizens' Intention to Continuously Use Smart City Services.

El Barachi, M., Salim, T.A., Nyadzayo, M.W., Mathew, S., Badewi, A., Amankwah-Amoah, J., 2022b. The relationship between citizen readiness and the intention to continuously use smart city services: mediating effects of satisfaction and discomfort. Technology in Society 71, 102115.

El Barachi, M., Salman, S., Mathew, S., 2022c. A sensor-embedded smart carton for the real-time monitoring of perishable foods' lifetime. In: 2022 7th International Conference on Smart and Sustainable Technologies (SpliTech). IEEE, pp. 1–8.

Ferro-Escobar, R., Vacca-González, H., Gómez-Castillo, H., 2022. Smart and sustainable cities in collaboration with IoT: the Singapore success case. In: Machine Learning for Smart Environments/Cities: An IoT Approach. Springer, pp. 213–243.

Government Technology, 2023. California utilities deploy smart water meters amid drought. https://www.govtech.com/civic/california-utilities-deploy-smart-water-meters-amid-drought. (Accessed 24 March 2024).

Gunatilaka, D., 2021. An iot-enabled acoustic sensing platform for noise pollution monitoring. In: 2021 IEEE 12th Annual Ubiquitous Computing, Electronics & Mobile Communication Conference (UEMCON). IEEE, pp. 0383–0389.

Gupta, H., Bhardwaj, D., Agrawal, H., Tikkiwal, V.A., Kumar, A., 2019. An iot based air pollution monitoring system for smart cities. In: 2019 IEEE International Conference on Sustainable Energy Technologies and Systems (ICSETS). IEEE, pp. 173–177.

Herranz, A., 2020. Success story: smart litter bins in Seoul. https://tomorrow.city/success-story-smart-litter-bins-in-seoul/. (Accessed 24 March 2024).

IoT M2M Council, 2022. Pedestrian crossing uses iot to improve safety. https://www.iotm2mcouncil.org/iot-library/news/smart-cities-news/pedestrian-crossing-uses-iot-to-improve-safety/. (Accessed 24 March 2024).

Jahanbakht, M., Xiang, W., Hanzo, L., Azghadi, M.R., 2021. Internet of underwater things and big marine data analytics—a comprehensive survey. IEEE Communications Surveys and Tutorials 23 (2), 904–956.

Kaginalkar, A., Kumar, S., Gargava, P., Niyogi, D., 2021. Review of urban computing in air quality management as smart city service: an integrated iot, ai, and cloud technology perspective. Urban Climate 39, 100972.

Li, Y., Zhang, S., Zhu, G., Huang, Z., Wang, R., Duan, X., Wang, Z., 2023. A cnn-based wearable system for driver drowsiness detection. Sensors 23 (7), 3475.

Maamar, Z., Baker, T., Faci, N., Al-Khafajiy, M., Ugljanin, E., Atif, Y., Sellami, M., 2019. Weaving cognition into the Internet-of-Things: application to water leaks. Cognitive Systems Research 56, 233–245.

Makker, S.R., 2016. Overcoming foggy notions of privacy: how data minimization will enable privacy in the Internet of Things. UMKC L. Rev. 85, 895.

Mathew, S.S., Atif, Y., Sheng, Q.Z., Maamar, Z., 2014. Building sustainable parking lots with the web of things. Personal and Ubiquitous Computing 18, 895–907.

NextBigThing, 2022. Iot and the battle against biodiversity loss: a powerful solution for a pressing challenge. https://nextbigthing.ag/blog/iot-and-the-battle-against-biodiversity-loss-a-powerful-solution-for-a-pressing-challenge/. (Accessed 24 March 2024).

Patil, P., 2017. Smart iot based system for vehicle noise and pollution monitoring. In: 2017 International Conference on Trends in Electronics and Informatics (ICEI). IEEE, pp. 322–326.

Perera, C., Rana, O., Goossens, B., Orozco-ter Wengel, P., 2019. Internet of things for efficient wildlife conservation: challenges and opportunities.

Ringenson, T., Höjer, M., 2016. Smart city planning and environmental aspects: lessons from seven cities. In: ICT for Sustainability 2016. Atlantis Press, pp. 159–166.

Rodier, C.J., Shaheen, S.A., 2010. Transit-based smart parking: an evaluation of the San Francisco bay area field test. Transportation Research. Part C, Emerging Technologies 18 (2), 225–233.

Rosil, M., 2022. Smart city solutions: waste management in cities. https://euristiq.com/waste-management-in-cities. (Accessed 24 March 2024).

Šabanovič, E., Žuraulis, V., Prentkovskis, O., Skrickij, V., 2020. Identification of road-surface type using deep neural networks for friction coefficient estimation. Sensors 20 (3), 612.

Shukla, S., Hait, S., 2022. Smart waste management practices in smart cities: current trends and future perspectives. In: Advanced Organic Waste Management. Elsevier, pp. 407–424.

SmartSight, 2020. Smart waste management: IoT solutions for sustainable cities. https://www.smartsight.in/industry-insights/smart-waste-management-iot-solutions-for-sustainable-cities/. (Accessed 24 March 2024).

The NBS, 2023. Introducing the smart crossing – a new kind of pedestrian crossing. https://www.thenbs.com/knowledge/introducing-the-smart-crossing-a-new-kind-of-pedestrian-crossing. (Accessed 24 March 2024).

TheMayor.EU, 2020. Smart bins reduce waste collection by up to 85. https://www.themayor.eu/en/a/view/smart-bins-reduce-waste-collection-by-up-to-85-1879. (Accessed 24 March 2024).

Tsesis, A., 2019. Data subjects' privacy rights: regulation of personal data retention and erasure. University of Colorado Law Review 90, 593.

Wilkie, A.C., Graunke, R.E., Cornejo, C., 2015. Food waste auditing at three Florida schools. Sustainability 7 (2), 1370–1387.

Xie, W., Lou, H., et al., 2022. Implementation of key technologies for a healthy food culture recommendation system using Internet of Things. Mobile Information Systems 2022.

CHAPTER

Connected mobility solutions

15

15.1 Introduction

In the transportation domain, connected mobility represents a shift towards digital transformation. This evolution leverages IoT and cloud computing to create an interconnected network, enabling vehicles, infrastructure, and individuals to engage and cooperate in real time. Through the utilization of connectivity tools, this ongoing development in the transportation sector improves safety, reduces environmental footprints, and enhances user satisfaction across various modes of travel.

As IoT devices make vehicles and road infrastructures connected to cloud platforms, vast volumes of data get analyzed from different sources, such as traffic conditions, weather updates, vehicle operations, and user interactions. Processing this data in the cloud optimizes traffic flow and anticipates safety risks (Mohanta et al., 2022).

Autonomous vehicles (AVs) operate IoT devices on wheels, thereby constantly producing and analyzing data. By linking this data to the cloud, AVs tap into computing resources that assist them in making intelligent choices, while maneuvering and engaging with other vehicles on the road. This two-tier data system enhances AV capabilities and allows sophisticated cloud-based services (He et al., 2014).

By looking at traffic patterns and information from within vehicles, connected transportation systems can predict possible hazards. For instance, if a road has a history of accidents under specific conditions, the system can preemptively reroute vehicles. Cloud-connected IoT systems can also utilize weather updates to modify vehicle operations, such as braking distances and speed limits. Moreover, IoT sensors regularly monitor vehicle conditions anticipating issues before they become expensive repairs (Srinivasan, 2018).

The shift from separate modes of transportation to interconnected data-driven systems marks a move towards the next level in vehicle navigation and transportation networks. In the past, transportation systems functioned independently with minimal sharing of information between various modes of transport and supporting-infrastructure. The enhanced connectivity and related automation in the vehicle industry and road structures have improved responses to potential hazards and decreased the severity of accidents. The progress in AI allows real-time processing of vast amounts of data within vehicles and traffic flow, enhancing safety through insights gained from driver behavior and surrounding traffic patterns (Lim et al., 2021).

Accelerating Digital Transformation with the Cloud and the Internet of Things (IoT)
https://doi.org/10.1016/B978-0-44-322217-7.00023-2

The network of communication links between vehicles and infrastructure forms a web of interconnected devices. With the advancement of 5G technology, it is predicted that over half of the vehicles on the road will be connected by 2025 increasing to 77% by 2030 (Ericsson, 2021). To keep up with the challenges and opportunities brought about by the combination of IoT and cloud computing, automotive industry manufacturers are increasingly teaming up with or taking over companies that specialize in mobility solutions. These collaborations are designed to reduce expenses and risks related to cutting edge mobility solutions and user involvement (Fard and Brugeman, 2019).

In this chapter, we explore the advancements in transportation to examine upcoming trends in connected mobility and observe how IoT and cloud technology are influencing the transportation sector evolution. We review aspects of vehicle connectivity by investigating different solutions for mobility and transportation. The commercial aspects of connected intelligent vehicles are also discussed. Lastly, we present examples that demonstrate connected mobility in practice, revealing a future where automation, electrification, and data-driven personalized vehicle interaction, are transforming our travel experiences and urban landscapes.

15.2 Understanding mobility services and transportation logistics

In transportation domains, one needs to grasp the distinction between mobility services and transportation logistics. Although they share a relationship, they serve distinct purposes in terms of transportation movement and organization. This section elucidates these variances towards their contribution to the broader landscape of innovative mobility solutions.

15.2.1 Mobility services

Assisting people in traveling effectively between locations through various transportation methods is the essence of mobility services. This encompasses travels via shared mobility solutions, such as ride sharing and public transportation networks. These services ensure that personal travel is convenient and accessible for all individuals. Important elements consist of the following:

- **Personal travel:** This encompasses vehicles, bicycles, scooters, and other individual modes of transportation. Pedestrians are also fundamental to mobility.
- **Shared mobility services:** Multiple individuals may share a single vehicle, which may involve car sharing, bike sharing, ride hailing services, such as Uber and Lyft, and emerging options, for example, scooters. These services lower the number of vehicles on the roads, particularly in urban core areas, resulting in reduced traffic and further transportation alternatives.

- **Public transit:** Public transportation encompasses mass transit systems, such as buses, trams, subways, and trains. They operate in urban transportation systems and thereby offering efficient and eco-friendly travel choices for a significant population.
- **On-demand mobility services:** Such services cater to tailored solutions, such as responsive transit and ride hailing accessed via mobile applications.

The use of technology in mobility services is on the rise, aiming to enhance user satisfaction, raise efficiency and support eco-friendly transportation approaches. By combining IoT and cloud computing, companies can track activities in real time, analyze mobility data for movement predictions, and allocate resources more effectively. This leads to the development of cities with better urban transportation options.

15.2.2 Transportation logistics

Transportation logistics, on the other hand, focuses on the movement and management of goods and services. This encompasses the planning, implementation, and control of the efficient, effective forward and reverse flow and storage of goods, services, and related information. Key components include the following:

- **Goods transportation:** Moving items from one location to another requires utilizing means, such as trucks, ships, trains, and planes. This process encompasses both domestic deliveries and international cargo operations.
- **Supply chain management:** Managing the supply chain involves supervising all aspects, starting from acquiring materials to delivering final products. This encompasses procurement, production, distribution, and inventory control.
- **Logistics infrastructure:** This involves the infrastructure used to facilitate transportation operations, such as storage facilities, distribution hubs, ports, and railway terminals. The system lowers chances of disruptions and maintain the seamless movement of products.
- **Fleet management:** Involves overseeing fleets of vehicles utilized for transporting merchandise. This encompasses functions such as maintaining the vehicles, planning routes, managing fuel usage, and adherence to regulations.
- **Last-mile delivery:** In the delivery process phase, products are transported from a hub to their ultimate location. This step supports e-commerce and city logistics, which often require strategies to address issues such as traffic jams and effective deliveries.

IoT and cloud computing benefit transportation logistics by raising visibility levels, optimizing routes, enhancing inventory management, and facilitating real-time communication across the supply chain. These advances result in streamlined operations, reduced expenses, and increased customer satisfaction.

A logistics company that utilizes IoT and cloud computing sensors placed on delivery trucks can offer real-time information on the trucks whereabouts, traffic situations, and route effectiveness. This information is transmitted to a cloud-based platform for analysis to enhance routing, cut down on fuel usage, and enhance delivery times. Furthermore, real-time monitoring of warehouse inventory levels ensures stock management and timely order fulfillment. The fusion of cloud technologies leads to efficient operations through dependable deliveries.

15.3 Evolution of connected mobility

15.3.1 Projected trends in connected mobility

The future of connected mobility projects certain trends, which reshape the landscape of transportation. Table 15.1 illustrates key milestones and expectations for the coming decades. The advancements in shared automated electric vehicle fleets is expected to make up a substantial portion of auto passenger miles by 2030. This trend reflects a shift towards more sustainable modes of transport and signals a change from traditional exclusive car ownership models, favoring shared, on-demand services.

Table 15.1 Key developments in mobility services (2010–2020).

Year	Milestone	Description
2010	Introduction of 4G	The widespread rollout of 4G networks improved connectivity speeds, enabling better real-time data transfer for navigation and vehicle communication systems.
2012	Electric vehicles adoption	The significant increase in electric vehicles adoption, driven by improvements in battery technology and support from governmental policies, is realized.
2014	Smart city initiatives	The launching of smart city initiatives, which integrate IoT technologies into road infrastructure, traffic management, and public transportation, is accomplished.
2018	Connectivity standards	The introduction and adoption of vehicle-to-everything (V2X) communication standards, which allow vehicles to interact with each other and road infrastructure.
2020	Expansion of ride-sharing	Ride-sharing applications and platforms became more prevalent, offering new modalities of connected urban transportation.

By 2035, the role of new mobility technologies in driving economic value within the auto industry is expected to rise, giving new opportunities to electronics and software suppliers. This move towards digital solutions will redefine vehicle functionality, safety, and user experience. By 2040, data-driven travel services are bound to become the norm to access transport systems. Such developments usher a larger trend towards smart, connected cities, where mobility is integrated into the fabric of urban life (Fard and Brugeman, 2019).

Table 15.2 Projected trends in connected mobility. Adapted from (Fard and Brugeman, 2019).

Year	Projected trend	Description
2030	Shared automated electric vehicle fleets	▪ 25% of all auto passenger miles traveled. ▪ 20% of all vehicles sold. ▪ Majority of shared vehicles on the road have at least 50% of utilization.
2035	New mobility technologies	▪ 40% of auto industry profits. ▪ Providers of connectivity solutions and related software will be instrumental in advancing mobility technologies.
2040	Shared services	▪ Real-time data related to shared services in connected mobility will increase from 4% in 2015 to 25% in 2040.

The projected trends in Table 15.2 offer an outlook into a future where mobility is shaped by an integrated approach to transportation with solutions that are sustainable, and user-centric.

15.3.2 Core components of vehicle connectivity

Vehicle connectivity is a shift from isolated, mechanical transport machines to today's intelligent, interconnected systems that blur the lines between vehicles, their environment, and the digital space. This transformation aims at enhancing the driving experience, thereby improving safety and optimizing vehicle management through a network of integrated systems, as illustrated in Fig. 15.1.

In-vehicle connectivity

Connectivity drives data and a conceptual visualization of the sophisticated data hierarchy and interaction within a vehicle connectivity system, which is structured following the standard Vehicle Signal Specification (VSS) model (Alliance, 2021) is illustrated in Fig. 15.2. A common vehicle data model, such as VSS, is a prominent advancement of connected vehicle technologies to provide a standardized approach to structuring and defining vehicle data, which is essential for interoperability, efficiency, and safety, as well as for enhancing user experience.

This effort fosters a cooperative ecosystem that benefits all stakeholders, from manufacturers to end-users, and propels the vehicle industry forward by ensuring that vehicles can communicate in an increasingly connected transportation landscape. Earlier on, the industry adopted AUTOSAR (automotive open system architecture) as an open and standardized automotive architecture. The primary goal of AUTOSAR was to enable the development of reusable and transferable software and functions across different vehicles and platforms. With the increasing integration of electronic control units (ECUs), a standardized interface to these hardware abstracts differences across manufacturers to facilitate collaboration between manufacturers and suppliers.

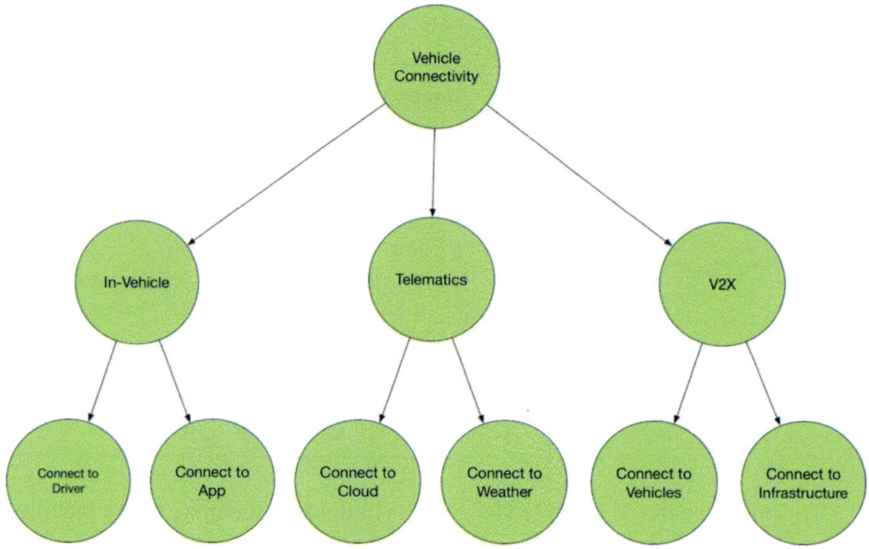

FIGURE 15.1

Vehicle connectivity.

VSS provides further a higher level of abstraction to categorize different signals and states within a vehicle, from the status of doors to driver monitoring systems, as show in Fig. 15.2.

A proposed extension to VSS extends the vehicle data model to connect with driver to monitor state that could influence driving behavior. This enhancement to the in-vehicle connectivity ecosystem illustrated in the hierarchical data model of Fig. 15.2 integrates driver state as part of the vehicle's overall data schema, emphasizing the vehicle's understanding of the driver's condition and ensuring a safe driving experience.

This proposed addition to VSS captures various signals related to the driver's condition, such as drowsiness and distraction, which can be detected through onboard cameras. Visual distraction is a prominent contributing factor to unsafe driving, inducing levels of inattention to critical driving activities (Cunningham and Regan, 2018). The fusion of driver physiological data and vehicle dynamics data is expected to increase the precision of safety risk computation, which is communicated to the advanced driver assistance systems to mitigate unsafe driving situations (Rezaei and Sabzevari, 2009), as illustrated in Fig. 15.3. Advances in safety score formulation (Arbabzadeh and Jafari, 2017) includes context identification (Fernandez-Rojas et al., 2019) and visualization of driving performance, building trust in driving assistance systems.

The purpose of this fusion is to explore machine learning techniques used to analyze driving patterns that could lead to the discovery and correction of unsafe driving behaviors (Shahverdy et al., 2020). The correlation of multiple data sources made

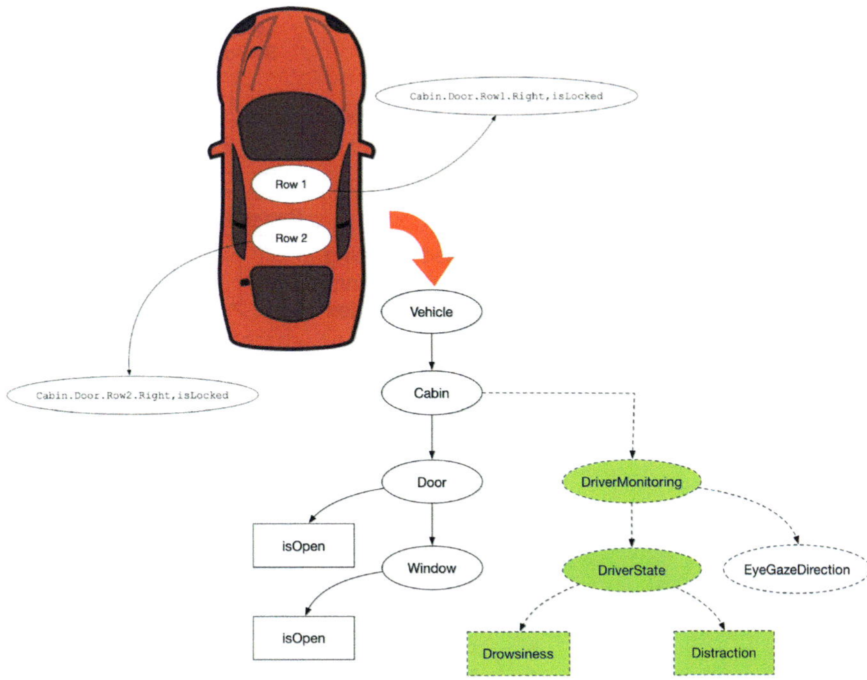

FIGURE 15.2

Vehicle cabin data modeling.

available today by car manufacturer technologies support data-driven driving safety analysis, which could identify risk factors used both to anticipate hazardous situations and aggregated to educate drivers.

Telematics data

Telematics encompasses telecommunications and informatics within connected transportation by enabling continuous flow of data exchange between vehicles and the cloud. Through telematics, vehicles are transformed into data-centric platforms capable of optimizing their own operation and enhancing the driving experience. With cloud connectivity, vehicles can transmit vast amounts of operational data to remote servers, where advanced analytics can unveil patterns into vehicle health and driving styles. These remote services include features such as remote diagnostics, vehicle and driver tracking, and OTA updates for vehicle software. Access to dynamic weather data allows telematics systems to inform driving systems of impending weather conditions, advising drivers on route changes or adjustments in driving behavior. The integration of weather data into vehicle systems contributes to proactive safety measures. This enhanced capability facilitates real-time traffic updates, smart routing, and even the aggregation of vehicle data to support urban planning and smart city initiatives.

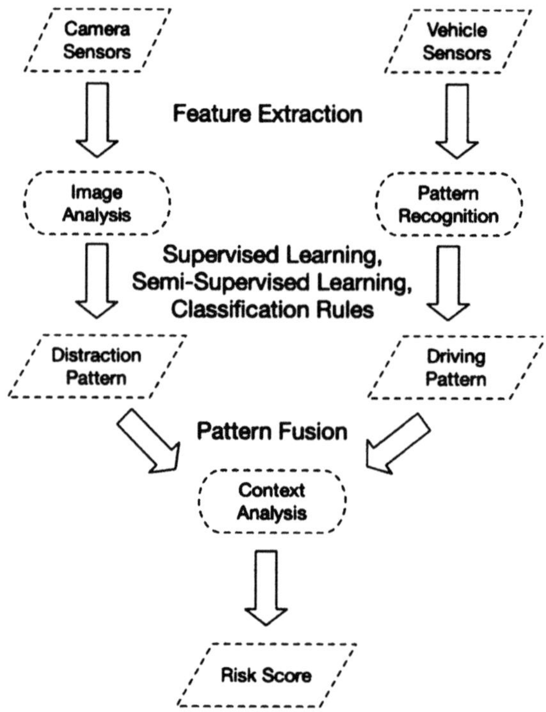

FIGURE 15.3

Multimodal pattern analysis for safety risk computation.

External communication systems (V2X)

The convergence of transportation and connectivity raised the role of external communication systems. These systems, collectively termed vehicle-to-everything (V2X) enable vehicles to communicate with the outside world, including other vehicles, road infrastructure, pedestrians, and the broader road actors. V2I extends this communication capability to the road's infrastructure. Vehicles can receive and respond to signals from traffic lights, road signs, parking sensors, and other road infrastructure components. This communication channel facilitates a data flow that enhances safety by providing timely alerts about traffic conditions, including construction zones and other roadway hazards.

With the goal of safeguarding those who share the road, V2P focuses on protecting pedestrians. There are several ways to capture these road actors, such as pole-mounted cameras that track all road actors including vehicles, pedestrians, and cyclists; or, by communicating directly with smartphones, vehicles can warn pedestrians of potential dangers, and likewise, pedestrians can alert drivers to their presence (Kabil et al., 2022).

15.3.3 Software-defined vehicle

Vehicle APIs facilitate communications between ADAS, mobile applications, cloud services, and the vehicle's embedded systems. These APIs transform the vehicle into an integrated platform of intelligent services and functions. They act as gateways, allowing various software components and external applications to interact with the vehicle's systems and sensors. APIs gather and process data on driving patterns to customize driver assistance features, ensure greater safety, and personalize insurance rates based on individual driving habits.

ADAS is empowered with access to API-provided real-time data to make informed decisions, which optimize passenger safety. Vehicle APIs play a role in V2X communications also, allowing the vehicle to invoke APIs to interact with city infrastructure and traffic systems. Similarly, vehicle APIs enable ADAS to utilize external computational power, such as cloud-based processing, to enhance its capabilities. Mobile applications can also use these APIs to interact with the vehicle, offering users remote control over certain features related to vehicle data.

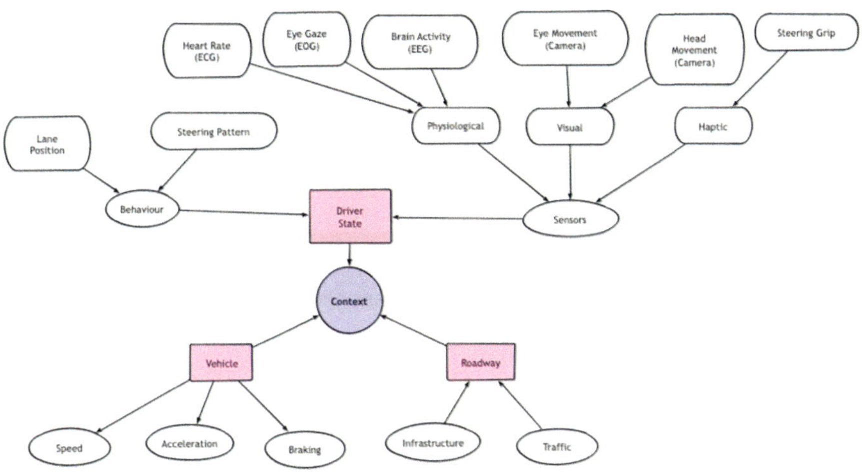

FIGURE 15.4

Multimodal data for software-defined vehicle.

The cloud plays a significant role in software-defined vehicles as a platform for data processing and storage to determine the context of driving (Fig. 15.4). Vehicle APIs enable the integration of cloud services, which can aggregate data from various sources for a comprehensive analysis that drives actionable processes. The confluence of data in the cloud results in a comprehensive context, allowing a vehicle to adjust ADAS settings to change driving patterns based on traffic and the driver's condition, as illustrated in (Fig. 15.4). Furthermore, the illustration underscores the need for standardization in how data is modeled, accessed, and used within software-defined vehicle ecosystem. Standards such as VSS are employed to ensure that data from different vehicles and systems can be integrated and correctly interpreted.

15.4 Transformation of connected transportation

15.4.1 Evolution of connected transportation over the past decade

The last decade has seen substantial growth in connected transportation, marked by technology advances and policy changes. Table 15.3 summarizes these developments. In the last decade, the landscape of transportation has undergone groundbreaking technological advancements and a global push towards sustainability and digitalization. The introduction of 4G networks and the surge in electric vehicle adoption marked the beginning of this transformation.

Table 15.3 outlines some milestones in the evolution of connected transportation from 2010 to 2020. Each step reflects a more connected, efficient, and environmentally friendly transportation ecosystem. These milestones underscore the rapid pace of change and the potential for even greater transformation in the years to come. The widespread rollout of 4G networks enhanced connectivity and real-time data transfer, which is further pushed by the significant adoption of electric vehicles. Table 15.3 outlines a trajectory of technological milestones and regulatory frameworks, which have collectively fostered the growth of connected transportation systems worldwide.

Table 15.3 Key developments in transportation logistics (2010–2020).

Year	Milestone	Description
2010	Introduction of 4G	Enhanced real-time data transfer for logistics and fleet management through improved connectivity speeds is attained.
2014	Smart city initiatives	The implementation of IoT technologies into logistics infrastructure to improve the efficiency of goods movement and supply chain management is realized.
2016	Autonomous vehicle testing	Pilot programs for autonomous delivery vehicles and trucks, integrating self-driving technology into logistics, are developed.
2018	Connectivity standards	Introduction of V2X communication standards that allow logistics vehicles to interact with each other and transportation infrastructure is realized.
2020	Last-mile delivery innovations	The expansion of drone and robot delivery services to optimize last-mile logistics are accomplished.

15.4.2 The integration of IoT and cloud in transportation

Connectivity models span in- vehicle to the external environment, thereby enhancing safety, efficiency, and user experience in mobility ecosystems. The resulting data model enables the vehicle API perception (Aust, 2022), which allows real-time diagnostics of vehicle status data by proactively invoking vehicle sensors to anticipate tire pressure, engine performance, and brake conditions. Applications can alert drivers to necessary maintenance or immediate safety concerns.

External connectivity enables dynamic, real-time interaction between vehicles and their surroundings, and V2X communication as a triune holds the potential to revolutionize road safety, traffic efficiency, and the overall driving experience. This shift towards creating a fully integrated and cooperative road network reduces the risk of accidents and fatalities on the road. By allowing vehicles to "speak" to each other (V2V) and to road infrastructure (V2I), such as traffic signals and signs, drivers and autonomous systems can receive early warnings about potential hazards. These indicators include upcoming traffic congestion, accidents, hazardous road conditions, and the presence of pedestrians or cyclists at crossings, thereby facilitating taking preventative actions that minimize the likelihood of collisions (Zang et al., 2019).

15.5 Mobility solutions

We discuss real-world examples that illustrate the practical application of connected mobility, such as in-vehicle connectivity, V2X communication, software-defined vehicles, and the impact of vehicle APIs. These case studies demonstrate the benefits and challenges of connected mobility solutions.

15.5.1 Mobility as a service (MaaS)

Mobility as a service (MaaS) brings together transportation options, such as transit, ride sharing, bike sharing, and car rentals, into one convenient on demand service, thereby transforming how people move around cities. This integrated platform offers users hassle-free travel experiences.

Whim in Helsinki, Finland

Whim, which was introduced in Helsinki stands out as one of the pioneering MaaS platforms globally. This innovative platform enables individuals to organize and manage all their transportation requirements conveniently from an app. Users have the flexibility to select from modes of transportation, such as transit, taxi services, rental cars, and bicycles, all seamlessly integrated into a unified payment system. The apps versatility in providing both subscription packages and pay-as-you-go alternatives has significantly enhanced the ease and personalization of travel experiences.

Moovel in Stuttgart, Germany

Moovel a company is a Daimler subsidiary, which provides an MaaS platform in Stuttgart. Their app combines mobility options, such as transit, car sharing, and bike sharing. Real-time information and convenient payment methods are offered by Moovel to improve user experience and lower reliance on owning vehicles, which encourages eco city travels.

15.5.2 In-vehicle connectivity

Improving the driving experience by connecting a vehicle to services and apps involves offering assistance to drivers with their own state monitoring for safety and providing navigation and entertainment alternatives, while self-diagnosing vehicles for any preventive measures.

Smart Eye in Gothenburg, Sweden

Smart Eye offers edge eye tracking technology, using onboard AI-powered cameras, providing driver monitoring systems (DMS) that observe and analyze driver state and actions. The system monitors eye movements, head positioning, and facial expressions, to detect signs of fatigue, distraction, or lack of attention. When unsafe driving behavior is detected, the system notifies the driver, or even intervene by adjusting the vehicles speed or recommending a rest break. This innovative technology is being integrated into car models to improve safety measures and minimize accidents resulting from driver mistakes.

General Motors' OnStar system

General Motors OnStar system offers safety features, emergency assistance, navigation services, and remote diagnostics, within the vehicle. By connecting vehicles to a support hub, OnStar provides assistance in situations such as accidents, car thefts, or other urgent incidents. This setup showcases the benefits of in-car connectivity in improving safety with convenient assistance options for drivers.

15.6 Transportation solutions

In today's changing city landscapes, with the incorporation of IoT and cloud computing within transportation systems, traffic management and vehicle fleets' maintenance are improving in efficiency. Next, we discuss transportation solutions that showcase how these technologies are being used in practice. Illustrating this transformation with smart city traffic control systems and predictive maintenance for vehicle fleets case studies, we learn how data-driven approaches facilitated by IoT and cloud convergence, are reshaping transportation and logistics.

15.6.1 Smart city traffic management system

A metropolitan area that implements a smart city traffic management system may use V2I models to optimize traffic flow and reduce congestion. For example, this implementation includes equipping traffic lights and signage with sensors that communicate with passing vehicle. Data from various sources, including mobile apps and roadway sensors, is further aggregated and analyzed in the cloud to predict traffic patterns and suggest route optimizations. This connectivity model can be found in several urban environment examples.

Copenhagen, Denmark

Copenhagen's intelligent traffic systems control traffic lights and manage traffic flow. The city uses sensors and Bluetooth connections to collect data from buses and bikes, aiming to prioritize public transport and create green waves for cyclists (Koubeck et al., 2017). The result is a reduction in travel times for buses and increased safety and convenience for cyclists.

Pittsburgh, USA

Pittsburgh implemented the Surtrac traffic signal control system, an AI-powered adaptive traffic signal control technology, which optimizes traffic flow for all modes of transportation in real time, reducing travel time, and wait times at intersections (Smith et al., 2013).

Barcelona, Spain

Barcelona, with its commitment to becoming a smart city, has integrated a smart parking system called Fastprk in its Les Corts District. This system, developed by Worldsensing, utilizes wireless sensors to detect and signal the availability of parking spaces to drivers, aiming to reduce congestion and CO2 emissions by making parking more efficient. These sensors are installed under the asphalt and communicate the status of parking spaces to a mobile app, thereby guiding drivers directly to open spots and streamlining the parking process (Liao, 2020).

Singapore

Singapore's intelligent transport systems (ITS) encompass a range of applications: from electronic road pricing and smart parking to traffic management. The city-state uses a sophisticated network of cameras and sensors to manage congestion and has one of the world's most advanced traffic analytics systems. One key element of Singapore's intelligent transportation system is the integrated, real-time traffic information system known as i-Transport (Dinh, 2019). This system centralizes data from a network of expressways and road tunnels using sensors. i-Transport gathers real-time data for traffic monitoring and incident management.

15.6.2 Predictive maintenance for fleet vehicles

A logistics company employs a predictive maintenance system using vehicle APIs to monitor the health of its fleet. On-board diagnostics track vehicle performance data, which is processed to predict maintenance needs. The system schedules maintenance automatically, thereby optimizing vehicle uptime and reducing the risk of unexpected breakdowns.

UPS's ORION system

United Parcel Service (UPS) is globally known as one of the logistics companies renowned for its fleet of delivery vehicles that demand ongoing maintenance. To minimize downtime and reduce operational costs, UPS needed a way to predict maintenance issues before they led to vehicle breakdowns. UPS implemented its on-road integrated optimization and navigation (ORION) system (Horner, 2016). Although primarily used for optimizing delivery routes, ORION system also analyzes vehicle sensors data to monitor the fleet health.

Using telematics, ORION collects diagnostic trouble codes (DTCs) from vehicles to identify issues, ranging from critical engine components to braking systems. This allows for scheduled maintenance before a breakdown occurs. By tracking battery performance and voltage levels, the system can also predict battery life and schedule replacements before failure, which is critical for delivery reliability.

DHL's smart trucking initiative

DHL, an international courier, package delivery, and express mail service, has been investing in smart logistics solutions for its extensive fleet management. DHL aims to enhance the efficiency of its transportation services, while reducing maintenance-related costs and improving safety. DHL implemented a smart trucking initiative, which includes a predictive maintenance program. By equipping their trucks with IoT devices, data regarding vehicle health is collected and analyzed. The collected data provides predictive analytics on engine performance, flagging potential issues, such as fuel system problems or exhaust control malfunctions, before they become major repairs (Diwan, 2016).

15.7 Business aspects of smart vehicles and connected transportation

Advances in connected vehicles and interconnected transportation systems represent more than a technological shift; they also signify a substantial transformation in business strategies and economic frameworks. This section examines the impacts induced by incorporating IoT and cloud computing in the mobility and transportation industry, which are disrupting traditional business models and fostering economic prospects.

15.7.1 Business models

The automotive industry is rapidly adopting business models that incorporate IoT and cloud computing utilization within the their delivered products and services. These strategies offer ways to provide value to customers and create long-lasting revenue streams for the industry.

Subscription services

A new trend in business involves offering subscription services for contemporary vehicle features. Rather than buying them, customers can opt for a subscription to unlock advanced functionalities, such as autonomous driving, improved navigation tools, and enriched entertainment systems. For example, customers can download new entertainment apps directly to their vehicles through the subscription service. Vehicle manufacturers ensure continuous revenue, while enabling consumers to experience the technological innovations without having to invest in brand new vehicles.

Data-driven services

Connected vehicle data can be monetized by enabling car makers to offer maintenance alerts, insurance options tailored to usage patterns, and personalized onboard or location specific functions. By analyzing how people drive, the state of their vehicles and their preferences, businesses can provide services that improve the driving experience and ensure safety.

Pay-per-use and fleet management

Businesses can take advantage of connected vehicle technology to introduce models such as pay-per-use in fleet management. Offering vehicles based on a pay-per-mile system is especially appealing to logistics firms. Advanced fleet management solutions that offer benefits such as real-time monitoring, route planning optimization, and timely maintenance scheduling, improve business effectiveness.

15.7.2 Economic impact

Incorporating transportation technologies is expected to influence the economy into creating new possibilities, across different industries.

Automotive industry

The move towards connected vehicles and transportation is leading to substantial transformations in the automotive sector. Conventional car makers are evolving into technology focused firms, making investments in software creation and cloud solutions. This change is stimulating the need for abilities and knowledge resulting in job growth in advanced technology fields.

Electronics and software suppliers

With the increasing connectivity and autonomy of vehicles, there is a rising need for related electronic parts and software solutions. This surge in demand for electronics manufacturers and software developers boost businesses focusing on sensors, semiconductors, and AI algorithms, to further lead advances and economic prosperity in these sectors.

Insurance industry

Connected vehicles have made usage-based insurance (UBI) models more popular. Insurers use vehicle data to provide customized premiums reflecting driving habits, vehicle usage, and real-time risk evaluation. This method does not only provide customers with fairer pricing, but also promotes safer driving practices.

Environmental benefits and sustainability

The shift towards self-driving cars is playing a crucial role in promoting environmental conservation. Decreased emissions, improved traffic management, and effective energy utilization stand out as prominent advantages of intelligent transportation. These enhancements are aligned with initiatives that address climate change issues; they foster economic growth within the eco-friendly technology industry.

15.8 The future of connected mobility and transportation

The future of connected mobility promises a profound transformation in the landscapes of personal and public transportation. The maturation of autonomous driving technology transforms the act of driving itself, whereby vehicles equipped with advanced sensors, AI, and machine learning will require little to no human intervention. The automotive industry is rapidly shifting towards a future where a majority of new vehicles are electric, supported by a robust infrastructure of charging stations and propelled by governmental incentives.

V2X communication will become more prevalent. This development extends to include communication with pedestrians, cyclists, and smart city systems, enabling a safer and more efficient mobility ecosystem. Mobility as a service (MaaS) platforms, with on-demand, integrated transportation services that combine public transport, will likely dominate. This integration promises optimized traffic flow, energy savings, and enhanced public safety, contributing to the overall quality of urban life.

The wealth of data generated by connected vehicles will be used to personalize the travel experience. Machine learning algorithms will tailor everything: from route planning to in-vehicle functions and safety, aligning with individual preferences and real-time conditions.

References

Alliance, G., 2021. Vehicle signal specification, vss. https://github.com/GENIVI/vehicle_signal_specification.

Arbabzadeh, N., Jafari, M., 2017. A data-driven approach for driving safety risk prediction using driver behavior and roadway information data. IEEE Trans. Intell. Transp. Syst. 19 (2), 446–460.

Aust, S., 2022. Vehicle api and service catalog for next generation mobility. In: 2022 25th International Symposium on Wireless Personal Multimedia Communications (WPMC). IEEE, pp. 418–423.

Cunningham, M.L., Regan, M.A., 2018. Driver Distraction and Inattention. Safe Mobility: Challenges, Methodology and Solutions, vol. 11. Emerald Publishing, Limited, pp. 57–82.

Dinh, T.T., 2019. Managing traffic congestion in a city: a study of Singapore's experiences. In: Research Gate, vol. 1.

Diwan, M., 2016. Internet of things in logistics: towards autonomous logistics & smart logistics entities. In: International Maritime Transport and Logistic Conference. https://marlog.aast.edu/archive/2016/pdf/Papers/s06p02.pdf.

Ericsson, 2021. Charting the future of connected cars and mobility with 5g. https://www.ericsson.com/en/blog/2021/6/charting-the-future-of-connected-cars-and-mobility-with-5g. (Accessed 4 September 2024).

Fard, Z.B., Brugeman, V.S., 2019. Technology Roadmap: Intelligent Mobility Technologies. Center for Automotive Research, p. 6.

Fernandez-Rojas, R., Perry, A., Singh, H., Campbell, B., Elsayed, S., Hunjet, R., Abbass, H.A., 2019. Contextual awareness in human-advanced-vehicle systems: a survey. IEEE Access 7, 33304–33328.

He, W., Yan, G., Da Xu, L., 2014. Developing vehicular data cloud services in the IoT environment. IEEE Transactions on Industrial Informatics 10 (2), 1587–1595.

Horner, P., 2016. Edelman award: 'Orion' delivers success for ups: revolutionary routing system boosts driver efficiency, cost savings, customer service and the environment. OR/MS Today 43 (3), 22–26.

Kabil, A., Rabieh, K., Kaleem, F., Azer, M.A., 2022. Vehicle to pedestrian systems: survey, challenges and recent trends. IEEE Access 10, 123981–123994.

Koubeck, A.M., Hunt, A., Bickham, S.C., Stuart, S.A., 2017. Breaking the cycle of congestion: an examination of bicycle traffic in Copenhagen, Saatavissa. https://digitalcommons.wpi.edu/iqp-all/348.

Liao, R., 2020. Smart mobility: challenges and trends. In: Toward Sustainable and Economic Smart Mobility: Shaping e Future of Smart Cities, vol. 10, No. 1.

Lim, K.L., Whitehead, J., Jia, D., Zheng, Z., 2021. State of data platforms for connected vehicles and infrastructures. Communications in Transportation Research 1, 100013.

Mohanta, B.K., Jena, D., Mohapatra, N., Ramasubbareddy, S., Rawal, B.S., 2022. Machine learning based accident prediction in secure IoT enable transportation system. Journal of Intelligent & Fuzzy Systems 42 (2), 713–725.

Rezaei, M., Sabzevari, R., 2009. Multisensor Data Fusion Strategies for Advanced Driver Assistance Systems. I-Tech Education and Publishing.

Shahverdy, M., Fathy, M., Berangi, R., Sabokrou, M., 2020. Driver behavior detection and classification using deep convolutional neural networks. Expert Systems with Applications 149, 113240.

Smith, S., Barlow, G., Xie, X.-F., Rubinstein, Z., 2013. Smart urban signal networks: initial application of the surtrac adaptive traffic signal control system. In: Proceedings of the International Conference on Automated Planning and Scheduling, vol. 23, pp. 434–442.

Srinivasan, A., 2018. IoT cloud based real time automobile monitoring system. In: 2018 3rd IEEE International Conference on Intelligent Transportation Engineering (ICITE). IEEE, pp. 231–235.

Zang, J., Towhidlou, V., Shikh-Bahaei, M., 2019. Collision avoidance in v2x communication networks. In: 2019 IEEE Wireless Communications and Networking Conference Workshop (WCNCW). IEEE, pp. 1–6.

CHAPTER

IoT-cloud business case studies and investment roadmap for sustainable digital transformation

16

16.1 Introduction

The fusion of IoT and cloud computing is driving the ongoing digital transformation sweeping across industries worldwide. This chapter captures the tangible benefits and economic impacts of IoT-cloud solutions, illustrating how this technological synergy is a practical enabler of efficiency, innovation, and value creation. The vast data generated by IoT devices is leveraged by the scalable processing capabilities of the cloud to unlock new levels of operational efficiency, product development, and customer engagement across business and public services.

Throughout the chapters of this book, we have explored fresh ideas and exciting prospects built around the concepts introduced at the start of the book surrounding IoT ecosystems, security challenges, and initiatives aimed at digital transformation. Across these chapters, we explored strategies for extracting and transmitting data to cloud platforms, while also considering the business advantages that emerge when edge, fog, and cloud computing intersect, with the emergence of 5G networks. Our discussion involved interoperability requirements and cooperative practices underscoring the significance of cohesive ecosystems in realizing the potential offered by digital transformations.

This chapter aims to showcase practical applications and reveal forward-looking strategies, emphasizing the tangible benefits and economic impacts that IoT and cloud synergies provide for efficiency, innovation, and value creation across various industries. This concluding chapter shifts towards revealing a roadmap for strategic investment to unlock these innovative benefits. This roadmap is a guide and a blueprint for stakeholders aiming to transform their operational, strategic, and sustainability agendas.

The process of identifying, evaluating, and deploying strategic investments in the IoT and cloud landscape is dissected through successful case studies across diverse sectors. In crafting this investment roadmap, we address the critical elements of risk assessment, stakeholder engagement, and the alignment of technological initiatives with broader organizational goals. The roadmap will also highlight the importance

Accelerating Digital Transformation with the Cloud and the Internet of Things (IoT)
https://doi.org/10.1016/B978-0-44-322217-7.00024-4

of agility in investment strategies to adapt to the rapid technological evolution and fluctuating market demands so that businesses remain competitive and relevant.

16.2 Synthesis of IoT and cloud computing impact

This section distills the essence of digital transformation journeys, focusing on sustainability, innovation, and resilience that have emerged from the continuum of cloud computing to IoT.

16.2.1 The paradigm of sustainability

IoT and cloud computing are fundamental enablers of sustainability in contemporary digital transformation. These technological advances are propelling a future where efficiency, environment protection, and resource conservation are seamlessly integrated into daily operations and strategic planning.

The potential for IoT and cloud technologies to drive sustainability initiatives is boundless. Sensors technology, data analytics, and cloud infrastructure continue to evolve, leading to reducing emissions and enhancing energy efficiency, while promoting the sustainable use of natural resources. IoT and cloud computing are leading eco-friendly sustainable innovations: from smart agriculture practices that optimize water and fertilizer use to intelligent energy systems that balance consumption with renewable sources.

Energy and resources

IoT and cloud computing have transformed approaches to conservation and optimization of the planet's vital resources. Eco-consciousness practices have been enabled to redefine sustainability for generations to come (Benkhelifa et al., 2014). Digital transparency through IoT-induced information encourages consumers towards more environmentally responsible choices.

The potent combination of IoT connectivity and cloud, which makes information accessible online, is influencing consumer behavior. Fueled by the abundance of data from IoT devices, individuals are made ware regarding the environmental impact of their consumption patterns. For example, smart home devices, which monitor energy usage, offer users real-time feedback on their consumption habits, encouraging a shift towards more energy-efficient practices (Wijaya et al., 2023).

The advent of IoT-based precision farming illustrate the profound impact enabled by an intricate network of sensors and other IoT devices. Farmers gain the ability to monitor soil moisture levels, crop health, and environmental conditions, which once analyzed through cloud-based platforms, farmers are informed to irrigate, fertilize, or apply pest control measures in optimal ways (Fastellini and Schillaci, 2020). This method has proven to drastically reduce resource waste, while increasing crop yields, as evidenced from farms in California's Central Valley, which leveraged precision agriculture to combat drought conditions to sustain farming practices, even in the face of climatic adversities (Marklein et al., 2017).

Similarly, the manufacturing sector monitors and manages the environmental footprint of production processes. IoT sensors deployed across manufacturing facilities collect data on energy consumption, waste generation, and emissions in real time (Ajumo et al., 2019). Once fed into cloud-based analytics systems, this information enables manufacturers to implement environmentally corrective measures (ElMaraghy et al., 2021).

Environmental monitoring

IoT sensors and cloud analytics contribute to sustainable urban and rural environments. Interconnected sensors collect vast amounts of data on various environmental parameters, including air quality and water levels, to support precise monitoring and timely decision-making aimed at mitigating environmental challenges (Ang and Seng, 2016). The fusion of IoT with cloud computing enhances data collection and analysis to share environmental impacts across platforms and stakeholders, driving eco-awareness and collective action towards sustainability (Ramírez-Moreno et al., 2021).

Cities such as Beijing and London have implemented extensive networks of IoT sensors across the cityscape to continuously monitor pollutants, such as PM2.5, NO2, and CO levels. Sensors transmit data to cloud-based analytics platform to determine pollution hotspots and infer trends over time (Jiyal and Saini, 2020). The patterns derived from this data inform policy decisions, such as traffic regulation and industrial emissions control, and are made accessible to the public through apps and websites, thereby enabling individuals to make informed decisions about their outdoor activities. For instance, the "Plume Air Report" leverages such data to provide live air quality tracking and forecasts, empowering residents with the information needed to protect their health (Plume Labs, 2023).

Another critical safety application is in flood monitoring and management, where IoT and cloud analytics were instrumented in disaster management. In flood-prone areas, sensors placed along rivers, coastlines, and urban water systems collect data on water levels, flow rates, and precipitation. This information is analyzed using cloud computing, enabling early warning systems, which alert communities and authorities to imminent floods, allowing for timely evacuations and preparations. The city of Venice, Italy, for example, has implemented the MOSE project (Modulo Sperimentale Elettromeccanico), integrating IoT sensors with a barrier system to monitor sea levels and automatically activate flood gates when a high tide is predicted, protecting the historic city from flooding (Maggi, 2024).

16.2.2 The engine of innovation

We have seen how IoT devices and cloud analytics are fundamental drivers of innovation. In the domain of healthcare, the introduction of IoT wearables, coupled with the analytical operations of cloud computing, has reshaped patient care, turning data into actionable patterns for personalized treatment. Similarly, Industry 4.0, with IoT and cloud technologies, is spearheading automation, predictive maintenance, and the innovative use of digital twins.

Industry 4.0

A standout example of Industry 4.0 in action is Siemens' deployment of digital twins, virtual replicas of physical manufacturing systems, to simulate, predict, and optimize the production process before any physical changes are made. This IoT approach employs sensors and cloud analytics to reduce downtime and enhance product quality by observing adjustments in the virtual model to be tested and optimized.

The goal is to simulate entire production processes and workflows to mitigate inefficiencies and potential errors before they occur in the real world (Tao et al., 2019). For example, in their electronics manufacturing services, Siemens utilizes digital twins to test and optimize the assembly processes of printed circuit boards (PCBs) virtually. This reduces the need for physical prototypes, significantly cutting down development time and costs (Tao et al., 2018).

Energy sector innovation

IoT and cloud computing catalyzes innovation in how energy is generated, distributed, and consumed. Siemens is harnessing the power of digital twins in power plants and renewable energy installations. These virtual replicas of physical assets, such as wind turbines, are dynamic systems that mirror their physical counterparts. This technology is a paradigm shift in renewable energy assets' management (Demircan and Akyüz, 2019).

Smart grids offer the capacity to adapt electricity supply based on demand fluctuations. By examining data gathered throughout the grid power, energy companies can anticipate peak demand periods, redirect energy to areas requiring it most, which reduces inefficiencies and mitigates the risk of outages caused by overload conditions. IoT devices act as the sensory organs and nerve endings of smart grids, scattered throughout the energy infrastructure. They continuously collect vast amounts of data on electricity consumption, production rates, and operational conditions from various points across the grid. This data originates from smart meters in homes, sensors on power lines, and weather stations, which predict environmental impacts on energy production and demand. The intelligent operations of smart grids are provisioned from IoT data (Saleem et al., 2019).

Advanced algorithms and machine learning models running in the cloud can forecast demand with high accuracy, enabling energy providers to preemptively adjust the supply, reroute power efficiently, and balance the grid's load. The seamless integration of IoT and cloud facilitates the smart power grid's ability to dynamically adjust the electricity supply. When analytics algorithms running in the cloud detect an significant peak demand period, the smart grid can automatically increase power supply from available sources or redirect energy from areas of low demand to those of high demand. Conversely, during low demand periods, power generation is reduced or excess of energy is stored in batteries for future use. This capability in dynamically adjusting supply and demand minimizes waste, prevents grid overloads, and avoids outages. The result of this enhancement is increased efficiency and reliability of energy distribution.

16.2.3 The framework of resilience

Resilience is the ability to recover from setbacks, but encompasses also a more comprehensive approach to anticipating challenges, adapting strategies, and thriving in the face of disruptions. The integration of IoT and cloud computing technologies enhances the resilience of organizations, and societies at large, by building a robust framework of resilience, by instrument data monitoring, analytics, and adaptive response mechanisms. For instance, in the manufacturing sector, IoT sensors can detect anomalies in equipment performance early, and cloud-based analytics can predict potential failures. This approach ensures continuity in production processes, thereby minimizing downtime and maintaining productivity, even in the face of unforeseen disruptions (Sterbenz, 2017).

Building resilience through data analytics

Data generated by IoT devices and analyzed through cloud computing platforms accelerate organizations decision-making capabilities. These data-driven strategies enable effective responses to changing market conditions, consumer behaviors, and potential risks. In the retail industry, for example, IoT-enabled inventory management systems, combined with cloud analytics, can optimize stock levels, predict demand surges, and ensure supply chain resilience against disruptions.

Amazon's fulfillment centers employ thousands of robots that work in harmony, driven by IoT technologies. These robots are tasked with moving goods around the warehouse, guided by sensors and navigation systems that track their location and the location of items dynamically (Bogue, 2016). This IoT infrastructure generates enormous volumes of data regarding inventory movement, storage efficiency, and order processing.

The data collected by these IoT devices are then transmitted to Amazon's cloud computing platforms, where powerful analytics tools take over. Machine learning algorithms run predictive analytics at Amazon's cloud systems to identify patterns that predict future demand, to optimize inventory levels accordingly. Amazon is thus empowered to adjust its stock levels, ensuring that popular items are readily available and reducing the risk of overstocking less popular products.

The integration of these IoT and cloud-based generated analytics enable further strategies to changing market conditions. For instance, if cloud analytics predict a surge in demand for a specific item, the system can preemptively reallocate robots and human workers to focus on picking and packing that item, speeding up order fulfillment. Similarly, if a potential supply chain disruption is detected, such as delays from suppliers or increased shipping times, the system can adjust inventory orders and distribution strategies to mitigate the impact. This IoT and cloud-powered approach to inventory management illustrates data-driven approaches to enhance supply chain resilience (Chakraborty and Das, 2021). These innovative approaches support high levels of customer satisfaction by ensuring that products are always in stock, and orders are fulfilled and shipped promptly, even during fluctuating demand and potential supply chain challenges.

Facilitating systemic resilience

On a larger scale, IoT and cloud computing contribute to systemic resilience by interconnecting various components of infrastructure, enabling them to respond collectively to challenges. Smart grid technologies illustrate well this concept. IoT sensors distributed throughout the grid collect data on energy consumption and supply, while cloud platforms analyze this data to manage and distribute energy resources efficiently. This interconnected system adjusts dynamically to changes, such as power outages or renewable energy fluctuations, ensuring a stable and resilient energy supply for communities (Körner et al., 2022).

16.3 Advanced business cases

We delve into the strategic methodologies that underpinned IoT and cloud successful implementation through a curated selection of case studies. We will examine partnerships that have broken new ground, solutions that have scaled to meet growing demands, and the cross-sectoral impacts that illustrate the transformative potential of IoT and cloud integration. This exploration is designed to offer readers a comprehensive understanding of how these advanced technologies are driving efficiency, sustainability, and growth across the global digital landscape to justify related investments.

16.3.1 Innovative partnerships

Innovative partnerships represent a cornerstone for driving profound innovation. Collaborations between tech companies and sectors, such as agriculture, manufacturing, and healthcare, harness the transformative power of IoT and cloud computing to address complex domain challenges to unlock new efficiencies and open new avenues for growth and sustainability.

The importance of such partnerships lies in the complementary strengths. Tech companies offer advanced technological capabilities, including expertise in IoT and cloud computing, which many traditional industries lack. Conversely, these traditional sectors provide deep industry knowledge, practical aspects, and access to specific domain challenges, which IoT and cloud-related technologies can address. By bridging the gap between technological potential and domain applications, these partnerships catalyze the development of tailored solutions that can significantly enhance operational processes, product offerings, and customer experiences.

Furthermore, these collaborations develop a mechanism for technology transfer to disseminate digital innovations across various sectors. Environments of mutual learning and experimentation are elaborated in a manner that facilitates tech companies fine-tuning their solutions in response to practical feedback, and traditional industries can accelerate their digital transformation practices. Next, we explore specific case studies that highlight the successful outcomes of such innovative partnerships, demonstrating how the strategic alliance of IoT and cloud technologies with domain sectors has led to breakthrough innovations and set new benchmarks for what can be achieved through creative collaborations.

Precision farming

In an effort to address the challenges of increasing agricultural productivity, while conserving resources, a tech company, renowned for its IoT solutions, can partner with agricultural firms known for diverse crop cultivation. The agricultural firms seek to enhance crop yields and optimize resource management practices in the face of changing climate conditions and growing food demand. They need a solution that could provide precise, data-driven exploitation of soil conditions across their diverse cultivation areas.

The tech company's IoT expertise develops a precision farming solution through this proposed partnership, utilizing an array of IoT sensors placed throughout agricultural fields. These sensors are designed to monitor soil moisture levels, nutrient content, and other environmental factors. The data collected by these sensors is then transmitted to a cloud-based platform, where advanced analytics algorithms generate actionable patterns and recommendations, such as optimal irrigation and fertilization and crop rotation strategies.

The above scenario is reflected in reality by John Deere, a leading manufacturer of agricultural machinery, which partnered with Granular, a company specializing in farm management software, to integrate advanced IoT and cloud computing technologies into farming practices. This collaboration aimed to enhance precision agriculture, focusing on optimizing crop yields and resource management (Counterpoint Research, 2023).

Insurance sector

Bosch electronics and engineering partnered with Munich Re, one of the world's leading insurance companies, to transform the insurance sector through IoT and cloud computing technologies (Munich Re, 2018). This collaboration aimed to develop innovative insurance solutions that leverage data to assess risks and customize insurance products.

Utilizing Bosch's IoT sensors, the partnership monitors insured assets, ranging from industrial machinery to smart home devices. These sensors collect data on usage patterns, environmental conditions, and potential risk factors. Munich Re leverages cloud computing to analyze the collected data from Bosch's IoT devices to accurately assess risks, predicting potential issues before they occur, and customizing insurance policies based on actual data rather than estimations.

Google Cloud and Mayo Clinic in healthcare

Google Cloud services, partnered with Mayo Clinic, a prestigious healthcare organization, to transform healthcare delivery through advanced cloud computing and AI technologies. This collaboration aimed to improve patient care and enhance clinical outcomes, as well as to support healthcare research (Mayo Clinic, 2023).

Google Cloud's secure and scalable infrastructure allowed Mayo Clinic to develop a platform that integrates patient data across various systems. This consolidation enables advanced data analysis and machine learning applications to improve diagnosis and treatment. By applying Google's cutting-edge AI and machine learning technologies to vast datasets, Mayo Clinic is able to accelerate medical research, which results in new treatments and better understanding of complex diseases. The partnership aims also to use AI to personalize patient care, from tailored treatment plans, which improve patient engagement and communication, to ensuring that patients receive the most effective care that is tailored to their specific needs.

16.3.2 Scaling solutions

The ability to scale IoT and cloud solutions aims to maximize the investment impact and sustain business growth. Scaling effectively allows companies to extend their reach, enhance service offerings, and enter new markets. However, the scaling process comes with its unique set of challenges, including managing increasing volumes of data, ensuring system reliability, while complying with legal regulations pertaining to global data privacy procedures. Yet, addressing these challenges is essential for successful scaling to transform a promising solution into a global market leader.

Fitbit: scaling wearable health monitoring globally

Fitbit started as a small start-up in 2007 and quickly became a leader in wellness sector with its wearable technology (Fitbit, 2024). Their devices track various health metrics, such as steps taken, heart rate, and sleep patterns, which are analyzed to provide actionable health indicators (Tan, 2018).

Fitbit utilized cloud computing to manage and analyze vast amounts of data generated by its devices worldwide. This scalable solution allowed them to handle growing data volumes, as their user base expanded. With its global reach, Fitbit had to ensure international data protection regulations' compliance, including GDPR and HIPAA. Thus stringent data security measures and privacy policies were implemented in FitBit range of products and services to protect user information.

16.3.3 Cross-sector impact

Objective: To explore how IoT and cloud technologies have facilitated value creation across different sectors, emphasizing their versatility and wide-ranging benefits.

Smart cities: Cisco and the City of Barcelona partnership

The partnership between Cisco and the City of Barcelona aimed to transform Barcelona into a global reference model for sustainable urban development. This collaboration focused on creating a blueprint for modern urban development through initiatives such as the Smart City Campus and the development of functional technological applications to improve the city's efficiency and the quality of services. The joint partnership included the creation of a City Protocol to measure sustainability in the city (Gascó et al., 2016).

Cisco worked with Barcelona to install an extensive network of IoT sensors across the city. These sensors collected data on traffic, waste management, street lighting, and water usage. Cisco's cloud processes the data collected from IoT devices to optimize city services. For example, intelligent traffic systems reduced congestion, and smart lighting systems conserved energy. The collaboration between Cisco and the City of Barcelona illustrates how public-private partnerships can drive innovation in urban development, thereby benefiting citizens and the environment.

16.3.4 Cross-sectoral impact

By facilitating the seamless integration of data and systems, the convergence of IoT and cloud technologies holds the remarkable potential to generate value across multiple sectors. Synergies that can significantly enhance efficiency, sustainability, and quality of life are made visible to stakeholders and policy makers. Next, we explore how holistic approaches to IoT and cloud integration can catalyze transformative impacts that benefit various sectors simultaneously and contribute to broader societal and environmental goals.

The Port of Rotterdam's digital twin

The Port of Rotterdam embarked on an ambitious project to create a digital twin of the entire port area. This initiative employ IoT and cloud technologies to optimize shipping operations, enhance safety, and improve environmental sustainability (Boyles, 2019).

In a partnership with IBM, IoT sensors deployed across the port to monitor vessel movements, dock availability, and cargo handling operations. Cloud-based analytics process this data to optimize logistics, reduce turnaround times for ships, and enhance overall supply chain efficiency. The digital twin integrates environmental data, including water and air quality metrics from IoT sensors, to ensure operations comply with sustainability standards. The Port of Rotterdam's digital twin illustrates the transformative power of IoT and cloud computing across the maritime, environmental, and safety sectors. This cross-sectoral innovation not only boosts the port's operational efficiency and competitiveness but also sets new standards for sustainability and safety in the maritime industry.

Smart ambulances in Dubai

In an innovative cross-sectoral project, a collaboration between healthcare services and transportation authorities utilized IoT and cloud technologies to drastically improve emergency medical response times in urban areas. Dubai's Health Authority initiated the Smart Ambulance project to enhance emergency medical services. The link enabled through the integration of IoT and cloud technologies, between healthcare and transportation, improves patient outcomes and optimizes emergency response.

Each ambulance is equipped with IoT devices that monitor patient vitals during transit. This data is continuously uploaded to a cloud platform, which allows medical staff to prepare for immediate intervention upon the patient's arrival. The ambulances are connected to Dubai's smart traffic management system via cloud computing. This system receives real-time traffic updates and calculates the fastest route to the hospital, considering current traffic conditions. Traffic lights are dynamically controlled to create green corridors, reducing ambulance travel time (GulfNews, 2020).

16.4 Crafting a future-ready investment roadmap

The importance of investing in emerging technologies, while navigating funding models and financial instruments, is paramount to develop adaptable strategies for future technology advances. This section guides businesses through the investment roadmap in IoT and cloud technologies to support digital transformation efforts and foster stakeholder engagement. We focus on navigating investment in emerging technologies, understanding diverse funding models, crafting adaptable future strategies, and involving stakeholders in the investment process. The aim is to help organizations make strategic decisions that meet their immediate goals and enhance their adaptability in a rapidly changing digital environment.

16.4.1 Investment in emerging technologies

This section discusses strategic investment considerations for organizations seeking to harness the power of IoT and cloud technologies for digital transformation. The potential risks and rewards associated with investing in cutting-edge tech are emphasized to support organizations balancing business objectives and market trends.

Risk assessment

It is important yo understand the investment risks associated with emerging technologies aiming to leverage IoT and cloud computing for digital transformation as outlined next.

- **Technological obsolescence:** The risk of a technology becoming outdated as newer, more advanced options become available need to be assessed. This risk can result in sunk costs and the need for additional investments to stay competitive.

- **Integration:** These challenges arise when new technologies must be seamlessly incorporated into existing systems, which may require significant effort and resources to ensure compatibility and functionality.
- **Security vulnerabilities:** In sum, these constitute a critical concern, as emerging technologies can introduce new threats and require robust measures to protect data and systems from cybersecurity breaches. It is necessary to acknowledging and mitigating these risks by developing a strategic investment plan, which minimizes potential threats and maximizes the return on investment in the rapidly evolving digital landscape.

Return on investment (ROI)

Evaluating the potential ROI of investments in emerging technologies, such as IoT and cloud computing, involves analyzing both quantitative and qualitative benefits. Quantitatively, businesses should assess direct financial metrics, such as cost savings, revenue growth, and payback periods. Qualitative, considerations might include improved brand reputation and competitive advantage. Techniques, for example, cost-benefit analysis, scenario planning, and pilot projects can provide outlooks into these areas.

Stakeholder engagement

Engaging stakeholders in technology investment initiatives ensures alignment and support. This engagement involves transparent communication with investors, customers, and partners about the potential impacts, benefits, and risks of emerging technologies. Building consensus and fostering collaboration enhance the likelihood of successful implementation and adoption.

16.4.2 Funding models and financial instruments

Investment in emerging technologies should incorporate principles of agility, scalability, and strategic alignment. Agile investment approaches enable organizations to adapt rapidly to technological advancements and market changes. Scalability ensures that investments can grow with the business, avoiding limitations on expansion. Strategic alignment guarantees that investments are in line with the overall business objectives, thereby driving growth and innovation. The diverse funding models and financial instruments available for supporting investments in emerging technologies, such as IoT and cloud computing could include:

Equity financing

This method is particularly favored in the tech industry, where startups rely on venture capital to scale their innovative IoT and cloud solutions. By offering equity, startups secure the necessary funding for growth and benefit from the expertise and networks of their investors. This approach accelerates the development and commercialization of cutting-edge technologies, fast-tracking startups' transition from early-stage ventures to significant market players.

Government grants and subsidies

These government-initiated programs are designed to support sectors critical to national and global priorities by providing financial assistance that does not require repayment. Engaging in these program opportunities offer a significant boost to projects focused on integrating IoT and cloud technologies, enabling them to achieve their objectives with reduced financial risk and enhanced public collaboration.

Crowdfunding

Platforms such as Kickstarter and Indiegogo offer tech entrepreneurs avenues to secure funding directly from the public (Huang et al., 2022). Solution-providers present their ideas to a global audience using these platforms, and validate their concepts through community engagement. One notable such project is QOOLA, a wearable air conditioner that can cool or heat the wearer, offering personal temperature control and air purification (ProductHype, 2022). Another innovative project is SunnySide, a smart lunchbox that keeps food fresh for up to 20 hours and can heat or cool meals on the go, powered by solar energy (ProductHype, 2022). These projects highlight the creative applications of IoT in enhancing everyday life and convenience.

Strategic partnerships and joint ventures

Joint ventures between startups and larger corporations or industry partners can significantly accelerate the development and market penetration of IoT and cloud solutions. These collaborations often provide startups with necessary financial support, access to established networks, expertise, and resources. Large companies innovate more rapidly and tap into novel technologies developed by agile startups.

16.4.3 Developing a future-ready roadmap

Developing a future-ready roadmap requires a structured approach, which is both strategic and adaptable, to effectively integrate emerging technologies, such as IoT and cloud computing. This approach starts with an assessment of current resources and capabilities. It is important to engage in a continuous analysis of the market and technology trends to understand how these advances drive business goals. Setting clear, measurable objectives for digital transformation efforts ensures that the roadmap is aligned with the organization's strategic vision. The development of the roadmap should outline specific actions, timelines, and milestones, while incorporating flexibility levels to adapt to new trends. The allocation of necessary investments and resources, alongside ongoing stakeholder engagement, foster an inclusive and supportive environment for change.

16.5 Synthesis of key themes and takeaways

This section consolidates the themes from the entire book, providing an outlook of how the combination of IoT and cloud technology can digitally transform different industries.

Cloud-to-things continuum

In the first chapter, the groundwork was set for grasping how IoT and cloud computing technologies work together to enable digital transformation. The building blocks of the cloud to things continuum is presented with business challenges. The connection between IoT's data creation and the clouds processing power was pointed out as a driving force for digital transformation.

IoT platforms for digital transformation

In the second chapter, the focus shifted to cloud-based IoT platforms. How they contribute to driving digital transformation? The discussion emphasized the significance of scalable platforms, which are capable of managing large volumes of data, while enabling real-time analytics. Instances of effective deployment across various industries were also showcased.

Enabling digital transformation

In Chapter 3, we investigated the approaches and techniques for leading transformation attempts. The focus was on matching IoT and cloud technologies with business goals to nurture a data-driven culture when handling informed key decisions.

Driving IoT data to the cloud

In Chapter 4, the discussion centered on approaches for transferring IoT data to the cloud, highlighting the significance of edge computing, fog computing, and 5G networks, in maintaining fast response times, strong dependability, and scalability of IoT applications.

Unlocking value with the cloud-to-things continuum

In Chapter 5, the importance of the edge-fog-cloud continuum and the emergence of 5G networks in driving business value was emphasized. The chapter investigated these driving forces to facilitate data processing and improve decision-making abilities, while introducing groundbreaking services.

Interoperability for sustainable digital transformation

In Chapter 6, the importance of interoperability in driving sustainability throughout a digital transformation journey was highlighted. The chapter stressed the significance of standardization and open structures to seamlessly implement and combine of IoT and cloud technologies.

Enterprise IoT

In Chapter 7, we showcased instances of cross-platforms collaborations, which involve data and resource sharing between IoT and cloud platforms. We discussed the integration of AI and IoT within enterprises to enable businesses to provide better value. Case studies demonstrate how AI-enabled enterprise IoT models can optimize operations and personalize customer experiences.

IoT-cloud security

In Chapter 8, the security aspects of IoT and cloud setups were stressed to signify the role of strong security protocols in safeguarding data privacy. Strategies to manage risks effectively and to implement secure IoT systems, in addition to protecting the data they produce, were also addressed.

Vulnerabilities in IoT

Identifying cyber vulnerability in IoT and cloud systems and providing strategies to mitigate them formed the scope of Chapter 9. The importance of anticipating threats and proactively taking preventive security measures to safeguard IoT environments was stressed.

IoT security best practices and standards

Chapter 10 discussed the recommended methods and guidelines for maintaining security in IoT and cloud systems. The significance of following industry norms, establishing thorough security measures, and prioritizing security patching exercises was emphasized for companies' security operations.

Smart citizenship

In Chapter 11, the opportunities for IoT and cloud technologies to elevate digital citizenship were explored. These technologies improve services that boost citizen engagement to thrive in growing eco-urban environments.

Driving change

In Chapter 12, we discussed the theory of change (ToC) framework, which leverages the cloud and IoT technologies through a range of "as a service" integrations, in various industrial domains. We showcased actual achievements and innovative approaches to improve productivity, customer experience, and sustainability.

IoT in healthcare

Chapter 13 revealed the impact of IoT and cloud-driven innovations in the healthcare sector. These technological advances are highlighted for their role, in transforming patients' experience when receiving diagnoses and treatment to meet personal expectations, while improving accessibility to healthcare.

IoT for social good

In Chapter 14, the impacts of IoT and cloud technologies on public sector services are demonstrated to bring about positive social changes. Projects that harness these technologies to address community issues, enhance public services, and raise the well being level of residents, were particularly emphasized.

Connected mobility solutions

In Chapter 15, the focus was on the integration of connectivity in mobility and transportation services. Trends highlighting the shift towards electric vehicle fleets, shared mobility and advances in transportation technologies, fueled by data centric analysis, are explored. The discussion also featured examples showcasing connected mobility and transportation solutions in everyday scenarios.

16.6 Conclusion

We have explored practical applications, strategic investments, and the profound impact of these technologies across various sectors. We have shown the gained operational efficiency to drive innovation and ensure resilience through the synergies between IoT and cloud computing; in addition, we revealed a blueprint for a more sustainable and innovative future that sees light through an investment roadmap. Through the practical applications and strategic investments in IoT and cloud technologies, the need for agile, scalable, and strategically aligned investments was emphasized. The future integration of quantum computing and other emerging technologies with IoT and cloud computing will open new horizons for innovation, sustainability, and resilience. Thus the proposed roadmap is designed to guide stakeholders through such evolving digital landscape, ensuring investments yield immediate benefits but also position organizations for long-term success in a rapidly evolving digital landscape.

References

Ajumo, S.G., Opara, F., Nosiri, O.C., Oguichen, T.C., 2019. Development of an IoT based process plant emission controller. International Journal of Scientific Engineering and Science 3 (4), 69–75.

Ang, L.-M., Seng, K.P., 2016. Big sensor data applications in urban environments. Big Data Research 4, 1–12.

Benkhelifa, E., Abdel-Maguid, M., Ewenike, S., Heatley, D., 2014. The Internet of Things: the eco-system for sustainable growth. In: 2014 IEEE/ACS 11th International Conference on Computer Systems and Applications (AICCSA). IEEE, pp. 836–842.

Bogue, R., 2016. Growth in e-commerce boosts innovation in the warehouse robot market. Industrial Robot: An International Journal 43 (6), 583–587.

Boyles, R., 2019. How the port of Rotterdam is using ibm digital twin technology to transform itself from the biggest to the smartest. https://innovacion.apba.es/digital-twin-technology-to-improve-port-operations-port-of-rotterdam-roadmap-and-use-case-2/. (Accessed 24 March 2024).

Chakraborty, B., Das, S., 2021. Introducing a new supply chain management concept by hybridizing topsis, IoT and cloud computing. Journal of the Institution of Engineers (India): Series C 102 (1), 109–119.

Counterpoint Research, 2023. John Deere: paving the way for connected agriculture. https://www.counterpointresearch.com/insights/john-deere-connected-agriculture/. (Accessed 24 March 2024).

Demircan, B., Akyüz, E., 2019. IoT and cloud based remote monitoring of wind turbine. Celal Bayar University Journal of Science 15 (4), 337–342.

ElMaraghy, H., Monostori, L., Schuh, G., ElMaraghy, W., 2021. Evolution and future of manufacturing systems. CIRP Annals 70 (2), 635–658.

Fastellini, G., Schillaci, C., 2020. Precision farming and IoT case studies across the world. In: Agricultural Internet of Things and Decision Support for Precision Smart Farming. Elsevier, pp. 331–415.

Fitbit, 2024. The fitbit app. https://www.fitbit.com/global/us/technology/fitbit-app. (Accessed 24 March 2024).

Gascó, M., Trivellato, B., Cavenago, D., 2016. How do southern European cities Foster innovation? Lessons from the experience of the smart city approaches of Barcelona and Milan. In: Smarter as the New Urban Agenda: A Comprehensive View of the 21st Century City, pp. 191–206.

GulfNews, 2020. UAE ambulances to turn signals green, have e-link with hospitals. https://gulfnews.com/uae/uae-ambulances-to-turn-signals-green-have-e-link-with-hospitals-1.69322305. (Accessed 24 March 2024).

Huang, S., Pickernell, D., Battisti, M., Nguyen, T., 2022. Signalling entrepreneurs' credibility and project quality for crowdfunding success: cases from the kickstarter and indiegogo environments. Small Business Economics, 1–21.

Jiyal, S., Saini, R.K., 2020. Prediction and monitoring of air pollution using Internet of Things (IoT). In: 2020 Sixth International Conference on Parallel, Distributed and Grid Computing (PDGC). IEEE, pp. 57–60.

Körner, M.-F., Sedlmeir, J., Weibelzahl, M., Fridgen, G., Heine, M., Neumann, C., 2022. Systemic risks in electricity systems: a perspective on the potential of digital technologies. Energy Policy 164, 112901.

Maggi, B., 2024. Living and adapting to climate change in coastal areas. a case study on citizens' perception of an infrastructure: the mose in Venice. The Egyptian Journal of Environmental Change. In press.

Marklein, A.R., Riley, W.J., Grant, R.F., Mezbahuddin, S., Mekonnen, Z.A., Liu, Y., Ying, S., 2017. Modeling applications for precision agriculture in the California central valley. In: AGU Fall Meeting Abstracts, vol. 2017. GC33I–05.

Mayo Clinic, 2023. Mayo clinic selects Google as strategic partner for health care innovation, cloud computing. https://newsnetwork.mayoclinic.org/discussion/mayo-clinic-selects-google-as-strategic-partner-for-health-care-innovation-cloud-computing/. (Accessed 24 March 2024).

Munich Re, 2018. New business models for the connected industry: Munich Re and Bosch agree partnership. https://www.munichre.com/en/company/media-relations/media-information-and-corporate-news/corporate-news/2018/2018-02-22-new-business-models-for-the-connected-industry-munich-re-and-bosch-agree-partnership.html. (Accessed 24 March 2024).

Plume Labs,, 2023. 'City by city, a view of what the world is breathing', https://plumelabs.com/en/air/. Plume Labs provides an air quality monitoring solution that leverages AI and sensor data to provide real-time and forecasted air pollution information city by city. This allows tracking live air quality levels and generating forecasts to empower people to take actions to protect their health.

ProductHype, 2022. The 13 best kickstarter projects of 2022. https://producthype.co/best-kickstarter-projects-2022/. (Accessed 24 March 2023).

Ramírez-Moreno, M.A., Keshtkar, S., Padilla-Reyes, D.A., Ramos-López, E., García-Martínez, M., Hernández-Luna, M.C., Mogro, A.E., Mahlknecht, J., Huertas, J.I., Peimbert-García, R.E., et al., 2021. Sensors for sustainable smart cities: a review. Applied Sciences 11 (17), 8198.

Saleem, Y., Crespi, N., Rehmani, M.H., Copeland, R., 2019. Internet of things-aided smart grid: technologies, architectures, applications, prototypes, and future research directions. IEEE Access 7, 62962–63003.

Sterbenz, J.P., 2017. Smart city and IoT resilience, survivability, and disruption tolerance: challenges, modelling, and a survey of research opportunities. In: 2017 9th International Workshop on Resilient Networks Design and Modeling (RNDM). IEEE, pp. 1–6.

Tan, M., 2018. How I analyzed the data from my fitbit to improve my overall health. https://www.freecodecamp.org/news/how-i-analyzed-the-data-from-my-fitbit-to-improve-my-overall-health-a2e36426d8f9/. (Accessed 24 March 2024).

Tao, F., Zhang, M., Liu, Y., Nee, A.Y., 2018. Digital twin workshop: a new communication mechanism for resolving conflicts between design and production. CIRP Annals 67 (1), 29–32. This article cites and discusses a Siemens whitepaper titled “Digital Twin: Manufacturing Excellence Through Virtual Plant Replication” which covers Siemens’ perspectives and applications of digital twins in manufacturing.

Tao, F., Zhang, M., Nee, A.Y.C., 2019. Digital Twin Driven Smart Manufacturing. Academic Press.

Wijaya, A.P., Prananta, W., Febriatmoko, B., 2023. Does Internet information enhance the intention to switch? Evidence shifting to eco-friendly products. Jurnal Organisasi dan Manajemen 19 (2), 345–359.

Index

D

9780443222177